Programming in C++

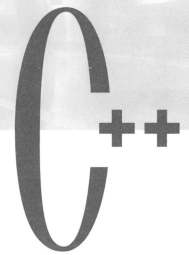

SECOND EDITION

Nell Dale
University of Texas, Austin

Chip Weems
University of Massachusetts, Amherst

Mark Headington
University of Wisconsin–La Crosse

JONES AND BARTLETT PUBLISHERS
Sudbury, Massachusetts
BOSTON   TORONTO   LONDON   SINGAPORE

World Headquarters
Jones and Bartlett Publishers
40 Tall Pine Drive
Sudbury, MA 01776
978-443-5000
info@jbpub.com
www.jbpub.com

Jones and Bartlett Publishers Canada
2406 Nikanna Road
Mississauga, Ontario
Canada L5C 2W6

Jones and Bartlett Publishers International
Barb House, Barb Mews
London W6 7PA
UK

Library of Congress Cataloging-in-Publication Data

Dale, Nell B.
    Programming in C++ / Nell Dale, Chip Weems, Mark Headington.--2nd ed.
      p. cm.
    ISBN 0-7637-1424-0
      1. C++ (Computer program language) I. Weems, Chip. II. Headington, Mark R. III.
Title.
QA76.73.C153 D35 2000
005.13'3--dc21   00-044385

Cover image © Wonderfile, Inc.

Chief Executive Officer: Clayton Jones
Chief Operating Officer: Don W. Jones, Jr.
Executive V.P., Publisher: Tom Manning
V.P., College Editorial Director: Brian L. McKean
V.P., Managing Editor: Judith H. Hauck
V.P., Design and Production: Anne Spencer
V.P., National Sales Manager: Paul Shepardson
Director of Manufacturing and Inventory Control: Therese Bräuer
Senior Acquisitions Editor: Michael Stranz
Development and Product Manager: Amy Rose
Senior Marketing Manager: Jennifer Jacobson
Interactive Technology Product Manager: W. Scott Smith
Editorial/Production Assistant: Amanda Green
Cover Design: Night & Day Design
Composition: Northeast Compositors, Inc.
Text Design: Anne Spencer
Printing and Binding: Courier Westford
Cover printing: John Pow Company, Inc.

This book was typeset in Quark 4.1 on a Macintosh G4. The font families used were Rotis Sans Serif, Rotis Serif, Industria, and Prestige Elite. The first printing was printed on 50 lb. Decision 94 opaque.

Printed in the United States of America
04 03 02 01 00   10 9 8 7 6 5 4 3 2 1

To you, and to all of our students for whom it has begun and without whom it would never have been completed.

N.D.   C.W.   M.H.

The first edition of *Programming in C++* was prepared in response to requests for a straightforward, no-frills introduction to C++. Although this second edition incorporates numerous changes, including reorganization of chapter material, one thing has not changed: our commitment to the student. As always, our efforts are directed toward making the sometimes difficult concepts of computer science more accessible to all students.

This edition of *Programming in C++* continues to reflect our experience that topics once considered too advanced can be taught in the first course. For example, preconditions and postconditions are used in the context of the algorithm walk-through, in the development of testing strategies, and as interface documentation for user-written functions. Data abstraction and abstract data types (ADTs) are explained in conjunction with the C++ class mechanism, forming a natural lead-in to object-oriented programming.

Changes in the Second Edition

The second edition incorporates the following changes:

- *Conformance to ISO/ANSI standard C++*. ISO/ANSI standard C++ (officially approved in July 1998) is used throughout the book, including relevant portions of the new C++ standard library. However, readers with pre-standard C++ compilers are also supported. A new appendix discusses how to modify the textbook's programs to compile and run successfully with an earlier compiler.
- *An earlier introduction to classes, data abstraction, and object-oriented concepts*. Chapters 11–16 of the first edition have been reorganized into the following Chapters 11–15:
  11 Structured Types, Data Abstraction, and Classes
  12 Arrays
  13 Array-Based Lists
  14 Object-Oriented Software Development
  15 Recursion

The visible changes are the deletion of two chapters ("Records" and "Multidimensional Arrays"), whose contents have been merged into Chapters 11 and 12, respectively, and the movement of material on classes and data abstraction (covered in Chapter 15 of the first edition) to Chapter 11. With this reorganization, the concept of the C++ class as both a structuring mechanism and a tool for abstraction now comes earlier in the book.

Introducing classes before arrays has several benefits. In their first exposure to composite types, many students find it easier to comprehend accessing a component by name rather than by position. Chapter 12 on arrays can now rather easily introduce the idea of an array of class objects or an array of structs. Also, Chapter 13, which deals with the list as an ADT, can now be handled in a better way, namely, encapsulating both the data representation (an array) and the length variable within a class, rather than the first edition's approach of using two loosely coupled variables (an array and a separate length variable) to represent the list. Finally, with three chapters' worth of exposure to classes and objects, students reading Chapter 14 can focus on the more difficult aspects of the chapter: inheritance, composition, and dynamic binding.

A natural result of this reorganization is that the chapter "Object-Oriented Software Development" comes earlier in the sequence: Chapter 14 rather than the first edition's Chapter 15.

C++ and Object-Oriented Programming

Some educators reject the C++ language as too permissive and too conducive to writing cryptic, unreadable programs. Our experience does not support this view, *provided that the use of language features is modeled appropriately.* We have found that with careful instruction in software engineering and a programming style that is straightforward, disciplined, and free of intricate language features, students can learn to use C++ to produce clear, readable code.

It must be emphasized that although we use C++ as a vehicle for teaching computer science concepts, the book is not a language manual and does not attempt to cover all of C++. Certain language features—templates, exceptions, operator overloading, default arguments, and mechanisms for advanced forms of inheritance, to name a few—are omitted in an effort not to overwhelm the beginning student with too much too fast.

There are diverse opinions about when to introduce the topic of object-oriented programming (OOP). Some educators advocate an immersion in OOP from the very beginning, whereas others (for whom this book is intended) favor a more heterogeneous approach in which both functional decomposition and object-oriented design are presented as design tools. The chapter organization of *Programming in C++* reflects a transitional approach to OOP. Although we provide an early preview of object-oriented design in Chapter 4, we delay a focused discussion until Chapter 14. The sequence of topics in Chapters 1 through 13 mirrors our belief that OOP is best understood after a firm grounding in algorithm design, control abstraction, and data abstraction with classes.

Features

Web Links Special Web icons found throughout the book prompt students to visit the text's companion Web site located at www.jbpub.com/dale for additional information about selected topics. These Web Links give students instant access to real-world applications of material presented in the text. The Web Links are updated on a regular basis to ensure that students receive the most recent information available on the Internet.

Goals Each chapter begins with a list of learning objectives for the student. These goals are reinforced and tested in the end-of-chapter exercises.

Programming Examples Included in most chapters, programming examples present a problem and discuss its solution. We then code the solution in C++. We also show sample test data and output and follow up with a discussion of program testing.

Testing and Debugging These sections consider the implications of the chapter material with regard to testing of programs. They conclude with a list of testing and debugging hints.

Quick Checks These questions test the student's recall of major points associated with the chapter goals. Upon reading each question, the student immediately should know the answer, which he or she can then verify by glancing at the answers at the end of the section. The page number on which the concept is discussed appears at the end of each question so that the student can review the material in the event of an incorrect response.

Exam Preparation Exercises To help the student prepare for tests, these questions usually have objective answers and are designed to be answerable with a few minutes of work. Answers to selected questions are given in the back of the book, and the remaining questions are answered in the *Instructor's Guide*.

Programming Warm-up Exercises These questions provide the student with experience in writing C++ code fragments. The student can practice the syntactic constructs in each chapter without the burden of writing a complete program.

Programming Problems These exercises require the student to design solutions and write complete programs.

Supplements

Instructor's Guide and Test Bank The *Instructor's Guide* features chapter-by-chapter teaching notes, answers to the balance of the exercises, and a compilation of exam questions with answers. The *Instructor's Guide* is available to adopters on request from Jones and Bartlett.

Instructor's ToolKit CD-ROM Also available to adopters upon request from the publisher is a powerful teaching tool entitled "Instructor's ToolKit." This CD-ROM contains an electronic version of the *Instructor's Guide,* a computerized test bank, PowerPoint lecture presentations, and the complete programs from the text (see below).

Programs The programs contain the source code for all of the complete programs that are found within the textbook. They are available on the Instructor's ToolKit CD-ROM and also as a free download for instructors and students from the publisher's web site: www.jbpub.com/disks. The programs from all the Programming Examples, plus several programs that appear in the chapter bodies, are included. Fragments or snippets of program code are not included nor are the solutions to the chapter-ending "Programming Problems." These program files can be viewed or edited using any standard text editor, but in order to compile and run the programs, a C++ compiler must be used.

Integrated Web Site This Web site features integrated Web Links from the textbook, the complete programs from the text, and Appendix D entitled "Using this Book with a Prestandard Version of C++," which describes the changes needed to allow the programs in the textbook to run successfully with a prestandard compiler.

Student Lecture Companion: A Note-Taking Guide Designed from the PowerPoint presentations developed for this text, the Student Lecture Companion is an invaluable tool for learning. The notebook is designed to encourage students to focus their energies on listening to the lecture as they fill in additional details. The skeletal outline concept helps students organize their notes and readily recognize the important concepts in each chapter.

A Laboratory Course in C++, Second Edition Written by Nell Dale, this lab manual follows the organization of the second edition of the text. The lab manual is designed to allow the instructor maximum flexibility and may be used in both open and closed laboratory settings. Each chapter contains three types of activities: Prelab, Inlab, and Postlab. Each lesson is broken into exercises that thoroughly demonstrate the concept covered in the chapter. A disk that contains the programs, program shells (partial programs), and data files accompanies the lab manual.

Acknowledgments

We would like to thank the many individuals who have helped us in the preparation of this second edition. We are indebted to the members of the faculties of the Computer Science Departments at the University of Texas at Austin, the University of Massachusetts at Amherst, and the University of Wisconsin–La Crosse.

We extend special thanks to Jeff Brumfield for developing the syntax template metalanguage and allowing us to use it in the text.

For their many helpful suggestions, we thank the lecturers, teaching assistants, consultants, and student proctors who run the courses for which this book was written, and the students themselves.

We are grateful to the following people who took the time to review the manuscript for the parent textbook, *Programming and Problem Solving with C++, Second Edition:* J. Ken Collier, Northern Arizona State; Lee Cornell, Mankato State University; Charles Dierbach, Towsen University; Judy Etchison, Collin County Community College; David Galles, University of San Francisco; Susan Gauch, University of Kansas; Wagar Haque, University of Northern British Columbia; Ilga Higbee, Black Hawk College; Jeanine Ingber, University of New Mexico; Paula Jech, Pennsylvania State University; Hikyoo Koh, Lamar University; I. Stephen Leach, Florida State University; Joseph Marti, College of the Canyons; Kenrick Mock, Oregon State University; Viera Proulx, Northeastern University; Howard Pyron, University of Missouri–Rolla; Dennis Ray, Old Dominion University; Sujan Sarkar, Santa Rosa Junior College; Lynn Stauffer, Sonoma State University; Greg Steuben, Rensselaer Polytechnic Institute.

We also thank Bobbie Lewis and Mike and Sigrid Wile along with the many people at Jones and Bartlett who contributed so much, especially J. Michael Stranz, Amy Rose, Jennifer Jacobson, Anne Spencer, and W. Scott Smith.

Anyone who has ever written a book—or is related to someone who has—can appreciate the amount of time involved in such a project. To our families—all the Dale clan and the extended Dale family (too numerous to name); to Lisa, Charlie, and Abby; to Anne, Brady, and Kari—thanks for your tremendous support and indulgence.

N. D.
C. W.
M. H.

contents

Overview of Programming and Problem Solving

- To understand what a computer program is.
- To be able to list the basic stages involved in writing a computer program.
- To understand what an algorithm is.
- To learn what a high-level programming language is.
- To be able to describe what a compiler is and what it does.
- To understand the compilation and execution processes.
- To learn what the major components of a computer are and how they work together.
- To be able to distinguish between hardware and software.
- To learn about some of the basic ethical issues confronting computing professionals.
- To be able to choose an appropriate problem-solving method for developing an algorithmic solution to a problem.

1.1 Overview of Programming

What Is Programming?

Much of human behavior and thought is characterized by logical sequences. Since infancy, you have been learning how to act, how to do things. And you have learned to expect certain behavior from other people.

Much of what you do unconsciously you once had to learn. Watch how a baby concentrates on putting one foot before the other while learning to walk. Then watch a group of three-year-olds playing tag.

On a broader scale, mathematics never could have been developed without logical sequences of steps for solving problems and proving theorems. Mass production never would have worked without operations taking place in a certain order. Our whole civilization is based on the order of things and actions.

Programming Planning or scheduling the performance of a task or an event.

Computer A programmable device that can store, retrieve, and process data.

Computer programming The process of planning a sequence of steps for a computer to follow.

Computer program A sequence of instructions to be performed by a computer.

We create order, both consciously and unconsciously, through a process we call **programming**. This book is concerned with the programming of one of our tools, the **computer**.

Just as a concert program lists the order in which the players perform pieces, a **computer program** lists the sequence of steps the computer performs. From now on, when we use the words *programming* and *program*, we mean *computer programming* and *computer program*.

The computer allows us to do tasks more efficiently, quickly, and accurately than we could by hand—if we could do them by hand at all. In order to use this powerful tool, we must specify what we want done and the order in which we want it done. We do this through programming.

How Do We Write a Program?

To write a sequence of instructions for a computer to follow, we must go through a two-phase process: *problem solving* and *implementation* (see Figure 1–1).

Problem-Solving Phase

1. *Analysis and specification.* Understand (define) the problem and what the solution must do.

2. *General solution (algorithm).* Develop a logical sequence of steps that solves the problem.

3. *Verify.* Follow the steps exactly to see if the solution really does solve the problem.

Implementation Phase

1. *Concrete solution (program).* Translate the algorithm into a programming language.

PROBLEM-SOLVING PHASE   IMPLEMENTATION PHASE

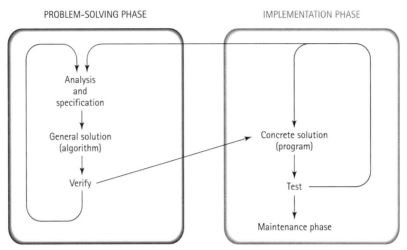

Figure 1–1 *Programming Process*

2. *Test.* Have the computer follow the instructions. Then manually check the results. If you find errors, analyze the program and the algorithm to determine the source of the errors, and then make corrections.

Once a program has been written, it enters a third phase: *maintenance.*

Maintenance Phase

1. *Use.* Use the program.
2. *Maintain.* Modify the program to meet changing requirements or to correct any errors that show up in using it.

The programmer begins the programming process by analyzing the problem and developing a general solution called an **algorithm.** Understanding and analyzing a problem take up much more time than Figure 1-1 implies. They are the heart of the programming process.

Algorithm A step-by-step procedure for solving a problem in a finite amount of time.

If our definitions of a computer program and an algorithm look similar, it is because all programs are algorithms. A program is simply an algorithm that has been written for a computer.

An algorithm is a verbal or written description of a logical sequence of actions. We use algorithms every day. Recipes, instructions, and directions are all examples of algorithms that are not programs.

When you start your car, you follow a step-by-step procedure. The algorithm might look something like this:

1. Insert the key.
2. Make sure the transmission is in Park (or Neutral).
3. Depress the gas pedal.
4. Turn the key to the start position.
5. If the engine starts within six seconds, release the key to the ignition position.
6. If the engine doesn't start in six seconds, release the key and gas pedal, wait ten seconds, and repeat Steps 3 through 6, but not more than five times.
7. If the car doesn't start, call the garage.

Without the phrase "but not more than five times" in Step 6, you could be trying to start the car forever. Why? Because if something is wrong with the car, repeating Steps 3 through 6 over and over again will not start it. This kind of never-ending situation is called an *infinite loop*. If we leave the phrase "but not more than five times" out of Step 6, the procedure does not fit our definition of an algorithm. An algorithm must terminate in a finite amount of time for all possible conditions.

Suppose a programmer needs an algorithm to determine an employee's weekly wages. The algorithm reflects what would be done by hand:

1. Look up the employee's pay rate.
2. Determine the number of hours worked during the week.
3. If the number of hours worked is less than or equal to 40, multiply the number of hours by the pay rate to calculate regular wages.
4. If the number of hours worked is greater than 40, multiply 40 by the pay rate to calculate regular wages, and then multiply the difference between the number of hours worked and 40 by 1½ times the pay rate to calculate overtime wages.
5. Add the regular wages to the overtime wages (if any) to determine total wages for the week.

The steps the computer follows are often the same steps you would use to do the calculations by hand.

After developing a general solution, the programmer tests the algorithm, walking through each step mentally or manually. If the algorithm doesn't work, the programmer repeats the problem-solving process, analyzing the problem again and coming up with another algorithm. Often the second algorithm is just a variation of the first. When the programmer is satisfied with the algorithm, he or she translates it into a **programming language**. We use the C++ programming language in this book.

> **Programming language** A set of rules, symbols, and special words used to construct a computer program.

A programming language is a simplified form of English (with math symbols) that adheres to a strict set of grammatical rules. English is far too complicated a language for today's computers to follow. Programming languages, because they limit vocabulary and grammar, are much simpler.

Although a programming language is simple in form, it is not always easy to use. Try giving someone directions to the nearest airport using a vocabulary of no more than 45 words, and you'll begin to see the problem. Programming forces you to write very simple, exact instructions.

Translating an algorithm into a programming language is called *coding* the algorithm. The product of that translation—the program—is tested by running (*executing*) it on the computer. If the program fails to produce the desired results, the programmer must *debug* it—that is, determine what is wrong and then modify the program, or even the algorithm, to fix it. The combination of coding and testing an algorithm is called *implementation*.

Some people try to speed up the programming process by going directly from the problem definition to coding the program (see Figure 1-2). A shortcut here is very tempting and at first seems to save a lot of time. However, for many reasons that will become obvious to you as you read this book, this kind of shortcut actually takes *more* time and effort. Developing a general solution before you write a program helps you manage the problem, keep your thoughts straight, and avoid mistakes. If you don't take the time at the beginning to think out and polish your algorithm, you'll spend a lot of extra time debugging and revising your program.

Once a program has been put into use, it is often necessary to modify it. Modification may involve fixing an error that is discovered during the use of the program or changing the program in response to changes in the user's requirements. Each time the program is modified, it is necessary to repeat the problem-solving and implementation

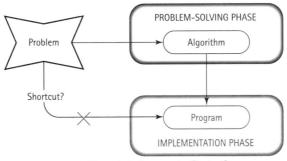

Figure 1-2 *Programming Shortcut?*

phases for those aspects of the program that change. This phase of the programming process is known as maintenance and actually accounts for the majority of the effort expended on most programs. For example, a program that is implemented in a few months may need to be maintained over a period of many years. Thus, it is a cost-effective investment of time to develop the initial problem solution and program implementation carefully. Together, the problem-solving, implementation, and maintenance phases constitute the program's *life cycle.*

In addition to solving the problem, implementing the algorithm, and maintaining the program, **documentation** is an important part of the programming process. Documentation includes written explanations of the problem being solved and the organization of the solution, comments embedded within the program itself, and user manuals that describe how to use the program. Most programs are worked on by many different people over a long period of time. Each of those people must be able to read and understand your code.

Documentation The written text and comments that make a program easier for others to understand, use, and modify.

After you write a program, you must give the computer the information or data necessary to solve the problem. **Information** is any knowledge that can be communicated, including abstract ideas and concepts such as "the earth is round." **Data** is information in a form the computer can use—for example, the numbers and letters making up the formulas that relate the earth's radius to its volume and surface area. But data is not restricted to numbers and letters. These days, computers also process data that represents sound (to be played through speakers), graphic images (to be displayed on a computer screen or printer), video (to be played on a VCR), and so forth.

Information Any knowledge that can be communicated.

Data Information in a form a computer can use.

Data Representation

In a computer, data is represented electronically by pulses of electricity. Electric circuits, in their simplest form, are either on or off. Usually a circuit that is on is represented by the number 1; a circuit that is off is represented by the number 0. Any kind of data can be represented by combinations of enough 1s and 0s. We simply have to choose which combination represents each piece of data we are using. For example, we could arbitrarily choose the pattern 1101000110 to represent the name C++.

Data represented by 1s and 0s is in *binary form.* The binary (base-2) number system uses only 1s and 0s to represent numbers. (The decimal [base-10] number system uses the digits 0 through 9.) The word *bit* (short for binary digit) refers to a single 1 or 0. The pattern 1101000110 thus has 10 bits. A binary number with 10 bits can represent 2^{10} (1024) different patterns. A *byte* is a group of 8 bits; it can represent 2^8 (256) patterns. Inside the computer, each character (such as the letter A, the letter g, or a question mark) is usually represented by a byte. Groups of 16, 32, and 64 bits are generally referred to as *words* (although the terms *short word* and *long word* are sometimes used to refer to 16-bit and 64-bit groups, respectively).

The process of assigning bit patterns to pieces of data is called *coding*—the same name we give to the process of translating an algorithm into a programming language. The names are the same because the only language that the first computers recognized was binary in form. Thus, in the early days of computers, programming meant translating both data and algorithms into patterns of 1s and 0s.

Fortunately, we no longer have to work with binary coding schemes. Today the process of coding is usually just a matter of writing down the data in letters, numbers, and symbols. The computer automatically converts these letters, numbers, and symbols into binary form. Still, as you work with computers, you will continually run into numbers that are related to powers of 2—numbers such as 256, 32,768, and 65,536—reminders that the binary number system is lurking somewhere nearby.

1.2   What Is a Programming Language?

The only programming language that a computer can directly execute is the primitive instruction set built into it—the **machine language**, or *machine code*. For example:

Machine language The language, made up of binary-coded instructions, that is used directly by the computer.

Instruction Name	Machine Language Form
Add	100101
Subtract	010011

Computer scientists develop high-level programming languages that are easier to use than machine code because they are closer to English and other natural languages (see Figure 1–3).

A program called a **compiler** translates a program written in a high-level language (C++, Pascal, FORTRAN, COBOL, or Ada, for example) into machine language. If you write a program in a high-level language, you can run it on any computer that has the appropriate compiler. This is possible because most high-level languages are *standardized*, which means that an official description of the language exists.*

Compiler A program that translates a high-level language into machine code.

A program in a high-level language is called a **source program.** To the compiler, a source program is just input data. It translates the source program into a machine language

Source program A program written in a high-level programming language.

---

*Some programming languages—LISP, Prolog, and many versions of BASIC, for example—are translated into machine language by an *interpreter* rather than a compiler. The difference between a compiler and an interpreter is outside the scope of this textbook, which focuses only on compiled languages.

Figure 1–3 *Levels of Abstraction*

Object program The machine language version of a source program.

program called an **object program**. Some compilers also output a *listing*—a copy of the program with error messages and other information inserted.

A benefit of standardized high-level languages is that they allow you to write *portable* (or *machine-independent*) code. A single C++ program can be used on different machines, whereas a program written in machine language is not portable from one computer to another.

It is important to understand that *compilation* and *execution* are two distinct processes. During compilation, the computer runs the compiler program. During execution, the object program is loaded into the computer's memory unit, replacing the compiler program. The computer then runs the object program, doing whatever the program instructs it to do (see Figure 1–4).

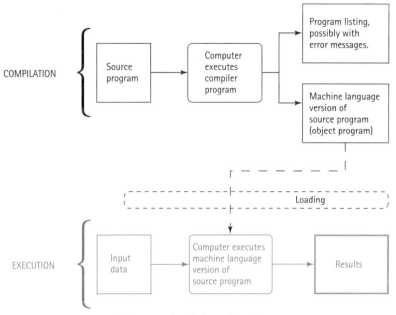

COMPILATION

Source program

Computer executes compiler program

Program listing, possibly with error messages.

Machine language version of source program (object program)

Loading

EXECUTION

Input data

Computer executes machine language version of source program

Results

Figure 1–4 *Compilation and Execution*

The instructions in a programming language reflect the operations a computer can perform. A computer can:

- transfer data from one place to another.
- input data from an input device (a keyboard, for example) and output data to an output device (a screen, for example).
- store data into and retrieve data from its memory and secondary storage (parts of a computer that we discuss in the next section).
- compare two data values for equality or inequality.
- perform arithmetic operations (addition and subtraction, for example) very quickly.

Programming languages require that we use certain *control structures* to express algorithms as programs. There are four basic ways of structuring statements (instructions) in most programming languages: sequentially, conditionally, repetitively, and with subprograms (see Figure 1-5). A *sequence* is a series of statements that are executed one after another. *Selection*, the conditional control structure, executes different statements depending on certain conditions. The repetitive control structure, the *loop*, repeats statements while certain conditions are met. The *subprogram* allows us to structure a program by breaking it into smaller units. Each of these ways of structuring statements controls the order in which the computer executes the statements, which is why they are called control structures.

SEQUENCE

SELECTION (also called *branch* or *decision*)

IF condition THEN statement1 ELSE statement2

LOOP (also called *repetition* or *iteration*)

WHILE condition DO statement1

SUBPROGRAM (also called *procedure, function, method,* or *subroutine*)

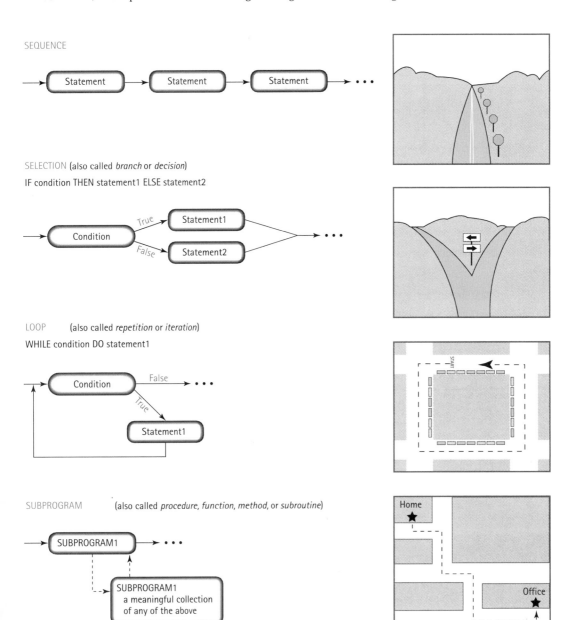

Figure 1–5 *Basic Structures of Programming Languages*

Imagine you're driving a car. Going down a straight stretch of road is like following a sequence of instructions. When you come to a fork in the road, you must decide which way to go and then take one or the other branch of the fork. This is what the computer does when it encounters a selection control structure (sometimes called a *branch* or *decision*) in a program. Sometimes you have to go around the block several times to find a place to park. The computer does the same sort of thing when it encounters a loop in a program.

A subprogram is a process that consists of multiple steps. Every day, for example, you follow a procedure to get from home to work. It makes sense, then, for someone to give you directions to a meeting by saying, "Go to the office, then go four blocks west" without specifying all the steps you have to take to get to the office. Subprograms allow us to write parts of our programs separately and then assemble them into final form. They can greatly simplify the task of writing large programs.

1.3 What Is a Computer?

You can learn how to write programs without knowing much about computers. But if you know something about the parts of a computer, you can better understand the effect of each instruction in a programming language.

Most computers have six basic components: the memory unit, the arithmetic/logic unit, the control unit, input devices, output devices, and auxiliary storage devices. Figure 1–6 is a stylized diagram of the basic components of a computer.

The **memory unit** is an ordered sequence of storage cells, each capable of holding a piece of data. Each memory cell has a distinct address to which we refer in order to store

> **Memory unit** Internal data storage in a computer.

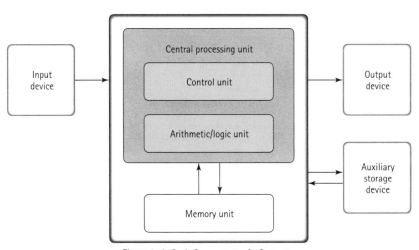

Figure 1–6 *Basic Components of a Computer*

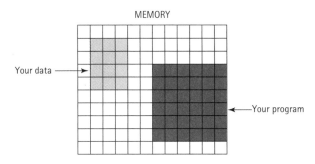

Figure 1–7 *Memory*

data into it or retrieve data from it. These storage cells are called *memory cells*, or *memory locations*.* The memory unit holds both data and instructions, as shown in Figure 1–7.

Central processing unit (CPU) The part of the computer that executes the instructions (program) stored in memory; made up of the arithmetic/logic unit and the control unit.

Arithmetic/logic unit (ALU) The component of the central processing unit that performs arithmetic and logical operations.

Control unit The component of the central processing unit that controls the actions of the other components.

Input/output (I/O) devices The parts of the computer that accept data to be processed (input) and present the results of that processing (output).

The part of the computer that follows instructions is called the **central processing unit (CPU)**. The CPU usually has two components. The **arithmetic/logic unit (ALU)** performs arithmetic operations (addition, subtraction, multiplication, and division) and logical operations (comparing two values). The **control unit** controls the actions of the other components so that program instructions are executed in the correct order.

For us to use computers, there must be some way of getting data into and out of them. **Input/output (I/O) devices** accept data to be processed (input) and present data values that have been processed (output). A keyboard is a common input device. Another is a *mouse,* a pointing device. A video display is a common output device, as are printers and liquid crystal display (LCD) screens. Some devices, such as a connection to a computer network, are used for both input and output.

For the most part, computers simply move and combine data in memory. The many types of computers differ primarily in the size of their memories, the speed with which data can be recalled, the efficiency with which data can be moved or combined, and limitations on I/O devices.

When a program is executing, the computer proceeds through a series of steps, the *fetch-execute cycle:*

1. The control unit retrieves (*fetches*) the next coded instruction from memory.

2. The instruction is translated into control signals.

---

*The memory unit is also referred to as RAM, an acronym for random access memory (so called because we can access any location at random).

3. The control signals tell the appropriate unit (arithmetic/logic unit, memory, I/O device) to perform (execute) the instruction.

4. The sequence repeats from Step 1.

Computers can have a wide variety of **peripheral devices** such as keyboards, printers, mice, and auxiliary storage devices. An **auxiliary storage device**, or *secondary storage device*, holds coded data for the computer until we actually want to use the data. Instead of inputting data every time, we can input it

> **Peripheral device** An input, output, or auxiliary storage device attached to a computer.
>
> **Auxiliary storage device** A device that stores data in encoded form outside the computer's main memory.

once and have the computer store it onto an auxiliary storage device. Typical auxiliary storage devices are disk drives and magnetic tape drives. A *disk drive* is a cross between a compact disc player and a tape recorder. It uses a thin disk made out of magnetic material. A read/write head (similar to the record/playback head in a tape recorder) travels across the spinning disk, retrieving or recording data. A *magnetic tape drive* is like a tape recorder and is most often used to *back up* (make a copy of) the data on a disk in case the disk is ever damaged.

Other examples of peripheral devices include the following:

- Scanners, which "read" visual images on paper and convert them into binary data
- CD-ROM (compact disc–read-only memory) drives, which read (but cannot write) data stored on removable compact discs
- CD-R (compact disc–recordable) drives, which can write to a particular CD once only but can read from it many times
- CD-RW (compact disc–rewritable) drives, which can both write to and read from a particular CD many times
- DVD-ROM (digital video disc [or digital versatile disc]–read-only memory) drives, which use CDs with far greater storage capacity than conventional CDs
- Modems (modulator/demodulators), which convert back and forth between binary data and signals that can be sent over conventional telephone lines
- Audio sound cards and speakers
- Voice synthesizers
- Digital cameras

> **Hardware** The physical components of a computer.
>
> **Software** Computer programs; the set of all programs available on a computer.
>
> **Interface** A shared boundary that allows independent systems to meet and act on or communicate with each other.

Together, all of these physical components are known as **hardware**. The programs that allow the hardware to operate are called **software**. Hardware usually is fixed in design; software is easily changed. In fact, the ease with which software can be manipulated is what makes the computer such a versatile, powerful tool.

In addition to the programs that we write or purchase, there are programs in the computer, called *system software,* that are designed to simplify the user/computer **interface,** making it easier for us to use the machine.

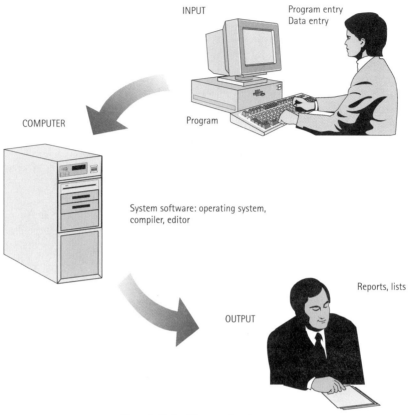

INPUT

Program entry
Data entry

COMPUTER

Program

System software: operating system,
compiler, editor

OUTPUT

Reports, lists

Figure 1–8 *User/Computer Interface*

Operating system A set of programs that manages all of
the computer's resources.

Editor An interactive program used to create and modify
source programs or data.

This set of programs includes the compiler as well as the operating system and the editor (see Figure 1–8). The **operating system** manages all of the computer's resources. It can input programs, call the compiler, execute object programs, and carry out any other system commands. The **editor** is an interactive program used to create and modify source programs or data.

Although solitary (*stand-alone*) computers are often used in private homes and small businesses, it is very common for many computers to be connected together, forming a *network*. A *local area network* (LAN) is one in which the computers are connected by wires and must be reasonably close together, as in a single office building. In a *wide area network* (WAN) or *long-haul network*, the computers can be far apart geographically and communicate through phone lines, fiber optic cable, and other media. The most well-known long-haul network is the Internet, which was originally devised as a means for universities, businesses, and government agencies to exchange research information. The Internet exploded in popularity with the establishment of the World Wide Web, a system of linked Internet computers that support specially formatted documents (*Web pages*) that contain text, graphics, audio, and video.

ISO/ANSI Standard C++

The C++ programming language was created in 1985. In the following years, the language began to evolve in slightly different ways in different C++ compilers. Although the fundamental features of C++ were nearly the same in all companies' compilers, one company might add a new language feature, whereas another would not. As a result, C++ programs were not always portable from one compiler to the next. The programming community agreed that the language needed to be standardized, and a joint committee of the International Standards Organization (ISO) and the American National Standards Institute (ANSI) began the long process of creating a C++ language standard. After several years of discussion and debate, the ISO/ANSI language standard for C++ was officially approved in mid-1998. Most of the current C++ compilers support the ISO/ANSI standard (hereafter called *standard C++*). To assist you if you are using a pre-standard compiler, throughout the book we point out discrepancies between older language features and new ones that may affect how you write your programs.

1.4   Ethics and Responsibilities in the Computing Profession

Every profession operates with a set of ethics that help to define the responsibilities of people who practice the profession. In this section we examine some common situations encountered in the computing profession that raise particular ethical issues.

Software Piracy

Computer software is easy to copy. But just like books, software is usually copyrighted. It is illegal to copy software without the permission of its creator. Such copying is called **software piracy.**

Software piracy The unauthorized copying of software for either personal use or use by others.

Copyright laws exist to protect the creators of software (and books and art) so that they can make a profit from the effort and money spent developing the software. If people make unauthorized copies of the software, then the company loses those sales and either has to raise its prices to compensate or spend less money to develop improved versions of the software—in either case, a desirable piece of software becomes harder to obtain.

Computing professionals have an ethical obligation to not engage in software piracy and to try to stop it from occurring. You should never copy software without permission. If someone asks you for a copy of a piece of software, you should refuse to supply it. If someone says that he or she just wants to "borrow" the software to "try it out," tell that person that he or she is welcome to try it out on your machine (or at a retailer's shop) but not to make a copy.

This rule isn't restricted to duplicating copyrighted software; it includes plagiarism of all or part of code that belongs to anyone else. If someone gives you permission to copy some of his or her code, then, just like any responsible writer, you should acknowledge that person with a citation in the code.

Privacy of Data

Suppose your job includes managing the company payroll database. In that database are the names and salaries of the employees in the company. You might be tempted to poke around in the database to see how your salary compares with your associates; however, this act is unethical and an invasion of your associates' right to privacy, because this information is confidential. Any information about a person that is not clearly public should be considered confidential. An example of public information is a phone number listed in a telephone directory. Private information includes any data that has been provided with an understanding that it will be used only for a specific purpose (such as the data on a credit card application).

A computing professional has a responsibility to avoid taking advantage of special access that he or she may have to confidential data. The professional also has a responsibility to guard that data from unauthorized access. Guarding data can involve such simple things as shredding old printouts, keeping backup copies in a locked cabinet, and not using passwords that are easy to guess (such as a name or word) as well as more complex measures such as *encryption* (keeping data stored in a secret coded form).

Use of Computer Resources

The computer is an unusual resource because it is valuable only when a program is running. Thus, the computer's time is really the valuable resource. There is no significant physical difference between a computer that is working and one that is sitting idle. By contrast, a car is in motion when it is working. Thus, unauthorized use of a computer is different from unauthorized use of a car. If one person uses another's car without permission, that individual must take possession of it physically—that is, steal it. If someone uses a computer without permission, the computer isn't physically stolen, but just as in the case of car theft, the owner is being deprived of a resource that he or she is paying for.

For some people, theft of computer resources is a game—like joyriding in a car. The thief really doesn't want the resources, just the challenge of breaking through a computer's security system and seeing how far he or she can get without being caught. Success gives a thrilling boost to this sort of person's ego. Many computer thieves think that their actions are acceptable if they do no harm, but whenever real work is displaced from the computer by such activities, then harm is clearly being done. If nothing else, the thief is trespassing in the computer owner's property.

Sometimes computer thieves leave behind programs that act as time bombs to cause harm long after they have gone. Another kind of program that may be left is a virus—a program that replicates itself, often with the goal of spreading to other computers.

Viruses can be benign, causing no other harm than to use up some resources. Others can be destructive and cause widespread damage to data. Incidents have occurred in which viruses have cost millions of dollars in lost computer time and data.

Virus A computer program that replicates itself, often with the goal of spreading to other computers without authorization, and possibly with the intent of doing harm.

Computing professionals have an ethical responsibility never to use computer resources without permission, including activities such as doing personal work on an employer's computer. We also have a responsibility to help guard resources to which we have access–by using unguessable passwords and keeping them secret, by watching for signs of unusual computer use, by writing programs that do not provide loopholes in a computer's security system, and so on.

Software Engineering

The reliability of a computer depends on the care that is taken in writing its software. Errors in a program can have serious consequences, as the following examples of real incidents involving software errors illustrate. An error in the control software of the F–18 jet fighter caused it to flip upside down the first time it flew across the equator. A radiation therapy machine killed several patients because a software error caused the machine to operate at full power when the operator typed certain commands too quickly.

Even when the software is used in less critical situations, errors can have significant effects. Examples of such errors include the following:

- An error in a statistical program that causes a scientist to draw a wrong conclusion and publish a paper that must later be retracted
- An error in a tax preparation program that produces an incorrect return, leading to a fine

Programmers thus have a responsibility to develop software that is free from errors. The process that is used to develop correct software is known as **software engineering.**

Software engineering The application of traditional engineering methodologies and techniques to the development of software.

Software engineering has many aspects. The software life cycle described at the beginning of this chapter outlines the stages in the development of software. Different techniques are used at each of these stages. We address many of the techniques in this text. In Chapter 4 we introduce methodologies for developing correct algorithms.

1.5 Problem–Solving Techniques

You solve problems every day, often unaware of the process you are going through. In a learning environment, you usually are given most of the information you need: a clear statement of the problem, the necessary input, and the required output. In real life, the process is not always so simple. You often have to define the problem yourself and then decide what information you have to work with and what the results should be.

After you understand and analyze a problem, you must come up with a solution—an algorithm. Most of your experience with algorithms is in the context of *following* them. You follow a recipe, play a game, assemble a toy. In the problem-solving phase of computer programming, you will be *designing* algorithms, not following them. This means you must be conscious of the strategies you use to solve problems in order to apply them to programming problems.

Ask Questions

If you are given a task orally, you ask questions—When? Why? Where?—until you understand exactly what you have to do. If your instructions are written, you might put question marks in the margin, or in some other way indicate that the task is not clear. Your questions may be answered by a later paragraph, or you might have to discuss them with the person who gave you the task.

These are some of the questions you might ask in the context of programming:

- What do I have to work with—that is, what is my data?
- What do the data items look like?
- How much data is there?
- How will I know when I have processed all the data?
- What should my output look like?
- How many times is the process going to be repeated?
- What special error conditions might come up?

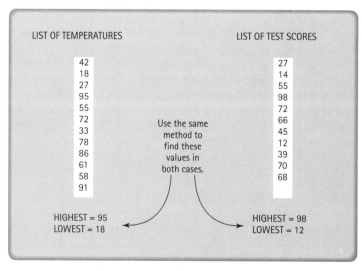

Figure 1–9 *Look for Things That Are Familiar*

Look for Things That Are Familiar

Never reinvent the wheel. If a solution exists, use it. If you've solved the same or a similar problem before, just repeat your solution.

In programming, certain problems occur again and again in different guises. A good programmer immediately recognizes a subtask he or she has solved before and plugs in the solution. For example, finding the daily high and low temperatures is really the same problem as finding the highest and lowest grades on a test. You want the largest and smallest values in a set of numbers (see Figure 1–9).

Solve by Analogy

Often a problem reminds you of a similar problem you have seen before. You may find solving the problem at hand easier if you remember how you solved the other problem. In other words, draw an analogy between the two problems. As you work your way through the new problem, you come across things that are different than they were in the old problem, but usually these are just details that you can deal with one at a time.

Analogy is really just a broader application of the strategy of looking for things that are familiar. When you are trying to find an algorithm for solving a problem, don't limit yourself to computer-oriented solutions. Step back and try to get a larger view of the problem. Don't worry if your analogy doesn't match perfectly–the only reason for using an analogy is that it gives you a place to start (see Figure 1–10). The best programmers are people who have broad experience solving all kinds of problems.

Means–Ends Analysis

Often the beginning state and the ending state are given; the problem is to define a set of actions that can be used to get from one to the other. Suppose you want to go from Boston, Massachusetts, to Austin, Texas. You know the beginning state (you are in Boston) and the ending state (you want to be in Austin). The problem is how to get from one to the other. In this example, you have lots of choices. You can fly, walk, hitchhike, ride a bike, or whatever. The method you choose depends on your circumstances. If you're in a hurry, you'll probably decide to fly.

A library catalog system can give insight into how to organize a parts inventory.

Figure 1–10 *Analogy*

Once you've narrowed down the set of actions, you have to work out the details. It may help to establish intermediate goals that are easier to meet than the overall goal. Let's say there is a really cheap, direct flight to Austin out of Newark, New Jersey. You might decide to divide the trip into legs: Boston to Newark and then Newark to Austin. Your intermediate goal is to get from Boston to Newark. Now you only have to examine the means of meeting that intermediate goal (see Figure 1–11).

The overall strategy of means-ends analysis is to define the ends and then to analyze your means of getting between them. The process translates easily to computer programming. You begin by writing down what the input is and what the output should be. Then you consider the actions a computer can perform and choose a sequence of actions that can transform the input into the output.

Divide and Conquer

We often break up large problems into smaller units that are easier to handle. Cleaning the whole house may seem overwhelming; cleaning the rooms one at a time seems much more manageable. The same principle applies to programming. We break up a large problem into smaller pieces that we can solve individually (see Figure 1–12). In fact, the functional decomposition and object-oriented methodologies, which we describe in Chapter 4, are based on the principle of divide and conquer.

The Building-Block Approach

Another way of attacking a large problem is to see if any solutions for smaller pieces of the problem exist. It may be possible to put some of these solutions together end to end to solve most of the big problem. This strategy is just a combination of the look-for-familiar-things and divide-and-conquer approaches. You look at the big problem and see that it can be divided into smaller problems for which solutions already exist. Solving the big problem is just a matter of putting the existing solutions together, like mortaring together blocks to form a wall (see Figure 1–13).

Start: Boston **Goal:** Austin	**Means:** *Fly*, walk, hitchhike, bike, drive, sail, bus
Start: Boston **Goal:** Austin	**Revised Means:** Fly to Chicago and then Austin; *fly to Newark and then Austin:* fly to Atlanta and then Austin
Start: Boston **Intermediate Goal:** Newark **Goal:** Austin	**Means to Intermediate Goal:** *Commuter flight*, walk, hitchhike, bike, drive, sail, bus
Solution: Take commuter flight to Newark and then catch cheap flight to Austin	

Figure 1–11 *Means-Ends Analysis*

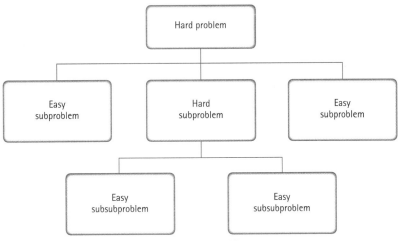

Figure 1-12 *Divide and Conquer*

Merging Solutions

Another way to combine existing solutions is to merge them on a step-by-step basis. For example, to compute the average of a list of values, we must both sum and count the values. If we already have separate solutions for summing values and for counting values, we can combine them. But if we first do the summing and then do the counting, we have to read the list twice. We can save steps if we merge these two solutions: Read a value and then add it to the running total and add 1 to our count before going on to

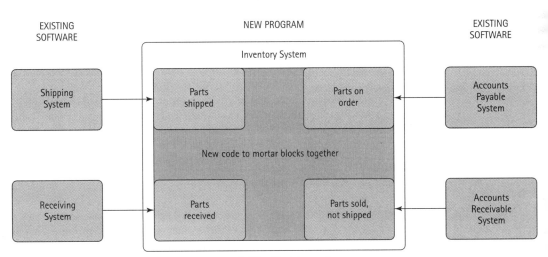

Figure 1-13 *Building-Block Approach*

the next value. Whenever the solutions to subproblems duplicate steps, think about merging them instead of joining them end to end.

Mental Blocks: The Fear of Starting

Writers are all too familiar with the experience of staring at a blank page, not knowing where to begin. Programmers have the same difficulty when they first tackle a big problem. They look at the problem and it seems overwhelming.

Remember that you always have a way to begin solving any problem: Write it down on paper in your own words so that you understand it. Once you paraphrase the problem, you can focus on each of the subparts individually instead of trying to tackle the entire problem at once. This process gives you a clearer picture of the overall problem. It helps you see pieces of the problem that look familiar or that are analogous to other problems you have solved, and it pinpoints areas where something is unclear, where you need more information.

As you write down a problem, you tend to group things together into small, understandable chunks, which may be natural places to split the problem up—to divide and conquer. Your description of the problem may collect all of the information about data and results into one place for easy reference. Then you can see the beginning and ending states necessary for means-ends analysis.

Most mental blocks are caused by not really understanding the problem. Rewriting the problem in your own words is a good way to focus on the subparts of the problem, one at a time, and to understand what is required for a solution.

Algorithmic Problem Solving

Coming up with a step-by-step procedure for solving a particular problem is not always a cut-and-dried process. In fact, it is usually a trial-and-error process requiring several attempts and refinements. We test each attempt to see if it really solves the problem. If it does, fine. If it doesn't, we try again. Solving any nontrivial problem typically requires a combination of the techniques we've described.

Remember that the computer can only do certain things (see p. 9). Your primary concern, then, is how to make the computer transform, manipulate, calculate, or process the input data to produce the desired output. If you keep in mind the allowable instructions in your programming language, you won't design an algorithm that is difficult or impossible to code.

Summary

Computer programming is the process of planning a sequence of steps for a computer to follow. It involves a problem-solving phase and an implementation phase. After analyzing a problem, we develop and test a general solution (algorithm). This general solution becomes a concrete solution—our program—when we write it in a high-level programming language. The sequence of instructions that makes up our program is then compiled into machine code, the language the computer uses. After correcting any errors ("bugs") that show up during testing, our program is ready to use.

Once we begin to use the program, it enters the maintenance phase. Maintenance involves correcting any errors discovered while the program is being used and changing the program to reflect changes in the user's requirements.

Data and instructions are represented as binary numbers (numbers consisting of just 1s and 0s) in electronic computers. The process of converting data and instructions into a form usable by the computer is called coding.

A programming language reflects the range of operations a computer can perform. The basic control structures in a programming language—sequence, selection, loop, and subprogram—are based on these fundamental operations. In this text, you will learn to write programs in the high-level programming language called C++.

Computers are composed of six basic parts: the memory unit, the arithmetic/logic unit, the control unit, input and output devices, and auxiliary storage devices. The arithmetic/logic unit and control unit together are called the central processing unit. The physical parts of the computer are called hardware. The programs that are executed by the computer are called software.

System software is a set of programs designed to simplify the user/computer interface. It includes the compiler, the operating system, and the editor.

Computing professionals are guided by a set of ethics, as are members of other professions. Among the responsibilities that we have are copying software only with permission and including attribution to other programmers when we make use of their code, guarding the privacy of confidential data, using computer resources only with permission, and carefully engineering our programs so that they work correctly.

We've said that problem solving is an integral part of the programming process. Although you may have little experience programming computers, you have lots of experience solving problems. The key is to stop and think about the strategies you use to solve problems, and then to use those strategies to devise workable algorithms. Among those strategies are asking questions, looking for things that are familiar, solving by analogy, applying means-ends analysis, dividing the problem into subproblems, using existing solutions to small problems to solve a larger problem, merging solutions, and paraphrasing the problem in order to overcome a mental block.

The computer is widely used today in science, engineering, business, government, medicine, consumer goods, and the arts. Learning to program in C++ can help you use this powerful tool effectively.

chapter 2

C++ Syntax and Semantics, and the Program Development Process

- ■ To understand how a C++ program is composed of one or more subprograms (functions).

- ■ To be able to read syntax templates in order to understand the formal rules governing C++ programs.

- ■ To be able to create and recognize legal C++ identifiers.

- ■ To be able to declare named constants and variables of type `char` and `string`.

- ■ To be able to distinguish reserved words in C++ from user-defined identifiers.

- ■ To be able to assign values to variables.

- ■ To be able to construct simple string expressions made up of constants, variables, and the concatenation operator.

- ■ To be able to construct a statement that writes to an output stream.

- ■ To be able to determine what is printed by a given output statement.

- ■ To be able to use comments to clarify your programs.

- ■ To be able to construct simple C++ programs.

2.1 The Elements of C++ Programs

In this chapter, we start looking at the rules and symbols that make up the C++ programming language. We also review the steps required to create a program and make it work on a computer.

C++ Program Structure

In Chapter 1, we said that subprograms allow us to write parts of our program separately and then assemble them into final form. In C++, all subprograms are referred to as **functions**, and a C++ program is a collection of one or more functions. Each function performs some particular task, and collectively they all cooperate to solve the entire problem.

Function A subprogram in C++.

Every C++ program must have a function named main. Execution of the program always begins with the main function. You can think of main as the master and the other functions as the servants. When main wants the function Square to perform a task, main *calls* (or *invokes*) Square. When the Square function completes execution of its statements, it obediently returns control to the master, main, so the master can continue executing.

Let's look at an example of a C++ program with three functions: main, Square, and Cube. Don't be too concerned with the details in the program—just observe its overall look and structure.

```
#include <iostream>

using namespace std;
```

```
int Square( int );
int Cube( int );

int main()
{
    cout << "The square of 27 is " << Square(27) << endl;
    cout << "and the cube of 27 is " << Cube(27) << endl;
    return 0;
}

int Square( int n )
{
    return n * n;
}

int Cube( int n )
{
    return n * n * n;
}
```

In each of the three functions, the left brace ({) and right brace (}) mark the beginning and end of the statements to be executed. Statements appearing between the braces are known as the *body* of the function.

Execution of a program always begins with the first statement of the main function. In our program, the first statement is

```
cout << "The square of 27 is " << Square(27) << endl;
```

This is an output statement that causes information to be printed on the computer's screen. You will learn how to construct output statements like this later in the chapter. Briefly, this statement prints two items. The first is the message

```
The square of 27 is
```

The second item to be printed is the value obtained by calling (invoking) the Square function, with the value 27 as the number to be squared. As the servant, the Square function performs its task of squaring the number and sending the computed result (729) back to its *caller*, the main function. Now main can continue executing by printing the value 729 and proceeding to its next statement.

In a similar fashion, the second statement in main prints the message

```
and the cube of 27 is
```

and then invokes the Cube function and prints the result, 19683. The complete output produced by executing this program is, therefore,

```
The square of 27 is 729
and the cube of 27 is 19683
```

Both `Square` and `Cube` are examples of *value-returning functions*. A value-returning function returns a single value to its caller. The word `int` at the beginning of the first line of the `Square` function

```
int Square( int n )
```

states that the function returns an integer value.

Now look at the `main` function again. You'll see that the first line of the function is

```
int main()
```

The word `int` indicates that `main` is a value-returning function that should return an integer value. And it does. After printing the square and cube of 27, `main` executes the statement

```
return 0;
```

to return the value 0 to its caller. But who calls the `main` function? The answer is: the computer's operating system.

When you work with C++ programs, the operating system is considered to be the caller of the `main` function. The operating system expects `main` to return a value (the *exit status*) when `main` finishes executing. By convention, a return value of 0 means everything went OK. A return value of anything else (typically 1, 2, ...) means something went wrong. Later in this book we look at situations in which you might want to return a value other than 0 from `main`. For the time being, we always conclude the execution of `main` by returning the value 0.

We have looked briefly at the overall appearance of a C++ program—a collection of one or more functions, including `main`. We have also mentioned what is special about the `main` function—it is a required function, execution begins there, and it returns a value to the operating system. Now it's time to begin looking at the details of the C++ language.

Syntax and Semantics

A programming language is a set of rules, symbols, and special words used to construct a program. There are rules for both **syntax** (grammar) and **semantics** (meaning).

Syntax is a formal set of rules that defines exactly what combinations of letters, numbers, and symbols can be used in a programming language. There is no room for ambiguity in the syntax of a programming language because the computer can't think; it doesn't "know what we mean."

Syntax rules are the blueprints we use to build instructions in a program. They allow us to take the elements of a programming language—the basic building blocks of the language—and assemble them into *constructs*, syntactically correct structures. If our program violates any of the rules of the language—by misspelling a crucial word or leaving out an important comma, for instance—the program is said to have *syntax errors* and cannot compile correctly until we fix them.

Syntax The formal rules governing how valid instructions are written in a programming language.

Semantics The set of rules that determines the meaning of instructions written in a programming language.

Metalanguages

Metalanguage is the word *language* with the prefix *meta-*, which means "beyond" or "more comprehensive." A metalanguage is a language that goes beyond a normal language by allowing us to speak precisely about that language. It is a language for talking about languages.

One of the oldest computer-oriented metalanguages is *Backus-Naur Form* (BNF), which is named for John Backus and Peter Naur, who developed it in 1960. BNF syntax definitions are written out using letters, numbers, and special symbols. For example, an *identifier* (a name for something in a program) in C++ must be at least one letter or underscore (_), which may or may not be followed by additional letters, underscores, or digits. The BNF definition of an identifier in C++ is

```
<Identifier> ::= <Nondigit> | <Nondigit> <NondigitOrDigitSequence>
<NondigitOrDigitSequence> ::= <NondigitOrDigit> | <NondigitOrDigit> <NondigitOrDigitSequence>
<NondigitOrDigit> ::= <Nondigit> | <Digit>
<Nondigit> ::= _ | A | B | C | D | E | F | G | H | I | J | K | L | M | N | O | P | Q | R | S | T | U | V | W | X | Y | Z |
               a | b | c | d | e | f | g | h | i | j | k | l | m | n | o | p | q | r | s | t | u | v | w | x | y | z
<Digit> ::= 0 | 1 | 2 | 3 | 4 | 5 | 6 | 7 | 8 | 9
```

where the symbol ::= is read "is defined as," the symbol | means "or," the symbols < and > are used to enclose words called *nonterminal symbols* (symbols that still need to be defined), and everything else is called a *terminal symbol*.

The first line of the definition reads as follows: "An identifier is defined as either a nondigit or a nondigit followed by a nondigit-or-digit sequence." This line contains nonterminal symbols that must be defined. In the second line, the nonterminal symbol NondigitOrDigitSequence is defined as either a NondigitOrDigit or a NondigitOrDigit followed by another NondigitOrDigitSequence. The self-reference in the definition is a roundabout way of saying that a NondigitOrDigitSequence can be a series of one or more nondigits or digits. The third line defines NondigitOrDigit to be either a Nondigit or a Digit. In the fourth and last lines, we finally encounter terminal symbols, which define Nondigit to be an underscore or any upper- or lowercase letter and Digit as any one of the numeric symbols 0 through 9.

BNF is an extremely simple language, but that simplicity leads to syntax definitions that can be long and difficult to read. In this text, we introduce another metalanguage, called a *syntax template*. Syntax templates show at a glance the form a C++ construct takes.

One final note: Metalanguages only show how to write instructions that the compiler can translate. They do not define what those instructions do (their semantics). Formal languages for defining the semantics of a programming language exist, but they are beyond the scope of this text. Throughout this book, we describe the semantics of C++ in English.

Syntax Templates

In this book, we write the syntax rules for C++ using *syntax templates*. A syntax template is a generic example of the C++ construct being defined. Graphic conventions show which portions are optional and which can be repeated. A boldface word or symbol is a literal word or symbol in the C++ language. A nonboldface word can be replaced by another template. A curly brace is used to indicate a list of items, from which one item can be chosen.

Let's look at an example. This template defines an identifier in C++:

Identifier

The shading indicates a part of the definition that is optional. The three dots (...) mean that the preceding symbol or shaded block can be repeated. Thus, an identifier in C++ must begin with a letter or underscore and is optionally followed by one or more letters, underscores, or digits.

Remember that a word not in boldface type can be replaced with another template. These are the templates for Letter and Digit:

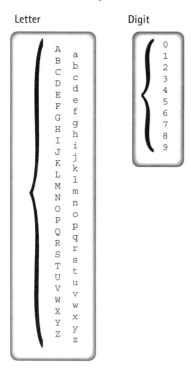

In these templates, the braces again indicate lists of items from which any one item can be chosen. So a letter can be any one of the upper- or lowercase letters, and a digit can be any of the numeric characters 0 through 9.

Now let's look at the syntax template for the C++ `main` function:

MainFunction

```
int main()
{
    Statement
    ⋮
}
```

The `main` function begins with the word `int`, followed by the word `main` and then left and right parentheses. This first line of the function is the *heading*. After the heading, the left brace signals the start of the statements in the function (its body). The shading and the three dots indicate that the function body consists of zero or more statements. (In this diagram we have placed the three dots vertically to suggest that statements usually are arranged vertically, one above the next.) Finally, the right brace indicates the end of the function.

In principle, the syntax template allows the function body to have no statements at all. In practice, however, the body should include a Return statement because the word `int` in the function heading states that `main` returns an integer value. Thus, the shortest C++ program is

```
int main()
{
    return 0;
}
```

As you might guess, this program does absolutely nothing useful when executed!

As we introduce C++ language constructs throughout the book, we use syntax templates to display the proper syntax.

When you finish this chapter, you should know enough about the syntax and semantics of statements in C++ to write simple programs. But before we can write statements, we must look at how names are written in C++ and at some of the elements of a program.

Naming Program Elements: Identifiers

Identifiers are used in C++ to name things— things such as subprograms and places in the computer's memory. Identifiers are made up of letters (A–Z, a–z), digits (0–9), and the underscore character (_), but must begin with a letter or underscore.

> **Identifier** A name associated with a function or data object and used to refer to that function or data object.

Remember that an identifier *must* start with a letter or underscore:

Identifier

(Identifiers beginning with an underscore have special meanings in some C++ systems, so it is best to begin an identifier with a letter.)

Here are some examples of valid identifiers:

```
sum_of_squares  J9  box_22A  GetData  Bin3D4  count
```

And here are some examples of invalid identifiers and the reasons why they are invalid:

Invalid Identifier	Explanation
40Hours	Identifiers cannot begin with a digit.
Get Data	Blanks are not allowed in identifiers.
box-22	The hyphen (–) is a math symbol (minus) in C++.
cost_in_$	Special symbols such as $ are not allowed.
int	The word int is predefined in the C++ language.

Reserved word A word that has special meaning in C++; it cannot be used as a programmer-defined identifier.

The last identifier in the table, int, is an example of a **reserved word**. Reserved words have specific uses in C++; you cannot use them as programmer-defined identifiers. Appendix A lists all of the reserved words in C++.

Using Meaningful, Readable Identifiers

The names we use to refer to things in our programs are totally meaningless to the computer. The computer behaves in the same way whether we call the value 3.14159265 pi or cake, as long as we always call it the same thing. However, it is much easier for somebody to figure out how a program works if we choose names that make sense.

C++ is a *case-sensitive* language. Uppercase letters are different from lowercase letters. The identifiers

```
PRINTTOPPORTION  printtopportion  pRiNtToPpOrTiOn  PrintTopPortion
```

are four distinct names and are not interchangeable in any way. As you can see, the last of these forms is the easiest to read. In this book, we use combinations of uppercase letters, lowercase letters, and underscores in identifiers. We explain our conventions for choosing between uppercase and lowercase as we proceed through this chapter.

Now that we've seen how to write identifiers, we look at some of the things that C++ allows us to name.

Data and Data Types

Where does a program get the data it needs to operate? Data is stored in the computer's memory. Each memory location has a unique address we refer to when we store or retrieve data. The actual address of each location in memory is a binary number in a machine language code. In C++ we use identifiers to name memory locations; the compiler then translates them into binary for us. This is one of the advantages of a high-level programming language: It frees us from having to keep track of the numeric addresses of the memory locations in which our data and instructions are stored. In C++, each piece of data must be of a specific data type. The data type determines how the data is represented in the computer and the kinds of processing the computer can perform on it.

> **Data type** A specific set of data values, along with a set of operations on those values.

Some types of data are used so frequently that C++ defines them for us. Examples of these *standard* (or *built-in*) *types* are int (for working with integer numbers), float (for working with real numbers having decimal points), and char (for working with character data).

Additionally, C++ allows programmers to define their own data types—*programmer-defined* (or *user-defined*) *types*. Beginning in Chapter 10, we show you how to define your own data types.

In this chapter, we focus on two data types—one for representing data consisting of a single character, the other for representing strings of characters. In the next chapter, we examine the numeric types (such as int and float) in detail.

The char Data Type The built-in type char describes data consisting of one alphanumeric character—a letter, a digit, or a special symbol:

```
'A'    'a'    '8'    '2'    '+'    '-'    '$'    '?'    '*'    ' '
```

Each machine uses a particular *character set*, the set of alphanumeric characters it can represent. (See Appendix E for some sample character sets.) Notice that each character is enclosed in single quotes (apostrophes). The C++ compiler needs the quotes to differentiate, say, between the character data '8' and the integer value 8 because the two are stored differently inside the machine. Notice also that the blank, ' ', is a valid character.

You wouldn't want to add the character 'A' to the character 'B' or subtract the character '3' from the character '8', but you might want to compare character values. Each character set has a *collating sequence*, a predefined ordering of all the characters. Although this sequence varies from one character set to another, 'A' always compares less than 'B', 'B' less than 'C', and so forth. And '1' compares less than '2', '2' less than '3', and so on.

The `string` *Data Type*   Whereas a value of type `char` is limited to a single character, a *string* is a sequence of characters, such as a word, name, or sentence, enclosed in double quotes. For example, the following are strings in C++:

```
"Problem Solving"     "C++"      "Programming and "     "     .     "
```

A string must be typed entirely on one line. For example, the string

```
"This string is invalid because it
is typed on more than one line."
```

is not valid because it is split across two lines.

The quotes are not considered to be part of the string but are simply there to distinguish the string from other parts of a C++ program. For example, `"amount"` (in double quotes) is the character string made up of the letters *a, m, o, u, n,* and *t* in that order. On the other hand, `amount` (without the quotes) is an identifier, perhaps the name of a place in memory. The symbols `"12345"` represent a string made up of the characters *1, 2, 3, 4,* and *5* in that order. If we write `12345` without the quotes, it is an integer quantity that can be used in calculations.

A string containing no characters is called the *null string* (or *empty string*). We write the null string using two double quotes with nothing (not even spaces) between them:

```
""
```

The null string is not equivalent to a string of spaces; it is a special string that contains no characters.

To work with string data, this book uses a data type named `string`. This data type is not part of the C++ language (that is, it is not a built-in type). Rather, `string` is a programmer-defined type that is supplied by the C++ *standard library*, a large collection of prewritten functions and data types that any C++ programmer can use. Operations on `string` data include comparing the values of strings, searching a string for a particular character, and joining one string to another. We look at some of these operations later in this chapter and cover additional operations in subsequent chapters.

Naming Elements: Declarations

Identifiers can be used to name both constants and variables. In other words, an identifier can be the name of a memory location whose contents are not allowed to change or it can be the name of a memory location whose contents can change.

How do we tell the computer what an identifier represents? By using a **declaration**, a statement that associates a name (an identifier) with a description of an element in a C++ program (just as a dictionary definition associates a name with a description of the

Declaration A statement that associates an identifier with a data object, a function, or a data type so that the programmer can refer to that item by name.

thing being named). In a declaration, we name an identifier and what it represents. For example, the declaration

```
int empNum;
```

announces that empNum is the name of a variable whose contents are of type int. When we declare a variable, the compiler picks a location in memory to be associated with the identifier and automatically keeps track of it for us.

In C++, each identifier can represent just one thing (except under special circumstances, which we talk about in Chapters 7 and 8). Every identifier you use in a program must be different from all others.

Constants and variables are collectively called *data objects*. Both data objects and the actual instructions in a program are stored in various memory locations. You have seen that a group of instructions—a function—can be given a name. A name also can be associated with a programmer-defined data type.

In C++, you must declare every identifier before it is used. This allows the compiler to verify that the use of the identifier is consistent with what it was declared to be. If you declare an identifier to be a constant and later try to change its value, the compiler detects this inconsistency and issues an error message.

There is a different form of declaration statement for each kind of data object, function, or data type in C++. The forms of declarations for variables and constants are introduced here; others are covered in later chapters.

Variables While a program is executing, different values may be stored in the same memory location at different times. This kind of memory location is called a **variable,** and its content is the *variable value*. The symbolic

> **Variable** A location in memory, referenced by an identifier, that contains a data value that can be changed.

name that we associate with a memory location is the *variable name* or *variable identifier* (see Figure 2-1). In practice, we often refer to the variable name more briefly as the *variable*.

Declaring a variable means specifying both its name and its data type. This tells the compiler to associate a name with a memory location whose contents are of a specific

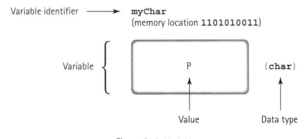

Figure 2–1 *Variable*

type (for example, `char` or `string`). The following statement declares `myChar` to be a variable of type `char`:

```
char myChar;
```

A declaration always ends with a semicolon.

In C++, a variable can contain a data value only of the type specified in its declaration. Thus, the variable `myChar` can contain *only* a `char` value. If the C++ compiler comes across an instruction that tries to store a `float` value into `myChar`, it generates extra instructions to convert the `float` value to the proper type. In Chapter 3, we examine how such type conversions take place.

It is possible to declare several variables in one statement:

```
char letter, middleInitial, ch;
```

Here, all three variables are declared to be `char` variables. Our preference, though, is to declare each variable with a separate statement:

```
char letter;
char middleInitial;
char ch;
```

With this form it is easier, when modifying a program, to add new variables to the list or delete ones you no longer want.

Declaring each variable with a separate statement also allows you to attach comments to the right of each declaration, as we do here:

```
float payRate;      // Employee's pay rate
float hours;        // Hours worked
float wages;        // Wages earned
float total;        // Total company payroll
int   empNum;       // Employee ID number
```

These declarations tell the compiler to reserve memory space for four `float` variables—`payRate`, `hours`, `wages`, and `total`—and one `int` variable, `empNum`. The comments (the words written after the `//` on each line) explain to someone reading the program what each variable represents.

Now that we've seen how to declare variables in C++, let's look at how to declare constants.

Constants All single characters (enclosed in single quotes) and strings (enclosed in double quotes) are constants.

```
'A'    '@'    "Howdy boys"    "Please enter an employee number:"
```

In C++, as in mathematics, a constant is something whose value never changes. When we use the actual value of a constant in a program, we are using a **literal value** (or *literal*).

Literal value Any constant value written in a program.

Named constant (symbolic constant) A location in memory, referenced by an identifier, that contains a data value that cannot be changed.

An alternative to the literal constant is the **named constant** (or **symbolic constant**), which is introduced in a declaration statement. A named constant is just another way of representing a literal value. Instead of using the literal value in an instruction, we give it a name in a declaration statement, then use that name in the instruction. For example, we can write an instruction that prints the title of this book using the literal string `"Programming in C++"`. Or we can declare a named constant called `BOOK_TITLE` that equals the same string and then use the constant name in the instruction. That is, we can use either

```
"Programming in C++"
```

or

```
BOOK_TITLE
```

in the instruction.

Using the literal value of a constant may seem easier than giving it a name and then referring to it by that name. But, in fact, named constants make a program easier to read because they make the meaning of literal constants clearer. Named constants also make it easier to change a program later on.

Here we see some example constant declarations. Notice that the reserved word `const` begins the declaration, and an equal sign (=) appears between the identifier and the literal value.

```
const string STARS = "********";
const char   BLANK = ' ';
const string BOOK_TITLE = "Programming in C++";
const string MESSAGE = "Error condition";
```

As we have done above, many C++ programmers capitalize the entire identifier of a named constant and separate the English words with an underscore. The idea is to let the reader quickly distinguish between variable names and constant names when they appear in the middle of a program.

Capitalization of Identifiers

Programmers often use capitalization as a quick visual clue to what an identifier represents. Different programmers adopt different conventions for using uppercase letters and lowercase letters.

The conventions we use in this book are as follows:

- For variables, we begin with a lowercase letter and capitalize each successive word.

  ```
  lengthInYards    middleInitial    hours
  ```

- Names of programmer-written functions and programmer-defined data types (which we examine later in the book) are capitalized in the same way but they begin with capital letters.

  ```
  CalcPay(payRate, hours, wages)    Cube(27)    MyDataType
  ```

  However, C++ expects every program to have a function named `main`—all in lowercase letters—so we cannot name it `Main`. Nor can we use `Char` for the built-in data type `char`. C++ reserved words use all lowercase letters, as do most of the identifiers declared in the standard library (such as `string`).
- For named constants, we capitalize every letter and use underscores to separate the English words.

  ```
  BOOK_TITLE    OVERTIME    MAX_LENGTH
  ```

C++ does not require this particular style of capitalizing identifiers. You may wish to capitalize in a different fashion, but be consistent throughout your program. It can be confusing or misleading if you use inconsistent capitalization.

Taking Action: Executable Statements

Up to this point, we've looked at ways of declaring data objects in a program. Now we turn our attention to ways of performing operations on data.

Assignment statement A statement that stores the value of an expression into a variable.

Assignment The value of a variable can be set or changed through an **assignment statement**. For example,

```
lastName = "Lincoln";
```

assigns the string value `"Lincoln"` to the variable `lastName` (that is, it stores the sequence of characters "Lincoln" into the memory associated with the variable named `lastName`).

Here's the syntax template for an assignment statement:

AssignmentStatement

> Variable = Expression ;

The semantics (meaning) of the assignment operator (=) is "store"; the value of the **expression** is *stored* into the variable. Any previous value in the variable is destroyed and replaced by the value of the expression.

Expression An arrangement of identifiers, literals, and operators that can be evaluated to compute a value of a given type.

Evaluate To compute a new value by performing a specified set of operations on given values.

Only one variable can be on the left-hand side of an assignment statement. An assignment statement is *not* like a math equation $(x + y = z + 4)$; the expression (what is on the right-hand side of the assignment operator) is **evaluated,** and the resulting value is stored into the single variable on the left of the assignment operator. A variable keeps its assigned value until another statement stores a new value into it.

Given the declarations

```
string firstName;
string middleName;
string lastName;
string title;
char    middleInitial;
char    letter;
```

the following assignment statements are valid:

```
firstName = "Abraham";
middleName = firstName;
middleName = "";
lastName = "Lincoln";
title = "President";
middleInitial = ' ';
letter = middleInitial;
```

However, these assignments are not valid:

Invalid Assignment Statement	Reason
`middleInitial = "A.";`	`middleInitial` is of type `char`; `"A."` is a string.
`letter = firstName;`	`letter` is of type `char`; `firstName` is of type string.
`firstName = Thomas;`	`Thomas` is an undeclared identifier.
`"Edison" = lastName;`	Only a variable can appear to the left of =.
`lastName = ;`	The expression to the right of = is missing.

String Expressions   Although we can't perform arithmetic on strings, the `string` data type provides a special string operation, called *concatenation*, that uses the + operator. The result of concatenating (joining) two strings is a new string containing the characters from both strings. For example, given the statements

```
string bookTitle;
string phrase1;
string phrase2;

phrase1 = "Programming and ";
phrase2 = "Problem Solving";
```

we could write

```
bookTitle = phrase1 + phrase2;
```

This statement retrieves the value of `phrase1` from memory and concatenates the value of `phrase2` to form a new, temporary string containing the characters

```
"Programming and Problem Solving"
```

This temporary string (which is of type `string`) is then assigned to (stored into) `book-Title`.

The order of the strings in the expression determines how they appear in the resulting string. If we instead write

```
bookTitle = phrase2 + phrase1;
```

then `bookTitle` contains

```
"Problem SolvingProgramming and "
```

Concatenation works with named `string` constants, literal strings, and `char` data as well as with `string` variables. The only restriction is that at least one of the operands of the + operator *must* be a `string` variable or named constant (so you cannot use expressions like "Hi" + "there" or 'A' + 'B'). For example, if we have declared the following constants:

```
const string WORD1 = "rogramming";
const string WORD3 = "Solving";
const string WORD5 = "C++";
```

then we could write the following assignment statement:

```
bookTitle = 'P' + WORD1 + " and Problem " + WORD3 + " with " + WORD5;
```

As a result, `bookTitle` contains the string

```
"Programming and Problem Solving with C++"
```

The preceding example demonstrates how we can combine identifiers, `char` data, and literal strings in a concatenation expression. Of course, if we simply want to assign the complete string to `bookTitle`, we can do so directly:

```
bookTitle = "Programming and Problem Solving with C++";
```

But occasionally we encounter a situation in which we want to add some characters to an existing string value. Suppose that `bookTitle` already contains `"Programming and Problem Solving"` and that we wish to complete the title. We could use a statement of the form

```
bookTitle = bookTitle + " with C++";
```

Such a statement retrieves the value of `bookTitle` from memory, concatenates the string `" with C++"` to form a new string, and then stores the new string back into `bookTitle`. The new string replaces the old value of `bookTitle` (which is destroyed).

Keep in mind that concatenation works only with values of type `string`. Even though an arithmetic plus sign is used for the operation, we cannot concatenate values of numeric data types, such as `int` and `float`, with strings.

If you are using pre–standard C++ (any version of C++ prior to the ISO/ANSI standard) and your standard library does not provide the `string` type, see Section D.1 of Appendix D for a discussion of how to proceed.

Output In C++ we write out the values of variables and expressions by using a special variable named `cout` (pronounced "see-out") along with the *insertion operator* (<<):

```
cout << "Hello";
```

This statement displays the characters `Hello` on the *standard output device*, usually the video display screen.

The variable `cout` is predefined in C++ systems to denote an *output stream*. You can think of an output stream as an endless sequence of characters going to an output device. In the case of `cout`, the output stream goes to the standard output device.

The insertion operator << (often pronounced as "put to") takes two operands. Its left-hand operand is a stream expression (in the simplest case, just a stream variable such as `cout`). Its right-hand operand is an expression, which could be as simple as a literal string:

```
cout << "The title is ";
cout << bookTitle + ", 2nd Edition";
```

The insertion operator converts its right-hand operand to a sequence of characters and inserts them into (or, more precisely, appends them to) the output stream. Notice how the << points in the direction the data is going—*from* the expression written on the right *to* the output stream on the left.

You can use the << operator several times in a single output statement. Each occurrence appends the next data item to the output stream. For example, we can write the preceding two output statements as

```
cout << "The title is " << bookTitle + ", 2nd Edition";
```

If bookTitle contains "American History", both versions produce the same output:

```
The title is American History, 2nd Edition
```

The following output statements yield the output shown. These examples assume that the char variable ch contains the value '2', the string variable firstName contains "Marie", and the string variable lastName contains "Curie".

Statement	What Is Printed (□means blank)
cout << ch;	2
cout << "ch = " << ch;	ch□=□2
cout << firstName + " " + lastName;	Marie□Curie
cout << firstName << lastName;	MarieCurie
cout << firstName << ' ' << lastName;	Marie□Curie
cout << "ERROR MESSAGE";	ERROR□MESSAGE
cout << "Error=" << ch;	Error=2

An output statement prints literal strings exactly as they appear. To let the computer know that you want to print a literal string—not a named constant or variable—you must remember to use double quotes to enclose the string. If you don't put quotes around a string, you'll probably get an error message (such as "UNDECLARED IDENTIFIER") from the C++ compiler. If you want to print a string that includes a double quote, you must type a backslash (\) character and a double quote, with no space between them. For example, to print the characters

```
Al "Butch" Jones
```

the output statement looks like this:

```
cout << "Al \"Butch\" Jones";
```

Normally, successive output statements cause the output to continue along the same line of the display screen. The sequence

```
cout << "Hi";
cout << "there";
```

writes the following to the screen, all on the same line:

```
Hithere
```

To print the two words on separate lines, we can do this:

```
cout << "Hi" << endl;
cout << "there" << endl;
```

The output from these statements is

```
Hi
there
```

The identifier endl (meaning "end line") is a special C++ feature called a *manipulator*. We discuss manipulators in the next chapter. For now, the important thing to note is that endl lets you finish an output line and go on to the next line whenever you wish.

Beyond Minimalism: Adding Comments to a Program

All you need to create a working program is the correct combination of declarations and executable statements. The compiler ignores comments, but they are of enormous help to anyone who must read the program. Comments can appear anywhere in a program except in the middle of an identifier, a reserved word, or a literal constant.

C++ comments come in two forms. The first is any sequence of characters enclosed by the /* */ pair. The compiler ignores anything within the pair. Here's an example:

```
string idNumber;    /* Identification number of the aircraft */
```

The second, and more common, form begins with two slashes (//) and extends to the end of that line of the program:

```
string idNumber;    // Identification number of the aircraft
```

The compiler ignores anything after the two slashes.

Writing fully commented programs is good programming style. A comment should appear at the beginning of a program to explain what the program does:

```
// This program computes the weight and balance of a Beechcraft
// Starship-1 airplane, given the amount of fuel, number of
// passengers, and weight of luggage in fore and aft storage.
// It assumes that there are two pilots and a standard complement
// of equipment, and that passengers weigh 170 pounds each
```

Another good place for comments is in constant and variable declarations, where the comments explain how each identifier is used. In addition, comments should introduce each major step in a long program and should explain anything that is unusual or difficult to read (for example, a lengthy formula).

It is important to make your comments concise and to arrange them in the program so that they are easy to see and it is clear what they refer to. If comments are too long or crowd the statements in the program, they make the program more difficult to read—just the opposite of what you intended!

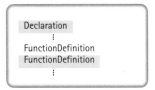

Program Construction

We have looked at basic elements of C++ programs: identifiers, declarations, variables, constants, expressions, statements, and comments. Now let's see how to collect these elements into a program. As you saw earlier, C++ programs are made up of functions, one of which must be named `main`. A program also can have declarations that lie outside of any function. The syntax template for a program looks like this:

Program

```
Declaration
      ⋮
FunctionDefinition
FunctionDefinition
      ⋮
```

A function definition consists of the function heading and its body, which is delimited by left and right braces:

FunctionDefinition

```
Heading
{
    Statement
        ⋮
}
```

Here's an example of a program with just one function, the `main` function:

```
//***********************************************************************
// PrintName program
// This program prints a name in two different formats
```

```
//**********************************************************************
#include <iostream>
#include <string>

using namespace std;

const string FIRST = "Herman";    // Person's first name
const string LAST = "Smith";      // Person's last name
const char   MIDDLE = 'G';        // Person's middle initial

int main()
{
    string firstLast;     // Name in first-last format
    string lastFirst;     // Name in last-first format

    firstLast = FIRST + " " + LAST;
    cout << "Name in first-last format is " << firstLast << endl;

    lastFirst = LAST + ", " + FIRST + ", ";
    cout << "Name in last-first-initial format is ";
    cout << lastFirst << MIDDLE << '.' << endl;

    return 0;
}
```

The program begins with a comment that explains what the program does. Immediately after the comment, the following lines appear:

```
#include <iostream>
#include <string>

using namespace std;
```

The #include lines instruct the C++ system to insert into our program the contents of the files named iostream and string. The first file contains information that C++ needs in order to output values to a stream such as cout. The second file contains information about the programmer-defined data type string. We discuss the purpose of these #include lines and the using statement a little later in the chapter.

Next come declarations of the constants FIRST, LAST, and MIDDLE. Comments explain how they are used. The rest of the program is the function definition for our main function. The first line is the function heading: the reserved word int, the name of the function, and then opening and closing parentheses. (The parentheses inform the compiler that main is the name of a function, not a variable or named constant.) The body of the function includes the declarations of two variables, firstLast and last-First, followed by a list of executable statements. Our main function finishes by returning 0 as the function value.

Notice how we use spacing in the program to make it easy to read. We use blank lines to separate statements into related groups, and we indent the body of the `main` function. The compiler doesn't require us to format the program this way; we do so only to make it more readable.

Blocks (Compound Statements)

The body of a function is an example of a *block* (or *compound statement*). This is the syntax template for a block:

Block

A block is just a sequence of zero or more statements enclosed (delimited) by a { } pair. Thus, we can redefine a function definition as a Heading followed by a Block. In later chapters we define the syntax of Heading in detail. In the case of the `main` function, Heading is simply

```
int main()
```

Here is the syntax template for a statement, limited to the C++ statements discussed in this chapter:

Statement

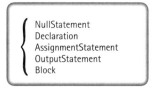

A statement can be empty (the *null statement*). The null statement is just a semicolon (;). It does absolutely nothing at execution time; execution just proceeds to the next statement. It is not used often.

As the syntax template shows, a statement also can be a declaration, an executable statement, or even a block. The latter means that you can use an entire block wherever a single statement is allowed. In later chapters in which we introduce the syntax for branching and looping structures, this fact is very important.

We use blocks often, especially as parts of other statements. Leaving out a { } pair can dramatically change the meaning as well as the execution of a program. This is why we always indent the statements inside a block—the indentation makes a block easy to spot in a long, complicated program.

Notice in the syntax templates for Block and Statement that there is no mention of semicolons. Yet the PrintName program contains many semicolons. It turns out that each declaration, assignment statement, and output statement is defined separately to end with a semicolon. However, the syntax template for Block shows no semicolon after the right brace. The rule for using semicolons in C++, then, is quite simple: Terminate each statement *except* a compound statement (block) with a semicolon.

One more thing about blocks and statements: According to the syntax template for a statement, a declaration is officially considered to be a statement. A declaration, therefore, can appear wherever an executable statement can. In a block, we can mix declarations and executable statements if we wish:

```
{
    char ch;
    ch = 'A';
    cout << ch;
    string str;
    str = "Hello";
    cout << str;
}
```

It's far more common, though, for programmers to group the declarations together before the start of the executable statements:

```
{
    char    ch;
    string str;

    ch = 'A';
    cout << ch;
    str = "Hello";
    cout << str;
}
```

The C++ Preprocessor

Imagine that you are the C++ compiler. You are presented with the following program. You are to check it for syntax errors and, if there are none, translate it into machine language.

```
int main()
{
```

```
        cout << "Happy Birthday" << endl;
        return 0;
}
```

You, the compiler, recognize the identifier int as a C++ reserved word and the identifier main as the name of a required function. But what about the identifiers cout and endl? The programmer has not declared them as variables or named constants, and they are not reserved words. You have no choice but to issue an error message and give up.

To fix this program, the first thing we must do is insert a line near the top that says

```
#include <iostream>
```

just as we did in the PrintName program (as well as in the sample program at the beginning of this chapter).

The line says to insert the contents of a file named iostream into the program. This file contains declarations of cout, endl, and other items needed to perform stream input and output. The #include line is not handled by the C++ compiler but by a program known as the *preprocessor*.

The preprocessor concept is fundamental to C++. The preprocessor is a program that acts as a filter during the compilation phase. Your source program passes through the preprocessor on its way to the compiler (see Figure 2-2).

A line beginning with a pound sign (#) is not considered to be a C++ language statement (and thus is not terminated by a semicolon). It is called a *preprocessor directive*. The preprocessor expands an #include directive by physically inserting the contents of the named file into your source program. A file whose name appears in an #include directive is called a *header file*. Header files contain constant, variable, data type, and function declarations needed by a program.

In the directives

```
#include <iostream>
#include <string>
```

the angle brackets < > are required. They tell the preprocessor to look for the files in the standard *include directory*—a location in the computer system that contains all the header files that are related to the C++ standard library. The file iostream contains declarations of input/output facilities, and the file string contains declarations about the string data type. In Chapter 3, we make use of standard header files other than iostream and string.

Figure 2-2 *C++ Preprocessor*

In the C language and in pre-standard C++, the standard header files end in the suffix .h (for example, iostream.h), where the *h* suggests "header file." In ISO/ANSI C++, the standard header files no longer use the .h suffix.

An Introduction to Namespaces

In our Happy Birthday program, even if we add the preprocessor directive #include <iostream>, the program will not compile. The compiler *still* doesn't recognize the identifiers cout and endl. The problem is that the header file iostream (and, in fact, every standard header file) declares all of its identifiers to be in a *namespace* called std:

```
namespace std
{
    ⋮   ←   Declarations of variables, data types, and so forth
}
```

An identifier declared within a namespace block can be accessed directly only by statements within that block. To access an identifier that is "hidden" inside a namespace, the programmer has several options. We describe two options here. Chapter 8 describes namespaces in more detail.

The first option is to use a *qualified name* for the identifier. A qualified name consists of the name of the namespace, then the :: operator (the *scope resolution operator*), and then the desired identifier:

```
std::cout
```

With this approach, our program looks like the following:

```
#include <iostream>

int main()
{
    std::cout << "Happy Birthday" << std::endl;
    return 0;
}
```

Notice that both cout and endl must be qualified.

The second option is to use a statement called a *using directive:*

```
using namespace std;
```

When we place this statement near the top of the program before the main function, we make *all* the identifiers in the std namespace accessible to our program without having to qualify them:

```
#include <iostream>
```

```
using namespace std;

int main()
{
    cout << "Happy Birthday" << endl;
    return 0;
}
```

This second option is the one we used in the PrintName program and the sample program at the beginning of the chapter. In many of the following chapters, we continue to use this method. However, in Chapter 8 we discuss why it is not advisable to use the method in large programs.

If you are using a pre-standard C++ compiler that does not recognize namespaces and the newer header files (iostream, string, and so forth), you should turn to Section D.2 of Appendix D for a discussion of incompatibilities.

2.3 More About Output

We can control both the horizontal and vertical spacing of our output to make it more appealing (and understandable). Let's look first at vertical spacing.

Creating Blank Lines

We control vertical spacing by using the endl manipulator in an output statement. You have seen that a sequence of output statements continues to write characters across the current line until an endl terminates the line. Here are some examples:

Statements	Output Produced*
cout << "Hi there, "; cout << "Lois Lane. " << endl; cout << "Have you seen "; cout << "Clark Kent?" << endl;	Hi there, Lois Lane. Have you seen Clark Kent?
cout << "Hi there, " << endl; cout << "Lois Lane. " << endl; cout << "Have you seen " << endl; cout << "Clark Kent?" << endl;	Hi there, Lois Lane. Have you seen Clark Kent?
cout << "Hi there, " << endl; cout << "Lois Lane. "; cout << "Have you seen " << endl; cout << "Clark Kent?" << endl;	Hi there, Lois Lane. Have you seen Clark Kent?

*The output lines are shown next to the output statement that ends each of them. There are no blank lines in the actual output from those statements.

What do you think the following statements print out?

```
cout << "Hi there, " << endl;
cout << endl;
cout << "Lois Lane." << endl;
```

The first output statement causes the words *Hi there,* to be printed; the `endl` causes the screen cursor to go to the next line. The next statement prints nothing but goes on to the next line. The third statement prints the words *Lois Lane.* and terminates the line. The resulting output is the three lines

```
Hi there,

Lois Lane.
```

Whenever you use an `endl` immediately after another `endl`, a blank line is produced. As you might guess, three consecutive uses of `endl` produce two blank lines, four consecutive uses produce three blank lines, and so forth.

Note that we have a great deal of flexibility in how we write an output statement in a C++ program. We could combine the three preceding statements into two statements:

```
cout << "Hi there, " << endl << endl;
cout << "Lois Lane." << endl;
```

In fact, we could do it all in one statement. One possibility is

```
cout << "Hi there, " << endl << endl << "Lois Lane." << endl;
```

Here's another:

```
cout << "Hi there, " << endl << endl
     << "Lois Lane." << endl;
```

The last example shows that you can spread a single C++ statement onto more than one line of the program. The compiler treats the semicolon, not the physical end of a line, as the end of a statement.

Inserting Blanks Within a Line

To control the horizontal spacing of the output, one technique is to send extra blank characters to the output stream. (Remember that the blank character, generated by pressing the spacebar on a keyboard, is a perfectly valid character in C++.)

For example, to produce this output:

```
*    *    *    *    *    *    *    *    *

*    *    *    *    *    *    *    *    *    *

*    *    *    *    *    *    *    *    *
```

you would use these statements:

```
cout << "   *    *    *    *    *    *    *    *    *" << endl << endl;
cout << " *    *    *    *    *    *    *    *    *" << endl << endl;
cout << "   *    *    *    *    *    *    *    *" << endl;
```

All of the blanks and asterisks are enclosed in double quotes, so they print literally as they are written in the program. The extra endl manipulators give you the blank lines between the rows of asterisks.

If you want blanks to be printed, you *must* enclose them in quotes. The statement

```
cout << '*' <<                              '*';
```

produces the output

```
* *
```

Despite all of the blanks we included in the output statement, the asterisks print side by side because the blanks are not enclosed by quotes.

Programming Example

Contest Letter

Problem   You've taken a job with a company that is running a promotional contest. They want you to write a program to print a personalized form letter for each of the contestants. As a first effort, they want to get the printing of the letter straight for just one name. Later on, they plan to have you extend the program to read a mailing list file, so the output should use variables in which the name appears in the letter.

Output   A form letter with a name inserted at the appropriate points so that it appears to be a personal letter.

Discussion   The marketing department for the company has written the letter already. Your job is to write a program that prints it out. The majority of the letter must be entered verbatim into a series of output statements, with a person's name inserted at the appropriate places.

In some places the letter calls for printing the full name, in others it uses a title (such as Mr. or Mrs.), and in others it uses just the first name. Because you plan to eventually use a data file that provides each name in four parts (title, first name, middle initial, last name), you decide that this preliminary program should start with a set of named `string` constants containing the four parts of a name. The program can then use concatenation expressions to form `string` variables in the different formats required by the letter. In that way, all the name strings can be created before the output statements are executed.

The form letter requires the name in four formats: the full name with the title, the last name preceded by the title, the first name alone, and the first and last names without the title or middle initial. Here is the algorithmic solution:

Define Constants

```
TITLE = "Dr."
FIRST_NAME = "Margaret"
MIDDLE_INITIAL = "H"
LAST_NAME = "Sklaznick"
```

Create First Name with Blank

```
Set first = FIRST_NAME + " "
```

Create Full Name

```
Set fullName = TITLE + " " + first + MIDDLE_INITIAL
Set fullName = fullName + ". " + LAST_NAME
```

Create First and Last Name

Set firstLast = first + LAST_NAME

Create Title and Last Name

Set titleLast = TITLE + " " + LAST_NAME

Print the Form Letter

Series of output statements containing the text of the letter
with the names inserted in the appropriate places

From the algorithm we can create tables of constants and variables that help us write the declarations in the program.

Constants

Name	Value	Description
TITLE	"Dr."	Salutary title for the name
FIRST_NAME	"Margaret"	First name of addressee
MIDDLE_INITIAL	"H"	Middle initial of addressee
LAST_NAME	"Sklaznick"	Last name of addressee

Variables

Name	Data Type	Description
first	string	Holds the first name plus a blank
fullName	string	Complete name, including title
firstLast	string	First name and last name
titleLast	string	Title followed by the last name

Now we're ready to write the program. Let's call it FormLetter. We can take the declarations from the tables and create the executable statements from the algorithm and the draft of the letter. We also include comments as necessary.

(The following program is written in ISO/ANSI standard C++. If you are working with pre-standard C++, see the alternate version of the program in the PRE_STD directory of the program disk, available at the publisher's Web site, www.jbpub.com/disks.)

```cpp
//************************************************************************
// FormLetter program
// This program prints a form letter for a promotional contest.
// It uses the four parts of a name to build name strings in four
// different formats to be used in personalizing the letter
//************************************************************************
#include <iostream>
#include <string>

using namespace std;

const string TITLE = "Dr.";              // Salutary title
const string FIRST_NAME = "Margaret";    // First name of addressee
const string MIDDLE_INITIAL = "H";       // Middle initial
const string LAST_NAME = "Sklaznick";    // Last name of addressee

int main()
{
    string first;       // Holds the first name plus a blank
    string fullName;    // Complete name, including title
    string firstLast;   // First name and last name
    string titleLast;   // Title followed by the last name

    // Create first name with blank

    first = FIRST_NAME + " ";

    // Create full name

    fullName = TITLE + " " + first + MIDDLE_INITIAL;
    fullName = fullName + ". " + LAST_NAME;

    // Create first and last name

    firstLast = first + LAST_NAME;

    // Create title and last name

    titleLast = TITLE + " " + LAST_NAME;

    // Print the form letter

    cout << fullName << " is a GRAND PRIZE WINNER!!!!!!" << endl
         << endl;
```

```
cout << "Dear " << titleLast << "," << endl << endl;
cout << "Yes it's true! " << firstLast << " has won our"
     << endl;
cout << "GRAND PRIZE — your choice of a 42-INCH* COLOR"
     << endl;
cout << "TELEVISION or a FREE WEEKEND IN NEW YORK CITY.**"
     << endl;
cout << "All that you have to do to collect your prize is"
     << endl;
cout << "attend one of our fun-filled all-day presentations"
     << endl;
cout << "on the benefits of owning a timeshare condominium"
     << endl;
cout << "trailer at the Happy Acres Mobile Campground in"
     << endl;
cout << "beautiful Panhard, Texas! Now " << first << "I realize"
     << endl;
cout << "that the three-hour drive from the nearest airport"
     << endl;
cout << "to Panhard may seem daunting at first, but isn't"
     << endl;
cout << "it worth a little extra effort to receive such a"
     << endl;
cout << "FABULOUS PRIZE? So why wait? Give us a call right"
     << endl;
cout << "now to schedule your visit and collect your" << endl;
cout << "GRAND PRIZE!" << endl << endl;
cout << "Most Sincerely," << endl << endl;
cout << "Argyle M. Sneeze" << endl << endl << endl << endl;
cout << "* Measured around the circumference of the packing"
     << endl;
cout << "crate. ** Includes air fare and hotel accommodations."
     << endl;
cout << "Departure from Nome, Alaska; surcharge applies to"
     << endl;
cout << "other departure airports. Accommodations within"
     << endl;
cout << "driving distance of New York City at the Cheap-O-Tel"
     << endl;
cout << "in Plattsburgh, NY." << endl;
return 0;
}
```

The output from the program is

```
Dr. Margaret H. Sklaznick is a GRAND PRIZE WINNER!!!!!!

Dear Dr. Sklaznick,

Yes it's true! Margaret Sklaznick has won our
GRAND PRIZE — your choice of a 42-INCH* COLOR
TELEVISION or a FREE WEEKEND IN NEW YORK CITY.**
All that you have to do to collect your prize is
attend one of our fun-filled all-day presentations
on the benefits of owning a timeshare condominium
trailer at the Happy Acres Mobile Campground in
beautiful Panhard, Texas! Now Margaret I realize
that the three-hour drive from the nearest airport
to Panhard may seem daunting at first, but isn't
it worth a little extra effort to receive such a
FABULOUS PRIZE? So why wait? Give us a call right
now to schedule your visit and collect your
GRAND PRIZE!

Most Sincerely,

Argyle M. Sneeze



* Measured around the circumference of the packing
crate. ** Includes air fare and hotel accommodations.
Departure from Nome, Alaska; surcharge applies to
other departure airports. Accommodations within
driving distance of New York City at the Cheap-O-Tel
in Plattsburgh, NY.
```

Testing and Debugging

1. Every identifier that isn't a C++ reserved word must be declared. If you use a name that hasn't been declared—either by your own declaration statements or by including a header file—you get an error message.

2. If you try to declare an identifier that is the same as a reserved word in C++, you get an error message from the compiler. See Appendix A for a list of reserved words.

3. C++ is a case-sensitive language. Two identifiers that are capitalized differently are treated as two different identifiers. The word `main` and all C++ reserved words use only lowercase letters.

4. To use identifiers from the standard library, such as `cout` and `string`, you must either (a) give a qualified name such as `std::cout` or (b) put a `using` directive near the top of your program:

```
using namespace std;
```

5. Check for mismatched quotes in `char` and string literals. Each `char` literal begins and ends with an apostrophe (single quote). Each string literal begins and ends with a double quote.

6. Be sure to use only the apostrophe (') to enclose `char` literals. Most keyboards also have a reverse apostrophe (`), which is easily confused with the apostrophe. If you use the reverse apostrophe, the compiler issues an error message.

7. To use a double quote within a literal string, use the two symbols \" in a row. If you use just a double quote, it ends the string, and the compiler then sees the remainder of the string as an error.

8. In an assignment statement, be sure that the identifier to the left of = is a variable and not a named constant.

9. In assigning a value to a `string` variable, the expression to the right of = must be a `string` expression, a literal string, or a `char`.

10. In a concatenation expression, at least one of the two operands of + must be of type `string`. For example, the operands cannot both be literal strings or `char` values.*

11. Make sure your statements end in semicolons (except compound statements, which do not have a semicolon after the right brace).

---

*The invalid concatenation expression `"Hi" + "there"` results in a syntax error message such as "INVALID POINTER ADDITION." This can be confusing, especially because the topic of pointers is not covered in this book.

Summary

In this text, we write the syntax (grammar) rules of C++ statements using syntax templates. We describe the semantics (meaning) of C++ statements in English.

Identifiers are used in C++ to name things. Some identifiers, called reserved words, have predefined meanings in the language; others are created by the programmer. The identifiers you invent are restricted to those *not* reserved by the C++ language. Reserved words are listed in Appendix A.

Identifiers are associated with memory locations by declarations. A declaration may give a name to a location whose value does not change (a constant) or to one whose value can change (a variable). Every constant and variable has an associated data type. C++ provides many built-in data types, the most common of which are int, float, and char. Additionally, C++ permits programmer-defined types such as the string type from the standard library.

The assignment operator is used to change the value of a variable by assigning it the value of an expression. At execution time, the expression is evaluated and the result is stored into the variable. With the string type, the plus sign (+) is an operator that concatenates two strings. A string expression can concatenate any number of strings to form a new string value.

Program output is accomplished by means of the output stream variable cout, along with the insertion operator (<<). Each insertion operation sends output data to the standard output device. When an endl manipulator appears instead of a data item, the computer terminates the current output line and goes on to the next line.

Output should be clear, understandable, and neatly arranged. Messages in the output should describe the significance of values. Blank lines (produced by successive uses of the endl manipulator) and blank spaces within lines help to organize the output and improve its appearance.

A C++ program is a collection of one or more function definitions (and optionally some declarations outside of any function). One of the functions *must* be named main. Execution of a program always begins with the main function. Collectively, the functions all cooperate to produce the desired results.

Quick Check

The Quick Check is intended to help you decide if you've met the goals set forth at the beginning of each chapter. If you understand the material in the chapter, the answer to each question should be fairly obvious. After reading a question, check your response against the answers listed at the end of the Quick Check. If you don't know an answer or don't understand the answer that's provided, turn to the page(s) listed at the end of the question to review the material.

1. Every C++ program consists of at least how many functions? (p. 28)
2. Use the following syntax template to decide whether your last name is a valid C++ identifier. (pp. 30–31)

Identifier

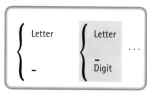

3. Write a C++ constant declaration that gives the name ZED to the value 'Z'. (pp. 37)
4. Which of the following words are reserved words in C++? (*Hint:* Look in Appendix A.)

```
const   pi   float   integer   sqrt
```

(pp. 31–32)
5. Declare a char variable named letter and a string variable named street. (pp. 35–36)
6. Assign the value "Elm" to the string variable street. (pp. 38–39)
7. Write an output statement to print out the title of this book (*Programming in C++*). (pp. 41–43)
8. What does the following code segment print out?

```
string str;

str = "Abraham";
cout << "The answer is " << str + "Lincoln" << endl;
```

(pp. 40–43)
9. The following program code is incorrect. Rewrite it, using correct syntax for the comment.

```
string address;   / Employee's street address,
                  / including apartment
```

(pp. 43–44)
10. Fill in the blanks in this program.

```
#include _____

#include _____

using _____

const string TITLE = "Mr";    // First part of salutary title
```

```
int _____()

_____

    string guest1;    // First guest

    string guest2;    // Second guest

    guest1 _____ TITLE + ". Jones";

    guest2 _____ TITLE + "s. Smith";

    _____ << "The guests in attendance were" _____ endl;

    _____ << guest1 << " and ";

    _____ << guest2 _____ endl;

    return _____;

_____
```

(pp. 44–50)

11. Show precisely the output produced by running the program in Question 10 above.
12. If you want to print the word *Hello* on one line and then print a blank line, how many consecutive `endl` manipulators should you insert after the output of `"Hello"`? (pp. 50–52)

Answers   1. A program must have at least one function—the `main` function.
2. Unless your last name is hyphenated, it probably is a valid C++ identifier.
3. `const char ZED = 'Z';`   4. `const, float`
5. `char letter;`
   `string street;`
6. `street = "Elm";`
7. `cout << "Programming in C++" << endl;`
8. The answer is AbrahamLincoln
9. `string address;   // Employee's street address,`
   `                  // including apartment`

   or

   `string address;   /* Employee's street address, */`
   `                  /* including apartment       */`

10.
```
#include <iostream>
#include <string>

using namespace std;

const string TITLE = "Mr";    // First part of salutary title

int main()
{
    string guest1;    // First guest
    string guest2;    // Second guest

    guest1 = TITLE + ". Jones";
    guest2 = TITLE + "s. Smith";
    cout << "The guests in attendance were" << endl;
    cout << guest1 << " and ";
    cout << guest2 << endl;
    return 0;
}
```

11. The guests in attendance were
    Mr. Jones and Mrs. Smith

12. Two consecutive endl manipulators are necessary.

Exam Preparation Exercises

1. Mark the following identifiers either valid or invalid.

		Valid	Invalid
a.	item#1	_____	_____
b.	data	_____	_____
c.	y	_____	_____
d.	3Set	_____	_____
e.	PAY_DAY	_____	_____
f.	bin-2	_____	_____
g.	num5	_____	_____
h.	Sq Ft	_____	_____

2. Given these four syntax templates:

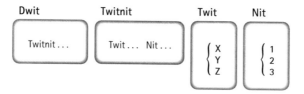

mark the following "Dwits" either valid or invalid.

		Valid	Invalid
a.	XYZ	_____	_____
b.	123	_____	_____
c.	X1	_____	_____
d.	23Y	_____	_____
e.	XY12	_____	_____
f.	Y2Y	_____	_____
g.	ZY2	_____	_____
h.	XY23X1	_____	_____

3. Match each of the following terms with the correct definition (1 through 15) given below. There is only one correct definition for each term.

_____ a. program   _____ g. variable
_____ b. algorithm   _____ h. constant
_____ c. compiler   _____ i. memory
_____ d. identifier   _____ j. syntax
_____ e. compilation phase   _____ k. semantics
_____ f. execution phase   _____ l. block

(1) A symbolic name made up of letters, digits, and underscores but not beginning with a digit
(2) A place in memory where a data value that cannot be changed is stored
(3) A program that takes a program written in a high-level language and translates it into machine code
(4) An input device
(5) The time spent planning a program
(6) Grammar rules
(7) A sequence of statements enclosed by braces
(8) Meaning
(9) A program that translates machine language instructions into C++ code
(10) When the machine code version of a program is being run
(11) A place in memory where a data value that can be changed is stored
(12) When a program in a high-level language is converted into machine code
(13) A part of the computer that can hold both program and data
(14) A step-by-step procedure for solving a problem in a finite amount of time
(15) A sequence of instructions that enables a computer to perform a particular task

4. Which of the following are reserved words and which are programmer-defined identifiers?

		Reserved	Programmer-Defined
a.	char	_____	_____
b.	sort	_____	_____
c.	INT	_____	_____
d.	long	_____	_____
e.	Float	_____	_____

5. Reserved words can be used as variable names. (True or False?)
6. In a C++ program consisting of just one function, that function can be named either `main` or `Main`. (True or False?)
7. If `s1` and `s2` are `string` variables containing `"blue"` and `"bird"`, respectively, what output does each of the following statements produce?
   a. `cout << "s1 = " << s1 << "s2 = " << s2 << endl;`
   b. `cout << "Result:" << s1 + s2 << endl;`
   c. `cout << "Result:  " << s1 + s2 << endl;`
   d. `cout << "Result:  " << s1 << ' ' << s2 << endl;`
8. Show precisely what is output by the following statement.

```
cout << "A rolling" << endl
     << "stone" << endl << endl
     << "gathers" << endl
     << endl << endl << endl << "no"
     << "moss" << endl;
```

9. How many characters can be stored into a variable of type `char`?
10. How many characters are in the null string?
11. A variable of type `string` can be assigned to a variable of type `char`. (True or False?)
12. A literal string can be assigned to a variable of type `string`. (True or False?)
13. What is the difference between the literal string `"computer"` and the identifier `computer`?
14. What is output by the following code segment? (All variables are of type `string`.)

```
street = "Elm St.";
address = "1425B";
city = "Amaryllis";
state = "Iowa";
firstLine = address + ' ' + street;
cout << firstLine << endl;
cout << city;
cout << ", " << state << endl;
```

15. Identify the syntax errors in the following program.

```
// This program is full of errors
#include <iostream

constant string FIRST : Martin";
constant string MID : "Luther;
constant string LAST : King
```

```
int main
{
    string name;
    character initial;

    name = Martin + Luther + King;
    initial = MID;
    LAST = "King Jr.";
    count << 'Name = ' << name << endl;
    cout << mid
    cout << endl;
```

16. In the FormLetter program, explain what takes place in each of the two statements that assign values to the `string` variable `fullName`.

Programming Warm-up Exercises

1. Write an output statement that prints your name.
2. Write three consecutive output statements that print the following three lines:

```
The moon
is
blue.
```

3. Write declaration statements to declare three variables of type `string` and two variables of type `char`. The `string` variables should be named `make`, `model`, and `color`. The `char` variables should be named `plateType` and `classification`.
4. Write a series of output statements that print out the values in the variables declared in Exercise 3. The values should each appear on a separate line, with a blank line between the `string` and `char` values. Each value should be preceded by an identifying message on the same line.
5. Change the PrintName program (pages 44–45) so that it also prints the name in the format

   First-name Middle-initial. Last-name

   Make `MIDDLE` a `string` constant rather than a `char` constant. Define a new `string` variable to hold the name in the new format and assign it the string using the existing named constants, any literal strings that are needed for punctuation and spacing, and concatenation operations. Print the string, labeled appropriately.
6. Write C++ output statements that produce exactly the following output.

a. Four score
   and seven years ago
b. Four score
   and seven
   years ago
c. Four score
   and

   seven
   years ago
d. Four
      score
         and
   seven
      years
         ago

7. Enter and run the following program. Be sure to type it exactly as it appears here.

```
//******************************************************************
// HelloWorld program
// This program prints two simple messages
//******************************************************************
#include <iostream>
#include <string>

using namespace std;

const string MSG1 = "Hello world.";

int main()
{
    string msg2;

    cout << MSG1 << endl;
    msg2 = MSG1 + " " + MSG1 + " " + MSG1;
    cout << msg2 << endl;
    return 0;
}
```

8. Change the FormLetter program so that your name is printed in the appropriate places in the letter. (*Hint:* You need to change only four lines in the program.)

Programming Problems

1. Write a C++ program that prints your initials in large block letters, each letter made up of the same character it represents. The letters should be a minimum of seven printed lines high and should appear all in a row. For example, if your initials were DOW, your program should print out

```
DDDDDDD              OOOOO            W       W
D      D            O     O           W       W
D      D           O       O          W       W
D      D           O       O          W   W   W
D      D           O       O          W  W W  W
D      D            O     O           W W   W W
DDDDDDD              OOOOO             WW     WW
```

    Be sure to include appropriate comments in your program, choose meaningful identifiers, and use indentation as we do in the programs in this chapter.

2. Write a program that simulates the child's game "My Grandmother's Trunk." In this game, the players sit in a circle, and the first player names something that goes in the trunk: "In my grandmother's trunk, I packed a pencil." The next player restates the sentence and adds something new to the trunk: "In my grandmother's trunk, I packed a pencil and a red ball." Each player in turn adds something to the trunk, attempting to keep track of all the items that are already there.

    Your program should simulate just five turns in the game. Starting with the null string, simulate each player's turn by concatenating a new word or phrase to the existing string, and print the result on a new line. The output should be formatted as follows:

```
In my grandmother's trunk, I packed
a flower.
In my grandmother's trunk, I packed
a flower and a shirt.
In my grandmother's trunk, I packed
a flower and a shirt and a cup.
In my grandmother's trunk, I packed
a flower and a shirt and a cup and a blue marble.
In my grandmother's trunk, I packed
a flower and a shirt and a cup and a blue marble and a ball.
```

3. Write a program that prints its own grading form. The program should output the name and number of the class, the name and number of the programming assignment, your name and student number, and labeled spaces for scores

reflecting correctness, quality of style, late deduction, and overall score. An example of such a form is the following:

```
CS-101 Introduction to Programming and Problem Solving

Programming Assignment 1

Sally A. Student
ID Number 431023877

Grade Summary:

    Program Correctness:
    Quality of Style:
    Late Deduction:
    Overall Score:
    Comments:
```

Numeric Types, Expressions, and Output

In Chapter 2, we examined enough C++ syntax to be able to construct simple programs using assignment and output. In this chapter we continue to write programs that use assignment and output, but we concentrate on additional built-in data types: int and float. These numeric types are supported by numerous operators that allow us to construct complex arithmetic expressions. We show how to make expressions even more powerful by using *library functions*—prewritten functions that are part of every C++ system.

We also return to the subject of formatting the output. In particular, we consider the special features that C++ provides for formatting numbers in the output. We finish by looking at some additional operations on string data.

3.1 Overview of C++ Data Types

The C++ built-in data types are organized into simple types, structured types, and address types (see Figure 3-1). This chapter concentrates on the integral and floating types. Details of the other types come later in the book. First we look at the integral types (those used primarily to represent integers), and then we consider the floating types (used to represent real numbers containing decimal points).

3.2 Numeric Data Types

You already are familiar with the basic concepts of integer and real numbers in math. However, as used on a computer, the corresponding data types have certain limitations, which we now consider.

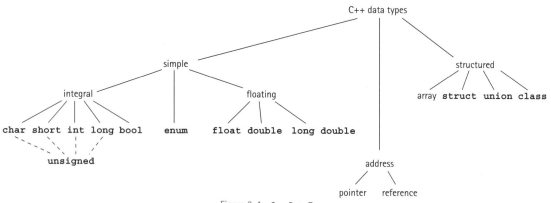

Figure 3-1 *C++ Data Types*

Integral Types

The data types `char`, `short`, `int`, and `long` are known as integral types (or integer types) because they refer to integer values—whole numbers with no fractional part. (We postpone talking about the remaining integral type, `bool`, until Chapter 5.)

In C++, the simplest form of integer value is a sequence of one or more digits:

```
22   16   1   498   0   4600
```

Commas are not allowed.

In most cases, a minus sign preceding an integer value makes the integer negative:

```
-378   -912
```

The exception is when you explicitly add the reserved word `unsigned` to the data type name:

```
unsigned int
```

An `unsigned` integer value is assumed to be only positive or zero. The `unsigned` types are used primarily in specialized situations. With a few exceptions later in this chapter, we rarely use `unsigned` in this book.

The data types `char`, `short`, `int`, and `long` are intended to represent different sizes of integers, from smaller (fewer bits) to larger (more bits). The sizes are machine dependent (that is, they may vary from machine to machine). For one particular machine, we might picture the sizes this way:

`char` memory cell ☐

`short` memory cell ☐

`int` memory cell ☐

`long` memory cell ☐

On another machine, the size of an `int` might be the same as the size of a `long`. In general, the more bits there are in the memory cell, the larger the integer value that can be stored.

Although we used the `char` type in Chapter 2 to store character data such as `'A'`, there are reasons why C++ classifies `char` as an integral type. Chapter 10 discusses the reasons.

You nearly always use `int` for manipulating integer values, but sometimes you have to use `long` if your program requires values larger than the maximum `int` value. (On some personal computers, the range of `int` values is from `-32768` through `+32767`. More commonly, `int`s range from `-2147483648` through `+2147483647`.) If your program tries to compute a value larger than your machine's maximum value, the result is *integer overflow*. Some machines give you an error message when overflow occurs, but others don't. We talk more about overflow in later chapters.

One caution about integer values in C++: A literal constant beginning with a zero is taken to be an octal (base-8) number instead of a decimal (base-10) number. If you write

```
015
```

the C++ compiler takes this to mean the decimal number 13. If you aren't familiar with the octal number system, don't worry about why an octal 15 is the same as a decimal 13. The important thing to remember is not to start a decimal integer constant with a zero (unless you simply want the number 0, which is the same in both octal and decimal). In Chapter 10, we discuss the various integral types in more detail.

Floating-Point Types

Floating-point types (or floating types), the second major category of simple types in C++, are used to represent real numbers. Floating-point numbers have an integer part and a fractional part, with a decimal point in between. Either the integer part or the fractional part, but not both, may be missing. Here are some examples:

```
18.0    127.54    0.57    4.    193145.8523    .8
```

Starting `0.57` with a zero does not make it an octal number. It is only with integer values that a leading zero indicates an octal number.

Just as the integral types in C++ come in different sizes (`char`, `short`, `int`, and `long`), so do the floating-point types. In increasing order of size, the floating-point types are `float`, `double` (meaning double precision), and `long double`. Again, the exact sizes are machine dependent. Each larger size potentially gives us a wider range of values and more precision (the number of significant digits in the number), but at the expense of more memory space to hold the number.

Floating-point values also can have an exponent, as in scientific notation. Instead of writing 3.504×10^{12}, in C++ we write `3.504E12`. The E means exponent of base 10. The number preceding the letter E doesn't need to include a decimal point. Here are some examples of floating-point numbers in scientific notation:

```
1.74536E-12    3.652442E4    7E20
```

Most programs don't need the `double` and `long double` types. The `float` type usually provides sufficient precision and range of values for floating-point numbers. Even personal computers provide `float` values with a precision of six or seven significant digits and a maximum value of about `3.4E+38`.

Computers cannot always represent floating-point numbers exactly. You learned in Chapter 1 that the computer stores all data in binary (base-2) form. Many floating-point values can only be approximated in the binary number system. Don't be surprised if your program prints out the number 4.8 as 4.7999998. In most cases, slight inaccuracies in the rightmost fractional digits are to be expected and are not the result of programmer error.

3.3 Declarations for Numeric Types

Just as with the types `char` and `string`, we can declare named constants and variables of type `int` and `float`. Such declarations use the same syntax as before, except that the literals and the names of the data types are different.

Named Constant Declarations

In the case of named constant declarations, the literal values in the declarations are numeric instead of being characters in single or double quotes. For example, here are some constant declarations that define values of type `int` and `float`. For comparison, declarations of `char` and `string` values are included.

```
const float  PI = 3.14159;
const float  E = 2.71828;
const int    MAX_SCORE = 100;
const int    MIN_SCORE = -100;
const char   LETTER = 'W';
const string NAME = "Elizabeth";
```

Although character and string literals are put in quotes, literal integers and floating-point numbers are not, because there is no chance of confusing them with identifiers. Why? Because identifiers must start with a letter or underscore, and numbers must start with a digit or sign.

Using Named Constants Instead of Literals

It's a good idea to use named constants instead of literals. In addition to making your program more readable, named constants can make your program easier to modify.

C++ allows us to declare constants with different names but the same value. If a value has different meanings in different parts of a program, it makes sense to declare and use a constant with an appropriate name for each meaning.

Named constants also are reliable; they protect us from mistakes. If you mistype the name PI as PO, the C++ compiler tells you that the name PO has not been declared. On the other hand, even though we recognize that the number 3.14149 is a mistyped version of pi (3.14159), the number is perfectly acceptable to the compiler. It won't warn us that anything is wrong.

It's a good idea to add comments to constant declarations as well as variable declarations. For example:

```
const float MAX_HOURS = 40.0; // Maximum normal work hours
const float OVERTIME = 1.5;   // Overtime pay rate factor
```

Variable Declarations

We declare numeric variables the same way in which we declare `char` and `string` variables, except that we use the names of numeric types. The following are valid variable declarations:

```
int    studentCount;    // Number of students
int    sumOfScores;     // Sum of their scores
float  average;         // Average of the scores
char   grade;           // Student's letter grade
string stuName;         // Student's name
```

Given the declarations

```
int    num;
int    alpha;
float  rate;
char   ch;
```

the following are appropriate assignment statements:

Variable	Expression
alpha =	2856;
rate =	0.36;
ch =	'B';
num =	alpha;

In each of these assignment statements, the data type of the expression matches the data type of the variable to which it is assigned. Later in the chapter we see what happens if the data types do not match.

3.4 Simple Arithmetic Expressions

Now that we have looked at declaration and assignment, we consider how to calculate with values of numeric types. Calculations are performed with expressions. We first look at simple expressions that involve at most one operator so that we may examine each operator in detail. Then, we move on to compound expressions that combine multiple operations.

Arithmetic Operators

Expressions are made up of constants, variables, and operators. The following are all valid expressions:

```
alpha + 2   rate - 6.0   4 - alpha   rate   alpha * num
```

The operators allowed in an expression depend on the data types of the constants and variables in the expression. The *arithmetic operators* are

+	Unary plus
-	Unary minus
+	Addition
-	Subtraction
*	Multiplication
/ {	Floating-point division (floating-point result)
	Integer division (no fractional part)
%	Modulus (remainder from integer division)

The first two operators are **unary operators**—they take just one operand. The remaining five are **binary operators**, taking two operands. Unary plus and minus are used as follows:

> **Unary operator** An operator that has just one operand.
> **Binary operator** An operator that has two operands.

```
-54   +259.65   -rate
```

Programmers rarely use the unary plus. Without any sign, a numeric constant is assumed to be positive anyway.

You may not be familiar with integer division and modulus (%). Let's look at them more closely. Note that % is used only with integers. When you divide one integer by another, you get an integer quotient and a remainder. Integer division gives only the integer quotient, and % gives only the remainder. (If either operand is negative, the sign of the remainder may vary from one C++ compiler to another.)

$$
\begin{array}{ll}
3 \leftarrow 6/2 & 3 \leftarrow 7/2 \\
2\,\overline{)6} & 2\,\overline{)7} \\
\underline{6} & \underline{6} \\
0 \leftarrow 6\%2 & 1 \leftarrow 7\%2
\end{array}
$$

In contrast, floating-point division yields a floating-point result. The expression

```
7.0 / 2.0
```

yields the value 3.5.

Here are some expressions using arithmetic operators and their values:

Expression	Value
3 + 6	9
3.4 - 6.1	−2.7
2 * 3	6
8 / 2	4
8.0 / 2.0	4.0
8 / 8	1
8 / 9	0
8 / 7	1
8 % 8	0
8 % 9	8
8 % 7	1
0 % 7	0
5 % 2.3	error (both operands must be integers)

Be careful with division and modulus. The expressions `7.0 / 0.0`, `7 / 0`, and `7 % 0` all produce errors. The computer cannot divide by zero.

Because variables are allowed in expressions, the following are valid assignments:

```
alpha = num + 6;        num = alpha * 2;        alpha = alpha + 1;
alpha = num / 2;        num = 6 % alpha;        num = num + alpha;
```

As we saw with assignment statements involving `string` expressions, the same variable can appear on both sides of the assignment operator. In the case of

```
num = num + alpha;
```

the value in `num` and the value in `alpha` are added together, and then the sum of the two values is stored back into `num`, replacing the previous value stored there. This example shows the difference between mathematical equality and assignment. The mathematical equality

$$num = num + alpha$$

is true only when *alpha* equals 0. The assignment statement

```
num = num + alpha;
```

is valid for *any* value of `alpha`.

Here's a simple program that uses arithmetic expressions:

```
//*******************************************************************
// FreezeBoil program
// This program computes the midpoint between
// the freeezing and boiling points of water
//*******************************************************************
#include <iostream>

using namespace std;

const float FREEZE_PT = 32.0;    // Freezing point of water
const float BOIL_PT = 212.0;     // Boiling point of water

int main()
{
    float avgTemp;               // Holds the result of averaging
                                 //   FREEZE_PT and BOIL_PT

    cout << "Water freezes at " << FREEZE_PT << endl;
    cout << " and boils at " << BOIL_PT << " degrees." << endl;

    avgTemp = FREEZE_PT + BOIL_PT;
    avgTemp = avgTemp / 2.0;

    cout << "Halfway between is ";
    cout << avgTemp << " degrees." << endl;

    return 0;
}
```

The program begins with a comment that explains what the program does. Next comes a declaration section where we define the constants FREEZE_PT and BOIL_PT. The body of the `main` function includes a declaration of the variable `avgTemp` and then a sequence of executable statements. These statements print a message, add FREEZE_PT and BOIL_PT, divide the sum by 2, and finally print the result.

Increment and Decrement Operators

In addition to the arithmetic operators, C++ provides increment and decrement operators:

```
++      Increment
--      Decrement
```

These are unary operators that take a single variable name as an operand. For integer and floating-point operands, the effect is to add 1 to (or subtract 1 from) the operand. If `num` currently contains the value 8, the statement

```
num++;
```

causes `num` to contain 9. You can achieve the same effect by writing the assignment statement

```
num = num + 1;
```

but C++ programmers typically prefer the increment operator.

The ++ and -- operators can be either *prefix operators*

```
++num;
```

or *postfix operators*

```
num++;
```

Both of these statements behave in exactly the same way; they add 1 to whatever is in `num`. The choice between the two is a matter of personal preference.

C++ allows the use of ++ and -- in the middle of a larger expression:

```
alpha = num++ * 3;
```

In this case, the postfix form of ++ does *not* give the same result as the prefix form. In Chapter 10, we explain the ++ and -- operators in detail. In the meantime, you should use them only to increment or decrement a variable as a separate, stand-alone statement.

3.5 Compound Arithmetic Expressions

The expressions we've used so far have contained at most a single arithmetic operator. We also have been careful not to mix integer and floating-point values in the same expression. Now we look at more complicated expressions—ones that are composed of several operators and ones that contain mixed data types.

Precedence Rules

Arithmetic expressions can be made up of many constants, variables, operators, and parentheses. In what order are the operations performed? For example, in the assignment statement

```
avgTemp = FREEZE_PT + BOIL_PT / 2.0;
```

is `FREEZE_PT + BOIL_PT` calculated first or is `BOIL_PT / 2.0` calculated first?

The basic arithmetic operators (unary +, unary -, + for addition, - for subtraction, * for multiplication, / for division, and % for modulus) are ordered the same way mathematical operators are, according to *precedence rules:*

Highest precedence level:	Unary + Unary -
Middle level:	* / %
Lowest level:	+ -

Because division has higher precedence than addition, the expression in the example above is implicitly parenthesized as

```
FREEZE_PT + (BOIL_PT / 2.0)
```

That is, we first divide `BOIL_PT` by 2.0 and then add `FREEZE_PT` to the result.

You can change the order of evaluation by using parentheses. In the statement

```
avgTemp = (FREEZE_PT + BOIL_PT) / 2.0;
```

`FREEZE_PT` and `BOIL_PT` are added first, and then their sum is divided by 2.0. We evaluate subexpressions in parentheses first and then follow the precedence of the operators.

When an arithmetic expression has several binary operators with the same precedence, their *grouping order* (or *associativity*) is from left to right. The expression

```
int1 - int2 + int3
```

means (`int1` - `int2`) + `int3`, not `int1` - (`int2` + `int3`). As another example, we would use the expression

```
(float1 + float2) / float1 * 3.0
```

to evaluate the expression in parentheses first, then divide the sum by `float1`, and multiply the result by 3.0. Below are some more examples.

Expression	Value
`10 / 2 * 3`	15
`10 % 3 - 4 / 2`	-1
`5.0 * 2.0 / 4.0 * 2.0`	5.0
`5.0 * 2.0 / (4.0 * 2.0)`	1.25
`5.0 + 2.0 / (4.0 * 2.0)`	5.25

In C++, all unary operators (such as unary + and unary -) have right-to-left associativity. Though this fact may seem strange at first, it turns out to be the natural grouping order. For example, - + x means - (+ x) rather than the meaningless (- +) x.

Type Coercion and Type Casting

Integer values and floating-point values are stored differently inside a computer's memory. The pattern of bits that represents the constant 2 does not look at all like the pattern of bits representing the constant 2.0. What happens if we mix integer and floating-point values together in an assignment statement or an arithmetic expression? Let's look first at assignment statements.

Assignment Statements   If you make the declarations

```
int   someInt;
float someFloat;
```

then `someInt` can hold *only* integer values, and `someFloat` can hold *only* floating-point values. The assignment statement

```
someFloat = 12;
```

may seem to store the integer value 12 into `someFloat`, but this is not true. The computer refuses to store anything other than a `float` value into `someFloat`. The compiler inserts extra machine language instructions that first convert 12 into 12.0 and then store 12.0 into `some-Float`. This implicit (automatic) conversion of a value from one data type to another is known as **type coercion**.

Type coercion The implicit (automatic) conversion of a value from one data type to another.

The statement

```
someInt = 4.8;
```

also causes type coercion. When a floating-point value is assigned to an `int` variable, the fractional part is truncated (cut off). As a result, `someInt` is assigned the value 4.

With both of the assignment statements above, the program would be less confusing for someone to read if we avoided mixing data types:

```
someFloat = 12.0;
someInt = 4;
```

More often, it is not just constants but entire expressions that are involved in type coercion. Storing the result of an `int` expression into a `float` variable generally doesn't cause loss of information; a whole number such as 24 can be represented in floating-point form as 24.0. However, storing the result of a floating-point expression into an `int` variable can cause loss of information because the fractional part is truncated. It is easy to overlook the assignment of a floating-point expression to an `int` variable when we try to discover why our program is producing the wrong answers.

To make our programs as clear (and error free) as possible, we can use explicit **type casting** (or **type conversion**). A C++ *cast operation* consists of a data type name and then, within parentheses, the expression to be converted:

> **Type casting** The explicit conversion of a value from one data type to another; also called type conversion.

```
someFloat = float(3 * someInt + 2);
someInt = int(5.2 / someFloat - anotherFloat);
```

Both of the statements

```
someInt = someFloat + 8.2;
someInt = int(someFloat + 8.2);
```

produce identical results. The only difference is in clarity. With the cast operation, it is perfectly clear to the programmer and to others reading the program that the mixing of types is intentional, not an oversight. Countless errors have resulted from unintentional mixing of types.

Note that there is a nice way to round off rather than truncate a floating-point value before storing it into an `int` variable. Here's how:

```
someInt = int(someFloat + 0.5);
```

With pencil and paper, see for yourself what gets stored into `someInt` when `someFloat` contains 4.7. Now try it again, assuming `someFloat` contains 4.2. (This technique of rounding by adding 0.5 assumes that `someFloat` is a positive number.)

Arithmetic Expressions So far we have been talking about mixing data types across the assignment operator (=). It's also possible to mix data types within an expression:

```
someInt * someFloat
4.8 + someInt - 3
```

Such expressions are called **mixed type** (or **mixed mode**) **expressions.**

Mixed type expression An expression that contains operands of different data types; also called mixed mode expression.

Whenever an integer value and a floating-point value are joined by an operator, implicit type coercion occurs as follows.

1. The integer value is temporarily coerced to a floating-point value.

2. The operation is performed.

3. The result is a floating-point value.

Let's examine how the machine evaluates the expression 4.8 + someInt - 3, where someInt contains the value 2. First, the operands of the + operator have mixed types, so the value of someInt is coerced to 2.0. (This conversion is only temporary; it does not affect the value that is stored in someInt.) The addition takes place, yielding a value of 6.8. Next, the subtraction (-) operator joins a floating-point value (6.8) and an integer value (3). The value 3 is coerced to 3.0, the subtraction takes place, and the result is the floating-point value 3.8.

Just as with assignment statements, you can use explicit type casts within expressions to lessen the risk of errors. Writing expressions such as

```
float(someInt) * someFloat
4.8 + float(someInt - 3)
```

makes it clear what your intentions are.

Explicit type casts are not only valuable for program clarity, but also are mandatory in some cases for correct programming. Given the declarations

```
int     sum;
int     count;
float average;
```

suppose that sum and count currently contain 60 and 80, respectively. If sum represents the sum of a group of integer values and count represents the number of values, let's find the average value:

```
average = sum / count;     // Wrong
```

Unfortunately, this statement stores the value 0.0 into average. Here's why. The expression to the right of the assignment operator is not a mixed type expression. Both operands of the / operator are of type int, so integer division is performed. 60 divided by 80 yields the integer value 0. Next, the machine implicitly coerces 0 to the value 0.0

before storing it into `average`. The way to find the average correctly, as well as clearly, is this:

```
average = float(sum) / float(count);
```

This statement gives us floating-point division instead of integer division. As a result, the value 0.75 is stored into `average`.

As a final remark about type coercion and type conversion, you may have noticed that we have concentrated only on the `int` and `float` types. It is also possible to stir `char` values, `short` values, and `double` values into the pot. The results can be confusing and unexpected. In Chapter 10, we return to the topic with a more detailed discussion. In the meantime, you should avoid mixing values of these types within an expression.

3.6 Function Calls and Library Functions

Value-Returning Functions

At the beginning of Chapter 2, we showed a program consisting of three functions: `main`, `Square`, and `Cube`. Here is a portion of the program:

```
int main()
{
    cout << "The square of 27 is " << Square(27) << endl;
    cout << "and the cube of 27 is " << Cube(27) << endl;
    return 0;
}

int Square( int n )
{
    return n * n;
}

int Cube( int n )
{
    return n * n * n;
}
```

We said that all three functions are value-returning functions. `Square` returns to its caller a value—the square of the number sent to it. `Cube` returns a value—the cube of the number sent to it. And `main` returns to the operating system a value—the program's exit status.

Let's focus for a moment on the `Cube` function. The `main` function contains a statement

```
cout << " and the cube of 27 is " << Cube(27) << endl;
```

In this statement, the master (`main`) causes the servant (`Cube`) to compute the cube of 27 and give the result back to `main`. The sequence of symbols

```
Cube(27)
```

is a **function call** or **function invocation**. The computer temporarily puts the `main` function on hold and starts the `Cube` function running. When `Cube` has finished doing its work, the computer goes back to `main` and picks up where it left off.

Function call (function invocation) The mechanism that transfers control to a function.

In the above function call, the number 27 is known as an *argument* (or *actual parameter*). Arguments make it possible for the same function to work on many different values. For example, we can write statements like these:

```
cout << Cube(4);
cout << Cube(16);
```

Here's the syntax template for a function call:

FunctionCall

FunctionName (ArgumentList)

Argument list A mechanism by which functions communicate with each other.

The **argument list** is a way for functions to communicate with each other. Some functions, like `Square` and `Cube`, have a single argument in the argument list. Other functions, like `main`, have no arguments in the list. And some functions have two, three, or more arguments in the argument list, separated by commas.

Value-returning functions are used in expressions in much the same way that variables and constants are. The value computed by a function simply takes its place in the expression. For example, the statement

```
someInt = Cube(2) * 10;
```

stores the value 80 into `someInt`. First the `Cube` function is executed to compute the cube of 2, which is 8. The value 8—now available for use in the rest of the expression—is multiplied by 10. Note that a function call has higher precedence than multiplication, which makes sense if you consider that the function result must be available before the multiplication takes place.

Here are several facts about value-returning functions:

- The function call is used within an expression; it does not appear as a separate statement.
- The function computes a value (*result*) that is then available for use in the expression.
- The function returns exactly one result—no more, no less.

The Cube function expects to be given (or *passed*) an argument of type int. What happens if the caller passes a float argument? The answer is that the compiler applies implicit type coercion. The function call Cube(6.9) computes the cube of 6, not 6.9.

Although we have been using literal constants as arguments to Cube, the argument could just as easily be a variable or named constant. In fact, the argument to a value-returning function can be any expression of the appropriate type. In the statement

```
alpha = Cube(int1 * int1 + int2 * int2);
```

the expression in the argument list is evaluated first, and only its result is passed to the function. For example, if int1 contains 3 and int2 contains 5, the above function call passes 34 as the argument to Cube.

An expression in a function's argument list can even include calls to functions. For example, we could use the Square function to rewrite the above assignment statement as follows:

```
alpha = Cube(Square(int1) + Square(int2));
```

Library Functions

Certain computations, such as taking square roots or finding the absolute value of a number, are very common in programs. To make the programmer's life easier, every C++ system includes a standard library—a large collection of prewritten functions that perform such computations. Here is a small sample of some standard library functions:

Header File*	Function	Argument Type(s)	Result Type	Result (Value Returned)
<cstdlib>	abs(i)	int	int	Absolute value of i
<cmath>	cos(x)	float	float	Cosine of x (x is in radians)
<cmath>	fabs(x)	float	float	Absolute value of x
<cstdlib>	labs(j)	long	long	Absolute value of j
<cmath>	pow(x, y)	float	float	x raised to the power y (if x = 0.0, y must be positive; if x ≤ 0.0, y must be a whole number)
<cmath>	sin(x)	float	float	Sine of x (x is in radians)
<cmath>	sqrt(x)	float	float	Square root of x (x ≥ 0.0)

*The names of these header files are not the same as in pre-standard C++. If you are working with pre-standard C++, see Section D.2 of Appendix D.

Technically, the entries in the table marked float should all say double. These library functions perform their work using double-precision floating-point values. But because of type coercion, the functions still work when you pass float values to them.

Using a library function is easy. First, you place an #include directive near the top of your program, specifying the appropriate header file. This directive causes the C++

preprocessor to insert declarations into your program that give the compiler some information about the function. Then, whenever you want to use the function, you just make a function call.* Here's an example:

```
#include <iostream>
#include <cmath>        // For sqrt() and fabs()

using namespace std;
   ⋮
float alpha;
float beta;
   ⋮
alpha = sqrt(7.3 + fabs(beta));
```

Remember from Chapter 2 that all identifiers in the standard library are in the namespace std. If we omit the using directive from the above code, we must use qualified names for the library functions (std::sqrt, std::fabs, and so forth).

The C++ standard library provides dozens of functions for you to use. Appendix C lists a much larger selection than we have presented here. You should glance briefly at this appendix now, keeping in mind that much of the terminology and C++ language notation will make sense only after you have read further into the book.

Void Functions

In this chapter, the only kind of function that we have looked at is the **value-returning function.** C++ provides another kind of function as well. If you look at the following function definition for CalcPay you see that it begins with the word void instead of a data type like int or float:

```
void CalcPay( ... )
{
     ⋮
}
```

Value-returning function A function that returns a single value to its caller and is invoked from within an expression.

Void function (procedure) A function that does not return a function value to its caller and is invoked as a separate statement.

CalcPay is an example of a function that doesn't return a value to its caller. Instead, it just performs some action and then returns. We refer to a function like this as a *non-value-returning function,* a *void-returning function,* or, simply, a **void function.** In many programming languages, a void function is known as a **procedure.**

Void functions are invoked differently from value-returning functions. With a value-returning function,

---

*Some systems require you to specify a particular compiler option if you use the math functions. For example, with some versions of UNIX, you must add the option -1m when compiling your program.

the function call appears in an expression. With a void function, the function call is a separate, stand-alone statement. Function `main` would call the `CalcPay` function like this:

```
CalcPay(payRate, hours, wages);
```

From the caller's perspective, a call to a void function has the flavor of a command or built-in instruction:

```
DoThis(x, y, z);
DoThat();
```

In contrast, a call to a value-returning function doesn't look like a command; it looks like a value in an expression:

```
y = 4.7 + Cube(x);
```

For the next few chapters, we won't be writing our own functions (except `main`). Instead, we'll be concentrating on how to use existing functions, including functions for performing stream input and output. Some of these functions are value-returning functions; others are void functions. Again, we emphasize the difference in how you invoke these two kinds of functions: A call to a value-returning function occurs in an expression, whereas a call to a void function occurs as a separate statement.

3.7 Formatting the Output

To format a program's output means to control how it appears visually on the screen or on a printer. In Chapter 2, we considered two kinds of output formatting: creating extra blank lines by using the `endl` manipulator and inserting blanks within a line by putting extra blanks into literal strings. In this section, we examine how to format the output values themselves.

Integers and Strings

By default, consecutive integer and string values are output with no spaces between them. If the variables i, j, and k contain the values 15, 2, and 6, respectively, the statement

```
cout << "Results: " << i << j << k;
```

outputs the stream of characters

```
Results: 1526
```

Without spacing between the numbers, this output is difficult to interpret.

To separate the output values, you could print a single blank (as a `char` constant) between the numbers:

```
cout << "Results: " << i << ' ' << j << ' ' << k;
```

This statement produces the output

```
Results: 15 2 6
```

If you want even more spacing between items, use literal strings containing blanks, as we discussed in Chapter 2:

```
cout << "Results: " << i << "    " << j << "    " << k;
```

Here, the resulting output is

```
Results: 15    2    6
```

Another way to control the horizontal spacing of the output is to use *manipulators*. For some time now, we have been using the `endl` manipulator to terminate an output line. In C++, a manipulator is a rather curious thing that behaves like a function but travels in the disguise of a data object. Like a function, a manipulator causes some action to occur. But like a data object, a manipulator can appear in the midst of a series of insertion operations:

```
cout << someInt << endl << someFloat;
```

Manipulators are used *only* in input and output statements.

The C++ standard library supplies many manipulators, but for now we look at only five of them: `endl`, `setw`, `fixed`, `showpoint`, and `setprecision`. The `endl`, `fixed`, and `showpoint` manipulators come "for free" when we #include the header file `iostream` to perform I/O. The other two manipulators, `setw` and `setprecision`, require that we also #include the header file `iomanip`:

```
#include <iostream>
#include <iomanip>

using namespace std;
    ⋮
cout << setw(5) << someInt;
```

The manipulator setw—meaning "set width"—lets us control how many character positions the next data item should occupy when it is output. (setw is only for formatting numbers and strings, not char data.) The argument to setw is an integer expression called the *fieldwidth specification;* the group of character positions is called the *field.* The next data item to be output is printed *right-justified* (filled with blanks on the left to fill up the field).

Let's look at some examples. Assuming two int variables have been assigned values as follows:

```
ans = 33;
num = 7132;
```

then the following output statements produce the output shown to their right.

Statement	Output (□ means blank)
1. cout << setw(4) << ans << setw(5) << num << setw(4) << "Hi";	□□33□7132□□Hi ‾4‾ ‾‾5‾‾ ‾4‾
2. cout << setw(2) << ans << setw(4) << num << setw(2) << "Hi";	337132Hi ‾2‾ ‾4‾ ‾2‾
3. cout << setw(6) << ans << setw(3) << "Hi" << setw(5) << num;	□□□□33□Hi□7132 ‾‾6‾‾ ‾3‾ ‾5‾
4. cout << setw(7) << "Hi" << setw(4) << num;	□□□□□Hi7132 ‾‾7‾‾ ‾4‾
5. cout << setw(1) << ans << setw(5) << num;	33□7132 ↑ ‾5‾ Field automatically expands to fit the two-digit value

In (1), each value is specified to occupy enough positions so that there is at least one space separating them. In (2), the values all run together because the fieldwidth specified for each value is just large enough to hold the value. This output obviously is not very readable. It's better to make the fieldwidth larger than the minimum size required so that some space is left between values. In (3), there are extra blanks for readability; in (4), there are not. In (5), the fieldwidth is not large enough for the value in ans, so it automatically expands to make room for all of the digits.

Setting the fieldwidth is a one-time action. It holds only for the very next item to be output. After this output, the fieldwidth resets to 0, meaning "extend the field to exactly as many positions as are needed." In the statement

```
cout << "Hi" << setw(5) << ans << num;
```

the fieldwidth resets to 0 after `ans` is output. As a result, we get the output

```
Hi   337132
```

Floating-Point Numbers

You can specify a fieldwidth for floating-point values just as for integer values. But you must remember to allow for the decimal point when you specify the number of character positions. The value 4.85 requires four output positions, not three. If x contains the value 4.85, the statement

```
cout << setw(4) << x << endl
     << setw(6) << x << endl
     << setw(3) << x << endl;
```

produces the output

```
4.85
  4.85
4.85
```

In the third line, a fieldwidth of 3 isn't sufficient, so the field automatically expands to accommodate the number.

There are several other issues related to output of floating-point numbers. First, large floating-point values are printed in scientific (E) notation. The value 123456789.5 may print on some systems as

```
1.23457E+08
```

You can use the manipulator named `fixed` to force all subsequent floating-point output to appear in decimal form rather than scientific notation:

```
cout << fixed << 3.8 * x;
```

Second, if the number is a whole number, C++ doesn't print a decimal point. The value 95.0 prints as

```
95
```

To force decimal points to be displayed in subsequent floating-point output, even for whole numbers, you can use the manipulator `showpoint`:

```
cout << showpoint << floatVar;
```

(If you are using a pre-standard version of C++, the `fixed` and `showpoint` manipulators may not be available. See Section D.3 of Appendix D for an alternative way of achieving the same results.)

Third, you often would like to control the number of *decimal places* (digits to the right of the decimal point) that are displayed. If your program is supposed to print the 5% sales tax on a certain amount, the statement

```
cout << "Tax is $" << price * 0.05;
```

may output

```
Tax is $17.7435
```

Here, you clearly would prefer to display the result to two decimal places. To do so, use the `setprecision` manipulator as follows:

```
cout << fixed << setprecision(2) << "Tax is $" << price * 0.05;
```

Provided that `fixed` has already been specified, the argument to `setprecision` specifies the desired number of decimal places. Unlike `setw`, which applies only to the very next item printed, the value sent to `setprecision` remains in effect for all subsequent output (until you change it with another call to `setprecision`). Here are some examples of using `setprecision` in conjunction with `setw`:

Value of x	Statement	Output (□ means blank)
	`cout << fixed;`	
310.0	`cout << setw(10)`	
	`     << setprecision(2) << x;`	`□□□□310.00`
310.0	`cout << setw(10)`	
	`     << setprecision(5) << x;`	`□310.00000`
310.0	`cout << setw(7)`	
	`     << setprecision(5) << x;`	`310.00000` (expands to nine positions)
4.827	`cout << setw(6)`	
	`     << setprecision(2) << x;`	`□□4.83` (last displayed digit is rounded off)
4.827	`cout << setw(6)`	
	`     << setprecision(1) << x;`	`□□□4.8` (last displayed digit is rounded off)

Again, the total number of print positions is expanded if the fieldwidth specified by `setw` is too narrow. However, the number of positions for fractional digits is controlled entirely by the argument to `setprecision`.

The following table summarizes the manipulators we have discussed in this section. Manipulators without arguments are available through the header file `iostream`. Those with arguments require the header file `iomanip`.

Header File	Manipulator	Argument Type	Effect
`<iostream>`	`endl`	None	Terminates the current output line
`<iostream>`	`showpoint`	None	Forces display of decimal point in floating-point output
`<iostream>`	`fixed`	None	Suppresses scientific notation in floating-point output
`<iomanip>`	`setw(n)`	`int`	Sets fieldwidth to n*
`<iomanip>`	`setprecision(n)`	`int`	Sets floating-point precision to n digits

*`setw` is only for numbers and strings, not `char` data. Also, `setw` applies only to the very next output item, after which the fieldwidth is reset to 0 (meaning "use only as many positions as are needed").

Program Formatting

As far as the compiler is concerned, C++ statements are *free format*. However, it is extremely important that your programs be readable, both for your sake and for the sake of anyone else who has to examine them. When you write an outline for an English paper, you follow certain rules of indentation to make it readable. Similar rules can make your programs easier to read. Take a look at the following program for computing the cost per square foot of a house. It compiles and runs correctly, but it does not conform to any formatting standards.

```
// HouseCost program
// This program computes the cost per square foot of
    // living space for a house, given the dimensions of
// the house, the number of stories, the size of the
// nonliving space, and the total cost less land
#include <iostream>
#include <iomanip>// For setw() and setprecision()
using namespace
std;
const float WIDTH = 30.0; // Width of the house
    const float LENGTH = 40.0; // Length of the house
const float STORIES = 2.5; // Number of full stories
const float NON_LIVING_SPACE = 825.0;// Garage, closets, etc.
const float PRICE = 150000.0; // Selling price less land
int main() { float grossFootage;// Total square footage
    float livingFootage;       // Living area
```

```
float costPerFoot;      // Cost/foot of living area
   cout << fixed << showpoint;    // Set up floating-pt.
//   output format
grossFootage = LENGTH * WIDTH * STORIES; livingFootage =
grossFootage - NON_LIVING_SPACE; costPerFoot = PRICE /
livingFootage; cout << "Cost per square foot is "
<< setw(6) << setprecision(2) << costPerFoot << endl;
return 0; }
```

Now look at the same program with proper formatting:

```
//*******************************************************************
// HouseCost program
// This program computes the cost per square foot of
// living space for a house, given the dimensions of
// the house, the number of stories, the size of the
// nonliving space, and the total cost less land
//*******************************************************************
#include <iostream>
#include <iomanip>     // For setw() and setprecision()
using namespace std;
const float WIDTH = 30.0;                // Width of the house
const float LENGTH = 40.0;               // Length of the house
const float STORIES = 2.5;               // Number of full stories
const float NON_LIVING_SPACE = 825.0;    // Garage, closets, etc.
const float PRICE = 150000.0;            // Selling price less land
int main()
{
    float grossFootage;         // Total square footage
    float livingFootage;        // Living area
    float costPerFoot;          // Cost/foot of living area
    cout << fixed << showpoint;             // Set up floating-pt.
                                            //   output format
    grossFootage = LENGTH * WIDTH * STORIES;
    livingFootage = grossFootage - NON_LIVING_SPACE;
    costPerFoot = PRICE / livingFootage;
    cout << "Cost per square foot is "
         << setw(6) << setprecision(2) << costPerFoot << endl;
    return 0;
}
```

Need we say more?

Appendix F talks about programming style. Use it as a guide when you are writing programs.

3.8 Additional `string` Operations

Now that we have introduced numeric types and function calls, we can take advantage of additional features of the `string` data type. In this section, we introduce four functions that operate on strings: `length`, `size`, `find`, and `substr`.

The `length` and `size` Functions

The `length` function, when applied to a `string` variable, returns an unsigned integer value that equals the number of characters currently in the string. If `myName` is a `string` variable, a call to the `length` function looks like this:

```
myName.length()
```

You specify the name of a `string` variable (here, `myName`), then a dot (period), and then the function name and argument list. The `length` function requires no arguments to be passed to it, but you still must use parentheses to signify an empty argument list. Also, `length` is a value-returning function, so the function call must appear within an expression:

```
string firstName;
string fullName;

firstName = "Alexandra";
cout << firstName.length() << endl;        // Prints 9
fullName = firstName + " Jones";
cout << fullName.length() << endl;         // Prints 15
```

Perhaps you are wondering about the syntax in a function call like

```
firstName.length()
```

This expression uses a C++ notation called *dot notation*. There is a dot (period) between the variable name `firstName` and the function name `length`. Certain programmer-defined data types, such as `string`, have functions that are tightly associated with them, and dot notation is required in the function calls. If you forget to use dot notation, writing the function call as

```
length()
```

you get a compile-time error message, something like "UNDECLARED IDENTIFIER." The compiler thinks you are trying to call an ordinary function named `length`, not the `length` function associated with the `string` type. In Chapter 4, we discuss the meaning behind dot notation.

Some people refer to the length of a string as its *size*. To accommodate both terms, the `string` type provides a function named `size`. Both `firstName.size()` and `firstName.length()` return the same value.

We said that the `length` function returns an unsigned integer value. If we want to save the result into a variable `len`, as in

```
len = firstName.length();
```

then what should we declare the data type of `len` to be? To keep us from having to guess whether `unsigned int` or `unsigned long` is correct for the particular compiler we're working with, the `string` type defines a data type `size_type` for us to use:

```
string firstName;
string::size_type len;

firstName = "Alexandra";
len = firstName.length();
```

Notice that we must use the qualified name `string::size_type` (just as we do with identifiers in namespaces) because the definition of `size_type` is otherwise hidden inside the definition of the `string` type.

Before leaving the `length` and `size` functions, we should make a remark about capitalization of identifiers. In the guidelines given in Chapter 2, we said that in this book we begin the names of programmer-defined functions and data types with upper-case letters. We follow this convention when we write out own functions and data types in later chapters. However, we have no control over the capitalization of items supplied by the C++ standard library. Identifiers in the standard library generally use all-lower-case letters.

The find Function

The `find` function searches a string to find the first occurrence of a particular substring and returns an unsigned integer value (of type `string:: size_type`) giving the result of the search. The substring, passed as an argument to the function, can be a literal string or a `string` expression. If `str1` and `str2` are of type `string`, the following are valid function calls:

```
str1.find("the")        str1.find(str2)        str1.find(str2 + "abc")
```

In each case above, `str1` is searched to see if the specified substring can be found within it. If so, the function returns the position in `str1` where the match begins. (Positions are numbered starting at 0, so the first character in a string is in position 0, the second is in position 1, and so on.) For a successful search, the match must be exact, including identical capitalization. If the substring could not be found, the function returns the special value `string::npos`, a named constant meaning "not a position within the string." (`string::npos` is the largest possible value of type `string::size_type`, a number like `4294967295` on many machines. This value is suitable for "not a valid position" because the `string` operations do not let any string become this long.)

Given the code segment

```
string phrase;
string::size_type position;

phrase = "The dog and the cat";
```

the statement

```
position = phrase.find("the");
```

assigns to `position` the value 12, whereas the statement

```
position = phrase.find("rat");
```

assigns to `position` the value `string::npos`, because there was no match.

The argument to the `find` function can also be a `char` value. In this case, `find` searches for the first occurrence of that character within the string and returns its position (or `string::npos`, if the character was not found). For example, the code segment

```
string theString;

theString = "Abracadabra";
cout << theString.find('a');
```

outputs the value 3, which is the position of the first occurrence of a lowercase *a* in `theString`.

Below are some more examples of calls to the `find` function, assuming the following code segment has been executed:

```
string str1;
string str2;
```

```
str1 = "Programming and Problem Solving";
str2 = "gram";
```

Function Call	Value Returned by Function
str1.find("and")	12
str1.find("Programming")	0
str2.find("and")	string::npos
str1.find("Pro")	0
str1.find("ro" + str2)	1
str1.find("Pr" + str2)	string::npos
str1.find(' ')	11

Notice in the fourth example that there are two copies of the substring "Pro" in str1, but find returns only the position of the first copy. Also notice that the copies can be either separate words or parts of words—find merely tries to match the sequence of characters given in the argument list. The final example demonstrates that the argument can be as simple as a single character, even a single blank.

The substr Function

The substr function returns a particular substring of a string. Assuming myString is of type string, here is a sample function call:

```
myString.substr(5, 20)
```

The first argument is an unsigned integer that specifies a position within the string, and the second is an unsigned integer that specifies the length of the desired substring. The function returns the piece of the string that starts with the specified position and continues for the number of characters given by the second argument. Note that substr doesn't change myString; it returns a new, temporary string value that is a copy of a portion of the string. Below are some examples, assuming the statement

```
myString = "Programming and Problem Solving";
```

has been executed.

Function Call	String Contained in Value Returned by Function
myString.substr(0, 7)	"Program"
myString.substr(7, 8)	"ming and"
myString.substr(10, 0)	""
myString.substr(24, 40)	"Solving"
myString.substr(40, 24)	None. Program terminates with an execution error message.

In the third example, specifying a length of 0 produces the null string as the result. The fourth example shows what happens if the second argument specifies more characters than are present after the starting position: `substr` returns the characters from the starting position to the end of the string. The last example illustrates that the first argument, the position, must not be beyond the end of the string.

Because `substr` returns a value of type `string`, you can use it with the concatenation operator (+) to copy pieces of strings and join them together to form new strings. The `find` and `length` functions can be useful in determining the location and end of a piece of a string to be passed to `substr` as arguments.

Here is a code segment that uses several of the `string` operations:

```
string fullName;
string name;
string::size_type startPos;

fullName = "Jonathan Alexander Peterson";
startPos = fullName.find("Peterson");
name = "Mr. " + fullName.substr(startPos, 8);
cout << name << endl;
```

This code outputs `Mr. Peterson` when it is executed. First it stores a string into the variable `fullName`, and then it uses `find` to locate the start of the name `Peterson` within the string. Next, it builds a new string by concatenating the literal `"Mr. "` with the characters `Peterson`, which are copied from the original string. Last, it prints out the new string. As we see in later chapters, string operations are an important aspect of many computer programs.

The following table summarizes the `string` operations we have looked at in this chapter.

Function Call (s is of type string)	Argument Type(s)	Result Type	Result (Value Returned)
s.length() s.size()	None	string::size_type	Number of characters in the string
s.find(arg)	string, literal string, or char	string::size_type	Starting position in s where arg was found. If not found, result is string::npos
s.substr(pos,len)	string::size_type	string	Substring of at most len characters, starting at position pos of s. If len is too large, it means "to the end" of string s. If pos is too large, execution of the program is terminated.*

*Technically, if pos is too large, the program generates what is called an out-of-range *exception*—a topic we do not discuss at this time. Unless we write additional program code to deal explicitly with this out-of-range exception, the program simply terminates with a message such as "ABNORMAL PROGRAM TERMINATION."

Understanding Before Changing

When you are in the middle of getting a program to run and you come across an error, it's tempting to start changing parts of the program to try to make it work. *Don't!* You'll nearly always make things worse. It's essential that you understand what is causing the error and carefully think through the solution. The only thing you should try is running the program with different data to determine the pattern of the unexpected behavior.

There is no magic trick that can automatically fix a program. If the compiler tells you that a semicolon or a right brace is missing, you need to examine the program and determine precisely what the problem is. Perhaps you accidentally typed a colon instead of a semicolon. Or maybe there's an extra left brace.

If the source of a problem isn't immediately obvious, a good rule of thumb is to leave the computer and go somewhere where you can quietly look over a printed copy of the program. Studies show that people who do all of their debugging away from the computer actually get their programs to work in less time *and in the end produce better programs* than those who continue to work on the machine—more proof that there is still no mechanical substitute for human thought.*

*Basili, V. R., and Selby, R. W., "Comparing the Effectiveness of Software Testing Strategies," *IEEE Trans. on Software Engineering* SE-13, no. 12 (1987): 1278–1296.

Programming Example

Map Measurements

Problem   You're spending a day in the city. You plan to visit the natural history museum, a record store, a gallery, and a bookshop, and then go to a concert. You have a tourist map that shows where these places are located. You want to determine how far apart they are and how far you'll walk during the entire day. Then you can decide when it would be better to take a taxi. According to the map's legend, one inch on the map equals one quarter of a mile on the ground.

Output   The distance between each of the places and the total distance, rounded to the nearest tenth of a mile. The values on which the calculations are based should also be printed for verification purposes.

Discussion You can measure the distances between two points on the map with a ruler. The program must output miles, so you need to multiply the number of inches by 0.25. You then write down the figure, rounded to the nearest tenth of a mile. When you've done this for each pair of places, you add the distances to get the total mileage. This is essentially the algorithm we use in the program.

The only tricky part is how to round a value to the nearest tenth of a mile. In this chapter, we showed how to round a floating-point value to the nearest integer by adding 0.5 and using a type cast to truncate the result:

```
int(floatValue + 0.5)
```

To round to the nearest tenth, we first multiply the value by 10, round the result to the nearest integer, and then divide by 10 again. For example, if floatValue contains 5.162, then

```
float(int(floatValue * 10.0 + 0.5)) / 10.0
```

gives 5.2 as its result.

Let's treat all of the quantities as named constants so that it is easier to change the program later. From measuring the map, you know that the distance from the museum to the record store is 1.5 inches, from the record store to the gallery is 2.3 inches, from the gallery to the bookshop is 5.9 inches, and from the bookshop to the concert is 4.0 inches. Here is the program:

```
//**************************************************************
// Walk program
// This program computes the mileage (rounded to tenths of a mile)
// for each of four distances between points in a city, given
// the measurements on a map with a scale of one inch equal to
// one quarter of a mile
//**************************************************************
#include <iostream>
#include <iomanip>      // For setprecision()

using namespace std;

const float DISTANCE1 = 1.5;        // Measurement for first distance
const float DISTANCE2 = 2.3;        // Measurement for second distance
const float DISTANCE3 = 5.9;        // Measurement for third distance
const float DISTANCE4 = 4.0;        // Measurement for fourth distance
const float SCALE = 0.25;           // Map scale (miles per inch)
```

```cpp
int main()
{
    float totMiles;        // Total of rounded mileages
    float miles;           // An individual rounded mileage

    cout << fixed << showpoint            // Set up floating-pt.
         << setprecision(1);              //    output format

    // Initialize the total miles

    totMiles = 0.0;

    // Compute miles for each distance on the map

    miles = float(int(DISTANCE1 * SCALE * 10.0 + 0.5)) / 10.0;
    cout << "For a measurement of " << DISTANCE1
         << " the first distance is " << miles << " mile(s) long."
         << endl;
    totMiles = totMiles + miles;

    miles = float(int(DISTANCE2 * SCALE * 10.0 + 0.5)) / 10.0;
    cout << "For a measurement of " << DISTANCE2
         << " the second distance is " << miles << " mile(s) long."
         << endl;
    totMiles = totMiles + miles;

    miles = float(int(DISTANCE3 * SCALE * 10.0 + 0.5)) / 10.0;
    cout << "For a measurement of " << DISTANCE3
         << " the third distance is " << miles << " mile(s) long."
         << endl;
    totMiles = totMiles + miles;

    miles = float(int(DISTANCE4 * SCALE * 10.0 + 0.5)) / 10.0;
    cout << "For a measurement of " << DISTANCE4
         << " the fourth distance is " << miles << " mile(s) long."
         << endl;
    totMiles = totMiles + miles;

    // Print the total miles

    cout << endl;
    cout << "Total mileage for the day is " << totMiles << " miles."
         << endl;
    return 0;
}
```

The output from the program is

```
For a measurement of 1.5 the first distance is 0.4 mile(s) long.
For a measurement of 2.3 the second distance is 0.6 mile(s) long.
For a measurement of 5.9 the third distance is 1.5 mile(s) long.
For a measurement of 4.0 the fourth distance is 1.0 mile(s) long.

Total mileage for the day is 3.5 miles.
```

Testing and Debugging

1. An `int` constant other than 0 should not start with a zero. If it starts with a zero, it is an octal (base-8) number.

2. Watch out for integer division. The expression `47/100` yields 0, the integer quotient. This is one of the major sources of wrong output in C++ programs.

3. When using the `/` and `%` operators, remember that division by zero is not allowed.

4. Double-check every expression according to the precedence rules to be sure that the operations are performed in the desired order.

5. Avoid mixing integer and floating-point values in expressions. If you must mix them, consider using explicit type casts to reduce the chance of mistakes.

6. For each assignment statement, check that the expression result has the same data type as the variable to the left of the assignment operator (=). If not, consider using an explicit type cast for clarity and safety. And remember that storing a floating-point value into an `int` variable truncates the fractional part.

7. For every library function you use in your program, be sure to `#include` the appropriate header file.

8. Examine each call to a library function to see that you have the right number of arguments and that the data types of the arguments are correct.

9. With the `string` type, positions of characters within a string are numbered starting at 0, not 1.

10. If the cause of an error in a program is not obvious, leave the computer and study a printed copy. Change your program only after you understand the source of the error.

Summary

C++ provides several built-in numeric data types, of which the most commonly used are int and float. The integral types are based on the mathematical integers, but the computer limits the range of integer values that can be represented. The floating-point types are based on the mathematical notion of real numbers. As with integers, the computer limits the range of floating-point numbers that can be represented. Also, it limits the number of digits of precision in floating-point values. We can write literals of type float in several forms, including scientific (E) notation.

Much of the computation of a program is performed in arithmetic expressions. Expressions can contain more than one operator. The order in which the operations are performed is determined by precedence rules. In arithmetic expressions, multiplication, division, and modulus are performed first, then addition and subtraction. Multiple binary (two-operand) operations of the same precedence are grouped from left to right. You can use parentheses to override the precedence rules.

Expressions may include function calls. C++ supports two kinds of functions: value-returning functions and void functions. A value-returning function is called by writing its name and argument list as part of an expression. A void function is called by writing its name and argument list as a complete C++ statement.

The C++ standard library is an integral part of every C++ system. The library contains many prewritten data types, functions, and other items that are accessed by using #include directives to the C++ preprocessor.

The setw, showpoint, fixed, and setprecision manipulators control the appearance of values in the output. These manipulators do *not* affect the values actually stored in memory, only their appearance when output.

The format of the program itself should be clear and readable. C++ is a free-format language. A consistent style that uses indentation, blank lines, and spaces within lines helps you (and other programmers) understand and work with your programs.

Quick Check

1. Write a C++ constant declaration that gives the name PI to the value 3.14159. (p. 73)
2. Declare an int variable named count and a float variable named sum. (p. 74)
3. You want to divide 9 by 5.
   a. How do you write the expression if you want the result to be the floating-point value 1.8?
   b. How do you write it if you want only the integer quotient? (pp. 74–77)
4. What is the value of the following C++ expression?

   5 % 2

   (pp. 75–77)

5. What is the result of evaluating the expression

```
(1 + 2 * 2) / 2 + 1
```

(pp. 78–80)

6. How would you write the following formula as a C++ expression that produces a floating-point value as a result? (pp. 78–80)

$$\frac{9}{5}C + 32$$

7. Add type casts to the following statements to make the type conversions clear and explicit. Your answers should produce the same results as the original statements. (pp. 80–83)
   a. `someFloat = 5 + someInt;`
   b. `someInt = 2.5 * someInt / someFloat;`

8. You want to compute the square roots and absolute values of some floating-point numbers.
   a. Which C++ library functions would you use? (pp. 85–86)
   b. Which header file(s) must you #include in order to use these functions?

9. Which part of the following function call is its argument list? (p. 84)

```
Square(someInt + 1)
```

10. In the statement

```
alpha = 4 * Beta(gamma, delta) + 3;
```

would you conclude that Beta is a value-returning function or a void function? (pp. 84–87)

11. In the statement

```
Display(gamma, delta);
```

would you conclude that Display is a value-returning function or a void function? (pp. 84–87)

12. Assume the float variable pay contains the value 327.66101. Using the fixed, setw, and setprecision manipulators, what output statement would you use to print pay in dollars and cents with three leading blanks? (pp. 88–92)

13. If the string variable str contains the string "Now is the time", what is output by the following statement? (pp. 94–98)

```
cout << str.length() << ' ' << str.substr(1, 2) << endl;
```

14. Reformat the following program to make it clear and readable. (pp. 92–93)

```
//*******************************************************************
                    // SumProd program
   // This program computes the sum and product of two integers
//*******************************************************************
#include <iostream>
using namespace std;
const int INT1=20;const int INT2=8;int main() { cout <<
"The sum of " << INT1 << " and "
<< INT2 << " is " << INT1+INT2 << endl;cout
<< "Their product is " << INT1*INT2 << endl;return 0; }
```

15. What should you do if a program fails to run correctly and the reason for the error is not immediately obvious? (p. 99)

Answers 1. `const float PI = 3.14159;`
2. `int    count;`
   `float sum;`
3. a. `9.0 / 5.0` b. `9 / 5`   4. The value is 1.   5. The result is 3.
6. `9.0 / 5.0 * c + 32.0`   7. a. `someFloat = float(5 + someInt);`
b. `someInt = int(2.5 * float(someInt) / someFloat);` 8. a. `sqrt` and
`fabs` b. `math`   9. `someInt + 1`   10. A value-returning function
11. A void function
12. `cout << fixed << setw(9) << setprecision(2) << pay;` 13. 15 ow
14.
```
//*******************************************************************
// SumProd program
// This program computes the sum and product of two integers
//*******************************************************************
#include <iostream>

using namespace std;

const int INT1 = 20;
const int INT2 = 8;

int main()
{
    cout << "The sum of " << INT1 << " and " << INT2
         << " is " << INT1 + INT2 << endl;
    cout << "Their product is " << INT1 * INT2 << endl;
    return 0;
}
```

15. Get a fresh printout of the program, leave the computer, and study the program until you understand the cause of the problem. Then correct the algorithm and the program as necessary before you go back to the computer and make any changes in the program file.

Exam Preparation Exercises

1. Mark the following constructs either valid or invalid. Assume all variables are of type int.

	Valid	Invalid
a. x * y = c;	_____	_____
b. y = con;	_____	_____
c. const int x : 10;	_____	_____
d. int x;	_____	_____
e. a = b % c;	_____	_____

2. If alpha and beta are int variables with alpha containing 4 and beta containing 9, what value is stored into alpha in each of the following? Answer each part independently of the others.
   a. alpha = 3 * beta;
   b. alpha = alpha + beta;
   c. alpha++;
   d. alpha = alpha / beta;
   e. alpha--;
   f. alpha = alpha + alpha;
   g. alpha = beta % 6;

3. Compute the value of each legal expression. Indicate whether the value is an integer or a floating-point value. If the expression is not legal, explain why.

	Integer	Floating Point
a. 10.0 / 3.0 + 5 * 2	_____	_____
b. 10 % 3 + 5 % 2	_____	_____
c. 10 / 3 + 5 / 2	_____	_____
d. 12.5 + (2.5 / (6.2 / 3.1))	_____	_____
e. -4 * (-5 + 6)	_____	_____
f. 13 % 5 / 3	_____	_____
g. (10.0 / 3.0 % 2) / 3	_____	_____

4. What value is stored into the int variable result in each of the following?
   a. result = 15 % 4;
   b. result = 7 / 3 + 2;
   c. result = 2 + 7 * 5;
   d. result = 45 / 8 * 4 + 2;
   e. result = 17 + (21 % 6) * 2;
   f. result = int(4.5 + 2.6 * 0.5);

5. If a and b are int variables with a containing 5 and b containing 2, what output does each of the following statements produce?
   a. cout << "a = " << a << "b = " << b << endl;
   b. cout << "Sum:" << a + b << endl;

c. `cout << "Sum:   " << a + b << endl;`
d. `cout << a / b << " feet" << endl;`

6. What does the following program print?

```
#include <iostream>

using namespace std;

const int LBS = 10;

int main()
{
    int   price;
    int   cost;
    char  ch;

    price = 30;
    cost = price * LBS;
    ch = 'A';
    cout << "Cost is " << endl;
    cout << cost << endl;
    cout << "Price is " << price << "Cost is " << cost << endl;
    cout << "Grade " << ch << " costs " << endl;
    cout << cost << endl;
    return 0;
}
```

7. Translate the following C++ code into algebraic notation. (All variables are `float` variables.)

```
y = -b + sqrt(b * b - 4.0 * a * c);
```

8. Given the following program fragment:

```
int    i;
int    j;
float z;

i = 4;
j = 17;
z = 2.6;
```

determine the value of each following expression. If the result is a floating-point value, include a decimal point in your answer.

    a. `i / float(j)`
    b. `1.0 / i + 2`
    c. `z * j`
    d. `i + j % i`
    e. `(1 / 2) * i`
    f. `2 * i + j - i`
    g. `j / 2`
    h. `2 * 3 - 1 % 3`
    i. `i % j / i`
    j. `int(z + 0.5)`

9. To use each of the following statements, a C++ program must #include which header file(s)?
     a. `cout << x;`
     b. `int1 = abs(int2);`
     c. `y = sqrt(7.6 + x);`
     d. `cout << y << endl;`
     e. `cout << setw(5) << someInt;`

10. Evaluate the following expressions. If the result is a floating-point number, include a decimal point in your answer.
      a. `fabs(-9.1)`
      b. `sqrt(49.0)`
      c. `3 * int(7.8) + 3`
      d. `pow(4.0, 2.0)`
      e. `sqrt(float(3 * 3 + 4 * 4))`
      f. `sqrt(fabs(-4.0) + sqrt(25.0))`

11. Show precisely the output of the following C++ program. Use a ▯ to indicate each blank.

```
#include <iostream>
#include <iomanip>    // For setw()

using namespace std;

int main()
{
    char  ch;
    int   n;
    float y;

    ch = 'A';
    cout << ch;
    ch = 'B';
    cout << ch << endl;
    n = 413;
    y = 21.8;
```

```
        cout << setw(5) << n << " is the value of n" << endl;
        cout << setw(7) << y << " is the value of y" << endl;
        return 0;
    }
```

12. Given that x is a `float` variable containing 14.3827, show the output of each statement below. Use a ⬚ to indicate each blank. (Assume that `cout << fixed` has already executed.)

    a. `cout << "x is" << setw(5) << setprecision(2) << x;`
    b. `cout << "x is" << setw(8) << setprecision(2) << x;`
    c. `cout << "x is" << setw(0) << setprecision(2) << x;`
    d. `cout << "x is" << setw(7) << setprecision(3) << x;`

13. Given the statements

    ```
    string heading;
    string str;

    heading = "Exam Preparation Exercises";
    ```

    what is the output of each code segment below?

    a. `cout << heading.length();`
    b. `cout << heading.substr(6, 10);`
    c. `cout << heading.find("Ex");`
    d. `str = heading.substr(2, 24);`
       `cout << str.find("Ex");`
    e. `str = heading.substr(heading.find("Ex") + 2, 24);`
       `cout << str.find("Ex");`
    f. `str = heading.substr(heading.find("Ex") + 2,`
       `                     heading.length() - heading.find("Ex") +`
       `                     2);`
       `cout << str.find("Ex");`

14. Formatting a program incorrectly causes an error. (True or False?)

15. What is the advantage of using named constants instead of literal constants in the Walk program?

16. In the Walk program, a particular pattern of statements is repeated four times with small variations. Identify the repeating pattern. Next, circle those parts of the statements that vary with each repetition.

Programming Warm-up Exercises

1. Change the program in Exam Preparation Exercise 6 so that it prints the cost for 15 pounds.

2. Write an assignment statement to calculate the sum of the numbers from 1 through n using Gauss's formula:

$$sum = \frac{n(n+1)}{2}$$

Store the result into the int variable sum.

3. Given the declarations

```
int    i;
int    j;
float  x;
float  y;
```

write a valid C++ expression for each of the following algebraic expressions.

a. $\dfrac{x}{y} - 3$ e. $\dfrac{i}{j}$ (the floating-point result)

b. $(x+y)(x-y)$ f. $\dfrac{i}{j}$ (the integer quotient)

c. $\dfrac{1}{x+y}$ g. $\dfrac{\dfrac{x+y}{3} - \dfrac{x-y}{5}}{4x}$

d. $\dfrac{1}{x} + y$

4. Given the declarations

```
int    i;
long   n;
float  x;
float  y;
```

write a valid C++ expression for each of the following algebraic expressions. Use calls to library functions wherever they are useful.

a. $|i|$ (absolute value)   e. $\dfrac{x^3}{y}$

b. $|n|$ f. $\sqrt{x^6 + y^5}$

c. $|x + y|$ g. $\left(x + \sqrt{y}\right)^7$

d. $|x| + |y|$

5. Write expressions to compute both solutions for the quadratic formula. The formula is

$$\frac{-b \pm \sqrt{b^2 - 4ac}}{2a}$$

The ± means "plus or minus" and indicates that there are two solutions to the equation: one in which the result of the square root is added to –b and one in which the result is subtracted from –b. Assume all variables are `float` variables.

6. Enter the following program into your computer and run it. In the initial comments, replace the items within parentheses with your own information. (Omit the parentheses.)

```
//************************************
// Programming Assignment (assignment number)
// (your name)
// (date program was run)
// (description of the problem)
//************************************
#include <iostream>

using namespace std;

const float DEBT = 300.0;       // Original value owed
const float PMT = 22.4;         // Payment
const float INT_RATE = 0.02;    // Interest rate

int main()
{
    float charge;       // Interest times debt
    float reduc;        // Amount debt is reduced
    float remaining;    // Remaining balance

    charge = INT_RATE * DEBT;
    reduc = PMT - charge;
    remaining = DEBT - reduc;
    cout << "Payment: " << PMT
         << " Charge: " << charge
         << " Balance owed: " << remaining << endl;
    return 0;
}
```

7. Enter the following program into your computer and run it. Add comments, using the pattern shown in Exercise 6 above. (Notice how hard it is to tell what the program does without the comments.)

```cpp
#include <iostream>

using namespace std;

const int TOT_COST = 1376;
const int POUNDS = 10;
const int OUNCES = 12;

int main()
{
    int    totOz;
    float uCost;

    totOz = 16 * POUNDS;
    totOz = totOz + OUNCES;
    uCost = TOT_COST / totOz;
    cout << "Cost per unit: " << uCost << endl;
    return 0;
}
```

8. Complete the following C++ program. The program should find and output the perimeter and area of a rectangle, given the length and the width. Be sure to label the output. And don't forget to use comments.

```cpp
//**************************************************
// Rectangle program
// This program finds the perimeter and the area
// of a rectangle, given the length and width
//**************************************************
#include <iostream>

using namespace std;

int main()
{
    float length;       // Length of the rectangle
    float width;        // Width of the rectangle
    float perimeter;    // Perimeter of the rectangle
    float area;         // Area of the rectangle

    length = 10.7;
    width = 5.2;
```

9. Write an expression whose result is the position of the first occurrence of the characters "res" in a string variable named sentence. If the variable contains the first sentence of this question, then what is the result? (Look at the sentence carefully!)

10. Write a sequence of C++ statements to output the positions of the second and third occurrences of the characters "res" in the string variable named sentence. You may assume that there are always at least three occurrences in the variable. (*Hint:* Use the substr function to create a new string whose contents are the portion of sentence following an occurrence of "res".)

11. Modify the Walk program to include a round-off factor so that the rounding of miles can be modified easily. Currently, the program uses a literal constant (10.0) in several places to round miles to the nearest tenth, requiring us to make multiple changes if we want a different round-off factor.

12. Should the round-off factor in Exercise 11 be a constant or a variable? Explain.

Programming Problems

1. C++ systems provide a header file climits, which contains declarations of constants related to the specific compiler and machine on which you are working. Two of these constants are INT_MAX and INT_MIN, the largest and smallest int values for your particular computer. Write a program to print out the values of INT_MAX and INT_MIN. The output should identify which value is INT_MAX and which value is INT_MIN. Be sure to include appropriate comments in your program, and use indentation as we do in the programs in this chapter.

2. Write a program that outputs three lines, labeled as follows:

```
7 / 4 using integer division equals   <result>
7 / 4 using floating-point division equals   <result>
7 modulo 4 equals   <result>
```

where <result> stands for the result computed by your program. Use named constants for 7 and 4 everywhere in your program (including the output statements) to make the program easy to modify. Be sure to include appropriate comments in your program, choose meaningful identifiers, and use indentation as we do in the programs in this chapter.

3. Write a C++ program that converts a Celsius temperature to its Fahrenheit equivalent. The formula is

$$Fahrenheit = \frac{9}{5} Celsius + 32$$

Make the Celsius temperature a named constant so that its value can be changed easily. The program should print both the value of the Celsius temperature and its Fahrenheit equivalent, with appropriate identifying messages. Be sure to include appropriate comments in your program, choose meaningful identifiers, and use indentation as we do in the programs in this chapter.

4. Write a program to calculate the diameter, the circumference, and the area of a circle with a radius of 6.75. Assign the radius to a `float` variable, and then output the radius with an appropriate message. Declare a named constant `PI` with the value 3.14159. The program should output the diameter, the circumference, and the area, each on a separate line, with identifying labels. Print each value to five decimal places within a total fieldwidth of 10. Be sure to include appropriate comments in your program, choose meaningful identifiers, and use indentation as we do in the programs in this chapter.

5. You have bought a car, taking out a loan with an annual interest rate of 9%. You will make 36 monthly payments of $165.25 each. You want to keep track of the remaining balance you owe after each monthly payment. The formula for the remaining balance is

$$bal_k = pmt\left[\frac{1-(1+i)^{k-n}}{i}\right]$$

where

bal_k = balance remaining after the kth payment
k = payment number (1, 2, 3, ...)
pmt = amount of the monthly payment
i = interest rate per month (annual rate ÷ 12)
n = total number of payments to be made

Write a program to calculate and print the balance remaining after the first, second, and third monthly car payments. Before printing these three results, the program should output the values on which the calculations are based (monthly payment, interest rate, and total number of payments). Label all output with identifying messages, and print all money amounts to two decimal places. Be sure to include appropriate comments in your program, choose meaningful identifiers, and use indentation as we do in the programs in this chapter.

Program Input and the Software Design Process

- To be able to construct input statements to read values into a program.

- To be able to determine the contents of variables assigned values by input statements.

- To be able to write appropriate prompting messages for interactive programs.

- To know when noninteractive input/output is appropriate and how it differs from interactive input/output.

- To be able to write programs that use data files for input and output.

- To understand the basic principles of object-oriented design.

- To be able to apply the functional decomposition methodology to solve a simple problem.

- To be able to take a functional decomposition and code it in C++, using self-documenting code.

A program needs data on which to operate. We have been writing all of the data values in the program itself, in literal and named constants. If this were the only way we could enter data, we would have to rewrite a program each time we wanted to apply it to a different set of values. In this chapter, we look at ways of entering data into a program while it is running.

Once we know how to input data, process the data, and output the results, we can begin to think about designing more complicated programs. We have talked about general problem-solving strategies and writing simple programs. For a simple problem, it's easy to choose a strategy, write the algorithm, and code the program. But as problems become more complex, we have to use a more organized approach. In the second part of this chapter, we look at two general methodologies for developing software: object-oriented design and functional decomposition.

4.1 Getting Data into Programs

One of the biggest advantages of computers is that a program can be used with many different sets of data. To do so, we must keep the data separate from the program until the program is executed. Then instructions in the program copy values from the data set into variables in the program. After storing these values into the variables, the program can perform calculations with them.

The process of placing values from an outside data set into variables in a program is called *input*. In widely used terminology, the computer is said to *read* outside data into the variables. The data for the program can come from an input device or from a file on an auxiliary storage device. We look at file input later in this chapter; here we consider the *standard input device,* the keyboard.

Input Streams and the Extraction Operator (>>)

The concept of a stream is fundamental to input and output in C++. As we stated in Chapter 3, you can think of an output stream as an endless sequence of characters going from your program to an output device. Likewise, think of an *input stream* as an endless sequence of characters coming into your program from an input device.

The header file iostream contains, among other things, the definitions of two data types: istream and ostream. These are data types representing input streams and output streams, respectively. The header file also contains declarations that look like this:

```
istream cin;
ostream cout;
```

The first declaration says that cin (pronounced "see-in") is a variable of type istream. The second says that cout (pronounced "see-out") is a variable of type ostream. Furthermore, cin is associated with the standard input device (the keyboard), and cout is associated with the standard output device (usually the display screen).

As you have already seen, you can output values to `cout` by using the insertion operator (<<), which is sometimes pronounced "put to":

```
cout << 3 * price;
```

In a similar fashion, you can input data from `cin` by using the *extraction operator* (>>), sometimes pronounced "get from":

```
cin >> cost;
```

When the computer executes this statement, it inputs the next number you type on the keyboard (425, for example) and stores it into the variable `cost`.

The extraction operator >> takes two operands. Its left-hand operand is a stream expression (in the simplest case, just the variable `cin`). Its right-hand operand is a variable into which we store the input data. For the time being, we assume the variable is of a simple type (`char`, `int`, `float`, and so forth). Later in the chapter we discuss the input of string data.

You can use the >> operator several times in a single input statement. Each occurrence extracts (inputs) the next data item from the input stream. For example, there is no difference between the statement

```
cin >> length >> width;
```

and the pair of statements

```
cin >> length;
cin >> width;
```

Using a sequence of extractions in one statement is a convenience for the programmer.

When you are new to C++, you may get the extraction operator (>>) and the insertion operator (<<) reversed. Here is an easy way to remember which one is which: Always begin the statement with either `cin` or `cout`, and use the operator that points in the direction in which the data is going. The statement

```
cout << someInt;
```

sends data from the variable `someInt` *to* the output stream. The statement

```
cin >> someInt;
```

sends data from the input stream *to* the variable `someInt`.

Unlike the items specified in an output statement, which can be constants, variables, or complicated expressions, the items specified in an input statement can *only* be variable names. Why? Because an input statement indicates where input data values should be stored. Only variable names refer to memory locations where we can store values while a program is running.

When you enter input data at the keyboard, you must be sure that each data value is appropriate for the data type of the variable in the input statement.

Data Type of Variable in an >> Operation	Valid Input Data
char	A single printable character other than a blank
int	An int literal constant, optionally preceded by a sign
float	An int or float literal constant (possibly in scientific, E, notation), optionally preceded by a sign

Notice that when you input a number into a float variable, the input value doesn't have to have a decimal point. The integer value is automatically coerced to a float value. Any other mismatches, such as trying to input a float value into an int variable or a char value into a float variable, can lead to unexpected and sometimes serious results. Later in this chapter we discuss what might happen.

When looking for the next input value in the stream, the >> operator skips any leading *whitespace characters*. Whitespace characters are blanks and certain nonprintable characters such as the character that marks the end of a line. (We talk about this end-of-line character in the next section.) After skipping these characters, the >> operator proceeds to extract the desired data value from the input stream. If this data value is a char value, input stops as soon as a single character is input. If the data value is int or float, input of the number stops at the first character that is inappropriate for the data type, such as a whitespace character. Here are some examples, where i, j, and k are int variables, ch is a char variable, and x is a float variable:

Statement	Data	Contents After Input
1. cin >> i;	32	i = 32
2. cin >> i >> j;	4 60	i = 4, j = 60
3. cin >> i >> ch >> x;	25 A 16.9	i = 25, ch = 'A', x = 16.9
4. cin >> i >> ch >> x;	25	
	A	
	16.9	i = 25, ch = 'A', x = 16.9
5. cin >> i >> ch >> x;	25A16.9	i = 25, ch = 'A', x = 16.9
6. cin >> i >> j >> x;	12 8	i = 12, j = 8
		(Computer waits for a third number)
7. cin >> i >> x;	46 32.4 15	i = 46, x = 32.4
		(15 is held for later input)

Examples (1) and (2) are straightforward examples of integer input. Example (3) shows that you do not use quotes around character data values when they are input. Example

(4) demonstrates how the process of skipping whitespace characters includes going on to the next line of input if necessary. Example (5) shows that the first character encountered that is inappropriate for a numeric data type ends the number. Input for the variable i stops at the input character A, after which the A is stored into ch, and then input for x stops at the end of the input line. Example (6) shows that if you are at the keyboard and haven't entered enough values to satisfy the input statement, the computer waits for more data. Example (7) shows that if more values are entered than there are variables in the input statement, the extra values remain waiting in the input stream until they can be read by the next input statement. If there are extra values left when the program ends, the computer disregards them.

The Reading Marker and the Newline Character

To help explain stream input in more detail, we introduce the concept of the *reading marker*. The reading marker works like a bookmark, but instead of marking a place in a book, it keeps track of the point in the input stream where the computer should continue reading. The reading marker indicates the next character waiting to be read. The extraction operator >> leaves the reading marker on the character following the last piece of data that was input.

Each input line has an invisible end-of-line character (the *newline character*) that tells the computer where one line ends and the next begins. To find the next input value, the >> operator crosses line boundaries (newline characters) if it has to.

Where does the newline character come from? What is it? The answer to the first question is easy. When you are working at a keyboard, you generate a newline character each time you hit the Return or Enter key. Your program also generates a newline character when it uses the endl manipulator in an output statement. The endl manipulator outputs a newline, telling the screen cursor to go to the next line. The answer to the second question varies from computer system to computer system. The newline character is a nonprintable control character that the system recognizes as meaning the end of a line, whether it's an input line or an output line.

In a C++ program, you can refer directly to the newline character by using the two symbols \n, a backslash and an n with no space between them. Although \n consists of two symbols, it refers to a single character—the newline character. Just as you can store the letter *A* into a char variable ch like this:

```
ch = 'A';
```

so you can store the newline character into a variable:

```
ch = '\n';
```

Let's look at some examples using the reading marker and the newline character. In the following table, i is an int variable, ch is a char variable, and x is a float variable. The input statements produce the results shown. The part of the input stream printed in color is what has been extracted by input statements. The reading marker, denoted by the shaded block, indicates the next character waiting to be read. The \n denotes the newline character.

Statements	Contents After Input	Marker Position in the Input Stream
1.		25 A 16.9\n
cin >> i;	i = 25	25 A 16.9\n
cin >> ch;	ch = 'A'	25 A 16.9\n
cin >> x;	x = 16.9	25 A 16.9\n
2.		25\n
		A\n
		16.9\n
cin >> i;	i = 25	25\n
		A\n
		16.9\n
cin >> ch;	ch = 'A'	25\n
		A\n
		16.9\n
cin >> x;	x = 16.9	25\n
		A\n
		16.9\n
3.		25A16.9\n
cin >> i;	i = 25	25A16.9\n
cin >> ch;	ch = 'A'	25A16.9\n
cin >> x;	x = 16.9	25A16.9\n

Reading Character Data with the `get` Function

As we have discussed, the >> operator skips leading whitespace characters in the input stream. Suppose that ch1 and ch2 are char variables and the program executes the statement

```
cin >> ch1 >> ch2;
```

If the input stream consists of

```
R 1
```

then the extraction operator stores 'R' into ch1, skips the blank, and stores '1' into ch2. (Note that the char value '1' is not the same as the int value 1. The two are stored completely differently in a computer's memory. The extraction operator interprets the same data in different ways, depending on the data type of the variable that's being filled.)

What if we had wanted to input *three* characters from the input line: the R, the blank, and the 1? With the extraction operator, it's not possible. Whitespace characters such as blanks are skipped over.

The `istream` data type provides a second way in which to read character data, in addition to the `>>` operator. You can use the `get` function, which inputs the very next character in the input stream without skipping any whitespace. Its call looks like this:

```
cin.get(someChar);
```

The `get` function is associated with the `istream` data type, and you must use dot notation to make a function call. (Recall that we used dot notation in Chapter 3 to invoke certain functions associated with the `string` type. Later in this chapter we explain the reason for dot notation.) To use the `get` function, you give the name of an `istream` variable (here, `cin`), then a dot (period), and then the function name and argument list. Notice that the call to `get` uses the syntax for calling a void function, not a value-returning function. The function call is a complete statement; it is not part of a larger expression.

The effect of the above function call is to input the next character waiting in the stream—even if it is a whitespace character like a blank—and store it into the variable `someChar`. The argument to the `get` function *must* be a variable, not a constant or arbitrary expression; we must tell the function where we want it to store the input character.

Using the `get` function, we now can input all three characters of the input line

```
R 1
```

We can use three consecutive calls to the `get` function:

```
cin.get(ch1);
cin.get(ch2);
cin.get(ch3);
```

or we can do it this way:

```
cin >> ch1;
cin.get(ch2);
cin >> ch3;
```

The first version is probably a bit clearer for someone to read and understand.

Here are some more examples of character input using both the `>>` operator and the `get` function. `ch1`, `ch2`, and `ch3` are all `char` variables. As before, `/n` denotes the newline character.

Statements	Contents After Input	Marker Position in the Input Stream
1.		A B\n
		CD\n
cin >> ch1;	ch1 = 'A'	A B\n
		CD\n
cin >> ch2;	ch2 = 'B'	A B\n
		CD\n
cin >> ch3;	ch3 = 'C'	A B\n
		CD\n

Statements	Contents After Input	Marker Position in the Input Stream
2.		A B\n
		CD\n
cin.get(ch1);	ch1 = 'A'	A B\n
		CD\n
cin.get(ch2);	ch2 = ' '	A B\n
		CD\n
cin.get(ch3);	ch3 = 'B'	A B\n
		CD\n

Statements	Contents After Input	Marker Position in the Input Stream
3.		A B\n
		CD\n
cin >> ch1;	ch1 = 'A'	A B\n
		CD\n
cin >> ch2;	ch2 = 'B'	A B\n
		CD\n
cin.get(ch3);	ch3 = '\n'	A B\n
		CD\n

Skipping Characters with the `ignore` Function

Most of us have a specialized tool lying in a kitchen drawer or in a toolbox. It gathers dust and cobwebs because we almost never use it. But when we suddenly need it, we're glad we have it. The `ignore` function associated with the `istream` type is like this specialized tool. You rarely have occasion to use `ignore`, but when you need it, you're glad it's available.

The `ignore` function is used to skip (read and discard) characters in the input stream. It is a function with two arguments, called like this:

```
cin.ignore(200, '\n');
```

The first argument is an `int` expression; the second, a `char` value. This particular function call tells the computer to skip the next 200 input characters *or* to skip characters until a newline character is read, whichever comes first.

Here are some examples that use a `char` variable `ch` and three `int` variables, `i`, `j`, and `k`:

Statements	Contents After Input	Marker Position in the Input Stream
1.		957 34 1235\n 128 96\n
`cin >> i >> j;`	i = 957, j = 34	957 34 1235\n 128 96\n
`cin.ignore(100, '\n');`		957 34 1235\n 128 96\n
`cin >> k;`	k = 128	957 34 1235\n 128 96\n

2.
`cin >> ch;`
`cin.ignore(100, 'B');`
`cin >> i;`
	ch = 'A'
	
	i = 16
		A 22 B 16 C 19\n
		A 22 B 16 C 19\n
		A 22 B 16 C 19\n
		A 22 B 16 C 19\n

3.
`cin.ignore(2, '\n');`
`cin >> ch;`
	
	ch = 'C'
		ABCDEF\n
		ABCDEF\n
		ABCDEF\n

Example (1) shows the most common use of the `ignore` function, which is to skip the rest of the data on the current input line. Example (2) demonstrates the use of a character other than '\n' as the second argument. We skip over all input characters until a *B* has been found, then read the next input number into `i`. In both (1) and (2), we are focusing on the second argument to the `ignore` function, and we arbitrarily choose any large number, such as 100, for the first argument. In (3), we change our focus and concentrate on the first argument. Our intention is to skip the next two input characters on the current line.

Reading String Data

To input a character string into a `string` variable, we have two options. The first is to use the extraction operator (`>>`). When reading input characters into a `string` variable, the `>>` operator skips any leading whitespace characters such as blanks and newlines. It then reads successive characters into the variable, stopping at the first *trailing* whitespace character (which is not consumed, but remains as the first character waiting in the input stream). For example, assume we have the following code:

```
string firstName;
string lastName;

cin >> firstName >> lastName;
```

If the input stream initially looks like this (where ☐ denotes a blank):

☐☐Mary☐Smith☐☐☐18

then our input statement stores the four characters `Mary` into `firstName`, stores the five characters `Smith` into `lastName`, and leaves the input stream as

☐☐☐18

Although the `>>` operator is widely used for string input, it has a potential drawback: it cannot be used to input a string that has blanks within it. (Remember that it stops reading as soon as it encounters a whitespace character.) This fact leads us to the second option for performing string input: the `getline` function. A call to this function looks like this:

```
getline(cin, myString);
```

The function call, which does not use dot notation, requires two arguments. The first is an input stream variable (here, `cin`) and the second is a `string` variable. The `getline` function does not skip leading whitespace characters and continues until it reaches the newline character '\n'. That is, `getline` reads and stores an entire input line, embedded blanks and all. Note that with `getline`, the newline character *is* consumed (but is not stored into the string variable). Given the code segment

```
string inputStr;

getline(cin, inputStr);
```

and the input line

☐☐Mary☐Smith☐☐☐18

the result of the call to `getline` is that all 17 characters on the input line (including blanks) are stored into `inputStr`, and the reading marker is positioned at the beginning of the next input line.

The following table summarizes the differences between the `>>` operator and the `getline` function when reading string data into `string` variables.

Statement	Skips Leading Whitespace?	Stops Reading When?
`cin >> inputStr;`	Yes	When a trailing whitespace character is encountered (which is *not* consumed)
`getline(cin, inputStr);`	No	When '\n' is encountered (which *is* consumed)

4.2 Interactive Input/Output

An interactive program is one in which the user communicates directly with the computer. Many of the programs that we write are interactive. There is a certain "etiquette" involved in writing interactive programs that has to do with instructions for the user to follow.

To get data into an interactive program, we begin with *input prompts,* printed messages that explain what the user should enter. Without these messages, the user has no idea what data values to type. In many cases, a program also should print out all of the data values typed in so that the user can verify that they were entered correctly. Printing out the input values is called *echo printing.* Here's a program segment showing the proper use of prompts:

```
cout << "Enter the part number:" << endl;              // Prompt
cin >> partNumber;
cout << "Enter the quantity of this part ordered:"     // Prompt
     << endl;
cin >> quantity;
cout << "Enter the unit price for this part:"          // Prompt
     << endl;
cin >> unitPrice;
totalPrice = quantity * unitPrice;
cout << "Part " << partNumber                          // Echo print
     << ", quantity " << quantity
     << ", at $ " << setprecision(2) << unitPrice
     << " each" << endl;
cout << "totals $ " << totalPrice << endl;
```

And here's the output, with the user's input shown in color:

```
Enter the part number:
4671
Enter the quantity of this part ordered:
10
Enter the unit price for this part:
27.25
Part 4671, quantity 10, at $ 27.25 each
totals $ 272.50
```

The amount of information you should put into your prompts depends on who is going to be using a program. If you are writing a program for people who are not familiar with computers, your messages should be more detailed. For example, "Type a four-digit part number, then press the key marked Enter." If the program is going to be used frequently by the same people, you might shorten the prompts: "Enter PN" and "Enter

Qty." If the program is for very experienced users, you can prompt for several values at once and have them type all of the values on one input line:

```
Enter PN, Qty, Unit Price:
4176 10 27.25
```

In programs that use large amounts of data, this method saves the user keystrokes and time. However, it also makes it easier for the user to enter values in the wrong order.

Prompts are not the only way in which programs interact with users. It can be helpful to have a program print out some general instructions at the beginning ("Press Enter after typing each data value. Enter a negative number when done."). When data is not entered in the correct form, a message that indicates the problem should be printed. For users who haven't worked much with computers, it's important that these messages be informative and "friendly." The message

```
ILLEGAL DATA VALUES!!!!!!!
```

is likely to upset an inexperienced user. Moreover, it doesn't offer any constructive information. A much better message would be

```
That is not a valid part number.
Part numbers must be no more than four digits long.
Please reenter the number in its proper form:
```

In Chapter 5, we introduce the statements that allow us to test for erroneous data.

4.3 Noninteractive Input/Output

Although we tend to use examples of interactive I/O in this text, many programs are written using noninteractive I/O. A common example of noninteractive I/O on large computer systems is *batch processing*. In batch processing, the user and the computer do not interact while the program is running. This method is most effective when a program is going to input or output large amounts of data. An example of batch processing is a program that inputs a file containing semester grades for thousands of students and prints grade reports to be mailed out.

When a program must read in many data values, the usual practice is to prepare them ahead of time, storing them into a disk file. This allows the user to go back and make changes or corrections to the data as necessary before running the program. When a program is designed to print lots of data, the output can be sent directly to a high-speed printer or another disk file. After the program has been run, the user can examine the data at leisure. In the next section, we discuss input and output with disk files.

Programs designed for noninteractive I/O do not print prompting messages for input. It is a good idea, however, to echo print each data value that is read. Echo printing allows the person reading the output to verify that the input values were prepared correctly. Because noninteractive programs tend to print large amounts of data, their output often is in the form of a table—columns with descriptive headings.

Most C++ programs are written for interactive use. But the flexibility of the language allows you to write noninteractive programs as well. The biggest difference is in the input/output requirements. Noninteractive programs are generally more rigid about the organization and format of the input and output data.

4.4   File Input and Output

In everything we've done so far, we've assumed that the input to our programs comes from the keyboard and that the output from our programs goes to the screen. We look now at input/output to and from files.

Files

A file is a named area in secondary storage that holds a collection of information (for example, the program code we have typed into the editor). The information in a file usually is stored on an auxiliary storage device, such as a disk. Our programs can read data from a file in the same way they read data from the keyboard, and they can write output to a disk file in the same way they write output to the screen.

Why would we want a program to read data from a file instead of the keyboard? If a program is going to read a large quantity of data, it is easier to enter the data into a file with an editor than to enter it while the program is running. With the editor, we can go back and correct mistakes. Also, we do not have to enter the data all at once; we can take a break and come back later. And if we want to rerun the program, having the data stored in a file allows us to do so without retyping the data.

Why would we want the output from a program to be written to a disk file? The contents of a file can be displayed on a screen or printed. This gives us the option of looking at the output over and over again without having to rerun the program. Also, the output stored in a file can be read into another program as input.

Using Files

If we want a program to use file I/O, we have to do four things:

1. Request the preprocessor to include the header file `fstream`.
2. Use declaration statements to declare the file streams we are going to use.
3. Prepare each file for reading or writing by using a function named `open`.
4. Specify the name of the file stream in each input or output statement.

Including the Header File `fstream`   Suppose we want the Walk program (p. 100) to read data from a file and to write its output to a file. The first thing we must do is use the preprocessor directive

```
#include <fstream>
```

Through the header file `fstream`, the C++ standard library defines two data types, `ifstream` and `ofstream` (standing for *input file stream* and *output file stream*). Consistent with the general idea of streams in C++, the `ifstream` data type represents a stream of characters coming from an input file, and `ofstream` represents a stream of characters going to an output file.

All of the `istream` operations you have learned about—the extraction operator (>>), the `get` function, and the `ignore` function—are also valid for the `ifstream` type. And all of the `ostream` operations, such as the insertion operator (<<) and the `endl`, `setw`, and `setprecision` manipulators, apply also to the `ofstream` type. To these basic operations, the `ifstream` and `ofstream` types add some more operations designed specifically for file I/O.

Declaring File Streams   In a program, you declare stream variables the same way that you declare any variable—you specify the data type and then the variable name:

```
int       someInt;
float     someFloat;
ifstream  inFile;
ofstream  outFile;
```

(You don't have to declare the stream variables `cin` and `cout`. The header file `iostream` already does this for you.)

For our Walk program, let's name the input and output file streams `inData` and `outData`. We declare them like this:

```
ifstream inData;        // Holds map distances in inches
ofstream outData;       // Holds walking distances in miles
```

Note that the `ifstream` type is for input files only, and the `ofstream` type is for output files only. With these data types, you cannot read from and write to the same file.

Opening Files   The third thing we have to do is prepare each file for reading or writing, an act called *opening a file*. Opening a file causes the computer's operating system to perform certain actions that allow us to proceed with file I/O.

In our example, we want to read from the file stream `inData` and write to the file stream `outData`. We open the relevant files by using the statements

```
inData.open("walk.dat");
outData.open("results.dat");
```

which are both function calls. In each function call, the argument is a literal string enclosed by quotes. The first statement is a call to a function named open, which is associated with the ifstream data type. The second is a call to another function (also named open) associated with the ofstream data type. As we have seen earlier, we use dot notation (as in inData.open) to call certain library functions that are tightly associated with data types.

Exactly what does an open function do? First, it associates a stream variable used in your program with a physical file on disk. Our first function call creates a connection between the stream variable inData and the actual disk file, named walk.dat. (Names of file streams must be identifiers; they are variables in your program. But some computer systems do not use this syntax for file names on disk. For example, many systems allow or even require a dot within a file name.) Similarly, the second function call associates the stream variable outData with the disk file results.dat. Associating a program's name for a file (outData) with the actual name for the file (results.dat) is much the same as associating a program's name for the standard output device (cout) with the actual device (the screen).

The next thing the open function does depends on whether the file is an input file or an output file. With an input file, the open function sets the file's reading marker to the first piece of data in the file. (Each input file has its own reading marker.)

With an output file, the open function checks to see whether the file already exists. If the file doesn't exist, open creates a new, empty file for you. If the file already exists, open erases the old contents of the file. Then the writing marker is set at the beginning of the empty file (see Figure 4-1). As output proceeds, each successive output operation advances the writing marker to add data to the end of the file.

Because the reason for opening files is to *prepare* the files for reading or writing, you must open the files before using any input or output statements that refer to the files. In a program, it's a good idea to open files right away to be sure that the files are prepared before the program attempts any file I/O.

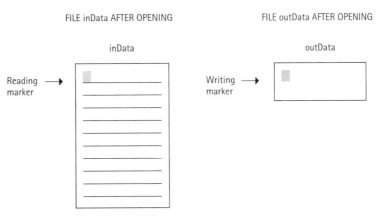

FILE inData AFTER OPENING   FILE outData AFTER OPENING

inData   outData

Reading →   Writing →
marker   marker

Figure 4-1 *The Effect of Opening a File*

```
      ⋮
int main()
{

      ⋮        } Declarations


   // Open the files

   inData.open("walk.dat");
   outData.open("results.dat");
      ⋮
}
```

Specifying File Streams in Input/Output Statements There is just one more thing we have to do in order to use files. As we said earlier, all `istream` operations are also valid for the `ifstream` type, and all `ostream` operations are valid for the `ofstream` type. So, to read from or write to a file, all we need to do in our input and output statements is substitute the appropriate file stream variable for `cin` or `cout`. In our Walk program, we would use a statement like

```
inData >> distance1 >> distance2 >> distance3 >> distance4 >> scale;
```

to instruct the computer to read data from the file `inData` instead of from `cin`. Similarly, all of the output statements that write to the file `outData` would specify `outData`, not `cout`, as the destination:

```
outData << "Total mileage for the day is " << totMiles << " miles."
        << endl;
```

What is nice about C++ stream I/O is that we have a uniform syntax for performing I/O operations, regardless of whether we're working with the keyboard and screen, with files, or with other I/O devices.

An Example Program Using Files

The reworked Walk program is shown below. Now it reads its input from the file `inData` and writes its output to the file `outData`. Compare this program with the original version on page 100 and notice that the named constants have disappeared because the data is now input at execution time. Notice also that to set up the floating-point output format, the `fixed`, `showpoint`, and `setprecision` manipulators are applied to the `outData` stream variable, not to `cout`.

```
//**********************************************************************
// Walk program
// This program computes the mileage (rounded to tenths of a mile)
```

```
// for each of four distances between points in a city, given
// the measurements on a map with a scale whose value is also
// input
//********************************************************************
#include <iostream>
#include <iomanip>    // For setprecision()
#include <fstream>    // For file I/O

using namespace std;

int main()
{
    float    distance1;      // Measurement for first distance
    float    distance2;      // Measurement for second distance
    float    distance3;      // Measurement for third distance
    float    distance4;      // Measurement for fourth distance
    float    scale;          // Map scale (miles per inch)
    float    totMiles;       // Total of rounded mileages
    float    miles;          // An individual rounded mileage
    ifstream inData;         // Holds map distances in inches
    ofstream outData;        // Holds walking distances in miles

    outData << fixed << showpoint           // Set up floating-pt.
            << setprecision(1);             //    output format

    // Open the files

    inData.open("walk.dat");
    outData.open("results.dat");

    // Get data

    inData >> distance1 >> distance2 >> distance3 >> distance4
           >> scale;

    // Initialize the total miles

    totMiles = 0.0;

    // Compute miles for each distance on the map

    miles = float(int(distance1 * scale * 10.0 + 0.5)) / 10.0;
    outData << "For a measurement of " << distance1
            << " the first distance is " << miles
            << " mile(s) long." << endl;
```

```
totMiles = totMiles + miles;

miles = float(int(distance2 * scale * 10.0 + 0.5)) / 10.0;
outData << "For a measurement of " << distance2
        << " the second distance is " << miles
        << " mile(s) long." << endl;
totMiles = totMiles + miles;

miles = float(int(distance3 * scale * 10.0 + 0.5)) / 10.0;
outData << "For a measurement of " << distance3
        << " the third distance is " << miles
        << " mile(s) long." << endl;
totMiles = totMiles + miles;

miles = float(int(distance4 * scale * 10.0 + 0.5)) / 10.0;
outData << "For a measurement of " << distance4
        << " the fourth distance is " << miles
        << " mile(s) long." << endl;
totMiles = totMiles + miles;

// Print the total miles

outData << endl;
outData << "Total mileage for the day is " << totMiles
        << " miles." << endl;
return 0;
}
```

Before running the program, you would use the editor to create and save a file walk.dat to serve as input. The contents of the file might look like this:

```
1.5 2.3 5.9 4.0 0.25
```

In writing the new Walk program, what happens if you mistakenly specify cout instead of outData in one of the output statements? Nothing disastrous; the output of that one statement merely goes to the screen instead of the output file. And what if, by mistake, you specify cin instead of inData in the input statement? The consequences are not as pleasant. When you run the program, the computer will appear to go dead (to *hang*). Here's the reason: Execution reaches the input statement and the computer waits for you to enter the data from the keyboard. But you don't know that the computer is waiting. There's no message on the screen prompting you for input, and you are assuming (wrongly) that the program is getting its input from a data file. So the computer waits, and you wait, and the computer waits, and you wait. Every programmer at one time or another has had the experience of thinking the computer has hung, when, in fact, it is working just fine, silently waiting for keyboard input.

Run-Time Input of File Names

Until now, our examples of opening a file for input have included code similar to the following:

```
ifstream inFile;

inFile.open("datafile.dat");
    ⋮
```

The open function associated with the ifstream data type requires an argument that specifies the name of the actual data file on disk. By using a literal string, as in the example above, the file name is fixed at compile time. Therefore, the program works only for this one particular disk file.

We often want to make a program more flexible by allowing the file name to be determined at *run time*. A common technique is to prompt the user for the name of the file, read the user's response into a variable, and pass the variable as an argument to the open function. In principle, the following code should accomplish what we want. Unfortunately, the compiler does not allow it.

```
ifstream inFile;
string    fileName;

cout << "Enter the input file name: ";
cin >> fileName;
inFile.open(fileName);                  // Compile-time error
```

The problem is that the open function does not expect an argument of type string. Instead, it expects a *C string*. A C string (so named because it originated in the C language, the forerunner of C++) is a limited form of string whose properties we discuss much later in the book. A literal string, such as "datafile.dat", happens to be a C string and thus is acceptable as an argument to the open function.

To make the above code work correctly, we need to convert a string variable to a C string. The string data type provides a value-returning function named c_str that is applied to a string variable as follows:

```
fileName.c_str()
```

This function returns the C string that is equivalent to the one contained in the file-Name variable. (The original string contained in fileName is not changed by the function call.) The primary purpose of the c_str function is to allow programmers to call library functions that expect C strings, not string strings, as arguments.

Using the c_str function, we can code the run-time input of a file name as follows:

```
ifstream inFile;
string    fileName;
```

```
cout << "Enter the input file name: ";
cin >> fileName;
inFile.open(fileName.c_str());
```

4.5 Input Failure

When a program inputs data from the keyboard or an input file, errors can occur. Let's suppose that we're executing a program. It prompts us to enter an integer value, but we absentmindedly type some letters of the alphabet. The input operation fails because of the invalid data. In C++ terminology, the cin stream has entered the *fail state*. Once a stream has entered the fail state, any further I/O operations using that stream are considered to be null operations—that is, they have no effect at all. Unfortunately for us, *the computer does not halt the program or give any error message.* The computer just continues executing the program, silently ignoring each additional attempt to use that stream.

Invalid data is the most common reason for input failure. When your program inputs an int value, it is expecting to find only digits in the input stream, possibly preceded by a plus or minus sign. If there is a decimal point somewhere within the digits, does the input operation fail? Not necessarily; it depends on where the reading marker is. Let's look at an example.

Assume that a program has int variables i, j, and k, whose contents are currently 10, 20, and 30, respectively. The program now executes the following two statements:

```
cin >> i >> j >> k;
cout << "i: " << i << "   j: " << j << "   k: " << k;
```

If we type these characters for the input data:

```
1234.56 7 89
```

then the program produces this output:

```
i: 1234   j: 20   k: 30
```

Let's see why.

Remember that when reading int or float data, the extraction operator >> stops reading at the first character that is inappropriate for the data type (whitespace or otherwise). In our example, the input operation for i succeeds. The computer extracts the first four characters from the input stream and stores the integer value 1234 into i. The reading marker is now on the decimal point:

```
1234.56 7 89
```

The next input operation (for j) fails; an int value cannot begin with a decimal point. The cin stream is now in the fail state, and the current value of j (20) remains unchanged. The third input operation (for k) is ignored, as are all the rest of the statements in our program that read from cin.

Another way to make a stream enter the fail state is to try to open an input file that doesn't exist. Suppose that you have a data file on your disk named myfile.dat. In your program you have the following statements:

```
ifstream inFile;

inFile.open("myfil.dat");
inFile >> i >> j >> k;
```

In the call to the open function, you misspelled the name of your disk file. At run time, the attempt to open the file fails, so the stream inFile enters the fail state. The next three input operations (for i, j, and k) are null operations. Without issuing any error message, the program proceeds to use the (unknown) contents of i, j, and k in calculations. The results of these calculations are certain to be puzzling.

The point of this discussion is not to make you nervous about I/O but to make you aware. The Testing and Debugging section at the end of this chapter offers suggestions for avoiding input failure, and Chapters 5 and 6 introduce program statements that let you test the state of a stream.

4.6   Software Design Methodologies

The programs we have written thus far were short and straightforward because the problems to be solved were simple. We are ready to write programs for more complicated problems, but first we need to step back and look at the overall process of programming.

As you learned in Chapter 1, the programming process consists of a problem-solving phase and an implementation phase. The problem-solving phase includes *analysis* (analyzing and understanding the problem to be solved) and *design* (designing a solution to the problem). Given a complex problem—one that results in a 10,000-line program, for example—it's simply not reasonable to skip the design process and go directly to writing C++ code. What we need is a systematic way of designing a solution to a problem, no matter how complicated the problem is.

In the remainder of this chapter, we describe two important design methodologies: *functional decomposition* and *object-oriented design*. These methodologies help you create solutions that can be easily implemented as C++ programs. The resulting programs are readable, understandable, and easy to debug and modify.

One software design methodology that is in widespread use is known as **object-oriented design (OOD)**. In the next two sections, we present the essential concepts of OOD; we expand our treatment of the approach later in the book. OOD is often used in conjunction

Object-oriented design   A technique for developing software in which the solution is expressed in terms of objects—self-contained entities composed of data and operations on that data.

Functional decomposition   A technique for developing software in which the problem is divided into more easily handled subproblems, the solutions of which create a solution to the overall problem.

with the other methodology that we discuss in this chapter, **functional decomposition**.

OOD focuses on entities (*objects*) consisting of data and operations on the data. In OOD, we solve a problem by identifying the components that make up a solution and identifying how those components interact with each other through operations on the data that they contain. The result is a design for a set of objects that can be assembled to form a solution to a problem. In contrast, functional decomposition views the solution to a problem as a task to be accomplished. It focuses on the sequence of operations that are required to complete the task. When the problem requires a sequence of steps that is long or complex, we divide it into subproblems that are easier to solve.

The choice of which methodology we use depends on the problem at hand. If you look at a problem and see that it is natural to think about it in terms of a collection of component parts, then it's appropriate to use OOD to solve it. For example, a banking problem may require a `checkingAccount` object with associated operations `OpenAccount`, `WriteCheck`, `MakeDeposit`, and `IsOverdrawn`. The `checkingAccount` object consists of not only data (the account number and current balance, for example) but also these operations, all bound together into one unit.

On the other hand, if you find that it is natural to think of the solution to the problem as a series of steps, then functional decomposition is appropriate. For example, when computing some statistical measures on a large set of real numbers, it is natural to decompose the problem into a sequence of steps that read a value, perform calculations, and then repeat the sequence. The C++ language and the standard library supply all of the operations that we need, and we simply write a sequence of those operations to solve the problem.

4.7   What Are Objects?

Let's take a closer look at what objects are and how they work before we examine OOD further. We said earlier that an object is a collection of data together with associated operations. Several programming languages, called *object-oriented programming languages*, have been created specifically to support OOD. Examples are C++, Java, Smalltalk, CLOS, Eiffel, and Object-Pascal. In these languages, a *class* is a programmer-defined data type from which objects are created. Although we did not say it at the time, we have been using classes and objects to perform input and output in C++. `cin` is an object of a data type (class) named `istream`, and `cout` is an object of a class `ostream`. As we explained earlier, the header file `iostream` defines the classes `istream` and `ostream` and also declares `cin` and `cout` to be objects of those classes:

```
istream cin;
ostream cout;
```

Similarly, the header file `fstream` defines classes `ifstream` and `ofstream`, from which you can declare your own input file stream and output file stream objects.

Another example you have seen already is `string`—a programmer-defined class from which you create objects by using declarations such as

```
string lastName;
```

In Figure 4-2, we picture the `cin` and `lastName` objects as entities that have a private part and a public part. The private part includes data and functions that the user cannot access and doesn't need to know about in order to use the object. The public part, shown as ovals in the side of the object, represents the object's *interface*. The interface consists of operations that are available to programmers wishing to use the object. In C++, public operations are written as functions and are known as *member functions*. Except for operations using symbols such as << and >>, a member function is invoked by giving the name of the class object, then a dot, and then the function name and argument list:

```
cin.ignore(100, '\n');
cin.get(someChar);
cin >> someInt;
len = lastName.length();
pos = lastName.find('A');
```

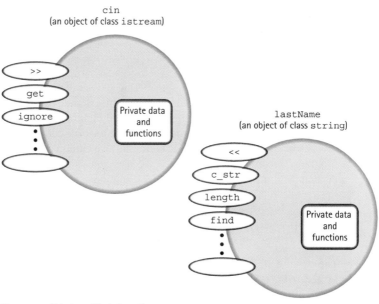

Figure 4-2 *Objects and Their Operations*

4.8   Object-Oriented Design

The first step in OOD is to identify the major objects in the problem, together with their associated operations. The final problem solution is ultimately expressed in terms of these objects and operations.

OOD leads to programs that are collections of objects. Each object is responsible for one part of the entire solution, and the objects communicate by accessing each other's member functions. There are many libraries of prewritten classes, including the C++ standard library, public libraries (called *freeware* or *shareware*), libraries that are sold commercially, and libraries that are developed by companies for their own use. In many cases, it is possible to browse through a library, choose classes you need for a problem, and assemble them to form a substantial portion of your program. Putting existing pieces together in this fashion is an excellent example of the building-block approach we discussed in Chapter 1.

When there isn't a suitable class available in a library, it is necessary to define a new class. We see how this is done in Chapter 11. The design of a new class begins with the specification of its interface. We must decide what operations are needed on the outside of the class to make its objects useful. Once the interface is defined, we can design the implementation of the class, including all of its private members.

Sometimes you discover a class in a library that is almost right for your purpose but is missing some key feature. OOD addresses this situation with a concept called *inheritance,* which allows you to adapt an existing class to meet your particular needs. You can use inheritance to add features to a class (or restrict the use of existing features) without having to inspect and modify its source code. Inheritance is considered such an integral part of object-oriented programming that a separate term, *object-based programming,* is used to describe programming with objects but not inheritance.

In Chapter 14, we see how to define classes that inherit members from existing classes. Together, OOD, class libraries, and inheritance can dramatically reduce the time and effort required to design, implement, and maintain large software systems.

In this section, we have presented only an introduction to OOD. A more complete discussion requires knowledge of topics that we explore in later chapters. Until then, our programs are relatively small, so we use object-based programming and functional decomposition to arrive at our problem solutions.

4.9   Functional Decomposition

The second design technique we use is functional decomposition (it's also called *structured design, top-down design, stepwise refinement,* and *modular programming).* In functional decomposition, we work from the abstract (a list of the major steps in our solution) to the particular (algorithmic steps that can be translated directly into C++ code). You can also think of this as working from a high-level solution, leaving the details of implementation unspecified, down to a fully detailed solution.

The easiest way to solve a problem is to give it to someone else and say, "Solve this problem." This is the most abstract level of a problem solution: a single-statement solution that encompasses the entire problem without specifying any of the details of implementation. It's at this point that we programmers are called in. Our job is to turn the abstract solution into a concrete solution, a program.

If the solution clearly involves a series of major steps, we break it down (decompose it) into pieces. In the process, we move to a lower level of abstraction—that is, some of the implementation details (but not too many) are now specified. Each of the major steps becomes an independent subproblem that we can work on separately. In a very large project, one person (the *chief architect* or *team leader*) formulates the subproblems and then gives them to other members of the programming team, saying, "Solve this problem." In the case of a small project, we give the subproblems to ourselves. Then we choose one subproblem at a time to solve. We may break the chosen subproblem into another series of steps that, in turn, become smaller subproblems. Or we may identify components that are naturally represented as objects. The process continues until each subproblem cannot be divided further or has an obvious solution.

Why do we work this way? Why not simply write out all of the details? Because it is much easier to focus on one problem at a time. For example, suppose you are working on part of a program to output certain values and discover that you need a complex formula to calculate an appropriate fieldwidth for printing one of the values. Calculating fieldwidths is not the purpose of this part of the program. If you shift your focus to the calculation, you are likely to forget some detail of the overall output process. What you do is write down an abstract step—"Calculate the fieldwidth required"—and go on with the problem at hand. Once you've written the major steps, you can go back to solving the step that does the calculation.

By subdividing the problem, you create a hierarchical structure called a *tree structure*. Each level of the tree is a complete solution to the problem that is less abstract (more detailed) than the level above it. Figure 4-3 shows a generic solution tree for a problem. Steps that are shaded have enough implementation details to be translated directly into C++ statements. These are *concrete steps*. Those that are not shaded are *abstract steps;* they reappear as subproblems in the next level down. Each box in the figure represents a *module*. Modules are the basic building blocks in a functional decomposition. The diagram in Figure 4-3 is also called a *module structure chart*.

Like OOD, functional decomposition uses the divide-and-conquer approach to problem solving. Both techniques break up large problems into smaller units that are easier to handle. The difference is that in OOD the units are objects, whereas the units in functional decomposition are modules representing algorithms.

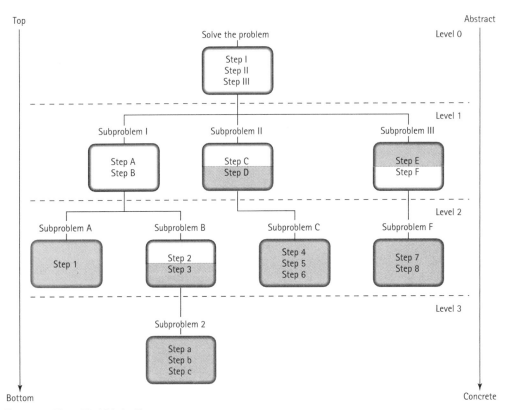

Figure 4-3 *Hierarchical Solution Tree*

Modules

A module begins life as an abstract step in the next-higher level of the solution tree. It is completed when it solves a given subproblem—that is, when it specifies a series of steps that does the same thing as the higher-level abstract step.

In a properly written module, all of the concrete steps should directly address the given subproblem; abstract steps are used only for significant new subproblems. Each module should do just one thing and do it well. Knowing which details to make concrete and which to leave abstract is a matter of experience, circumstance, and personal style. For example, you might decide to include a fieldwidth calculation in a printing module if there isn't so much detail in the rest of the module that it becomes confusing. On the other hand, if the calculation is performed several times, it makes sense to write it as a separate module and just refer to it each time you need it.

Writing Modules   Here's one approach to writing modules:

1. Think about how you would solve the subproblem by hand.

2. Begin writing down the major steps.

3. If a step is simple enough that you can see how to implement it directly in C++, it is at the concrete level; it doesn't need any further refinement.

4. If you have to think about implementing a step as a series of smaller steps or as several C++ statements, it is still at an abstract level.

5. If you are trying to write a series of steps and start to feel overwhelmed by details, you probably are bypassing one or more levels of abstraction. Stand back and look for pieces that you can write as more abstract steps.

As you work your way down the solution tree, you make a series of design decisions. If a decision proves awkward or wrong (and many times it does!), you can backtrack (go back up the tree to a higher-level module) and try something else. You don't have to scrap your whole design—only the small part you are working on.

Pseudocode   You'll find it easier to implement a design if you write the steps in pseudocode. *Pseudocode* is a mixture of English statements and C++-like control structures that can be translated easily into C++. (We show an example of using pseudocode in the programming example at the end of this chapter.) When a concrete step is written in pseudocode, it should be possible to rewrite it directly as a C++ statement in a program.

A Perspective on Design

We have looked at two design methodologies, object-oriented design and functional decomposition. Until we learn about additional C++ language features that support OOD, we use functional decomposition (and object-based programming) in the next several chapters to come up with our problem solutions.

An important perspective to keep in mind is that functional decomposition and OOD are not separate, disjoint techniques. OOD decomposes a problem into objects. Objects not only contain data but also have associated operations. The operations on objects require algorithms. Sometimes the algorithms are complicated and must be decomposed into subalgorithms by using functional decomposition. Experienced programmers are familiar with both methodologies and know when to use one or the other, or a combination of the two.

Remember that the problem-solving phase of the programming process takes time. If you spend the bulk of your time analyzing and designing a solution, then coding and implementing the program take relatively little time.

Now let's look at a programming example that demonstrates functional decomposition.

Documentation

As you create your functional decomposition or object-oriented design, you are developing documentation for your program. *Documentation* includes the written problem specifications, design, development history, and actual code of a program.

Good documentation helps other programmers read and understand a program and is invaluable when software is being debugged and modified (maintained). If you haven't looked at your program for six months and need to change it, you'll be happy that you documented it well. Of course, if someone else has to use and modify your program, documentation is indispensable.

Documentation is both external and internal to the program. External documentation includes the specifications, the development history, and the design documents. Internal documentation includes the program format and **self-documenting code**—meaningful identifiers and comments. You can use the pseudocode from the design process as comments in your programs.

Self-documenting code   Program code containing meaningful identifiers as well as judiciously used clarifying comments.

This kind of documentation may be sufficient for someone reading or maintaining your programs. However, if a program is going to be used by people who are not programmers, you must provide a user's manual as well.

Be sure to keep documentation up-to-date. Indicate any changes you make in a program in all of the pertinent documentation. Use self-documenting code to make your programs more readable.

Programming Example

Stretching a Canvas

Problem   You are taking an art class in which you are learning to make your own painting canvas by stretching the cloth over a wooden frame and stapling it to the back of the frame. For a given size of painting, you must determine how much wood to buy for the frame, how large a piece of canvas to purchase, and the cost of the materials.

Input Four floating-point numbers: the length and width of the painting, the cost per inch of the wood, and the cost per square foot of the canvas.

Output Prompting messages, the input data (echo print), the length of wood to buy, the dimensions of the canvas, the cost of the wood, the cost of the canvas, and the total cost of the materials.

Discussion The length of the wood is twice the sum of the length and width of the painting. The cost of the wood is simply its length times its cost per inch.

According to the art instructor, the dimensions of the canvas are the length and width of the painting, each with 5 inches added (for the part that wraps around to the back of the frame). The area of the canvas in square inches is its length times its width. However, we are given the cost for a square foot of the canvas. Thus, we must divide the area of the canvas by the number of square inches in a square foot (144) before multiplying by the cost.

Assumptions The input values are positive (checking for erroneous data is not done).

Functional Decomposition in Pseudocode

Main Module	**Level 0**
Get length and width	
Get wood cost	
Get canvas cost	
Compute dimensions and costs	
Print dimensions and costs	

Get Length and Width	**Level 1**
Print "Enter length and width of painting:"	
Read length, width	

Get Wood Cost	
Print "Enter cost per inch of the framing wood in dollars:"	
Read woodCost	

Get Canvas Cost	
Print "Enter cost per square foot of canvas in dollars:"	
Read canvasCost	

Compute Dimensions and Costs

Set lengthOfWood = (length + width) * 2

Set canvasWidth = width + 5

Set canvasLength = length + 5

Set canvasAreaInches = canvasWidth * canvasLength

Set canvasAreaFeet = canvasAreaInches / 144.0

Set totWoodCost = lengthOfWood * woodCost

Set totCanvasCost = canvasAreaFeet * canvasCost

Set totCost = totWoodCost + totCanvasCost

Print Dimensions and Costs

Print "For a painting", length, "in. long and", width, "in. wide,"

Print "you need to buy", lengthOfWood, "in. of wood, and"

Print "the canvas must be", canvasLength, "in. long and",
        canvasWidth, "in. wide."

Print "Given a wood cost of $", woodCost, "per in."

Print "and a canvas cost of $", canvasCost, "per sq. ft.,"

Print "the wood will cost $", totWoodCost, ','

Print "the canvas will cost $", totCanvasCost, ','

Print "and the total cost of materials will be $", totCost, '.'

Module Structure Chart:

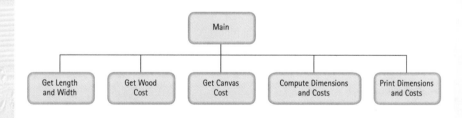

Here is the complete program. Notice how we've used the module names as comments.

(The following program is written in ISO/ANSI standard C++. If you are working with pre-standard C++, see the alternate version of the program in the PRE_STD directory of the program disk, available at the publisher's Web site, www.jbpub.com/disks.)

```
//**********************************************************************
// Canvas program
// This program computes the dimensions and costs of materials
// to build a painting canvas of given dimensions. The user is
// asked to enter the length and width of the painting and the
// costs of the wood (per inch) and canvas (per square foot)
//**********************************************************************
#include <iostream>
#include <iomanip>    // For setprecision()

using namespace std;

const float SQ_IN_PER_SQ_FT = 144.0;    // Square inches per
                                        //   square foot
int main()
{
    float length;            // Length of painting in inches
    float width;             // Width of painting in inches
    float woodCost;          // Cost of wood per inch in dollars
    float canvasCost;        // Cost of canvas per square foot
    float lengthOfWood;      // Amount of wood to buy
    float canvasWidth;       // Width of canvas to buy
    float canvasLength;      // Length of canvas to buy
    float canvasAreaInches;  // Area of canvas in square inches
    float canvasAreaFeet;    // Area of canvas in square feet
    float totCanvasCost;     // Total cost of canvas being bought
    float totWoodCost;       // Total cost of wood being bought
    float totCost;           // Total cost of materials

    cout << fixed << showpoint;              // Set up floating-pt.
                                             //   output format


    // Get length and width

    cout << "Enter length and width of painting:" << endl;
    cin >> length >> width;

    // Get wood cost

    cout << "Enter cost per inch of the framing wood in dollars:"
         << endl;
    cin >> woodCost;
```

```
// Get canvas cost

cout << "Enter cost per square foot of canvas in dollars:"
     << endl;
cin >> canvasCost;

// Compute dimensions and costs

lengthOfWood = (length + width) * 2;
canvasWidth = width + 5;
canvasLength = length + 5;
canvasAreaInches = canvasWidth * canvasLength;
canvasAreaFeet = canvasAreaInches / SQ_IN_PER_SQ_FT;
totWoodCost = lengthOfWood * woodCost;
totCanvasCost = canvasAreaFeet * canvasCost;
totCost = totWoodCost + totCanvasCost;

// Print dimensions and costs

cout << endl << setprecision(1);
cout << "For a painting " << length << " in. long and "
     << width << " in. wide," << endl;
cout << "you need to buy " << lengthOfWood << " in. of wood,"
     << " and" << endl;
cout << "the canvas must be " << canvasLength << " in. long"
     << " and " << canvasWidth << " in. wide." << endl;

cout << endl << setprecision(2);
cout << "Given a wood cost of $" << woodCost << " per in."
     << endl;
cout << "and a canvas cost of $" << canvasCost
     << " per sq. ft.," << endl;
cout << "the wood will cost $" << totWoodCost << ',' << endl;
cout << "the canvas will cost $" << totCanvasCost << ','
     << endl;
cout << "and the total cost of materials will be $" << totCost
     << '.' << endl;
return 0;
}
```

This is an interactive program. The data values are input while the program is executing. If the user enters this data:

```
24.0 36.0 0.08 2.80
```

then the dialogue with the user looks like this:

```
Enter length and width of painting:
24.0 36.0
Enter cost per inch of the framing wood in dollars:
0.08
Enter cost per square foot of canvas in dollars:
2.80

For a painting 24.0 in. long and 36.0 in. wide,
you need to buy 120.0 in. of wood, and
the canvas must be 29.0 in. long and 41.0 in. wide.

Given a wood cost of $0.08 per in.
and a canvas cost of $2.80 per sq. ft.,
the wood will cost $9.60,
the canvas will cost $23.12,
and the total cost of materials will be $32.72.
```

Testing and Debugging

An important part of implementing a program is testing it (checking the results). From here on, these Testing and Debugging sections offer tips on how to test your programs and what to do if a program doesn't work the way you expect. But don't wait until you've found a bug to read the Testing and Debugging sections. It's much easier to prevent bugs than to fix them.

When testing programs that input data, it's possible for input operations to fail. And when input fails, the computer doesn't issue a warning message but simply continues executing, ignoring any further input operations. The two most common reasons for input failure are invalid data and the *end-of-file error.*

An end-of-file error occurs when the program has read all of the input data available in the file and needs more data to fill the variables in its input statements. It might be that the data file simply was not prepared properly. Perhaps it contains fewer data items than the program requires. Or perhaps the format of the input data is wrong. Leaving out whitespace between numeric values is guaranteed to cause trouble. For example, we may want a data file to contain three integer values—25, 16, and 42. Look what happens with this data:

```
2516   42
```

and this code:

```
inFile >> i >> j >> k;
```

The first two input operations use up the data in the file, leaving the third with no data to read. The stream `inFile` enters the fail state, so k isn't assigned a new value and the computer quietly continues executing.

If the data file is prepared correctly and there is still an end-of-file error, the problem is in the program logic. For some reason, the program is attempting too many input operations. It could be a simple oversight such as specifying too many variables in a particular input statement. It could be a misuse of the `ignore` function, causing values to be skipped inadvertently. Or it could be a serious flaw in the algorithm. You should check all of these possibilities.

The other major source of input failure, invalid data, has several possible causes. The most common is an error in the preparation or entry of the data. Numeric and character data mixed inappropriately in the input can cause the input stream to fail if it is supposed to read a numeric value but the reading marker is positioned at a character that isn't allowed in the number. Another cause is using the wrong variable name (which happens to be of the wrong data type) in an input statement. Declaring a variable to be of the wrong data type is a variation on the problem. Last, leaving out a variable (or including an extra one) in an input statement can cause the reading marker to end up positioned on the wrong type of data.

Another oversight, one that doesn't cause input failure but causes programmer frustration, is to use `cin` or `cout` in an I/O statement when you meant to specify a file stream. If you mistakenly use `cin` instead of an input file stream, the program stops and waits for input from the keyboard. If you mistakenly use `cout` instead of an output file stream, you get unexpected output on the screen.

By giving you a framework that can help you organize and keep track of the details involved in designing and implementing a program, functional decomposition (and, later, object-oriented design) should help you avoid many of these errors in the first place.

Testing and Debugging Hints

1. Input and output statements always begin with the name of a stream object, and the >> and << operators point in the direction in which the data is going. The statement

   ```
   cout << n;
   ```

   sends data *to* the output stream `cout`, and the statement

   ```
   cin >> n;
   ```

   sends data *to* the variable n.

2. When a program inputs from or outputs to a file, be sure each I/O statement from or to the file uses the name of the file stream, not `cin` or `cout`.

3. The `open` function associated with an `ifstream` or `ofstream` object requires a C string as an argument. The argument cannot be a `string` object. At this point in the book, the argument can only be (a) a literal string or (b) the C string returned by the function call `myString.c_str()`, where `myString` is of type `string`.

4. When you open a data file for input, make sure that the argument to the `open` function supplies the correct name of the file as it exists on disk.

5. When reading a character string into a `string` object, the `>>` operator stops at, *but does not consume,* the first trailing whitespace character.

6. Be sure that each input statement specifies the correct number of variables and that each of those variables is of the correct data type.

7. If your input data is mixed (character and numeric values), be sure to deal with intervening blanks.

8. Echo print the input data to verify that each value is where it belongs and is in the proper format. (This is crucial, because an input failure in C++ doesn't produce an error message or terminate the program.)

9. Remember that the extraction operator (`>>`) skips whitespace characters. If you need to input these characters, you must use the `get` function.

Summary

Programs operate on data. If data and programs are kept separate, the same program can be run with different sets of input data.

The extraction operator (`>>`) inputs data from the keyboard or a file, storing the data into the variable specified as its right-hand operand. The extraction operator skips any leading whitespace characters to find the next data value in the input stream. The `get` function does not skip leading whitespace characters; it inputs the very next character and stores it into the `char` variable specified in its argument list. Both `>>` and `get` leave the reading marker positioned at the next character to be read. The next input operation begins at the point indicated by the marker.

The newline character (denoted by `\n` in a C++ program) marks the end of a data line. You create a newline character each time you press the Return or Enter key. Your program generates a newline each time you use the `endl` manipulator or explicitly output the `\n` character. Newline is a control character; it does not print. It controls the movement of the screen cursor or the position of a line on a printer.

Interactive programs prompt the user for each data entry and directly inform the user of results and errors. Designing interactive dialogue is an exercise in the art of communication.

Noninteractive input/output allows data to be prepared in advance and allows the program to run again with the same data if a problem crops up during processing.

Data files often are used for noninteractive processing. To use these files, you must do four things: (1) include the header file `fstream`, (2) declare the file streams along with your other variable declarations, (3) prepare the files for reading or writing by calling the `open` function, and (4) specify the name of the file stream in each input or output statement that uses it.

Object-oriented design and functional decomposition are methodologies for tackling nontrivial programming problems. Object-oriented design produces a problem solution by focusing on objects and their associated operations. The first step is to identify the

major objects in the problem and choose appropriate operations on those objects. The result of the design process is a program consisting of self-contained objects that manage their own data and communicate by invoking each other's operations.

Functional decomposition begins with an abstract solution that then is divided into major steps. Each step becomes a subproblem that is analyzed and subdivided further. A concrete step is one that can be translated directly into C++; those steps that need more refining are abstract steps. A module is a collection of concrete and abstract steps that solves a subproblem.

Careful attention to program design, program formatting, and documentation produces highly structured and readable programs.

Quick Check

1. Write a C++ statement that inputs values from the standard input stream into two `float` variables, x and y. (pp. 116–119)
2. Your program is reading from the standard input stream. The next three characters waiting in the stream are a blank, a blank, and the letter *A*. Indicate what character is stored into the `char` variable ch by each of the following statements. (Assume the same initial stream contents for each.)
   a. `cin >> ch;`
   b. `cin.get(ch);`
   (pp. 119–122)
3. An input line contains a person's first, middle, and last names, separated by spaces. To read the entire name into a single `string` variable, which is appropriate: the `>>` operator or the `getline` function? (pp. 123–124)
4. Input prompts should acknowledge the user's experience.
   a. What sort of message would you have a program print to prompt a novice user to input a Social Security number?
   b. How would you change the wording of the prompting message for an experienced user? (pp. 125–126)
5. If a program is going to input 1000 numbers, is interactive input appropriate? (pp. 126–127)
6. What four things must you remember to do in order to use data files in a C++ program? (pp. 127–130)
7. How many levels of abstraction are there in a functional decomposition before you reach the point at which you can begin coding a program? (pp. 138–141)
8. Modules are the building blocks of functional decomposition. What are the building blocks of object-oriented design? (pp. 135–139)

Answers 1. `cin >> x >> y;` 2. a. 'A' b. ' ' (a blank) 3. The `getline` function 4. a. `Please type a nine-digit Social Security number, then press the key marked Enter.` b. `Enter SSN.` 5. No. Batch input is more appropriate for programs that input large amounts of data. 6. (1) Include the header file `fstream`. (2) Declare the file streams along with your other variable declarations. (3) Call the `open` function to prepare each file for reading or writing. (4) Specify the name of the file stream in each I/O statement that uses it. 7. There is no fixed number of levels of abstraction. You keep refining the solution through as many levels as necessary until the steps are all concrete. 8. The building blocks are objects, each of which has associated operations.

Exam Preparation Exercises

1. What is the main advantage of having a program input its data rather than writing all the data values as constants in the program?
2. Given these two lines of data:

```
17  13
7  3  24  6
```

and this input statement:

```
cin >> int1 >> int2 >> int3;
```

   a. What is the value of each variable after the statement is executed?
   b. What happens to any leftover data values in the input stream?
3. The newline character signals the end of a line.
   a. How do you generate a newline character when typing input data at the keyboard?
   b. How do you generate a newline character in a program's output?
4. When reading `char` data from an input stream, what is the difference between using the `>>` operator and using the `get` function?
5. Integer values can be read from the input data into `float` variables. (True or False?)
6. You may use either spaces or newlines to separate numeric data values being entered into a C++ program. (True or False?)
7. Consider this input data:

```
14  21  64
19  67  91
73  89  27
23  96  47
```

   What are the values of the `int` variables a, b, c, and d after the following program segment is executed?

```
cin >> a;
cin.ignore(200, '\n');
cin >> b >> c;
cin.ignore(200, '\n');
cin >> d;
```

8. Given the input data

```
123W 56
```

what is printed by the output statement when the following code segment is executed?

```
int1 = 98;
int2 = 147;
cin >> int1 >> int2;
cout << int1 << ' ' << int2;
```

9. Given the input data

```
11 12.35 ABC
```

what is the value of each variable after the following statements are executed? Assume that i is of type int, x is of type float, and ch1 is of type char.
   a. `cin >> i >> x >> ch1 >> ch1;`
   b. `cin >> ch1 >> i >> x;`
10. Consider the input data

```
40 Tall Pine Drive
Sudbury, MA 01776
```

and the program code

```
string address;

cin >> address;
```

After the code is executed,
   a. what string is contained in `address`?
   b. where is the reading marker positioned?
11. Answer Exercise 10 again, replacing the input statement with

```
getline(cin, address);
```

12. Define the following terms as they apply to interactive input/output.
   a. Input prompt
   b. Echo printing
13. Correct the following program so that it reads a value from the file stream `inData` and writes it to the file stream `outData`.

```
#include <iostream>

using namespace std;
```

```
int main()
{
    int       n;
    ifstream inData;

    outData.open("results.dat");
    cin >> n;
    outData << n << endl;
    return 0;
}
```

14. Use your corrected version of the program in Exercise 13 to answer the following questions.
    a. If the file stream `inData` initially contains the value 144, what does it contain after the program is executed?
    b. If the file stream `outData` is initially empty, what are its contents after the program is executed?

15. List three characteristics of programs that are designed using a highly organized methodology such as functional decomposition or object-oriented design.

16. The `get` and `ignore` functions are member functions of the `istream` class. (True or False?)

17. The `find` and `substr` functions are member functions of the `string` class. (True or False?)

18. The `getline` function is a member function of the `string` class. (True or False?)

19. In the Canvas problem, look at the module structure chart and identify each level 1 module as an input module, a computational module, or an output module.

20. Redraw the module structure chart for the Canvas program so that level 1 contains modules named Get Data, Compute Values, and Print Results. Decide whether each of the level 1 modules in the original module structure chart corresponds directly to one of the three new modules or if it fits best as a level 2 module under one of the three. In the latter case, add the level 2 modules to the new module structure chart in the appropriate places.

Programming Warm-up Exercises

1. Your program has three `char` variables: `ch1`, `ch2`, and `ch3`. Given the input data

   A   B   C\n

   write the input statement(s) required to store the A into `ch1`, the B into `ch2`, and the C into `ch3`. Note that each pair of input characters is separated by two blanks.

2. Change your answer to Exercise 1 so that the A is stored into `ch1` and the next two blanks are stored into `ch2` and `ch3`.

3. Write a single input statement that reads the input lines

```
10.25    7.625\n
8.5\n
1.0\n
```

and stores the four values into the `float` variables `length1`, `height1`, `length2`, and `height2`.

4. Write a series of statements that input the first letter of each of the following names into the `char` variables `chr1`, `chr2`, and `chr3`.

```
Peter\n
Kitty\n
Kathy\n
```

5. Write a set of variable declarations and a series of input statements to read the following lines of data into variables of the appropriate type. You can make up the variable names. Notice that the values are separated from one another by a single blank and that there are no blanks to the left of the first character on each line.

```
A 100 2.78 g 14\n
207.98 w q 23.4 92\n
R 42 L 27 R 63\n
```

6. Write a program segment that reads nine integer values from a file and writes them to the screen, three numbers per output line. The file is organized one value to a line.

7. Write a code segment for an interactive program to input values for a person's age, height, and weight and the initials of his or her first and last names. The numeric values are all integers. Assume that the person using the program is a novice user. How would you rewrite the code for an experienced user?

8. Fill in the blanks in the following program, which should read four values from the file stream `dataIn` and output them to the file stream `resultsOut`.

```
#include _____
#include _____
using _____
int main()
{
    int        val1;
    int        val2;
    int        val3;
```

```
int                 val4;
_____         dataIn;
ofstream            _____;
_____         ("myinput.dat");
_____         ("myoutput.dat");
_____         >> val1 >> val2 >> val3 >> val4;
_____         << val1 << val2 << val3 << val4 << endl;
return 0;
}
```

9. Modify the program in Exercise 8 so that the name of the input file is prompted for and read in from the user at run time instead of being specified as a literal string.

10. Use functional decomposition to write an algorithm for starting the engine of an automobile with a manual transmission.

11. Use functional decomposition to write an algorithm for logging on to your computer system and entering and running a program. The algorithm should be simple enough for a novice user to follow.

12. The quadratic formula is

$$x = \frac{-b \pm \sqrt{b^2 - 4ac}}{2a}$$

Use functional decomposition to write an algorithm to read the three coefficients of a quadratic polynomial from a file (inQuad) and write the two floating-point solutions to another file (outQuad). Assume that the discriminant (the portion of the formula inside the square root) is nonnegative. You may use the standard library function sqrt. (Express your solution as pseudocode, not as a C++ program.)

13. Modify the Canvas program so that it reads the input data from a file rather than the keyboard. At run time, prompt the user for the name of the file containing the data.

Programming Problems

1. Write a functional decomposition and a C++ program to read an invoice number, quantity ordered, and unit price (all integers) and compute the total price. The program should write out the invoice number, quantity, unit price, and total price with identifying phrases. Format your program with consistent indentation, and use appropriate comments and meaningful identifiers. Write the program to be run interactively, with informative prompts for each data value.

2. How tall is a rainbow? Because of the way in which light is refracted by water droplets, the angle between the level of your eye and the top of a rainbow is always the same. If you know the distance to the rainbow, you can multiply it

by the tangent of that angle to find the height of the rainbow. The magic angle is 42.3333333 degrees. The C++ standard library works in radians, however, so you have to convert the angle to radians with this formula:

$$radians = degrees \times \frac{\pi}{180}$$

where π equals 3.14159265.

Through the header file `cmath`, the C++ standard library provides a tangent function named `tan`. This is a value-returning function that takes a floating-point argument and returns a floating-point result:

```
x = tan(someAngle);
```

If you multiply the tangent by the distance to the rainbow, you get the height of the rainbow.

Write a functional decomposition and a C++ program to read a single floating-point value—the distance to the rainbow—and compute the height of the rainbow. The program should print the distance to the rainbow and its height, with phrases that identify which number is which. Display the floating-point values to four decimal places. Format your program with consistent indentation, and use appropriate comments and meaningful identifiers. Write the program so that it prompts the user for the input value.

3. Sometimes you can see a second, fainter rainbow outside a bright rainbow. This second rainbow has a magic angle of 52.25 degrees. Modify the program in Problem 2 so that it prints the height of the main rainbow, the height of the secondary rainbow, and the distance to the main rainbow, with a phrase identifying each of the numbers.

4. Write a program that reads a person's name in the format First Middle Last and then prints each of the names on a separate line. Following the last name, the program should print the initials for the name. For example, given the input `James Tiberius Kirk`, the program should output

```
James
Tiberius
Kirk
JTK
```

Assume that the first name begins in the first position on a line (there are no leading blanks) and that the names are separated from each other by a single blank.

Conditions, Logical Expressions, and Selection Control Structures

- To be able to construct a simple logical (Boolean) expression to evaluate a given condition.

- To be able to construct a complex logical expression to evaluate a given condition.

- To be able to construct an If-Then-Else statement to perform a specific task.

- To be able to construct an If-Then statement to perform a specific task.

- To be able to construct a set of nested If statements to perform a specific task.

- To be able to determine the precondition and postcondition for a module and to use them to perform an algorithm walk-through.

- To be able to trace the execution of a C++ program.

- To be able to test and debug a C++ program.

So far, the statements in our programs have been executed in their physical order, one after the other. But what if we want the computer to execute the statements in some other order? Suppose we want to check the validity of input data and then perform a calculation or print an error message, not both. To do so, we must be able to ask a question and then, based on the answer, choose one or another course of action.

The If statement allows us to execute statements in an order that is different from their physical order. We can ask a question with it and do one thing if the answer is yes (true) or another if the answer is no (false). In the first part of this chapter, we deal with asking questions; in the second part, we deal with the If statement itself.

5.1 Flow of Control

The order in which statements are executed in a program is called the *flow of control*. In a sense, the computer is under the control of one statement at a time. When a statement has been executed, control is turned over to the next statement (like a baton being passed in a relay race).

Control structure A statement used to alter the normally sequential flow of control.

Flow of control is normally sequential (see Figure 5-1). When we want the flow of control to be nonsequential, we use **control structures**, special statements that transfer control to a statement other than the one that physically comes next.

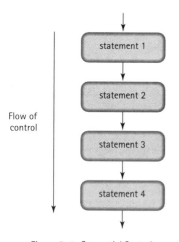

Figure 5-1 *Sequential Control*

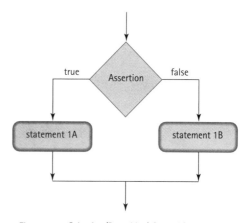

Figure 5-2 *Selection (Branching) Control Structure*

Selection

We use a selection (or branching) control structure when we want the computer to choose between alternative actions. We make an assertion, a claim that is either true or false. If the assertion is true, the computer executes one statement. If it is false, it executes another (see Figure 5–2).

Suppose the computer must decide whether or not a worker has earned overtime pay. It does this by testing the assertion that the person has worked more than 40 hours. If the assertion is true, the computer follows the instructions for computing overtime pay. If the assertion is false, the computer simply computes the regular pay. Before we examine selection control structures in C++, let's look closely at how we get the computer to make decisions.

5.2 Conditions and Logical Expressions

To ask a question in C++, we make an assertion. The computer *evaluates* the assertion, checking it against some internal condition (the values stored in certain variables, for instance) to see whether it is true or false.

The `bool` Data Type

In C++, the `bool` data type is a built-in type consisting of just two values, the constants `true` and `false`. The reserved word `bool` is short for Boolean (pronounced 'B$\overline{OO}$L-$\overline{e}$-un).* Boolean data is used for testing conditions in a program so that the computer can make decisions (with a selection control structure).

We declare variables of type `bool` the same way we declare variables of other types, that is, by writing the name of the data type and then an identifier:

```
bool dataOK;    // True if the input data is valid
bool done;      // True if the process is done
bool taxable;   // True if the item has sales tax
```

Each variable of type `bool` can contain one of two values: `true` or `false`. It's important to understand right from the beginning that `true` and `false` are not variable names and they are not strings. They are special constants in C++ and, in fact, are reserved words.

(The C language does not have a `bool` data type, and prior to the ISO/ANSI C++ language standard, neither did C++. If you are working with pre-standard C++, see Section D.4 of Appendix D for more information about defining your own `bool` type so that you can work with the programs in this book.)

---

*The word *Boolean* is a tribute to George Boole, a nineteenth-century English mathematician who described a system of logic using variables with just two values, True and False.

Logical Expressions

In C++, assertions take the form of *logical expressions* (also called *Boolean expressions*). A logical expression is made up of logical values and operations. Every logical expression has one of two values: true or false. Here are some examples of logical expressions:

- A Boolean variable or constant
- An expression followed by a relational operator followed by an expression
- A logical expression followed by a logical operator followed by a logical expression

Let's look at each of these in detail.

Boolean Variables and Constants   As we have seen, a Boolean variable is a variable declared to be of type `bool`, and it can contain either the value `true` or the value `false`. For example, if `dataOK` is a Boolean variable, then

```
dataOK = true;
```

is a valid assignment statement.

Relational Operators   Another way of assigning a value to a Boolean variable is to set it equal to the result of comparing two expressions with a *relational operator*. Relational operators test a relationship between two values.

Let's look at an example. In the following program fragment, `lessThan` is a Boolean variable and `i` and `j` are `int` variables:

```
cin >> i >> j;
lessThan = (i < j);   // Assigns true to lessThan if i < j
```

By comparing two values, we assert that a relationship (like "less than") exists between them. If the relationship does exist, the assertion is true; if not, it is false. These are the relationships we can test for in C++:

Operator	Relationship Tested
==	Equal to
!=	Not equal to
>	Greater than
<	Less than
>=	Greater than or equal to
<=	Less than or equal to

An expression followed by a relational operator followed by an expression is called a *relational expression*. The result of a relational expression is of type `bool`. For example, if `x` is 5 and `y` is 10, the following expressions all have the value `true`:

```
x == 5        y > x        y >= x
x != y        x < y        x <= y
```

If x is the character 'M' and y is 'R', the values of the expressions are still `true` because the relational operator <, used with letters, means "comes before in the alphabet," or, more properly, "comes before in the collating sequence of the character set." For example, in the widely used ASCII character set, all of the uppercase letters are in alphabetical order, as are the lowercase letters, but all of the uppercase letters come before the lowercase letters. So

```
'M' < 'R'   and    'm' < 'r'
```

have the value `true`, but

```
'm' < 'R'
```

has the value `false`.

Of course, we have to be careful about the data types of things we compare. The safest approach is to always compare `int`s with `int`s, `float`s with `float`s, `char`s with `char`s, and so on. If you mix data types in a comparison, implicit type coercion takes place just as in arithmetic expressions. If an `int` value and a `float` value are compared, the computer temporarily coerces the `int` value to its `float` equivalent before making the comparison. As with arithmetic expressions, it's wise to use explicit type casting to make your intentions known:

```
someFloat >= float(someInt)
```

If you compare a `bool` value with a numeric value (probably by mistake), the value `false` is temporarily coerced to the number 0, and `true` is coerced to 1. Therefore, if `boolVar` is a `bool` variable, the expression

```
boolVar < 5
```

yields `true` because 0 and 1 both are less than 5.

Until you learn more about the `char` type in Chapter 10, be careful to compare `char` values only with other `char` values. For example, the comparisons

```
'0' < '9'   and   0 < 9
```

are appropriate, but

```
'0' < 9
```

generates an implicit type coercion and a result that probably isn't what you expect.

We can use relational operators not only to compare variables or constants, but also to compare the values of arithmetic expressions. In the following table, we compare the results of adding 3 to x and multiplying y by 10 for different values of x and y.

Value of x	Value of y	Expression	Result
12	2	x + 3 <= y * 10	true
20	2	x + 3 <= y * 10	false
7	1	x + 3 != y * 10	false
17	2	x + 3 == y * 10	true
100	5	x + 3 > y * 10	true

Caution: It's easy to confuse the assignment operator (=) and the == relational operator. These two operators have very different effects in a program. Some people pronounce the relational operator as "equals-equals" to remind themselves of the difference.

Comparing Strings Recall from Chapter 4 that string is a class—a programmer-defined type from which you declare variables that are more commonly called objects. Contained within each string object is a character string. The string class is designed such that you can compare these strings using the relational operators. Syntactically, the operands of a relational operator can either be two string objects, as in

```
myString < yourString
```

or a string object and a C string:

```
myString >= "Johnson"
```

However, the operands cannot both be C strings.

Comparison of strings follows the collating sequence of the machine's character set (ASCII, for instance). When the computer tests a relationship between two strings, it begins with the first character of each, compares them according to the collating sequence, and if they are the same, repeats the comparison with the next character in each string. The character-by-character test proceeds until either a mismatch is found or the final characters have been compared and are equal. If all their characters are equal, then the two strings are equal. If a mismatch is found, then the string with the character that comes before the other is the "lesser" string.

For example, given the statements

```
string word1;
string word2;
word1 = "Tremendous";
word2 = "Small";
```

the relational expressions in the following table have the indicated values.

Expression	Value	Reason
`word1 == word2`	`false`	They are unequal in the first character.
`word1 > word2`	`true`	'T' comes after 'S' in the collating sequence.
`word1 < "Tremble"`	`false`	Fifth characters don't match, and 'b' comes before 'e'.
`word2 == "Small"`	`true`	They are equal.
`"cat" < "dog"`	Unpredictable	The operands cannot both be C strings.*

*The expression is syntactically legal in C++ but results in a *pointer* comparison, not a string comparison. Pointers are not discussed in this book.

In most cases, the ordering of strings corresponds to alphabetical ordering. But when strings have mixed-case letters, we can get nonalphabetical results. For example, in a phone book we expect to see Macauley before MacPherson, but the ASCII collating sequence places all uppercase letters before the lowercase letters, so the string `"MacPherson"` compares as less than `"Macauley"`. To compare strings for strict alphabetical ordering, all the characters must be in the same case. In a later chapter we show an algorithm for changing the case of a string.

If two strings with different lengths are compared and the comparison is equal up to the end of the shorter string, then the shorter string compares as less than the longer string. For example, if `word2` contains `"Small"`, the expression

```
word2 < "Smaller"
```

yields `true`, because the strings are equal up to their fifth character position (the end of the string on the left), and the string on the right is longer.

Logical Operators In mathematics, the *logical* (or *Boolean*) *operators* AND, OR, and NOT take logical expressions as operands. C++ uses special symbols for the logical operators: `&&` (for AND), `||` (for OR), and `!` (for NOT). By combining relational operators with logical operators, we can make more complex assertions. For example, suppose we want to determine whether a final score is greater than 90 *and* a midterm score is greater than 70. In C++, we would write the expression this way:

```
finalScore > 90 && midtermScore > 70
```

The AND operation (`&&`) requires both relationships to be true in order for the overall result to be true. If either or both of the relationships are false, the entire result is false.

The OR operation (`||`) takes two logical expressions and combines them. If *either* or *both* are true, the result is true. Both values must be false for the result to be false. Now we can determine whether the midterm grade is an A or the final grade is an A. If either the midterm grade or the final grade equals A, the assertion is true. In C++, we write the expression like this:

```
midtermGrade == 'A' || finalGrade == 'A'
```

The `&&` and `||` operators are binary (two-operand) operators. The NOT operator (`!`) is a unary (one-operand) operator. It precedes a single logical expression and gives its opposite as the result. If (`grade == 'A'`) is false, then `!(grade == 'A')` is true. NOT gives us a convenient way of reversing the meaning of an assertion. For example,

`!(hours > 40)`   is the equivalent of   `hours <= 40`

In some contexts, the first form is clearer; in others, the second makes more sense.

The following pairs of expressions are equivalent:

Expression	Equivalent Expression
`!(a == b)`	`a != b`
`!(a == b || a == c)`	`a != b && a != c`
`!(a == b && c > d)`	`a != b || c <= d`

Take a close look at these expressions to be sure you understand why they are equivalent. Try evaluating them with some values for a, b, c, and d. Notice the pattern: The expression on the left is just the one to its right with `!` added and the relational and logical operators reversed (for example, `==` instead of `!=` and `||` instead of `&&`). Remember this pattern. It allows you to rewrite expressions in the simplest form.*

Logical operators can be applied to the results of comparisons. They also can be applied directly to variables of type `bool`. For example, instead of writing

`isElector = (age >= 18 && district == 23);`

to assign a value to the Boolean variable `isElector`, we could use two intermediate Boolean variables, `isVoter` and `isConstituent`:

```
isVoter = (age >= 18);
isConstituent = (district == 23);
isElector = isVoter && isConstituent;
```

The next two tables summarize the results of applying `&&` and `||` to a pair of logical expressions (represented here by Boolean variables x and y).

---

* In Boolean algebra, the pattern is formalized by a theorem called *DeMorgan's law*.

Value of x	Value of y	Value of x && y
true	true	true
true	false	false
false	true	false
false	false	false

Value of x	Value of y	Value of x || y
true	true	true
true	false	true
false	true	true
false	false	false

The following table summarizes the results of applying the ! operator to a logical expression (represented by Boolean variable x).

Value of x	Value of !x
true	false
false	true

Technically, the C++ operators !, &&, and || are not required to have logical expressions as operands. Their operands can be of any simple data type, even floating-point types. If an operand is not of type bool, its value is temporarily coerced to type bool as follows: A 0 value is coerced to false, and any nonzero value is coerced to true. Throughout this text we apply the logical operators only to logical expressions, not to arithmetic expressions.

Caution: It's easy to confuse the logical operators && and || with two other C++ operators, & and |. We don't discuss the & and | operators here, but we'll tell you that they are used for manipulating individual bits within a memory cell—a role quite different from that of the logical operators. If you accidentally use & instead of &&, or | instead of ||, you won't get an error message from the compiler, but your program probably will compute wrong answers. Some programmers pronounce && as "and-and" and || as "or-or" to avoid making mistakes.

Short-Circuit Evaluation   Consider the logical expression

```
i == 1 && j > 2
```

Short-circuit (conditional) evaluation Evaluation of a logical expression in left-to-right order with evaluation stopping as soon as the final truth value can be determined.

C++ uses **short-circuit** (or **conditional**) evaluation of logical expressions. Evaluation proceeds from left to right, and the computer stops evaluating subexpressions as soon as possible—that is, as soon as it knows the truth value of the entire expression. How can the computer know if a lengthy logical expression yields true or false if it doesn't examine all the subexpressions? Let's look first at the AND operation.

An AND operation yields the value true only if both of its operands are true. In the expression above, suppose that the value of i happens to be 95. The first subexpression yields false, so it isn't necessary even to look at the second subexpression. The computer stops evaluation and produces the final result of false.

With the OR operation, the left-to-right evaluation stops as soon as a subexpression yielding true is found. Remember that an OR produces a result of true if either one or both of its operands are true. Given this expression:

```
c <= d || e == f
```

if the first subexpression is true, evaluation stops and the entire result is true. The computer doesn't waste time with an unnecessary evaluation of the second subexpression.

Precedence of Operators

In Chapter 3, we discussed the rules of precedence that govern the evaluation of arithmetic expressions. C++'s rules of precedence also govern relational and logical operators. Here's a list showing the order of precedence for the arithmetic, relational, and logical operators (with the assignment operator thrown in as well):

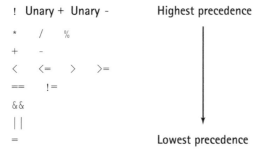

! Unary + Unary -	Highest precedence
* / %	
+ -	
< <= > >=	
== !=	
&&	
||	
=	Lowest precedence

Operators on the same line in the list have the same precedence. If an expression contains several operators with the same precedence, most of the operators group (or *associate*) from left to right. For example, the expression

```
a / b * c
```

means (a / b) * c, not a / (b * c). However, the unary operators (!, unary +, unary -)
group from right to left. Although you'd never have occasion to use this expression:

```
!!badData
```

the meaning of it is !(!badData) rather than the meaningless (!!)badData. Appendix B, "Precedence of Operators," lists the order of precedence for all operators in C++.

Parentheses are used to override the order of evaluation in an expression. If you're
not sure whether parentheses are necessary, use them anyway. The compiler disregards
unnecessary parentheses. So if they clarify an expression, use them.

One final comment about parentheses: C++, like other programming languages,
requires that parentheses always be used in pairs. Whenever you write a complicated
expression, take a minute to go through and pair up all of the opening parentheses with
their closing counterparts.

Relational Operators with Floating-Point Types

So far, we've talked only about comparing int, char, and string values. Here we look
at float values.

Do not compare floating-point numbers for equality. Because small errors in the
rightmost decimal places are likely to arise when calculations are performed on floating-point numbers, two float values rarely are exactly equal. For example, consider
the following code that uses two float variables named oneThird and x:

```
oneThird = 1.0 / 3.0;
x = oneThird + oneThird + oneThird;
```

We would expect x to contain the value 1.0, but it probably doesn't. The first assignment statement stores an *approximation* of 1/3 into oneThird, perhaps 0.333333. The
second statement stores a value like 0.999999 into x. If we now ask the computer to
compare x with 1.0, the comparison yields false.

Instead of testing floating-point numbers for equality, we test for near equality. To
do so, we compute the difference between the two numbers and test to see if the result
is less than some maximum allowable difference. For example, we often use comparisons like this:

```
fabs(r - s) < 0.00001
```

where fabs is the floating-point absolute value function from the C++ standard library.
The expression fabs(r - s) computes the absolute value of the difference between
two float variables r and s. If the difference is less than 0.00001, the two numbers are
close enough to call them equal. We discuss this problem with floating-point accuracy
in more detail in Chapter 10.

Common Mistakes

Many errors in logical expressions stem from our tendency to take shortcuts in English. We might ask whether the midterm grade or the final grade is an A, but if we write this directly in C++ as

```
midtermGrade || finalGrade == 'A'
```

we get erroneous results because the || operator is connecting a char value (midtermGrade) and a logical expression (finalGrade == 'A'). The two operands of || should be logical expressions. So, we must write

```
midtermGrade == 'A' || finalGrade == 'A'
```

Similarly, asking if i equals 3 or 4 cannot be written as

```
i == 3 || 4
```

Instead, we must write

```
i == 3 || i == 4
```

Mathematicians use the notation

$$12 < y < 24$$

to mean "y is between 12 and 24," but translating this directly to C++ has a different effect. First, the relation $12 < y$ is evaluated, giving the result true or false. The computer then coerces this result to 1 or 0 in order to compare it with the number 24. Because both 1 and 0 are less than 24, the result is always true. The correct C++ translation is

```
12 < y && y < 24
```

5.3 The If Statement

Now that we've seen how to write logical expressions, let's use them to alter the normal flow of control in a program. The *If statement* is the fundamental control structure that allows branches in the flow of control. With it, we can ask a question and choose a course of action: *If* a certain condition exists, *then* perform one action, *else* perform a different action.

The If-Then-Else Form

In C++, the If statement comes in two forms: the *If-Then-Else* form and the *If-Then* form. Let's look first at the If-Then-Else. Here is its syntax template:

IfStatement (the If-Then-Else form)

```
if  ( Expression )
        Statement1A
else
        Statement1B
```

The expression in parentheses can be of any simple data type. Almost without exception, this will be a logical (Boolean) expression; if not, its value is implicitly coerced to type `bool`. At run time, the computer evaluates the expression. If the value is `true`, the computer executes Statement1A. If the value of the expression is `false`, Statement1B is executed. Statement1A often is called the *then-clause;* Statement1B, the *else-clause.* Figure 5–3 illustrates the flow of control of the If-Then-Else. In the figure, Statement2 is the next statement in the program after the entire If statement.

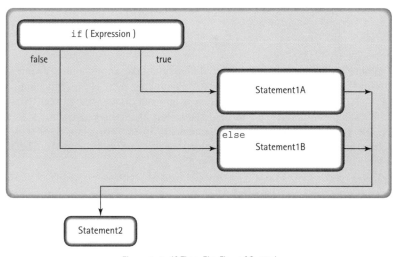

Figure 5–3 *If-Then-Else Flow of Control*

Notice that a C++ If statement uses the reserved words `if` and `else` but does not include the word *then*. Still, we use the term If-Then-Else because it corresponds to how we say things in English: "*If* something is true, *then* do this, *else* do that."

The code fragment below shows how to write an If statement in a program. Observe the indentation of the then-clause and the else-clause, which makes the statement easier to read. And notice the placement of the statement following the If statement.

```
if (hours <= 40.0)
    pay = rate * hours;
else
    pay = rate * (40.0 + (hours - 40.0) * 1.5);
cout << pay;
```

In terms of instructions to the computer, the above code fragment says, "If `hours` is less than or equal to 40.0, compute the regular pay and then go on to execute the output statement. But if `hours` is greater than 40, compute the regular pay and the overtime pay, and then go on to execute the output statement."

As another example of an If-Then-Else, suppose we want to determine where in a `string` variable the first occurrence (if any) of the letter *A* is located. Recall from Chapter 3 that the `string` class has a member function named `find`, which returns the position where the item was found (or the named constant `string::npos` if the item wasn't found). The following code outputs the result of the search:

```
string myString;
string::size_type pos;
   ⋮
pos = myString.find('A');
if (pos == string::npos)
    cout << "No 'A' was found" << endl;
else
    cout << "An 'A' was found in position " << pos << endl;
```

Before we look any further at If statements, take another look at the syntax template for the If-Then-Else. According to the template, there is no semicolon at the end of an If statement. In both of the program fragments above—the worker's pay and string search examples—there seems to be a semicolon at the end of each If statement. However, the semicolons belong to the statements in the else-clauses in those examples; assignment statements end in semicolons, as do output statements. The If statement doesn't have its own semicolon at the end.

Blocks (Compound Statements)

In checking to avoid division-by-zero in an expression, suppose that when the divisor is equal to zero we want to do *two* things: print an error message *and* set a variable named `result` equal to a special value like 9999. We would need two statements in the same branch, but the syntax template seems to limit us to one.

What we really want to do is turn the else-clause into a *sequence* of statements. This is easy. Remember from Chapter 2 that the compiler treats the block

```
{
    ⋮
}
```

like a single statement. If you put a { } pair around the sequence of statements in a branch of the If statement, the sequence of statements becomes a single block. For example:

```
if (divisor != 0)
    result = dividend / divisor;
else
{
    cout << "Division by zero is not allowed." << endl;
    result = 9999;
}
```

If the value of `divisor` is 0, the computer both prints the error message and sets the value of `result` to 9999 before continuing with whatever statement follows the If statement.

Blocks can be used in both branches of an If-Then-Else. For example:

```
if (divisor != 0)
{
    result = dividend / divisor;
    cout << "Division performed." << endl;
}
else
{
    cout << "Division by zero is not allowed." << endl;
    result = 9999;
}
```

When you use blocks in an If statement, there's a rule of C++ syntax to remember: *Never use a semicolon after the right brace of a block.* Semicolons are used only to terminate simple statements such as assignment statements, input statements, and output statements. In the examples above, there is no semicolon after the right brace that signals the end of each block.

The If-Then Form

Sometimes you run into a situation where you want to say, "*If* a certain condition exists, *then* perform some action; otherwise, don't do anything." In other words, you want the computer to skip a sequence of instructions if a certain condition isn't met. You could do this by leaving the `else` branch empty, using only the null statement:

```
if (a <= b)
    c = 20;
else
    ;
```

Better yet, you can simply leave off the `else` part. The resulting statement is the If-Then form of the If statement. This is its syntax template:

IfStatement (the If-Then form)

```
if    ( Expression )
      Statement
```

Here's an example of an If-Then. Notice the indentation and the placement of the statement that follows the If-Then.

```
if (age < 18)
    cout << "Not an eligible ";
cout << "voter." << endl;
```

This statement means that if `age` is less than 18, first print "Not an eligible " and then print "voter." If `age` is not less than 18, skip the first output statement and go directly to print "voter."

As in an If-Then-Else, the branch in an If-Then can be a block. For example, let's say you are writing a program to compute income taxes. One of the lines on the tax form reads "Subtract line 23 from line 17 and enter result on line 24; if result is less than zero, enter zero and check box 24A." You can use an If-Then to do this in C++:

```
result = line17 - line23;
if (result < 0.0)
{
    cout << "Check box 24A" << endl;
    result = 0.0;
}
line24 = result;
```

This code does exactly what the tax form says it should. It computes the result of subtracting line 23 from line 17. Then it looks to see if `result` is less than 0. If it is, the fragment prints a message telling the user to check box 24A and then sets `result` to 0. Finally, the calculated result (or 0, if the result is less than 0) is stored into a variable named `line24`.

What happens if we leave out the left and right braces in the code fragment above? Let's look at it:

```
result = line17 - line23;                  // Incorrect version
if (result < 0.0)
    cout << "Check box 24A" << endl;
    result = 0.0;
line24 = result;
```

Despite the way we have indented the code, the compiler takes the then-clause to be a single statement—the output statement. If `result` is less than 0, the computer executes the output statement, then sets `result` to 0, and then stores `result` into `line24`. So far, so good. But if `result` is initially greater than or equal to 0, the computer skips the then-clause and proceeds to the statement following the If statement—the assignment statement that sets `result` to 0. The outcome is that `result` ends up as 0 no matter what its initial value was! The moral here is not to rely on indentation alone; you can't fool the compiler. If you want a compound statement for a then- or else-clause, you must include the left and right braces.

A Common Mistake

Earlier we warned against confusing the `=` operator and the `==` operator. Here is an example of a mistake that every C++ programmer is guaranteed to make at least once in his or her career:

```
cin >> n;
if (n = 3)                         // Wrong
    cout << "n equals 3";
else
    cout << "n doesn't equal 3";
```

This code segment *always* prints out

```
n equals 3
```

no matter what was input for `n`.

Here is the reason: We've used the wrong operator in the If test. The expression `n = 3` is not a logical expression; it's called an *assignment expression*. (If an assignment is written as a separate statement ending with a semicolon, it's an assignment *statement*.) An assignment expression has a *value* (above, it's 3) and a *side effect* (storing 3 into `n`). In the If statement of our example, the computer finds the value of the tested expression to be 3. Because 3 is a nonzero value and thus is coerced to `true`, the then-clause is executed, no matter what the value of `n` is. Worse yet, the side effect of the assignment expression is to store 3 into `n`, destroying what was there.

Our intention is not to focus on assignment expressions; we discuss their use later in the book. What's important now is that you see the effect of using = when you meant to use ==. The program compiles correctly but runs incorrectly. When debugging a faulty program, always look at your If statements to see whether you've made this particular mistake.

5.4 Nested If Statements

There are no restrictions on what the statements in an If can be. Therefore, an If within an If is OK. In fact, an If within an If within an If is legal. The only limitation here is that people cannot follow a structure that is too involved, and readability is one of the marks of a good program.

When we place an If within an If, we are creating a *nested control structure*. Control structures nest much like mixing bowls do, with smaller ones tucked inside larger ones. Here's an example, written in pseudocode:

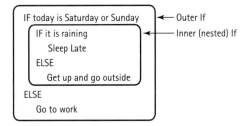

In general, any problem that involves a *multiway branch* (more than two alternative courses of action) can be coded using nested If statements. For example, to print out the name of a month given its number, we could use a sequence of If statements (unnested):

```
if (month == 1)
    cout << "January";
if (month == 2)
    cout << "February";
if (month == 3)
    cout << "March";
    ⋮
if (month == 12)
    cout << "December";
```

But the equivalent nested If structure,

```
if (month == 1)
    cout << "January";
else
    if (month == 2)                // Nested If
        cout << "February";
    else
        if (month == 3)            // Nested If
            cout << "March";
        else
            if (month == 4)            // Nested If
                ⋮
```

is more efficient because it makes fewer comparisons. The first version—the sequence of independent If statements—always tests every condition (all 12 of them), even if the first one is satisfied. In contrast, the nested If solution skips all remaining comparisons after one alternative has been selected.

In the last example, notice how the indentation of the then- and else-clauses causes the statements to move continually to the right. Instead, we can use a special indentation style with deeply nested If-Then-Else statements to indicate that the complex structure is just choosing one of a set of alternatives. This general multiway branch is known as an *If-Then-Else-If* control structure:

```
if (month == 1)
    cout << "January";
else if (month == 2)           // Nested If
    cout << "February";
else if (month == 3)           // Nested If
    cout << "March";
else if (month == 4)           // Nested If
    ⋮
else
    cout << "December";
```

This style prevents the indentation from marching continuously to the right. But, more important, it visually conveys the idea that we are using a 12-way branch based on the variable month.

It's important to note one difference between the sequence of If statements and the nested If: More than one alternative can be taken by the sequence of Ifs, but the nested If can select only one. To see why this is important, consider the analogy of filling out a questionnaire. Some questions are like a sequence of If statements, asking you to circle all the items in a list that apply to you (such as all your hobbies). Other questions ask you to circle only one item in a list (your age group, for example) and are thus like a nested If structure. Both kinds of questions occur in programming problems. Being able to recognize which type of question is being asked permits you to immediately select the appropriate control structure.

Another particularly helpful use of the nested If is when you want to select from a series of consecutive ranges of values. For example, suppose that we want to print out an appropriate activity for the outdoor temperature, given the following table.

Activity	Temperature
Swimming	Temperature > 85
Tennis	$70 <$ temperature ≤ 85
Golf	$32 <$ temperature ≤ 70
Skiing	$0 <$ temperature ≤ 32
Dancing	Temperature ≤ 0

At first glance, you may be tempted to write a separate If statement for each range of temperatures. On closer examination, however, it is clear that these If conditions are interdependent. That is, if one of the statements is executed, none of the others should be executed. We really are selecting one alternative from a set of possibilities—just the sort of situation in which we can use a nested If structure as a multiway branch. The only difference between this problem and our earlier example of printing the month name from its number is that we must check ranges of numbers in the If expressions of the branches.

When the ranges are consecutive, we can take advantage of that fact to make our code more efficient. We arrange the branches in consecutive order by range. Then, if a particular branch has been reached, we know that the preceding ranges have been eliminated from consideration. Thus, the If expressions must compare the temperature to only the lowest value of each range.

```cpp
cout << "The recommended activity is ";
if (temperature > 85)
    cout << "swimming." << endl;
else if (temperature > 70)
    cout << "tennis." << endl;
else if (temperature > 32)
    cout << "golf." << endl;
else if (temperature > 0)
    cout << "skiing." << endl;
else
    cout << "dancing." << endl;
```

The Dangling `else`

When If statements are nested, you may find yourself confused about the `if-else` pairings. That is, to which `if` does an `else` belong? For example, suppose that if a student's average is below 60, we want to print "Failing"; if it is at least 60 but less than 70, we want to print "Passing but marginal"; and if it is 70 or greater, we don't want to print anything.

We code this information with an If-Then-Else nested within an If-Then:

```
if (average < 70.0)
    if (average < 60.0)
        cout << "Failing";
    else
        cout << "Passing but marginal";
```

How do we know to which `if` the `else` belongs? Here is the rule that the C++ compiler follows: In the absence of braces, an `else` is always paired with the closest preceding `if` that doesn't already have an `else` paired with it. We indented the code to reflect this pairing.

Suppose we write the fragment like this:

```
if (average >= 60.0)        // Incorrect version
    if (average < 70.0)
        cout << "Passing but marginal";
else
    cout << "Failing";
```

Here we want the `else` branch attached to the outer If statement, not the inner, so we indent the code as you see it. But indentation does not affect the execution of the code. Even though the `else` aligns with the first `if`, the compiler pairs it with the second `if`. An `else` that follows a nested If-Then is called a *dangling* `else`. It doesn't logically belong with the nested If but is attached to it by the compiler.

To attach the `else` to the first `if`, not the second, you can turn the outer then-clause into a block:

```
if (average >= 60.0)        // Correct version
{
    if (average < 70.0)
        cout << "Passing but marginal";
}
else
    cout << "Failing";
```

The { } pair indicates that the inner If statement is complete, so the `else` must belong to the outer `if`.

5.5 Testing the State of an I/O Stream

In Chapter 4, we talked about the concept of input and output streams in C++. We introduced the classes `istream`, `ostream`, `ifstream`, and `ofstream`. We said that any of the following can cause an input stream to enter the fail state:

- Invalid input data
- An attempt to read beyond the end of a file
- An attempt to open a nonexistent file for input

C++ provides a way to check whether a stream is in the fail state. In a logical expression, you simply use the name of the stream object (such as `cin`) as if it were a Boolean variable:

```
if (cin)
    ⋮
if ( !inFile )
    ⋮
```

Testing the state of a stream The act of using a C++ stream object in a logical expression as if it were a Boolean variable; the result is `true` if the last I/O operation on that stream succeeded, and `false` otherwise.

When you do this, you are said to be **testing the state of the stream.** The result of the test is either `true` (meaning the last I/O operation on that stream succeeded) or `false` (meaning the last I/O operation failed).

Conceptually, you want to think of a stream object in a logical expression as being a Boolean variable with a value `true` (the stream state is OK) or `false` (the state isn't OK).

Notice in the second If statement above that we typed spaces around the expression `!inFile`. The spaces are not required by C++ but are there for readability. Without the spaces, it is harder to see the exclamation mark: `if (!inFile)`.

In an If statement, the way you phrase the logical expression depends on what you want the then-clause to do. The statement

```
if (inFile)
    ⋮
```

executes the then-clause if the last I/O operation on `inFile` succeeded. The statement

```
if ( !inFile )
    ⋮
```

executes the then-clause if `inFile` is in the fail state. (And remember that once a stream is in the fail state, it remains so. Any further I/O operations on that stream are null operations.)

Here's an example that shows how to check whether an input file was opened successfully:

```
#include <iostream>
#include <fstream>     // For file I/O

using namespace std;

int main()
{
    int       height;
    int       width;
    ifstream inFile;

    inFile.open("mydata.dat");              // Attempt to open input file
    if ( !inFile )                          // Was it opened?
    {
        cout << "Can't open the input file.";  // No--print message
        return 1;                              // Terminate program
    }
    inFile >> height >> width;
    ⋮
    return 0;
}
```

In this program, we begin by attempting to open the disk file mydata.dat for input. Immediately, we check to see whether the attempt succeeded. If it was successful, the value of the expression !inFile in the If statement is false and the then-clause is skipped. The program proceeds to read data from the file.

Let's trace through the program again, assuming we weren't able to open the input file. Upon return from the open function, the stream inFile is in the fail state. In the If statement, the value of the expression !inFile is true. Thus, the then-clause is executed. The program prints an error message to the user and then terminates, returning an exit status of 1 to inform the operating system of an abnormal termination of the program. (Our choice of the value 1 for the exit status is purely arbitrary. Programmers sometimes use different values to signal different reasons for program termination. But most people just use the value 1.)

Whenever you open a data file for input, be sure to test the stream state before proceeding. If you forget to, and the computer cannot open the file, your program quietly continues executing and ignores any input operations on the file.

Programming Example

Warning Notices

Problem Write a program that calculates the average of three test grades and prints out a student's ID number, average, and whether or not the student is passing. Passing is a 60-point average or better. If the student is passing with less than a 70 average, the program should indicate that he or she is marginal.

Input Student ID number (of type `long`) followed by three test grades (of type `int`). On some personal computers, the maximum `int` value is `32767`. The student ID number is of type `long` (meaning long integer) to accommodate larger values such as nine-digit Social Security numbers.

Output

A prompt for input

The input values (echo print)

Student ID number, average grade, passing/failing message, marginal indication, and error message if any of the test scores are negative

Discussion To calculate the average, we have to read in the three test scores, add them, and divide by 3.

To print the appropriate message, we have to determine whether or not the average is below 60. If it is at least 60, we have to determine if it is less than 70.

If you were doing this by hand, you probably would notice if a test grade was negative and question it. If the semantics of your data imply that the values should be nonnegative, then your program should test to be sure they are. We test to make sure each grade is nonnegative, using a Boolean variable to report the result of the test. Here is the main module for our algorithm.

....

Main Module   **Level 0**

```
Get data
Test data
IF data OK
    Calculate average
    Print message indicating status
ELSE
    Print "Invalid Data: Score(s) less than zero."
```

Which of these steps require(s) expansion? *Get data*, *Test data*, and *Print message indicating status* all require multiple statements in order to solve their particular subproblem. On the other hand, we can translate *Print "Invalid Data: ..."* directly into a C++ output statement. What about the step *Calculate average?* We can write it as a single C++ statement, but there's another level of detail that we must fill in—the actual formula to be used. Because the formula is at a lower level of detail than the rest of the main module, we chose to expand *Calculate average* as a level 1 module.

Get Data   Level 1

> Prompt for input
> Read studentID, test1, test2, test3
> Print studentID, test1, test2, test3

Test Data

> IF test1 < 0 OR test2 < 0 OR test3 < 0
>> Set dataOK = false
> ELSE
>> Set dataOK = true

Calculate Average

> Set average = (test1 + test2 + test3) / 3.0

Print Message Indicating Status

> Print average
> IF average >= 60.0
>> Print "Passing"
>> IF average < 70.0
>>> Print " but marginal"
>> Print '.'
> ELSE
>> Print "Failing."

(The following program is written in ISO/ANSI standard C++. If you are working with pre-standard C++, see the alternate version of the program in the PRE_STD directory of the program disk, available at the publisher's Web site, www.jbpub.com/disks.)

```
//**********************************************************************
// Notices program
// This program determines (1) a student's average based on three
// test scores and (2) the student's passing/failing status
//**********************************************************************
#include <iostream>
#include <iomanip>      // For setprecision()

using namespace std;

int main()
{
    float average;       // Average of three test scores
    long  studentID;     // Student's identification number
    int   test1;         // Score for first test
    int   test2;         // Score for second test
    int   test3;         // Score for third test
    bool  dataOK;        // True if data is correct

    cout << fixed << showpoint;            // Set up floating-pt.
                                           //   output format

    // Get data

    cout << "Enter a Student ID number and three test scores:"
         << endl;
    cin >> studentID >> test1 >> test2 >> test3;
    cout << "Student number: " << studentID << "  Test Scores: "
         << test1 << ", " << test2 << ", " << test3 << endl;

    // Test data

    if (test1 < 0 || test2 < 0 || test3 < 0)
        dataOK = false;
    else
        dataOK = true;

    if (dataOK)
    {
        // Calculate average

        average = float(test1 + test2 + test3) / 3.0;
```

```
        // Print message

        cout << "Average score is "
            << setprecision(2) << average << "--";
        if (average >= 60.0)
        {
            cout << "Passing";                    // Student is passing
            if (average < 70.0)
                cout << " but marginal";          // But marginal
            cout << '.' << endl;
        }
        else                                      // Student is failing
            cout << "Failing." << endl;
    }
    else                                          // Invalid data
        cout << "Invalid Data:  Score(s) less than zero." << endl;

    return 0;
}
```

Here's a sample run of the program. Again, the input is in color.

```
Enter a Student ID number and three test scores:
9483681  73  62  68
Student Number: 9483681  Test Scores: 73, 62, 68
Average score is 67.67--Passing but marginal.
```

And here's a sample run with invalid data:

```
Enter a Student ID number and three test scores:
9483681  73  -10  62
Student Number: 9483681  Test Scores: 73, -10, 62
Invalid Data:  Score(s) less than zero.
```

Testing and Debugging

In Chapter 1, we discussed the problem-solving and implementation phases of computer programming. Testing is an integral part of both phases. Here we test both phases of the process used to develop the Notices program. Testing in the problem-solving phase is done after the solution is developed but before it is implemented. In the implementation phase, we test after the algorithm is translated into a program, and again after the program has compiled successfully. The compilation itself constitutes another stage of testing that is performed automatically.

Testing in the Problem-Solving Phase: The Algorithm Walk-Through

Determining Preconditions and Postconditions To test during the problem-solving phase, we do a *walk-through* of the algorithm. For each module in the functional decomposition, we establish an assertion called a precondition and another called a postcondition. A **precondition** is an assertion that must be true before a module is executed in order for the module to execute correctly. A **postcondition** is an assertion that should be true after the module has executed, if it has done its job correctly. To test a module, we "walk through" the algorithmic steps to confirm that they produce the required postcondition, given the stated precondition.

Precondition An assertion that must be true before a module begins executing.

Postcondition An assertion that must be true after a module has executed.

Our algorithm has five modules: the main module, Get Data, Test Data, Calculate Average, and Print Message Indicating Status. Usually there is no precondition for a main module. Our main module's postcondition is that it outputs the correct results, given the correct input. More specifically, the postcondition for the main module is

- the computer has input four integer values into `studentID`, `test1`, `test2`, and `test3`.
- the input values have been echo printed.
- if the input is invalid, an error message has been printed; otherwise, the average of the last three input values has been printed, along with the message "Passing" if the average is greater than or equal to 70.0, "Passing but marginal." if the average is less than 70.0 and greater than or equal to 60.0, or "Failing." if the average is less than 60.0.

Because Get Data is the first module executed in the algorithm and because it does not assume anything about the contents of the variables it is about to manipulate, it has no precondition. Its postcondition is that it has input four integer values into `studentID`, `test1`, `test2`, and `test3`.

The precondition for module Test Data is that `test1`, `test2`, and `test3` have been assigned meaningful values. Its postcondition is that `dataOK` contains `true` if the values in `test1`, `test2`, and `test3` are nonnegative; otherwise, `dataOK` contains `false`.

The precondition for module Calculate Average is that `test1`, `test2`, and `test3` contain meaningful values. Its postcondition is that the variable named `average` contains the mean (the average) of `test1`, `test2`, and `test3`.

The precondition for module Print Message Indicating Status is that `average` contains the mean of the values in `test1`, `test2`, and `test3`. Its postcondition is that the value in `average` has been printed, along with the message "Passing" if the average is greater than or equal to 70.0, "Passing but marginal." if the average is less than 70.0 and greater than or equal to 60.0, or "Failing." if the average is less than 60.0.

Performing the Algorithm Walk-Through   Now that we've established the preconditions and postconditions, we walk through the main module. At this point, we are concerned only with the steps in the main module, so for now we assume that each lower-level module executes correctly. At each step, we must determine the current conditions. If the step is a reference to another module, we must verify that the precondition of that module is met by the current conditions.

We begin with the first statement in the main module. Get Data does not have a precondition, and we assume that Get Data satisfies its postcondition that it correctly inputs four integer values into `studentID`, `test1`, `test2`, and `test3`.

The precondition for module Test Data is that `test1`, `test2`, and `test3` are assigned values. This must be the case if Get Data's postcondition is true. Again, because we are concerned only with the step at level 0, we assume that Test Data satisfies its postcondition that `dataOK` contains `true` or `false`, depending on the input values.

Next, the If statement checks to see if `dataOK` is `true`. If it is, the algorithm performs the then-clause. Assuming that Calculate Average correctly calculates the mean of `test1`, `test2`, and `test3` and that Print Message Indicating Status prints the average and the appropriate message, then the If statement's then-clause is correct. If the value in `dataOK` is `false`, the algorithm performs the else-clause and prints an error message.

We now have verified that the main (level 0) module is correct, assuming the level 1 modules are correct. The next step is to examine each module at level 1 and answer this question: If the level 2 modules (if any) are assumed to be correct, does this level 1 module do what it is supposed to do? We simply repeat the walk-through process for each module, starting with its particular precondition. In this example, there are no level 2 modules, so the level 1 modules must be complete.

Get Data correctly reads in four values—`studentID`, `test1`, `test2`, and `test3`—thereby satisfying its postcondition. (The next refinement is to code this instruction in C++. Whether it is coded correctly or not is *not* an issue in this phase; we deal with the code when we perform testing in the implementation phase.)

Test Data checks to see if all three of the variables contain nonnegative scores. The If condition correctly uses OR operators to combine the relational expressions so that if any of them are `true`, the then-clause is executed. It thus assigns `false` to `dataOK` if any of the numbers are negative; otherwise, it assigns `true`. The module therefore satisfies its postcondition.

Calculate Average sums the three test scores, divides the sum by 3.0, and assigns the result to `average`. The required postcondition therefore is true.

Print Message Indicating Status outputs the value in `average`. It then tests whether `average` is greater than or equal to 60.0. If so, "Passing" is printed and it then tests whether `average` is less than 70.0. If so, the words "but marginal" are added after "Passing". On the other hand, if `average` is less than 60.0, the message "Failing." is printed. Thus the module satisfies its postcondition.

Once we've completed the algorithm walk-through, we have to correct any discrepancies and repeat the process. When we know that the modules do what they are supposed to do, we start translating the algorithm into our programming language.

A standard postcondition for any program is that the user has been notified of invalid data. You should *validate* every input value for which any restrictions apply. A data-validation If statement tests an input value and outputs an error message if the value is not acceptable. (We validated the data when we tested for negative scores in the Notices program.) The best place to validate data is immediately after it is input. To satisfy the data-validation postcondition, the Warning Notices algorithm also should test the input values to ensure that they aren't too large.

For example, if the maximum score on a test is 100, then module Test Data should check for values in `test1`, `test2`, and `test3` that are greater than 100. The printing of the error message also should be modified to indicate the particular error condition that occurred. It would be best if it also specified the score that is invalid. Such a change makes it clear that Test Data should be the module to print the error messages. If Test Data prints the error message, then the If-Then-Else in the main module can be rewritten as an If-Then.

Testing in the Implementation Phase

Now that we've talked about testing in the problem-solving phase, we turn to testing in the implementation phase. In this phase, you need to test at several points.

Code Walk-Through   After the code is written, you should go over it line by line to be sure that you've faithfully reproduced the algorithm—a process known as a *code walk-through*. In a team programming situation, you ask other team members to walk through the algorithm and code with you, to double-check the design and code.

Execution Trace   You also should take some actual values and hand-calculate what the output should be by doing an *execution trace* (or *hand trace*). When the program is executed, you can use these same values as input and check the results.

The computer is a very literal device—it does exactly what we tell it to do, which may or may not be what we want it to do. We try to make sure that a program does what we want by tracing the execution of the statements.

We use the following nonsense program to demonstrate the technique. We keep track of the values of the program variables on the right-hand side. Variables with undefined values are indicated with a dash. When a variable is assigned a value, that value is listed in the appropriate column.

Statement	Value of		
	a	b	c
`const int x = 5;`			
`int main()`			
`{`			
`    int a, b, c;`	—	—	—
`    b = 1;`	—	1	—
`    c = x + b;`	—	1	6
`    a = x + 4;`	9	1	6
`    a = c;`	6	1	6
`    b = c;`	6	6	6
`    a = a + b + c;`	18	6	6
`    c = c % x;`	18	6	1
`    c = c * a;`	18	6	18
`    a = a % b;`	0	6	18
`    cout << a << b << c;`	0	6	18
`    return 0;`	0	6	18
`}`			

Now that you've seen how the technique works, let's apply it to the Notices program. We list only the executable statement portion here. The input values are 6483, 73, 62, and 60. (The table is on page 188.)

The then-clause of the first If statement is not executed for this input data, so we do not fill in any of the variable columns to its right. The same situation occurs with the else-clauses in the other If statements. The test data causes only the then-clauses to be executed. We always create columns for all of the variables, even if we know that some will stay empty. Why? Because it's possible that later we'll encounter an erroneous reference to an empty variable; having a column for the variable reminds us to check for just such an error.

When a program contains branches, it's a good idea to retrace its execution with different input data so that each branch is traced at least once. In the next section, we describe how to develop data sets that test each of a program's branches.

Statement	Value of					
	test1	test2	test3	average	dataOK	studentID
`cout << "Enter a Student ID number and three "`						
`    << "test scores:" << endl;`	—	—	—	—	—	—
`cin >> studentID >> test1 >> test2 >> test3;`	73	62	60	—	—	6483
`cout << "Student number: " << studentID`						
`    << "  Test Scores: " << test1 << ", "`						
`    << test2 << ", " << test3 << endl;`	73	62	60	—	—	6483
`if (test1 < 0 || test2 < 0 || test3 < 0)`	73	62	60	—	—	6483
`    dataOK = false;`						
`else`						
`    dataOK = true;`	73	62	60	—	true	6483
`if (dataOK)`	73	62	60	—	true	6483
`{`						
`    average = float(test1 + test2 + test3) /`						
`        3.0;`	73	62	60	67.67	true	6483
`    cout << "Average score is "`						
`        << setprecision(2) << average << "--";`	73	62	60	67.67	true	6483
`    if (average >= 60.0)`	73	62	60	67.67	true	6483
`    {`						
`        cout << "Passing";`	73	62	60	67.67	true	6483
`        if (average < 70.0)`	73	62	60	67.67	true	6483
`            cout << " but marginal";`	73	62	60	67.67	true	6483
`        cout << '.' << endl;`	73	62	60	67.67	true	6483
`    }`						
`    else`						
`        cout << "Failing." << endl;`						
`}`						
`else`						
`    cout << "Invalid Data:  Score(s) less "`						
`        << "than zero." << endl;`						
`return 0;`	73	62	60	67.67	true	6483

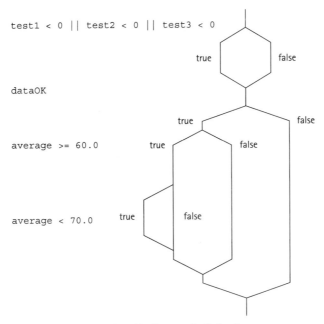

```
test1 < 0 || test2 < 0 || test3 < 0
```

dataOK

average >= 60.0

average < 70.0

Figure 5-4 *Branching Structure for Notices Program*

Testing Selection Control Structures To test a program with branches, we need to execute each branch at least once and verify the results. For example, in the Notices program there are four If-Then-Else statements (see Figure 5-4). We need a series of data sets to test the different branches. For example, the following sets of input values for test1, test2, and test3 cause all of the branches to be executed:

	test1	test2	test3
Set 1	100	100	100
Set 2	60	60	63
Set 3	50	50	50
Set 4	−50	50	50

Figure 5-5 shows the flow of control through the branching structure of the Notices program for each of these data sets. Set 1 is valid and gives an average of 100, which is passing and not marginal. Set 2 is valid and gives an average of 61, which is passing but marginal. Set 3 is valid and gives an average of 50, which is failing. Set 4 has an invalid test grade, which generates an error message.

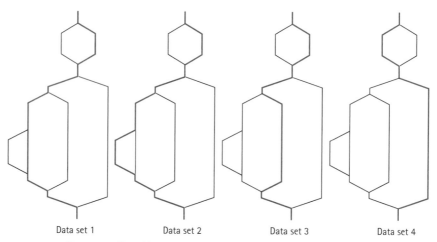

Data set 1   Data set 2   Data set 3   Data set 4

Figure 5–5 *Flow of Control Through Notices Program for Each of Four Data Sets*

The approach to testing that we've used here is called *code coverage* because the test data is designed by looking at the code of the program. Another approach to testing, *data coverage,* attempts to test as many allowable data values as possible without regard to the program code. Complete data coverage is impractical for many programs.

Often, testing is a combination of these two strategies. Instead of trying every possible data value, we examine the code and look for ranges of values for which processing is identical. Then we test the values at the boundaries and, sometimes, a value in the middle of each range. For example, a simple condition such as

```
alpha < 0
```

divides the integers into two ranges:

1. INT_MIN through –1
2. 0 through INT_MAX*

Thus, we should test the four values INT_MIN, –1, 0, and INT_MAX. A compound condition such as

```
alpha >= 0 && alpha <= 100
```

---

*INT_MAX and INT_MIN are constants declared in the header file climits. They represent the largest and smallest possible int values, respectively, on your particular computer and C++ compiler.

divides the integers into three ranges:

1. `INT_MIN` through −1
2. 0 through 100
3. 101 through `INT_MAX`

Thus, we have six values to test. In addition, to verify that the relational operators are correct, we should test for values of 1 (> 0) and 99 (< 100).

Conditional branches are only one factor in developing a testing strategy. We consider more of these factors in later chapters.

The Test Plan

We've discussed strategies and techniques for testing programs, but how do you approach the testing of a specific program? You do it by designing and implementing a **test plan**—a document that specifies the test cases that should be tried, the reason for each test case, and the expected output. **Implementing a test plan** involves running the program using the data specified by the test cases in the plan and checking and recording the results.

Test plan   A document that specifies how a program is to be tested.

Test plan implementation   Using the test cases specified in a test plan to verify that a program outputs the predicted results.

The test plan should be developed together with the functional decomposition. As you create each module, write out its precondition and postcondition and note the test data required to verify them. Consider code coverage and data coverage to see if you've left out tests for any aspects of the program (if you've forgotten something, it probably also indicates that a precondition or postcondition is incomplete).

The following table shows a partial test plan for the Notices program. It has eight test cases. The first test case is just to check that the program echo prints its input properly. The next three cases test the different paths through the program for valid data. Three more test cases check that each of the scores is appropriately validated by separately entering an invalid score for each. The last test case checks the boundary where a score is considered valid—when it is 0. We could further expand this test plan to check the valid data boundary separately for each score by providing three test cases in which one score in each case is 0. We also could test the boundary conditions of the different paths for valid data. That is, we could check that averages of exactly 60 and 70, and slightly higher and slightly lower, produce the desired output.

Test Plan for Notices Program

Reason for Test Case	Input Values	Expected Output	Observed Output
Echo-print check	9999, 100, 100, 100	Student Number: 9999 Test Scores: 100, 100, 100	

Note to implementor: Once echo printing has been checked, it is omitted from the expected output column in subsequent test cases, but still appears in the program's output.

Passing scores	9999, 80, 70, 90	Average score is 80.00-- Passing.	
Passing but marginal scores	9999, 55, 65, 75	Average score is 65.00-- Passing but marginal.	
Failing scores	9999, 30, 40, 50	Average score is 40.00-- Failing.	
Invalid data, Test 1	9999, –1, 20, 30	Invalid Data: Score(s) less than zero.	
Invalid data, Test 2	9999, 10, –1, 30	Invalid Data: Score(s) less than zero.	
Invalid data, Test 3	9999, 10, 20, –1	Invalid Data: Score(s) less than zero.	
Boundary of valid data	9999, 0, 0, 0	Average score is 0.00 -- Failing.	

Implementing a test plan does not guarantee that a program is completely correct. It means only that a careful, systematic test of the program has not demonstrated any bugs. If you try to test a program without a plan and depend only on luck, you may completely miss the fact that a program contains numerous errors. Developing and implementing a written test plan, on the other hand, casts a wide net that is much more likely to find errors.

Tests Performed Automatically During Compilation and Execution

Once a program is coded and test data has been prepared, it is ready for compiling. The compiler has two responsibilities: to report any errors and (if there are no errors) to translate the program into object code.

Errors can be syntactic or semantic. The compiler finds syntactic errors. For example, the compiler warns you when reserved words are misspelled, identifiers are undeclared, semicolons are missing, and operand types are mismatched. But it won't find all of your typing errors. If you type > instead of <, you won't get an error message; instead, you get erroneous results when you test the program. It's up to you to design a test plan and carefully check the code to detect errors of this type.

Semantic errors (also called *logic errors*) are mistakes that give you the wrong answer. They are more difficult to locate than syntactic errors and usually surface when a program is executing. C++ detects only the most obvious semantic errors—those that result in an invalid operation (dividing by zero, for example). Although semantic errors sometimes are caused by typing errors, they are more often a product of a faulty algorithm design. The lack of checking for test scores over 100 that we found in the algorithm walk-through for the Warning Notices problem is a typical semantic error.

By walking through the algorithm and the code, tracing the execution of the program, and developing a thorough test strategy, you should be able to avoid, or at least quickly locate, semantic errors in your programs.

Testing and Debugging Hints

1. C++ has three pairs of operators that are similar in appearance but very different in effect: == and =, && and &, and || and |. Double-check all of your logical expressions to be sure you're using the "equals-equals," "and-and," and "or-or" operators.

2. If you use extra parentheses for clarity, be sure that the opening and closing parentheses match up. To verify that parentheses are properly paired, start with the innermost pair and draw a line connecting them. Do the same for the others, working your way out to the outermost pair. For example,

```
if (((total/scores) > 50) && ((total/(scores - 1)) < 100))
```

Here is a quick way to tell whether you have an equal number of opening and closing parentheses. The scheme uses a single number (the "magic number"), whose value initially is 0. Scan the expression from left to right. At each opening parenthesis, add 1 to the magic number; at each closing parenthesis, subtract 1. At the final closing parenthesis, the magic number should be 0. For example,

```
if ((( total/scores) > 50) && ((total/(scores - 1)) < 100))
   0   123                   2   1    23        4       32      10
```

3. Don't use =< to mean "less than or equal to"; only the symbol <= works. Likewise, => is invalid for "greater than or equal to"; you must use >= for this operation.

4. In an If statement, remember to use a { } pair if the then-clause or else-clause is a sequence of statements. And be sure not to put a semicolon after the right brace.

5. Echo print all input data. By doing so, you know that your input values are what they are supposed to be.

6. Test for bad data. If a data value must be positive, use an If statement to test the value. If the value is negative or 0, an error message should be printed; otherwise, processing should continue. For example, module Test Data in the Notices program

could be rewritten to test for scores greater than 100 as follows (this change also requires that we remove the `else` branch in the main module):

```
dataOK = true;
if (test1 < 0 || test2 < 0 || test3 < 0)
{
    cout << "Invalid Data:  Score(s) less than zero." << endl;
    dataOK = false;
}
if (test1 > 100 || test2 > 100 || test3 > 100)
{
    cout << "Invalid Data:  Score(s) greater than 100." << endl;
    dataOK = false;
}
```

These If statements test the limits of reasonable scores, and the rest of the program continues only if the data values are reasonable.

7. Take some sample values and try them by hand as we did for the Notices program. (There's more on this method in Chapter 6.)

8. If your program reads data from an input file, it should verify that the file was opened successfully. Immediately after the call to the `open` function, an If statement should test the state of the file stream.

9. If your program produces an answer that does not agree with a value you've calculated by hand, try these suggestions:

   a. Redo your arithmetic.

   b. Recheck your input data.

   c. Carefully go over the section of code that does the calculation. If you're in doubt about the order in which the operations are performed, insert clarifying parentheses.

   d. Check for integer overflow. The value of an `int` variable may have exceeded `INT_MAX` in the middle of a calculation. Some systems give an error message when this happens, but most do not.

   e. Check the conditions in branching statements to be sure that the correct branch is taken under all circumstances.

Summary

Using logical expressions is a way of asking questions while a program is running. The program evaluates each logical expression, producing the value `true` if the expression is true or the value `false` if the expression is not true.

The If statement allows you to take different paths through a program based on the value of a logical expression. The If-Then-Else is used to choose between two courses of action; the If-Then is used to choose whether or not to take a particular course of action. The branches of an If-Then or If-Then-Else can be any statement, simple or compound. They can even be other If statements.

The algorithm walk-through requires us to define a precondition and a postcondition for each module in an algorithm. Then we need to verify that those assertions are true at the beginning and end of each module. By testing our design in the problem-solving phase, we can eliminate errors that can be more difficult to detect in the implementation phase.

An execution trace is a way of finding program errors once we've entered the implementation phase. It's a good idea to trace a program before you run it, so that you have some sample results against which to check the program's output. A written test plan is an essential part of any program development effort.

Quick Check

1. Write a C++ expression that compares the variable `letter` to the constant 'Z' and yields `true` if `letter` is less than 'Z'. (pp. 159–163)
2. Write a C++ expression that yields `true` if `letter` is between 'A' and 'Z' inclusive. (pp. 159–166)
3. What form of the If statement would you use to make a C++ program print out "Is an uppercase letter" if the value in `letter` is between 'A' and 'Z' inclusive, and print out "Is not an uppercase letter" if the value in `letter` is outside that range? (pp. 168–170)
4. What form of the If statement would you use to make a C++ program print out "Is a digit" only if the value in the variable `someChar` is between '0' and '9' inclusive? (pp. 172–174)
5. On a telephone, each of the digits 2 through 9 has a segment of the alphabet associated with it. What kind of control structure would you use to decide which segment a given letter falls into and to print out the corresponding digit? (pp. 174–177)
6. What is one postcondition that every program should have? (pp. 184–186)
7. In what phase of the program development process should you carry out an execution trace? (pp. 186–188)
8. You've written a program that prints out the corresponding digit on a phone, given a letter of the alphabet. Everything seems to work right except that you can't get the digit '5' to print out; you keep getting the digit '6'. What steps would you take to find and fix this bug? (pp. 189–191)
9. How do we satisfy the postcondition that the user has been notified of invalid data values? (pp. 184–186)

Answers   1. `letter < 'Z'`   2. `letter >= 'A' && letter <= 'Z'`   3. The If-Then-Else form   4. The If-Then form   5. A nested If statement   6. The user has been notified of invalid data values.   7. The implementation phase   8. Carefully review the section of code that should print out '5'. Check the branching condition and the output statement there. Try some sample values by hand.   9. The program must validate every input for which any restrictions apply and print an error message if the data violates any of the restrictions.

Exam Preparation Exercises

1. Given these values for the Boolean variables x, y, and z:

   ```
   x = true, y = false, z = true
   ```

   evaluate the following logical expressions. In the blank next to each expression, write a T if the result is `true` or an F if the result is `false`.

   _____ a. `x && y || x && z`
   _____ b. `(x || !y) && (!x || z)`
   _____ c. `x || y && z`
   _____ d. `!(x || y) && z`

2. Given these values for variables i, j, p, and q:

   ```
   i = 10, j = 19, p = true, q = false
   ```

   add parentheses (if necessary) to the expressions below so that they evaluate to true.

   a. `i == j || p`
   b. `i >= j || i <= j && p`
   c. `!p || p`
   d. `!q && q`

3. Given these values for the `int` variables i, j, m, and n:

   ```
   i = 6, j = 7, m = 11, n = 11
   ```

   what is the output of the following code?

   ```
   cout << "Madam";
   if (i < j)
       if (m != n)
           cout << "How";
       else
           cout << "Now";
   cout << "I'm";
   if (i >= m)
       cout << "Cow";
   else
       cout << "Adam";
   ```

4. Given the `int` variables `x`, `y`, and `z`, where `x` contains 3, `y` contains 7, and `z` contains 6, what is the output from each of the following code fragments?

a.
```
if (x <= 3)
     cout << x + y << endl;
  cout << x + y << endl;
```

b.
```
if (x != -1)
       cout << "The value of x is " << x << endl;
  else
       cout << "The value of y is " << y << endl;
```

c.
```
if (x != -1)
  {
     cout << x << endl;
     cout << y << endl;
     cout << z << endl;
  }
  else
     cout << "y" << endl;
     cout << "z" << endl;
```

5. Given this code fragment:

```
if (height >= minHeight)
   if (weight >= minWeight)
      cout << "Eligible to serve." << endl;
   else
      cout << "Too light to serve." << endl;
else
   if (weight >= minWeight)
      cout << "Too short to serve." << endl;
   else
      cout << "Too short and too light to serve." << endl;
```

a. What is the output when `height` exceeds `minHeight` and `weight` exceeds `minWeight`?

b. What is the output when `height` is less than `minHeight` and `weight` is less than `minWeight`?

6. Match each logical expression in the left column with the logical expression in the right column that tests for the same condition.

```
_____  a. x < y && y < z      (1) !(x != y) && y == z
_____  b. x > y && y >= z     (2) !(x <= y || y < z)
_____  c. x != y || y == z    (3) (y < z || y == z) || x == y
_____  d. x == y || y <= z    (4) !(x >= y) && !(y >= z)
_____  e. x == y && y == z    (5) !(x == y && y != z)
```

7. The following expressions make sense but are invalid according to C++'s rules of syntax. Rewrite them so that they are valid logical expressions. (All the variables are of type `int`.)

a. `x < y <= z`

b. `x`, `y`, and `z` are greater than 0

c. `x` is equal to neither `y` nor `z`

d. `x` is equal to `y` and `z`

8. Given these values for the Boolean variables `x`, `y`, and `z`:

    `x = true, y = true, z = false`

    indicate whether each expression is `true` (T) or `false` (F).

    _____ a. `!(y || z) || x`

    _____ b. `z && x && y`

    _____ c. `! y || (z || !x)`

    _____ d. `z || (x && (y || z))`

    _____ e. `x || x && z`

9. For each of the following problems, decide which is more appropriate, an If-Then-Else or an If-Then. Explain your answers.

    a. Students who are candidates for admission to a college submit their SAT scores. If a student's score is equal to or above a certain value, print a letter of acceptance for the student. Otherwise, print a rejection notice.

    b. For employees who work more than 40 hours a week, calculate overtime pay and add it to their regular pay.

    c. In solving a quadratic equation, whenever the value of the discriminant (the quantity under the square root sign) is negative, print out a message noting that the roots are complex (imaginary) numbers.

    d. In a computer-controlled sawmill, if a cross section of a log is greater than certain dimensions, adjust the saw to cut 4-inch by 8-inch beams; otherwise, adjust the saw to cut 2-inch by 4-inch studs.

10. What causes the error message "UNEXPECTED ELSE" when this code fragment is compiled?

```
if (mileage < 24.0)
{
    cout << "Gas ";
    cout << "guzzler.";
};
else
    cout << "Fuel efficient.";
```

11. The following code fragment is supposed to print "Type AB" when Boolean variables `typeA` and `typeB` are both `true`, and print "Type 0" when both variables are `false`. Instead it prints "Type 0" whenever just one of the variables is `false`. Insert a { } pair to make the code segment work the way it should.

```
if (typeA || typeB)
    if (typeA && typeB)
        cout << "Type AB";
else
    cout << "Type 0";
```

12. The nested If structure below has five possible branches depending on the values read into `char` variables `ch1`, `ch2`, and `ch3`. To test the structure, you need five sets of data, each set using a different branch. Create the five test data sets.

```
cin >> ch1 >> ch2 >> ch3;
if (ch1 == ch2)
    if (ch2 == ch3)
        cout << "All initials are the same." << endl;
    else
        cout << "First two are the same." << endl;
else if (ch2 == ch3)
    cout << "Last two are the same." << endl;
else if (ch1 == ch3)
    cout << "First and last are the same." << endl;
else
    cout << "All initials are different." << endl;
```

a. Test data set 1:   ch1 = _____   ch2 = _____   ch3 = _____
b. Test data set 2:   ch1 = _____   ch2 = _____   ch3 = _____
c. Test data set 3:   ch1 = _____   ch2 = _____   ch3 = _____
d. Test data set 4:   ch1 = _____   ch2 = _____   ch3 = _____
e. Test data set 5:   ch1 = _____   ch2 = _____   ch3 = _____

13. If `x` and `y` are Boolean variables, do the following two expressions test the same condition?

```
x != y
(x || y) && !(x && y)
```

14. The following If condition is made up of three relational expressions:

```
if (i >= 10 && i <= 20 && i != 16)
    j = 4;
```

If `i` contains the value 25 when this If statement is executed, which relational expression(s) does the computer evaluate? (Remember that C++ uses short-circuit evaluation.)

15. Could the data validation test in the Notices program be changed to the following:

```
dataOK = (test1 + test2 + test3) >= 0;
```

Explain.

Programming Warm-up Exercises

1. Declare `eligible` to be a Boolean variable, and assign it the value `true`.
2. Write a statement that sets the Boolean variable `available` to `true` if `numberOrdered` is less than or equal to `numberOnHand` minus `number-Reserved`.

3. Write a statement containing a logical expression that assigns `true` to the Boolean variable `isCandidate` if `satScore` is greater than or equal to 1100, `gpa` is not less than 2.5, and `age` is greater than 15. Otherwise, `isCandidate` should be `false`.

4. Given the declarations

```
bool leftPage;
int  pageNumber;
```

write a statement that sets `leftPage` to `true` if `pageNumber` is even. (*Hint:* Consider what the remainders are when you divide different integers by 2.)

5. Write an If statement (or a series of If statements) that assigns to the variable `biggest` the greatest value contained in variables `i`, `j`, and `k`. Assume the three values are distinct.

6. Rewrite the following sequence of If-Thens as a single If-Then-Else.

```
if (year % 4 == 0)
    cout << year << " is a leap year." << endl;
if (year % 4 != 0)
{
    year = year + 4 - year % 4;
    cout << year << " is the next leap year." << endl;
}
```

7. Simplify the following program segment, taking out unnecessary comparisons. Assume that `age` is an `int` variable.

```
if (age > 64)
    cout << "Senior voter";
if (age < 18)
    cout << "Under age";
if (age >= 18 && age < 65)
    cout << "Regular voter";
```

8. The following program fragment is supposed to print out the values 25, 60, and 8, in that order. Instead, it prints out 50, 60, and 4. Why?

```
length = 25;
width = 60;
if (length = 50)
    height = 4;
else
    height = 8;
cout << length << ' ' << width << ' ' << height << endl;
```

9. The following C++ program segment is almost unreadable because of the inconsistent indentation and the random placement of left and right braces. Fix the indentation and align the braces properly.

```
// This is a nonsense program
if (a > 0)
if (a < 20)
        {
    cout << "A is in range." << endl;
b = 5;
    }
        else
            {
cout << "A is too large." << endl;
    b = 3;
}
    else
cout << "A is too small." << endl;
  cout << "All done." << endl;
```

10. Given the `float` variables x1, x2, y1, y2, and m, write a program segment to find the slope of a line through the two points (x1, y1) and (x2, y2). Use the formula

$$m = \frac{y1 - y2}{x1 - x2}$$

to determine the slope of the line. If x1 equals x2, the line is vertical and the slope is undefined. The segment should write the slope with an appropriate label. If the slope is undefined, it should write the message "Slope undefined."

11. Given the `float` variables a, b, c, root1, root2, and discriminant, write a program segment to determine whether the roots of a quadratic polynomial are real or complex (imaginary). If the roots are real, find them and assign them to root1 and root2. If they are complex, write the message "No real roots."

The formula for the solution to the quadratic equation is

$$\frac{-b \pm \sqrt{b^2 - 4ac}}{2a}$$

The $\pm$ means "plus or minus" and indicates that there are two solutions to the equation: one in which the result of the square root is added to $-b$ and one in which the result is subtracted from $-b$. The roots are real if the discriminant (the quantity under the square root sign) is not negative.

12. The following program reads data from an input file without checking to see if the file was opened successfully. Insert statements that print an error message and terminate the program if the file cannot be opened.

```
#include <iostream>
#include <fstream>     // For file I/O

using namespace std;

int main()
{
    int      m;
    int      n;
    ifstream info;

    info.open("indata.dat");
    info >> m >> n;
    cout << "The sum of " << m << " and " << n
         << " is " << m + n << endl;
    return 0;
}
```

13. Modify the Notices program so that it prints "Passing with high marks." if the value in `average` is above 90.0.
14. If the Notices program is modified to input and average four scores, what changes (if any) to the control structures are required?
15. Change the Notices program so that it checks each of the test scores individually and prints error messages indicating which of the scores is invalid and why.

Programming Problems

1. Using functional decomposition, write a C++ program that inputs a single letter and prints out the corresponding digit on the telephone. The letters and digits on a telephone are grouped this way:

2 = ABC	4 = GHI	6 = MNO	8 = TUV
3 = DEF	5 = JKL	7 = PRS	9 = WXY

No digit corresponds to either Q or Z. For these two letters, your program should print a message indicating that they are not used on a telephone.

The program might operate like this:

```
Enter a single letter, and I will tell you what the
corresponding digit is on the telephone.
R
The digit 7 corresponds to the letter R on the telephone.
```

Here's another example:

```
Enter a single letter, and I will tell you what the
corresponding digit is on the telephone.
Q
There is no digit on the telephone that corresponds to Q.
```

Your program should print a message indicating that there is no matching digit for any nonalphabetic character the user enters. Also, the program should recognize only uppercase letters. Include the lowercase letters with the invalid characters.

Prompt the user with an informative message for the input value, as shown above. The program should echo-print the input letter as part of the output.

Use proper indentation, appropriate comments, and meaningful identifiers throughout the program.

2. People who deal with historical dates use a number called the *Julian day* to calculate the number of days between two events. The Julian day is the number of days that have elapsed since January 1, 4713 B.C. For example, the Julian day for October 16, 1956, is 2435763. There are formulas for computing the Julian day from a given date and vice versa.

One very simple formula computes the day of the week from a given Julian day:

$$day\ of\ the\ week = (Julian\ day + 1)\ \%\ 7$$

where % is the C++ modulus operator. This formula gives a result of 0 for Sunday, 1 for Monday, and so on up to 6 for Saturday. For Julian day 2435763, the result is 2 (a Tuesday). Your job is to write a C++ program that inputs a Julian day, computes the day of the week using the formula, and then prints out the name of the day that corresponds to that number. If the maximum int value on your machine is small (32767, for instance), use the long data type instead of int. Be sure to echo-print the input data and to use proper indentation and comments.

Your output might look like this:

```
Enter a Julian day number:
2451545
Julian day number 2451545 is a Saturday.
```

3. You can compute the date for any Easter Sunday from 1982 to 2048 as follows (all variables are of type int):

a is year % 19
b is year % 4
c is year % 7
d is (19 * a + 24) % 30
e is (2 * b + 4 * c + 6 * d + 5) % 7
Easter Sunday is March (22 + d + e)*

---

*Notice that this formula can give a date in April.

Write a program that inputs the year and outputs the date (month and day) of Easter Sunday for that year. Echo-print the input as part of the output. For example:

```
Enter the year (for example, 1999):
1985
Easter is Sunday, April 7, in 1985.
```

4. The algorithm for computing the date of Easter can be extended easily to work with any year from 1900 to 2099. There are four years—1954, 1981, 2049, and 2076—for which the algorithm gives a date that is seven days later than it should be. Modify the program for Problem 3 to check for these years and subtract 7 from the day of the month. This correction does not cause the month to change. Be sure to change the documentation for the program to reflect its broadened capabilities.

5. Write a C++ program that calculates and prints the diameter, the circumference, or the area of a circle, given the radius. The program inputs two data items. The first is a character—'D' (for diameter), 'C' (for circumference), or 'A' (for area)—to indicate the calculation needed. The next data value is a floating-point number indicating the radius of the particular circle.

The program should echo-print the input data. The output should be labeled appropriately and formatted to two decimal places. For example, if the input is

```
A 6.75
```

your program should print something like this:

```
The area of a circle with radius 6.75 is 143.14.
```

Here are the formulas you need:

Diameter = $2r$
Circumference = $2\pi r$
Area of a circle = πr^2

where r is the radius. Use 3.14159265 for π.

Looping

- To be able to construct syntactically correct While loops.

- To be able to construct count-controlled loops with a While statement.

- To be able to construct event-controlled loops with a While statement.

- To be able to use the end-of-file condition to control the input of data.

- To be able to use flags to control the execution of a While statement.

- To be able to construct counting loops with a While statement.

- To be able to construct summing loops with a While statement.

- To be able to choose the correct type of loop for a given problem.

- To be able to construct nested While loops.

- To be able to choose data sets that test a looping program comprehensively.

In Chapter 5, we saw how to select different statements for execution using the If statement.

A **loop** executes the same statement (simple or compound) over and over, as long as a condition or set of conditions is satisfied.

> **Loop** A control structure that causes a statement or group of statements to be executed repeatedly.

In this chapter, we discuss different kinds of loops and how they are constructed using the While statement. We also discuss *nested loops* (loops that contain other loops).

6.1 The While Statement

The While statement, like the If statement, tests a condition. Here is the syntax template for the While statement:

WhileStatement

```
while ( Expression )
    Statement
```

and this is an example of one:

```
while (inputVal != 25)
    cin >> inputVal;
```

The While statement is a looping control structure. The statement to be executed each time through the loop is called the *body* of the loop. In the example above, the body of the loop is the input statement that reads in a value for `inputVal`. This While statement says to execute the body repeatedly as long as the input value does not equal 25. The While statement is completed (hence, the loop stops) when `inputVal` equals 25. The effect of this loop, then, is to consume and ignore all the values in the input stream until the number 25 is read.

Just like the condition in an If statement, the condition in a While statement can be an expression of any simple data type. Nearly always, it is a logical (Boolean) expression; if not, its value is implicitly coerced to type `bool` (recall that a zero value is coerced to `false`, and any nonzero value is coerced to `true`). The While statement says, "If the value of the expression is `true`, execute the body and then go back and test the expression again. If the expression's value is `false`, skip the body." The loop body is thus executed over and over as long as the expression is `true` when it is tested. When the expression is `false`, the program skips the body and execution continues at the statement immediately following the loop. Of course, if the expression is `false` to begin with, the body is not even executed. Figure 6–1 shows the flow of control of the While statement, where Statement1 is the body of the loop and Statement2 is the statement following the loop.

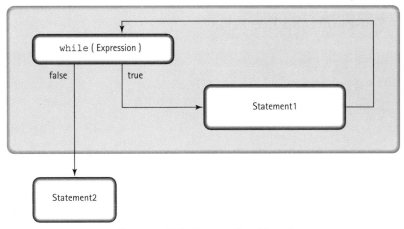

Figure 6–1 *While Statement Flow of Control*

The body of a loop can be a compound statement (block), which allows us to execute any group of statements repeatedly. Most often we use While loops in the following form:

```
while (Expression)
{
    ⋮
}
```

In this structure, if the expression is `true`, the entire sequence of statements in the block is executed, and then the expression is checked again. If it is still `true`, the statements are executed again. The cycle continues until the expression becomes `false`.

Figure 6–2 emphasizes the difference between If and While.

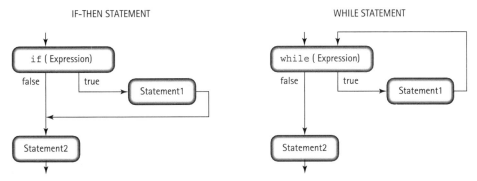

Figure 6–2 *A Comparison of If and While*

6.2 Phases of Loop Execution

The body of a loop is executed in several phases:

Loop entry The point at which the flow of control reaches the first statement inside a loop.

Iteration An individual pass through, or repetition of, the body of a loop.

Loop test The point at which the While expression is evaluated and the decision is made either to begin a new iteration or skip to the statement immediately following the loop.

Loop exit The point at which the repetition of the loop body ends and control passes to the first statement following the loop.

Termination condition The condition that causes a loop to be exited.

- The moment that the flow of control reaches the first statement inside the loop body is the **loop entry.**
- Each time the body of a loop is executed, a pass is made through the loop. This pass is called an **iteration.**
- Before each iteration, control is transferred to the **loop test** at the beginning of the loop.
- When the last iteration is complete and the flow of control has passed to the first statement following the loop, the program has **exited the loop.** The condition that causes a loop to be exited is the **termination condition.** In the case of a While loop, the termination condition is that the While expression becomes `false`.

Notice that the loop exit occurs only at one point: when the loop test is performed. Even though the termination condition may become satisfied midway through the execution of the loop, the current iteration is completed before the computer checks the While expression again.

The concept of looping is fundamental to programming. In this chapter, we spend some time looking at typical kinds of loops and ways of implementing them with the While statement. These looping situations come up again and again when you are analyzing problems and designing algorithms.

6.3 Loops Using the While Statement

Count-controlled loop A loop that executes a specified number of times.

Event-controlled loop A loop that terminates when something happens inside the loop body to signal that the loop should be exited.

In solving problems, you will come across two major types of loops: **count-controlled loops,** which repeat a specified number of times, and **event-controlled loops,** which repeat until something happens within the loop.

If you are making an angel food cake and the recipe reads "Beat the mixture 300 strokes," you are executing a count-controlled loop. If you are making a pie crust and the recipe reads "Cut with a pastry blender until the mixture resembles coarse meal," you are executing an event-controlled loop; you don't know ahead of time the exact number of loop iterations.

Count-Controlled Loops

A count-controlled loop uses a variable we call the *loop control variable* in the loop test. Before we enter a count-controlled loop, we have to *initialize* (set the initial value of) the loop control variable and then test it. Then, as part of each iteration of the loop, we must *increment* (increase by 1) the loop control variable. Here's an example:

```
loopCount = 1;                  // Initialization
while (loopCount <= 10)         // Test
{
    .
    .                           // Repeated actions
    .
    loopCount++;                // Incrementation
}
```

Here `loopCount` is the loop control variable. It is set to 1 before loop entry. The While statement tests the expression

```
loopCount <= 10
```

and executes the loop body as long as the expression is `true`. The dots inside the compound statement represent a sequence of statements to be repeated. The last statement in the loop body increments `loopCount`. Variables that are used this way are called *counters*. In our example, `loopCount` is incremented with each iteration of the loop— we use it to count the iterations. The loop control variable of a count-controlled loop is always a counter.

When designing loops, it is the programmer's responsibility to see that the condition to be tested is set correctly (initialized) before the While statement begins. The programmer also must make sure that the condition changes within the loop so that it eventually becomes `false`; otherwise, the loop is never exited.

A loop that never exits is called an *infinite loop* because, in theory, the loop executes forever. In the code above, omitting the incrementation of `loopCount` at the bottom of the loop leads to an infinite loop; the While expression is always `true` because the value of `loopCount` is forever 1. If your program goes on running for much longer than you expect it to, chances are that you've created an infinite loop. You may have to issue an operating system command to stop the program.

Event-Controlled Loops

There are several kinds of event-controlled loops: sentinel-controlled, end-of-file-controlled, and flag-controlled. In all of these loops, the termination condition depends on some event occurring while the loop body is executing.

Sentinel-Controlled Loops Loops often are used to read in and process long lists of data. Each time the loop body is executed, a new piece of data is read and processed.

Often a special data value, called a *sentinel* or *trailer value*, is used to signal the program that there is no more data to be processed. Looping continues as long as the data value read is *not* the sentinel. In other words, reading the sentinel value is the event that controls the looping process.

A sentinel value must be something that never shows up in the normal input to a program. For example, if a program reads calendar dates, we could use February 31 as a sentinel value:

```
cin >> month >> day;                    // Get a date--priming read
while ( !(month == 2 && day == 31) )
{
        :                               // Process it
    cin >> month >> day;                // Get the next date
}
```

This segment reads the first data pair prior to entering the loop (we refer to this as a *priming read*). If it is not the sentinel, it gets processed. At the end of the loop, the next data set is read in, and we go back to the beginning of the loop. If the new data set is not the sentinel, it gets processed just like the first. When the sentinel value is read, the While expression becomes `false` and the loop exits (*without* processing the sentinel).

Many times the problem dictates the value of the sentinel. For example, if the problem does not allow data values of 0, then the sentinel value should be 0. When you process `char` data one line of input at a time, the newline character (`'\n'`) often serves as the sentinel. Here's a code segment that reads and prints all of the characters on an input line (`inChar` is of type `char`):

```
cin.get(inChar);                        // Get first character
while (inChar != '\n')
{
    cout << inChar;                     // Echo it
    cin.get(inChar);                    // Get next character
}
```

(Notice that for this particular task we must use the `get` function, not the `>>` operator, to input a character. Remember that the `>>` operator skips whitespace characters—including blanks and newlines—to find the next data value in the input stream. In this example, we want to input *every* character, even a blank and especially the newline character.)

In a sentinel-controlled loop, what happens if you forget to enter the sentinel value? In an interactive program, the loop executes again, prompting for input. At that point, you can enter the sentinel value, but your program logic may be wrong if you already entered what you thought was the sentinel value. If the input to the program is from a file, once all the data has been read from the file, the loop body is executed again. However, there isn't any data left—because the computer has reached the end of the file—so the file stream enters the fail state. In the next section, we describe a way to use the end-of-file situation as an alternative to using a sentinel.

Before we go on, we mention an issue that is related not to the design of loops but to C++ language usage. In Chapter 5, we talked about the common mistake of using the assignment operator (=) instead of the relational operator (==) in an If condition. This same mistake can happen when you write While statements. See what happens when we use the wrong operator in the following example. (The second number of each input pair is used as a sentinel. It equals 1 for every data pair *except* the last. For the last pair, it equals 0, meaning there is no more data.)

```
cin >> dataValue >> sentinel;
while (sentinel = 1)                    // Whoops--wrong operator
{
    ⋮
    cin >> dataValue >> sentinel;
}
```

This mistake creates an infinite loop. The While expression is now an assignment expression, not a relational expression. The expression's value is 1 (interpreted in the loop test as `true` because it's nonzero), and its side effect is to store the value 1 into `sentinel`, replacing the value that was just input into the variable. Because the While expression is always `true`, the loop never stops.

End-of-File-Controlled Loops   After a program has read the last piece of data from an input file, the computer is at the end of the file (EOF, for short). At this moment, the stream state is all right. But if we try to input even one more data value, the stream goes into the fail state. We can use this fact to our advantage. To write a loop that inputs an unknown number of data items, we can use the failure of the input stream as a form of sentinel.

In Chapter 5, we described how to test the state of an I/O stream. In a logical expression, we use the name of the stream as though it were a Boolean variable:

```
if (inFile)
    ⋮
```

In a test like this, the result is `true` if the most recent I/O operation succeeded, or `false` if it failed. In a While statement, testing the state of a stream works the same way. Suppose we have a data file containing integer values. If `inData` is the name of the file stream in our program, here's a loop that reads and echoes all of the data values in the file:

```
inData >> intVal;                       // Get first value
while (inData)                          // While the input succeeded ...
{
    cout << intVal << endl;             // Echo it
    inData >> intVal;                   // Get next value
}
```

Let's trace this code, assuming there are three values in the file: 10, 20, and 30. The priming read inputs the value 10. The While condition is `true` because the input succeeded. Therefore, the computer executes the loop body. First the body prints out the value 10, and then it inputs the second data value, 20. Looping back to the loop test, the expression `inData` is `true` because the input succeeded. The body executes again, printing the value 20 and reading the value 30 from the file. Looping back to the test, the expression is `true`. Even though we are at the end of the file, the stream state is still OK—the previous input operation succeeded. The body executes a third time, printing the value 30 and executing the input statement. This time, the input statement fails; we're trying to read beyond the end of the file. The stream `inData` enters the fail state. Looping back to the loop test, the value of the expression is `false` and we exit the loop.

When we write EOF-controlled loops like the one above, we are expecting that the end of the file is the reason for stream failure. But keep in mind that *any* input error causes stream failure. The above loop terminates, for example, if input fails because of invalid characters in the input data. This fact emphasizes again the importance of echo printing. It helps us verify that all the data was read correctly before the EOF was encountered.

Is it possible to use an EOF-controlled loop when we read from the standard input device (via the `cin` stream) instead of a data file? On many systems, yes. With the UNIX operating system, you can type Ctrl-D (that is, you hold down the Ctrl key and tap the D key) to signify end-of-file during interactive input. With the MS-DOS operating system, the end-of-file keystrokes are Ctrl-Z (or sometimes Ctrl-D). Other systems use similar keystrokes.

Flag-Controlled Loops A *flag* is a Boolean variable that is used to control the logical flow of a program. We can set a Boolean variable to `true` before a While loop; then, when we want to stop executing the loop, we reset it to `false`. That is, we can use the Boolean variable to record whether or not the event that controls the process has occurred. For example, the following code segment reads and sums values until the input value is negative. (`nonNegative` is the Boolean flag; all of the other variables are of type `int`.)

```
sum = 0;
nonNegative = true;              // Initialize flag
while (nonNegative)
{
    cin >> number;
    if (number < 0)              // Test input value
        nonNegative = false;     // Set flag if event occurred
    else
        sum = sum + number;
}
```

Notice that we can code sentinel-controlled loops with flags. In fact, this code uses a negative value as a sentinel.

Looping Subtasks

We have been looking at ways to use loops to affect the flow of control in programs. But looping by itself does nothing. The loop body must perform a task in order for the loop to accomplish something. In this section, we look at three tasks—counting, summing, and keeping track of a previous value—that often are used in loops.

Counting A common task in a loop is to keep track of the number of times the loop has been executed. For example, the following program fragment reads and counts input characters until it comes to a period. (inChar is of type char; count is of type int.) The loop in this example has a counter variable, but the loop is not a count-controlled loop because the variable is not being used as a loop control variable.

```
count = 0;                          // Initialize counter
cin.get(inChar);                    // Read the first character
while (inChar != '.')
{
    count++;                        // Increment counter
    cin.get(inChar);                // Get the next character
}
```

After the loop is finished, count contains one less than the number of characters read. That is, it counts the number of characters up to, but not including, the sentinel value (the period). Notice that if a period is the first character, the loop body is not entered and count contains a 0, as it should. We use a priming read here because the loop is sentinel-controlled.

The counter variable in this example is called an **iteration counter** because its value equals the number of iterations through the loop.

> **Iteration counter** A counter variable that is incremented with each iteration of a loop.

According to our definition, the loop control variable of a count-controlled loop is an iteration counter. However, as you've just seen, not all iteration counters are loop control variables.

Summing Another common looping task is to sum a set of data values. Notice in the following example that the summing operation is written the same way, regardless of how the loop is controlled.

```
sum = 0;                            // Initialize the sum
count = 1;
while (count <= 10)
{
    cin >> number;                  // Input a value
    sum = sum + number;             // Add the value to sum
    count++;
}
```

We initialize sum to 0 before the loop starts so that the first time the loop body executes, the statement

```
sum = sum + number;
```

adds the current value of sum (0) to number to form the new value of sum. After the entire code fragment has executed, sum contains the total of the ten values read, count contains 11, and number contains the last value read.

Keeping Track of a Previous Value Sometimes we want to remember the previous value of a variable. Suppose we want to write a program that counts the number of not-equal operators (!=) in a file that contains a C++ program. We can do so by simply counting the number of times an exclamation mark (!) followed by an equal sign (=) appears in the input. One way in which to do this is to read the input file one character at a time, keeping track of the two most recent characters, the current value and the previous value. In each iteration of the loop, a new current value is read and the old current value becomes the previous value. When EOF is reached, the loop is finished. Here's a loop that counts not-equal operators in this way:

```
count = 0;                    // Initialize counter
inFile.get(prevChar);         // Initialize previous value
inFile.get(currChar);         // Initialize current value
while (inFile)                // While previous input succeeded ...
{
    if (currChar == '=' &&    // Test for event
        prevChar == '!')
        count++;              // Increment counter
    prevChar = currChar;      // Replace previous value
                              //    with current value
    inFile.get(currChar);     // Get next value
}
cout << count << " != operators were found." << endl;
```

Event counter A variable that is incremented each time a particular event occurs.

The counter in this example is an **event counter**; it is initialized to 0 and incremented only when a certain event occurs. The counter in the previous example was an *iteration counter*; it was initialized to 1 and incremented during each iteration of the loop.

Study this loop carefully. It's going to come in handy. There are many problems in which you must keep track of the last value read in addition to the current value.

6.4 How to Design Loops

It's one thing to understand how a loop works when you look at it and something else again to design a loop that solves a given problem. In this section, we look at how to design loops. We can divide the design process into two tasks: designing the control flow and designing the processing in the loop. We break each task into three phases: the task itself, initialization, and update. It's also important to specify the state of the program when it exits the loop.

There are seven different points to consider in designing a loop:

1. What is the condition that ends the loop?
2. How should the condition be initialized?
3. How should the condition be updated?
4. What is the process being repeated?
5. How should the process be initialized?
6. How should the process be updated?
7. What is the state of the program on exiting the loop?

We use these questions as a checklist. The first three help us design the parts of the loop that control its execution. The next three help us design the processing within the loop. The last question reminds us to make sure that the loop exits in an appropriate manner.

Designing the Flow of Control

The most important step in loop design is deciding what should make the loop stop. If the termination condition isn't well thought out, there's the potential for infinite loops and other mistakes. So here is our first question:

• What is the condition that ends the loop?

This question usually is answered through examination of the problem statement. The following table lists some examples.

Key Phrase in Problem Statement	Termination Condition
"Sum 365 temperatures"	The loop ends when a counter reaches 365 (count-controlled loop).
"Process all the data in the file"	The loop ends when EOF occurs (EOF-controlled loop).
"The end of the data is indicated by a negative test score"	The loop ends when a negative input value is encountered (sentinel-controlled loop).

Now we are ready to ask the next two questions:

• How should the condition be initialized?
• How should the condition be updated?

The answers depend on the type of termination condition.

For count-controlled loops that use an iteration counter, these are the answers to the questions:

- Initialize the iteration counter to 1.
- Increment the iteration counter at the end of each iteration.

When a loop uses an event counter, these are the answers to the questions:

- Initialize the event counter to 0.
- Increment the event counter each time the event occurs.

For sentinel-controlled loops, we answer our questions this way:

- Open the file, if necessary, and input a value before entering the loop (priming read).
- Input a new value for processing at the end of each iteration.

EOF-controlled loops require the same initialization as sentinel-controlled loops. Updating the loop condition means the loop must keep reading data.

For flag-controlled loops, the answers to our questions are these:

- Initialize the flag variable to `true` or `false`, as appropriate.
- Update the flag variable as soon as the condition changes.

Because the update depends on what the process does, at times we have to design the process before we can decide how to update the condition.

Designing the Process Within the Loop

Next, we fill in the details of the process. In designing the process, we first must decide what we want a single iteration to do.

- What is the process being repeated?

To answer this question, we have to take another look at the problem statement. The definition of the problem may require the process to sum up data values or to keep a count of data values that satisfy some test. For example:

Count the number of integers in the file `howMany`.

This statement tells us that the process to be repeated is a counting operation.

We can now design the parts of the process that are necessary for it to be repeated correctly. We add steps to take into account the fact that the loop executes more than once. This part of the design typically involves initializing certain variables before the loop and then reinitializing or updating them before each subsequent iteration.

- How should the process be initialized?
- How should the process be updated?

For example, if the process within a loop requires that several different counts and sums be performed, each must have its own statements to initialize variables, increment counting variables, or add values to sums. Just deal with each counting or summing operation by itself—that is, first write the initialization statement, and then write the incrementing or summing statement. After you've done this for one operation, you go on to the next.

The Loop Exit

Now we have to consider the consequences of our design and double-check its validity.

- What is the state of the program on exiting the loop?

For example, suppose we've used an event counter and that later processing depends on the number of events. It's important to be sure (with an algorithm walk-through) that the value left in the counter is the exact number of events—that it is not off by 1.

Designing correct loops depends as much on experience as it does on the application of design methodology. At this point, you may want to read through the programming example at the end of the chapter to see how the loop design process is applied to a real problem.

6.5 Nested Logic

In Chapter 5, we described nested If statements. It's also possible to nest While statements. Both While and If statements contain statements and are, themselves, statements. So the body of a While statement or the branch of an If statement can contain other While and If statements. By nesting, we can create complex control structures.

Suppose we want to count the number of commas on a line of input data, repeating it for all the lines in a file. We put an EOF-controlled loop around a sentinel-controlled loop:

```
cin.get(inChar);                   // Initialize outer loop
while (cin)                        // Outer loop test
{
    commaCount = 0;               // Initialize inner loop
                                  //    (Priming read is taken care of
                                  //     by outer loop's priming read)
    while (inChar != '\n')        // Inner loop test
    {
        if (inChar == ',')
            commaCount++;
        cin.get(inChar);          // Update inner termination condition
    }
    cout << commaCount << endl;
    cin.get(inChar);              // Update outer termination condition
}
```

In this code, notice that we have omitted the priming read for the inner loop. The priming read for the outer loop has already "primed the pump." It would be a mistake to include another priming read just before the inner loop; the character read by the outer priming read would be destroyed before we could test it.

Let's examine the general pattern of a simple nested loop. The dots represent places where the processing and update may take place in the outer loop.

```
Initialize outer loop
while ( Outer loop condition )
{
        ⋮
        ┌─────────────────────────────────────────┐
        │ Initialize inner loop                     │
        │ while ( Inner loop condition )            │
        │ {                                         │
        │     Inner loop processing and update      │
        │ }                                         │
        └─────────────────────────────────────────┘
        ⋮
}
```

Notice that each loop has its own initialization, test, and update. It's possible for an outer loop to do no processing other than to execute the inner loop repeatedly. On the other hand, the inner loop might be just a small part of the processing done by the outer loop; there could be many statements preceding or following the inner loop.

Let's look at another example. For nested count-controlled loops, the pattern looks like this (where outCount is the counter for the outer loop, inCount is the counter for the inner loop, and limit1 and limit2 are the number of times each loop should be executed):

```
outCount = 1;                      // Initialize outer loop counter
while (outCount <= limit1)
{
    ⋮
    inCount = 1;                   // Initialize inner loop counter
    while (inCount <= limit2)
    {
        ⋮
```

```
        inCount++;                 // Increment inner loop counter
    }
    ⋮
    outCount++;                    // Increment outer loop counter
}
```

Here, both the inner and outer loops are count-controlled loops, but the pattern can be used with any combination of loops.

Designing Nested Loops

To design a nested loop, we begin with the outer loop. The process being repeated includes the nested loop as one of its steps. Because that step is more complex than a single statement, our functional decomposition methodology tells us to make it a separate module. We can come back to it later and design the nested loop just as we would any other loop.

Of course, nested loops themselves can contain nested loops (called *doubly nested loops*), which can contain nested loops (*triply nested loops*), and so on. You can use this design process for any number of levels of nesting. The trick is to defer details by using the functional decomposition methodology—that is, focus on the outermost loop first and treat each new level of nested loop as a module within the loop that contains it.

It's also possible for the process within a loop to include more than one loop. For example, here's an algorithm that reads and prints people's names from a file, omitting the middle name in the output:

```
Read and print first name (ends with a comma)
WHILE NOT EOF
        Read and discard characters from middle name (ends with a comma)
        Read and print last name (ends at newline)
        Output newline
        Read and print first name (ends with a comma)
```

The steps for reading the first name, middle name, and last name require us to design three separate loops. All of these loops are sentinel-controlled.

This kind of complex control structure would be difficult to read if written out in full. There are simply too many variables, conditions, and steps to remember at one time. In the next two chapters, we examine the control structure that allows us to break programs down into more manageable chunks—the subprogram.

As a final note about nested loops, it is important to keep in mind that the time it takes the computer to execute a deeply nested loop will be proportional to the product of the number of iterations at each level of the nested structure. For example, if we nest loops that count from 1 to 1000 four levels deep, the innermost loop body will execute 1,000,000,000,000 times. Such a loop would take several hours to execute on a typical computer.

Programming Example

Average Income by Gender

Problem You've been hired by a law firm that is working on a sex discrimination case. Your firm has obtained a file of income data. As a first pass in the analysis of this data, you've been asked to compute the average income for females and the average income for males.

Input A file, incFile, of floating-point salary amounts, with one amount per line. Each amount is preceded by a character ('F' for female, 'M' for male). This code is the first character on each input line and is followed by a blank, which separates the code from the amount.

Output

All the input data (echo print)
The number of females and their average income
The number of males and their average income

Discussion The problem breaks down into three main steps. First, we have to process the data, counting and summing the salary amounts for each sex. Next, we compute the averages. Finally, we have to print the calculated results.

The first step is the most difficult. It involves a loop with several subtasks. We use our checklist of questions to develop these subtasks in detail.

1. *What is the condition that ends the loop?* The termination condition is EOF on the file incFile. It leads to the following loop test (in pseudocode).

   WHILE NOT EOF on incFile

2. *How should the condition be initialized?* We must open the file for input, and a priming read must take place.

3. *How should the condition be updated?* We must input a new data line with a gender code and amount at the end of each iteration. Here's the resulting algorithm:

```
Open incFile for input (and verify the attempt)
Read sex and amount from incFile
WHILE NOT EOF on incFile
  : (Process being repeated)
  Read sex and amount from incFile
```

4. *What is the process being repeated?* From our knowledge of how to compute an average, we know that we have to count the number of amounts and divide this number into the sum of the amounts. Because we have to do this separately for females and males, the process consists of four parts: counting the females and summing their incomes, and then counting the males and summing their incomes. We develop each of these in turn.

5. *How should the process be initialized?* femaleCount and femaleSum should be set to zero. maleCount and maleSum should also be set to zero.

6. *How should the process be updated?* When a female income is input, femaleCount is incremented and the income is added to femaleSum. Otherwise, an income is assumed to be for a male, so maleCount is incremented and the amount is added to maleSum.

7. *What is the state of the program on exiting the loop?* The file stream incFile is in the fail state, femaleCount contains the number of input values preceded by 'F', femaleSum contains the sum of the values preceded by 'F', maleCount contains the number of values not preceded by 'F', and maleSum holds the sum of those values.

From the description of how the process is updated, we can see that the loop must contain an If-Then-Else structure, with one branch for female incomes and the other for male incomes. Each branch must increment the correct event counter and add the income amount to the correct total. After the loop has exited, we have enough information to compute and print the averages, dividing each total by the corresponding count.

Assumptions   There is at least one male and one female among all the data sets. The only gender codes in the file are 'M' and 'F'—any other codes are counted as 'M'. (This last assumption invalidates the results if there are any illegal codes in the data.)

Now we can write the program. (The following program is written in ISO/ANSI standard C++. If you are working with pre-standard C++, see the alternate version of the program in the PRE_STD directory of the program disk, available at the publisher's Web site, www.jbpub.com/disks.)

```cpp
//******************************************************************
// Incomes program
// This program reads a file of income amounts classified by
// gender and computes the average income for each gender
//******************************************************************
#include <iostream>
#include <iomanip>    // For setprecision()
#include <fstream>    // For file I/O
#include <string>     // For string type
```

```cpp
using namespace std;

int main()
{
    char      sex;             // Coded 'F' = female, 'M' = male
    int       femaleCount;     // Number of female income amounts
    int       maleCount;       // Number of male income amounts
    float     amount;          // Amount of income for a person
    float     femaleSum;       // Total of female income amounts
    float     maleSum;         // Total of male income amounts
    float     femaleAverage;   // Average female income
    float     maleAverage;     // Average male income
    ifstream  incFile;         // File of income amounts
    string    fileName;        // External name of file

    cout << fixed << showpoint              // Set up floating-pt.
         << setprecision(2);                //   output format

    // Separately count females and males, and sum incomes

    // Initialize ending condition

    cout << "Name of the income data file: ";
    cin >> fileName;
    incFile.open(fileName.c_str());         // Open input file
    if ( !incFile )                         //   and verify attempt
    {
        cout << "** Can't open input file **" << endl;
        return 1;
    }
    incFile >> sex >> amount;               // Perform priming read

    // Initialize process

    femaleCount = 0;
    femaleSum = 0.0;
    maleCount = 0;
    maleSum = 0.0;

    while (incFile)
    {
        // Update process

        cout << "Sex: " << sex << " Amount: " << amount << endl;
        if (sex == 'F')
        {
            femaleCount++;
            femaleSum = femaleSum + amount;
        }
```

```
        else
        {
            maleCount++;
            maleSum = maleSum + amount;
        }

        // Update ending condition

        incFile >> sex >> amount;
    }

    // Compute average incomes

    femaleAverage = femaleSum / float(femaleCount);
    maleAverage = maleSum / float(maleCount);

    // Output results

    cout << "For " << femaleCount << " females, the average "
         << "income is " << femaleAverage << endl;
    cout << "For " << maleCount << " males, the average "
         << "income is " << maleAverage << endl;
    return 0;
}
```

Testing   With an EOF-controlled loop, the obvious test cases are a file with data and an empty file. We should test input values of both 'F' and 'M' for the gender, and try some typical data (so we can compare the results with our hand-calculated values) and some atypical data (to see how the process behaves). An atypical data set for testing a counting operation is an empty file, which should result in a count of zero. Any other result for the count indicates an error. For a summing operation, atypical data might include negative or zero values.

The Incomes program is not designed to handle empty files or negative income values. An empty file causes both `femaleCount` and `maleCount` to equal zero at the end of the loop. Although this is correct, the statements that compute average income cause the program to crash because they divide by zero. A negative income would be treated like any other value, even though it is probably a mistake.

To correct these problems, we should insert If statements to test for the error conditions at the appropriate points in the program. When an error is detected, the program should print an error message instead of carrying out the usual computation.

Testing and Debugging

Loop-Testing Strategy

Even if a loop has been properly designed and verified, it is still important to test it rigorously because the chance of an error creeping in during the implementation phase is always present. Because loops allow us to input many data sets in one run, and because each iteration may be affected by preceding ones, the test data for a looping program is usually more extensive than for a program with just sequential or branching statements. To test a loop thoroughly, we must check for the proper execution of both a single iteration and multiple iterations.

Remember that a loop has seven parts (corresponding to the seven questions in our checklist). A test strategy must test each part. Although all seven parts aren't implemented separately in every loop, the checklist reminds us that some loop operations serve multiple purposes, each of which should be tested. For example, the incrementing statement in a count-controlled loop may be updating both the process and the ending condition, so it's important to verify that it performs both actions properly with respect to the rest of the loop.

To test a loop, we try to devise data sets that could cause the variables to go out of range or leave the files in improper states that violate either the loop postcondition (an assertion that must be true immediately after loop exit) or the postcondition of the module containing the loop.

It's also good practice to test a loop for four special cases: (1) when the loop is skipped entirely, (2) when the loop body is executed just once, (3) when the loop executes some normal number of times, and (4) when the loop fails to exit.

Statements following a loop often depend on its processing. If a loop can be skipped, those statements may not execute correctly. If it's possible to execute a single iteration of a loop, the results can show whether the body performs correctly in the absence of the effects of previous iterations, which can be very helpful when you're trying to isolate the source of an error. Obviously, it's important to test a loop under normal conditions, with a wide variety of inputs. If possible, you should test the loop with real data in addition to mock data sets. Count-controlled loops should be tested to be sure they execute exactly the right number of times. And finally, if there is any chance that a loop might never exit, your test data should try to make that happen.

Test Plans Involving Loops

In Chapter 5, we introduced formal test plans and discussed the testing of branches. Those guidelines still apply to programs with loops, but here we provide some additional guidelines that are specific to loops.

To simplify our testing of loops, we often want to observe the values of the variables associated with the loop at the start of each iteration. How can we observe the values of variables while a program is running? Two common techniques are the use of the system's *debugger* program and the use of extra output statements designed solely for debugging purposes. We discuss these techniques in the next section, Testing and Debugging Hints.

Now let's look at some test cases that are specific to the different types of loops that we've seen in this chapter.

Count-Controlled Loops When a loop is count-controlled, you should include a test case that specifies the output for all the iterations. It may help to add an extra column to the test plan that lists the iteration number. If the loop reads data and outputs a result, then each input value should produce a different output to make it easier to spot errors. For example, in a loop that is supposed to read and print 100 data values, it is easier to tell that the loop executes the correct number of iterations when the values are 1, 2, 3, ..., 100 than if they are all the same.

Event-Controlled Loops In an event-controlled loop, you should test the situation in which the event occurs before the loop, in the first iteration, and in a typical number of iterations. For example, if the event is that EOF occurs, then try an empty file, a file with one data set, and another with several data sets. If your testing involves reading from test files, you should attach printed copies of the files to the test plan and identify each in some way so that the plan can refer to them. It also helps to identify where each iteration begins in the Input and Expected Output columns of the test plan.

When the event is the input of a sentinel value, you need the following test cases: the sentinel is the only data set, the sentinel follows one data set, and the sentinel follows a typical number of data sets. Given that sentinel-controlled loops involve a priming read, it is especially important to verify that the first and last data sets are processed properly.

Testing and Debugging Hints

1. Plan your test data carefully to test all sections of a program.
2. Beware of infinite loops, in which the expression in the While statement never becomes `false`. The symptom: the program doesn't stop.

   If you have created an infinite loop, check your logic and the syntax of your loops. Be sure there's no semicolon immediately after the right parenthesis of the While condition:

```
while (Expression);          // Wrong
    Statement
```

This semicolon causes an infinite loop in most cases; the compiler thinks the loop body is the null statement (the do-nothing statement composed only of a semicolon). In a count-controlled loop, make sure the loop control variable is incremented within the loop. In a flag-controlled loop, make sure the flag eventually changes.

And, as always, watch for the = versus == problem in While conditions as well as in If conditions. The line

```
while (someVar = 5)        // Wrong (should be ==)
```

produces an infinite loop. The value of the assignment (not relational) expression is always 5, which is interpreted as `true`.

3. Check the loop termination condition carefully and be sure that something in the loop causes it to be met. Watch closely for values that cause one iteration too many or too few (the "off-by-1" syndrome).

4. Remember to use the `get` function rather than the `>>` operator in loops that are controlled by detection of a newline character.

5. Perform an algorithm walk-through to verify that all of the appropriate preconditions and postconditions occur in the right places.

6. Trace the execution of the loop by hand with a code walk-through. Simulate the first few passes and the last few passes very carefully to see how the loop really behaves.

7. Use a *debugger* if your system provides one. A debugger is a program that runs your program in "slow motion," allowing you to execute one instruction at a time and to examine the contents of variables as they change. If you haven't already done so, check to see if a debugger is available on your system.

8. If all else fails, use *debug output statements*—output statements inserted into a program to help debug it. They output messages that indicate the flow of execution in the program or report the values of variables at certain points in the program.

    For example, if you want to know the value of variable `beta` at a certain point in a program, you could insert this statement:

```
cout << "beta = " << beta << endl;
```

If this output statement is in a loop, you will get as many values of `beta` output as there are iterations of the body of the loop.

    After you have debugged your program, you can remove the debug output statements or just precede them with `//` so that they'll be treated as comments. (This practice is referred to as *commenting out* a piece of code.) You can remove the double slashes if you need to use the statements again.

9. An ounce of prevention is worth a pound of debugging. Use the checklist questions to design your loop correctly at the outset. It may seem like extra work, but it pays off in the long run.

Summary

The While statement is a looping construct that allows the program to repeat a statement as long as the value of an expression is `true`. When the value of the expression becomes `false`, the body of the loop is skipped and execution continues with the first statement following the loop.

With the While statement, you can construct several types of loops that you will use again and again. These types of loops fall into two categories: count-controlled loops and event-controlled loops.

In a count-controlled loop, the loop body is repeated a specified number of times.

Event-controlled loops continue executing until something inside the body signals that the looping process should stop. Event-controlled loops include those that test for a sentinel value in the data, for end-of-file, or for a change in a flag variable.

Sentinel-controlled loops are input loops that use a special data value as a signal to stop reading. EOF-controlled loops are loops that continue to input (and process) data values until there is no more data. In a flag-controlled loop, you must set the flag before the loop begins, test it in the While expression, and change it somewhere in the body of the loop.

A counter is a variable that is used for counting. It may be the loop control variable in a count-controlled loop, an iteration counter in a counting loop, or an event counter that counts the number of times a particular condition occurs in a loop.

Summing is a looping operation that keeps a running total of certain values.

When you design a loop, there are seven points to consider: how the termination condition is initialized, tested, and updated; how the process in the loop is initialized, performed, and updated; and the state of the program upon exiting the loop. By answering the checklist questions, you can bring each of these points into focus.

To design a nested loop structure, begin with the outermost loop. When you get to where the inner loop must appear, make it a separate module and come back to its design later.

The process of testing a loop is based on the answers to the checklist questions and the patterns the loop might encounter (for example, executing a single iteration, multiple iterations, an infinite number of iterations, or no iterations at all).

Quick Check

1. Write the first line of a While statement that loops until the value of the Boolean variable `done` becomes `true`. (pp. 206–208)
2. What are the four parts of a count-controlled loop? (pp. 208–209)
3. Should you use a priming read with an EOF-controlled loop? (pp. 211–212)
4. How is a flag variable used to control a loop? (p. 212)
5. What is the difference between a counting operation in a loop and a summing operation in a loop? (pp. 212–214)
6. What is the difference between a loop control variable and an event counter? (pp. 212–214)

7. What kind of loop would you use in a program that reads the closing price of a stock for each day of the week? (pp. 214–217)
8. How would you extend the loop in Question 7 to make it read prices for 52 weeks? (pp. 217–220)
9. How would you test a program that is supposed to count the number of females and the number of males in a data set? (Assume that females are coded with 'F' in the data; males, with 'M'.) (pp. 223–225)

Answers 1. `while ( !done )` 2. The process being repeated, plus initializing, testing, and incrementing the loop control variable 3. Yes 4. The flag is set outside the loop. The While expression checks the flag, and an If inside the loop resets the flag when the termination condition occurs. 5. A counting operation increments by a fixed value with each iteration of the loop; a summing operation adds unknown values to the total. 6. A loop control variable controls the loop; an event counter simply counts certain events during execution of the loop. 7. Because there are five days in a business week, you would use a count-controlled loop that runs from 1 to 5. 8. Nest the original loop inside a count-controlled loop that runs from 1 to 52. 9. Run the program with data sets that have a different number of females and males, only females, only males, illegal values (other characters), and an empty input file.

Exam Preparation Exercises

1. In one or two sentences, explain the difference between loops and branches.
2. What does the following loop print out? (`number` is of type `int`.)

```
number = 1;
while (number < 11)
{
    number++;
    cout << number << endl;
}
```

3. By rearranging the order of the statements (don't change the way they are written), make the loop in Exercise 2 print the numbers from 1 through 10.
4. When the following code is executed, how many iterations of the loop are performed?

```
number = 2;
done = false;
while ( !done )
{
    number = number * 2;
    if (number > 64)
        done = true;
}
```

5. What is the output of this nested loop structure?

```
i = 4;
while (i >= 1)
{
    j = 2;
    while (j >= 1)
    {
        cout << j << ' ';
        j--;
    }
    cout << i << endl;
    i--;
}
```

6. The following code segment is supposed to write out the even numbers between 1 and 15. (n is an int variable.) It has two flaws in it.

```
n = 2;
while (n != 15)
{
    n = n + 2;
    cout << n << ' ';
}
```

a. What is the output of the code as written?
b. Correct the code so that it works as intended.

7. The following code segment is supposed to copy one line from the standard input device to the standard output device.

```
cin.get(inChar);
while (inChar != '\n')
{
    cin.get(inChar);
    cout << inChar;
}
```

a. What is the output if the input line consists of the characters ABCDE?
b. Rewrite the code so that it works properly.

8. Does the following program segment need any priming reads? If not, explain why. If so, add the input statement(s) in the proper place. (letter is of type char.)

```
while (cin)
{
    while (letter != '\n')
    {
```

(continued on next page)

```
        cout << letter;
        cin.get(letter);
    }
    cout << endl;
    cout << "Another line read ..." << endl;
    cin.get(letter);
}
```

9. What sentinel value would you choose for a program that reads telephone numbers as integers?

10. Consider this program:

```
#include <iostream>

using namespace std;

const int LIMIT = 8;

int main()
{
    int    sum;
    int    i;
    int    number;
    bool finished;

    sum = 0;
    i = 1;
    finished = false;
    while (i <= LIMIT && !finished)
    {
        cin >> number;
        if (number > 0)
            sum = sum + number;
        else if (number == 0)
            finished = true;
        i++;
    }
    cout << "End of test. " << sum << ' ' << number << endl;
    return 0;
}
```

and these data values:

```
5   6   -3   7   -4   0   5   8   9
```

a. What are the contents of sum and number after exit from the loop?

b. Do the data values fully test the program? Explain your answer.

11. Here is a simple count-controlled loop:

```
count = 1;
while (count < 20)
    count++;
```

a. List three ways of changing the loop so that it executes 20 times instead of 19.

b. Which of those changes makes the value of count range from 1 through 21?

12. What is the output of the following program segment? (All variables are of type int.)

```
i = 1;
while (i <= 5)
{
    sum = 0;
    j = 1;
    while (j <= i)
    {
        sum = sum + j;
        j++;
    }
    cout << sum << ' ';
    i++;
}
```

Programming Warm-up Exercises

1. Write a program segment that sets a Boolean variable dangerous to true and stops reading data if pressure (a float variable being read in) exceeds 510.0. Use dangerous as a flag to control the loop.

2. Write a program segment that counts the number of times the integer 28 occurs in a file of 100 integers.

3. Write a nested loop code segment that produces this output:

```
1
1 2
1 2 3
1 2 3 4
```

4. Write a program segment that reads a file of student scores for a class (any size) and finds the class average.

5. Write a program segment that reads in integers and then counts and prints out the number of positive integers and the number of negative integers. If a value is 0, it should not be counted. The process should continue until end-of-file occurs.

6. Write a program segment that adds up the even integers from 16 through 26, inclusive.

7. Write a program segment that prints out the sequence of all the hour and minute combinations in a day, starting with 1:00 A.M. and ending with 12:59 A.M.

8. Rewrite the code segment for Exercise 7 so that it prints the times in ten-minute intervals, arranged as a table with six columns and 24 rows.

9. Write a code segment that inputs one line of data containing an unknown number of character strings that are separated by spaces. The final value on the line is the sentinel string End. The segment should output the number of strings on the input line (excluding End), the number of strings that contained at least one letter *e*, and the percentage of strings that contained at least one *e*. (*Hint*: To determine if *e* occurs in a string, use the find function of the string class.)

10. Extend the code segment of Exercise 9 so that it processes all the lines in a data file inFile and prints the three pieces of information for each input line.

11. Modify the code segment of Exercise 10 so that it also keeps a count of the total number of strings in the file and the total number of strings containing at least one *e*. (Again, do not count the sentinel string on each line.) When EOF is reached, print the three pieces of information for the entire file.

12. Change the Incomes program so that it does the following:
   a. Prints an error message when a negative income value is input and then goes on processing any remaining data. The erroneous data should not be included in any of the calculations. Thoroughly test the modified program with your own data sets.
   b. Does not crash when there are no males in the input file or no females (or the file is empty). Instead, it should print an appropriate error message. Test the revised program with your own data sets.
   c. Rejects data sets that are coded with a letter other than 'F' or 'M' and prints an error message before continuing to process the remaining data. The program also should print a message indicating the number of erroneous data sets encountered in the file.

13. Develop a thorough set of test data for the Incomes program as modified in Exercise 12.

14. Modify the Incomes program so that it reports the highest and lowest incomes for each gender.

15. Develop a thorough set of test data for the Incomes program as modified in Exercise 14.

Programming Problems

1. Write a functional decomposition and a C++ program that inputs an integer and a character. The output should be a diamond composed of the character and extending the width specified by the integer. For example, if the integer is 11 and the character is an asterisk (*), the diamond would look like this:

```
          *
        * * *
      * * * * *
    * * * * * * *
  * * * * * * * * *
* * * * * * * * * * *
  * * * * * * * * *
    * * * * * * *
      * * * * *
        * * *
          *
```

If the input integer is an even number, it should be increased to the next odd number. Use meaningful variable names, proper indentation, appropriate comments, and good prompting messages.

2. Write a functional decomposition and a C++ program that inputs an integer larger than 1 and calculates the sum of the squares from 1 to that integer. For example, if the integer equals 4, the sum of the squares is 30 (1 + 4 + 9 + 16). The output should be the value of the integer and the sum, properly labeled. The program should repeat this process for several input values. A negative input value signals the end of the data.

3. Using functional decomposition, write a program that prints out the approximate number of words in a file of text. For our purposes, this is the same as the number of gaps following words. A *gap* is defined as one or more spaces in a row, so a sequence of spaces counts as just one gap. The newline character also counts as a gap. Anything other than a space or newline is considered to be part of a word. For example, there are 13 words in this sentence, according to our definition. The program should echo print the data.

   Solve this problem with two different programs:

   a. Use a `string` object into which you input each word as a string. This approach is quite straightforward.

   b. Assume the `string` class does not exist, and input the data one character at a time. This approach is more complicated. (*Hint*: Only count a space as a gap if the previous character read is something other than a space.)

Use meaningful variable names, proper indentation, and appropriate comments. Thoroughly test the programs with your own data sets.

Functions

■ To be able to write a program that uses functions to reflect the structure of your functional decomposition.

■ To be able to write a module of your own design as a void function.

■ To be able to define a void function to do a specified task.

■ To be able to distinguish between value and reference parameters.

■ To be able to use arguments and parameters correctly.

■ To be able to do the following tasks, given a functional decomposition of a problem:

■ Determine what the parameter list should be for each module.

■ Determine which parameters should be reference parameters and which should be value parameters.

■ Code the program correctly.

■ To be able to define and use local variables correctly.

■ To be able to write a program that uses multiple calls to a single function.

You have been using C++ functions since we introduced standard library routines such as `sqrt` and `abs` in Chapter 3. So far, we have not considered how the programmer can create his or her own functions other than `main`. That is the topic of this chapter and the next.

You might wonder why we waited until now to look at user-defined subprograms. The reason, and the major purpose for using subprograms, is to help organize and simplify larger programs. Until now, our programs have been relatively small and simple, so we didn't need to write subprograms. Now that we've covered the basic control structures, we are ready to introduce subprograms so that we can begin writing larger and more complex programs.

7.1 Functional Decomposition with Void Functions

Recall from Chapter 3 that there are two kinds of subprograms that the C++ language works with: value-returning functions and void functions. In this chapter, we concentrate exclusively on creating our own void functions. In Chapter 8, we examine how to write value-returning functions.

From the early chapters on, you have been designing your programs as collections of modules. Many of these modules are naturally implemented as *user-defined void functions*. We now look at how to turn the modules in your algorithms into user-defined void functions.

Writing Modules as Void Functions

It is quite simple to turn a module into a void function in C++. Basically, a void function looks like the `main` function except that the function heading uses `void` rather than `int` as the data type of the function. Additionally, the body of a void function does not contain a statement like

```
return 0;
```

as does `main`. A void function does not return a function value to its caller.

Let's look at a program using void functions. A friend of yours is returning from a long trip, and you want to write a program that prints the following message:

```
* * * * * * * * * * * * * *
* * * * * * * * * * * * * *
  Welcome Home!
* * * * * * * * * * * * * *
* * * * * * * * * * * * * *
* * * * * * * * * * * * * *
* * * * * * * * * * * * * *
```

Here is a design for the program, following the style we introduced in the Programming Example in Chapter 4.

Main   Level 0

Print two lines of asterisks
Print "Welcome Home!"
Print four lines of asterisks

Print 2 Lines   Level 1

Print "***************"
Print "***************"

Print 4 Lines

Print "***************"
Print "***************"
Print "***************"
Print "***************"

If we write the two level 1 modules as void functions, the main function is simply

```
int main()
{
    Print2Lines();
    cout << "Welcome Home!" << endl;
    Print4Lines();
    return 0;
}
```

Notice how similar this code is to the main module of our functional decomposition. It contains two function calls—one to a function named Print2Lines and another to a function named Print4Lines. Both of these functions have empty argument lists.

The following code should look familiar to you, but look carefully at the function heading.

```
void Print2Lines()                              // Function heading
{
    cout << "***************" << endl;
    cout << "***************" << endl;
}
```

This segment is a *function definition.* A function definition is the code that extends from the function heading to the end of the block that is the body of the function. The function heading begins with the word `void`, signaling the compiler that this is not a value-returning function. The body of the function executes some ordinary statements and does *not* finish with a `return` statement to return a function value.

Now look again at the function heading. Following the function name is an empty argument list—that is, there is nothing between the parentheses. Later we see what goes inside the parentheses if a function uses arguments. Now let's put `main` and the other two functions together to form a complete program.

```cpp
//*******************************************************************
// Welcome program
// This program prints a "Welcome Home" message
//*******************************************************************
#include <iostream>

using namespace std;

void Print2Lines();                        // Function prototypes
void Print4Lines();

int main()
{
    Print2Lines();                         // Function call
    cout << " Welcome Home!" << endl;
    Print4Lines();                         // Function call
    return 0;
}

//*******************************************************************

void Print2Lines()                         // Function heading

// This function prints two lines of asterisks
{
    cout << "***************" << endl;
    cout << "***************" << endl;
}

//*******************************************************************

void Print4Lines()                         // Function heading

// This function prints four lines of asterisks
{
    cout << "***************" << endl;
```

```
    cout << "***************" << endl;
    cout << "***************" << endl;
    cout << "***************" << endl;
}
```

C++ function definitions can appear in any order. We could have chosen to place the `main` function last instead of first, but C++ programmers typically put `main` first and any supporting functions after it.

In the Welcome program, the two statements just before the `main` function are called *function prototypes*. These declarations are necessary because of the C++ rule requiring you to declare an identifier before you can use it. Our `main` function uses the identifiers `Print2Lines` and `Print4Lines`, but the definitions of those functions don't appear until later. We must supply the function prototypes to inform the compiler in advance that `Print2Lines` and `Print4Lines` are the names of functions, that they do not return function values, and that they have no arguments. We say more about function prototypes later in the chapter.

Because the Welcome program is so simple to begin with, it may seem more complicated with its modules written as functions. However, it is clear that it much more closely resembles our functional decomposition. This is especially true of the `main` function. As our programs grow to include many modules nested several levels deep, the ability to read a program in the same manner as a functional decomposition aids greatly in the development and debugging process.

7.2   An Overview of User-Defined Functions

Now that we've seen an example of how a program is written with functions, let's look briefly and informally at some of the more important points of function construction and use.

Flow of Control in Function Calls

We said that C++ function definitions can be arranged in any order, although `main` usually appears first. During compilation, the functions are translated in the order in which they physically appear. When the program is executed, however, control begins at the first statement in the `main` function, and the program proceeds in logical sequence. When a function call is encountered, logical control is passed to the first statement in that function's body. The statements in the function are executed in logical order. After the last one is executed, control returns to the point immediately following the function call. Because function calls alter the logical order of execution, functions are considered control structures.

In the Welcome program, execution begins with the first executable statement in the `main` function (the call to `Print2Lines`). When `Print2Lines` is called, control passes to its first statement and subsequent statements in its body. After the last statement in `Print2Lines` has executed, control returns to the `main` function at the point following the call (the output statement that prints "Welcome Home!").

Function Parameters

Looking at the Welcome program, you can see that the `Print2Lines` and `Print4Lines` functions differ only in the number of lines that they print. Do we really need two different functions in this program? Maybe we should write only one function that prints *any* number of lines, where the "any number of lines" is passed as an argument by the caller (`main`). Here is a second version of the program, which uses only one function to do the printing. We call it NewWelcome.

```
//*******************************************************************
// NewWelcome program
// This program prints a "Welcome Home" message
//*******************************************************************
#include <iostream>

using namespace std;

void PrintLines( int );                      // Function prototype

int main()
{
    PrintLines(2);
    cout << " Welcome Home!" << endl;
    PrintLines(4);
    return 0;
}


//*******************************************************************

void PrintLines( int numLines )

// This function prints lines of asterisks, where
// numLines specifies how many lines to print

{
    int count;       // Loop control variable

    count = 1;
    while (count <= numLines)
    {
        cout << "****************" << endl;
        count++;
    }
}
```

In the function heading of `PrintLines`, the code between the parentheses is a *parameter declaration.* As you learned in earlier chapters, arguments represent a way for two functions to communicate with each other. Arguments enable the calling function to input (pass) values to another function to use in its processing and—in some cases—to allow the called function to output (return) results to the caller. The items listed in the call to a function are the **arguments.** The variables declared in the function heading are the **parameters.** (Some programmers use the pair of terms *actual argument* and *formal argument* instead of *argument* and *parameter.*

> **Argument** A variable or expression listed in a call to a function; also called *actual argument* or *actual parameter.*
>
> **Parameter** A variable declared in a function heading; also called *formal argument* or *formal parameter.*

Others use the term *actual parameter* in place of *argument,* and *formal parameter* in place of *parameter.*) Notice that the `main` function in the code above is a *parameterless* function.

In the NewWelcome program, the arguments in the two function calls are the constants 2 and 4, and the parameter in the `PrintLines` function is named `numLines`. The `main` function first calls `PrintLines` with an argument of 2. When control is turned over to `PrintLines`, the parameter `numLines` is initialized to 2. Within `PrintLines`, the count-controlled loop executes twice and the function returns. The second time `PrintLines` is called, the parameter `numLines` is initialized to the value of the argument, 4. The loop executes four times, after which the function returns.

The NewWelcome program brings up a second major reason for using functions— namely, a function can be called from many places in the `main` function (or from other functions). Use of multiple calls can save a great deal of effort in coding many problem solutions. If a task must be done in more than one place in a program, we can avoid repetitive coding by writing it as a function and then calling it wherever we need it.

7.3 Syntax and Semantics of Void Functions

Function Call (Invocation)

To call (or invoke) a void function, we use its name as a statement, with the arguments in parentheses following the name. A **function call** in a program results in the execution of the body of the called function. This is the syntax template of a function call to a void function:

> **Function call (to a void function)** A statement that transfers control to a void function. In C++, this statement is the name of the function, followed by a list of arguments.

FunctionCall (to a void function)

```
FunctionName ( ArgumentList ) ;
```

According to the syntax template for a function call, the argument list is optional. A function is not required to have arguments. However, as the syntax template also shows, the parentheses are required even if the argument list is empty.

If there are two or more arguments in the argument list, you must separate them with commas. Here is the syntax template for ArgumentList:

ArgumentList

When a function call is executed, the arguments are passed to the parameters according to their positions, left to right, and control is then transferred to the first executable statement in the function body. When the last statement in the function has executed, control returns to the point from which the function was called.

Function Declarations and Definitions

In C++, you must declare every identifier before it can be used. In the case of functions, a function's declaration must physically precede any function call.

A function declaration announces to the compiler the name of the function, the data type of the function's return value (either `void` or a data type like `int` or `float`), and the data types of the parameters it uses. The NewWelcome program shows a total of three function declarations. The first declaration (the statement labeled "Function prototype") does not include the body of the function. The remaining two declarations—for `main` and `PrintLines`—include bodies for the functions.

Function prototype   A function declaration without the body of the function.

Function definition   A function declaration that includes the body of the function.

In C++ terminology, a function declaration that omits the body is called a **function prototype,** and a declaration that does include the body is a **function definition.** Note that all definitions are declarations, but not all declarations are definitions.

The rule throughout C++ is that you can declare an item as many times as you wish, but you can define it only once. In the NewWelcome program, we could include many function prototypes for `PrintLines` (though we'd have no reason to), but only one function definition is allowed.

Function Prototypes   We have said that the definition of the `main` function usually appears first in a program, followed by the definitions of all other functions. To satisfy the requirement that identifiers be declared before they are used, C++ programmers typically place all function prototypes near the top of the program, before the definition of `main`.

A function prototype (known as a *forward declaration* in some languages) specifies in advance the data type of the function value to be returned (or the word `void`) and the data types of the parameters. A prototype for a void function has the following form:

FunctionPrototype (for a void function)

> **void** FunctionName (ParameterList) ;

As you can see in the syntax template, no body is included for the function, and a semicolon terminates the declaration. The parameter list is optional and has the form:

ParameterList (in a function prototype)

> Datatype **&** VariableName , DataType **&** VariableName . . .

The ampersand (`&`) attached to the name of a data type is optional and has a special significance that we cover later in the chapter.

In a function prototype, the parameter list must specify the data types of the parameters, but their names are optional. You could write either

```
void DoSomething( int, float );
```

or

```
void DoSomething( int velocity, float angle );
```

Sometimes it's useful for documentation purposes to supply names for the parameters, but the compiler ignores them.

Function Definitions   You learned in Chapter 2 that a function definition consists of two parts: the function heading and the function body, which is syntactically a block (compound statement). Here's the syntax template for a function definition, specifically, for a void function:

FunctionDefinition (for a void function)

> **void** FunctionName (ParameterList)
> {
>   Statement
>   ⋮
>
> }

Notice that the function heading does *not* end in a semicolon the way a function prototype does. It is a common syntax error to put a semicolon at the end of the line.

The syntax of the parameter list differs slightly from that of a function prototype in that you *must* specify the names of all the parameters. Also, it's our style preference (but not a language requirement) to declare each parameter on a separate line:

ParameterList (in a function definition)

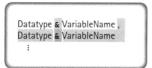

```
Datatype & VariableName ,
Datatype & VariableName
    ⋮
```

Local Variables

Because a function body is a block, any function—not only the `main` function—can include variable declarations within its body. These variables are called **local variables** because they are accessible only within the block in which they are declared. As far as the calling code is concerned, they don't exist. If you tried to print the contents of a local variable from another function, a compile-time error such as "UNDECLARED IDENTI-FIER" would occur. You saw an example of a local variable in the NewWelcome program—the `count` variable declared within the `PrintLines` function.

Local variable   A variable declared within a block and not accessible outside of that block.

In contrast to local variables, variables declared outside of all the functions in a program are called *global variables*. We return to the topic of global variables in Chapter 8.

Local variables occupy memory space only while the function is executing. At the moment the function is called, memory space is created for its local variables. When the function returns, its local variables are destroyed.* Therefore, every time the function is called, its local variables start out with their values undefined. Because every call to a function is independent of every other call to that same function, you must initialize the local variables within the function itself. And because local variables are destroyed when the function returns, you cannot use them to store values between calls to the function.

The following code segment illustrates each of the parts of the function declaration and calling mechanism that we have discussed.

---

*We'll see an exception to this rule in the next chapter.

```
#include <iostream>

using namespace std;

void TryThis( int, int, float );        // Function prototype

int main()                              // Function definition
{
    int    int1;                        // Variables local to main
    int    int2;
    float someFloat;
    ⋮
    TryThis(int1, int2, someFloat);     // Function call with three
                                        //    arguments
    ⋮
}

void TryThis( int    param1,            // Function definition with
              int    param2,            //    three parameters
              float param3 )
{
    int    i;                           // Variables local to TryThis
    float x;
    ⋮
}
```

The Return Statement

The main function uses the statement

```
return 0;
```

to return the value 0 (or 1 or some other value) to its caller, the operating system. Every value-returning function must return its function value this way.

A void function does not return a function value. Control returns from the function when it "falls off" the end of the body—that is, after the final statement has executed. As you saw in the NewWelcome program, the PrintLines function simply prints some lines of asterisks and then returns.

Alternatively, there is a second form of the Return statement. It looks like this:

```
return;
```

This statement is valid *only* for void functions. It can appear anywhere in the body of the function; it causes control to exit the function immediately and return to the caller.

Naming Void Functions

When you choose a name for a void function, keep in mind how calls to it will look. A call is written as a statement; therefore, it should sound like a command or an instruction to the computer. Try to choose a name that is an imperative verb or has an imperative verb as part of it. (In English, an imperative verb is one representing a command: *Listen! Look! Do something!*) For example, the statement

```
Lines(3);
```

has no verb to suggest that it's a command. Adding the verb *Print* makes the name sound like a command:

```
PrintLines(3);
```

Header Files

From the very beginning, we have been using #include directives to insert the contents of header files into our programs:

```
#include <iostream>
#include <cmath>       // For sqrt() and fabs()
#include <fstream>     // For file I/O
#include <climits>     // For INT_MAX and INT_MIN
```

Exactly what do these header files contain?

It turns out that there is nothing magical about header files. Their contents are just a series of C++ declarations. There are declarations of items such as named constants (INT_MAX, INT_MIN), classes (istream, ostream, string), and objects (cin, cout). But most of the items in a header file are function prototypes.

Suppose that your program needs to use the library function sqrt in a statement like this:

```
y = sqrt(x);
```

Every identifier must be declared before it can be used. If you forget to #include the header file cmath, the compiler gives you an "UNDECLARED IDENTIFIER" error message. The file cmath contains function prototypes for sqrt and other math-oriented library functions. With this header file included in your program, the compiler not only knows that the identifier sqrt is the name of a function but it also can verify that your function call is correct with respect to the number of arguments and their data types.

Header files save you the trouble of writing all of the library function prototypes yourself at the beginning of your program. With just one line—the #include directive—you cause the preprocessor to go out and find the header file and insert the prototypes into your program.

7.4 Parameters

When a function is executed, it uses the arguments given to it in the function call. How is this done? The answer to this question depends on the nature of the parameters. C++ supports two kinds of parameters: **value parameters** and **reference parameters**. With a value parameter, which is declared without an ampersand (&) at the end of the data type name, the function receives a copy of the argument's value. With a reference parameter, which is declared by adding an ampersand to the data type name, the function receives the location (memory address) of the caller's argument. Before we examine in detail the difference between these two kinds of parameters, let's look at an example of a function heading with a mixture of reference and value parameter declarations.

> **Value parameter** A parameter that receives a copy of the value of the corresponding argument.
>
> **Reference parameter** A parameter that receives the location (memory address) of the caller's argument.

```
void Example( int&   param1,    // A reference parameter
              int    param2,    // A value parameter
              float param3 )    // Another value parameter
```

With simple data types—int, char, float, and so on—a value parameter is the default (assumed) kind of parameter. In other words, if you don't do anything special (add an ampersand), a parameter is assumed to be a value parameter. To specify a reference parameter, you have to go out of your way to do something extra (attach an ampersand).

The following table summarizes the usage of arguments and parameters.

Item	Usage
Argument	Appears in a function *call*. The corresponding parameter may be either a reference or a value parameter.
Value parameter	Appears in a function *heading*. Receives a *copy* of the value of the corresponding argument.
Reference parameter	Appears in a function *heading*. Receives the *address* of the corresponding argument.

Let's look at both kinds of parameters, starting with value parameters.

Value Parameters

Because value parameters are passed copies of their arguments, anything that has a value may be passed to a value parameter. This includes constants, variables, and even arbitrarily complicated expressions. (The expression is simply evaluated and a copy of the result is sent to the corresponding value parameter.) For the `PrintLines` function, the following function calls are all valid:

```
PrintLines(3);
PrintLines(lineCount);
PrintLines(2 * abs(10 - someInt));
```

There must be the same number of arguments in a function call as there are parameters in the function heading.* Also, each argument should have the same data type as the parameter in the same position. Notice how each parameter in the following example is matched to the argument in the same position (the data type of each argument below is what you would assume from its name):

Function heading: `void ShowMatch(float num1, int num2, char letter)`

Function call: `ShowMatch(floatVariable, intVariable, charVariable);`

If the matched items are not of the same data type, implicit type coercion takes place. For example, if a parameter is of type `int`, an argument that is a `float` expression is coerced to an `int` value before it is passed to the function. As usual in C++, you can avoid unintended type coercion by using an explicit type cast or, better yet, by not mixing data types at all.

As we have stressed, a value parameter receives a copy of the argument, and therefore the caller's argument is protected from being accessed directly or changed. When a function returns, the contents of its value parameters are destroyed, along with the contents of its local variables. The difference between value parameters and local variables is that the values of local variables are undefined when a function starts to execute, whereas value parameters are automatically initialized to the values of the corresponding arguments.

Because the contents of value parameters are destroyed when the function returns, they cannot be used to return information to the calling code. What if we *do* want to return information by modifying the caller's arguments? We must use the second kind of parameter available in C++: reference parameters. Let's look at these now.

---

*This statement is not the whole truth. C++ has a special language feature—*default parameters*—that lets you call a function with fewer arguments than parameters. We do not cover default parameters in this book.

Reference Parameters

A reference parameter is one that you declare by attaching an ampersand to the name of its data type. It is called a reference parameter because the called function can refer to the corresponding argument directly. Specifically, the function is allowed to inspect *and modify* the caller's argument.

When a function is invoked using a reference parameter, it is the *location* (memory address) of the argument, not its value, that is passed to the function. There is only one copy of the information, and it is used by both the caller and the called function. When a function is called, the argument and the parameter become synonyms for the same location in memory. Whatever value is left by the called function in this location is the value that the caller will find there. Therefore, you must be careful when using a reference parameter because any change made to it affects the argument in the calling code.

Only a variable can be passed as an argument to a reference parameter because a function can assign a new value to the argument. (In contrast, remember that an arbitrarily complicated expression can be passed to a value parameter.) Suppose that we have a function with the following heading:

```
void DoThis( float val,      // Value parameter
             int&  count )   // Reference parameter
```

Then the following function calls are all valid.

```
DoThis(someFloat, someInt);
DoThis(9.83, intCounter);
DoThis(4.9 * sqrt(y), myInt);
```

In the DoThis function, the first parameter is a value parameter, so any expression is allowed as the argument. The second parameter is a reference parameter, so the argument *must* be a variable name. The statement

```
DoThis(y, 3);
```

generates a compile-time error because the second argument isn't a variable name.

There is another important difference between value and reference parameters when it comes to matching arguments with parameters. With value parameters, we said that implicit type coercion occurs if the matched items have different data types (the value of the argument is coerced, if possible, to the data type of the parameter). In contrast, with reference parameters, the matched items *must* have exactly the same data type.

The following table summarizes the appropriate forms of arguments.

Parameter	Argument
Value parameter	A variable, constant, or arbitrary expression (type coercion may take place)
Reference parameter	A variable *only*, of exactly the same data type as the parameter

Finally, it is the programmer's responsibility to make sure that the argument list and parameter list match up semantically as well as syntactically. Similarly, if a function has two parameters of the same data type, you must be careful that the arguments are in the right order. If they are in the wrong order, no syntax error will result, but the answers will be wrong.

Argument-Passing Mechanisms

There are three major ways of passing arguments to and from subprograms. C++ supports only two of these mechanisms; however, it's useful to know about all three in case you have occasion to use them in another language.

C++ reference parameters employ a mechanism called a *pass by address* or *pass by location*. A memory address is passed to the function. Another name for this is a *pass by reference* because the function can refer directly to the caller's variable that is specified in the argument list.

C++ value parameters are an example of a *pass by value*. The function receives a copy of the value of the caller's argument. Passing by value can be less efficient than passing by address because the value of an argument may occupy many memory locations (as we see in Chapter 11), whereas an address usually occupies only a single location. For the simple data types `int`, `char`, `bool`, and `float`, the efficiency of either mechanism is about the same.

A third method of passing arguments is called a *pass by name*. The argument is passed to the function as a character string that must be interpreted by special runtime support software (called a *thunk*) supplied by the compiler. Passing by name is the least efficient of the three argument-passing mechanisms and is supported by the ALGOL and LISP programming languages, but not by C++.

There are two different ways of matching arguments with parameters, although C++ supports only one of them. Most programming languages, C++ among them, match arguments and parameters by their relative positions in the argument and parameter lists. This is called *positional matching, relative matching,* or *implicit matching.* A few languages, such as Ada, also support *explicit* or *named matching.* In explicit matching, the argument list specifies the name of the parameter to be associated with each argument. Explicit matching allows arguments to be written in any order in the function call. The real advantage is that each call documents precisely which values are being passed to which parameters.

7.5 Designing Functions

We've looked at some examples of functions and defined the syntax of function prototypes and function definitions. But how do we design functions? First, we need to be more specific about what functions do. We've said that they allow us to organize our programs more like our functional decompositions, but what really is the advantage of doing that?

The body of a function is like any other segment of code except that it is contained in a separate block within the program. Isolating a segment of code in a separate block means that its implementation details can be "hidden" from view. As long as you know how to call a function and what its purpose is, you can use it without looking at the code inside the function body. For example, you don't know how the code for a library function like `sqrt` is written (its implementation is hidden from view), yet you still can use it effectively.

The specification of what a function does and how it is invoked defines its **interface** (see Figure 7–1). By hiding a module implementation, or **encapsulating** the module, we can make changes to it without changing the `main` function, as long as the interface remains the same. For example, you might rewrite the body of a function using a more efficient algorithm.

Interface   A shared boundary that permits independent systems to meet and act on or communicate with each other. Also, the formal description of the purpose of a subprogram and the mechanism for communicating with it.

Encapsulation   Hiding a module implementation in a separate block with a formally specified interface.

Encapsulation is what we do in the functional decomposition process when we postpone the solution of a difficult subproblem. We write down its purpose, its precondition and postcondition, and what information it takes and returns, and then we write the rest of our design as if the subproblem had already been solved. We could hand this interface specification to someone else, and that person could develop a function for us that solves the subproblem. We needn't be concerned about how it works, as long as it conforms to the interface specification. Interfaces and encapsulation are the basis for *team programming,* in which a group of programmers work together to solve a large problem.

Thus, designing a function can (and should) be divided into two tasks: designing the interface and designing the implementation. We already know how to design an implementation—it is a segment of code that corresponds to an algorithm. To design the interface, we focus on the *what,* not the *how.* We must define the behavior of the function (what it does) and the mechanism for communicating with it.

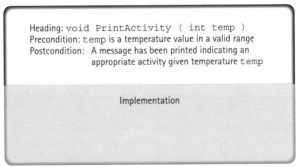

```
Heading: void PrintActivity ( int temp )
Precondition: temp is a temperature value in a valid range
Postcondition:  A message has been printed indicating an
                 appropriate activity given temperature temp


                         Implementation
```

Figure 7–1   *Function Interface (Visible) and Implementation (Hidden)*

You already know how to specify formally the behavior of a function. Because a function corresponds to a module, its behavior is defined by the precondition and postcondition of the module. All that remains is to define the mechanism for communicating with the function. To do so, make a list of the following items:

1. *Incoming values* that the function receives from the caller.
2. *Outgoing values* that the function produces and returns to the caller.
3. *Incoming/outgoing values*—values the caller has that the function changes (receives and returns).

Decide which identifiers inside the module match the values in this list. These identifiers become the variables in the parameter list for the function. Then the parameters are declared in the function heading. All other variables that the function needs are local and must be declared within the body of the function. This process is repeated for all the modules at each level.

Let's look more closely at designing the interface. First we examine function preconditions and postconditions. After that, we consider in more detail the notion of incoming, outgoing, and incoming/outgoing parameters.

Writing Assertions as Program Comments

We have been writing module preconditions and postconditions as informal, English-language assertions. From now on, we include preconditions and postconditions as comments to document the interfaces of C++ functions. Here's an example:

```
void PrintAverage( float sum,
                   int   count )

// Precondition:
//     sum is assigned  &&  count > 0
// Postcondition:
//     The average sum/count has been output on one line

{
    cout << "Average is " << sum / float(count) << endl;
}
```

The precondition is an assertion describing everything that the function requires to be true at the moment the caller invokes the function. The postcondition describes the state of the program at the moment the function finishes executing.

You can think of the precondition and postcondition as a contract. The contract states that if the precondition is true at function entry, then the postcondition must be true at function exit. The *caller* is responsible for ensuring the precondition, and the *function code* must ensure the postcondition. If the caller fails to satisfy its part of the contract (the precondition), the contract is off; the function cannot guarantee that the postcondition will be true.

Above, the precondition warns the caller to make sure that sum has been assigned a meaningful value and to be sure that count is positive. If this precondition is true, the function guarantees it will satisfy the postcondition. If count isn't positive when PrintAverage is invoked, the effect of the function is undefined. (For example, if count equals 0, the postcondition surely isn't satisfied—the program crashes!)

Sometimes the caller doesn't need to satisfy any precondition before calling a function. In this case, the precondition can be written as the value true or simply omitted. In the following example, no precondition is necessary:

```
void Get2Ints( int& int1,
               int& int2 )

// Postcondition:
//     User has been prompted to enter two integers
//   && int1 == first input value
//   && int2 == second input value

{
    cout << "Please enter two integers: ";
    cin >> int1 >> int2;
}
```

In assertions written as C++ comments, we use either && or AND to denote the logical AND operator, either || or OR to denote a logical OR, either ! or NOT to denote a logical NOT, and == to denote "equals." (Notice that we do *not* use = to denote "equals." Even when we write program comments, we want to keep C++'s == operator distinct from the assignment operator.)

There is one final notation we use when we express assertions as program comments. Preconditions implicitly refer to values of variables at the moment the function is invoked. Postconditions implicitly refer to values at the moment the function returns. But sometimes you need to write a postcondition that refers to parameter values that existed at the moment the function was invoked. To signify "at the time of entry to the function," we attach the symbol @entry to the end of the variable name. Below is an example of the use of this notation. The Swap function exchanges, or swaps, the contents of its two parameters.

```
void Swap( int& firstInt,
           int& secondInt )

// Precondition:
//     firstInt and secondInt are assigned
// Postcondition:
//     firstInt == secondInt@entry
//   && secondInt == firstInt@entry
```

```
{
    int temporaryInt;

    temporaryInt = firstInt;
    firstInt = secondInt;
    secondInt = temporaryInt;
}
```

Documenting the Direction of Data Flow

Data flow The flow of information from the calling code to a function and from the function back to the calling code.

Another helpful piece of documentation in a function interface is the direction of **data flow** for each parameter in the parameter list. Data flow is the flow of information between the function and its caller. We said earlier that each parameter can be classified as an *incoming* parameter, an *outgoing* parameter, or an *incoming/outgoing* parameter. (Some programmers refer to these as *input* parameters, *output* parameters, and *input/output* parameters.)

For an incoming parameter, the direction of data flow is one-way—into the function. The function inspects and uses the current value of the parameter but does not modify it. In the function heading, we attach the comment

```
/* in */
```

to the declaration of the parameter. (Remember that C++ comments come in two forms. The first starts with two slashes and extends to the end of the line. The second form encloses a comment between /* and */ and allows us to embed a comment within a line of code.) Here is the PrintAverage function with comments added to the parameter declarations:

```
void PrintAverage( /* in */ float sum,
                   /* in */ int   count )

// Precondition:
//      sum is assigned  &&  count > 0
// Postcondition:
//      The average sum/count has been output on one line

{
    cout << "Average is " << sum / float(count) << endl;
}
```

Passing by value is appropriate for each parameter that is incoming only. As you can see in the function body, PrintAverage does not modify the values of the parameters sum and count. It merely uses their current values. The direction of data flow is one-way—into the function.

The data flow for an outgoing parameter is one-way—out of the function. The function produces a new value for the parameter without using the old value in any way. The comment /* out */ identifies an outgoing parameter. Here we've added comments to the Get2Ints function heading:

```
void Get2Ints( /* out */ int& int1,
               /* out */ int& int2 )
```

Passing by reference must be used for an outgoing parameter. If you look back at the body of Get2Ints, you'll see that the function stores new values into the two variables (by means of the input statement), replacing whatever values they originally contained.

Finally, the data flow for an incoming/outgoing parameter is two-way—into and out of the function. The function uses the old value and also produces a new value for the parameter. We use /* inout */ to document this two-way direction of data flow. Here is an example of a function that uses two parameters, one of them incoming only and the other one incoming/outgoing:

```
void Calc( /* in */    int  alpha,
           /* inout */ int& beta  )

// Precondition:
//    alpha and beta are assigned
// Postcondition
//    beta == beta@entry * 7 - alpha

{
    beta = beta * 7 - alpha;
}
```

This function first inspects the incoming value of beta so that it can evaluate the expression to the right of the equal sign. Then it stores a new value into beta by using the assignment operation. The data flow for beta is therefore considered a two-way flow of information. A pass by value is appropriate for alpha (it's incoming only), but a pass by reference is required for beta (it's an incoming/outgoing parameter).

Formatting Function Headings

From here on, we follow a specific style when coding our function headings. Comments appear next to the parameters to explain how each parameter is used. Also, embedded comments indicate which of the three data flow categories each parameter belongs to (In, Out, or Inout).

```
void Print( /* in */    float val,    // Value to be printed
            /* inout */ int&  count )  // Number of lines printed
                                       //   so far
```

We use comments in the form of rows of asterisks (or dashes or some other character) before and after a function to make the function stand out from the surrounding code. Each function also has its own block of introductory comments, just like those at the start of a program, as well as its precondition and post-condition.

It's important to put as much care into documenting each function as you would into the documentation at the beginning of a program.

The following table summarizes the correspondence between a parameter's data flow and the appropriate argument-passing mechanism.

Data Flow for a Parameter	Argument-Passing Mechanism
Incoming	Pass by value
Outgoing	Pass by reference
Incoming/outgoing	Pass by reference

There are exceptions to the guidelines in this table. C++ requires that I/O stream objects be passed by reference because of the way streams and files are implemented. We encounter another exception in Chapter 12.

Conceptual Versus Physical Hiding of a Function Implementation

In many programming languages, the encapsulation of an implementation is purely conceptual. If you want to know how a function is implemented, you simply look at the function body. C++, however, permits function implementations to be written and stored separately from the main function.

Larger C++ programs are usually split up and stored into separate files on a disk. One file might contain just the source code for the main function; another file, the source code for one or two functions invoked by main; and so on. This organization is called a *multifile program*. To translate the source code into object code, the compiler is invoked for each file independently of the others, possibly at different times. A program called the *linker* then collects all the resulting object code into a single executable program.

When you write a program that invokes a function located in another file, it isn't necessary for that function's source code to be available. All that's required is for you to include a function prototype so that the compiler can check the syntax of the call to the function. After the compiler is done, the linker finds the object code for that function and links it with your main function's object code. We do this kind of thing all the time when we invoke library functions. C++ systems supply only the object code, not the source code, for library functions like sqrt. The source code for their implementations are physically hidden from view.

Later in the book, you learn how to write multifile programs and hide implementations physically. In the meantime, conscientiously avoid writing code that depends on the internal workings of a function.

Programming Example

Comparison of Furniture-Store Sales

Problem A new regional sales manager for the Chippendale Furniture Stores has just come into town. She wants to see a monthly, department-by-department comparison, in the form of bar graphs, of the two Chippendale stores in town. The daily sales for each department are kept in each store's accounting files. Data on each store is stored in the following form:

Department ID number
Number of business days for the department
Daily sales for day 1
Daily sales for day 2
⋮
Daily sales for last day in period
Department ID number
Number of business days for the department
Daily sales for day 1
⋮

The bar graph is to be printed in the following form:

```
Bar Graph Comparing Departments of Store #1 and Store #2

Store  Sales in 1,000s of dollars
  #    0         5         10        15        20        25
       |.........|.........|.........|.........|.........|

       Dept 1030
  1    ***********************
       Dept 1030
  2    *****************************************************
  
       Dept 1210
  1    ***************************************************************
       Dept 1210
  2    ***********************************************
  
       Dept 2040
  1    **********************************************************
       Dept 2040
  2    *******************************
```

As you can see from the bar graph, each star represents $500 in sales. No stars are printed if a department's sales are less than or equal to $250.

Input   Two data files (`store1` and `store2`), each containing the following values for each department:

Department ID number (`int`)
Number of business days (`int`)
Daily sales (several `float` values)

Output   A bar graph showing total sales for each department.

Discussion   Reading the input data from both files is straightforward. To make the program flexible, we'll prompt the user for the names of the disk files, read the names as strings, and associate the strings with file stream objects (let's call them `store1` and `store2`). We need to read a department ID number, the number of business days, and the daily sales for that department. After processing each department, we can read the data for the next department, continuing until we run out of departments (EOF is encountered). Because the reading process is the same for both `store1` and `store2`, we can use one function for reading both files. All we have to do is pass the appropriate file stream as an argument to the function. We want total sales for each department, so this function has to sum the daily sales for a department as they are read. A function can be used to print the output heading. Another function can be used to print out each department's sales for the month in graphic form.

There are three loops in this program: one in the `main` function (to read and process the file data), one in the function that gets the data for one department (to read all the daily sales amounts), and one in the function that prints the bar graph (to print the stars in the graph). The loop for the `main` function tests for EOF on *both* `store1` and `store2`. One graph for each store must be printed for each iteration of this loop.

The loop for the `GetData` function requires an iteration counter that ranges from 1 through the number of days for the department. Also, a summing operation is needed to total the sales for the period.

At first glance, it might seem that the loop for the `PrintData` function is like any other counting loop, but let's look at how we would do this process by hand. Suppose we want to print a bar for the value 1850. We first make sure the number is greater than 250, then print a star and subtract 500 from the original value. We check again to see if the new value is greater than 250, then print a star and subtract 500. This process repeats until the resulting value is less than or equal to 250. Thus, the loop requires a counter that is decremented by 500 for each iteration, with a termination value of 250 or less. A star is printed for each iteration of the loop.

Function `PrintHeading` does not receive any values from `main`, nor does it return any. Thus, its parameter list is empty.

Function `GetData` receives the file stream object from `main` and returns it, modified, after having read some values. The function also returns to `main` the values of the department ID and its sales for the month. Thus, `GetData` has three parameters: the file stream object (with data flow Inout), department ID (data flow Out), and department sales (data flow Out).

Function `PrintData` must receive the department ID, store number, and department sales from the `main` function to print the bar graph for an input record. Therefore, the function has those three items as its parameters, all with data flow In.

We include one more function named `OpenForInput`. This function receives a file stream object, prompts the user for the name of the associated disk file, and attempts to open the file. The function returns the file stream object to its caller, either successfully opened or in the fail state (if the file could not be opened). The single parameter to this function—the file stream object—therefore has data flow Inout.

Assumptions Each file is in order by department ID. Both stores have the same departments.

Module Structure Chart Because we are expressing our modules as C++ functions, the module structure chart now includes the names of parameters and uses arrows to show the direction of data flow.

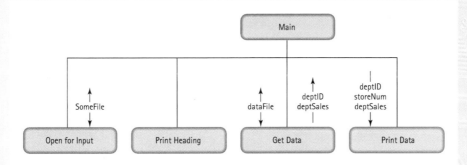

(The following program is written in ISO/ANSI standard C++. If you are working with pre-standard C++, see the alternate version of the program in the PRE_STD directory of the program disk, available at the publisher's Web site, www.jbpub.com/disks.)

```
//*************************************************************************
// Graph program
// This program generates bar graphs of monthly sales
// by department for two Chippendale furniture stores, permitting
// department-by-department comparison of sales
//*************************************************************************
#include <iostream>
#include <iomanip>     // For setw()
#include <fstream>     // For file I/O
#include <string>      // For string type
```

```cpp
using namespace std;

void GetData( ifstream&, int&, float& );
void OpenForInput( ifstream& );
void PrintData( int, int, float );
void PrintHeading();

int main()
{
    int      deptID1;         // Department ID number for Store 1
    int      deptID2;         // Department ID number for Store 2
    float    sales1;          // Department sales for Store 1
    float    sales2;          // Department sales for Store 2
    ifstream store1;          // Accounting file for Store 1
    ifstream store2;          // Accounting file for Store 2

    cout << "For Store 1," << endl;
    OpenForInput(store1);
    cout << "For Store 2," << endl;
    OpenForInput(store2);
    if ( !store1 || !store2 )               // Make sure files
        return 1;                           //   were opened

    PrintHeading();

    GetData(store1, deptID1, sales1);       // Priming reads
    GetData(store2, deptID2, sales2);
    while (store1 && store2)                // While not EOF...
    {
        cout << endl;
        PrintData(deptID1, 1, sales1);      // Process Store 1
        PrintData(deptID2, 2, sales2);      // Process Store 2
        GetData(store1, deptID1, sales1);
        GetData(store2, deptID2, sales2);
    }
    return 0;
}

//*******************************************************************

void OpenForInput( /* inout */ ifstream& someFile )     // File to be
                                                        //  opened
// Prompts the user for the name of an input file
// and attempts to open the file
```

```
// Postcondition:
//     The user has been prompted for a file name
//  && IF the file could not be opened
//         An error message has been printed
// Note:
//     Upon return from this function, the caller must test
//     the stream state to see if the file was successfully opened

{
    string fileName;    // User-specified file name

    cout << "Input file name: ";
    cin >> fileName;
    someFile.open(fileName.c_str());
    if ( !someFile )
        cout << "** Can't open " << fileName << " **" << endl;
}

//***********************************************************************

void PrintHeading()

// Prints the title for the bar chart, a heading, and the numeric
// scale for the chart.  The scale uses one mark per $500

// Postcondition:
//     The heading for the bar chart has been printed

{
    cout
      << "Bar Graph Comparing Departments of Store #1 and Store #2"
      << endl << endl
      << "Store  Sales in 1,000s of dollars" << endl
      << " #     0         5        10        15        20        25"
      << endl
      << "        |.........|.........|.........|.........|.........|"
      << endl;
}

//***********************************************************************

void GetData( /* inout */ ifstream& dataFile,   // Input file
              /* out */    int&      deptID,     // Department number
              /* out */    float&    deptSales ) // Department's
                                                 //   monthly sales
```

```
// Takes an input accounting file as a parameter, reads the
// department ID number and number of days of sales from that file,
// then reads one sales figure for each of those days, computing a
// total sales figure for the month.  This figure is returned in
// deptSales.  (If input of the department ID fails due to
// end-of-file, deptID and deptSales are undefined.)

// Precondition:
//     dataFile has been successfully opened
//  && For each department, the file contains a department ID,
//     number of days, and one sales figure for each day
// Postcondition:
//     IF input of deptID failed due to end-of-file
//         deptID and deptSales are undefined
//     ELSE
//         The data file reading marker has advanced past one
//         department's data
//      && deptID == department ID number as read from the file
//      && deptSales == sum of the sales values for the department

{
    int   numDays;  // Number of business days in the month
    int   day;      // Loop control variable for reading daily sales
    float sale;     // One day's sales for the department

    dataFile >> deptID;
    if ( !dataFile )              // Check for EOF
        return;                   // If so, exit the function

    dataFile >> numDays;
    deptSales = 0.0;
    day = 1;                      // Initialize loop control variable
    while (day <= numDays)
    {
        dataFile >> sale;
        deptSales = deptSales + sale;
        day++;                    // Update loop control variable
    }
}


//******************************************************************

void PrintData( /* in */ int   deptID,     // Department ID number
                /* in */ int   storeNum,   // Store number
                /* in */ float deptSales )  // Total sales for the
                                            //    department
```

```
// Prints the department ID number, the store number, and a
// bar graph of the sales for the department.  The bar graph
// is printed at a scale of one mark per $500

// Precondition:
//     deptID contains a valid department number
//   && storeNum contains a valid store number
//   && 0.0 <= deptSales <= 25000.0
// Postcondition:
//     A line of the bar chart has been printed with one * for
//     each $500 in sales, with remainders over $250 rounded up
//   && No stars have been printed for sales <= $250

{
    cout << setw(12) << "Dept " << deptID << endl;
    cout << setw(3) << storeNum << "        ";
    while (deptSales > 250.0)
    {
        cout << '*' ;                      // Print '*' for each $500
        deptSales = deptSales - 500.0;     // Update loop control
    }                                      //    variable
    cout << endl;
}
```

Testing   We should test this program with data files that contain the same number of data sets for both stores and with data files that contain different numbers of data sets for both stores. The case in which one or both of the files are empty also should be tested. The test data should include a set that generates a monthly sales figure of $0.00 and one that generates more than $25,000 in sales. We also should test the program to see what it does with negative days, negative sales, and mismatched department IDs. This series of tests would reveal that for this program to work correctly for the furniture-store employees who are to use it, we should add several checks for invalid data.

The main function of the Graph program not only reflects our functional decomposition but also contains multiple calls to OpenForInput, GetData, and PrintData. The resulting program is shorter and more readable than one in which the code for each function is physically duplicated.

Testing and Debugging

The parameters declared by a function and the arguments that are passed to the function by the caller must satisfy the interface to the function. Errors that occur with the use of functions often are due to an incorrect use of the interface between the calling code and the called function.

One source of errors is mismatched argument lists and parameter lists. The C++ compiler ensures that the lists have the same number of items and that they are compatible in type. It's the programmer's responsibility, however, to verify that each argument list contains the correct items. This is a matter of comparing the parameter declarations to the argument list in every call to the function. This job is much easier if the function heading gives each parameter a distinct name and describes its purpose in a comment. You can avoid mistakes in writing an argument list by using descriptive variable names in the calling code to suggest exactly what information is being passed to the function.

Another source of error is the failure to ensure that the precondition for a function is met before it is called. For example, if a function assumes that the input file is not at EOF when it is called, then the calling code must ensure that this is true before making the call to the function. If a function behaves incorrectly, review its precondition, then trace the program execution up to the point of the call to verify the precondition. You can waste a lot of time trying to locate an error in a correct function when the error is really in the part of the program prior to the call.

If the arguments match the parameters and the precondition is correctly established, then the source of the error is most likely in the function itself. Trace the function to verify that it transforms the precondition into the proper postcondition. Check that all local variables are initialized properly. Parameters that are supposed to return data to the caller must be declared as reference parameters (with an & symbol attached to the data type name).

An important technique for debugging a function is to use your system's debugger program, if one is available, to step through the execution of the function. If a debugger is not available, you can insert debug output statements to print the values of the arguments immediately before and after calls to the function. It also may help to print the values of all local variables at the end of the function. This information provides a snapshot of the function (a picture of its status at a particular moment in time) at its two most critical points, which is useful in verifying hand traces.

To test a function thoroughly, you must arrange the incoming values so that the precondition is pushed to its limits; then the postcondition must be verified. For example, if a function requires a parameter to be within a certain range, try calling the function with values in the middle of that range and at its extremes.

Testing a function also involves trying to arrange the data to *violate* its precondition. If the precondition can be violated, then errors may crop up that appear to be in the function being tested, when they are really in the main function or another function. For example, function PrintData in the Graph program assumes that a department's sales do not exceed $25,000. If a figure of $250,000 is entered by mistake, the main function does not check this number before the call, and the function tries to print a row of 500 stars. When this happens, you might assume that PrintData has gone haywire, but it's the main function's fault for not checking the validity of the data. (The program should perform this test in function GetData.) Thus, a side effect of one function can multiply and give the appearance of errors elsewhere in a program. We take a closer look at the concept of side effects in the next chapter.

The `assert` Library Function

We have discussed how function preconditions and postconditions are useful for debugging (by checking that the precondition of each function is true prior to a function call, and by verifying that each function correctly transforms the precondition into the postcondition) and for testing (by pushing the precondition to its limits and even violating it). To state the preconditions and postconditions for our functions, we've been writing the assertions as program comments:

```
// Precondition:
//     studentCount > 0
```

All comments, of course, are ignored by the compiler. They are not executable statements; they are for humans to examine.

On the other hand, the C++ standard library gives us a way in which to write *executable assertions*. Through the header file `cassert`, the library provides a void function named `assert`. This function takes a logical (Boolean) expression as an argument and halts the program if the expression is false. Here's an example:

```
#include <cassert>
   ⋮
assert(studentCount > 0);
average = sumOfScores / studentCount;
```

The argument to the `assert` function must be a valid C++ logical expression. If its value is `true`, nothing happens; execution continues on to the next statement. If its value is `false`, execution of the program terminates immediately with a message stating (a) the assertion as it appears in the argument list, (b) the name of the file containing the program source code, and (c) the line number in the program. In the example above, if the value of `studentCount` is less than or equal to 0, the program halts after printing a message like this:

```
Assertion failed: studentCount > 0, file myprog.cpp, line 48
```

(This message is potentially confusing. It doesn't mean that `studentCount` *is* greater than 0. In fact, it's just the opposite. The message tells you that the assertion `studentCount > 0` is *false*.)

Executable assertions have a profound advantage over assertions expressed as comments: the effect of a false assertion is highly visible (the program terminates with an error message). The `assert` function is therefore valuable in software testing. A program under development might be filled with calls to the `assert` function to help identify where errors are occurring. If an assertion is false, the error message gives the precise line number of the failed assertion.

Additionally, there is a way to "remove" the assertions without really removing them. If you use the preprocessor directive ⌗define NDEBUG before including the header file cassert, like this:

```
⌗define NDEBUG
⌗include <cassert>
    ⋮
```

then all calls to the assert function are ignored when you run the program. (NDEBUG stands for "No debug," and a ⌗define directive is a preprocessor feature that we don't discuss right now.) After program testing and debugging, programmers often like to "turn off" debugging statements yet leave them physically present in the source code in case they might need the statements later. Inserting the line ⌗define NDEBUG turns off assertion checking without having to remove the assertions.

As useful as the assert function is, it has two limitations. First, the argument to the function must be expressed as a C++ logical expression. We can turn the comment

```
//   0.0 <= deptSales <= 25000.0
```

into an executable assertion with the statement

```
assert(0.0 <= deptSales && deptSales <= 25000.0);
```

But there is no easy way to turn the comment

```
//   For each department, the file contains a department ID,
//   number of days, and one sales figure for each day
```

into a C++ logical expression.

The second limitation is that the assert function is appropriate only for testing a program that is under development. A production program (one that has been completed and released to the public) must be robust and must furnish helpful error messages to the user of the program. You can imagine how baffled a user would be if the program suddenly quit and displayed an error message such as

```
Assertion failed: sysRes <= resCount, file newproj.cpp, line 298
```

Despite these limitations, you should consider using the assert function as a regular tool for testing and debugging your programs.

Testing and Debugging Hints

1. Follow documentation guidelines carefully when writing functions (see Appendix F). As your programs become more complex and therefore prone to errors, it

becomes increasingly important to adhere to documentation and formatting standards.

2. Provide a function prototype near the top of your program for each function you've written. Make sure that the prototype and its corresponding function heading are an *exact* match (except for the absence of parameter names in the prototype).

3. Be sure to put a semicolon at the end of a function prototype. But do *not* put a semicolon at the end of the function heading in a function definition. Because function prototypes look so much like function headings, it's common to get one of them wrong.

4. Be sure the parameter list gives the data type of each parameter.

5. Use value parameters unless a result is to be returned through a parameter. Reference parameters can change the contents of the caller's argument; value parameters cannot.

6. In a parameter list, be sure the data type of each reference parameter ends with an ampersand (&). Without the ampersand, the parameter is a value parameter.

7. Make sure that the argument list of every function call matches the parameter list in number and order of items, and be very careful with their data types. The compiler will trap any mismatch in the number of arguments. But if there is a mismatch in data types, there may be no compile-time error. Specifically, with a pass by value, a type mismatch can lead to implicit type coercion rather than a compile-time error.

8. Remember that an argument matching a reference parameter *must* be a variable, whereas an argument matching a value parameter can be any expression that supplies a value of the same data type (except as noted in Hint 7).

Summary

C++ allows us to write programs in modules expressed as functions. The structure of a program, therefore, can parallel its functional decomposition even when the program is complicated. To make your `main` function look exactly like level 0 of your functional decomposition, simply write each lower-level module as a function. The `main` function then executes these other functions in logical sequence.

Functions communicate by means of two lists: the parameter list (which specifies the data type of each identifier) in the function heading, and the argument list in the calling code. The items in these lists must agree in number and position, and they should agree in data type.

Part of the functional decomposition process involves determining what data must be received by a lower-level module and what information must be returned from it. The names of these data items, together with the precondition and postcondition of a module, define its interface. The names of the data items become the parameter list, and the module name becomes the name of the function. With void functions, a call to the function is accomplished by writing the function's name as a statement, enclosing the appropriate arguments in parentheses.

C++ has two kinds of parameters: reference and value. Reference parameters have data types ending in & in the parameter list, whereas value parameters do not. Parameters that return values from a function must be reference parameters. All others should be value parameters. This minimizes the risk of errors, because only a copy of the value of an argument is passed to a value parameter, and thus the argument is protected from change.

In addition to the variables declared in its parameter list, a function may have local variables declared within it. These variables are accessible only within the block in which they are declared. Local variables must be initialized each time the function containing them is called because their values are destroyed when the function returns.

You may call functions from more than one place in a program. The positional matching mechanism allows the use of different variables as arguments to the same function. Multiple calls to a function, from different places and with different arguments, can simplify greatly the coding of many complex programs.

Quick Check

1. If a design has one level 0 module and three level 1 modules, how many C++ functions is the program likely to have? (pp. 236–239)
2. Does a C++ function have to be declared before it can be used in a function call? (p. 239)
3. What is the difference between a function declaration and a function definition in C++? (pp. 242–244)
4. Given the function heading

```
void QuickCheck( int    size,
                 float& length,
                 char   initial )
```

indicate which parameters are value parameters and which are reference parameters. (p. 247)
5. a. What would a call to the `QuickCheck` function look like if the arguments were the variables `radius` (a `float`), `number` (an `int`), and `letter` (a `char`)? (pp. 241–242)
   b. How is the matchup between these arguments and the parameters made? What information is actually passed from the calling code to the `QuickCheck` function, given these arguments? (pp. 247–250)
   c. Which of these arguments is (are) protected from being changed by the `QuickCheck` function? (pp. 247–250)
6. Where in a function are local variables declared, and what are their initial values equal to? (pp. 244–245)
7. You are designing a program and you need a void function that reads any number of floating-point values and returns their average. The number of values to be read is in an integer variable named `dataPoints`, declared in the calling code.
   a. How many parameters should there be in the parameter list, and what should their data type(s) be? (pp. 250–252)

b. Which parameter(s) should be passed by reference and which should be passed by value? (pp. 250–256)

8. Describe one way in which you can use a function to simplify the coding of an algorithm. (p. 241)

Answers   1. Four (including `main`) 2. Yes 3. A definition is a declaration that includes the function body. 4. `length` is a reference parameter; `size` and `initial` are value parameters. 5. a. `QuickCheck(number, radius, letter)`; b. The matchup is done on the basis of the variables' positions in each list. Copies of the values of `size` and `initial` are passed to the function; the location (memory address) of `length` is passed to the function. c. `size` and `initial` are protected from change because only copies of their values are sent to the function. 6. In the block that forms the body of the function. Their initial values are undefined. 7. a. There should be two parameters: an `int` containing the number of values to be read and a `float` containing the computed average. b. The `int` should be a value parameter; the `float` should be a reference parameter. 8. The coding may be simplified if the function is called from more than one place in the program.

Exam Preparation Exercises

1. Define the following terms:

   function call   parameter
   argument list   argument
   parameterless function   local variable

2. Identify the following items in the program fragment shown below.

   function prototype   function definition
   function heading   parameters
   arguments   function call
   local variables   function body

```
void Test( int, int, int );

int main()
{
    int a;
    int b;
    int c;
    ⋮
    Test(a, c, b);
    Test(b, a, c);
    ⋮
}
```

(continued on next page)

```
void Test( int d,
           int e,
           int f )
{
    int g;
    int h;
    ⋮
}
```

3. For the program in Exercise 2, fill in the blanks below with variable names to show the matching that takes place between the arguments and parameters in each of the two calls to the Test function.

First Call to Test		Second Call to Test	
Parameter	Argument	Parameter	Argument
1. _____	_____	1. _____	_____
2. _____	_____	2. _____	_____
3. _____	_____	3. _____	_____

4. What is the output of the following program?

```
#include <iostream>

using namespace std;

void Print( int, int );

int main()
{
    int n;

    n = 3;
    Print(5, n);
    Print(n, n);
    Print(n * n, 12);
    return 0;
}

void Print( int a,
            int b )
{
    int c;

    c = 2 * a + b;
    cout << a << ' ' << b << ' ' << c << endl;
}
```

5. Using a reference parameter (passing by reference), the called function can obtain the initial value of an argument as well as change the value of the argument. (True or False?)

6. Using a value parameter, the value of a variable can be passed to a function and used for computation there without any modification of the caller's argument. (True or False?)

7. Given the declarations

```
const int ANGLE = 90;

char letter;
int  number;
```

indicate whether each of the following arguments would be valid using a pass by value, a pass by reference, or both.

a. `letter`
b. `ANGLE`
c. `number`
d. `number + 3`
e. `23`
f. `ANGLE * number`
g. `abs(number)`

8. A variable named `widgets` is stored in memory location 13571. When the statements

```
widgets = 23;
Drop(widgets);
```

are executed, what information is passed to the parameter in the `Drop` function? (Assume the parameter is a reference parameter.)

9. Assume that, in Exercise 8, the parameter within the `Drop` function is named `clunkers`. After the function body performs the assignment

```
clunkers = 77;
```

what is the value in `widgets`? in `clunkers`?

10. Using the data values

```
3 2 4
```

show what is printed by the following program.

```
#include <iostream>

using namespace std;

void Test( int&, int&, int& );
```

(continued on next page)

```
int main()
{
    int a;
    int b;
    int c;

    Test(a, b, c);
    b = b + 10;
    cout << "The answers are " << b << ' ' << c << ' ' << a;
    return 0;
}

void Test( int& z,
           int& x,
           int& a )
{
    cin >> z >> x >> a;
    a = z * x + a;
}
```

11. The program below has a function named `Change`. Fill in the values of all variables before and after the function is called. Then fill in the values of all variables after the return to the `main` function. (If any value is undefined, write *U* instead of a number.)

```
#include <iostream>

using namespace std;

void Change( int, int& );

int main()
{
    int a;
    int b;

    a = 10;
    b = 7;
    Change(a, b);
    cout << a << ' ' << b << endl;
    return 0;
}

void Change( int  x,
             int& y )
```

```
{
    int b;

    b = x;
    y = y + b;
    x = y;
}
```

Variables in `main` just before `Change` is called:

a _____

b _____

Variables in `Change` at the moment control enters the function:

x _____

y _____

b _____

Variables in `main` after return from `Change`:

a _____

b _____

12. Show the output of the following program.

```
#include <iostream>

using namespace std;

void Test( int&, int );

int main()
{
    int d;
    int e;

    d = 12;
    e = 14;
    Test(d, e);
    cout << "In the main function after the first call, "
        << "the variables equal " << d << ' ' << e << endl;
    d = 15;
    e = 18;
    Test(e, d);
    cout << "In the main function after the second call, "
        << "the variables equal " << d << ' ' << e << endl;
    return 0;
}
```

(continued on next page)

```
void Test( int& s,
           int   t )
{
    s = 3;
    s = s + 2;
    t = 4 * s;
    cout << "In function Test, the variables equal "
         << s << ' ' << t << endl;
}
```

13. Number the marked statements in the following program to show the order in which they are executed (the logical order of execution).

```
#include <iostream>

using namespace std;

void DoThis( int&, int& );

int main()
{
    int number1;
    int number2;

_____  cout << "Exercise ";
_____  DoThis(number1, number2);
_____  cout << number1 << ' ' << number2 << endl;
            return 0;
}

void DoThis( int& value1,
             int& value2 )
{
    int value3;

_____  cin >> value3 >> value1;
_____  value2 = value1 + 10;
}
```

14. If the program in Exercise 13 were run with the data values 10 and 15, what would be the values of the following variables just before execution of the Return statement in the main function?

number1 _____ number2 _____ value3 _____

Programming Warm-up Exercises

1. Write the function heading for a void function named `PrintMax` that accepts a pair of integers and prints out the greater of the two. Document the data flow of each parameter with `/* in */`, `/* out */`, or `/* inout */`.

2. Write the heading for a void function that corresponds to the following list.

   Rocket Simulation Module

Incoming	thrust (floating point)
Incoming/Outgoing	weight (floating point)
Incoming	timeStep (integer)
Incoming	totalTime (integer)
Outgoing	velocity (floating point)
Outgoing	outOfFuel (Boolean)

3. Write a void function that reads in a specified number of `float` values and returns their average. A call to this function might look like

   ```
   GetMeanOf(5, mean);
   ```

   where the first argument specifies the number of values to be read, and the second argument contains the result. Document the data flow of each parameter with `/* in */`, `/* out */`, or `/* inout */`.

4. Given the function heading

   ```
   void Halve( /* inout */ int& firstNumber,
               /* inout */ int& secondNumber )
   ```

   write the body of the function so that when it returns, the original values in `firstNumber` and `secondNumber` are halved.

5. Add comments to the preceding `Halve` function that state the function precondition and postcondition.

6. a. Write a single void function to replace the repeated pattern of statements you identified in Exam Preparation Exercise 16 of Chapter 3. Document the data flow of the parameters with `/* in */`, `/* out */`, or `/* inout */`. Include comments giving the function precondition and postcondition.

   b. Show the function calls with arguments.

7. a. Write a void function that reads in data values of type `int` (`heartRate`) until a normal heart rate (from 60 through 80) is read or EOF occurs. The function has one parameter, named `normal`, that contains `true` if a normal heart rate was read or `false` if EOF occurred.

   b. Write a statement that invokes your function. You may use the same variable name for the argument and the parameter.

8. Consider the following function definition.

   ```
   void Rotate( /* inout */ int& firstValue,
                /* inout */ int& secondValue,
                /* inout */ int& thirdValue )
   ```

```
{
    int temp;

    temp = firstValue;
    firstValue = secondValue;
    secondValue = thirdValue;
    thirdValue = temp;
}
```

   a. Add comments to the function that tell a reader what the function does and what is the purpose of each parameter and local variable.

   b. Write a program that reads three values into variables, echo prints them, calls the `Rotate` function with the three variables as arguments, and then prints the arguments after the function returns.

9. Modify the function in Exercise 8 to perform the same sort of operation on four values. Modify the program you wrote for part b of Exercise 8 to work with the new version of this function.

10. Write a void function named `CountUpper` that counts the number of uppercase letters on one line of input. The function should return this number to the calling code in a parameter named `upCount`.

11. Write a void function named `AddTime` that has three parameters: `hours`, `minutes`, and `elapsedTime`. `elapsedTime` is an integer number of minutes to be added to the starting time passed in through `hours` and `minutes`. The resulting new time is returned through `hours` and `minutes`. Here is an example, assuming that the arguments are also named `hours`, `minutes`, and `elapsedTime`:

Before Call to `AddTime`	After Call to `AddTime`
hours = 12	hours = 16
minutes = 44	minutes = 2
elapsedTime = 198	elapsedTime = 198

12. Write a void function named `GetNonBlank` that returns the first nonblank character it encounters in the standard input stream. In your function, use the `cin.get` function to read each character. (This `GetNonBlank` function is just for practice. It's unnecessary because you could use the `>>` operator, which skips leading blanks, to accomplish the same result.)

13. Write a void function named `SkipToBlank` that skips all characters in the standard input stream until a blank is encountered. In your function, use the `cin.get` function to read each character. (This function is just for practice. There's already a library function, `cin.ignore`, that allows you to do the same thing.)

14. Modify the function in Exercise 13 so that it returns a count of the number of characters that were skipped.

15. Write a separate function for the Graph program that creates a bar of asterisks in a `string` object, given a sales figure.

16. Rewrite the existing `PrintData` function so that it calls the function you wrote for Exercise 15.

Programming Problems

1. Using functions, rewrite the program developed for Programming Problem 3 in Chapter 6. The program is to determine the number of words encountered in the input stream. For the sake of simplicity, we define a word to be any sequence of characters except whitespace characters (such as blanks and newlines). Words can be separated by any number of whitespace characters. A word can be any length, from a single character to an entire line of characters. If you are writing the program to read data from a file, then it should echo print the input. For an interactive implementation, you do not need to echo print for this program.

   For example, for the following data, the program would indicate that 26 words were entered.

   ```
   This isn't exactly an example of g00d english, but it
   does demonstrate that a w0rd is just a se@uence of
   characters            with0u+ any blank$.   #####   .......
   ```

   As with Programming Problem 3 in Chapter 6, solve this problem with two different programs:

   a. Use a `string` object into which you input each word as a string.

   b. Assume the `string` class does not exist, and input the data one character at a time. (*Hint:* Consider turning the `SkipToBlank` function of Programming Warm-up Exercise 13 into a `SkipToWhitespace` function.)

   Now that your programs are becoming more complex, it is even more important for you to use proper indentation and style, meaningful identifiers, and appropriate comments.

2. Write a C++ program that reads characters representing binary (base-2) numbers from a data file and translates them to decimal (base-10) numbers. The binary and decimal numbers should be output in two columns with appropriate headings. Here is a sample of the output:

   ```
   Binary Number   Decimal Equivalent
       1                   1
      10                   2
      11                   3
   10000                  16
   10101                  21
   ```

   There is only one binary number per input line, but an arbitrary number of blanks can precede the number. The program must read the binary numbers one character at a time. As each character is read, the program multiplies the total decimal value by 2 and adds either 1 or 0, depending on the input character. The program should check for bad data; if it encounters anything except a 0 or a 1, it should output the message "Bad digit on input."

As always, use appropriate comments, proper documentation and coding style, and meaningful identifiers throughout this program. You must decide which of your design modules should be coded as functions to make the program easier to understand.

3. Develop a functional decomposition and write a C++ program to print a calendar for one year, given the year and the day of the week that January 1 falls on. It may help to think of this task as printing 12 calendars, one for each month, given the day of the week on which a month starts and the number of days in the month. Each successive month starts on the day of the week that follows the last day of the preceding month. Days of the week should be numbered 0 through 6 for Sunday through Saturday. Years that are divisible by 4 are leap years. (Determining leap years actually is more complicated than this, but for this program it will suffice.) Here is a sample run for an interactive program:

```
What year do you want a calendar for?
2002
What day of the week does January 1 fall on?
(Enter 0 for Sunday, 1 for Monday, etc.)
2

            2002

          January
    S   M   T   W   T   F   S
   --------------------
            1   2   3   4   5
    6   7   8   9  10  11  12
   13  14  15  16  17  18  19
   20  21  22  23  24  25  26
   27  28  29  30  31

          February
    S   M   T   W   T   F   S
   --------------------
                            1   2
    3   4   5   6   7   8   9
   10  11  12  13  14  15  16
   17  18  19  20  21  22  23
   24  25  26  27  28

            .

            .

            .
```

```
        December
  S   M   T   W   T   F   S
  - - - - - - - - - - - - - - - - - - - -
  1   2   3   4   5   6   7
  8   9  10  11  12  13  14
 15  16  17  18  19  20  21
 22  23  24  25  26  27  28
 29  30  31
```

When writing your program, be sure to use proper indentation and style, meaningful identifiers, and appropriate comments.

4. In this problem, you are to design and implement a Roman numeral calculator. The subtractive Roman numeral notation commonly in use today (such as IV, meaning 4) was used only rarely during the time of the Roman Republic and Empire. For ease of calculation, the Romans most frequently used a purely additive notation in which a number was simply the sum of its digits (4 equals IIII, in this notation). Each number starts with the digit of highest value and ends with the digit of smallest value. This is the notation we use in this problem.

Your program inputs two Roman numbers and an arithmetic operator and prints out the result of the operation, also as a Roman number. The values of the Roman digits are as follows:

I	1
V	5
X	10
L	50
C	100
D	500
M	1000

Thus, the number MDCCCCLXXXXVIIII represents 1999. The arithmetic operators that your program should recognize in the input are +, – , *, and /. These should perform the C++ operations of integer addition, subtraction, multiplication, and division.

One way of approaching this problem is to convert the Roman numbers into decimal integers, perform the required operation, and then convert the result back into a Roman number for printing. The following is a sample run of the program:

```
Enter the first number:
MCCXXVI
The first number is 1226
Enter the second number:
LXVIIII
```

```
The second number is 69
Enter the desired arithmetic operation:
+
The sum of MCCXXVI and LXVIIII is MCCLXXXXV (1295)
```

Your program should use proper style and indentation, appropriate comments, and meaningful identifiers. It also should check for errors in the input, such as illegal digits or arithmetic operators, and take appropriate actions when these are found. The program also might check to ensure that the numbers are in purely additive form—that is, digits are followed only by digits of the same or lower value.

Scope, Lifetime, and More on Functions

- To be able to do the following tasks, given a C++ program composed of several functions:

  - Determine whether a variable is being referenced globally.

  - Determine which variables are local variables.

  - Determine which variables are accessible within a given block.

- To be able to determine the lifetime of each variable in a program.

- To understand and be able to avoid unwanted side effects.

- To know when to use a value-returning function.

- To be able to design and code a value-returning function for a specific task.

- To be able to invoke a value-returning function properly.

As programs get larger and more complicated, the number of identifiers in a program increases. Some of these identifiers we declare inside blocks. Other identifiers—function names, for example—we declare outside of any block. This chapter examines the C++ rules by which a function may access identifiers that are declared outside its own block. Using these rules, we return to the discussion of interface design that we began in Chapter 7.

Finally, we look at the second kind of subprogram provided by C++: the *value-returning function*. A value-returning function returns a single result—the function value—to the expression from which it was called. In this chapter, you learn how to write such functions.

8.1 Scope of Identifiers

As we saw in Chapter 7, local variables are those declared inside a block, such as the body of a function. Recall that local variables cannot be accessed outside the block that contains them. The same access rule applies to named constants: Local constants may be accessed only in the block in which they are declared.

Any block, not only a function body, can contain variable and constant declarations. For example, this If statement contains a block that declares a local variable n:

```
if (alpha > 3)
{
    int n;

    cin >> n;
    beta = beta + n;
}
```

As a local variable, n cannot be accessed by any statement outside the block.

Scope The region of program code where it is legal to reference (use) an identifier.

If we listed all the places from which an identifier could be accessed legally, we would describe that identifier's *scope of visibility* or *scope of access*, often just called its **scope**.

C++ defines several categories of scope for any identifier. We begin by describing three of these categories.

1. *Class scope.* This term refers to the data type called a *class*, which we introduced briefly in Chapter 4. We postpone a detailed discussion of class scope until Chapter 11.

2. *Local scope.* The scope of an identifier declared inside a block extends from the point of declaration to the end of that block. Also, the scope of a function parameter (formal parameter) extends from the point of declaration to the end of the block that is the body of the function.

3. *Global scope.* The scope of an identifier declared outside all functions and classes extends from the point of declaration to the end of the entire file containing the program code.

C++ function names have global scope. (There is an exception to this rule, which we discuss in Chapter 11 when we examine C++ classes.) Once a function name has been declared, the function can be invoked by any other function in the rest of the program. In C++, there is no such thing as a local function—that is, you cannot nest a function definition inside another function definition.

Global variables and constants are those declared outside all functions. When a function declares a local identifier with the same name as a global identifier, the local identifier takes precedence within the function. This principle is called **name precedence** or **name hiding**.

> **Name precedence**   The precedence that a local identifier in a function has over a global identifier with the same name in any references that the function makes to that identifier; also called *name hiding*.

Here's an example that uses both local and global declarations:

```cpp
#include <iostream>

using namespace std;

void SomeFunc( float );

const int a = 17;    // A global constant
int b;               // A global variable
int c;               // Another global variable

int main()
{
    b = 4;                  // Assignment to global b
    c = 6;                  // Assignment to global c
    SomeFunc(42.8);
    return 0;
}

void SomeFunc( float c )    // Prevents access to global c
{
    float b;                // Prevents access to global b

    b = 2.3;                // Assignment to local b
    cout << "a = " << a;    // Output global a (17)
    cout << " b = " << b;   // Output local b (2.3)
    cout << " c = " << c;   // Output local c (42.8)
}
```

In this example, function SomeFunc accesses global constant a but declares its own local variable b and parameter c. Thus, the output would be

```
a = 17 b = 2.3 c = 42.8
```

Local variable b takes precedence over global variable b, effectively hiding global b from the statements in function SomeFunc. Parameter c also blocks access to global variable c from within the function. Function parameters act just like local variables in this respect; that is, parameters have local scope.

Scope Rules

When you write C++ programs, you rarely declare global variables. There are negative aspects to using global variables, which we discuss later. But when a situation crops up in which you have a compelling need for global variables, it pays to know how C++ handles these declarations. The rules for accessing identifiers that aren't declared locally are called **scope rules**.

In addition to local and global access, the C++ scope rules define what happens when blocks are nested within other blocks. Anything declared in a block that contains a nested block is **nonlocal** to the inner block. (Global identifiers are nonlocal with respect to all blocks in the program.) If a block accesses any identifier declared outside its own block, it is a *nonlocal access*.

Scope rules The rules that determine where in the program an identifier may be accessed, given the point where that identifier is declared.

Nonlocal identifier With respect to a given block, any identifier declared outside that block.

Here are the detailed scope rules, excluding class scope and certain language features we have not yet discussed:

1. A function name has global scope. Function definitions cannot be nested within function definitions.
2. The scope of a function parameter is identical to the scope of a local variable declared in the outermost block of the function body.
3. The scope of a global variable or constant extends from its declaration to the end of the file, except as noted in rule 5.
4. The scope of a local variable or constant extends from its declaration to the end of the block in which it is declared. This scope includes any nested blocks, except as noted in rule 5.
5. The scope of an identifier does not include any nested block that contains a locally declared identifier with the same name (local identifiers have name precedence).

Here is a sample program that demonstrates C++ scope rules. To simplify the example, only the declarations and headings are spelled out. Note how the While-loop body labeled Block3, located within function `Block2`, contains its own local variable declarations.

```
// ScopeRules program

#include <iostream>

using namespace std;

void Block1( int, char& );
void Block2();
```

```
int  a1;           // One global variable
char a2;           // Another global variable

int main()
{
    ⋮
}

//*****************************************************************

void Block1( int    a1,          // Prevents access to global a1
             char& b2 )          // Has same scope as c1 and d2
{
    int c1;        // A variable local to Block1
    int d2;        // Another variable local to Block1
      ⋮
}

//*****************************************************************

void Block2()
{
    int a1;        // Prevents access to global a1
    int b2;        // Local to Block2; no conflict with b2 in Block1

    while (...)
    {              // Block3
        int c1;    // Local to Block3; no conflict with c1 in Block1
        int b2;    // Prevents nonlocal access to b2 in Block2; no
                   //  conflict with b2 in Block1
          ⋮
    }
}
```

Let's look at the ScopeRules program in terms of the blocks it defines and see just what these rules mean. Figure 8-1 shows the headings and declarations in the ScopeRules program with the scopes of visibility indicated by boxes.

Anything inside a box can refer to anything in a larger surrounding box, but outside-in references aren't allowed. Thus, a statement in Block3 could access any identifier declared in Block2 or any global variable. A statement in Block3 could not access identifiers declared in Block1 because it would have to enter the Block1 box from outside.

Notice that the parameters for a function are inside the function's box, but the function name itself is outside. If the name of the function were inside the box, no function could call another function. This demonstrates merely that function names are globally accessible.

Imagine the boxes in Figure 8-1 as rooms with walls made of two-way mirrors, with the reflective side facing out and the see-through side facing in. If you stood in the

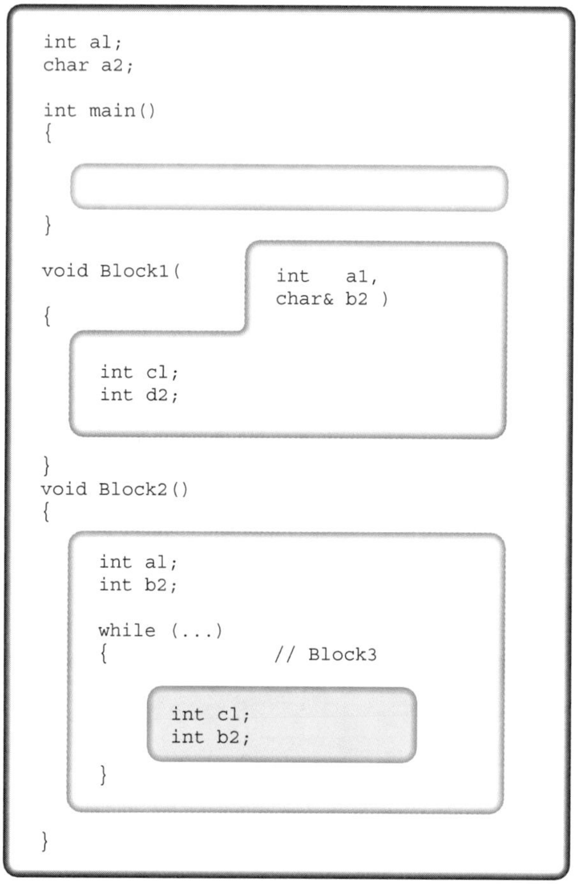

```
int a1;
char a2;

int main()
{


}
void Block1(              int    a1,
                         char& b2 )
       {
             int c1;
             int d2;



       }
void Block2()
{
             int a1;
             int b2;

             while (...)
             {                      // Block3

                     int c1;
                     int b2;

             }

}
```

Figure 8-1 *Scope Diagram for ScopeRules Program*

room for Block3, you would be able to see out through all the surrounding rooms to the declarations of the global variables (and anything between). You would not be able to see into any other rooms (such as Block1), however, because their mirrored outer surfaces would block your view. Because of this analogy, the term *visible* is often used in describing a scope of access. For example, variable a2 is visible throughout the program, meaning that it can be accessed from anywhere in the program.

Figure 8-1 does not tell the whole story; it represents only scope rules 1 through 4. We also must keep rule 5 in mind. Variable a1 is declared in three different places in the ScopeRules program. Because of name precedence, Block2 and Block3 access the a1 declared in Block2 rather than the global a1. Similarly, the scope of the variable b2 declared in Block2 does *not* include the "hole" created by Block3, because Block3 declares its own variable b2.

Name precedence is implemented by the compiler as follows. When an expression refers to an identifier, the compiler first checks the local declarations. If the identifier isn't local, the compiler works its way outward through each level of nesting until it finds an identifier with the same name. There it stops. If there is an identifier with the same name declared at a level even further out, it is never reached. If the compiler reaches the global declarations (including identifiers inserted by #include directives) and still can't find the identifier, an error message such as "UNDECLARED IDENTIFIER" is issued.

Such a message most likely indicates a misspelling or an incorrect capitalization, or it could mean that the identifier was not declared before the reference to it or was not declared at all. It may also indicate, however, that the blocks are nested so that the identifier's scope doesn't include the reference.

Variable Declarations and Definitions

In Chapter 7, you learned that C++ terminology distinguishes between a function declaration and a function definition. A function prototype is a declaration only—that is, it doesn't cause memory space to be reserved for the function. In contrast, a function declaration that includes the body is called a function definition. The compiler reserves memory for the instructions in the function body.

C++ applies the same terminology to variable declarations. A variable declaration becomes a variable definition if it also reserves memory for the variable. All of the variable declarations we have used from the beginning have been variable definitions. What would a variable declaration look like if it were *not* also a definition?

In the previous chapter, we talked about the concept of a multifile program, a program that physically occupies several files containing individual pieces of the program. C++ has a reserved word extern that lets you reference a global variable located in another file. A "normal" declaration such as

```
int someInt;
```

causes the compiler to reserve a memory location for someInt. On the other hand, the declaration

```
extern int someInt;
```

is an *external declaration*. It states that someInt is a global variable located in another file and that no storage should be reserved for it here. Header files such as iostream contain external declarations so that user programs can access important variables defined in system files. For example, iostream includes declarations like these:

```
extern istream cin;
extern ostream cout;
```

These declarations allow you to reference `cin` and `cout` as global variables in your program, but the variable definitions are located in another file supplied by the C++ system.

In C++ terminology, the statement

```
extern int someInt;
```

is a declaration but not a definition of `someInt`. It associates a variable name with a data type so that the compiler can perform type checking. But the statement

```
int someInt;
```

is both a declaration and a definition of `someInt`. It is a definition because it reserves memory for `someInt`. In C++, you can declare a variable or a function many times, but there can be only one definition.

Except in situations in which it's important to distinguish between declarations and definitions of variables, we'll continue to use the more general phrase *variable declaration* instead of the more specific *variable definition*.

Namespaces

For some time, we have been including the following `using` directive in our programs:

```
using namespace std;
```

What exactly is a namespace? As a general concept, *namespace* is another word for *scope*. However, as a specific C++ language feature, a namespace is a mechanism by which the programmer can create a named scope. For example, the standard header file `cstdlib` contains function prototypes for several library functions, one of which is the absolute value function, `abs`. The declarations are contained within a *namespace definition* as follows:

```
// In header file cstdlib:

namespace std
{
    ⋮
    int abs( int );
    ⋮
}
```

A namespace definition consists of the word `namespace`, then an identifier of the programmer's choice, and then the *namespace body* between braces. Identifiers declared within the namespace body are said to have *namespace scope*. Such identifiers cannot be accessed outside the body except by using one of three methods.

The first method, introduced in Chapter 2, is to use a qualified name: the name of the namespace, followed by the scope resolution operator (::), followed by the desired identifier. Here is an example:

```
#include <cstdlib>

int main()
{
    int alpha;
    int beta;
      ⋮
    alpha = std::abs(beta);    // A qualified name
      ⋮
}
```

The general idea is to inform the compiler that we are referring to the abs declared in the std namespace, not some other abs (such as a global function named abs that we might have written ourselves).

The second method is to use a statement called a *using declaration* as follows:

```
#include <cstdlib>

int main()
{
    int alpha;
    int beta;
    using std::abs;    // A using declaration
      ⋮
    alpha = abs(beta);
      ⋮
}
```

This using declaration allows the identifier abs to be used throughout the body of main as a synonym for the longer std::abs.

The third method—one with which we are familiar—is to use a using directive (not to be confused with a using declaration).

```
#include <cstdlib>

int main()
{
    int alpha;
    int beta;
    using namespace std;    // A using directive
      ⋮
    alpha = abs(beta);
      ⋮
}
```

With a `using` directive, *all* identifiers from the specified namespace are accessible, but only in the scope in which the `using` directive appears. In the last example, the `using` directive is in local scope (it's within a block), so identifiers from the `std` namespace are accessible only within `main`. On the other hand, if we put the `using` directive outside all functions (as we have been doing), like this:

```
#include <cstdlib>

using namespace std;

int main()
{
    ⋮
}
```

then the `using` directive is in global scope; consequently, identifiers from the `std` namespace are accessible globally.

Placing a `using` directive in global scope can be a convenience. For example, all of the functions we write can refer to identifiers such as `abs`, `cin`, and `cout` without our having to insert a `using` directive locally in each function. However, global `using` directives are considered a bad idea when creating large, multifile programs. Programmers often make use of several libraries, not just the C++ standard library, when developing complex software. Two or more libraries may, just by coincidence, use the same identifier for completely different purposes. If global `using` directives are employed, *name clashes* (multiple definitions of the same identifier) can occur because all the identifiers have been brought into global scope. (C++ programmers refer to this as "polluting the global namespace.") Over the next several chapters, we continue to use global `using` directives for the `std` namespace because our programs are relatively small and therefore name clashes aren't likely.

Given the concept of namespace scope, we refine our description of C++ scope categories as follows.

1. *Class scope.* This term refers to the data type called a *class*. We postpone a detailed discussion of class scope until Chapter 11.

2. *Local scope.* The scope of an identifier declared inside a block extends from the point of declaration to the end of that block. Also, the scope of a function parameter (formal parameter) extends from the point of declaration to the end of the block that is the body of the function.

3. *Namespace scope.* The scope of an identifier declared in a namespace definition extends from the point of declaration to the end of the namespace body, *and* its scope includes the scope of a `using` directive specifying that namespace.

4. *Global (or global namespace) scope.* The scope of an identifier declared outside all namespaces, functions, and classes extends from the point of declaration to the end of the entire file containing the program code.

Note that these are general descriptions of scope categories and not scope rules. The descriptions do not account for name hiding (the redefinition of an identifier within a nested block).

8.2 Lifetime of a Variable

A concept related to but separate from the scope of a variable is its **lifetime**—the period of time during program execution when an identifier actually has memory allocated to it.

Lifetime The period of time during program execution when an identifier has memory allocated to it.

We have said that storage for local variables is created (allocated) at the moment control enters a function. Then the variables are "alive" while the function is executing, and finally the storage is deallocated when the function exits. In contrast, the lifetime of a global variable is the same as the lifetime of the entire program. Memory is allocated only once, when the program begins executing, and is deallocated only when the entire program terminates. Observe that scope is a *compile-time* issue, but lifetime is a *run-time* issue.

In C++, an **automatic variable** is one whose storage is allocated at block entry and deallocated at block exit. A **static variable** is one whose storage remains allocated for the duration of the entire program. All global variables are static variables. By default, variables declared within a block are automatic variables. However, you can use the reserved word `static` when you declare a local variable. If you do so, the variable is a static variable and its lifetime persists from function call to function call:

Automatic variable A variable for which memory is allocated and deallocated when control enters and exits the block in which it is declared.

Static variable A variable for which memory remains allocated throughout the execution of the entire program.

```
void SomeFunc()
{
    float   someFloat;      // Destroyed when function exits
    static int someInt;     // Retains its value from call to call
      ⋮
}
```

It is usually better to declare a local variable as `static` than to use a global variable. Like a global variable, its memory remains allocated throughout the lifetime of the entire program. But unlike a global variable, its local scope prevents other functions in the program from tinkering with it.

Initializations in Declarations

One of the most common things we do in programs is first declare a variable and then, in a separate statement, assign an initial value to the variable. Here's a typical example:

```
int sum;

sum = 0;
```

C++ allows you to combine these two statements into one. The result is known as an *initialization in a declaration*. Here we initialize sum in its declaration:

```
int sum = 0;
```

In a declaration, the expression that specifies the initial value is called an *initializer*. Above, the initializer is the constant 0. Implicit type coercion takes place if the data type of the initializer is different from the data type of the variable.

An automatic variable is initialized to the specified value each time control enters the block:

```
void SomeFunc( int someParam )
{
    int i = 0;                      // Initialized each time
    int n = 2 * someParam + 3;      // Initialized each time
      ⋮
}
```

In contrast, initialization of a static variable (either a global variable or a local variable explicitly declared static) occurs only once, the first time control reaches its declaration. Here's an example in which two local static variables are initialized only once (the first time the function is called):

```
void AnotherFunc( int param )
{
    static char ch = 'A';        // Initialized only once
    static int  m  = param + 1;  // Initialized only once
      ⋮
}
```

Although an initialization gives a variable an initial value, it is perfectly acceptable to reassign it another value during program execution.

There are differing opinions about initializing a variable in its declaration. Some programmers never do it, preferring to keep an initialization close to the executable statements that depend on that variable. For example,

```
int loopCount;
    ⋮
loopCount = 1;
while (loopCount <= 20)
{
    ⋮
}
```

If this loop were also nested inside another loop, then initialization of loopCount *must* be done just before the while. Otherwise, loopCount would not be reinitialized on subsequent iterations of the outer loop. In this situation, relying only on initialization in the declaration is a common error.

Other programmers maintain that a frequent cause of program errors is forgetting to initialize variables before using their contents; initializing each variable in its declaration eliminates these errors. Most programmers seem to take a position somewhere between these two extremes.

8.3 Interface Design

We return now to the issue of interface design, which we first discussed in Chapter 7. Recall that the data flow through a function interface can take three forms: incoming only, outgoing only, and incoming/outgoing. Any item that can be classified as purely incoming should be coded as a value parameter. Items in the remaining two categories (outgoing and incoming/outgoing) must be reference parameters; the only way the function can deposit results into the caller's arguments is to have the addresses of those arguments. For emphasis, we repeat the following table from Chapter 7.

Data Flow for a Parameter	Argument-Passing Mechanism
Incoming	Pass by value
Outgoing	Pass by reference
Incoming/outgoing	Pass by reference

As we said in the last chapter, there are exceptions to the guidelines in this table. C++ requires that I/O stream objects be passed by reference because of the way streams and files are implemented. We encounter another exception in Chapter 12.

Sometimes it is tempting to skip the interface design step when writing a function, letting it communicate with other functions by referencing global variables. Don't! Without the interface design step, you would actually be creating a poorly structured and undocumented interface. Except in well-justified circumstances, the use of global variables is a poor programming practice that can lead to program errors. These errors are extremely hard to locate and usually take the form of unwanted side effects.

Side Effects

Suppose you made a call to the `sqrt` library function in your program:

```
y = sqrt(x);
```

You expect the call to `sqrt` to do one thing only: compute the square root of the variable `x`. You'd be surprised if `sqrt` also changed the value of your variable `x` because `sqrt`, by definition, does not make such changes. This would be an example of an unexpected and unwanted side effect.

> **Side effect** Any effect of one function on another that is not a part of the explicitly defined interface between them.

Side effects are sometimes caused by a combination of reference parameters and careless coding in a function. Perhaps an assignment statement in the function stores a temporary result into one of the reference parameters, accidentally changing the value of an argument back in the calling code. As we mentioned before, using value parameters avoids this type of side effect by preventing the change from reaching the argument.

Side effects also can occur when a function accesses a global variable. An error in the function might cause the value of a global variable to be changed in an unexpected way, causing an error in other functions that access that variable.

The symptoms of a side-effect error are misleading because the trouble shows up in one part of the program when it really is caused by something in another part. To avoid such errors, the only external effect that a function should have is to transfer information through the well-structured interface of the parameter list (see Figure 8-2). If functions access nonlocal variables *only* through their parameter lists, and if all incoming-only parameters are value parameters, then each function is essentially isolated from other parts of the program and side effects cannot occur.

When a function is free of side effects, we can treat it as an independent module and reuse it in other programs. It is hazardous or impossible to reuse functions with side effects.

Global Constants

Contrary to what you might think, it is acceptable to reference named constants globally. Because the values of global constants cannot be changed while the program is running, no side effects can occur.

There are two advantages to referencing constants globally: ease of change, and consistency. If you need to change the value of a constant, it's easier to change only one global declaration than to change a local declaration in every function. By declaring a constant in only one place, we also ensure that all parts of the program use exactly the same value.

This is not to say that you should declare *all* constants globally. If a constant is needed in only one function, then it makes sense to declare it locally within that function.

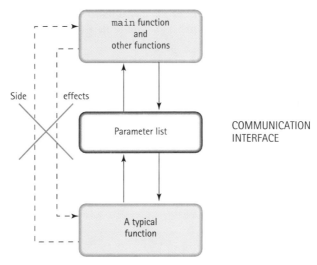

Figure 8-2 *Side Effects*

8.4 Value-Returning Functions

Up to now we have been writing void functions. We now turn our attention to value-returning functions. You already know several value-returning functions supplied by the C++ standard library: `sqrt`, `abs`, `fabs`, and others. From the caller's perspective, the main difference between void functions and value-returning functions is that a call to a void function is a complete statement; a call to a value-returning function is part of an expression.

From a design perspective, value-returning functions are used when there is only one result returned by a function and that result is to be used directly in an expression. For example, suppose we are writing a program that calculates a prorated refund of tuition for students who withdraw in the middle of a semester. As part of the program we must calculate the day number, which is the number associated with each day of the year if you count sequentially from January 1. December 31 has the day number 365, except in leap years, when it is 366. For example, if a semester begins on 1/3/01 and ends on 5/17/01, the calculation is as follows.

The day number of 1/3/01 is 3
The day number of 5/17/01 is 137
The length of the semester is 137 − 3 + 1 = 135

We add 1 to the difference of the days because we count the first day as part of the period.

Let's write the calculation of the day number as a value-returning function named Day that returns the day number of a date in a given year. The calling code for our function might look like this:

```
start = Day (startMonth, startDay, startYear);
last = Day (lastMonth, lastDay, lastYear);
semesterLength = last - start + 1;
```

Here's the function definition for Day. Don't worry about how Day works; for now, you should concentrate on its syntax and structure.

```
int Day( /* in */ int month,        // Month number, 1 - 12
         /* in */ int dayOfMonth,    // Day of month, 1 - 31
         /* in */ int year       )   // Year. For example, 2001

// This function computes the day number within a year, given
// the date. It accounts correctly for leap years.

// Precondition:
//     1 <= month <= 12
//  && dayOfMonth is in valid range for the month
//  && year is assigned
// Postcondition:
//     Function value == day number in the range 1 - 365
//                       (or 1 - 366 for a leap year)

{
    int correction = 0;   // Correction factor to account for leap
                          //    year and months of different lengths

    // Test for leap year

    if (year % 4 == 0 && (year % 100 != 0 || year % 400 == 0))
        if (month >= 3)              // If date is after February 29
            correction = 1;          //    then add one for leap year

    // Correct for different-length months

    if (month == 3)
        correction = correction - 1;
    else if (month == 2 || month == 6 || month == 7)
        correction = correction + 1;
    else if (month == 8)
        correction = correction + 2;
    else if (month == 9 || month == 10)
        correction = correction + 3;
```

```
        else if (month == 11 || month == 12)
            correction = correction + 4;
        return (month - 1) * 30 + correction + dayOfMonth;
}
```

The first thing to note is that the function definition looks like a void function, except that the heading begins with the data type `int` instead of the word `void`. The second thing to observe is the Return statement at the end, which includes an integer expression between the word `return` and the semicolon.

A value-returning function returns one value, not through a parameter but by means of a Return statement. The data type at the beginning of the heading declares the type of value that the function returns. This data type is called the *function type,* although a more precise term is **function value type** (or *function return type* or *function result type*).

Function value type   The data type of the result value returned by a function.

The last statement in the `Day` function evaluates the expression

```
(month - 1) * 30 + correction + dayOfMonth
```

and returns the result as the function value.

You now have seen two forms of the Return statement. The form

```
return;
```

is valid *only* in void functions. It causes control to exit the function immediately and return to the caller. The second form is

```
return Expression;
```

This form is valid *only* in a value-returning function. It returns control to the caller, sending back the value of Expression as the function value. (If the data type of Expression is different from the declared function type, its value is coerced to the correct type.)

In Chapter 7, we presented a syntax template for the function definition of a void function. We now update the syntax template to cover both void functions and value-returning functions:

FunctionDefinition

```
DataType FunctionName ( ParameterList )
{
    Statement
        ⋮
}
```

If DataType is the word `void`, the function is a void function; otherwise, it is a value-returning function. Notice from the shading in the syntax template that DataType is optional. If you omit the data type of a function, `int` is assumed. We mention this point only because you sometimes encounter programs where DataType is missing from the function heading. Many programmers do not consider this practice to be good programming style.

The parameter list for a value-returning function has exactly the same form as for a void function: a list of parameter declarations, separated by commas. Also, a function prototype for a value-returning function looks just like the prototype for a void function except that it begins with a data type instead of `void`.

Let's look at another example of a value-returning function. The C++ standard library provides a power function, `pow`, that raises a floating-point number to a floating-point power. The library does not supply a power function for `int` values, so let's build one of our own. The function receives two integers, x and n (where $n \geq 0$), and computes x^n. We use a simple approach, multiplying repeatedly by x. Because the number of iterations is known in advance, a count-controlled loop is appropriate. The loop counts down to 0 from the initial value of n. For each iteration of the loop, x is multiplied by the previous product.

```
int Power( /* in */ int x,      // Base number
           /* in */ int n )     // Power to raise base to

// This function computes x to the n power

// Precondition:
//      x is assigned  &&  n >= 0  &&  (x to the n) <= INT_MAX
// Postcondition:
//      Function value == x to the n power

{
    int result;      // Holds intermediate powers of x

    result = 1;
    while (n > 0)
    {
        result = result * x;
        n--;
    }
    return result;
}
```

Notice the notation we use in the postcondition of a value-returning function. Because a value-returning function returns a single value, it is most concise if you simply state what that value equals. Except in complicated examples, the postcondition looks like this:

```
// Postcondition
//      Function value == ...
```

Boolean Functions

Value-returning functions are not restricted to returning numerical results. We can also use them, for example, to evaluate a condition and return a Boolean result. Boolean functions can be useful when a branch or loop depends on some complex condition. Rather than code the condition directly into the If or While statement, we can call a Boolean function to form the controlling expression.

The C++ standard library provides a number of helpful functions that let you test the contents of char variables. To use them, you #include the header file cctype. Here are some of the available functions; Appendix C contains a more complete list.

Header File	Function	Function Type	Function Value
`<cctype>`	`isalpha(ch)`	`int`	Nonzero, if ch is a letter ('A'–'Z', 'a'–'z'); 0, otherwise
`<cctype>`	`isalnum(ch)`	`int`	Nonzero, if ch is a letter or a digit ('A'–'Z', 'a'–'z', '0'–'9'); 0, otherwise
`<cctype>`	`isdigit(ch)`	`int`	Nonzero, if ch is a digit ('0'–'9'); 0, otherwise
`<cctype>`	`islower(ch)`	`int`	Nonzero, if ch is a lowercase letter ('a'–'z'); 0, otherwise
`<cctype>`	`isspace(ch)`	`int`	Nonzero, if ch is a whitespace character (blank, newline, tab, carriage return, form feed); 0, otherwise
`<cctype>`	`isupper(ch)`	`int`	Nonzero, if ch is an uppercase letter ('A'–'Z'); 0, otherwise

Although they return int values, the "is..." functions behave like Boolean functions. They return an int value that is nonzero (coerced to true in an If or While condition) or 0 (coerced to false in an If or While condition). These functions are convenient to use and make programs more readable. For example, the test

```
if (isalnum(inputChar))
```

is easier to read and less prone to error than if you coded the test the long way:

```
if (inputChar >= 'A' && inputChar <= 'Z' ||
    inputChar >= 'a' && inputChar <= 'z' ||
    inputChar >= '0' && inputChar <= '9'    )
```

In fact, this complicated logical expression doesn't work correctly on some machines. We'll see why when we examine character data in Chapter 10.

Naming Value-Returning Functions

In Chapter 7, we said that it's good style to use imperative verbs when naming void functions. This naming scheme, however, doesn't work well with value-returning functions. With a value-returning function, the function call represents a value within an expression. Things that represent values, such as variables and value-returning functions, are best given names that are nouns or, occasionally, adjectives. Examples of names that suggest values rather than actions are `SquareRoot`, `Cube`, `Factorial`, `StudentCount`, `SumOfSquares`, and `SocialSecurityNum`. As you see, they are all nouns or noun phrases.

Boolean value-returning functions (and variables) are often named using adjectives or phrases beginning with *Is*. A few examples are `Valid`, `Odd`, and `IsTriangle`.

Interface Design for Value-Returning Functions

The interface to a value-returning function is designed in much the same way as for a void function. We simply write down a list of what the function needs and what it must return. Because value-returning functions return only one value, there is only one item labeled "outgoing" in the list: the function return value. Everything else in the list is labeled "incoming," and there aren't any "incoming/outgoing" parameters.

Returning more than one value from a value-returning function (by modifying the caller's arguments) is a side effect and should be avoided. If your interface design calls for multiple values to be returned, then you should use a void function.

A rule of thumb is never to use reference parameters in the parameter list of a value-returning function, but to use value parameters exclusively. An exception is the case in which an I/O stream object is passed to a value-returning function. Remember that C++ allows a stream object to be passed only to a reference parameter. Within a value-returning function, the only operation that should be performed is testing the state of the stream (for EOF or I/O errors). A value-returning function should not perform input or output operations. Such operations are considered to be side effects of the function. (We should point out that not everyone agrees with this point of view. Some programmers feel that performing I/O within a value-returning function is perfectly acceptable. You will find strong opinions on both sides of this issue.)

When to Use Value-Returning Functions

There aren't any formal rules for determining when to use a void function and when to use a value-returning function, but here are some guidelines:

1. If the module must return more than one value or modify any of the caller's arguments, do not use a value-returning function.

2. If the module must perform I/O, do not use a value-returning function. (This guideline is not universally agreed upon.)

3. If there is only one value returned from the module and it is a Boolean value, a value-returning function is appropriate.

4. If there is only one value returned and that value is to be used immediately in an expression, a value-returning function is appropriate.

5. When in doubt, use a void function. You can recode any value-returning function as a void function by adding an extra outgoing parameter to carry back the computed result.

6. If both a void function and a value-returning function are acceptable, use the one you feel more comfortable implementing.

Value-returning functions were included in C++ to provide a way of simulating the mathematical concept of a function. The C++ standard library supplies a set of commonly used mathematical functions through the header file `cmath`. A list of these appears in Appendix C.

Ignoring a Function Value

The C++ language lets you ignore the value returned by a value-returning function. For example, you could write the following statement in your program without any complaint from the compiler:

```
sqrt(x);
```

When this statement is executed, the value returned by `sqrt` is promptly discarded. This function call has no effect except to waste time by calculating a value that is never used.

Clearly, the above call to `sqrt` is a mistake. But C++ programmers occasionally write value-returning functions that allow the caller to ignore the function value. Such a function is sort of a hybrid between a void function and a value-returning function.

In this book, we don't write hybrid functions. We prefer to keep the concept of a void function distinct from a value-returning function. But there are two reasons why you should know about the topic of ignoring a function value. First, if you accidentally call a value-returning function as if it were a void function, the compiler won't prevent you from making the mistake. Second, you sometimes encounter this style of coding in other people's programs and in the C++ standard library. Several of the library functions are technically value-returning functions, but the function value is used merely to return something of secondary importance such as a status value.

Programming Example

Starship Weight and Balance

Problem The company you work for has just upgraded its fleet of corporate aircraft by adding the Beechcraft Starship-1. As with any airplane, it is essential that the pilot know the total weight of the loaded plane at takeoff and its center of gravity. If the plane weighs too much, it won't be able to lift off. If its center of gravity is outside the limits established for the plane, it might be impossible to control. Either situation can lead to a crash. You have been asked to write a program that determines the weight and center of gravity of this new plane, based on the number of crew members and passengers as well as the weight of the baggage, closet contents, and fuel.

Input Number of crew members, number of passengers, weight of closet contents, baggage weight, fuel in gallons.

Output Total weight, center of gravity.

Discussion As with most real-world problems, the basic solution is simple but is complicated by special cases. We use value-returning functions to hide the complexity so that the `main` function remains simple.

The total weight is basically the sum of the empty weight of the airplane plus the weight of each of the following: crew members, passengers, baggage, contents of the storage closet, and fuel. We use the standard average weight of a person, 170 pounds, to compute the total weight of the people. The weight of the baggage and the contents of the closet are given. Fuel weighs 6.7 pounds per gallon. Thus, the total weight is

totalWeight = emptyWeight + (crew + passengers) × 170 + baggage + closet + fuel × 6.7

To compute the center of gravity, each weight is multiplied by its distance from the front of the airplane, and the products—called *moment* arms or simply *moments*—are then summed and divided by the total weight (see Figure 8-3). The formula is thus

centerOfGravity = (emptyMoment + crewMoment + passengerMoment + cargoMoment + fuelMoment) / totalWeight

The Starship-1 manual gives the distance from the front of the plane to the crew's seats, closet, baggage compartment, and fuel tanks. There are four rows of passenger seats, so this calculation depends on where the individual passengers sit. We have to make some assumptions about how passengers arrange themselves. Each row has two seats. The most popular seats are in row 2 because they are near the entrance and face forward. Once row 2 is filled, passengers usually take seats in row 1, facing their traveling companions. Row 3 is usually the next to fill up, even though it faces backward, because row 4 is a fold-down bench seat that is

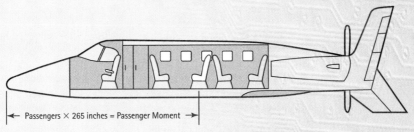

Figure 8-3 *A Passenger Moment Arm*

less comfortable than the armchairs in the forward rows. The following table gives the distance from the nose of the plane to each of the "loading stations."

Loading Station	Distance from Nose (inches)
Crew seats	143
Row 1 seats	219
Row 2 seats	265
Row 3 seats	295
Row 4 seats	341
Closet	182
Baggage	386

The distance for the fuel varies because there are several tanks, and the tanks are in different places. As fuel is added to the plane, it automatically flows into the different tanks so that the center of gravity changes as the tanks are filled. There are four formulas for computing the distance from the nose to the "center" of the fuel tanks, depending on how much fuel is being loaded into the plane. The following table lists these distance formulas.

Gallons of Fuel (G)	Distance (D) Formula
0–59	$D = 314.6 \times G$
60–360	$D = 305.8 + (\,-0.01233 \times (G - 60\,))$
361–520	$D = 303.0 + (\,0.12500 \times (G - 361\,))$
521–565	$D = 323.0 + (\,-0.04444 \times (G - 521\,))$

We define one value-returning function for each of the different moments, and we name these functions `CrewMoment`, `PassengerMoment`, `CargoMoment`, and `FuelMoment`. The center of gravity is then computed with the formula we gave earlier and the following arguments:

$$centerOfGravity = (CrewMoment(crew) + PassengerMoment(passengers) +$$
$$CargoMoment(closet, baggage) + FuelMoment(fuel) +$$
$$emptyMoment) / totalWeight$$

The empty weight of the Starship is 9887 pounds, and its empty center of gravity is 319 inches from the front of the airplane. Thus, the empty moment is 3,153,953 inch-pounds.

We now have enough information to write the algorithm to solve this problem. We'll use a void function to get the data. The `main` function then computes the total weight and uses our value-returning functions in its calculation of the center of gravity. It then prints these two results. In addition to printing the results, we'll also print a warning message that states the assumptions of the program and tells the pilot to double-check the results by hand if the weight or center of gravity is near the allowable limits. This warning message is printed by another void function.

Module Structure Chart   In the following chart, you'll see a new notation. The box corresponding to each value-returning function has an upward arrow originating at its right side. This arrow signifies the function value that is returned.

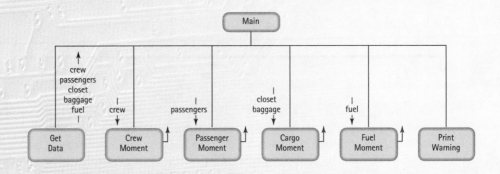

(The following program is written in ISO/ANSI standard C++. If you are working with pre-standard C++, see the alternate version of the program in the PRE_STD directory of the program disk, available at the publisher's Web site, `www.jbpub.com/disks`.)

```
//*********************************************************************
// Starship program
// This program computes the total weight and center of gravity
// of a Beechcraft Starship-1
//*********************************************************************
#include <iostream>
#include <iomanip> // For setw() and setprecision()
```

```cpp
using namespace std;

const float PERSON_WT = 170.0;          // Average person weighs
                                        //    170 lbs.
const float LBS_PER_GAL = 6.7;          // Jet-A weighs 6.7 lbs.
                                        //    per gal.
const float EMPTY_WEIGHT = 9887.0;      // Standard empty weight
const float EMPTY_MOMENT = 3153953.0;   // Standard empty moment

float CargoMoment( int, int );
float CrewMoment( int );
float FuelMoment( int );
void  GetData( int&, int&, int&, int&, int& );
float PassengerMoment( int );
void  PrintWarning();

int main()
{
    int   crew;            // Number of crew on board (1 or 2)
    int   passengers;      // Number of passengers (0 through 8)
    int   closet;          // Weight in closet (160 lbs. maximum)
    int   baggage;         // Weight of baggage (525 lbs. max.)
    int   fuel;            // Gallons of fuel (10 through 565 gals.)
    float totalWt;         // Total weight of the loaded Starship
    float centerOfGravity; // Center of gravity of loaded Starship

    cout << fixed << showpoint              // Set up floating-pt.
         << setprecision(2);                //    output format

    GetData(crew, passengers, closet, baggage, fuel);

    totalWt =
        EMPTY_WEIGHT + float(passengers + crew) * PERSON_WT +
        float(baggage + closet) + float(fuel) * LBS_PER_GAL;
    centerOfGravity =
        (CrewMoment(crew) + PassengerMoment(passengers) +
        CargoMoment(closet, baggage) + FuelMoment(fuel) +
        EMPTY_MOMENT) / totalWt;

    cout << "Total weight is " << totalWt << " pounds." << endl;
    cout << "Center of gravity is " << centerOfGravity
         << " inches from the front of the plane." << endl;
    PrintWarning();
    return 0;
}
```

```
//**********************************************************************

void GetData( /* out */ int& crew,         // Number of crew members
              /* out */ int& passengers,   // Number of passengers
              /* out */ int& closet,       // Weight of closet cargo
              /* out */ int& baggage,      // Weight of baggage
              /* out */ int& fuel      )   // Gallons of fuel

// Prompts for the input of crew, passengers, closet, baggage, and
// fuel values and returns the five values after echo printing them

// Postcondition:
//     All parameters (crew, passengers, closet, baggage, and fuel)
//     have been prompted for, input, and echo printed

{
    cout << "Enter the number of crew members." << endl;
    cin >> crew;
    cout << "Enter the number of passengers." << endl;
    cin >> passengers;
    cout << "Enter the weight, in pounds, of cargo in the" << endl
         << " closet, rounded up to the nearest whole number."
         << endl;
    cin >> closet;
    cout << "Enter the weight, in pounds, of cargo in the" << endl
         << " aft baggage compartment, rounded up to the" << endl
         << " nearest whole number." << endl;
    cin >> baggage;
    cout << "Enter the number of U.S. gallons of fuel" << endl
         << " loaded, rounded up to the nearest whole number."
         << endl;
    cin >> fuel;
    cout << endl;
    cout << "Starship loading data as entered:" << endl
         << "    Crew:          " << setw(6) << crew << endl
         << "    Passengers:    " << setw(6) << passengers << endl
         << "    Closet weight: " << setw(6) << closet << " pounds"
         << endl
         << "    Baggage weight:" << setw(6) << baggage << " pounds"
         << endl
         << "    Fuel:          " << setw(6) << fuel << " gallons"
         << endl << endl;
}

//**********************************************************************

float CrewMoment( /* in */ int crew )   // Number of crew members
```

```
// Computes the crew moment arm in inch-pounds

// Precondition:
//    crew == 1  OR  crew == 2
// Postcondition:
//    Function value == Crew moment arm, based on the crew parameter

{
    const float CREW_DISTANCE = 143.0;  // Distance to crew seats
                                        //    from front
    return float(crew) * PERSON_WT * CREW_DISTANCE;
}


//*********************************************************************


float PassengerMoment( /* in */ int passengers )    // Number of
                                                    //   passengers

// Computes the passenger moment arm in inch-pounds from the number
// of passengers.  Global constant PERSON_WT is used as the weight
// of each passenger.  It is assumed that the first two passengers
// sit in row 2, the second two in row 1, the next two in row 3,
// and remaining passengers sit in row 4

// Precondition:
//     0 <= passengers <= 8
// Postcondition:
//     Function value == Passenger moment arm, based on the
//                       passengers parameter

{
    const float ROW1_DIST = 219.0;  // Distance to row 1 seats
                                    //    from front
    const float ROW2_DIST = 265.0;  // Distance to row 2 seats
    const float ROW3_DIST = 295.0;  // Distance to row 3 seats
    const float ROW4_DIST = 341.0;  // Distance to row 4 seats

    float moment = 0.0;             // Running total of moment as
                                    //    rows are added

    if (passengers > 6)                      // For passengers 7 and 8
    {
        moment = moment +
                float(passengers - 6) * PERSON_WT * ROW4_DIST;
        passengers = 6;                       // 6 remain
    }
```

```cpp
    if (passengers > 4)                        // For passengers 5 and 6
    {
        moment = moment +
                float(passengers - 4) * PERSON_WT * ROW3_DIST;
        passengers = 4;                    // 4 remain
    }
    if (passengers > 2)                        // For passengers 3 and 4
    {
        moment = moment +
                float(passengers - 2) * PERSON_WT * ROW1_DIST;
        passengers = 2;                    // 2 remain
    }
    if (passengers > 0)                        // For passengers 1 and 2
        moment = moment +
                float(passengers) * PERSON_WT * ROW2_DIST;
    return moment;
}

//********************************************************************

float CargoMoment( /* in */ int closet,     // Weight in closet
                   /* in */ int baggage )   // Weight of baggage

// Computes the total moment arm for cargo

// Precondition:
//     0 <= closet <= 160  &&  0 <= baggage <= 525
// Postcondition:
//     Function value == Cargo moment arm, based on the closet and
//                       baggage parameters

{
    const float CLOSET_DIST = 182.0;    // Distance from front
                                        //    to closet
    const float BAGGAGE_DIST = 386.0;   // Distance from front
                                        //    to bagg. comp.
    return float(closet) * CLOSET_DIST +
           float(baggage) * BAGGAGE_DIST;
}

//********************************************************************

float FuelMoment( /* in */ int fuel )     // Fuel in gallons
```

```
// Computes the moment arm for fuel on board

// Precondition:
//     10 <= fuel <= 565
// Postcondition:
//     Function value == Fuel moment arm, based on the
//                       fuel parameter

{
    float fuelWt;           // Weight of fuel in pounds
    float fuelDistance;     // Distance from front of plane

    fuelWt = float(fuel) * LBS_PER_GAL;
    if (fuel < 60)
        fuelDistance = float(fuel) * 314.6;
    else if (fuel < 361)
        fuelDistance = 305.8 + (-0.01233 * float(fuel - 60));
    else if (fuel < 521)
        fuelDistance = 303.0 + ( 0.12500 * float(fuel - 361));
    else
        fuelDistance = 323.0 + (-0.04444 * float(fuel - 521));
    return fuelDistance * fuelWt;
}

//********************************************************************

void PrintWarning()

// Warns the user of assumptions made by the program
// and when to double-check the program's results

// Postcondition:
//     An informational warning message has been printed

{
    cout << endl
        << "Notice:  This program assumes that passengers" << endl
        << "  fill the seat rows in order 2, 1, 3, 4, and" << endl
        << "  that each passenger and crew member weighs "
        << PERSON_WT << " pounds." << endl
        << "  It also assumes that Jet-A fuel weighs "
        << LBS_PER_GAL << " pounds" << endl
        << "  per U.S. gallon.  The center of gravity" << endl
        << "  calculations for fuel are approximate.  If" << endl
        << "  the aircraft is loaded near its limits, the" << endl
```

```
           << "   pilot's operating handbook should be used" << endl
           << "   to compute weight and center of gravity" << endl
           << "   with more accuracy." << endl;
}
```

Testing Because someone could use the output of this program to make decisions that could result in property damage, injury, or death, it is essential to test the program thoroughly. In particular, it should be checked for maximum and minimum input values in different combinations. In addition, a wide range of test cases should be tried and verified against results calculated by hand. If possible, the program's output should be checked against sample calculations done by experienced pilots for actual flights.

Notice that the `main` function neglects to guarantee any of the function preconditions before calling the functions. If this program were actually to be used by pilots, it should have data validation checks added in the `GetData` function.

Testing and Debugging

One of the advantages of a modular design is that you can test it long before the code has been written for all of the modules. If we test each module individually, then we can assemble the modules into a complete program with much greater confidence that the program is correct. In this section, we introduce a technique for testing a module separately.

Stubs and Drivers

Suppose you were given the code for a module and your job was to test it. How would you test a single module by itself? First of all, it must be called by something (unless it is the `main` function). Second, it may have calls to other modules that aren't available to you. To test the module, you must fill in these missing links.

When a module contains calls to other modules, we can write dummy functions called **stubs** to satisfy those calls. A stub usually consists of an output statement that prints a message such as "Function such-and-such just got called." Even though the stub is a dummy, it allows us to determine whether the function is called at the right time by the `main` function or another function.

Stub A dummy function that assists in testing part of a program. A stub has the same name and interface as a function that actually would be called by the part of the program being tested, but it is usually much simpler.

A stub can also be used to print the set of values that are passed to it; this tells us whether or not the module being tested is supplying the correct information. Sometimes a stub assigns new values to its reference parameters to simulate data being read or results being computed in order to give the calling module something to keep working on. Because we can choose the values that are returned by the stub, we have better control over the conditions of the test run.

Driver A simple `main` function that is used to call a function being tested. The use of a driver permits direct control of the testing process.

In addition to supplying a stub for each call within the module, you must provide a dummy program—a **driver**—to call the module itself. A driver program contains the bare minimum of code required to call the module being tested.

By surrounding a module with a driver and stubs, you gain complete control of the conditions under which it executes. This allows you to test different situations and combinations that may reveal errors.

Testing and Debugging Hints

1. Make sure that variables used as arguments to a function are declared in the block where the function call is made.

2. Carefully define the precondition, postcondition, and parameter list to eliminate side effects. Variables used only in a function should be declared as local variables. *Do not* use global variables in your programs. (Exception: It is acceptable to reference `cin` and `cout` globally.)

3. If the compiler displays a message such as "UNDECLARED IDENTIFIER," check that the identifier isn't misspelled (and that it is, in fact, declared), that the identifier is declared before it is referenced, and that the scope of the identifier includes the reference to it.

4. If you intend to use a local name that is the same as a nonlocal name, a misspelling in the local declaration will wreak havoc. The C++ compiler won't complain, but will cause every reference to the local name to go to the nonlocal name instead.

5. Remember that the same identifier cannot be used in both the parameter list and the outermost local declarations of a function.

6. With a value-returning function, be sure the function heading and prototype begin with the correct data type for the function return value.

7. With a value-returning function, don't forget to use a statement

```
return Expression;
```

to return the function value. Make sure the expression is of the correct type, or implicit type coercion will occur.

8. Remember that a call to a value-returning function is part of an expression, whereas a call to a void function is a separate statement. (C++ softens this distinction, however, by letting you call a value-returning function as if it were a void function, ignoring the return value. Be careful here.)

9. In general, don't use reference parameters in the parameter list of a value-returning function. A reference parameter must be used, however, when an I/O stream object is passed as a parameter.

10. If necessary, use your system's debugger (or use debug output statements) to indicate when a function is called and if it is executing correctly. The values of the arguments can be displayed immediately before the call to the function (to show the incoming values) and immediately after (to show the outgoing values). You also may want to display the values of local variables in the function itself to indicate what happens each time it is called.

Summary

The scope of an identifier refers to the parts of the program in which it is visible. C++ function names have global scope, as do the names of variables and constants that are declared outside all functions and namespaces. Variables and constants declared within a block have local scope; they are not visible outside the block. The parameters of a function have the same scope as local variables declared in the outermost block of the function.

With rare exceptions, it is not considered good practice to declare global variables and reference them directly from within a function. All communication between the modules of a program should be through the argument and parameter lists (and via the function value sent back by a value-returning function). The use of global constants, on the other hand, is considered to be an acceptable programming practice because it adds consistency and makes a program easier to change while avoiding the pitfalls of side effects. Well-designed and well-documented functions that are free of side effects can often be reused in other programs. Many programmers keep a library of functions that they use repeatedly.

The lifetime of a variable is the period of time during program execution when memory is allocated to it. Global variables have static lifetime (memory remains allocated for the duration of the program's execution). By default, local variables have automatic lifetime (memory is allocated and deallocated at block entry and block exit). A local variable may be given static lifetime by using the word `static` in its declaration. This variable has the lifetime of a global variable but the scope of a local variable.

C++ allows a variable to be initialized in its declaration. For a static variable, the initialization occurs once only—when control first reaches its declaration. An automatic variable is initialized each time control reaches the declaration.

C++ provides two kinds of subprograms, void functions and value-returning functions. A value-returning function is called from within an expression and returns a single result that is used in the evaluation of the expression. For the function value to be returned, the last statement executed by the function must be a Return statement containing an expression of the appropriate data type.

All the scope rules, as well as the rules about reference and value parameters, apply to both void functions and value-returning functions. It is considered poor programming practice, however, to use reference parameters in a value-returning function definition. Doing so increases the potential for unintended side effects. (An exception is when I/O stream objects are passed as parameters.)

We can use stubs and drivers to test functions in isolation from the rest of a program. They are particularly useful in the context of team-programming projects.

Quick Check

1. a. How can you tell if a variable that is referenced inside a function is local or global? (pp. 282–287)
   b. Where are local variables declared? (pp. 282–287)

c. When does the scope of an identifier declared in block A exclude a block nested within block A? (pp. 282–287)

2. A program consists of two functions, `main` and `DoCalc`. A variable `x` is declared outside both functions. `DoCalc` declares two variables, `a` and `b`, within its body; `b` is declared as `static`. In what function(s) are each of `a`, `b`, and `x` visible, and what is the lifetime of each variable? (pp. 282–287, 291–293)

3. Why should you use value parameters whenever possible? Why should you avoid the use of global variables? (pp. 293–295, 300)

4. For each of the following, decide whether a value-returning function or a void function is the most appropriate implementation. (pp. 295–301)
   a. Selecting the larger of two values for further processing in an expression.
   b. Printing a paycheck.
   c. Computing the area of a hexagon.
   d. Testing whether an incoming value is valid and returning `true` if it is.
   e. Computing the two roots of a quadratic equation.

5. What would the heading for a value-returning function named `Min` look like if it had two `float` parameters, `num1` and `num2`, and returned a `float` result? (pp. 295–301)

6. What would a call to `Min` look like if the arguments were a variable named `deductions` and the literal `2000.0`? (pp. 295–301)

Answers 1. a. If the variable is not declared in either the body of the function or its parameter list, then the reference is global. b. Local variables are declared within a block (compound statement). c. When the nested block declares an identifier with the same name. 2. x is visible to both functions, but a and b are visible only within `DoCalc`. x and b are static variables; once memory is allocated to them, they are "alive" until the program terminates. a is an automatic variable; it is "alive" only while `DoCalc` is executing. 3. Both using value parameters and avoiding global variables will minimize side effects. Also, passing by value allows the arguments to be arbitrary expressions. 4. a. Value-returning function b. Void function c. Value-returning function d. Value-returning function e. Void function

5. `float Min( float num1,`
   `           float num2 )`

6. `smaller = Min(deductions, 2000.0);`

Exam Preparation Exercises

1. If a function contains a locally declared variable with the same name as a global variable, no confusion results because references to variables in functions are first interpreted as references to local variables. (True or False?)

2. Variables declared at the beginning of a block are accessible to all remaining statements in that block, including those in nested blocks (assuming the nested blocks don't declare local variables with the same names). (True or False?)

3. Define the following terms.

   local variable   scope
   global variable   side effects
   lifetime   name precedence (name hiding)

4. What is the output of the following C++ program? (This program is an example of poor interface design practices.)

```cpp
#include <iostream>

using namespace std;

void DoGlobal();
void DoLocal();
void DoReference( int& );
void DoValue( int );

int x;

int main()
{
    x = 15;
    DoReference(x);
    cout << "x = " << x << " after the call to DoReference."
         << endl;
    x = 16;
    DoValue(x);
    cout << "x = " << x << " after the call to DoValue."
         << endl;
    x = 17;
    DoLocal();
    cout << "x = " << x << " after the call to DoLocal."
         << endl;
    x = 18;
    DoGlobal();
    cout << "x = " << x << " after the call to DoGlobal."
         << endl;
    return 0;
}

void DoReference( int& a )
{
    a = 3;
}
```

```
void DoValue( int b )
{
    b = 4;
}

void DoLocal()
{
    int x;

    x = 5;
}

void DoGlobal()
{
    x = 7;
}
```

5. What is the output of the following program?

```
#include <iostream>
using namespace std;

void Test();

int main()
{
    Test();
    Test();
    Test();
    return 0;
}

void Test()
{
    int i = 0;
    static int j = 0;

    i++;
    j++;
    cout << i << ' ' << j << endl;
}
```

6. The following function calculates the sum of the integers from 1 through n. However, it has an unintended side effect. What is it?

```
void SumInts( int& n,
                int& sum )
{
    sum = 0;
    while (n >= 1)
    {
        sum = sum + n;
        n = n - 1;
    }
}
```

7. Given the function heading

```
bool HighTaxBracket( int inc,
                        int ded )
```

is the following statement a legal call to the function if income and deductions are of type int?

```
if (HighTaxBracket(income, deductions))
    cout << "Upper Class";
```

8. The statement

```
Power(k, 1, m);
```

is a call to the void function whose definition follows. Rewrite the function as a value-returning function, then write a function call that assigns the function value to the variable m.

```
void Power( float  base,
            int    exponent,
            float& answer   )
{
    int i;

    answer = 1.0;
    i = 1;
    while (i <= exponent)
    {
        answer = answer * base;
        i++;
    }
}
```

9. You are given the following `Test` function and a C++ program in which the variables a, b, c, and `result` are declared to be of type `float`. In the calling code, a = -5.0, b = 0.1, and c = 16.2. What is the value of `result` when each of the following calls returns?

```
float Test( float x,
            float y,
            float z )
{
    if (x > y || y > z)
        return 0.5;
    else
        return -0.5;
}
```

a. `result = Test(5.2, 5.3, 5.6);`
b. `result = Test(fabs(a), b, c);`

10. What is wrong with each of the following C++ function definitions?
   a.
```
void Test1( int m,
            int n )
{
    return 3 * m + n;
}
```
   b.
```
float Test2( int   i,
             float x )
{
    i = i + 7;
    x = 4.8 + float(i);
}
```

11. Explain why it is risky to use a reference parameter as a parameter of a value-returning function.

Programming Warm-up Exercises

1. The following program is written with very poor style. For one thing, global variables are used in place of arguments. Rewrite it without global variables, using good programming style.

```
#include <iostream>
using namespace std;
void MashGlobals();
int a, b, c;
int main()
{
cin >> a >> b >> c;
```

```
MashGlobals();
cout << "a=" << a << ' ' << "b=" << b << ' '
<< "c=" << c << endl;
return 0;
}
void MashGlobals()
{
int temp;
temp = a + b;
a = b + c;
b = temp;
}
```

2. Write the heading for a value-returning function `Epsilon` that receives two `float` parameters named `high` and `low` and returns a `float` result.

3. Write the heading for a value-returning function named `NearlyEqual` that receives three `float` parameters—`num1`, `num2`, and `difference`—and returns a Boolean result.

4. Given the heading you wrote in Exercise 3, write the body of the function. The function returns `true` if the absolute value of the difference between `num1` and `num2` is less than the value in `difference` and returns `false` otherwise.

5. Write a value-returning function named `CompassHeading` that returns the sum of its four `float` parameters: `trueCourse`, `windCorrAngle`, `variance`, and `deviation`.

6. Write a value-returning function named `FracPart` that receives a floating-point number and returns the fractional part of that number. Use a single parameter named `x`. For example, if the incoming value of `x` is 16.753, the function return value is 0.753.

7. Write a value-returning function named `Circumf` that finds the circumference of a circle given the radius. The formula for calculating the circumference of a circle is π multiplied by twice the radius. Use 3.14159 for π.

8. Given the function heading

```
float Hypotenuse( float side1,
                  float side2 )
```

write the body of the function to return the length of the hypotenuse of a right triangle. The parameters represent the lengths of the other two sides. The formula for the hypotenuse is

$$\sqrt{side\,1^2 + side\,2^2}$$

9. Write a value-returning function named `FifthPow` that returns the fifth power of its `float` parameter.

10. Write a value-returning function named `Min` that returns the smallest of its three integer parameters.

11. The following If conditions work correctly on most, but not all, machines. Rewrite them using the "is . . ." functions from the C++ standard library (header file `cctype`).

    a. `if (inChar >= '0' && inChar <= '9')`
          `DoSomething();`

    b. `if (inChar >= 'A' && inChar <= 'Z' ||`
          `    inChar >= 'a' && inChar <= 'z'   )`
          `DoSomething();`

    c. `if (inChar >= 'A' && inChar <= 'Z' ||`
          `    inChar >= '0' && inChar <= '9'   )`
          `DoSomething();`

    d. `if (inChar < 'a' || inChar > 'z')`
          `DoSomething();`

12. Write a Boolean value-returning function `IsPrime` that receives an integer parameter n, tests it to see if it is a prime number, and returns `true` if it is. (A prime number is an integer greater than or equal to 2 whose only divisors are 1 and the number itself.) A call to this function might look like this:

```
if (IsPrime(n))
    cout << n << " is a prime number.";
```

    (*Hint:* If n is not a prime number, it is exactly divisible by an integer in the range 2 through $\sqrt{n}$.)

13. Write a value-returning function named `Postage` that returns the cost of mailing a package, given the weight of the package in pounds and ounces and the cost per ounce.

14. In the Starship program, the `main` function neglects to guarantee any of the function preconditions before calling the functions. Modify the `GetData` function to validate the input data. When control returns from `GetData`, the `main` function should be able to assume that all the data values are within the proper ranges.

Programming Problems

1. If a principal amount P, for which the interest is compounded Q times per year, is placed in a savings account, then the amount of money in the account (the balance) after N years is given by the following formula, where I is the annual interest rate as a floating-point number:

$$balance = P \times \left(1 + \frac{I}{Q}\right)^{N \times Q}$$

    Write a C++ program that inputs the values for P, I, Q, and N and outputs the balance for each year up through year N. Use a value-returning function to compute the balance. Your program should prompt the user appropriately, label the output values, and have good style.

2. The distance to the landing point of a projectile, launched at an angle `angle` (in radians) with an initial velocity of `velocity` (in feet per second), ignoring air resistance, is given by the formula

$$distance = \frac{velocity^2 \times \sin(2 \times angle)}{32.2}$$

Write a C++ program that implements a game in which the user first enters the distance to a target. The user then enters the angle and velocity for launching a projectile. If the projectile comes within 0.1% of the distance to the target, the user wins the game. If the projectile doesn't come close enough, the user is told how far off the projectile is and is allowed to try again. If there isn't a winning input after five tries, then the user loses the game.

To simplify input for the user, your program should allow the angle to be input in degrees. The formula for converting degrees to radians is

$$radians = \frac{degrees \times 3.14159265}{180.0}$$

Each of the formulas in this problem should be implemented as a C++ value-returning function. Your program should prompt the user for input appropriately, label the output values, and have proper programming style.

3. Write a program that computes the number of days between two dates. One way of doing this is to have the program compute the Julian day number for each date and subtract one from the other. The Julian day number is the number of days that have elapsed since noon on January 1, 4713 B.C. The following algorithm can be used to calculate the Julian day number.

Given `year` (an integer, such as 2001), `month` (an integer from 1 through 12), and `day` (an integer from 1 through 31), if `month` is 1 or 2, then subtract 1 from `year` and add 12 to `month`.

If the date comes from the Gregorian calendar (later than October 15, 1582), then compute an intermediate result with the following formula (otherwise, let `intRes1` equal 0):

$$intRes1 = 2 - year / 100 + year / 400 \text{ (integer division)}$$

Compute a second intermediate result with the formula

$$intRes2 = int(365.25 \times year)$$

Compute a third intermediate result with the formula

$$intRes3 = int(30.6001 \times (month + 1))$$

Finally, the Julian day number is computed with the formula

$$julianDay = intRes1 + intRes2 + intRes3 + day + 1720994.5$$

Your program should make appropriate use of value-returning functions in solving this problem. These formulas require nine significant digits; you may have to use the integer type `long` and the floating-point type `double`. Your program should prompt appropriately for input (the two dates) if it is to be run interactively. Use proper style with appropriate comments.

Additional Control Structures

- To be able to write a Switch statement for a multi-way branching problem.

- To be able to write a Do-While statement and contrast it with a While statement.

- To be able to write a For statement as an alternative to a While statement.

- To understand the purpose of the Break and Continue statements.

- To be able to choose the most appropriate looping statement for a given problem.

In the preceding chapters, we introduced C++ statements for sequence, selection, loop, and subprogram structures. In some cases, we introduced more than one way of implementing these structures. For example, selection may be implemented by an If-Then structure or an If-Then-Else structure. The If-Then is sufficient to implement any selection structure, but C++ provides the If-Then-Else for convenience because the two-way branch is frequently used in programming.

This chapter introduces five new statements that are also nonessential to, but nonetheless convenient for, programming. One, the Switch statement, makes it easier to write selection structures that have many branches. Two new looping statements, For and Do-While, make it easier to program certain types of loops. The other two statements, Break and Continue, are control statements that are used as part of larger looping and selection structures.

9.1 The Switch Statement

Switch expression   The expression whose value determines which switch label is selected. It cannot be a floating-point or string expression.

The Switch statement is a selection control structure that allows us to list any number of branches. In other words, it is a control structure for multiway branches. The value of the **switch expression**—an expression whose value is matched with a label attached to a branch—determines which one of the branches is executed. For example, look at the following statement:

```
switch (letter)
{
    case 'X' : Statement1;
               break;
    case 'L' :
    case 'M' : Statement2;
               break;
    case 'S' : Statement3;
               break;
    default  : Statement4;
}
Statement5;
```

In this example, letter is the switch expression. The statement means "If letter is 'X', execute Statement1 and break out of the Switch statement, continuing with Statement5. If letter is 'L' or 'M', execute Statement2 and continue with Statement5. If letter is 'S', execute Statement3 and continue with Statement5. If letter is none of the characters mentioned, execute Statement4 and continue with Statement5." The Break statement causes an immediate exit from the Switch statement. We'll see shortly what happens if we omit the Break statements.

A switch expression must be of integral type—`char`, `short`, `int`, `long`, `bool`—or of `enum` type (we discuss `enum` in the next chapter). The *switch label* in front of each branch is either a *case label* or a *default label:*

SwitchLabel

```
case ConstantExpression :
default :
```

In a case label, ConstantExpression is an integral or `enum` expression whose operands must be literal or named constants. The following are examples of constant integral expressions (where `CLASS_SIZE` is a named constant of type `int`):

```
3
CLASS_SIZE
'A'
2 * CLASS_SIZE + 1
```

The data type of ConstantExpression is coerced, if necessary, to match the type of the switch expression.

In our opening example that tests the value of `letter`, the following are the case labels:

```
case 'X' :
case 'L' :
case 'M' :
case 'S' :
```

As that example shows, a single statement may be preceded by more than one case label. Each case value may appear only once in a given Switch statement. If a value appears more than once, a syntax error results. Also, there can be only one default label in a Switch statement.

The flow of control through a Switch statement goes like this. First, the switch expression is evaluated. If this value matches one of the values in a case label, control branches to the statement following that case label. From there, control proceeds sequentially until either a Break statement or the end of the Switch statement is encountered. If the value of the switch expression doesn't match any case value, then one of two things happens. If there is a default label, control branches to the statement following that label. If there is no default label, all statements within the Switch are skipped and control simply proceeds to the statement following the entire Switch statement.

The following Switch statement prints an appropriate comment based on a student's grade (grade is of type char):

```
switch (grade)
{
    case 'A' :
    case 'B' : cout << "Good Work";
               break;
    case 'C' : cout << "Average Work";
               break;
    case 'D' :
    case 'F' : cout << "Poor Work";
               numberInTrouble++;
               break;                 // Unnecessary, but a good habit
}
```

Notice that the final Break statement is unnecessary. But programmers often include it because it's easier to insert another case label at the end if a Break statement is already present.

If grade does not contain one of the specified characters, none of the statements within the Switch is executed. Unless a precondition of the Switch statement is that grade is definitely one of 'A', 'B', 'C', 'D', or 'F', it would be wise to include a default label to account for an invalid grade:

```
switch (grade)
{
    case 'A' :
    case 'B' : cout << "Good Work";
               break;
    case 'C' : cout << "Average Work";
               break;
    case 'D' :
    case 'F' : cout << "Poor Work";
               numberInTrouble++;
               break;
    default  : cout << grade << " is not a valid letter grade.";
               break;
}
```

A Switch statement with a Break statement after each case alternative behaves exactly like an If-Then-Else-If control structure. For example, our Switch statement is equivalent to the following code:

```
if (grade == 'A' || grade == 'B')
    cout << "Good Work";
else if (grade == 'C')
    cout << "Average Work";
```

```
else if (grade == 'D' || grade == 'F')
{
    cout << "Poor Work";
    numberInTrouble++;
}
else
    cout << grade << " is not a valid letter grade.";
```

Finally, we said we would look at what happens if you omit the Break statements inside a Switch statement. Let's rewrite our letter grade example without the Break statements:

```
switch (grade)    // Wrong version
{
    case 'A' :
    case 'B' : cout << "Good Work";
    case 'C' : cout << "Average Work";
    case 'D' :
    case 'F' : cout << "Poor Work";
               numberInTrouble++;
    default  : cout << grade << " is not a valid letter grade.";
}
```

If grade is 'A', the resulting output is this:

```
Good WorkAverage WorkPoor WorkA is not a valid letter grade.
```

Remember that after a branch is taken to a specific case label, control proceeds sequentially until either a Break statement or the end of the Switch statement is encountered. Forgetting a Break statement in a case alternative is a very common source of errors in C++ programs.

9.2 The Do-While Statement

The Do-While statement is a looping control structure in which the loop condition is tested at the end (bottom) of the loop. This format guarantees that the loop body executes at least once.

Here is the form of a Do-While statement:

```
do
{
    Statement1;
    Statement2;
        ⋮
    StatementN;
} while (Expression);
```

This statement means "Execute the statements between `do` and `while` as long as Expression still has the value `true` at the end of the loop." Note that the Do-While statement ends with a semicolon.

Let's compare a While loop and a Do-While loop that do the same task: They find the first period in a file of data. Assume that there is at least one period in the file.

While Solution

```
dataFile >> inputChar;
while (inputChar != '.')
    dataFile >> inputChar;
```

Do-While Solution

```
do
    dataFile >> inputChar;
while (inputChar != '.');
```

The While solution requires a priming read so that `inputChar` has a value before the loop is entered. This isn't required for the Do-While solution because the input statement within the loop is executed before the loop condition is evaluated.

Let's look at another example. Suppose a program needs to read a person's age interactively. The program requires that the age be positive. The following loops ensure that the input value is positive before the program proceeds any further.

While Solution

```
cout << "Enter your age: ";
cin >> age;
while (age <= 0)
{
    cout << "Your age must be positive." << endl;
    cout << "Enter your age: ";
    cin >> age;
}
```

Do-While Solution

```
do
{
    cout << "Enter your age: ";
    cin >> age;
    if (age <= 0)
        cout << "Your age must be positive." << endl;
} while (age <= 0);
```

Notice that the Do-While solution does not require the prompt and input steps to appear twice—once before the loop and once within it—but it does test the input value twice.

We can also use the Do-While to implement a count-controlled loop *if* we know in advance that the loop body should always execute at least once. Below are two versions of a loop to sum the integers from 1 through n.

While Solution	Do-While Solution

```
sum = 0;
counter = 1;
while (counter <= n)
{
    sum = sum + counter;
    counter++;
}
```

```
sum = 0;
counter = 1;
do
{
    sum = sum + counter;
    counter++;
} while (counter <= n);
```

If n is a positive number, both of these versions are equivalent. But if n is 0 or negative, the two loops give different results. In the While version, the final value of sum is 0 because the loop body is never entered. In the Do-While version, the final value of sum is 1 because the body executes once and *then* the loop test is made.

Because the While statement tests the condition before executing the body of the loop, it is called a *pretest loop*. The Do-While statement does the opposite and thus is known as a *posttest loop*. Figure 9-1 compares the flow of control in the While and Do-While loops.

After we look at two other new looping constructs, we offer some guidelines for determining when to use each type of loop.

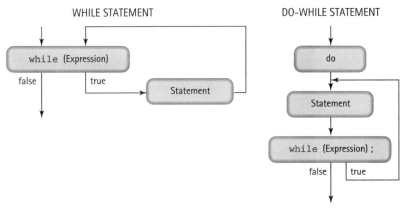

Figure 9-1 *Flow of Control: While and Do-While*

9.3 The For Statement

The For statement is designed to simplify the writing of count-controlled loops. The following statement prints out the integers from 1 through n:

```
for (count = 1; count <= n; count++)
    cout << count << endl;
```

This For statement means "Initialize the loop control variable `count` to 1. While `count` is less than or equal to n, execute the output statement and increment `count` by 1. Stop the loop after `count` has been incremented to n + 1."

In C++, a For statement is merely a compact notation for a While loop. In fact, the compiler essentially translates a For statement into an equivalent While loop as follows:

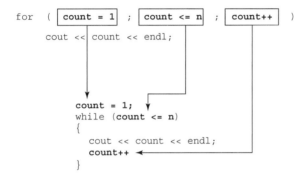

The syntax template for a For statement is

ForStatement

```
for (InitStatement Expression1 ;  Expression2 )
    Statement
```

Expression1 is the While condition. InitStatement can be one of the following: the null statement (just a semicolon), a declaration statement (which always ends in a semicolon), or an expression statement (an expression ending in a semicolon). Therefore, there is always a semicolon before Expression1. (This semicolon isn't shown in the syntax template because InitStatement always ends with its own semicolon.)

Most often, a For statement is written such that InitStatement initializes a loop control variable and Expression2 increments or decrements the loop control variable. Here are two loops that execute the same number of times (50):

```
for (loopCount = 1; loopCount <= 50; loopCount++)
   ⋮
for (loopCount = 50; loopCount >= 1; loopCount--)
   ⋮
```

Just like While loops, Do-While and For loops may be nested. For example, the nested For structure

```
for (lastNum = 1; lastNum <= 7; lastNum++)
{
    for (numToPrint = 1; numToPrint <= lastNum; numToPrint++)
        cout << numToPrint;
    cout << endl;
}
```

prints the following triangle of numbers.

```
1
12
123
1234
12345
123456
1234567
```

Although For statements are used primarily for count-controlled loops, C++ allows you to write *any* While loop by using a For statement. To use For loops intelligently, you should know the following facts.

1. In the syntax template, InitStatement can be the null statement, and Expression2 is optional. If Expression2 is omitted, there is no statement for the compiler to insert at the bottom of the loop. As a result, you could write the While loop

   ```
   while (inputVal != 999)
       cin >> inputVal;
   ```

   as the equivalent For loop

   ```
   for ( ; inputVal != 999; )
       cin >> inputVal;
   ```

2. According to the syntax template, Expression1—the While condition—is optional. If you omit it, the expression `true` is assumed. The loop

```
for ( ; ; )
    cout "Hi" << endl;
```

is equivalent to the While loop

```
while (true)
    cout << "Hi" << endl;
```

Both of these are infinite loops that print "Hi" endlessly.

3. The initializing statement, InitStatement, can be a declaration with initialization:

```
for (int i = 1; i <= 20; i++)
    cout << "Hi" << endl;
```

Here, the variable `i` has local scope, even though there are no braces creating a block. The scope of `i` extends only to the end of the For statement. Like any local variable, `i` is inaccessible outside its scope (that is, outside the For statement). Because `i` is local to the For statement, it's possible to write code like this:

```
for (int i = 1; i <= 20; i++)
    cout << "Hi" << endl;
for (int i = 1; i <= 100; i++)
    cout << "Ed" << endl;
```

This code does *not* generate a compile-time error (such as "MULTIPLY DEFINED IDENTIFIER"). We have declared two distinct variables named `i`, each of which is local to its own For statement.

As you can see, the For statement in C++ is a very flexible structure. Its use can range from a simple count-controlled loop to a general-purpose, "anything goes" While loop.

With For statements, our advice is to keep things simple. The trickier the code is, the harder it will be for another person (or you!) to understand your code and track down errors. In this book, we use For loops for count-controlled loops only.

9.4 The Break and Continue Statements

The Break statement, which we introduced with the Switch statement, is also used with loops. A Break statement causes an immediate exit from the innermost Switch, While,

Do-While, or For statement in which it appears. Notice the word *innermost*. If break is in a loop that is nested inside another loop, control exits the inner loop but not the outer.

One of the more common ways of using break with loops is to set up an infinite loop and use If tests to exit the loop. Suppose we want to input ten pairs of integers, performing data validation and computing the square root of the sum of each pair. For data validation, assume that the first number of each pair must be less than 100 and the second must be greater than 50. Also, after each input, we want to test the state of the stream for EOF. Here's a loop using Break statements to accomplish the task:

```
loopCount = 1;
while (true)
{
    cin >> num1;
    if ( !cin || num1 >= 100)
        break;
    cin >> num2;
    if ( !cin || num2 <= 50)
        break;
    cout << sqrt(float(num1 + num2)) << endl;
    loopCount++;
    if (loopCount > 10)
        break;
}
```

Note that we could have used a For loop to count from 1 to 10, breaking out of it as necessary. However, this loop is both count-controlled and event-controlled, so we prefer to use a While loop.

The above loop contains three distinct exit points. Some people oppose this style of programming, because having multiple exit points from a long block can make the code hard to follow. Is there any advantage to using an infinite loop in conjunction with break? To answer this question, let's rewrite the loop without using Break statements. The loop must terminate when num1 is invalid or num2 is invalid or loopCount exceeds 10. We'll use Boolean flags to signal invalid data in the While condition:

```
num1Valid = true;
num2Valid = true;
loopCount = 1;
while (num1Valid && num2Valid && loopCount <= 10)
{
    cin >> num1;
    if ( !cin || num1 >= 100)
        num1Valid = false;
    else
```

```
        {
            cin >> num2;
            if ( !cin || num2 <= 50)
                num2Valid = false;
            else
            {
                cout << sqrt(float(num1 + num2)) << endl;
                loopCount++;
            }
        }
    }
```

One could argue that the first version is easier to follow and understand than this second version. The primary task of the loop body—computing the square root of the sum of the numbers—is more prominent in the first version. In the second version, the computation is obscured by being buried within nested Ifs. The second version also has a more complicated control flow.

The disadvantage of using `break` with loops is that it can become a crutch for those who are too impatient to think carefully about loop design. It's easy to overuse (and abuse) the technique. A good rule of thumb is: Use `break` within loops only as a last resort. Specifically, use it only to avoid baffling combinations of multiple Boolean flags and nested Ifs.

Another statement that alters the flow of control in a C++ program is the Continue statement. This statement, valid only in loops, terminates the current loop iteration (but not the entire loop). It causes an immediate branch to the bottom of the loop—skipping the rest of the statements in the loop body—in preparation for the next iteration. Here is an example of a reading loop in which we want to process only the positive numbers in an input file:

```
for (dataCount = 1; dataCount <= 500; dataCount++)
{
    dataFile >> inputVal;
    if (inputVal <= 0)
        continue;
    cout << inputVal;
      ⋮
}
```

If `inputVal` is less than or equal to 0, control branches to the bottom of the loop. Then, as with any For loop, the computer increments `dataCount` and performs the loop test before going on to the next iteration.

The Continue statement is not used often, but we present it for completeness (and because you may run across it in other people's programs). Its primary purpose is to avoid obscuring the main process of the loop by indenting the process within an If statement. For example, the previous code would be written without a Continue statement as follows:

```
for (dataCount = 1; dataCount <= 500; dataCount++)
{
    dataFile >> inputVal;
    if (inputVal > 0)
    {
        cout << inputVal;
          ⋮
    }
}
```

Be sure to note the difference between `continue` and `break`. The Continue statement means "Abandon the current iteration of the loop, and go on to the next iteration." The Break statement means "Exit the entire loop immediately."

9.5   Guidelines for Choosing a Looping Statement

Here are some guidelines to help you decide when to use each of the three looping statements (While, Do-While, and For).

1. If the loop is a simple count-controlled loop, the For statement is a natural. Concentrating the three loop control actions—initialize, test, and increment/decrement—into one location (the heading of the For statement) reduces the chances of forgetting to include one of them.

2. If the loop is an event-controlled loop whose body should execute at least once, a Do-While statement is appropriate.

3. If the loop is an event-controlled loop and nothing is known about the first execution, use a While (or perhaps a For) statement.

4. When in doubt, use a While statement.

5. An infinite loop with Break statements sometimes clarifies the code but more often reflects an undisciplined loop design. Use it only after careful consideration of While, Do-While, and For.

Programming Example

Monthly Rainfall Averages

Problem Meteorologists have recorded monthly rainfall amounts at several sites throughout a region of the country. You have been asked to write an interactive program that lets the user enter one year's rainfall amounts at a particular site and prints out the average of the 12 values. After the data for a site is processed, the program asks whether the user would like to repeat the process for another recording site. A user response of 'y' means yes, and 'n' means no. The program must trap erroneous input data (negative values for rainfall amounts and invalid responses to the "Do you wish to continue?" prompt).

Input For each recording site, 12 floating-point rainfall amounts. For each "Do you wish to continue?" prompt, either a 'y' or an 'n'.

Output For each recording site, the floating-point average of the 12 rainfall amounts, displayed to two decimal places.

Discussion A solution to this problem requires several looping structures. At the topmost level of the design, we need a loop to process the data from all the sites. Each iteration must process one site's data, then ask the user whether to continue with another recording site. The program does not know in advance how many recording sites there are, so the loop cannot be a count-controlled loop. Although we can make any of For, While, or Do-While work correctly, we'll use a Do-While under the assumption that the user definitely wants to process at least one site's data. Therefore, we can set up the loop so that it processes the data from a recording site and then, at the *bottom* of the loop, decides whether to iterate again.

Another loop is required to input 12 monthly rainfall amounts and form their sum. A For loop is appropriate for this task, because we know that exactly 12 iterations must occur.

We'll need two more loops to perform data validation—one loop to ensure that a rainfall amount is nonnegative and another to verify that the user types only 'y' or 'n' when prompted to continue. As we saw earlier in the chapter, Do-While loops are well suited to this kind of data validation. We want the loop body to execute at least once, reading an input value and testing for valid data. As long as the user keeps entering invalid data, the loop continues. Control exits the loop only when the user finally gets it right.

Assumptions The user processes data for at least one site.

(The following program is written in ISO/ANSI standard C++. If you are working with pre-standard C++, see the alternate version of the program in the PRE_STD directory of the program disk, available at the publisher's Web site, www.jbpub.com/disks.)

```
//****************************************************************
// Rainfall program
// This program inputs 12 monthly rainfall amounts from a
```

```
// recording site and computes the average monthly rainfall.
// This process is repeated for as many recording sites as
// the user wishes.
//*********************************************************************
#include <iostream>
#include <iomanip>     // For setprecision()

using namespace std;

void Get12Amounts( float& );
void GetOneAmount( float& );
void GetYesOrNo( char& );

int main()
{
    float sum;          // Sum of 12 rainfall amounts
    char  response;     // User response ('y' or 'n')

    cout << fixed << showpoint           // Set up floating-pt.
         << setprecision(2);             //    output format

    do
    {
        Get12Amounts(sum);
        cout << endl << "Average rainfall is " << sum / 12.0
             << " inches" << endl << endl;
        cout << "Do you have another recording site? (y or n) ";
        GetYesOrNo(response);
    } while (response == 'y');
    return 0;
}

//*********************************************************************

void Get12Amounts( /* out */ float& sum )    // Sum of 12 rainfall
                                             // amounts

// Inputs 12 monthly rainfall amounts and returns their sum

// Postcondition:
//     12 rainfall amounts have been read and verified to be
//     nonnegative
//  && sum == sum of the 12 input values
```

```
        {
            int   count;        // Loop control variable
            float amount;       // Rainfall amount for one month

            sum = 0;
            for (count = 1; count <= 12; count++)
            {
                cout << "Enter rainfall amount " << count << ": ";
                GetOneAmount(amount);
                sum = sum + amount;
            }
        }


//*********************************************************************

void GetYesOrNo( /* out */ char& response )    // User response char

// Inputs a character from the user

// Postcondition:
//     response has been input (repeatedly, if necessary, along
//     with output of an error message)
//     && response == 'y' or 'n'

{
    do
    {
        cin >> response;
        if (response != 'y' && response != 'n')
            cout << "Please type y or n: ";
    } while (response != 'y' && response != 'n');
}


//*********************************************************************

void GetOneAmount( /* out */ float& amount )    // Rainfall amount
                                                // for one month

// Inputs one month's rainfall amount

// Postcondition:
//     amount has been input (repeatedly, if necessary, along
//     with output of an error message)
//     && amount >= 0.0
```

```
{
    do
    {
        cin >> amount;
        if (amount < 0.0)
            cout << "Amount cannot be negative. Enter again: ";
    } while (amount < 0.0);
}
```

Testing   We should test two separate aspects of the Rainfall program. First, we should verify that the program works correctly given valid input data. Supplying arbitrary rainfall amounts of 0 or greater, we must confirm that the program correctly adds up the values and divides by 12 to produce the average. Also, we should make sure that the program behaves correctly whether we type 'y' or 'n' when prompted to continue.

The second aspect to test is the data validation code that we included in the program. When prompted for a rainfall amount, we should type negative numbers repeatedly to verify that an error message is printed and that we cannot escape the Do-While loop until we eventually type a nonnegative number. Similarly, when prompted to type 'y' or 'n' to process another recording site, we must press several incorrect keys to exercise the loop in the GetYesOrNo function. Here's a sample run showing the testing of the data validation code:

```
Enter rainfall amount 1: 0
Enter rainfall amount 2: 0
Enter rainfall amount 3: 0
Enter rainfall amount 4: 3.4
Enter rainfall amount 5: 9.6
Enter rainfall amount 6: 1.2
Enter rainfall amount 7: -3.4
Amount cannot be negative. Enter again: -9
Amount cannot be negative. Enter again: -4.2
Amount cannot be negative. Enter again: 1.3
Enter rainfall amount 8: 0
Enter rainfall amount 9: 0
Enter rainfall amount 10: 0
Enter rainfall amount 11: 0
Enter rainfall amount 12: 0

Average rainfall is 1.29 inches

Do you have another recording site? (y or n) d
Please type y or n: q
Please type y or n: Y
Please type y or n: n
```

Testing and Debugging

The same testing techniques we used with While loops apply to Do-While and For loops. There are, however, a few additional considerations with these loops.

The body of a Do-While loop always executes at least once. Thus, you should try data sets that show the result of executing a Do-While loop the minimal number of times.

With a data-dependent For loop, it is important to test for proper results when the loop executes zero times. This occurs when the starting value is greater than the ending value (or less than the ending value if the loop control variable is being decremented).

When a program contains a Switch statement, you should test it with enough different data sets to ensure that each branch is selected and executed correctly. You should also test the program with a switch expression whose value is not in any of the case labels.

Testing and Debugging Hints

1. In a Switch statement, make sure there is a Break statement at the end of each case alternative. Otherwise, control "falls through" to the code in the next case alternative.

2. Case labels in a Switch statement are made up of values, not variables. They may, however, include named constants and expressions involving only constants.

3. A switch expression cannot be a floating-point or string expression, and case constants cannot be floating-point or string constants.

4. If there is a possibility that the value of the switch expression might not match one of the case constants, you should provide a `default` alternative.

5. Double-check long Switch statements to make sure that you haven't omitted any branches.

6. The Do-While loop is a posttest loop. If there is a possibility that the loop body should be skipped entirely, use a While statement or a For statement.

7. The For statement heading (the first line) always has three pieces within the parentheses. Most often, the first piece initializes a loop control variable, the second piece tests the variable, and the third piece increments or decrements the variable. The three pieces must be separated by semicolons. Any of the pieces can be omitted, but the semicolons still must be present.

8. With nested control structures, the Break statement can exit only one level of nesting—the innermost Switch or loop in which the `break` is located.

Summary

The Switch statement is a multiway selection statement. It allows the program to choose among a set of branches. A Switch containing Break statements can always be simulated by an If-Then-Else-If structure. If a Switch can be used, however, it often makes the code easier to read and understand. A Switch statement cannot be used with floating-point or string values in the case labels.

The Do-While is a general-purpose looping statement. It is like the While loop except that its test occurs at the end of the loop, guaranteeing at least one execution of the loop body. As with a While loop, a Do-While continues as long as the loop condition is `true`.

The For statement is also a general-purpose looping statement, but its most common use is to implement count-controlled loops. The initialization, testing, and incrementation (or decrementation) of the loop control variable are centralized in one location, the first line of the For statement.

The For, Do-While, and Switch statements are the ice cream and cake of C++. We can live without them if we absolutely must, but they are very nice to have.

Quick Check

1. Given a switch expression that is the `int` variable `nameVal`, write a Switch statement that prints your first name if `nameVal` = 1, your middle name if `nameVal` = 2, and your last name if `nameVal` = 3. (pp. 324–327)
2. How would you change the answer to Question 1 so that it prints an error message if the value is not 1, 2, or 3? (pp. 324–327)
3. What is the primary difference between a While loop and a Do-While loop? (pp. 327–329)
4. A certain problem requires a count-controlled loop that starts at 10 and counts down to 1. Write the heading (the first line) of a For statement that controls this loop. (pp. 330–332)
5. Within a loop, how does a Continue statement differ from a Break statement? (pp. 332–335)
6. What C++ looping statement would you choose for a loop that is both count-controlled and event-controlled and whose body might not execute even once? (p. 335)

Answers

1.
```
switch (nameVal)
{
    case 1 : cout << "Mary";
             break;
    case 2 : cout << "Lynn";
             break;
    case 3 : cout << "Smith";
             break;    // Not required
}
```

```
2.   switch (nameVal)
     {
         case 1  : cout << "Mary";
                   break;
         case 2  : cout << "Lynn";
                   break;
         case 3  : cout << "Smith";
                   break;
         default : cout << "Invalid name value.";
                   break;   // Not required
     }
```

3. The body of a Do-While always executes at least once; the body of a While may not execute at all. 4. `for (count = 10; count >= 1; count--)` 5. A Continue statement terminates the current iteration and goes on to the next iteration (if possible). A Break statement causes an immediate loop exit. 6. A While (or perhaps a For) statement.

Exam Preparation Exercises

1. Define the following terms:

   switch expression
   pretest loop
   posttest loop

2. A switch expression may be an expression that results in a value of type `int`, `float`, `bool`, or `char`. (True or False?)
3. The values in case labels may appear in any order, but duplicate case labels are not allowed within a given Switch statement. (True or False?)
4. All possible values for the switch expression must be included among the case labels for a given Switch statement. (True or False?)
5. Rewrite the following code fragment using a Switch statement.

```
if (n == 3)
    alpha++;
else if (n == 7)
    beta++;
else if (n == 10)
    gamma++;
```

6. What is printed by the following code fragment if n equals 3? (Be careful here.)

```
switch (n + 1)
{
    case 2  : cout << "Bill";
    case 4  : cout << "Mary";
    case 7  : cout << "Joe";
```

```
    case 9  : cout << "Anne";
    default : cout << "Whoops!";
}
```

7. If a While loop whose condition is `delta <= alpha` is converted into a Do-While loop, the loop condition of the Do-While loop is `delta > alpha`. (True or False?)

8. A Do-While statement always ends in a semicolon. (True or False?)

9. What is printed by the following program fragment, assuming the input value is 0? (All variables are of type `int`.)

```
cin >> n;
i = 1;
do
{
    cout << i;
    i++;
} while (i <= n);
```

10. What is printed by the following program fragment, assuming the input value is 0? (All variables are of type `int`.)

```
cin >> n;
for (i = 1; i <= n; i++)
    cout << i;
```

11. What is printed by the following program fragment? (All variables are of type `int`.)

```
for (i = 4; i >= 1; i--)
{
    for (j = i; j >= 1; j--)
        cout << j << ' ';
    cout << i << endl;
}
```

12. What is printed by the following program fragment? (All variables are of type `int`.)

```
for (row = 1; row <= 10; row++)
{
    for (col = 1; col <= 10 - row; col++)
        cout << '*';
    for (col = 1; col <= 2*row - 1; col++)
        cout << ' ';
    for (col = 1; col <= 10 - row; col++)
        cout << '*';
    cout << endl;
}
```

13. A Break statement located inside a Switch statement that is within a While loop causes control to exit the loop immediately. (True or False?)

Programming Warm-up Exercises

1. Write a Switch statement that does the following:

    If the value of grade is

    'A', add 4 to sum

    'B', add 3 to sum

    'C', add 2 to sum

    'D', add 1 to sum

    'F', print "Student is on probation"

2. Modify the code for Exercise 1 so that an error message is printed if grade does not equal one of the five possible grades.

3. Rewrite the Day function of Chapter 8 (pages 296–297), replacing the If-Then-Else-If structure with a Switch statement.

4. Write a program segment that reads and sums until it has summed ten data values or until a negative value is read, whichever comes first. Use a Do-While loop for your solution.

5. Rewrite the following code segment using a Do-While loop instead of a While loop.

```
cout << "Enter 1, 2, or 3: ";
cin >> response;
while (response < 1 || response > 3)
{
    cout << "Enter 1, 2, or 3: ";
    cin >> response;
}
```

6. Rewrite the following code segment using a While loop.

```
cin >> ch;
if (cin)
    do
    {
        cout << ch;
        cin >> ch;
    } while (cin);
```

7. Rewrite the following code segment using a For loop.

```
sum = 0;
count = 1;
while (count <= 1000)
{
    sum = sum + count;
    count++;
}
```

8. Rewrite the following For loop as a While loop.

```
for (m = 93; m >= 5; m--)
    cout << m << ' ' << m * m << endl;
```

9. Rewrite the following For loop using a Do-While loop.

```
for (k = 9; k <= 21; k++)
    cout << k << ' ' << 3 * k << endl;
```

10. Write a value-returning function that accepts two `int` parameters, `base` and `exponent`, and returns the value of `base` raised to the `exponent` power. Use a For loop in your solution.

11. Make the logic of the following loop easier to understand by using an infinite loop with Break statements.

```
sum = 0;
count = 1;
do
{
    cin >> int1;
    if ( !cin || int1 <= 0)
        cout << "Invalid first integer.";
    else
    {
        cin >> int2;
        if ( !cin || int2 > int1)
            cout << "Invalid second integer.";
        else
        {
            cin >> int3;
            if ( !cin || int3 == 0)
                cout << "Invalid third integer.";
            else
            {
                sum = sum + (int1 + int2) / int3;
                count++;
            }
        }
    }
} while (cin && int1 > 0 && int2 <= int1 && int3 != 0 &&
        count <= 100);
```

12. Rewrite the `GetYesOrNo` and `GetOneAmount` functions in the Rainfall program, replacing the Do-While loops with While loops.

13. Rewrite the `Get12Amounts` function in the Rainfall program, replacing the For loop with a Do-While loop.

14. Rewrite the `Get12Amounts` function in the Rainfall program, replacing the For loop with a While loop.

Programming Problems

1. Develop a functional decomposition and write a C++ program that inputs a two-letter abbreviation for one of the 50 states and prints out the full name of the state. If the abbreviation isn't valid, the program should print an error message and ask for an abbreviation again. The names of the 50 states and their abbreviations are given in the following table.

State	Abbreviation	State	Abbreviation
Alabama	AL	Montana	MT
Alaska	AK	Nebraska	NE
Arizona	AZ	Nevada	NV
Arkansas	AR	New Hampshire	NH
California	CA	New Jersey	NJ
Colorado	CO	New Mexico	NM
Connecticut	CT	New York	NY
Delaware	DE	North Carolina	NC
Florida	FL	North Dakota	ND
Georgia	GA	Ohio	OH
Hawaii	HI	Oklahoma	OK
Idaho	ID	Oregon	OR
Illinois	IL	Pennsylvania	PA
Indiana	IN	Rhode Island	RI
Iowa	IA	South Carolina	SC
Kansas	KS	South Dakota	SD
Kentucky	KY	Tennessee	TN
Louisiana	LA	Texas	TX
Maine	ME	Utah	UT
Maryland	MD	Vermont	VT
Massachusetts	MA	Virginia	VA
Michigan	MI	Washington	WA
Minnesota	MN	West Virginia	WV
Mississippi	MS	Wisconsin	WI
Missouri	MO	Wyoming	WY

(*Hint:* Use nested Switch statements, where the outer statement uses the first letter of the abbreviation as its switch expression.)

2. Write a functional decomposition and a C++ program that reads a date in numeric form and prints it in English. For example:

```
Enter a date in the form mm dd yyyy.
10  27  1942
October twenty-seventh, nineteen hundred forty-two.
```

Here is another example:

```
Enter a date in the form mm dd yyyy.
12  10  2010
December tenth, two thousand ten.
```

The program should print an error message for any invalid date, such as `2  29  1883` (1883 wasn't a leap year).

3. Write a C++ program that reads full names from an input file and writes the initials for the names to an output file stream named `initials`. For example, the input

```
John James Henry
```

should produce the output

```
JJH
```

The names are stored in the input file first name first, then middle name, then last name, separated by an arbitrary number of blanks. There is only one name per line. The first name or the middle name could be just an initial, or there may not be a middle name.

4. Write a functional decomposition and a C++ program that converts letters of the alphabet into their corresponding digits on the telephone. The program should let the user enter letters repeatedly until a 'Q' or a 'Z' is entered. (Q and Z are the two letters that are not on the telephone.) An error message should be printed for any nonalphabetic character that is entered.

The letters and digits on the telephone have the following correspondence.

```
ABC = 2    DEF  = 3    GHI = 4
JKL = 5    MNO  = 6    PRS = 7
TUV = 8    WXY  = 9
```

Here is an example:

```
Enter a letter: P
The letter P corresponds to 7 on the telephone.
Enter a letter: A
The letter A corresponds to 2 on the telephone.
Enter a letter: D
The letter D corresponds to 3 on the telephone.
Enter a letter: 2
Invalid letter. Enter Q or Z to quit.
Enter a letter: Z
Quit.
```

Simple Data Types: Built-In and User-Defined

- To be able to identify all of the simple data types provided by the C++ language.

- To become familiar with specialized C++ operators and expressions.

- To be able to distinguish between external and internal representations of character data.

- To understand how floating-point numbers are represented in the computer.

- To understand how the limited numeric precision of the computer can affect calculations.

- To be able to select the most appropriate simple data type for a given variable.

- To be able to declare and use an enumeration type.

- To be able to use the For and Switch statements with user-defined enumeration types.

- To be able to distinguish a named user-defined type from an anonymous user-defined type.

- To be able to create a user-written header file.

- To understand the concepts of type promotion and type demotion.

Until now, we have worked primarily with the data types int, char, bool, and float. These four data types are adequate for solving a wide variety of problems, but certain programs need other kinds of data. In this chapter, we take a closer look at all of the simple data types that are part of the C++ language. As part of this look, we discuss the limitations of the computer in doing calculations. We examine how these limitations can cause numerical errors and how to avoid such errors.

There are times when even the built-in data types cannot adequately represent all the data in a program. C++ has several mechanisms for creating *user-defined* data types; that is, we can define new data types ourselves. This chapter introduces one of these mechanisms, the enumeration type. In subsequent chapters, we introduce additional user-defined data types.

10.1 Built-In Simple Types

In Chapter 2, we defined a data type as a specific set of data values (which we call the *domain*) along with a set of operations on those values. For the int type, the domain is the set of whole numbers from INT_MIN through INT_MAX, and the allowable operations we have seen so far are +, –, *, /, %, ++, --, and the relational and logical operations. The domain of the float type is the set of all real numbers that a particular computer is capable of representing, and the operations are the same as those for the int type except that modulus (%) is excluded. For the bool type, the domain is the set consisting of the two values true and false, and the allowable operations are the logical (!, &&, ||) and relational operations. The char type, though used primarily to manipulate character data, is classified as an integral type because it uses integers in memory to stand for characters. Later in the chapter we see how this works.

Simple (atomic) data type A data type in which each value is atomic (indivisible).

The int, char, bool, and float types have a property in common. The domain of each type is made up of indivisible, or atomic, data values. Data types with this property are called **simple** (or **atomic**) **data types.** When we say that a value is atomic, we mean that it has no component parts that can be accessed individually. For example, a single character of type char is atomic, but the string "Good Morning" is not (it is composed of 12 individual characters).

Another way of describing a simple type is to say that only one value can be associated with a variable of that type. In contrast, a *structured type* is one in which an entire collection of values is associated with a single variable of that type. For example, a string object represents a collection of characters that are given a single name. Beginning in Chapter 11, we look at structured types.

Figure 10-1 displays the simple types that are built into the C++ language. In this figure, one of the types—enum—is not actually a single data type in the sense that int and float are data types. Instead, it is a mechanism with which we can define our own simple data types. We look at enum later in the chapter.

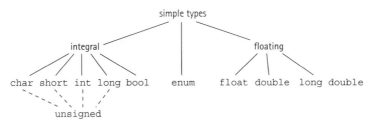

Figure 10-1 *C++ Simple Types*

The integral types `char`, `short`, `int`, and `long` represent nothing more than integers of different sizes. Similarly, the floating-point types `float`, `double`, and `long double` simply refer to floating-point numbers of different sizes. What do we mean by *sizes?*

In C++, sizes are measured in multiples of the size of a `char`. By definition, the size of a `char` is 1. On most computers, the 1 means one byte. (Recall from Chapter 1 that a byte is a group of eight consecutive bits [1s or 0s].)

Let's use the notation *sizeof*(SomeType) to denote the size of a value of type Some-Type. Then, by definition, *sizeof*(`char`) = 1. Other than `char`, the sizes of data objects in C++ are machine dependent. On one machine, it might be the case that

sizeof(`char`) = 1
sizeof(`short`) = 2
sizeof(`int`) = 4
sizeof(`long`) = 8

On another machine, the sizes might be as follows:

sizeof(`char`) = 1
sizeof(`short`) = 2
sizeof(`int`) = 2
sizeof(`long`) = 4

Despite these variations, the C++ language guarantees that the following statements are true:

- 1 = *sizeof*(`char`) ≤ *sizeof*(`short`) ≤ *sizeof*(`int`) ≤ *sizeof*(`long`).
- 1 ≤ *sizeof*(`bool`) ≤ *sizeof*(`long`).
- *sizeof*(`float`) ≤ *sizeof*(`double`) ≤ *sizeof*(`long double`).
- A `char` is at least 8 bits.
- A `short` is at least 16 bits.
- A `long` is at least 32 bits.

Range of values The interval within which values of a numeric type must fall, specified in terms of the largest and smallest allowable values.

For numeric data, the size of a data object determines its **range of values**. Let's look in more detail at the sizes, ranges of values, and literal constants for each of the built-in types.

Integral Types

Before looking at how the sizes of integral types affect their possible values, we remind you that the reserved word `unsigned` may precede the name of certain integral types—`unsigned char`, `unsigned short`, `unsigned int`, `unsigned long`. Values of these types are nonnegative integers with values from 0 through some machine-dependent maximum value. Although we rarely use unsigned types in this book, we include them in this discussion for thoroughness.

Ranges of Values The following table displays sample ranges of values for the `char`, `short`, `int`, and `long` data types and their `unsigned` variations.

Type	Size in Bytes*	Minimum Value*	Maximum Value*
char	1	−128	127
unsigned char	1	0	255
short	2	−32,768	32,767
unsigned short	2	0	65,535
int	2	−32,768	32,767
unsigned int	2	0	65,535
long	4	−2,147,483,648	2,147,483,647
unsigned long	4	0	4,294,967,295

* These values are for one particular machine. Your machine's values may be different.

C++ systems provide the header file `climits`, from which you can determine the maximum and minimum values for your machine. This header file defines the constants CHAR_MAX and CHAR_MIN, SHRT_MAX and SHRT_MIN, INT_MAX and INT_MIN, and LONG_MAX and LONG_MIN. The unsigned types have a minimum value of 0 and maximum values defined by `UCHAR_MAX`, `USHRT_MAX`, `UINT_MAX`, and `ULONG_MAX`. To find out the values specific to your computer, you could print them out like this:

```
#include <climits>
using namespace std;
    ⋮
cout << "Max. long = " << LONG_MAX << endl;
cout << "Min. long = " << LONG_MIN << endl;
    ⋮
```

Literal Constants   In C++, the valid `bool` constants are `true` and `false`. Integer constants can be specified in three different number bases: decimal (base 10), octal (base 8), and hexadecimal (base 16). Octal and hexadecimal values are used in system software (compilers, linkers, and operating systems, for example) to refer directly to individual bits in a memory cell. These manipulations of low-level objects in a computer are the subject of more advanced study and are outside the scope of this book.

The following table shows examples of integer constants in C++. Notice that an `L` or a `U` (either uppercase or lowercase) can be added to the end of a constant to signify `long` or `unsigned`, respectively.

Constant	Type	Remarks
1658	int	Decimal (base-10) integer.
03172	int	Octal (base-8) integer. Begins with 0 (zero). Decimal equivalent is 1658.
0x67A	int	Hexadecimal (base-16) integer. Begins with 0 (zero), then either x or X. Decimal equivalent is 1658.
65535U	unsigned int	Unsigned constants end in U or u.
421L	long	Explicit `long` constant. Ends in L or l.
53100	long	Implicit `long` constant, assuming the machine's maximum int is, say, 32767.
389123487UL	unsigned long	Unsigned `long` constants end in UL or LU in any combination of uppercase and lowercase letters.

Notice that this table presents only numeric constants for the integral types. We discuss `char` constants later in a separate section.

Floating-Point Types

Ranges of Values   Following is a table that gives sample ranges of values for the three floating-point types, `float`, `double`, and `long double`. In this table we show, for each type, the maximum positive value and the minimum positive value (a tiny fraction that is very close to 0). Negative numbers have the same range but the opposite sign. Ranges of values are expressed in exponential (scientific) notation, where 3.4E+38 means 3.4×10^{38}.

Type	Size in Bytes*	Minimum Positive Value*	Maximum Positive Value*
float	4	3.4E–38	3.4E+38
double	8	1.7E–308	1.7E+308
long double	10	3.4E–4932	1.1E+4932

*These values are for one particular machine. Your machine's values may be different.

The standard header file `cfloat` defines the constants `FLT_MAX` and `FLT_MIN`, `DBL_MAX` and `DBL_MIN`, and `LDBL_MAX` and `LDBL_MIN`. To determine the ranges of values for your machine, you could write a short program that prints out these constants.

Literal Constants   When you use a floating-point constant such as 5.8 in a C++ program, its type is assumed to be `double` (double precision). If you store the value into a `float` variable, the computer coerces its type from `double` to `float` (single precision). If you insist on a constant being of type `float` rather than `double`, you can append an F or an f at the end of the constant. Similarly, a suffix of L or l signifies a `long double` constant. Here are some examples of floating-point constants in C++:

Constant	Type	Remarks
6.83	double	By default, floating-point constants are of type `double`.
6.83F	float	Explicit `float` constants end in F or f.
6.83L	long double	Explicit `long double` constants end in L or l.
4.35E-9	double	Exponential notation, meaning 4.35×10^{-9}.

10.2 Additional C++ Operators

C++ has a rich, sometimes bewildering, variety of operators that allow you to manipulate values of the simple data types. Operators you have learned about so far include the assignment operator (=), the arithmetic operators (+, -, *, /, %), the increment and decrement operators (++, --), the relational operators (==, !=, <, <=, >, >=), and the logical operators (!, &&, ||). In certain cases, a pair of parentheses is also considered to be an operator—namely, the function call operator,

```
ComputeSum(x, y);
```

and the type cast operator,

```
y = float(someInt);
```

C++ also has many specialized operators that are seldom found in other programming languages. Here is a table of these additional operators. As you inspect the table, don't panic—a quick scan will do.

We won't be using most of these operators in this text, and we discuss them only briefly so that you will have some familiarity with them if you should encounter them in other people's programs.

Operator		Remarks
Combined assignment operators		
+=	Add and assign	
-=	Subtract and assign	
*=	Multiply and assign	
/=	Divide and assign	
Increment and decrement operators		
++	Pre-increment	Example: ++someVar
++	Post-increment	Example: someVar++
--	Pre-decrement	Example: --someVar
--	Post-decrement	Example: someVar--
Bitwise operators		Integer operands only
<<	Left shift	
>>	Right shift	
&	Bitwise AND	
|	Bitwise OR	
^	Bitwise EXCLUSIVE OR	
~	Complement (invert all bits)	
More combined assignment operators		Integer operands only
%=	Modulus and assign	
<<=	Shift left and assign	
>>=	Shift right and assign	
&=	Bitwise AND and assign	
|=	Bitwise OR and assign	
^=	Bitwise EXCLUSIVE OR and assign	
Other operators		
()	Cast	
sizeof	Size of operand in bytes	Form: sizeof Expr or sizeof(Type)
?:	Conditional operator	Form: Expr1 ? Expr2 : Expr3

The operators in this table, along with those you already know, comprise most—but not all—of the C++ operators. We introduce a few more operators in later chapters as the need arises.

Assignment Operators and Assignment Expressions

Assignment expression   A C++ expression with (1) a value and (2) the side effect of storing the expression value into a memory location.

C++ has several assignment operators. The equal sign (=) is the basic assignment operator. When combined with its two operands, it forms an **assignment expression** (*not* an assignment statement). Every assignment expression has a *value* and a *side effect,* namely, that the value is stored into the object denoted by the left-hand side. For example, the expression

```
delta = 2 * 12
```

Expression statement   A statement formed by appending a semicolon to an expression.

has the value 24 and the side effect of storing this value into delta. In C++, any expression becomes an expression statement when it is terminated by a semicolon. Therefore,

```
delta = 2 * 12;
```

is an expression statement (in this case, more commonly called an *assignment statement*).

Because an assignment is an expression, not a statement, you can use it anywhere an expression is allowed. Here is a statement that stores the value 20 into firstInt, the value 30 into secondInt, and the value 35 into thirdInt:

```
thirdInt = (secondInt = (firstInt = 20) + 10) + 5;
```

Some C++ programmers use this style of coding, but others find it hard to read and error-prone.

In Chapter 5, we cautioned against the mistake of using the = operator in place of the == operator:

```
if (alpha = 12)   // Wrong
    ⋮
else
    ⋮
```

The condition in the If statement is an assignment expression, not a relational expression. The value of the expression is 12 (interpreted in the If condition as true), so the else-clause is never executed. Worse yet, the side effect of the assignment expression is to store 12 into `alpha`, destroying its previous contents.

In addition to the = operator, C++ has several combined assignment operators (+=, *=, and the others listed in our table of operators). These operators have the following semantics:

Statement	Equivalent Statement
`i += 5;`	`i = i + 5;`
`pivotPoint *= n + 3;`	`pivotPoint = pivotPoint * (n + 3);`

The combined assignment operators are another example of "ice cream and cake." They are sometimes convenient for writing a line of code more compactly, but you can do just fine without them.

Increment and Decrement Operators

The increment and decrement operators (++ and --) operate only on variables, not on constants or arbitrary expressions. Suppose a variable `someInt` contains the value 3. The expression `++someInt` denotes pre-incrementation. The side effect of incrementing `someInt` occurs first, so the resulting value of the expression is 4. In contrast, the expression `someInt++` denotes post-incrementation. The value of the expression is 3, and *then* the side effect of incrementing `someInt` takes place. The following code illustrates the difference between pre- and post-incrementation:

```
int1 = 14;
int2 = ++int1;    // Increments int1, then assigns 15 to int2

int1 = 14;
int2 = int1++;    // Assigns 14 to int2, then increments int1
```

Using side effects in the middle of larger expressions is always a bit dangerous. It's easy to make semantic errors, and the code may be confusing to read. Look at this example:

```
a = (b = c++) * --d / (e += f++);
```

Some people make a game of seeing how much they can do in the fewest keystrokes possible. But they should remember that serious software development requires writing code that other programmers can read and understand. Overuse of side effects hinders this goal. By far the most common use of ++ and -- is to do the incrementation or decrementation as a separate expression statement:

```
count++;
```

Here, the value of the expression is unused, but we get the desired side effect of incrementing `count`.

Bitwise Operators

The bitwise operators listed in the operator table ($<<$, $>>$, &, |, and so forth) are used for manipulating individual bits within a memory cell. This book does not explore the use of these operators; the topic of bit-level operations is most often covered in a course on computer organization and assembly language programming. However, be aware that if you mistakenly write & for && or | for ||, your program will probably compile successfully but will produce erroneous results. Like writing = when you mean ==, this is a very common mistake in C++ programs.

The Cast Operation

You have seen that C++ is very liberal about letting the programmer mix data types in expressions, in assignment operations, in argument passing, and in returning a function value. Instead of relying on implicit type coercion, we have recommended using an explicit type cast to show that the type conversion is intentional:

```
intVar = int(floatVar);
```

In C++, the cast operation comes in two forms:

```
intVar = int(floatVar);     // Functional notation
intVar = (int) floatVar;    // Prefix notation. Parentheses required
```

The first form is called functional notation because it looks like a function call. It isn't really a function call (there is no subprogram named `int`), but it has the appearance of a function call. The second form, prefix notation, is the only form available in the C language; C++ added the functional notation.

Although most C++ programmers use the functional notation for the cast operation, there is one restriction on its use. The data type name must be a single identifier. If the type name consists of more than one identifier, you *must* use prefix notation. For example,

```
myVar = unsigned int(someFloat);    // Not valid
myVar = (unsigned int) someFloat;   // Valid
```

The `sizeof` Operator

The `sizeof` operator is a unary operator that yields the size, in bytes, of its operand. The operand can be a variable name, as in

```
sizeof someInt
```

or the operand can be the name of a data type, enclosed in parentheses:

```
sizeof(float)
```

You could find out the sizes of various data types on your machine by using code like this:

```
cout << "Size of a short is " << sizeof(short) << endl;
```

The ?: Operator

The last operator in our operator table is the ?: operator, sometimes called the conditional operator. It is a ternary (three-operand) operator with the following syntax:

ConditionalExpression

> Expression1 **?** Expression2 **:** Expression3

The computer evaluates Expression1. If the value is true, then the value of the entire expression is Expression2; otherwise, the value of the entire expression is Expression3. (Only one of Expression2 and Expression3 is evaluated.) A classic example of its use is to set a variable max equal to the larger of two variables a and b. Using an If statement, we would do it this way:

```
if (a > b)
    max = a;
else
    max = b;
```

With the ?: operator, we can use the following assignment statement:

```
max = (a > b) ? a : b;
```

In this example, we used parentheses around the expression being tested. These parentheses are unnecessary because, as we'll see shortly, the conditional operator has very low precedence. But it is customary to include the parentheses for clarity.

Operator Precedence

Following is a summary of operator precedence for the C++ operators we have encountered so far, excluding the bitwise operators. (Appendix B contains the complete list.) In the table, the operators are grouped by precedence level, and a horizontal line separates each precedence level from the next-lower level.

Precedence (highest to lowest)		
Operator	Associativity	Remarks
`()`	Left to right	Function call and function-style cast
`++ --`	Right to left	`++` and `--` as postfix operators
`++ -- !` Unary `+` Unary `-`	Right to left	`++` and `--` as prefix operators
`(cast)` `sizeof`	Right to left	
`*` `/` `%`	Left to right	
`+` `-`	Left to right	
`<` `<=` `>` `>=`	Left to right	
`==` `!=`	Left to right	
`&&`	Left to right	
`||`	Left to right	
`? :`	Right to left	
`=` `+=` `-=` `*=` `/=`	Right to left	

The column labeled *Associativity* describes grouping order. Within a precedence level, most operators group from left to right. For example,

```
a - b + c
```

means

```
(a - b) + c
```

Certain operators, though, group from right to left. Look at the assignment operators, for example. The expression

```
sum = count = 0
```

means

```
sum = (count = 0)
```

This associativity makes sense because the assignment operation is naturally a right-to-left operation.

10.3 Working with Character Data

We have been using `char` variables to store character data, such as the character 'A' or 'e' or '+':

```
char someChar;
   ⋮
someChar = 'A';
```

However, because `char` is an integral type and `sizeof(char)` equals 1, a `char` variable can store a small (usually one-byte) integer constant. For example,

```
char counter;
   ⋮
counter = 3;
```

On computers with a very limited amount of memory space, programmers sometimes use the `char` type to save memory when they are working with small integers.

A natural question to ask is, How does the computer know the difference between integer data and character data when the data is sitting in a memory cell? The answer is, The computer *can't* tell the difference! To explain this surprising fact, we must look more closely at how character data is stored in a computer.

Character Sets

Each computer uses a particular character set, the set of all possible characters with which it is capable of working. Two character sets widely in use today are the ASCII character set and the EBCDIC character set. ASCII is used by the vast majority of all computers, whereas EBCDIC is found primarily on IBM mainframe computers. ASCII consists of 128 different characters, and EBCDIC has 256 characters. Appendix E shows the characters that are available in these two character sets.

A more recently developed character set called *Unicode* allows many more distinct characters than either ASCII or EBCDIC. Unicode was invented primarily to accommodate the larger alphabets and symbols of various international human languages. In C++, the data type `wchar_t` rather than `char` is used for Unicode characters. In fact, `wchar_t` can be used for other, possibly infrequently used, "wide character" sets in addition to Unicode. In this book, we do not examine Unicode or the `wchar_t` type. We continue to focus our attention on the `char` type and the ASCII and EBCDIC character sets.

Whichever character set is being used, each character has an **external representation**—the way it looks on an I/O device like a printer—and an **internal representation**—the way it is stored inside the computer's memory. If you use the `char` constant 'A' in a C++ program, its external representation is the letter *A*. That is, if you print it out you see an *A*, as you would expect. Its internal representation, though, is an integer value. For example, the ASCII table in Appendix E shows that the character 'A' has internal representation 65.

> **External representation** The printable (character) form of a data value.
>
> **Internal representation** The form in which a data value is stored inside the memory unit.

Let's look again at the statement

```
someChar = 'A';
```

Assuming our machine uses the ASCII character set, the compiler translates the constant 'A' into the integer 65. We could also have written the statement as

```
someChar = 65;
```

Both statements have exactly the same effect—that of storing 65 into someChar. However, the second version is *not* recommended. It is not as understandable as the first version, and it is nonportable (the program won't work correctly on a machine that uses EBCDIC, which uses a different internal representation—193—for 'A').

Earlier we mentioned that the computer cannot tell the difference between character and integer data in memory. Both are stored internally as integers. However, when we perform I/O operations, the computer does the right thing—it uses the external representation that corresponds to the data type of the expression being printed. Look at this code segment, for example:

```
// This example assumes use of the ASCII character set
int   someInt = 97;
char someChar = 97;

cout << someInt << endl;
cout << someChar << endl;
```

When these statements are executed, the output is

```
97
a
```

When the << operator outputs someInt, it prints the sequence of characters 9 and 7. To output someChar, it prints the single character a. Even though both variables contain the value 97 internally, the data type of each variable determines how it is printed.

C++ char Constants

In C++, char constants come in two different forms. The first form, which we have been using regularly, is a single printable character enclosed by apostrophes (single quotes):

```
'A'    '8'    ')'    '+'
```

Notice that we said *printable* character. Character sets include both printable characters and *control characters* (or *nonprintable characters*). Control characters are not meant to be printed but are used to control the screen, printer, and other hardware devices. If you look at the ASCII character table, you see that the printable characters are those with integer values 32–126. The remaining characters (with values 0–31 and 127) are nonprintable control characters.

To accommodate control characters, C++ provides a second form of char constant: the *escape sequence*. An escape sequence is one or more characters preceded by a backslash (\). You are familiar with the escape sequence \n, which represents the newline character. Here is the complete description of the two forms of char constant in C++:

1. A single printable character—except an apostrophe (') or backslash (\)—enclosed by apostrophes.

2. One of the following escape sequences, enclosed by apostrophes:

\n	Newline (Line feed in ASCII)
\t	Horizontal tab
\v	Vertical tab
\b	Backspace
\r	Carriage return
\f	Form feed
\a	Alert (a bell or beep)
\\	Backslash
\'	Single quote (apostrophe)
\"	Double quote (quotation mark)
\0	Null character (all 0 bits)
\ddd	Octal equivalent (one, two, or three octal digits specifying the integer value of the desired character)
\xddd	Hexadecimal equivalent (one or more hexadecimal digits specifying the integer value of the desired character)

Even though an escape sequence is written as two or more characters, each escape sequence represents a single character in the character set. In the list of escape sequences above, the entries labeled *Octal equivalent* and *Hexadecimal equivalent* let you refer to any character in your machine's character set by specifying its integer value in either octal or hexadecimal form.

Note that you can use an escape sequence within a string just as you can use any printable character within a string. The statement

```
cout << "\aWhoops!\n";
```

beeps the beeper, displays Whoops!, and terminates the output line. The statement

```
cout << "She said \"Hi\"";
```

outputs She said "Hi" and does not terminate the output line.

Programming Techniques

What kinds of things can we do with character data in a program? The possibilities are endless and depend, of course, on the particular problem we are solving. But several techniques are so widely used that it's worth taking a look at them.

Comparing Characters In previous chapters, you have seen examples of comparing characters for equality. We have used tests such as

```
if (ch == 'a')   and   while (inputChar != '\n')
```

Characters can also be compared by using <, <=, >, and >=. For example, if the variable firstLetter contains the first letter of a person's last name, we can test to see if the last name starts with *A* through *H* by using this test:

```
if (firstLetter >= 'A' && firstLetter <= 'H')
```

On one level of thought, a test like this is reasonable if you think of < as meaning "comes before" in the character set and > as meaning "comes after." On another level, the test makes even more sense when you consider that the underlying representation of a character is an integer number. The machine literally compares the two integer values using the mathematical meaning of less than or greater than.

When you write a logical expression to check whether a character lies within a certain range of values, you sometimes have to keep in mind the character set your machine uses. A test like

```
if (ch >= 'a' && ch <= 'z')
```

works correctly on machines that use ASCII, but not on machines that use EBCDIC because the ordering of letters in EBCDIC is interspersed with control characters. A better approach is to take advantage of the "is..." functions supplied by the standard library through the header file cctype. If you replace the above If test with this one:

```
if (islower(ch))
```

then your program is more portable; the test works correctly on any machine, regardless of its character set. It's a good idea to become well acquainted with these character-testing library functions (Appendix C). They can save you time and help you to write more portable programs.

Converting Digit Characters to Integers Suppose you want to convert a digit that is read in character form to its numeric equivalent. Because the digit characters '0' through '9' are consecutive in both the ASCII and EBCDIC character sets, subtracting '0' from any digit in character form gives the digit in numeric form:

```
'0' - '0' = 0
'1' - '0' = 1
'2' - '0' = 2
    ⋮
```

Why would you want to do this? Recall that when the extraction operator (>>) reads data into an int variable, the input stream fails if an invalid character is encountered. (And once the stream has failed, no further input will succeed.) Suppose you're writing a program that prompts an inexperienced user to enter a number from 1 through 5. If the input variable is of type int and the user accidentally types a letter of the alphabet, the program is in trouble. To defend against this possibility, you might read the user's response as a character and convert it to a number, performing error checking along the way. Here's a code segment that demonstrates the technique:

```
#include <cctype>    // For isdigit()
using namespace std;
    :
void GetResponse( /* out */ int& response )
{
    char inChar;
    bool badData = false;

    do
    {
        cout << "Enter a number from 1 through 5: ";
        cin >> inChar;
        if ( !isdigit(inChar) )
            badData = true;                        // It's not a digit
        else
        {
            response = int(inChar - '0');
            if (response < 1 || response > 5)
                badData = true;                    // It's a digit, but
        }                                          // it's out of range
        if (badData)
            cout << "Please try again." << endl;
    } while (badData);
}
```

Converting to Lowercase and Uppercase When working with character data, you sometimes find that you need to convert a lowercase letter to uppercase, or vice versa. Fortunately, the programming technique required to do these conversions is easy—a simple call to a library function is all it takes. Through the header file cctype, the standard library provides not only the "is..." functions we have discussed, but also two value-returning functions named toupper and tolower. Here are their descriptions:

Header File	Function	Function Type	Function Value
<cctype>	toupper(ch)	char*	Uppercase equivalent of ch, if ch is a lowercase letter; ch, otherwise
<cctype>	tolower(ch)	char	Lowercase equivalent of ch, if ch is an uppercase letter; ch, otherwise

*Technically, both the argument and the return value are of type int. But conceptually, the functions operate on character data.

Notice that the value returned by each function is just the original character if the condition is not met. For example, tolower('M') returns the character 'm', whereas tolower('+') returns '+'.

A common use of these two functions is to let the user respond to certain input prompts by using either uppercase or lowercase letters. For example, if you want to allow either *Y* or *y* for a "Yes" response from the user, and either *N* or *n* for "No," you might do this:

```
#include <cctype>    // For toupper()
using namespace std;
    ⋮
cout << "Enter Y or N: ";
cin >> inputChar;
if (toupper(inputChar) == 'Y')
{
    ⋮
}
else if (toupper(inputChar) == 'N')
{
    ⋮
}
else
    PrintErrorMsg();
```

Accessing Characters Within a String In the last section, the code segment accepted a response of 'Y' or 'N' in uppercase or lowercase letters. If a problem requires the user to type the entire word *Yes* or *No* in any combination of uppercase and lowercase letters, the code becomes more complicated. Reading the user's response as a string into a string object named inputStr, we would need a lengthy If-Then-Else-If structure to compare inputStr to "yes", "Yes", "yEs", "yeS", and so on.

As an alternative, let's inspect only the first character of the input string, comparing it with 'Y', 'y', 'N', or 'n', and then ignore the rest of the string. The string class allows you to access an individual character in a string by giving its position number in square brackets:

StringObject [Position]

Within a string, the first character is at position 0, the second is at position 1, and so forth. Therefore, the value of Position must be greater than or equal to 0 and less than or equal to the string length minus 1. For example, if `inputStr` is a `string` object and `ch` is a `char` variable, the statement

```
ch = inputStr[2];
```

accesses the character at position 2 of the string (the third character) and copies it into `ch`.

Now we can sketch out the code for reading a "Yes" or "No" response, checking only the first letter of that response.

```
string inputStr;
   ⋮
cout << "Enter Yes or No: ";
cin >> inputStr;
if (toupper(inputStr[0]) == 'Y')
{
   ⋮
}
else if (toupper(inputStr[0]) == 'N')
{
   ⋮
}
else
    PrintErrorMsg();
```

10.4   More on Floating-Point Numbers

We have used floating-point numbers off and on since we introduced them in Chapter 2, but we have not examined them in depth. Floating-point numbers have special properties when used on the computer. Thus far, we've almost ignored these properties, but now it's time to consider them in detail.

Representation of Floating-Point Numbers

Let's assume we have a computer in which each memory location is the same size and is divided into a sign plus five decimal digits. When a variable or constant is defined, the location assigned to it consists of five digits and a sign. When an `int` variable or constant is defined, the interpretation of the number stored in that place is straightforward. When a `float` variable or constant is defined, the number stored there has both a whole number part and a fractional part, so it must be coded to represent both parts.

Let's see what such coded numbers might look like. The range of whole numbers we can represent with five digits is –99,999 through +99,999:

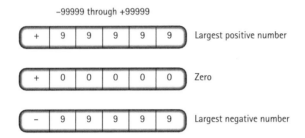

Our **precision** (the number of digits we can represent) is five digits, and each number within that range can be represented exactly.

Precision The maximum number of significant digits.

What happens if we allow one of those digits (the leftmost one, for example) to represent an exponent?

Then +82345 represents the number $+2345 \times 10^8$. The range of numbers we now can represent is much larger:

-9999×10^9 through 9999×10^9

NUMBER	POWER OF TEN NOTATION	CODED REPRESENTATION						VALUE
		Sign	Exp					
+99,999	$+9999 \times 10^1$	+	1	9	9	9	9	+99,990
		Sign	Exp					
–999,999	-9999×10^2	–	2	9	9	9	9	–999,900
		Sign	Exp					
+1,000,000	-1000×10^3	+	3	1	0	0	0	+1,000,000
		Sign	Exp					
–4,932,416	-4932×10^3	–	3	4	9	3	2	–4,932,000

Figure 10-2 *Coding Using Positive Exponents*

or

−9,999,000,000,000 through +9,999,000,000,000

However, our precision is now only four digits; that is, only four-digit numbers can be represented exactly in our system. What happens to numbers with more digits? The four leftmost digits are represented correctly, and the rightmost digits, or least significant digits, are lost (assumed to be 0). Figure 10-2 shows what happens. Note that 1,000,000 can be represented exactly but −4,932,416 cannot, because our coding scheme limits us to four **significant digits**.

Significant digits   Those digits from the first nonzero digit on the left to the last nonzero digit on the right (plus any 0 digits that are exact).

To extend our coding scheme to represent floating-point numbers, we must be able to represent negative exponents. Examples are

$7394 \times 10^{-2} = 73.94$

and

$22 \times 10^{-4} = .0022$

Because our scheme does not include a sign for the exponent, let's change it slightly. The existing sign becomes the sign of the exponent, and we add a sign to the far left to represent the sign of the number itself (see Figure 10-3).

All the numbers between -9999×10^9 and 9999×10^9 can now be represented accurately to four digits. Adding negative exponents to our scheme allows us to represent fractional numbers as small as 1×10^{-9}.

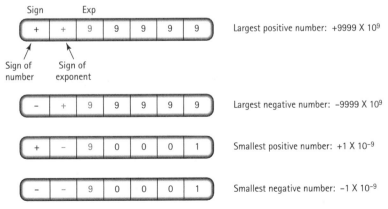

Figure 10-3 *Coding Using Positive and Negative Exponents*

Arithmetic with Floating-Point Numbers

When we use integer arithmetic, our results are exact. Floating-point arithmetic, however, is seldom exact. To understand why, let's add three floating-point numbers x, y, and z using our coding scheme.

First, we add x to y and then we add z to the result. Next, we perform the operations in a different order, adding y to z, and then adding x to that result. The associative law of arithmetic says that the two answers should be the same—but are they? Let's use the following values for x, y, and z:

$$x = -1324 \times 10^3 \quad y = 1325 \times 10^3 \quad z = 5424 \times 10^0$$

Here is the result of adding z to the sum of x and y:

$$
\begin{array}{lll}
(x) & -1324 \times 10^3 \\
(y) & \underline{1325 \times 10^3} \\
& 1 \times 10^3 & = 1000 \times 10^0 \\
\\
(x+y) & 1000 \times 10^0 \\
(z) & \underline{5424 \times 10^0} \\
& 6424 \times 10^0 & \leftarrow (x+y)+z
\end{array}
$$

Now here is the result of adding x to the sum of y and z:

$$
\begin{array}{lll}
(y) & 1325000 \times 10^0 \\
(z) & \underline{5424 \times 10^0} \\
& 1330424 \times 10^0 & = 1330 \times 10^3 \text{ (truncated to four digits)} \\
\\
(y+z) & 1330 \times 10^3 \\
(x) & \underline{-1324 \times 10^3} \\
& 6 \times 10^3 & = 6000 \times 10^0 \leftarrow x + (y + z)
\end{array}
$$

Representational error Arithmetic error that occurs when the precision of the true result of an arithmetic operation is greater than the precision of the machine.

These two answers are the same in the thousands place but are different thereafter. The error behind this discrepancy is called **representational error**.

Because of representational errors, it is unwise to use a floating-point variable as a loop control variable. Because precision may be lost in calculations involving floating-point numbers, it is difficult to predict when (or even *if*) a loop control variable of type `float` (or `double` or `long double`) will equal the termination value. A count-controlled loop with a floating-point control variable can behave unpredictably.

Also because of representational errors, you should never compare floating-point numbers for exact equality. Rarely are two floating-point numbers exactly equal, and thus you should compare them only for near equality. If the difference between the two numbers is less than some acceptable small value, you can consider them equal for the purposes of the given problem.

Underflow and Overflow   In addition to representational errors, there are two other problems to watch out for in floating-point arithmetic: *underflow* and *overflow*.

Underflow is the condition that arises when the value of a calculation is too small to be represented. Going back to our decimal representation, let's look at a calculation involving small numbers:

$$\begin{array}{r} 4210 \times 10^{-8} \\ \times\ 2000 \times 10^{-8} \\ \hline 8420000 \times 10^{-16} \ =\ 8420 \times 10^{-13} \end{array}$$

This value cannot be represented in our scheme because the exponent −13 is too small. Our minimum is −9. One way to resolve the problem is to set the result of the calculation to 0.0. Obviously, any answer depending on this calculation will not be exact.

Overflow is a more serious problem because there is no logical recourse when it occurs. For example, the result of the calculation

$$\begin{array}{r} 9999 \times 10^{9} \\ \times\ 1000 \times 10^{9} \\ \hline 9999000 \times 10^{18} \ =\ 9999 \times 10^{21} \end{array}$$

cannot be stored, so what should we do? To be consistent with our response to underflow, we could set the result to 9999×10^9 (the maximum representable value in this case). Yet this seems intuitively wrong. The alternative is to stop with an error message.

C++ does not define what should happen in the case of overflow or underflow. Different implementations of C++ solve the problem in different ways. You might try to cause an overflow with your system and see what happens. Some systems may print a run-time error message such as "FLOATING POINT OVERFLOW." On other systems, you may get the largest number that can be represented.

Although we are discussing problems with floating-point numbers, integer numbers also can overflow both negatively and positively. Most implementations of C++ ignore integer overflow. To see how your system handles the situation, you should try adding 1 to INT_MAX and −1 to INT_MIN. On most systems, adding 1 to INT_MAX sets the result to INT_MIN, a negative number.

Choosing a Numeric Data Type

A first encounter with all the numeric data types of C++ may leave you feeling overwhelmed. To help in choosing among them, here are some guidelines:

1. Use floating-point types *only* when you definitely need fractional values.

2. For ordinary integer data, use `int` instead of `char` or `short`. It's easy to make overflow errors with these smaller data types.
3. Use `long` only if the range of `int` values on your machine is too restrictive.
4. Use `double` and `long double` only if you need enormously large or small numbers, or if your machine's `float` values do not carry enough digits of precision.
5. Avoid the `unsigned` forms of integral types.

By following these guidelines, you'll find that the simple types you use most often are `int` and `float`, along with `char` for character data and `bool` for Boolean data. Only rarely do you need the longer and shorter variations of these fundamental types.

10.5 User-Defined Simple Types

The concept of a data type is fundamental to all of the widely used programming languages. One of the strengths of the C++ language is that it allows programmers to create new data types, tailored to meet the needs of a particular program. Much of the remainder of this book is about user-defined data types. In this section, we examine how to create our own simple types.

The Typedef Statement

The *Typedef statement* allows you to introduce a new name for an existing type. Its syntax template is

TypedefStatement

```
typedef ExistingTypeName NewTypeName;
```

Before the `bool` data type was part of the C++ language, many programmers used code like the following to simulate a Boolean type:

```
typedef int Boolean;
const int TRUE = 1;
const int FALSE = 0;
   ⋮
Boolean dataOK;
   ⋮
dataOK = TRUE;
```

In this code, the Typedef statement causes the compiler to substitute the word `int` for every occurrence of the word `Boolean` in the rest of the program.

The Typedef statement provides a very limited way of defining our own data types. In fact, Typedef does not create a new data type at all: It merely creates an additional name for an existing data type. As far as the compiler is concerned, the domain and operations of the above `Boolean` type are identical to the domain and operations of the `int` type.

Names of user-defined types obey the same scope rules that apply to identifiers in general. Most types like `Boolean` above are defined globally, although it is reasonable to define a new type within a subprogram if that is the only place it is used.

Enumeration Types

C++ allows the user to define a new simple type by listing (enumerating) the literal values that make up the domain of the type. These literal values must be *identifiers,* not numbers. The identifiers are separated by commas, and the list is enclosed in braces. Data types defined in this way are called **enumeration types.** Here's an example:

> **Enumeration type** A user-defined data type whose domain is an ordered set of literal values expressed as identifiers.

```
enum Days {SUN, MON, TUE, WED, THU, FRI, SAT};
```

This declaration creates a new data type named `Days`. Whereas Typedef merely creates a synonym for an existing type, an enumeration type like `Days` is truly a new type and is distinct from any existing type.

The values in the `Days` type—SUN, MON, TUE, and so forth—are called **enumerators.** The enumerators are *ordered,* in the sense that SUN < MON < TUE ... < FRI < SAT. When applying relational operators to enumerators, the relation that is tested is "comes before" or "comes after" in the ordering of the data type.

> **Enumerator** One of the values in the domain of an enumeration type.

Earlier we saw that the internal representation of a `char` constant is a nonnegative integer. The 128 ASCII characters are represented in memory as the integers 0 through 127. Values in an enumeration type are also represented internally as integers. By default, the first enumerator has the integer value 0, the second has the value 1, and so forth.

If there is some reason that you want different internal representations for the enumerators, you can specify them explicitly like this:

```
enum Days {SUN = 4, MON = 18, TUE = 9, ... };
```

There is rarely any reason to assign specific values to enumerators. With the `Days` type, we are interested in the days of the week, not in the way the machine stores them internally.

Because enumerators are, in essence, named constants, we capitalize the entire identifier. This is purely a style choice. Many C++ programmers use both uppercase and lowercase letters when they invent names for the enumerators.

The identifiers used as enumerators must follow the rules for any C++ identifier. For example,

```
enum Vowel {'A', 'E', 'I', 'O', 'U'};     // Error
```

is not legal because the items are not identifiers. The declaration

```
enum Places {1st, 2nd, 3rd};     // Error
```

is not legal because identifiers cannot begin with digits. In the declarations

```
enum Starch {CORN, RICE, POTATO, BEAN};
enum Grain {WHEAT, CORN, RYE, BARLEY, SORGHUM};     // Error
```

type `Starch` and type `Grain` are legal individually, but together they are not. Identifiers in the same scope must be unique. `CORN` cannot be defined twice.

Suppose you are writing a program for a veterinary clinic. The program must keep track of different kinds of animals. The following enumeration type might be used for this purpose.

Type identifier   Literal values in the domain
        ↓
```
enum Animals {RODENT, CAT, DOG, BIRD, REPTILE, HORSE, BOVINE, SHEEP};

Animals inPatient;   ⎫
Animals outPatient;  ⎬ Creation of two variables of type Animals
```

`RODENT` is a literal, one of the values in the data type `Animals`. Be sure you understand that `RODENT` is not a variable name. Instead, `RODENT` is one of the values that can be stored into the variables `inPatient` and `outPatient`. Let's look at the kinds of operations we might want to perform on variables of enumeration types.

Assignment   The assignment statement

```
inPatient = DOG;
```

does not assign to `inPatient` the character string "DOG", nor the contents of a variable named `DOG`. It assigns the *value* `DOG`, which is one of the values in the domain of the data type `Animals`.

Assignment is a valid operation, as long as the value being stored is of type `Animals`. Both of the statements

```
inPatient = DOG;
outPatient = inPatient;
```

are acceptable. Each expression on the right-hand side is of type `Animals`—`DOG` is a literal of type `Animals`, and `inPatient` is a variable of type `Animals`. Although we know that the underlying representation of `DOG` is the integer 2, the compiler prevents us from using this assignment:

```
inPatient = 2;   // Not allowed
```

Here is the precise rule:

Implicit type coercion is defined from an enumeration type to an integral type but not from an integral type to an enumeration type.

Applying this rule to the statements

```
someInt = DOG;   // Valid
inPatient = 2;   // Error
```

we see that the first statement stores 2 into `someInt` (because of implicit type coercion), but the second produces a compile-time error. The restriction against storing an integer value into a variable of type `Animals` is to keep you from accidentally storing an out-of-range value:

```
inPatient = 65;   // Error
```

Incrementation   Suppose that you want to "increment" the value in `inPatient` so that it becomes the next value in the domain:

```
inPatient = inPatient + 1;   // Error
```

This statement is illegal for the following reason. The right-hand side is OK because implicit type coercion lets you add `inPatient` to 1; the result is an `int` value. But the assignment operation is not valid because you can't store an `int` value into `inPatient`. The statement

```
inPatient++;   // Error
```

is also invalid because the compiler considers it to have the same semantics as the assignment statement above. However, you can escape the type coercion rule by using an *explicit* type conversion—a type cast—as follows:

```
inPatient = Animals(inPatient + 1);   // Correct
```

When you use the type cast, the compiler assumes that you know what you are doing and allows it.

Incrementing a variable of enumeration type is very useful in loops. Sometimes we need a loop that processes all the values in the domain of the type. We might try the following For loop:

```
Animals patient;

for (patient=RODENT; patient <= SHEEP; patient++)  // Error
    ⋮
```

However, as we explained previously, the compiler will complain about the expression patient++. To increment patient, we must use an assignment expression and a type cast:

```
for (patient=RODENT; patient <= SHEEP; patient=Animals(patient + 1))
    ⋮
```

The only caution here is that when control exits the loop, the value of patient is 1 *greater than* the largest value in the domain (SHEEP). If you want to use patient outside the loop, you must reassign it a value that is within the appropriate range for the Animals type.

Comparison   The most common operation performed on values of enumeration types is comparison. When you compare two values, their ordering is determined by the order in which you listed the enumerators in the type declaration. For instance, the expression

```
inPatient <= BIRD
```

has the value true if inPatient contains the value RODENT, CAT, DOG, or BIRD.

You can also use values of an enumeration type in a Switch statement. Because RODENT, CAT, and so on are literals, they can appear in case labels:

```
switch (inPatient)
{
    case RODENT  :
    case CAT     :
    case DOG     :
    case BIRD    : cout << "Cage ward";
                   break;
    case REPTILE : cout << "Terrarium ward";
                   break;
    case HORSE   :
    case BOVINE  :
    case SHEEP   : cout << "Barn";
}
```

Input and Output   Stream I/O is defined only for the basic built-in types (int, float, and so on), not for user-defined enumeration types. Values of enumeration types must be input or output indirectly.

To input values, one strategy is to read a string that spells one of the constants in the enumeration type. The idea is to input the string and translate it to one of the literals in the enumeration type by looking only at as many letters as are necessary to determine what it is. For example, the veterinary clinic program could read the kind of animal as a string, then assign one of the values of type Animals to that patient. *Cat, dog, horse,* and *sheep* can be determined by their first letter. *Bovine, bird, rodent,* and *reptile* cannot be determined until the second letter is examined. The following program fragment reads in a string representing an animal name and converts it to one of the values in type Animals.

```cpp
#include <cctype>    // For toupper()
#include <string>    // For string type
   ⋮
string animalName;
   ⋮
cin >> animalName;
switch (toupper(animalName[0]))
{
    case 'R' : if (toupper(animalName[1]) == 'O')
                   inPatient = RODENT;
               else
                   inPatient = REPTILE;
               break;
    case 'C' : inPatient = CAT;
               break;
    case 'D' : inPatient = DOG;
               break;
    case 'B' : if (toupper(animalName[1]) == 'I')
                   inPatient = BIRD;
               else
                   inPatient = BOVINE;
               break;
    case 'H' : inPatient = HORSE;
               break;
    default  :  inPatient = SHEEP;
}
```

Enumeration type values cannot be printed directly either. Printing is done by using a Switch statement that prints a character string corresponding to the value.

```
switch (inPatient)
{
    case RODENT  : cout << "Rodent";
                   break;
    case CAT     : cout << "Cat";
                   break;
    case DOG     : cout << "Dog";
                   break;
    case BIRD    : cout << "Bird";
                   break;
    case REPTILE : cout << "Reptile";
                   break;
    case HORSE   : cout << "Horse";
                   break;
    case BOVINE  : cout << "Bovine";
                   break;
    case SHEEP   : cout << "Sheep";
}
```

You might ask, Why not use just a pair of letters or an integer number as a code to represent each animal in a program? The answer is that we use enumeration types to make our programs more readable; they are another way to make the code more self-documenting.

Returning a Function Value   We have been using value-returning functions to compute and return values of built-in types such as `int`, `float`, and `char`:

```
int Power( int, int );
float CargoMoment( int );
```

C++ allows a function return value to be of *any* data type—built-in or user-defined—except an array (a data type we examine in later chapters).

In the last section, we wrote a Switch statement to convert an input string into a value of type `Animals`. Let's write a value-returning function that performs this task. Notice how the function heading declares the data type of the return value to be `Animals`.

```
Animals StrToAnimal( /* in */ string str )
{
    switch (toupper(str[0]))
    {
        case 'R' : if (toupper(str[1]) == 'O')
                        return RODENT;
                   else
                        return REPTILE;
```

```
        case 'C' : return CAT;
        case 'D' : return DOG;
        case 'B' : if (toupper(str[1]) == 'I')
                       return BIRD;
                   else
                       return BOVINE;
        case 'H' : return HORSE;
        default  : return SHEEP;
    }
}
```

In this function, why didn't we include a Break statement after each case alternative? Because when one of the alternatives executes a Return statement, control immediately exits the function. It's not possible for control to "fall through" to the next alternative.

Named and Anonymous Data Types

The enumeration types we have looked at, `Animals` and `Days`, are called **named types** because their declarations included names for the types. Variables of these new data types are declared separately using the type identifiers `Animals` and `Days`.

Named type   A user-defined type whose declaration includes a type identifier that gives a name to the type.

C++ also lets us introduce a new type directly in a variable declaration. Instead of the declarations

```
enum CoinType {NICKEL, DIME, QUARTER, HALF_DOLLAR};
enum StatusType {OK, OUT_OF_STOCK, BACK_ORDERED};

CoinType   change;
StatusType status;
```

we could write

```
enum {NICKEL, DIME, QUARTER, HALF_DOLLAR} change;
enum {OK, OUT_OF_STOCK, BACK_ORDERED} status;
```

A new type declared in a variable declaration is called an **anonymous type** because it does not have a name—that is, it does not have a type identifier associated with it.

Anonymous type   A type that does not have an associated type identifier.

If we can create a data type in a variable declaration, why bother with a separate type declaration that creates a named type? Named types, like named constants, make a program more readable, more understandable, and easier to modify. Also, declaring a type and declaring a variable of that type are two distinct concepts; it is best to keep them separate.

User-Written Header Files

As you create your own user-defined data types, you often find that a data type can be useful in more than one program. For example, you may be working on several programs that need an enumeration type consisting of the names of the 12 months of the year. Instead of typing the statement

```
enum Months
{
    JANUARY, FEBRUARY, MARCH, APRIL, MAY, JUNE,
    JULY, AUGUST, SEPTEMBER, OCTOBER, NOVEMBER, DECEMBER
};
```

at the beginning of every program that uses the `Months` type, you can put this statement into a separate file named, say, `months.h`. Then you use `months.h` just as you use system-supplied header files such as `iostream` and `cmath`. By using an `#include` directive, you ask the C++ preprocessor to insert the contents of the file physically into your program. (Although many C++ systems use the filename extension `.h` [or no extension at all] to denote header files, other systems use extensions such as `.hpp` or `.hxx`.)

When you enclose the name of a header file in angle brackets, as in

```
#include <iostream>
```

the preprocessor looks for the file in the standard *include directory*, a directory that contains all the header files supplied by the C++ system. On the other hand, you can enclose the name of a header file in double quotes, like this:

```
#include "months.h"
```

In this case, the preprocessor looks for the file in the programmer's current directory. This mechanism allows us to write our own header files that contain type declarations and constant declarations. We can use a simple `#include` directive instead of retyping the declarations in every program that needs them (see Figure 10-4).

10.6 More on Type Coercion

As you have learned over the course of several chapters, C++ performs implicit type coercion whenever values of different data types are used in the following:

1. Arithmetic and relational expressions
2. Assignment operations

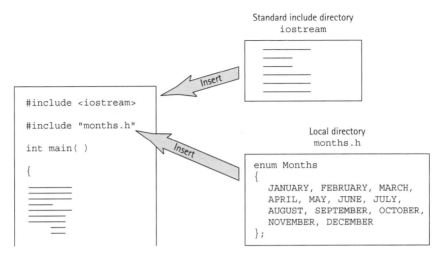

Figure 10-4 *Including Header Files*

3. Argument passing

4. Return of the function value from a value-returning function

For item 1–mixed type expressions–the C++ compiler follows one set of rules for type coercion. For items 2, 3, and 4, the compiler follows a second set of rules. Let's examine each of these two rules.

Type Coercion in Arithmetic and Relational Expressions

Suppose that an arithmetic expression consists of one operator and two operands–for example, 3.4*sum or var1/var2. If the two operands are of different data types, then one of them is temporarily **promoted** (or **widened**) to match the data type of the other. To understand exactly what promotion means, let's look at the rule for type coercion in an arithmetic expression.*

> **Promotion (widening)** The conversion of a value from a "lower" type to a "higher" type according to a programming language's precedence of data types.

Step 1: Each char, short, bool, or enumeration value is promoted (widened) to int. If both operands are now int, the result is an int expression.

---

*The rule we give for type coercion is a simplified version of the rule found in the C++ language definition. The complete rule has more to say about unsigned types, which we rarely use in this book.

Step 2: If Step 1 still leaves a mixed type expression, the following precedence of types is used:

lowest → highest

`int, unsigned int, long, unsigned long, float, double, long double`

The value of the operand of "lower" type is promoted to that of the "higher" type, and the result is an expression of that type.

A simple example is the expression `someFloat+2`. This expression has no `char`, `short`, `bool`, or enumeration values in it, so Step 1 still leaves a mixed type expression. In Step 2, `int` is a "lower" type than `float`, so the value 2 is coerced temporarily to the `float` value, say, 2.0. Then the addition takes place, and the type of the entire expression is `float`.

This description of type coercion also holds for relational expressions such as

`someInt <= someFloat`

The value of `someInt` is temporarily coerced to floating-point representation before the comparison takes place. The only difference between arithmetic expressions and relational expressions is that the resulting type of a relational expression is always `bool`— the value `true` or `false`.

Type Coercion in Assignments, Argument Passing, and Return of a Function Value

In general, promotion of a value from one type to another does not cause loss of information. On the other hand, **demotion** (or **narrowing**) of data values can potentially cause loss of information.

> **Demotion (narrowing)** The conversion of a value from a "higher" type to a "lower" type according to a programming language's precedence of data types. Demotion may cause corruption of data.

Consider an assignment operation

v = e

where *v* is a variable and *e* is an expression. Regarding the data types of *v* and *e*, there are three possibilities:

1. If the types of *v* and *e* are the same, no type coercion is necessary.
2. If the type of *v* is "higher" than that of *e* (using the type precedence we explained with promotion), then the value of *e* is promoted to *v*'s type before being stored into *v*.
3. If the type of *v* is "lower" than that of *e*, the value of *e* is demoted to *v*'s type before being stored into *v*.

Demotion may cause corruption of data:

- Demotion from a longer integral type to a shorter integral type (such as `long` to `int`) results in discarding the leftmost (most significant) bits in the binary number representation. The result may be a drastically different number.
- Demotion from a floating-point type to an integral type causes truncation of the fractional part (and an undefined result if the whole-number part will not fit into the destination variable). The result of truncating a negative number is machine dependent.
- Demotion from a longer floating-point type to a shorter floating-point type (such as `double` to `float`) may result in a loss of digits of precision.

Our description of type coercion in an assignment operation also holds for argument passing (the mapping of arguments onto parameters) and for returning a function value with a Return statement. For example, assume that INT_MAX on your machine is 32767 and that you have the following function:

```
void DoSomething( int n )
{
    ⋮
}
```

If the function is called with the statement

```
DoSomething(50000);
```

then the value 50000 (which is implicitly of type `long` because it is larger than INT_MAX) is demoted to a completely different, smaller value that fits into an `int` location. In a similar fashion, execution of the function

```
int SomeFunc( float x )
{
    ⋮
    return 70000;
}
```

causes demotion of the value 70000 to a smaller `int` value because `int` is the declared type of the function return value.

Programming Example

Rock, Paper, Scissors

Problem   Play the children's game Rock, Paper, Scissors. In this game, two people simultaneously choose one of the following: rock, paper, or scissors. The rules are as follows:

Rock breaks scissors; rock wins.
Paper covers rock; paper wins.
Scissors cut paper; scissors win.
All matching combinations are ties.
The overall winner is the player who wins the most individual games.

Input   A series of letters representing player A's plays (fileA, one letter per line) and a series of letters representing player B's plays (fileB, one letter per line), with each play indicated by 'R' (for Rock), 'P' (for Paper), or 'S' (for Scissors).

Output   For each game, the game number and the player who won that game; at the end, the total number of games won by each player, and the overall winner.

Discussion   We assume that everyone has played this game and understands it. Therefore, our discussion centers on how to simulate the game in a program.

In the algorithm we developed to read in animal names, we used as input a string containing the entire animal name and translated the string into a corresponding literal in an enumeration type. Here, we show an alternative approach. For input, we use a single character to stand for rock, paper, or scissors. We input 'R', 'P', or 'S' and convert the letter to a value of an enumeration type made up of the literals ROCK, PAPER, and SCISSORS.

Each player creates a file composed of a series of the letters 'R', 'P', and 'S', representing a series of individual games. A pair of letters is read, one from each file, and converted into the appropriate enumeration type literals. Let's call each literal a play. The plays are compared, and a winner is determined. The number of games won is incremented for the winning player each time. The game is over when there are no more plays (the files are empty).

Assumptions   The game is over when one of the files runs out of plays.

(The following program is written in ISO/ANSI standard C++. If you are working with pre-standard C++, see the alternate version of the program in the PRE_STD directory of the program disk, available at the publisher's Web site, www.jbpub.com/disks.)

```
//****************************************************************************
// Game program
// This program simulates the children's game Rock, Paper, and
// Scissors.  Each game consists of inputs from two players,
// coming from fileA and fileB.  A winner is determined for each
// individual game and for the games overall
//****************************************************************************
```

```cpp
#include <iostream>
#include <fstream>      // For file I/O

using namespace std;

enum PlayType {ROCK, PAPER, SCISSORS};

PlayType ConversionVal( char );
void GetPlays( ifstream&, ifstream&, PlayType&, PlayType&, bool& );
void PrintBigWinner( int, int );
void ProcessPlays( int, PlayType, PlayType, int&, int& );
void RecordAWin( char, int, int& );

int main()
{
    PlayType playForA;                  // Player A's play
    PlayType playForB;                  // Player B's play
    int      winsForA = 0;              // Number of games A wins
    int      winsForB = 0;              // Number of games B wins
    int      gameNumber = 0;            // Number of games played
    bool     legal;                     // True if play is legal
    ifstream fileA;                     // Player A's plays
    ifstream fileB;                     // Player B's plays

    // Open the input files

    fileA.open("filea.dat");
    fileB.open("fileb.dat");
    if ( !fileA || !fileB )
    {
        cout << "** Can't open input file(s) **" << endl;
        return 1;
    }

    // Play a series of games and keep track of who wins

    GetPlays(fileA, fileB, playForA, playForB, legal);
    while (fileA && fileB)
    {
        gameNumber++;
        if (legal)
            ProcessPlays(gameNumber, playForA, playForB, winsForA,
                    winsForB);
```

```
                else
                    cout << "Game number " << gameNumber
                            << " contained an illegal play." << endl;
                GetPlays(fileA, fileB, playForA, playForB, legal);
            }

            // Print overall winner

            PrintBigWinner(winsForA, winsForB);

            return 0;
        }


//***********************************************************************

        void GetPlays( /* inout */ ifstream& fileA,          // Plays for A
                       /* inout */ ifstream& fileB,          // Plays for B
                       /* out */   PlayType& playForA,       // A's play
                       /* out */   PlayType& playForB,       // B's play
                       /* out */   bool&     legal    )      // True if plays
                                                             //   are legal

        // Reads the players' plays from the data files, converts the plays
        // from char form to PlayType form, and reports whether the plays
        // are legal.  If end-of-file is encountered on either file, the
        // outgoing parameters are undefined.

        // Precondition:
        //      fileA and fileB have been successfully opened
        // Postcondition:
        //      IF input from either file failed due to end-of-file
        //          playForA, playForB, and legal are undefined
        //      ELSE
        //          Player A's play has been read from fileA and Player B's
        //          play has been read from fileB
        //       && IF both plays are legal
        //              legal == TRUE
        //           && playForA == PlayType equivalent of Player A's play
        //                          char
        //           && playForB == PlayType equivalent of Player B's play
        //                          char
        //          ELSE
        //              legal == FALSE
        //           && playForA and playForB are undefined
        {
            char charForA;      // Player A's input
```

```
    char charForB;        // Player B's input

    fileA >> charForA;            // Skip whitespace, including newline
    fileB >> charForB;
    if ( !fileA || !fileB)
        return;

    legal = (charForA=='R' || charForA=='P' || charForA=='S') &&
            (charForB=='R' || charForB=='P' || charForB=='S');
    if (legal)
    {
        playForA = ConversionVal(charForA);
        playForB = ConversionVal(charForB);
    }
}


//*******************************************************************

PlayType ConversionVal( /* in */ char someChar )   // Play character

// Converts a character into an associated PlayType value

// Precondition:
//      someChar == 'R' or 'P' or 'S'
// Postcondition:
//      Function value == ROCK, if someChar == 'R'
//                     == PAPER, if someChar == 'P'
//                     == SCISSORS, if someChar == 'S'

{
    switch (someChar)
    {
        case 'R': return ROCK;       // No break needed after
        case 'P': return PAPER;      //    return statement
        case 'S': return SCISSORS;
    }
}


//*******************************************************************

void ProcessPlays( /* in */     int      gameNumber,   // Game number
                   /* in */     PlayType playForA,      // A's play
                   /* in */     PlayType playForB,      // B's play
                   /* inout */ int&      winsForA,      // A's wins
                   /* inout */ int&      winsForB )     // B's wins
```

```
// Determines whether there is a winning play or a tie.  If there
// is a winner, the number of wins of the winning player is
// incremented.  In all cases, a message is written

// Precondition:
//     All arguments are assigned
// Postcondition:
//     IF Player A won
//        winsForA == winsForA@entry + 1
//     ELSE IF Player B won
//        winsForB == winsForB@entry + 1
// && A message, including gameNumber, has been written specifying
//     either a tie or a winner

{
    if (playForA == playForB)
        cout << "Game number " << gameNumber << " is a tie."
            << endl;
    else if (playForA == PAPER && playForB == ROCK ||
             playForA == SCISSORS && playForB == PAPER ||
             playForA == ROCK && playForB == SCISSORS)
        RecordAWin('A', gameNumber, winsForA);     // Player A wins
    else
        RecordAWin('B', gameNumber, winsForB);     // Player B wins
}

//*************************************************************************

void RecordAWin( /* in */    char player,        // Winning player
                 /* in */    int  gameNumber,    // Game number
                 /* inout */ int& numOfWins  )   // Win count

// Outputs a message telling which player has won the current game
// and updates that player's total

// Precondition:
//     player == 'A' or 'B'
//  && gameNumber and numOfWins are assigned
// Postcondition:
//     A winning message, including player and gameNumber, has
//     been written
//  && numOfWins == numOfWins@entry + 1
```

```
{
    cout << "Player " << player << " has won game number "
        << gameNumber << '.' << endl;
    numOfWins++;
}


//**********************************************************************

void PrintBigWinner( /* in */ int winsForA,     // A's win count
                     /* in */ int winsForB )    // B's win count

// Prints number of wins for each player and the
// overall winner (or tie)

// Precondition:
//      winsForA and winsForB are assigned
// Postcondition:
//      The values of winsForA and winsForB have been output
//      && A message indicating the overall winner (or a tie) has been
//      output

{

    cout << endl;
    cout << "Player A has won " << winsForA << " games." << endl;
    cout << "Player B has won " << winsForB << " games." << endl;
    if (winsForA > winsForB)
        cout << "Player A has won the most games." << endl;
    else if (winsForB > winsForA)
        cout << "Player B has won the most games." << endl;
    else
        cout << "Players A and B have tied." << endl;
}
```

Testing   We tested the Game program with the following files. They are listed side by side so that you can see the pairs that made up each game. Note that each combination of 'R', 'P', and 'S' is used at least once. In addition, there is an erroneous play character in each file.

fileA	fileB
R	R
S	S
S	S
R	S
R	P
P	P
P	P
R	S
S	T
A	P
P	S
P	R
S	P
R	S
R	S
P	P
S	R

Given the data in these files, the program produced the following output.

```
Game number 1 is a tie.
Game number 2 is a tie.
Game number 3 is a tie.
Player A has won game number 4.
Player B has won game number 5.
Game number 6 is a tie.
Game number 7 is a tie.
Player A has won game number 8.
Game number 9 contained an illegal play.
Game number 10 contained an illegal play.
Player B has won game number 11.
Player A has won game number 12.
Player A has won game number 13.
Player A has won game number 14.
Player A has won game number 15.
Game number 16 is a tie.
Player B has won game number 17.

Player A has won 6 games.
Player B has won 3 games.
Player A has won the most games.
```

An examination of the output shows it to be correct: Player A did win six games, player B did win three games, and player A won the most games. This one set of test data is not enough to test the program completely, though. It should be run with test data in which player B wins, player A and player B tie, fileA is longer than fileB, and fileB is longer than fileA.

Testing and Debugging

Floating-Point Data

When a problem requires the use of floating-point numbers that are extremely large, small, or precise, it is important to keep in mind the limitations of the particular system you are using. When testing a program that performs floating-point calculations, determine the acceptable margin of error beforehand, and then design your test data to try to push the program beyond those limits. Carefully check the accuracy of the computed results. (Remember that when you hand-calculate the correct results, a pocket calculator may have *less* precision than your computer system.) If the program produces acceptable results when given worst-case data, it probably performs correctly on typical data.

Coping with Input Errors

Several times in this book, we've had our programs test for invalid data and write an error message. Writing an error message is certainly necessary, but it is only the first step. We must also decide what the program should do next. The problem itself and the severity of the error should determine what action is taken in any error condition. The approach taken also depends on whether or not the program is being run interactively.

In a program that reads its data only from an input file, there is no interaction with the person who entered the data. The program, therefore, should try to adjust for the bad data items, if at all possible.

If the invalid data item is not essential, the program can skip it and continue; for example, if a program averaging test grades encounters a negative test score, it could simply skip the negative score. A message should be written stating that an invalid data item was encountered and outlining the steps that were taken. Such messages form an *exception report.*

If the data item is essential and no guess is possible, processing should be terminated. A message should be written to the user with as much information as possible about the invalid data item.

In an interactive environment, the program can prompt the user to supply another value. The program should indicate to the user what is wrong with the original data. Another possibility is to write out a list of actions and ask the user to choose among them.

These suggestions on how to handle bad data assume that the program recognizes bad data values. There are two approaches to error detection: passive and active. Passive error detection leaves it to the system to detect errors. This may seem easier, but the programmer relinquishes control of processing when an error occurs. An example of passive error detection is the system's division-by-zero error.

Active error detection means having the program check for possible errors and determine an appropriate action if an error occurs. An example of active error detection would be to read a value and use an If statement to see if the value is 0 before dividing it into another number.

Testing and Debugging Hints

1. Avoid using unnecessary side effects in expressions. The test

   ```
   if ((x = y) < z)
       ⋮
   ```

   is less clear and more prone to error than the equivalent sequence of statements

   ```
   x = y;
   if (y < z)
       ⋮
   ```

   Also, if you accidentally omit the parentheses around the assignment operation, like this:

   ```
   if (x = y < z)
   ```

   then, according to C++ operator precedence, x is not assigned the value of y. It is assigned the value 1 or 0 (the coerced value of the Boolean result of the relational expression y < z).

2. Programs that rely on a particular machine's character set may not run correctly on another machine. Check to see what character-handling functions are supplied by the standard library. Functions such as `tolower`, `toupper`, `isalpha`, and `iscntrl` automatically account for the character set being used.

3. Don't directly compare floating-point values for equality. Instead, check them for near equality. The tolerance for near equality depends on the particular problem you are solving.

4. Use integers if you are dealing with whole numbers only. Any integer can be represented exactly by the computer, as long as it is within the machine's allowable range of values. Also, integer arithmetic is faster than floating-point arithmetic on most machines.

5. Be aware of representational, overflow, and underflow errors. If possible, try to arrange calculations in your program to keep floating-point numbers from becoming too large or too small.

6. If your program increases the value of a positive integer and the result suddenly becomes a negative number, you should suspect integer overflow. On most computers, adding 1 to `INT_MAX` yields `INT_MIN`, a negative number.

7. Avoid mixing data types in expressions, assignment operations, argument passing, and the return of a function value. If you must mix types, explicit type casts can prevent unwelcome surprises caused by implicit type coercion.

8. Consider using enumeration types to make your programs more readable, understandable, and modifiable.

9. Avoid anonymous data typing. Give each user-defined type a name.

10. Enumeration type values cannot be input or output directly.

11. Type demotion can lead to decreased precision or corruption of data.

Summary

A data type is a set of values (the domain) along with the operations that can be applied to those values. Simple data types are data types whose values are atomic (indivisible).

The integral types in C++ are `char`, `short`, `int`, `long`, and `bool`. The most commonly used integral types are `int` and `char`. The `char` type can be used for storing small (usually one-byte) numeric integers or, more often, for storing character data. Character data includes both printable and nonprintable characters. Nonprintable characters—those that control the behavior of hardware devices—are expressed in C++ as escape sequences such as `\n`. Each character is represented internally as a nonnegative integer according to the particular character set (such as ASCII or EBCDIC) that a computer uses.

The floating-point types built into the C++ language are `float`, `double`, and `long double`. Floating-point representation permits numbers that are much larger or much smaller than those that can be represented with the integral types. Floating-point representation also allows us to perform calculations on numbers with fractional parts.

Representational errors can affect the accuracy of a program's computations. When using floating-point numbers, keep in mind that if two numbers are vastly different from each other in size, adding or subtracting them can produce the wrong answer. Remember, also, that the computer has a limited range of numbers that it can represent. If a program tries to compute a value that is too large or too small, an error message may result when the program executes.

C++ allows the programmer to define additional data types. The Typedef statement is a simple mechanism for renaming an existing type, although the result is not truly a new data type. An enumeration type, created by listing the identifiers that make up the domain, is a new data type that is distinct from any existing type. Values of an enumeration type may be assigned, compared in relational expressions, used as case labels in a Switch statement, passed as arguments, and returned as function values. Enumeration types are extremely useful in the writing of clear, self-documenting programs.

Quick Check

1. The C++ simple types are divided into integral types, floating-point types, and `enum` types. What are the five integral types (ignoring the `unsigned` variations) and the three floating-point types? (pp. 350–351)
2. What is the difference between an expression and an expression statement in C++? (pp. 356–357)
3. Assume that the following code segment is executed on a machine that uses the ASCII character set. What is the final value of the `char` variable `someChar`? Give both its external and internal representations. (pp. 360–362)

```
someChar = 'T';
someChar = someChar + 4;
```

4. Why is it inappropriate to use a variable of a floating-point type as a loop control variable? (pp. 367–371)

5. If a computer has four digits of precision, what would be the result of the following addition operation? (pp. 367–371)

400400.000 + 199.9

6. When choosing a data type for a variable that stores whole numbers only, why should `int` be your first choice? (pp. 371–372)

7. Declare an enumeration type named `AutoMakes`, consisting of the names of five of your favorite car manufacturers. (pp. 373–379)

8. Given the type declaration

```
enum VisibleColors
{
    RED, ORANGE, YELLOW, GREEN, BLUE, INDIGO, VIOLET
};
```

write the first line of a For statement that "counts" from RED through VIOLET. Use a loop control variable named `rainbow` that is of type `VisibleColors`. (pp. 373–379)

9. Why is it better to use a named type than an anonymous type? (p. 379)

10. Suppose that many of your programs need an enumeration type named `Days` and another named `Months`. If you place the type declarations into a file named `calendar.h`, what would an #include directive look like that inserts these declarations into a program? (p. 380)

11. In arithmetic and relational expressions, which of the following could occur: type promotion, type demotion, or both? (pp. 380–383)

Answers   1. The integral types are `char`, `short`, `int`, `long`, and `bool`. The floating-point types are `float`, `double`, and `long double`. 2. An expression becomes an expression statement when it is terminated by a semicolon. 3. The external representation is the letter *X;* the internal representation is the integer 88. 4. Because representational errors can cause the loop termination condition to be evaluated with unpredictable results. 5. 400500.000 (Actually, 4.005E+5) 6. Floating-point arithmetic is subject to numerical inaccuracies and is slower than integer arithmetic on most machines. Use of the smaller integral types, `char` and `short`, can more easily lead to overflow errors. The `long` type usually requires more memory than `int`, and the arithmetic is usually slower. 7. `enum AutoMakes {SAAB, JAGUAR, CITROEN, CHEVROLET, FORD};` 8. `for (rainbow = RED; rainbow <= VIOLET; rainbow = VisibleColors(rainbow + 1))` 9. Named types make a program more readable, more understandable, and easier to modify. 10. #include "calendar.h" 11. Type promotion

Exam Preparation Exercises

1. Every C++ compiler guarantees that `sizeof(int) < sizeof(long)`. (True or False?)

2. Classify each of the following as either an expression or an expression statement.

   a. `sum = 0`

   b. `sqrt(x)`

   c. `y = 17;`

   d. `count++`

3. Rewrite each statement as described.

   a. Using the += operator, rewrite the statement

   ```
   sumOfSquares = sumOfSquares + x * x;
   ```

   b. Using the decrement operator, rewrite the statement

   ```
   count = count - 1;
   ```

   c. Using a single assignment statement that uses the ?: operator, rewrite the statement

   ```
   if (n > 8)
       k = 32;
   else
       k = 15 * n;
   ```

4. What is printed by each of the following program fragments? (In both cases, `ch` is of type `char`.)

   a. `for (ch = 'd'; ch <= 'g'; ch++)`
       `cout << ch;`

   b. `ch = 'F';`
       `cout << ch << ' ' << int(ch);   // Assume ASCII`

5. What is printed by the following output statement?

   ```
   cout << "Notice that\nthe character \\ is a backslash.\n";
   ```

6. If a system supports ten digits of precision for floating-point numbers, what are the results of the following computations?

   a. 1.4E+12 + 100.0

   b. 4.2E-8 + 100.0

   c. 3.2E-5 + 3.2E+5

7. Define the following terms:
   significant digits
   overflow
   representational error

8. Given the type declaration

   ```
   enum Agents {SMITH, JONES, GRANT, WHITE};
   ```

does the expression JONES > GRANT have the value true or false?

9. Given the following declarations,

```
enum Perfumes {POISON, DIOR_ESSENCE, CHANEL_NO_5, COTY};
Perfumes sample;
```

indicate whether each statement below is valid or invalid.
   a. `sample = POISON;`
   b. `sample = 3;`
   c. `sample++;`
   d. `sample = Perfumes(sample + 1);`

10. Using the declarations

```
enum SeasonType {WINTER, SPRING, SUMMER, FALL};
SeasonType season;
```

indicate whether each statement below is valid or invalid.
   a. `cin >> season;`
   b. `if (season >= SPRING)`
      ⋮
   c. `for (season = WINTER; season <= SUMMER; season = `
      `                               SeasonType(season + 1))`

      ⋮

11. Given the following program fragment,

```
enum Colors {RED, GREEN, BLUE};

Colors myColor;
enum {RED, GREEN, BLUE} yourColor;
```

the data type of `myColor` is a named type, and the data type of `yourColor` is an anonymous type. (True or False?)

12. If you have written your own header file named `mytypes.h`, then the preprocessor directive

```
#include <mytypes.h>
```

is the correct way to insert the contents of the header file into a program. (True or False?)

13. In each of the following situations, indicate whether promotion or demotion occurs. (The names of the variables are meant to suggest their data types.)
   a. Execution of the assignment operation `someInt = someFloat`
   b. Evaluation of the expression `someFloat + someLong`
   c. Passing the argument `someDouble` to the parameter `someFloat`
   d. Execution of the following statement within an `int` function:

   ```
   return someShort;
   ```

14. Active error detection leaves error hunting to C++ and the operating system, whereas passive error detection requires the programmer to do the error hunting. (True or False?)

Programming Warm-up Exercises

1. Find out the maximum and minimum values for each of the C++ integral and floating-point types on your machine. These values are declared as named constants in the files `climits` and `cfloat` in the standard include directory.

2. Using a combination of printable characters and escape sequences within *one* literal string, write a single output statement that does the following in the order shown:
   - Prints `Hello`
   - Prints a (horizontal) tab character
   - Prints `There`
   - Prints two blank lines
   - Prints `"Ace"` (including the double quotes)

3. Write a While loop that copies all the characters (including whitespace characters) from an input file stream `inFile` to an output file stream `outFile`, except that every lowercase letter is converted to uppercase. Assume that both files have been opened successfully before the loop begins. The loop should terminate when end-of-file is detected.

4. Given the following declarations

   ```
   int   n;
   char ch1;
   char ch2;
   ```

   and given that `n` contains a two-digit number, translate `n` into two single characters such that `ch1` holds the higher-order digit, and `ch2` holds the lower-order digit. For example, if n = 59, `ch1` would equal '5', and `ch2` would equal '9'. Then output the two digits as characters in the same order as the original numbers. (*Hint:* Consider how you might use the / and % operators in your solution.)

5. In a program you are writing, a `float` variable `beta` potentially contains a very large number. Before multiplying `beta` by 100.0, you want the program to test whether it is safe to do so. Write an If statement that tests for a possible overflow *before* multiplying by 100.0. Specifically, if the multiplication would lead to overflow, print a message and don't perform the multiplication; otherwise, go ahead with the multiplication.

6. Declare an enumeration type for the course numbers of computer courses at your school.

7. Declare an enumeration type for the South American countries.

8. Declare an enumeration type for the work days of the week (Monday through Friday).

9. Write a value-returning function that converts the first two letters of a work day into the type declared in Exercise 8.

10. Write a void function that prints a value of the type declared in Exercise 8.

11. Using a loop control variable `today` of the type declared in Exercise 8, write a For loop that prints out all five values in the domain of the type. To print each value, invoke the function of Exercise 10.

12. Below is a function that is supposed to return the ratio of two integers, rounded up or down to the nearest integer.

```
int Ratio( /* in */ int int1,
           /* in */ int int2 )
{
    return float(int1) / float(int2);
}
```

Sometimes this function returns an incorrect result. Describe what the problem is in terms of type promotion or demotion and fix the problem.

13. Modify the Game program so that it prompts the user for the names of the two external files before opening them.

Programming Problems

1. Read in the lengths of the sides of a triangle and determine whether the triangle is isosceles (two sides are equal), equilateral (three sides are equal), or scalene (no sides are equal). Use an enumeration type whose enumerators are ISOSCELES, EQUILATERAL, and SCALENE.

   The lengths of the sides of the triangle are to be entered as integer values. For each set of sides, print out the kind of triangle or an error message saying that the three sides do not make a triangle. (For a triangle to exist, any two sides together must be longer than the remaining side.) Continue analyzing triangles until end-of-file occurs.

2. Write a C++ program that reads a single character from 'A' through 'Z' and produces output in the shape of a pyramid composed of the letters up to and including the letter that is input. The top letter in the pyramid should be 'A', and on each level, the next letter in the alphabet should fall between two copies of the letter that was introduced in the level above it. For example, if the input is 'E', the output looks like the following:

```
    A
   ABA
  ABCBA
 ABCDCBA
ABCDEDCBA
```

3. Read in a floating-point number character by character, ignoring any characters other than digits and a decimal point. Convert the valid characters into a single floating-point number and print the result. Your algorithm should convert the whole number part to an integer and the fractional part to an integer and combine the two integers as follows:

$$Set\ result = wholePart + fractionalPart / (10^{number\ of\ digits\ in\ fraction})$$

For example, 3A4.21P6 would be converted into 34 and 216, and the result would be the value of the sum

$$34 + \frac{216}{1000}$$

You may assume that the number has at least one digit on either side of the decimal point.

Structured Types, Data Abstraction, and Classes

- To be able to declare a record (struct) data type, a data structure whose components may be heterogeneous.

- To be able to access a member of a record variable.

- To be able to define a hierarchical record structure.

- To be able to access values stored in a hierarchical record variable.

- To understand the general concept of a C++ union type.

- To understand the difference between specification and implementation of an abstract data type.

- To be able to declare a C++ class type.

- To be able to declare class objects, given the declaration of a class type.

- To be able to write client code that invokes class member functions.

- To be able to implement class member functions.

- To understand how encapsulation and information hiding are enforced by the C++ compiler.

- To be able to organize the code for a C++ class into two files: the specification (.h) file and the implementation file.

- To be able to write a C++ class constructor

In the last chapter, we examined the concept of a data type and looked at how to define simple data types. In this chapter, we expand the definition of a data type to include structured types, which represent collections of components that are referred to by a single name. We begin with a discussion of structured types in general and then examine two structured types provided by the C++ language: the struct and the union.

Next, we introduce the concept of *data abstraction,* the separation of a data type's logical properties from its implementation. Data abstraction is important because it allows us to create data types not otherwise available in a programming language. Another benefit of data abstraction is the ability to produce *off-the-shelf software*—pieces of software that can be used over and over again in different programs either by the creator of the software or by any programmer wishing to use them.

The primary concept for practicing data abstraction is the *abstract data type.* In this chapter, we examine abstract data types in depth and introduce the C++ language feature designed expressly for creating abstract data types: the *class.*

11.1 Simple Versus Structured Data Types

In Chapter 10, we examined simple, or atomic, data types. A value in a simple type is a single data item; it cannot be broken down into component parts. For example, each int value is a single integer number and cannot be further decomposed. In contrast, a **structured data type** is one in which each value is a *collection* of component items. The entire collection is given a single name, yet each component can still be accessed individually. An example of a structured data type in C++ is the string class, used for creating and manipulating strings. When you declare a variable myString to be of type string, myString does not represent just one atomic data value; it represents an entire collection of characters. But each of the components in the string can be accessed individually (by using an expression such as myString[3], which accesses the char value at position 3).

Structured data type A data type in which each value is a collection of components and whose organization is characterized by the method used to access individual components. The allowable operations on a structured data type include the storage and retrieval of individual components.

Simple data types, both built-in and user-defined, are the building blocks for structured types. A structured type gathers together a set of component values and usually imposes a specific arrangement on them (see Figure 11-1). The method used to access the individual components of a structured type depends on how the components are arranged. As we discuss various ways of structuring data, we look at the corresponding access mechanisms.

Figure 11-2 shows the structured types available in C++. This figure is a portion of the complete diagram presented in Figure 3-1.

In this chapter, we examine the struct, union, and class types. Array data types are the topic of Chapter 12.

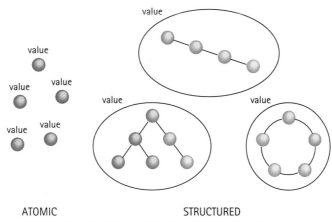

Figure 11-1 *Atomic (Simple) and Structured Data Types*

11.2   Records (C++ Structs)

In computer science, a **record** is a heterogeneous structured data type. By *heterogeneous,*
we mean that the individual components of a
record can be of different data types. Each
component of a record is called a **field** of the
record, and each field is given a name called
the *field name.* C++ uses its own terminology

> **Record (structure, in C++)**   A structured data type with a
> fixed number of components that are accessed by name.
> The components may be heterogeneous (of different types).
>
> **Field (member, in C++)**   A component of a record.

with records. A record is called a **structure**, the fields of a record are called **members** of
the structure, and each member has a *member name.*

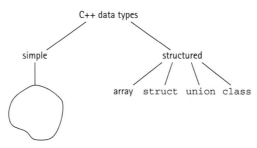

Figure 11-2 *C++ Structured Types*

In C++, record data types are most commonly declared according to the following syntax:

StructDeclaration

```
struct TypeName
{
     MemberList
};
```

where TypeName is an identifier giving a name to the data type, and MemberList is defined as

MemberList

```
DataType MemberName ;
DataType MemberName ;
          ⋮
```

The reserved word `struct` is an abbreviation for *structure,* the C++ term for a record. Because the word *structure* has many other meanings in computer science, we'll use *struct* or *record* to avoid any possible confusion about what we are referring to.

You probably recognize the syntax of a member list as being nearly identical to a series of variable declarations. Be careful: A `struct` declaration is a type declaration, and we still must declare variables of this type for any memory locations to be associated with the member names. As an example, let's use a struct to describe a student in a class. We want to store the first and last names, the overall grade point average prior to this class, the grade on programming assignments, the grade on quizzes, the final exam grade, and the final course grade.

```
// Type declarations

enum GradeType {A, B, C, D, F};

struct StudentRec
{
    string    firstName;
    string    lastName;
    float     gpa;           // Grade point average
    int       programGrade;  // Assume 0..400
    int       quizGrade;     // Assume 0..300
```

```
    int       finalExam;      // Assume 0..300
    GradeType courseGrade;
};

// Variable declarations

StudentRec firstStudent;
StudentRec student;
int        grade;
```

Notice, both in this example and in the syntax template, that a `struct` declaration ends with a semicolon. By now, you have learned not to put a semicolon after the right brace of a compound statement (block). However, the member list in a `struct` declaration is not considered to be a compound statement; the braces are simply required syntax in the declaration. A `struct` declaration, like all C++ declaration statements, must end with a semicolon.

`firstName`, `lastName`, `gpa`, `programGrade`, `quizGrade`, `finalExam`, and `courseGrade` are member names within the `struct` type `StudentRec`. These member names make up the member list. Note that each member name is given a type. Also, member names must be unique within a `struct` type, just as variable names must be unique within a block.

`firstName` and `lastName` are of type `string`. `gpa` is a `float` member. `programGrade`, `quizGrade`, and `finalExam` are `int` members. `courseGrade` is of an enumeration data type made up of the grades A through D and F.

None of these struct members are associated with memory locations until we declare a variable of the `StudentRec` type. `StudentRec` is merely a pattern for a struct (see Figure 11-3). The variables `firstStudent` and `student` are variables of type `StudentRec`.

Accessing Individual Components

To access an individual member of a struct variable, you give the name of the variable, followed by a dot (period), and then the member name. This expression is called a **member selector**. The syntax template is

Member selector   The expression used to access components of a struct variable. It is formed by using the struct variable name and the member name, separated by a dot (period).

MemberSelector

```
StructVariable . MemberName
```

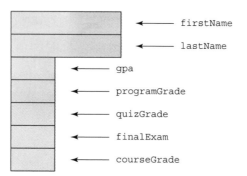

Figure 11-3 *Pattern for a Struct*

This syntax for selecting individual components of a struct is often called *dot notation.* To access the grade point average of `firstStudent`, we would write

`firstStudent.gpa`

To access the final exam score of `student`, we would write

`student.finalExam`

The component of a struct accessed by the member selector is treated just like any other variable of the same type. It may be used in an assignment statement, passed as an argument, and so on. Figure 11-4 shows the struct variable `student` with the member selector for each member. In this example, values are already stored in some of the components.

Let's demonstrate the use of these member selectors. Using our `student` variable, the following code segment reads in a final exam grade; adds up the program grade, the quiz grade, and the final exam grade; and then assigns a letter grade to the result.

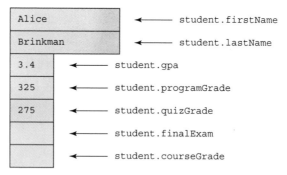

Figure 11-4 *Struct Variable* `student` *with Member Selectors*

```
cin >> student.finalExam;
grade = student.finalExam + student.programGrade +
        student.quizGrade;
if (grade >= 900)
    student.courseGrade = A;
else if (grade >= 800)
    student.courseGrade = B;
else
    ⋮
```

Aggregate Operations on Structs

In addition to accessing individual components of a struct variable, we can in some cases use **aggregate operations**. An aggregate operation is one that manipulates the struct as an entire unit.

> **Aggregate operation** An operation on a data structure as a whole, as opposed to an operation on an individual component of the data structure.

The following table summarizes the aggregate operations that are allowed on struct variables.

Aggregate Operation	Allowed on Structs?
I/O	No
Assignment	Yes
Arithmetic	No
Comparison	No
Argument passage	Yes, by value or by reference
Return as a function's return value	Yes

According to the table, one struct variable can be assigned to another. However, both variables must be declared to be of the same type. For example, given the declarations

```
StudentRec student;
StudentRec anotherStudent;
```

the statement

```
anotherStudent = student;
```

copies the entire contents of the struct variable `student` to the variable `anotherStudent`, member by member.

On the other hand, aggregate arithmetic operations and comparisons are not allowed (primarily because they wouldn't make sense):

```
student = student * anotherStudent;    // Not allowed
if (student < anotherStudent)          // Not allowed
```

Furthermore, aggregate I/O is not permitted:

```
cin >> student;                        // Not allowed
```

We must input or output a struct variable one member at a time:

```
cin >> student.firstName;
cin >> student.lastName;
   ⋮
```

According to the table, an entire struct can be passed as an argument, either by value or by reference, and a struct can be returned as the value of a value-returning function. Let's define a function that takes a StudentRec variable as a parameter.

The task of this function is to determine if a student's grade in a course is consistent with his or her overall grade point average (GPA). We define *consistent* to mean that the course grade corresponds correctly to the rounded GPA. The GPA is calculated on a four-point scale, where A is 4, B is 3, C is 2, D is 1, and F is 0. If the rounded GPA is 4 and the course grade is A, then the function returns true. If the rounded GPA is 4 and the course grade is not A, then the function returns false. Each of the other grades is tested in the same way.

The Consistent function is coded below. The parameter aStudent, a struct variable of type StudentRec, is passed by value.

```
bool Consistent( /* in */ StudentRec aStudent )
{
    int roundedGPA = int(aStudent.gpa + 0.5);

    switch (roundedGPA)
    {
        case 0: return (aStudent.courseGrade == F);
        case 1: return (aStudent.courseGrade == D);
        case 2: return (aStudent.courseGrade == C);
        case 3: return (aStudent.courseGrade == B);
        case 4: return (aStudent.courseGrade == A);
    }
}
```

More About Struct Declarations

To complete our initial look at C++ structs, we give a more complete syntax template for a `struct` type declaration:

StructDeclaration

```
struct TypeName
{
    MemberList
} VariableList ;
```

As you can see in the syntax template, two items are optional: TypeName (the name of the `struct` type being declared), and VariableList (a list of variable names between the right brace and the semicolon). Our examples thus far have declared a type name but have not included a variable list. The variable list allows you not only to declare a `struct` type but also to declare variables of that type, all in one statement.

In this book, we avoid combining variable declarations with type declarations, preferring to keep the two notions separate.

If you omit the type name but include the variable list, you create an anonymous type. The cautions given in Chapter 10 against anonymous typing of enumeration types apply to `struct` types as well.

Hierarchical Records

We have seen examples in which the components of a record are simple variables and strings. A component of a record can also be another record. Records whose components are themselves records are called **hierarchical records.**

> **Hierarchical record** A record in which at least one of the components is itself a record.

Let's look at an example in which a hierarchical structure is appropriate. A small machine shop keeps information about each of its machines. There is descriptive information, such as the identification number, a description of the machine, the purchase date, and the cost. Statistical information is also kept, such as the number of down days, the failure rate, and the date of last service. What is a reasonable way of representing all this information? First, let's look at a flat (nonhierarchical) record structure that holds this information.

```
struct MachineRec
{
    int     idNumber;
    string  description;
```

```
    float   failRate;
    int     lastServicedMonth;    // Assume 1..12
    int     lastServicedDay;      // Assume 1..31
    int     lastServicedYear;     // Assume 1900..2050
    int     downDays;
    int     purchaseDateMonth;    // Assume 1..12
    int     purchaseDateDay;      // Assume 1..31
    int     purchaseDateYear;     // Assume 1900..2050
    float   cost;
};
```

The `MachineRec` type has 11 members. There is so much detailed information here that it is difficult to quickly get a feeling for what the record represents. Let's see if we can reorganize it into a hierarchical structure that makes more sense. We can divide the information into two groups: information that changes and information that does not. There are also two dates to be kept: date of purchase and date of last service. These observations suggest use of a record describing a date, a record describing the statistical data, and an overall record containing the other two as components. The following type declarations reflect this structure.

```
struct DateType
{
    int month;    // Assume 1..12
    int day;      // Assume 1..31
    int year;     // Assume 1900..2050
};
struct StatisticsType
{
    float      failRate;
    DateType   lastServiced;
    int        downDays;
};
struct MachineRec
{
    int            idNumber;
    string         description;
    StatisticsType history;
    DateType       purchaseDate;
    float          cost;
};

MachineRec machine;
```

The contents of a machine record are now much more obvious. Two of the components of the `struct` type `MachineRec` are themselves structs: `purchaseDate` is of struct type DateType, and history is of struct type StatisticsType. One of the components of struct type StatisticsType is a struct of type DateType.

How do we access the components of a hierarchical structure such as this one? We build the accessing expressions (member selectors) for the members of the embedded structs from left to right, beginning with the struct variable name. Here are some expressions and the components they access:

Expression	Component Accessed
machine.purchaseDate	DateType struct variable
machine.purchaseDate.month	month member of a DateType struct variable
machine.purchaseDate.year	year member of a DateType struct variable
machine.history.lastServiced.year	year member of a DateType struct variable contained in a struct of type StatisticsType

Figure 11-5 is a pictorial representation of machine with values. Look carefully at how each component is accessed.

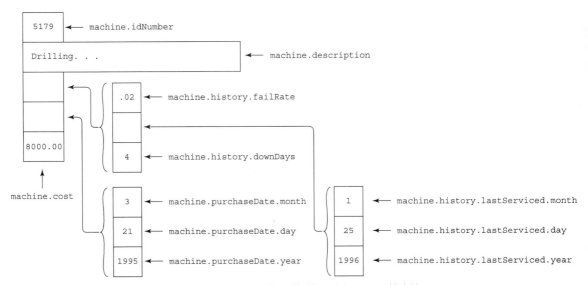

Figure 11-5 *Hierarchical Records in* machine *Variable*

11.3 Unions

In Figure 11-2, we presented a diagram showing the four structured types available in C++. We have discussed `struct` types and now look briefly at *union* types.

In C++, a union is defined to be a struct that holds only one of its members at a time during program execution. Here is a declaration of a `union` type and a union variable:

```
union WeightType
{
    long  wtInOunces;
    int   wtInPounds;
    float wtInTons;
};


WeightType weight;
```

The syntax for declaring a `union` type is identical to that of a `struct` type, except that the word `union` is substituted for `struct`.

At run time, the memory space allocated to the variable `weight` does *not* include room for three distinct components. Instead, `weight` can contain only one of the following: *either* a `long` value *or* an `int` value *or* a `float` value. The assumption is that the program will never need a weight in ounces, a weight in pounds, and a weight in tons simultaneously while executing. The purpose of a union is to conserve memory by forcing several values to use the same memory space, one at a time. The following code shows how the `weight` variable might be used.

```
weight.wtInTons = 4.83;
    ⋮
// Weight in tons is no longer needed. Reuse the memory space.

weight.wtInPounds = 35;
    ⋮
```

After the last assignment statement, the previous `float` value 4.83 is gone, replaced by the `int` value 35.

It's quite reasonable to argue that a union is not a data structure at all. It does not represent a collection of values; it represents only a single value from among several *potential* values. On the other hand, unions are grouped together with the structured types because of their similarity to structs.

There is much more to be said about unions, including subtle issues related to their declaration and usage. However, these issues are more appropriate in an advanced study of data structures and system programming. We have introduced unions only to present a complete picture of the structured types provided by C++ and to acquaint you with the general idea in case you encounter unions in other C++ programs.

11.4 Data Abstraction

As the software we develop becomes more complex, we design algorithms and data structures in parallel. We progress from the logical or abstract data structure envisioned at the top level through the refinement process until we reach the concrete coding in C++. We have illustrated two ways of representing the logical structure of a machine record in a shop inventory. The first used a record in which all the components were defined (made concrete) at the same time. The second used a hierarchical record in which the dates and statistics describing a machine's history were defined in lower-level records.

Let's look again at the two different ways in which we represented our logical data structure.

```
// *************** Version 1 ***************

struct MachineRec
{
    int     idNumber;
    string  description;
    float   failRate;
    int     lastServicedMonth;  // Assume 1..12
    int     lastServicedDay;    // Assume 1..31
    int     lastServicedYear;   // Assume 1900..2050
    int     downDays;
    int     purchaseDateMonth;  // Assume 1..12
    int     purchaseDateDay;    // Assume 1..31
    int     purchaseDateYear;   // Assume 1900..2050
    float   cost;
};


// *************** Version 2 ***************

struct DateType
{
    int month;  // Assume 1..12
    int day;    // Assume 1..31
    int year;   // Assume 1900..2050
};
```

```
struct StatisticsType
{
    float     failRate;
    DateType  lastServiced;
    int       downDays;
};
struct MachineRec
{
    int             idNumber;
    string          description;
    StatisticsType  history;
    DateType        purchaseDate;
    float           cost;
};
```

Which of these two representations is better? The second one is better for two reasons.

First, it groups elements together logically. The statistics and the dates are entities within themselves. We may want a date or a machine history in another record structure. If we define the dates and statistics only within `MachineRec` (as in the first structure), we would have to define them again for every other data structure that needs them, giving us multiple definitions of the same logical entity.

Second, the details of the entities (statistics and dates) are pushed down to a lower level in the second structure. The principle of deferring details to as low a level as possible should be applied to designing data structures as well as to designing algorithms. How a machine history or a date is represented is not relevant to our concept of a machine record, so the details need not be specified until it is time to write the algorithms to manipulate those members.

Pushing the implementation details of a data type to a lower level separates the logical description from the implementation. The separation of the logical properties of a data type from its implementation details is called **data abstraction**, which is a goal of effective programming and the foundation upon which abstract data types are built. (We explore the concept of abstract data types in the next section.)

Data abstraction The separation of a data type's logical properties from its implementation.

Eventually, all the logical properties must be defined in terms of concrete data types and routines written to manipulate them. If the implementation is properly designed, we can use the same routines to manipulate the structure in a wide variety of applications. For example, if we have a routine to compare dates, we can use that routine to compare dates representing days on which equipment was bought or maintained, or dates representing people's birthdays. The concept of designing a low-level structure and writing routines to manipulate it is the basis for C++ `class` types, which we examine later in the chapter.

11.5 Abstract Data Types

We live in a complex world. To cope with complexity, the human mind engages in *abstraction*—the act of separating the essential qualities of an idea or object from the details of how it works or is composed.

With abstraction, we focus on the *what*, not the *how*. For example, our understanding of automobiles is largely based on abstraction. Most of us know *what* the engine does (it propels the car), but fewer of us know—or want to know—precisely *how* the engine works internally. Abstraction allows us to discuss, think about, and use automobiles without having to know everything about how they work.

In the world of software design, it is now recognized that abstraction is an absolute necessity for managing immense, complex software projects. In introductory computer science courses, programs are usually small (perhaps 50 to 200 lines of code) and understandable in their entirety by one person. However, large commercial software products composed of hundreds of thousands—even millions—of lines of code cannot be designed without using abstraction in various forms. To manage complexity, software developers regularly use two important abstraction techniques: control abstraction and data abstraction.

Control abstraction is the separation of the logical properties of an action from its implementation. We engage in control abstraction whenever we write a function that reduces a complicated algorithm to an abstract action performed by a function call. By invoking a library function, as in the expression

```
4.6 + sqrt(x)
```

we depend only on the function's *specification*, a written description of what it does. We can use the function without having to know its *implementation* (the algorithms that accomplish the result).

Abstraction techniques also apply to data. Every data type consists of a set of values (the domain) along with a collection of allowable operations on those values. In the preceding section, we described data abstraction as the separation of a data type's logical properties from its implementation details. Data abstraction comes into play when we need a data type that is not built into the programming language. We can define the new data type as an **abstract data type** (ADT), concentrating only on its logical properties and deferring the details of its implementation.

> **Abstract data type** A data type whose properties (domain and operations) are specified independently of any particular implementation.

As with control abstraction, an abstract data type has both a specification (the *what*) and an implementation (the *how*). The specification of an ADT describes the characteristics of the data values as well as the behavior of each of the operations on those values. The user of the ADT needs to understand only the specification, not the implementation, in order to use it. Here's a very informal specification of a list ADT:

TYPE
    IntList
DOMAIN
    Each IntList value is a collection of up to 100 separate integer numbers.
OPERATIONS
    Insert an item into the list.
    Delete an item from the list.
    Search the list for an item.
    Return the current length of the list.
    Sort the list into ascending order.
    Print the list.

Notice the complete absence of implementation details. We have not mentioned how the data might actually be stored in a program or how the operations might be implemented. Concealing the implementation details reduces complexity for the user and also shields the user from changes in the implementation.

Below is the specification of another ADT, one that might be useful for representing time in a program.

TYPE
    TimeType
DOMAIN
    Each TimeType value is a time of day in the form of hours, minutes, and
    seconds.
OPERATIONS
    Set the time.
    Print the time.
    Increment the time by one second.
    Compare two times for equality.
    Determine if one time is "less than" (comes before) another.

The specification of an ADT defines abstract data values and abstract operations for the user. Ultimately, of course, the ADT must be implemented in program code. To implement an ADT, the programmer must do two things:

1. Choose a concrete **data representation** of the abstract data, using data types that already exist.

2. Implement each of the allowable operations in terms of program instructions.

Data representation The concrete form of data used to represent the abstract values of an abstract data type.

To implement the IntList ADT, we could choose a concrete data representation consisting of two items: a 100-element data structure (such as an *array*, the topic of the next chapter) and an int variable that keeps track of the current length of the list. To implement the IntList operations, we must create algorithms based on the chosen data representation. In the next two chapters, we discuss in detail the array data structure and its use in implementing list ADTs.

To implement the TimeType ADT, we might use three `int` variables for the data representation—one for the hours, one for the minutes, and one for the seconds. Or we might use three strings as the data representation. The specification of the ADT does not confine us to any particular data representation. As long as we satisfy the specification, we are free to choose among alternative data representations and their associated algorithms. Our choice may be based on time efficiency (the speed at which the algorithms execute), space efficiency (the economical use of memory space), or simplicity and readability of the algorithms. Over time, you will acquire knowledge and experience that help you decide which implementation is best for a particular context.

11.6 C++ Classes

In previous chapters, we have treated data values as passive quantities to be acted upon by functions. In Chapter 10, we viewed Rock, Paper, Scissors game plays as passive data, and we implemented operations as functions that took `PlayType` values as parameters. Similarly, earlier in this chapter we treated a student record as a passive quantity, using a struct as the data representation and implementing the operation `Consistent` as a function receiving a struct as a parameter (see Figure 11-6).

This separation of operations and data does not correspond very well with the notion of an abstract data type. After all, an ADT consists of *both* data values and operations on those values. It is preferable to view an ADT as defining an *active* data structure—one that combines both data and operations into a single, cohesive unit (see

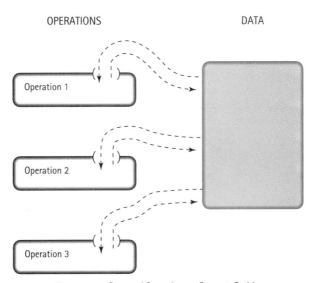

Figure 11-6 *Data and Operations as Separate Entities*

Figure 11-7 *Data and Operations Bound into a Single Unit*

Class A structured type in a programming language that is used to represent an abstract data type.

Class member A component of a class. Class members may be either data or functions.

Figure 11-7). C++ supports this view by providing a built-in structured type known as a **class.**

In Figure 11-2, we listed the four structured types available in the C++ language: the array, the struct, the union, and the class. A class is a structured type provided specifically for representing abstract data types. A class is similar to a struct but is nearly always designed so that its components (**class members**) include not only data but also functions that manipulate that data. Here is a C++ class declaration corresponding to the TimeType ADT that we defined in the previous section:

```
class TimeType
{
public:
    void Set( int, int, int );
    void Increment();
    void Write() const;
    bool Equal( TimeType ) const;
    bool LessThan( TimeType ) const;
private:
    int hrs;
    int mins;
    int secs;
};
```

(For now, you should ignore the word `const` appearing in some of the function prototypes. We explain this use of `const` later in the chapter.)

The `TimeType` class has eight members—five member functions (`Set`, `Increment`, `Write`, `Equal`, `LessThan`) and three member variables (`hrs`, `mins`, `secs`). As you might guess, the three member variables form the concrete data representation for the Time-Type ADT. The five member functions correspond to the operations we listed for the TimeType ADT: set the time (to the hours, minutes, and seconds passed as arguments to the Set function), increment the time by one second, print the time, compare two times for equality, and determine if one time is less than another. Although the Equal function compares two TimeType variables for equality, its parameter list has only one parameter—a TimeType variable. Similarly, the LessThan function has only one parameter, even though it compares two times. We'll see the reason later.

Like a struct declaration, the declaration of TimeType defines a data type but does not create variables of the type. Class variables (more often referred to as **class objects** or **class instances**) are created by using ordinary variable declarations:

> **Class object (class instance)** A variable of a class type.

```
TimeType startTime;
TimeType endTime;
```

Any software that declares and manipulates TimeType objects is called a **client** of the class.

> **Client** Software that declares and manipulates objects of a particular class.

As you look at the preceding declaration of the TimeType class, you can see the reserved words public and private, each followed by a colon. Data and/or functions declared between the words public and private constitute the public interface; clients can access these class members directly. Class members declared after the word private are considered private information and are inaccessible to clients. If client code attempts to access a private item, the compiler signals an error.

Private class members can be accessed only by the class's member functions. In the TimeType class, the private variables hrs, mins, and secs can be accessed only by the member functions Set, Increment, Write, Equal, and LessThan, not by client code. This separation of class members into private and public parts is a hallmark of ADT design. To preserve the properties of an ADT correctly, an instance of the ADT should be manipulated only through the operations that form the public interface. We have more to say about this issue later in the chapter.

Regarding public versus private accessibility, we can now describe more fully the difference between C++ structs and classes. C++ defines a struct to be a class whose members are all, by default, public. In contrast, members of a class are, by default, private. Furthermore, it is most common to use only data, not functions, as members of a struct. Note that you *can* declare struct members to be private and you *can* include member functions in a struct, but then you might as well use a class!

Classes, Class Objects, and Class Members

It is important to restate that a class is a type, not a data object. Like any type, a class is a pattern from which you create (or *instantiate*) many objects of that type. Think of a type as a cookie cutter and objects of that type as the cookies.

The declarations

```
TimeType time1;
TimeType time2;
```

create two objects of the `TimeType` class: `time1` and `time2`. Each object has its own copies of `hrs`, `mins`, and `secs`, the private data members of the class. At a given moment during program execution, `time1`'s copies of `hrs`, `mins`, and `secs` might contain the values 5, 30, and 10; and `time2`'s copies might contain the values 17, 58, and 2. Figure 11-8 is a visual image of the class objects `time1` and `time2`.

(In truth, the C++ compiler does not waste memory by placing duplicate copies of a member function—say, `Increment`—into both `time1` and `time2`. The compiler generates just one physical copy of `Increment`, and any class object executes this one copy of the function. Nevertheless, the diagram in Figure 11-8 is a good mental picture of two different class objects.)

Be sure you are clear about the difference between the terms *class object* and *class member*. Figure 11-8 depicts two objects of the `TimeType` class, and each object has eight members.

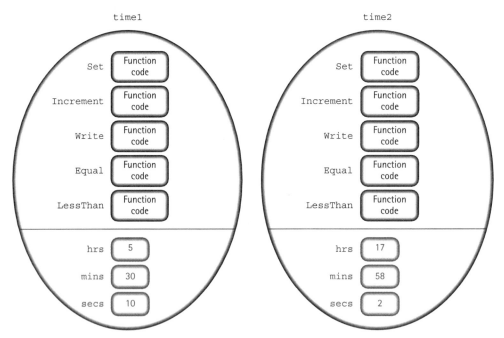

Figure 11-8 *Conceptual View of Two Class Objects*

Built-in Operations on Class Objects

In many ways, programmer-defined classes are like built-in types. You can declare as many objects of a class as you like. You can pass class objects as arguments to functions and return them as function values. Like any variable, a class object can be automatic (created each time control reaches its declaration and destroyed when control exits its surrounding block) or static (created once when control reaches its declaration and destroyed when the program terminates).

In other ways, C++ treats structs and classes differently from built-in types. Most of the built-in operations do not apply to structs or classes. You cannot use the + operator to add two TimeType objects, nor can you use the == operator to compare two Time-Type objects for equality.

Two built-in operations that are valid for struct and class objects are member selection (.) and assignment (=). As with structs, you select an individual member of a class by using dot notation. That is, you write the name of the class object, then a dot, then the member name. The statement

```
time1.Increment();
```

invokes the Increment function for the time1 object, presumably to add one second to the time stored in time1. The other built-in operation, assignment, performs aggregate assignment of one class object to another with the following semantics: If x and y are objects of the same class, then the assignment x = y copies the data members of y into x. Below is a fragment of client code that demonstrates member selection and assignment.

```
TimeType time1;
TimeType time2;
int      inputHrs;
int      inputMins;
int      inputSecs;

time1.Set(5, 20, 0);
// Assert: time1 corresponds to 5:20:0

cout << "Enter hours, minutes, seconds: ";
cin >> inputHrs >> inputMins >> inputSecs;
time2.Set(inputHrs, inputMins, inputSecs);

if (time1.LessThan(time2))
    DoSomething();

time2 = time1;                    // Member-by-member assignment
time2.Write();
// Assert: 5:20:0 has been output
```

Earlier we remarked that the `Equal` and `LessThan` functions have only one parameter each, even though they are comparing two `TimeType` objects. In the If statement of the previous code segment, we are comparing `time1` and `time2`. Because `LessThan` is a class member function, we invoke it by giving the name of a class object (`time1`), then a dot, then the function name (`LessThan`). Only one item remains unspecified: the class object with which `time1` should be compared (`time2`). Therefore, the `LessThan` function requires only one parameter, not two. Here is another way of explaining it: If a class member function represents a binary (two-operand) operation, the first operand appears to the left of the dot operator, and the second operand is in the parameter list. (To generalize, an *n*-ary operation has *n* – 1 operands in the parameter list. Thus, a unary operation—such as `Write` or `Increment` in the `TimeType` class—has an empty parameter list.)

In addition to member selection and assignment, a few other built-in operators are valid for class objects and structs. These operators are used for manipulating memory addresses and are not discussed in this book. For now, think of . and = as the only valid built-in operators.

From the very beginning, you have been working with C++ classes in a particular context: input and output. The standard header file `iostream` contains the declarations of two classes—`istream` and `ostream`—that manage a program's I/O. The C++ standard library declares `cin` and `cout` to be objects of these classes:

```
istream cin;
ostream cout;
```

The `istream` class has many member functions, two of which—the `get` function and the `ignore` function—you have already seen in statements like these:

```
cin.get(someChar);
cin.ignore(200, '\n');
```

As with any C++ class object, we use dot notation to select a particular member function to invoke.

You also have used C++ classes when performing file I/O. The header file `fstream` contains declarations for the `ifstream` and `ofstream` classes. The client code

```
ifstream dataFile;

dataFile.open("input.dat");
```

declares an `ifstream` class object named `dataFile`, then invokes the class member function `open` to try to open a file `input.dat` for input.

We do not examine in detail the `istream`, `ostream`, `ifstream`, and `ofstream` classes and all of their member functions. To study these would be beyond the goals of this book. What is important to recognize is that classes and objects are fundamental to all I/O activity in a C++ program.

Class Scope

We said earlier that member names must be unique within a struct. Additionally, in Chapter 8 we mentioned four kinds of scope in C++: local scope, global scope, name-space scope, and *class scope*. Class scope applies to the member names within structs, unions, and classes. To say that a member name has class scope means that the name is bound to that class (or struct or union). If the same identifier happens to be declared outside the class, the two identifiers are unrelated. Let's look at an example.

The TimeType class has a member function named Write. In the same program, another class (say, SomeClass) could also have a member function named Write. Fur-thermore, the program might have a global Write function that is completely unrelated to any classes. If the program has statements like

```
TimeType   checkInTime;
SomeClass someObject;
int        n;
   ⋮
checkInTime.Write();
someObject.Write();
Write(n);
```

then the C++ compiler has no trouble distinguishing among the three Write functions. In the first two function calls, the dot notation denotes class member selection. The first statement invokes the Write function of the TimeType class, and the second statement invokes the Write function of the SomeClass class. The final statement does not use dot notation, so the compiler knows that the function being called is the global Write function.

Information Hiding

Conceptually, a class object has an invisible wall around it. This wall, called the **abstraction barrier,** protects private data and functions from being accessed by client code. The barrier also prohibits the class object

> **Abstraction barrier**   The invisible wall around a class object that encapsulates implementation details. The wall can be breached only through the public interface.

from directly accessing data and functions outside the object. This barrier is a critical characteristic of classes and abstract data types.

For a class object to share information with the outside world (that is, with clients), there must be a gap in the abstraction barrier. This gap is the public interface—the class members declared to be public. The only way that a client can manipulate the internals of the class object is indirectly—through the operations in the public interface. Engineers have a similar concept called a **black box.** A

> **Black box**   An electrical or mechanical device whose inner workings are hidden from view.

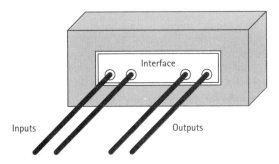

Figure 11-9 *A Black Box*

black box is a module or device whose inner workings are hidden from view. The user of the black box depends only on the written specification of *what* it does, not on *how* it does it. The user connects wires to the interface and assumes that the module works correctly by satisfying the specification (see Figure 11-9).

In software design, the black box concept is referred to as **information hiding**. Information hiding protects the user of a class from having to know all the details of its implementation. Information hiding also assures the class's implementor that the user cannot directly access any private code or data and compromise the correctness of the implementation. In this chapter, you'll see how to hide the implementations of class member functions by placing them in files that are separate from the client code.

> **Information hiding**   The encapsulation and hiding of implementation details to keep the user of an abstraction from depending on or incorrectly manipulating these details.

The creator of a C++ class is free to choose which members are private and which are public. However, making data members public (as in a struct) allows the client to inspect and modify the data directly. Because information hiding is so fundamental to data abstraction, most classes exhibit a typical pattern: The private part contains data, and the public part contains the functions that manipulate the data.

The TimeType class exemplifies this organization. The data members hrs, mins, and secs are private, so the compiler prohibits a client from accessing these members directly. The following client statement therefore results in a compile-time error:

```
TimeType checkInTime;

checkInTime.hrs = 9;     // Prohibited in client code
```

Because only the class's member functions can access the private data, the creator of the class can offer a reliable product, knowing that external access to the private data is impossible. If it is acceptable to let the client *inspect* (but not modify) private data members, a class might provide functions that access but do not change these values. The

`TimeType` class has three such functions: `Write`, `Equal`, and `LessThan`. Because these functions are not intended to modify the private data, they are declared with the word `const` following the parameter list:

```
void Write() const;
bool Equal( TimeType ) const;
bool LessThan( TimeType ) const;
```

C++ refers to these functions as *const member functions*. Within the body of a `const` member function, a compile-time error occurs if any statement tries to modify a private data member. Although not required by the language, it is good practice to declare as `const` those member functions that do not modify private data.

11.7 Specification and Implementation Files

An abstract data type consists of two parts: a specification and an implementation. The specification describes the behavior of the data type without reference to its implementation. The implementation creates an abstraction barrier by hiding the concrete data representation as well as the code for the operations.

The `TimeType` class declaration serves as the specification of `TimeType`. This declaration presents the public interface to the user in the form of function prototypes. To implement the `TimeType` class, we must provide function definitions (declarations with bodies) for all the member functions.

In C++, it is customary (though not required) to package the class declaration and the class implementation into separate files. One file—the *specification file*—is a header (`.h`) file containing only the class declaration. The second file—the *implementation file*—contains the function definitions for the class member functions. Let's look first at the specification file.

The Specification File

Below is the specification file for the `TimeType` class. On our computer system, we have named the file `timetype.h`. The class declaration is the same as we presented earlier, with one important exception: We include function preconditions and postconditions to specify the semantics of the member functions as unambiguously as possible for the user of the class.

```
//*****************************************************************
// SPECIFICATION FILE (timetype.h)
// This file gives the specification
// of a TimeType abstract data type
//*****************************************************************
```

```
class TimeType
{
public:
    void Set( /* in */ int hours,
              /* in */ int minutes,
              /* in */ int seconds );
        // Precondition:
        //    0 <= hours <= 23  &&  0 <= minutes <= 59
        //  && 0 <= seconds <= 59
        // Postcondition:
        //    Time is set according to the incoming parameters
        // NOTE:
        //    This function MUST be called prior to
        //    any of the other member functions

    void Increment();
        // Precondition:
        //    The Set function has been invoked at least once
        // Postcondition:
        //    Time has been advanced by one second, with
        //    23:59:59 wrapping around to 0:0:0

    void Write() const;
        // Precondition:
        //    The Set function has been invoked at least once
        // Postcondition:
        //    Time has been output in the form HH:MM:SS

    bool Equal( /* in */ TimeType otherTime ) const;
        // Precondition:
        //    The Set function has been invoked at least once
        //    for both this time and otherTime
        // Postcondition:
        //    Function value == true, if this time equals otherTime
        //                   == false, otherwise

    bool LessThan( /* in */ TimeType otherTime ) const;
        // Precondition:
        //    The Set function has been invoked at least once
        //    for both this time and otherTime
        //  && This time and otherTime represent times in the
        //    same day
        // Postcondition:
        //    Function value == true, if this time is earlier
        //                            in the day than otherTime
        //                   == false, otherwise
```

```
private:
    int hrs;
    int mins;
    int secs;
};
```

Notice the preconditions for the `Increment`, `Write`, `Equal`, and `LessThan` functions. It is the responsibility of the client to set the time before incrementing, printing, or testing it. If the client fails to set the time, the effect of each of these functions is undefined.

In principle, a specification file should not reveal any implementation details to the user of the class. The file should specify *what* each member function does without disclosing how it does it. However, as you can see in the class declaration, there is one implementation detail that is visible to the user: the concrete data representation of our ADT that is listed in the private part. However, the data representation is still considered hidden information in the sense that the compiler prohibits client code from accessing the data directly.

The Implementation File

The specification (.h) file for the `TimeType` class contains only the class declaration. The implementation file must provide the function definitions for all the class member functions. In the opening comments of the implementation file below, we document the file name as `timetype.cpp`. Your system may use a different file name suffix for source code files, perhaps `.c`, `.C`, or `.cxx`.

We recommend that you first skim the C++ code below, not being too concerned about the new language features such as prefixing the name of each function with the symbols

```
TimeType::
```

Immediately following the program code, we explain the new features. We omit the preconditions and postconditions here to save space, although they would normally be present in the implementation file.

```
//************************************************************************
// IMPLEMENTATION FILE (timetype.cpp)
// This file implements the TimeType member functions
//************************************************************************

#include "timetype.h"
#include <iostream>

using namespace std;
```

```
// Private members of class:
//      int hrs;
//      int mins;
//      int secs;

//*******************************************************************

void TimeType::Set( /* in */ int hours,
                    /* in */ int minutes,
                    /* in */ int seconds )
{
    hrs = hours;
    mins = minutes;
    secs = seconds;
}

//*******************************************************************

void TimeType::Increment()
{
    secs++;
    if (secs > 59)
    {
        secs = 0;
        mins++;
        if (mins > 59)
        {
            mins = 0;
            hrs++;
            if (hrs > 23)
                hrs = 0;
        }
    }
}

//*******************************************************************

void TimeType::Write() const
{
    if (hrs < 10)
        cout << '0';
    cout << hrs << ':';
    if (mins < 10)
        cout << '0';
```

```
        cout << mins << ':';
        if (secs < 10)
            cout << '0';
        cout << secs;
}

//*********************************************************************

bool TimeType::Equal( /* in */ TimeType otherTime ) const
{
    return (hrs == otherTime.hrs && mins == otherTime.mins &&
            secs == otherTime.secs);
}

//*********************************************************************

bool TimeType::LessThan( /* in */ TimeType otherTime ) const
{
    return (hrs < otherTime.hrs ||
            hrs == otherTime.hrs && mins < otherTime.mins ||
            hrs == otherTime.hrs && mins == otherTime.mins
                                 && secs < otherTime.secs);
}
```

This implementation file demonstrates several important points.

1. The file begins with the preprocessor directive

   ```
   #include "timetype.h"
   ```

   Both the implementation file and the client code must #include the specification file. Figure 11-10 pictures this shared access to the specification file. This sharing guarantees that all declarations related to an abstraction are consistent. That is, both client.cpp and timetype.cpp must reference the same declaration of the TimeType class located in timetype.h.

2. Near the top of the implementation file we have included a comment that restates the private members of the TimeType class.

   ```
   // Private members of class:
   //      int hrs;
   //      int mins;
   //      int secs;
   ```

   This comment reminds the reader that any references to these identifiers are references to the private class members.

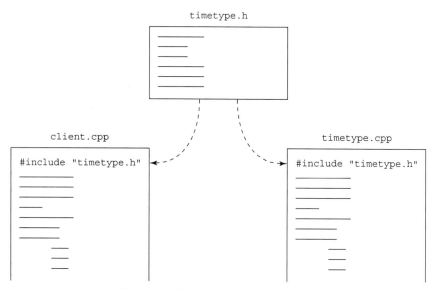

Figure 11-10 *Shared Access to a Specification File*

3. In the heading of each function definition, the name of the member function is pre-fixed by the class name (TimeType) and the C++ scope resolution operator (::). As we discussed earlier, it is possible for several different classes to have member functions with the same name, say, Write. In addition, there may be a global Write function that is not a member of any class. The scope resolution operator eliminates any uncertainty about which particular function is being defined.

4. Although clients of a class must use the dot operator to refer to class members (for example, startTime.Write()), members of a class refer to each other directly without using dot notation. Looking at the bodies of the Set and Increment functions, you can see that the statements refer directly to the member variables hrs, mins, and secs without using the dot operator.

   An exception to this rule occurs when a member function manipulates two or more class objects. Consider the Equal function. Suppose that the client code has two class objects, startTime and endTime, and uses the statement

```
if (startTime.Equal(endTime))
   ⋮
```

At execution time, the `startTime` object is the object for which the `Equal` function is invoked. In the body of the `Equal` function, the relational expression

```
hrs == otherTime.hrs
```

refers to class members of two different class objects. The unadorned identifier `hrs` refers to the `hrs` member of the class object for which the function is invoked (that is, `startTime`). The expression `otherTime.hrs` refers to the `hrs` member of the class object that is passed as a function argument: `endTime`.

5. `Write`, `Equal`, and `LessThan` do not modify the private data of the class. Because we have declared these to be `const` member functions, the compiler prevents them from assigning new values to the private data. The use of `const` is both an aid to the user of the class (as a visual signal that this function does not modify any private data) and an aid to the class implementor (as a way of preventing accidental modification of the data). Note that the word `const` must appear in both the function prototype (in the class declaration) and the heading of the function definition.

Compiling and Linking a Multifile Program

Now that we have created a specification file and an implementation file for our `TimeType` class, how do we (or any other programmer) make use of these files in our programs? Let's begin by looking at the notion of *separate compilation* of source code files.

In earlier chapters, we have referred to the concept of a multifile program—a program divided up into several files containing source code. In C++, it is possible to compile each of these files separately and at different times. The compiler translates each source code file into an object code file. Figure 11-11 shows a multifile program consisting of the source code files `myprog.cpp`, `file2.cpp`, and `file3.cpp`. We can compile each of these files independently, yielding object code files `myprog.obj`, `file2.obj`, and `file3.obj`. Although each `.obj` file contains machine language code, it is not yet in executable form. The system's linker program brings the object code together to form an executable program file. (In Figure 11-11, we use the file name suffixes `.cpp`, `.obj`, and `.exe`. Your C++ system may use different file name conventions.)

Files such as `file2.cpp` and `file3.cpp` typically contain function definitions for functions that are called by the code in `myprog.cpp`. An important benefit of separate compilation is that modifying the code in just one file requires recompiling only that file. The new `.obj` file is then relinked with the other existing `.obj` files. Of course, if a modification to one file affects the code in another file—for example, changing a function's interface by altering the number or data types of the function parameters—then the affected files also need to be modified and recompiled.

Returning to our `TimeType` class, let's assume we have used the system's editor to create the `timetype.h` and `timetype.cpp` files. Now we can compile `timetype.cpp` into object code. If we are working at the operating system's command line, we use a command similar to the following:

```
cc -c timetype.cpp
```

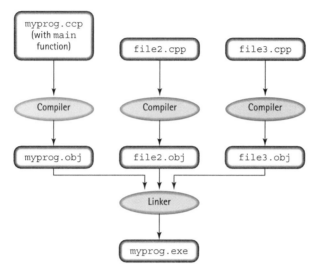

Figure 11-11 *Separate Compilation and Linking*

In this example, we assume that `cc` is the name of a command that invokes either the C++ compiler or the linker or both, depending on various options given on the command line. The command-line option `-c` means, on many systems, "compile but do not link." In other words, this command produces an object code file, say, `timetype.obj`, but does not attempt to link this file with any other file.

A programmer wishing to use the `TimeType` class will write code that #includes the file `timetype.h`, then declares and uses `TimeType` objects:

```
#include "timetype.h"
   ⋮
TimeType appointment;

appointment.Set(15, 30, 0);
appointment.Write();
   ⋮
```

If this client code is in a file named `diary.cpp`, an operating system command like

```
cc diary.cpp timetype.obj
```

compiles the client program into object code, links this object code with `timetype.obj`, and produces an executable program (see Figure 11-12).

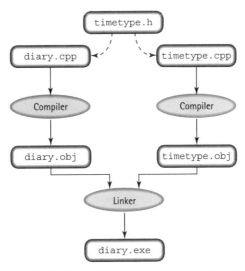

Figure 11-12 *Linking with the* `TimeType` *Implementation File*

The mechanics of compiling, linking, and executing vary from one computer system to another. Our examples using the `cc` command assume you are working at the operating system's command line. Many C++ systems provide an *integrated environment*—a program that bundles the editor, the compiler, and the linker into one package. Whichever environment you use—the command-line environment or an integrated environment—the overall process is the same: You compile the individual source code files into object code, link the object files into an executable program, then execute the program.

Before leaving the topic of multifile programs, we stress an important point. Referring to Figure 11-12, the files `timetype.h` and `timetype.obj` must be available to users of the `TimeType` class. The user needs to examine `timetype.h` to see what `Time-Type` objects do and how to use them. The user must also be able to link his or her program with `timetype.obj` to produce an executable program. But the user does *not* need to see `timetype.cpp`. The implementation of `TimeType` should be treated as a black box. The main purpose of abstraction is to simplify the programmer's job by reducing complexity. Users of an abstraction should not have to look at its implementation to learn how to use it, nor should they write programs that depend on implementation details. In the latter case, any changes in the implementation could "break" the user's programs.

11.8 Guaranteed Initialization with Class Constructors

The `TimeType` class we have been discussing has a weakness. It depends on the client to invoke the `Set` function before calling any other member function. For example, the `Increment` function's precondition is

```
// Precondition:
//     The Set function has been invoked at least once
```

If the client fails to invoke the `Set` function first, this precondition is false and the contract between the client and the function implementation is broken. Because classes nearly always encapsulate data, the creator of a class should not rely on the user to initialize the data. If the user forgets to do so, unpleasant results may occur.

C++ provides a mechanism, called a *class constructor,* to guarantee the initialization of a class object. A constructor is a member function that is implicitly invoked whenever a class object is created.

A constructor function has an unusual name: the name of the class itself. Let's change the `TimeType` class by adding two class constructors:

```cpp
class TimeType
{
public:
    void Set( int, int, int );
    void Increment();
    void Write() const;
    bool Equal( TimeType ) const;
    bool LessThan( TimeType ) const;
    TimeType( int, int, int );          // Constructor
    TimeType();                          // Constructor
private:
    int hrs;
    int mins;
    int secs;
};
```

This class declaration includes two constructors, differentiated by their parameter lists. The first has three `int` parameters, which, as we will see, are used to initialize the private data when a class object is created. The second constructor is parameterless and initializes the time to some default value, such as 0:0:0. A parameterless constructor is known in C++ as a *default constructor.*

Constructor declarations are unique in two ways. First, as we have mentioned, the name of the function is the same as the name of the class. Second, the data type of the function is omitted. The reason is that a constructor cannot return a function value. Its purpose is only to initialize a class object's private data.

In the implementation file, the function definitions for the two `TimeType` constructors might look like the following:

```
//*******************************************************************

TimeType::TimeType( /* in */ int initHrs,
                    /* in */ int initMins,
                    /* in */ int initSecs )
// Constructor

// Precondition:
//     0 <= initHrs <= 23  &&  0 <= initMins <= 59
//  && 0 <= initSecs <= 59
// Postcondition:
//     hrs == initHrs  &&  mins == initMins  &&  secs == initSecs

{
    hrs = initHrs;
    mins = initMins;
    secs = initSecs;
}


//*******************************************************************

TimeType::TimeType()

// Default constructor

// Postcondition:
//     hrs == 0  &&  mins == 0  &&  secs == 0

{
    hrs = 0;
    mins = 0;
    secs = 0;
}
```

Invoking a Constructor

Although a constructor is a member of a class, it is never invoked using dot notation. A constructor is automatically invoked whenever a class object is created. The client declaration

```
TimeType lectureTime(10, 30, 0);
```

includes an argument list to the right of the name of the class object being declared. When this declaration is encountered at execution time, the first (parameterized) constructor is automatically invoked, initializing the private data of `lectureTime` to the time 10:30:0. The client declaration

```
TimeType startTime;
```

has no argument list after the identifier `startTime`. The default (parameterless) constructor is implicitly invoked, initializing `startTime`'s private data to the time 0:0:0.

Remember that a declaration in C++ is a genuine statement and can appear anywhere among executable statements. Placing declarations among executable statements is extremely useful when creating class objects whose initial values are not known until execution time. Here's an example:

```
cout << "Enter appointment time in hours, minutes, and seconds: ";
cin >> hours >> minutes >> seconds;

TimeType appointmentTime(hours, minutes, seconds);

cout << "The appointment time is ";
appointmentTime.Write();
  ⋮
```

Revised Specification and Implementation Files for `TimeType`

By including constructors for the `TimeType` class, we are sure that each class object is initialized before any subsequent calls to the class member functions. One of the constructors allows the client code to specify an initial time; the other creates an initial time of 0:0:0 if the client does not specify a time. Because of these constructors, it is *impossible* for a `TimeType` object to be in an uninitialized state after it is created. As a result, we can delete from the `TimeType` specification file the warning to call `Set` before calling any other member functions. Also, we can remove all of the function preconditions that require `Set` to be called previously. Here is the revised `TimeType` specification file:

```
//***********************************************************************
// SPECIFICATION FILE (timetype.h)
// This file gives the specification
// of a TimeType abstract data type
//***********************************************************************

class TimeType
{
```

```
public:
    void Set( /* in */ int hours,
              /* in */ int minutes,
              /* in */ int seconds );
        // Precondition:
        //     0 <= hours <= 23  &&  0 <= minutes <= 59
        //  && 0 <= seconds <= 59
        // Postcondition:
        //     Time is set according to the incoming parameters

    void Increment();
        // Postcondition:
        //     Time has been advanced by one second, with
        //     23:59:59 wrapping around to 0:0:0

    void Write() const;
        // Postcondition:
        //     Time has been output in the form HH:MM:SS

    bool Equal( /* in */ TimeType otherTime ) const;
        // Postcondition:
        //     Function value == true, if this time equals otherTime
        //                    == false, otherwise

    bool LessThan( /* in */ TimeType otherTime ) const;
        // Precondition:
        //     This time and otherTime represent times in the
        //     same day
        // Postcondition:
        //     Function value == true, if this time is earlier
        //                             in the day than otherTime
        //                    == false, otherwise

    TimeType( /* in */ int initHrs,
              /* in */ int initMins,
              /* in */ int initSecs );
        // Precondition:
        //     0 <= initHrs <= 23  &&  0 <= initMins <= 59
        //  && 0 <= initSecs <= 59
        // Postcondition:
        //     Class object is constructed
        //  && Time is set according to the incoming parameters
```

```
        TimeType();
            // Postcondition:
            //      Class object is constructed  &&  Time is 0:0:0

private:
    int hrs;
    int mins;
    int secs;
};
```

To save space, we do not include the revised implementation file here. The only changes are as follows:

1. The inclusion of the function definitions for the two class constructors, which we presented earlier.

2. The deletion of all function preconditions stating that the Set function must be invoked previously.

At this point, you may wonder whether we need the Set function at all. After all, both the Set function and the parameterized constructor seem to do the same thing—set the time according to values passed as arguments—and the implementations of the two functions are essentially identical. The difference is that Set can be invoked for an existing class object whenever and as often as we wish, whereas the parameterized constructor is invoked once only—at the moment a class object is created. Therefore, we retain the Set function to provide maximum flexibility to clients of the class.

Guidelines for Using Class Constructors

The class is an essential language feature for creating abstract data types in C++. The class mechanism is a powerful design tool, but along with this power come rules for using classes correctly.

C++ has some very intricate rules about using constructors, many of which relate to language features we have not yet discussed. Below are some guidelines that are pertinent at this point.

1. A constructor cannot return a function value, so the function is declared without a return value type.

2. A class may provide several constructors. When a class object is declared, the compiler chooses the appropriate constructor according to the number and data types of the arguments to the constructor.

3. Arguments to a constructor are passed by placing the argument list immediately after the name of the class object being declared:

```
SomeClass anObject(arg1, arg2);
```

4. If a class object is declared without an argument list, as in the statement

```
SomeClass anObject;
```

then the effect depends upon what constructors (if any) the class provides.

If the class has no constructors at all, memory is allocated for `anObject` but its private data members are in an uninitialized state.

If the class does have constructors, then the default (parameterless) constructor is invoked if there is one. If the class has constructors but no default constructor, a syntax error occurs.

Before leaving the topic of constructors, we give you a brief preview of another special member function supported by C++: the *class destructor*. Just as a constructor is implicitly invoked when a class object is created, a destructor is implicitly invoked when a class object is destroyed—for example, when control leaves the block in which a local object is declared. A class destructor is named the same as a constructor except that the first character is a tilde (~):

```
class SomeClass
{
public:
    ⋮
    SomeClass();      // Constructor
    ~SomeClass();     // Destructor
private:
    ⋮
};
```

In this book, we won't be using destructors; the kinds of classes we'll be writing have no need to perform special actions at the moment a class object is destroyed. In more advanced coursework, you will learn about situations in which you need to use destructors.

Programming Example

Manipulating Dates

In this chapter, the machine shop example had a date as part of the data. In fact, the machine shop example had two dates: the date of purchase and the date of last service. Each time we needed a date, we defined it again. Let's stop this duplication of effort and do the job once and for all—let's write the code to support a date as an abstract data type.

Problem   Design and implement an ADT to represent a date. The informal specification of the ADT is given below.

TYPE
    DateType
DOMAIN
    Each DateType value is a single date after the year 1582 A.D. in the form of month, day, and year.
OPERATIONS
    Construct a new DateType instance.
    Set the date.
    Inspect the date's month.
    Inspect the date's day.
    Inspect the date's year.
    Print the date.
    Compare two dates for "before," "equal," or "after."
    Increment the date by one day.

Discussion   We create the DateType ADT in two stages: specification, followed by implementation. The result of the first stage is a C++ specification (.h) file containing the declaration of a DateType class. This file must describe for the user the precise semantics of each ADT operation. The informal specification given above would be unacceptable to the user of the ADT. The descriptions of the operations are too imprecise and ambiguous to be helpful to the user.

The second stage—implementation—requires us to (a) choose a concrete data representation for a date, and (b) implement each of the operations as a C++ function definition. The result is a C++ implementation file containing these function definitions.

Specification of the ADT   The domain of our ADT is the set of all dates after the year 1582 A.D. in the form of a month, a day, and a year. We restrict the year to be after 1582 A.D. in order to simplify the ADT operations (ten days were skipped in 1582 in switching from the Julian to the Gregorian calendar).

To represent the DateType ADT as program code, we use a C++ class named DateType. The ADT operations become public member functions of the class. Let's now specify the operations more carefully.

Construct a new DateType instance: For this operation, we use a C++ default constructor that initializes the date to January 1 of the year 1583. The client code can reset the date at any time using the "Set the date" operation.

Set the date: The client must supply three arguments for this operation: month, day, and year. Although we haven't yet determined a concrete data representation for a date, we must decide what data types the client should use for these arguments. We choose integers, where the month must be in the range 1 through 12, the day must be in the range 1 through the maximum number of days in the month, and the year must be greater than 1582. Notice that these range restrictions will become the precondition for invoking this operation.

Inspect the date's month, inspect the date's day, and inspect the date's year: All three of these operations give the client access, indirectly, to the private data. In the `DateType` class, we represent these operations as value-returning member functions with the following prototypes:

```
int Month();
int Day();
int Year();
```

Why do we need these operations? Why not simply let the data representation of the month, day, and year be public instead of private so that the client can access the values directly? The answer is that the client should be allowed to inspect *but not modify* these values. If the data were public, a client could manipulate the data incorrectly (such as incrementing January 31 to January 32), thereby compromising the correct behavior of the ADT.

Print the date: This operation prints the date on the standard output device in the following form:

```
January 12, 2001
```

Compare two dates: This operation compares two dates and determines whether the first one comes before the second one, they are the same, or the first one comes after the second one. To indicate the result of the comparison, we define an enumeration type with three values:

```
enum RelationType {BEFORE, SAME, AFTER};
```

Then we can code the comparison operation as a class member function that returns a value of type `RelationType`. Here is the function prototype:

```
RelationType ComparedTo( /* in */ DateType otherDate ) const;
```

Because this is a class member function, the date being compared to `otherDate` is the class object for which the member function is invoked. For example, the following client code tests to see whether `date1` comes before `date2`.

```
DateType date1;
DateType date2;
    ⋮
```

```
if (date1.ComparedTo(date2) == BEFORE)
    DoSomething();
```

Increment the date by one day: This operation advances the date to the next day. For example, given the date March 31, 2000, this operation changes the date to April 1, 2000.

We are now almost ready to write the C++ specification file for our `DateType` class. However, the class declaration requires us to include the private part—the private variables that are the concrete data representation of the ADT. Choosing a concrete data representation properly belongs in the ADT implementation phase, not the specification phase. But to satisfy the C++ class declaration requirement, we now choose a data representation. The simplest representation for a date is three `int` values—one each for the month, day, and year. Here, then, is the specification file containing the `DateType` class declaration (along with the declaration of the `RelationType` enumeration type).

```
//**********************************************************************
// SPECIFICATION FILE (datetype.h)
// This file gives the specification of a DateType abstract data
// type and provides an enumeration type for comparing dates
//**********************************************************************

enum RelationType {BEFORE, SAME, AFTER};

class DateType
{
public:
    void Set( /* in */ int newMonth,
              /* in */ int newDay,
              /* in */ int newYear  );
        // Precondition:
        //     1 <= newMonth <= 12
        //  && 1 <= newDay <= maximum no. of days in month newMonth
        //  && newYear > 1582
        // Postcondition:
        //     Date is set according to the incoming parameters

    int Month() const;
        // Postcondition:
        //     Function value == this date's month

    int Day() const;
        // Postcondition:
        //     Function value == this date's day
```

```
    int Year() const;
        // Postcondition:
        //      Function value == this date's year

    void Print() const;
        // Postcondition:
        //      Date has been output in the form
        //          month day, year
        //      where the name of the month is printed as a string

    RelationType ComparedTo( /* in */ DateType otherDate ) const;
        // Postcondition:
        //      Function value == BEFORE, if this date is
        //                                  before otherDate
        //                     == SAME, if this date equals otherDate
        //                     == AFTER, if this date is
        //                                  after otherDate

    void Increment();
        // Postcondition:
        //      Date has been advanced by one day

    DateType();
        // Postcondition:
        //      New DateType object is constructed with a
        //      month, day, and year of 1, 1, and 1583
private:
    int mo;
    int day;
    int yr;
};
```

Implementation of the ADT We have already chosen a concrete data representation for a date, shown in the specification file as the int variables mo, day, and yr. Now we must implement each class member function, placing the function definitions into a C++ implementation file named, say, datetype.cpp. As we implement the member functions, we also discuss testing strategies that can help to convince us that the implementations are correct.

To save space, we omit the function preconditions and postconditions that would normally be present in the implementation file.

The class constructor, Set, Month, Day, *and* Year *functions:* The implementations of these functions are so straightforward that no discussion is needed.

```cpp
//*********************************************************************
// IMPLEMENTATION FILE (datetype.cpp)
// This file implements the DateType member functions
//*********************************************************************
#include "datetype.h"
#include <iostream>

using namespace std;

// Private members of class:
//     int mo;
//     int day;
//     int yr;

int DaysInMonth( int, int );  // Prototype for auxiliary function

//*********************************************************************

DateType::DateType()

// Constructor

{
    mo = 1;
    day = 1;
    yr = 1583;
}

//*********************************************************************

void DateType::Set( /* in */ int newMonth,
                    /* in */ int newDay,
                    /* in */ int newYear  )
{
    mo = newMonth;
    day = newDay;
    yr = newYear;
}

//*********************************************************************

int DateType::Month() const
{
```

```
        return mo;
}

//********************************************************************

int DateType::Day() const
{
        return day;
}

//********************************************************************

int DateType::Year() const
{
        return yr;
}
```

Testing   The Month, Day, and Year functions can be used to verify that the class constructor and Set functions work correctly. The code

```
DateType someDate;

cout << someDate.Month() << ' ' << someDate.Day() << ' '
        << someDate.Year() << endl;
```

should print out 1 1 1583. To test the Set function, it is sufficient to set a DateType object to a few different values (obeying the precondition for the Set function), then print out the month, day, and year as above.

The Print function   The date is to be printed in the form month, day, comma, and year. Because the month is represented as an integer in the range 1 through 12, we can use a Switch statement to print out the month in word form.

```
//********************************************************************

void DateType::Print() const
{
        switch (mo)
        {
                case 1 : cout << "January";
                             break;
                case 2 : cout << "February";
                             break;
                case 3 : cout << "March";
                             break;
                case 4 : cout << "April";
                             break;
```

```
            case 5 : cout << "May";
                     break;
            case 6 : cout << "June";
                     break;
            case 7 : cout << "July";
                     break;
            case 8 : cout << "August";
                     break;
            case 9 : cout << "September";
                     break;
            case 10 : cout << "October";
                      break;
            case 11 : cout << "November";
                      break;
            case 12 : cout << "December";
        }
        cout << ' ' << day << ", " << yr;
}
```

Testing   In testing the `Print` function, we should print each month at least once. Both the year and the day should be tested at their end points and at several points between.

The `ComparedTo` function: If we were to compare two dates in our heads, we would look first at the years. If the years were different, we would immediately know which date came first. If the years were the same, we would look at the months. If the months were the same, we would have to look at the days. As so often happens, we can use this algorithm directly in our function.

```
//*************************************************************************

RelationType DateType::ComparedTo(
                        /* in */ DateType otherDate ) const

{
    if (yr < otherDate.yr)              // Compare years
        return BEFORE;
    if (yr > otherDate.yr)
        return AFTER;

    if (mo < otherDate.mo)              // Years are equal. Compare
        return BEFORE;                  //   months
    if (mo > otherDate.mo)
        return AFTER;
```

```
    if (day < otherDate.day)        // Years and months are equal.
        return BEFORE;              //   Compare days
    if (day > otherDate.day)
        return AFTER;

    return SAME;                    // Years, months, and days
}                                   //   are equal
```

Testing   In testing this function, we should ensure that each path is taken at least once. Programming Warm-up Exercises 13 and 14 ask you to design test data for this function and to write a driver that does the testing.

The `Increment` *function:* The algorithm to increment the date is similar to our earlier algorithm for incrementing a `TimeType` value by one second. If the current date plus 1 is still within the same month, we are done. If the current date plus 1 is within the next month, then we must increment the month and reset the day to 1. Finally, we must not forget to increment the year when the month changes from December to January.

  To determine whether the current date plus 1 is within the current month, we add 1 to the current day and compare this value with the maximum number of days in the current month. In this comparison, we must remember to check for leap year if the month is February.

  We can code the algorithm for finding the number of days in a month as a separate function—an auxiliary ("helper") function that is not a member of the `DateType` class. The number of days in February might need to be adjusted for leap year, so this function must receive as parameters both a month and a year.

```
//********************************************************************

void DateType::Increment()
{
    day++;
    if (day > DaysInMonth(mo, yr))
    {
        day = 1;
        mo++;
        if (mo > 12)
        {
            mo = 1;
            yr++;
        }
    }
}
```

```
//***********************************************************************

int DaysInMonth( /* in */ int month,
                 /* in */ int year  )

// Returns the number of days in month "month", taking
// leap year into account

// Precondition:
//     1 <= month <= 12   &&   year > 1582
// Postcondition:
//     Function value == number of days in month "month"

{
    switch (month)
    {
        case 1: case 3: case 5: case 7: case 8: case 10: case 12:
            return 31;
        case 4: case 6: case 9: case 11:
            return 30;
        case 2:    // It's February.  Check for leap year
            if ((year % 4 == 0 && year % 100 != 0) ||
                year % 400 == 0)
                return 29;
            else
                return 28;
    }
}
```

Testing To test the Increment function, we need to create a driver that calls the function with different values for the date. Values that cause the month to change must be tested, as well as values that cause the year to change. Leap year must be tested, including years with the last two digits 00.

A date is a logical entity for which we now have developed an implementation. We have designed, implemented, and tested a date ADT that we (or any programmer) can use whenever we have a date as part of our program data. If we discover in the future that additional operations on a date would be useful, we can implement, test, and add them to our set of date operations.

Programming Example

Birthday Calls

Problem Let's write a program to go through your address book and print the names and phone numbers of all the people who have birthdays within the next two weeks, so you can give them a call. Here, the "address book" is a data file containing information about your friends.

Input Today's date (from the keyboard); and a list of names, phone numbers, and birth dates (from file `friendFile`). Entries in this file are in the form

```
John Arbuthnot
(493) 384-2938
1/12/1970

Mary Smith
(123) 123-4567
10/12/1960
```

Output The names, phone numbers, and birthdays of any friends whose birthdays are within the next two weeks. A sample of the output is

```
John Arbuthnot
(493) 384-2938
January 12, 2001
```

Note that the date printed is the friend's next birthday, not the friend's birth date.

Discussion As we start our design phase for this problem, we call all the information about one person an *entry*. An entry consists of the following items: first name, last name, phone number, and birth date. To go any further, we must decide how we will represent these items as a C++ data structure. And we must design specific algorithms associated with our data structure.

Two of the items are names—that is, sequences of alphabetic characters. We can represent them as strings. The area code and local phone number could both be integer numbers, but we would like to store the hyphen that is between the third and fourth digits of the local number, because this is how phone numbers are usually printed. Therefore, we make the area code an integer, but we make the local phone number a string. (We assume that an area code is 100 or greater so that we don't have to worry about how to print leading zeros in area codes such as 052.) Because a phone number has two components—an area code and a local number—it makes sense to represent it as a struct:

```
struct PhoneType
{
    int     areaCode;
    string number;
};
```

Finally, we represent a birth date as a `DateType` object, where `DateType` is the class we developed in the preceding Programming Example.

Putting this all together, we define the following `struct` type to represent an entry for one person.

```
struct EntryType
{
    string     firstName;
    string     lastName;
    PhoneType  phone;
    DateType   birthDate;
};
```

`firstName`, `lastName`, `phone`, and `birthDate` are member names within the `struct` type `EntryType`. The members `firstName` and `lastName` are strings of type `string`, `phone` is a struct of type `PhoneType`, and `birthDate` is a class object of type `DateType`. Notice that `EntryType` is a hierarchical record type, because the `phone` member is also a record. A complete entry with values stored in a struct variable named `entry` is shown in Figure 11-13.

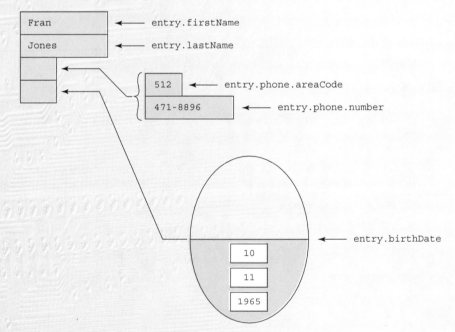

Figure 11-13 *Struct Variable* `entry`, *of type* `EntryType`

When looking for birthdays, we are interested in month and day only—the year is not important. If we were going through a conventional address book checking for birthdays by hand, we would write down the month and day of the date two weeks away and compare it to the month and day of each friend's birth date.

We can use the same algorithm in our program. Using the DateType class that we developed, the member function Increment can be used to calculate the date two weeks (14 days) from the current date. We can use the class member function ComparedTo to determine whether a friend's birthday lies between the current date and the date two weeks away, inclusive. How do we ignore the year? We set the year of each friend's birth date to the current year for the comparison. However, if the current date plus 14 days is in the next year, and the friend's birthday is in January, then we must set the year to the current year plus 1 for the comparison to work correctly.

Data Structures:

The DateType class, for manipulating dates.

A struct type PhoneType that stores an area code (integer) and a local phone number (string).

A struct type EntryType that stores a first name (string), a last name (string), a telephone number of type PhoneType, and a birth date of type DateType.

Below is the BirthdayCalls program. By using the preexisting DateType class, the program is significantly shorter and easier to understand than if it included all the code to manipulate dates. All we have to do is #include the header file datetype.h to make use of DateType class objects. To run the program, we link its object code file with the DateType object code file, the place where all the DateType implementation details are hidden.

(The following program is written in ISO/ANSI standard C++. If you are working with pre-standard C++, see the alternate version of the program in the PRE_STD directory of the program disk, available at the publisher's Web site, www.jbpub.com/disks.)

```
//*********************************************************************
// BirthdayCalls program
// A data file contains people's names, phone numbers, and birth
// dates.  This program reads a date from standard input, calculates
// a date two weeks away, and prints the names, phone numbers, and
// birthdays of all those in the file whose birthdays come on or
// before the date two weeks away
//*********************************************************************
#include "datetype.h"
#include <iostream>
#include <fstream>     // For file I/O
#include <string>      // For string type
```

```cpp
using namespace std;

struct PhoneType
{
    int     areaCode;
    string number;
};
struct EntryType
{
    string     firstName;
    string     lastName;
    PhoneType phone;
    DateType  birthDate;
};

void GetCurrentDate( DateType& );
void GetEntry( ifstream&, EntryType& );
void OpenForInput( ifstream& );
void PrintEntry( EntryType, DateType );

int main()
{
    ifstream  friendFile;      // Input file of friends' records
    EntryType entry;           // Current record from friendFile
                               //    being checked
    DateType  currentDate;     // Month, day, and year of current day
    DateType  birthday;        // Date of next birthday
    DateType  targetDate;      // Two weeks from current date
    int       birthdayYear;    // Year of next birthday
    int       count;           // Loop counter

    OpenForInput(friendFile);
    if ( !friendFile )
        return 1;

    GetCurrentDate(currentDate);
    targetDate = currentDate;
    for (count = 1; count <= 14; count++)
        targetDate.Increment();

    GetEntry(friendFile, entry);
    while (friendFile)
```

```
    {
        if (targetDate.Year() != currentDate.Year() &&
            entry.birthDate.Month() == 1)
          birthdayYear = targetDate.Year();
        else
          birthdayYear = currentDate.Year();
        birthday.Set(entry.birthDate.Month(), entry.birthDate.Day(),
                birthdayYear);
        if (birthday.ComparedTo(currentDate) >= SAME &&
            birthday.ComparedTo(targetDate) <= SAME)
          PrintEntry(entry, birthday);
        GetEntry(friendFile, entry);
    }
    return 0;
}


//****************************************************************

void OpenForInput( /* inout */ ifstream& someFile )      // File to be
                                                         // opened
// Prompts the user for the name of an input file
// and attempts to open the file

// Postcondition:
//      The user has been prompted for a file name
//   && IF the file could not be opened
//          An error message has been printed
// Note:
//      Upon return from this function, the caller must test
//      the stream state to see if the file was successfully opened

{

        .
        .         (Same as in Graph program of Chapter 7)
        .

}


//****************************************************************

void GetCurrentDate( /* out */ DateType& currentDate )   // Today's
                                                         //   date
// Reads the current date from standard input
```

```
// Postcondition:
//     User has been prompted for the current month, day, and year
//   && currentDate is set according to the input values

{
    int month;
    int day;
    int year;

    cout << "Enter current date as three integers, separated by"
         << " spaces: MM DD YYYY" << endl;
    cin >> month >> day >> year;
    currentDate.Set(month, day, year);
}

//*******************************************************************

void GetEntry(
    /* inout */ ifstream&  friendFile,    // Input file of records
    /* out */   EntryType& entry       )   // Next record from file

// Reads an entry from file friendFile

// Precondition:
//     friendFile is open for input
// Postcondition:
//     IF input of the firstName member failed due to end-of-file
//         entry is undefined
//     ELSE
//         All members of entry are filled with the values
//         for one person read from friendFile

{
    char dummy;    // Used to input and ignore certain characters
    int  month;
    int  day;
    int  year;

    friendFile >> entry.firstName;
    if ( !friendFile )
        return;
    friendFile >> entry.lastName;
```

```
    friendFile >> dummy                     // Consume '('
               >> entry.phone.areaCode
               >> dummy                      // Consume ')'
               >> entry.phone.number;

    friendFile >> month
               >> dummy                      // Consume '/'
               >> day
               >> dummy                      // Consume '/'
               >> year;
    entry.birthDate.Set(month, day, year);
}


//*******************************************************************


void PrintEntry( /* in */ EntryType entry,      // Friend's record
                 /* in */ DateType  birthday )   // Friend's birthday
                                                 //    this year
// Prints the name, phone number, and birthday

// Precondition:
//     entry is assigned
// Postcondition:
//     entry.firstName, entry.lastName, entry.phone, and birthday
//     have been printed

{
    cout << entry.firstName << ' ' << entry.lastName << endl;
    cout << '(' << entry.phone.areaCode << ") "
         << entry.phone.number << endl;
    birthday.Print();
    cout << endl << endl;
}
```

Testing   The only portions of this program that need to be checked are the `main` function and the input and output routines. The operations on dates have already been tested thoroughly.

The logic in the `main` function is straightforward. The test data should include birthdays less than two weeks away, exactly two weeks away, and more than two weeks away. The current date should include the cases in which two weeks away is within the same month, within the next month, and within the next year.

Testing and Debugging

Testing and debugging a C++ class amounts to testing and debugging each member function of the class. All of the techniques you have learned about—algorithm walk-throughs, code walk-throughs, hand traces, test drivers, verification of preconditions and postconditions, the system debugger, the `assert` function, and debug outputs—may be brought into play.

Consider how we might test this chapter's `TimeType` class. Here is the class declaration, abbreviated by leaving out the function preconditions and postconditions:

```
class TimeType
{
public:
    void Set( /* in */ int hours,
              /* in */ int minutes,
              /* in */ int seconds );
        // Precondition: ...
        // Postcondition: ...

    void Increment();
        // Postcondition: ...

    void Write() const;
        // Postcondition: ...

    bool Equal( /* in */ TimeType otherTime ) const;
        // Postcondition: ...

    bool LessThan( /* in */ TimeType otherTime ) const;
        // Precondition: ...
        // Postcondition: ...

    TimeType( /* in */ int initHrs,
              /* in */ int initMins,
              /* in */ int initSecs );
        // Precondition: ...
        // Postcondition: ...

    TimeType();
        // Postcondition: ...
private:
    int hrs;
    int mins;
    int secs;
};
```

To test this class fully, we must test each of the member functions. Let's step through the process of testing just one of them: the `Increment` function.

We implemented the `Increment` function as follows:

```
void TimeType::Increment()
{
    secs++;
    if (secs > 59)
    {
        secs = 0;
        mins++;
        if (mins > 59)
        {
            mins = 0;
            hrs++;
            if (hrs > 23)
                hrs = 0;
        }
    }
}
```

For test data, we should pick values of `hrs`, `mins`, and `secs` that ensure code coverage. To execute every path though the control flow, we need cases in which the following conditions occur:

1. The first If condition is false.
2. The first If condition is true and the second is false.
3. The first If condition is true, the second is true, and the third is false.
4. The first If condition is true, the second is true, and the third is true.

Below is a table displaying values of `hrs`, `mins`, and `secs` that correspond to these four cases. For each case we also write down what we hope will be the values of the variables after executing the algorithm.

	Initial Values			Expected Results		
Case	hrs	mins	secs	hrs	mins	secs
1	10	5	30	10	5	31
2	4	6	59	4	7	0
3	13	59	59	14	0	0
4	23	59	59	0	0	0

Finally, we write a test driver for the Increment function:

```cpp
#include <iostream>
#include "timetype.h"

using namespace std;

int main()
{
    TimeType time;
    int       hours;
    int       minutes;
    int       seconds;

    cout << "Enter a time (use hours < 0 to quit): ";
    cin >> hours >> minutes >> seconds;
    while (hours >= 0)
    {
        time.Set(hours, minutes, seconds);
        time.Increment();
        cout << "Incremented time is ";
        time.Write();
        cout << endl;
        cout << "Enter a time (use hours < 0 to quit): ";
        cin >> hours >> minutes >> seconds;
    }
    return 0;
}
```

The timetype.cpp implementation file only needs to contain function definitions for the following member functions: Set, Increment, Write, and the default constructor. The other member functions do not need to be implemented yet. Now we compile the test driver and timetype.cpp, link the two object files, and execute the program. For input data, we supply at least the four test cases discussed earlier. The program's output should match the desired results.

Now that we have tested the Increment function, we can apply the same steps to the remaining class member functions. We can create a separate test driver for each function, or we can write just one driver that tests all of the functions. The disadvantage of writing just one driver is that devising different combinations of input values to test several functions at once can quickly become complicated.

Before leaving the topic of testing a class, we must emphasize an important point. Even though a class has been tested thoroughly, it is still possible for errors to arise. Let's look at two examples using the TimeType class. The first example is the client statement

```cpp
time.Set(24, 0, 0);
```

The second example is the comparison

```
if (time1.LessThan(time2))
    ⋮
```

where the programmer intends `time1` to be 11:00:00 on a Wednesday and `time2` to be 1:20:00 on a Thursday. (The result of the test is `false`, not `true` as the programmer expects.) Do you see the problem? In each example, the client has violated the function precondition. The precondition of `Set` requires the first argument to have a value from 0 through 23. The precondition of `LessThan` requires the two times to be on the same day, not on two different days.

If a class has been well tested and there are errors when client code uses the class, always check the member function preconditions. You can waste many hours trying to debug a class member function when, in fact, the function is correct. The error may lie in the client code.

Testing and Debugging Hints

1. The declarations of `struct` and `class` types must end with semicolons.
2. Be sure to specify the full member selector when referencing a component of a struct variable or class object.
3. Avoid using anonymous `struct` types.
4. Regarding semicolons, the declarations and definitions of class member functions are treated the same as any C++ function. The member function prototype, located in the class declaration, ends with a semicolon. The function heading—the part of the function definition preceding the body—does not end with a semicolon.
5. When implementing a class member function, don't forget to prefix the function name with the name of the class and the scope resolution operator (::).

   ```
   void TimeType::Increment()
   {
       ⋮
   }
   ```

6. For now, the only built-in operations that apply to struct variables and class objects are member selection (.) and assignment (=). To perform other operations, such as comparing two struct variables or class objects, you must access the components individually (in the case of struct variables) or write class member functions (in the case of class objects).
7. If a class member function inspects but does not modify the private data, it is a good idea to make it a `const` member function.

8. A class member function does not use dot notation to access private members of the class object for which the function is invoked. In contrast, a member function *must* use dot notation to access the private members of a class object that is passed to it as an argument.

9. To avoid errors caused by uninitialized data, it is good practice to always include a class constructor when designing a class.

10. A class constructor is declared without a return value type and cannot return a function value.

11. If a client of a class has errors that seem to be related to the class, start by checking the preconditions of the class member functions. The errors may be in the client, not the class.

Summary

In addition to being able to create user-defined atomic data types, we can create structured data types. In a structured data type, a name is given to an entire group of components. With many structured types, the group can be accessed as a whole, or each individual component can be accessed separately.

The record is a data structure for grouping together heterogeneous data—data items that are of different types. Individual components of a record are accessed by name. In C++, records are referred to as *structures* or as *structs*. We can use a struct variable to refer to the struct as a whole, or we can use a member selector to access any individual member (component) of the struct. Entire structs of the same type may be assigned directly to each other, passed as arguments, or returned as function return values. Comparison of structs, however, must be done member by member. Reading and writing of structs must also be done member by member.

Data abstraction is a powerful technique for reducing the complexity and increasing the reliability of programs. Separating the properties of a data type from the details of its implementation frees the user of the type from having to write code that depends on a particular implementation of the type. This separation also assures the implementor of the type that client code cannot accidentally compromise a correct implementation.

An abstract data type (ADT) is a type whose specification is separate from its implementation. The specification announces the abstract properties of the type. The implementation consists of (a) a concrete data representation and (b) the implementations of the ADT operations. In C++, an ADT can be realized by using the class mechanism. A class is similar to a struct, but the members of a class are not only data but also functions. Class members can be designated as public or private. Most commonly, the private members are the concrete data representation of the ADT, and the public members are the functions corresponding to the ADT operations.

Among the public member functions of a class, the programmer often includes one or more class constructors—functions that are invoked automatically whenever a class object is created.

Separate compilation of program units is central to the separation of specification from implementation. The declaration of a C++ class is typically placed in a specification (.h) file, and the implementations of the class member functions reside in another file: the implementation file. The client code is compiled separately from the class implementation file, and the two resulting object code files are linked together to form an executable file. Through separate compilation, the user of an ADT can treat the ADT as an off-the-shelf component without ever seeing how it is implemented.

Quick Check

1. Write the type declaration for a `struct` data type named `PersonRec` with three members: `age`, `height`, and `weight`. All three members are intended to store integer values, with `height` and `weight` representing height in inches and weight in pounds, respectively. (pp. 403–409)

2. Assume a variable named `now`, of type `PersonRec`, has been declared. Write assignment statements to store into `now` the data for a 28-year old person measuring 5'6" and weighing 140 pounds. (pp. 403–409)

3. Declare a hierarchical record type named `HistoryRec` that consists of two members of type `PersonRec`. The members are named `past` and `present`. (pp. 409–411)

4. Assume a variable named `history`, of type `HistoryRec`, has been declared. Write assignment statements to store into the `past` member of `history` the data for a 15-year-old person measuring 5'0" and weighing 96 pounds. Write the assignment statement that copies the contents of variable `now` into the `present` member of `history`. (pp. 409–411)

5. What is the primary purpose of C++ `union` types? (pp. 412–413)

6. The specification of an ADT describes only its properties (the domain and allowable operations). To implement the ADT, what two things must a programmer do? (pp. 415–417)

7. Write a C++ class declaration for the following Checkbook ADT. Do not implement the ADT other than to include in the private part a concrete data representation for the current balance. All monetary amounts are to be represented as floating-point numbers.

> TYPE
> 　　Checkbook
> DOMAIN
> 　　Each instance of the Checkbook type is a value representing one customer's current checking account balance.
> OPERATIONS
> 　　Open the checking account, specifying an initial balance.
> 　　Write a check for a specified amount.
> 　　Deposit a specified amount into the checking account.
> 　　Return the current balance.

(pp. 417–419)

8. Write a segment of client code that declares two Checkbook objects, one for a personal checkbook and one for a business account. (pp. 417–419)

9. For the personal checkbook in Question 8, write a segment of client code that opens the account with an initial balance of $300.00, writes two checks for $50.25 and $150.00, deposits $87.34 into the account, and prints out the resulting balance. (pp. 419–422)

10. Implement the following Checkbook member functions. (pp. 427–431)
    a. Open
    b. WriteCheck
    c. CurrentBalance

11. A compile-time error occurs if a client of Checkbook tries to access the private class members directly. Give an example of such a client statement. (pp. 423–424)

12. In which file—the specification file or the implementation file—would the solution to Question 7 be located? In which file would the solution to Question 10 be located? (pp. 425–431)

13. For the Checkbook class, replace the Open function with two C++ class constructors. One (the default constructor) initializes the account balance to zero. The other initializes the balance to an amount passed as an argument. (pp. 434–439)
    a. Revise the class declaration.
    b. Implement the two class constructors.

Answers

1.
```
struct PersonRec
{
    int age;
    int height;
    int weight;
};
```

2.
```
now.age = 28;
now.height = 66;
now.weight = 140;
```

3.
```
struct HistoryRec
{
    PersonRec past;
    PersonRec present;
};
```

4.
```
history.past.age = 15;
history.past.height = 60;
history.past.weight = 96;
history.present = now;
```

5. The primary purpose is to save memory by forcing different values to share the same memory space, one at a time.

6. a. Choose a concrete data representation of the abstract data, using data types that already exist. b. Implement each of the allowable operations in terms of program instructions.

7.
```
class Checkbook
{
public:
    void Open( /* in */ float initBalance );
    void WriteCheck( /* in */ float amount );
    void Deposit( /* in */ float amount );
    float CurrentBalance() const;
private:
    float balance;
};
```

8.
```
Checkbook personalAcct;
Checkbook businessAcct;
```

9.
```
personalAcct.Open(300.0);
personalAcct.WriteCheck(50.25);
personalAcct.WriteCheck(150.0);
personalAcct.Deposit(87.34);
cout << '$' << personalAcct.CurrentBalance() << endl;
```

10. a.
```
void Checkbook::Open( /* in */ float initBalance )
{
    balance = initBalance;
}
```
   b.
```
void Checkbook::WriteCheck( /* in */ float amount )
{
    balance = balance - amount;
}
```
   c.
```
float Checkbook::CurrentBalance() const
{
    return balance;
}
```

11.
```
personalAcct.balance = 10000.0;
```

12. The C++ class declaration of Question 7 would be located in the specification file. The C++ function definitions of Question 10 would be located in the implementation file.

13. a.
```
class Checkbook
{
public:
    void WriteCheck( /* in */ float amount );
    void Deposit( /* in */ float amount );
    float CurrentBalance() const;
    Checkbook();
    Checkbook( /* in */ float initBalance );
```

```
    private:
        float balance;
    };
b.  Checkbook::Checkbook()
    {
        balance = 0.0;
    }
    Checkbook::Checkbook( /* in */ float initBalance )
    {
        balance = initBalance;
    }
```

Exam Preparation Exercises

1. Define the following terms that relate to records (structs in C++):
   record
   member
   member selector
   hierarchical record

2. Declare a `struct` type named `RecType` to contain an integer variable representing a person's number of dependents, a floating-point variable representing the person's salary, and a Boolean variable indicating whether the person has major medical insurance coverage (`true`) or basic company coverage only (`false`).

3. Using the second version of the `MachineRec` type in this chapter (p. 410), the code below is supposed to print a message if a machine has not been serviced within the current year. The code has an error. Correct the error by using a proper member selector in the If statement.

```
DateType    currentDate;
MachineRec  machine;
    ⋮
if (machine.lastServiced.year != currentDate.year)
    PrintMsg();
```

4. Given the declarations

```
struct NameType
{
    string first;
    string last;
};
struct AddrType
{
    string city;
    string state;
```

```
    long    zipCode;
};
struct PersonType
{
    NameType name;
    AddrType address;
};


PersonType person;
```

write C++ code that stores the following information into `person`:
Beverly Johnson
2638 Oak Dr.
La Crosse, WI 54601

5. The specification of an abstract data type (ADT) should not mention implementation details. (True or False?)

6. Below are some real-world objects you might want to represent in a program as ADTs. For each, give some abstract operations that might be appropriate. (Ignore the concrete data representation for each object.)

   a. A thesaurus

   b. An automatic dishwasher

   c. A radio-controlled model airplane

7. Consider the following C++ class declaration and client code:

Class Declaration	*Client Code*
`class SomeClass`	`SomeClass object1;`
`{`	`SomeClass object2;`
`public:`	`int       m;`
`    void Func1( int n );`	
`    int  Func2( int n ) const;`	`object1.Func1(3);`
`    void Func3();`	`m = object2.Func2(5);`
`private:`	
`    int someInt;`	
`};`	

   a. List all the identifiers that refer to data types (both built-in and programmer-defined).

   b. List all the identifiers that are names of class members.

   c. List all the identifiers that are names of class objects.

   d. List the names of all member functions that are allowed to inspect the private data.

   e. List the names of all member functions that are allowed to modify the private data.

(continued on next page)

f. In the implementation of `SomeClass`, which one of the following would be the correct function definition for `Func3`?

i.
```
void Func3()
{
    ⋮
}
```

ii.
```
void SomeClass::Func3()
{
    ⋮
}
```

iii.
```
SomeClass::void Func3()
{
    ⋮
}
```

8. If you do not use the reserved words `public` and `private`, all members of a C++ class are private and all members of a struct are public. (True or False?)

9. Define the following terms:
   instantiate
   `const` member function
   specification file
   implementation file

10. To the `TimeType` class we wish to add three operations: `CurrentHrs`, `CurrentMins`, and `CurrentSecs`. These operations simply return the current values of the private data to the client. We can amend the class declaration by inserting the following function prototypes into the public part:

```
int CurrentHrs() const;
    // Postcondition:
    //       Function value == hours part of the time of day

int CurrentMins() const;
    // Postcondition:
    //       Function value == minutes part of the time of day

int CurrentSecs() const;
    // Postcondition:
    //       Function value == seconds part of the time of day
```

Write the function definitions for these three functions as they would appear in the implementation file.

11. Answer the following questions about Figure 11-11, which illustrates the process of compiling and linking a multifile program.
    a. If only the file `myprog.cpp` is modified, which files must be recompiled?
    b. If only the file `myprog.cpp` is modified, which files must be relinked?

c. If only the files `file2.cpp` and `file3.cpp` are modified, which files must be recompiled? (Assume that the modifications do not affect existing code in `myprog.cpp`.)

d. If only the files `file2.cpp` and `file3.cpp` are modified, which files must be relinked? (Assume that the modifications do not affect existing code in `myprog.cpp`.)

12. Define the following terms:
separate compilation
C++ class constructor
default constructor

13. The following class has two constructors among its public member functions:

```
class SomeClass
{
public:
    float Func1() const;
      ⋮
    SomeClass( /* in */ float f );
        // Precondition:
        //     f is assigned
        // Postcondition:
        //     Private data is initialized to f
    SomeClass();
        // Postcondition:
        //     Private data is initialized to 8.6
private:
    float someFloat;
};
```

Write declarations for the following class objects.
a. An object `obj1`, initialized to 0.0.
b. An object `obj2`, initialized to 8.6.

14. The C++ compiler will signal a syntax error in the following class declaration. What is the error?

```
class SomeClass
{
public:
    void Func1( int n );
    int  Func2();
    int  SomeClass();
private:
    int privateInt;
};
```

Programming Warm-up Exercises

1. a. Write a `struct` declaration to contain the following information about a student:

   Name (string of characters)
   Social Security number (string of characters)
   Year (freshman, sophomore, junior, senior)
   Grade point average (floating-point number)
   Sex (M, F)

   b. Declare a struct variable of the type in part (a), and write a program segment that prints the information in each member of the variable.

2. a. Declare a `struct` type named `AptType` for an apartment locator service. The following information should be included:

   Landlord (string of characters)
   Address (string of characters)
   Bedrooms (integer)
   Price (floating-point number)

   b. Declare `anApt` to be a variable of type `AptType`.

   c. Write a function to read values into the members of a variable of type `AptType`. (The struct variable should be passed as an argument.) The order in which the data is read is the same as that of the items in the struct.

3. Write a hierarchical C++ `struct` declaration to contain the following information about a student:

   Name (string of characters)
   Student ID number
   Credit hours to date
   Number of courses taken
   Date first enrolled (month and year)
   Year (freshman, sophomore, junior, senior)
   Grade point average

   Each `struct` and enumeration type should have a separate type declaration.

4. You are writing the subscription renewal system for a magazine. For each subscriber, the system is to keep the following information:

   Name (first, last)
   Address (street, city, state, zip code)
   Expiration date (month, year)
   Date renewal notice was sent (month, day, year)
   Number of renewal notices sent so far
   Number of years for which subscription is being renewed (0 for renewal not yet received; otherwise, 1, 2, or 3 years)
   Whether or not the subscriber's name may be included in a mailing list for sale to other companies

   Write a hierarchical record type declaration to represent this information. Each subrecord should be declared separately as a named data type.

5. The `TimeType` class supplies two member functions, `Equal` and `LessThan`, that correspond to the relational operators `==` and `<`. Show how *client code* can simulate the other four relational operators (`!=`, `<=`, `>`, and `>=`) using only the `Equal` and `LessThan` functions. Specifically, express each of the following pseudocode statements in C++, where `time1` and `time2` are objects of type `TimeType`.

   a. IF time1 ≠ time2
       Set n = 1
   b. IF time1 ≤ time2
       Set n = 5
   c. IF time1 > time2
       Set n = 8
   d. IF time1 ≥ time2
       Set n = 5

6. In reference to Programming Warm-up Exercise 5, make life easier for the user of the `TimeType` class by adding new member functions `NotEqual`, `LessOrEqual`, `GreaterThan`, and `GreaterOrEqual` to the class.

   a. Show the function specifications (prototypes and preconditions and postconditions) as they would appear in the new class declaration.
   b. Write the function definitions as they would appear in the implementation file. (*Hint:* Instead of writing the algorithms from scratch, simply have the function bodies invoke the existing functions `Equal` and `LessThan`. And remember: Class members can refer to each other directly without using dot notation.)

7. Enhance the `TimeType` class by adding a new member function `WriteAmPm`. This function prints the time in 12-hour rather than 24-hour form, adding *AM* or *PM* at the end. Show the function specification (prototype and precondition and postcondition) as it would appear in the new class declaration. Then write the function definition as it would appear in the implementation file.

8. Add a member function named `Minus` to the `TimeType` class. This value-returning function yields the difference in seconds between the times represented by two class objects. Show the function specification (prototype and precondition and postcondition) as it would appear in the new class declaration. Then write the function definition as it would appear in the implementation file.

9. a. Design the data sets necessary to thoroughly test the `LessThan` function of the `TimeType` class.
   b. Write a driver and test the `LessThan` function using your test data.

10. a. Design the data sets necessary to thoroughly test the `Write` function of the `TimeType` class.
    b. Write a driver and test the `Write` function using your test data.

11. a. Design the data sets necessary to thoroughly test the `WriteAmPm` function of Programming Warm-Up Exercise 7.
    b. Write a driver and test the `WriteAmPm` function using your test data.

12. Reimplement the `TimeType` class so that the private data representation is a single variable:

```
long secs;
```

This variable represents time as the number of seconds since midnight. *Do not change the public interface in any way.* The user's view is still hours, minutes, and seconds, but the class's view is seconds since midnight.

Notice how this data representation simplifies the `Equal` and `LessThan` functions but makes the other operations more complicated by converting seconds back and forth to hours, minutes, and seconds. Use auxiliary functions, hidden inside the implementation file, to perform these conversions instead of duplicating the algorithms in several places.

13. Write a test plan for testing the `ComparedTo` function of the `DateType` class.

14. Write a driver to implement your test plan for the `ComparedTo` function.

15. In the BirthdayCalls program, we represented a person's area code as an `int` value. Printing an `int` area code works fine for North American phone numbers, where area codes are greater than 200. But international area codes may start with a zero. Our program would print an area code of 052 as 52. Suggest two ways of accommodating international area codes so that leading zeros are printed.

Programming Problems

1. The Emerging Manufacturing Company has just installed its first computer and hired you as a junior programmer. Your first program is to read employee pay data and produce two reports: (1) an error and control report, and (2) a report on pay amounts. The second report must contain a line for each employee and a line of totals at the end of the report.

Input:
Transaction File
Set of three job site number/name pairs
One line for each employee containing ID number, job site number, and number of hours worked

These data items have been presorted by ID number.

Master File
ID number
Name
Pay rate per hour
Number of dependents
Type of employee (1 is management, 0 is union)
Job site
Sex (M, F)

This file is ordered by ID number.

NOTE: (1) Union members, unlike management, get time and a half for hours over 40. (2) The tax formula for tax computation is as follows: If number of dependents is 1, tax rate is 15%. Otherwise, the tax rate is the greater of 2.5% and

$$\left[1 - \left(\frac{\textit{No. of dep.}}{\textit{No. of dep.} + 6}\right)\right] \times 15\%$$

Output:

Error and Control Report

Lists the input lines for which there is no corresponding master record, or where the employees' job site numbers do not agree with those in the master file. Continues processing with the next line of data.

Gives the total number of employee records that were processed correctly during the run.

Payroll Report (Labeled for Management)

Contains a line for each employee showing the name, ID number, job site name, gross pay, and net pay.

Contains a total line showing the total amount of gross pay and total amount of net pay.

2. A rational number is a number that can be expressed as a fraction whose numerator and denominator are integers. Examples of rational numbers are 0.75 (which is 3/4) and 1.125 (which is 9/8). The value π is not a rational number; it cannot be expressed as the ratio of two integers.

Working with rational numbers on a computer is often a problem. Inaccuracies in floating-point representation can yield imprecise results. For example, the result of the C++ expression

```
1.0 / 3.0 * 3.0
```

is likely to be a value like 0.999999 rather than 1.0.

Design, implement, and test a `Rational` class that represents a rational number as a pair of integers instead of a single floating-point number. The `Rational` class should have two class constructors. The first one lets the client specify an initial numerator and denominator. The other—the default constructor—creates the rational number 0, represented as a numerator of 0 and a denominator of 1. The segment of client code

```
Rational num1(1, 3);
Rational num2(3, 1);
Rational result;

cout << "The product of ";
num1.Write();
cout << " and ";
```

```
num2.Write();
cout << " is ";
result = num1.MultipliedBy(num2);
result.Write();
```

would produce the output

```
The product of 1/3 and 3/1 is 1/1
```

At the very least, you should provide the following operations:

- Constructors for explicit as well as default initialization of Rational objects.
- Arithmetic operations that add, subtract, multiply, and divide two Rational objects. These should be implemented as value-returning functions, each returning a Rational object.
- A Boolean operation that compares two Rational objects for equality.
- An output operation that displays the value of a Rational object in the form numerator/denominator.

Include any additional operations that you think would be useful for a rational number class.

3. A complex ("imaginary") number has the form $a + bi$, where i is the square root of -1. Here, a is called the real part and b is called the imaginary part. Alternatively, $a + bi$ can be expressed as the ordered pair of real numbers (a, b).

   Arithmetic operations on two complex numbers (a, b) and (c, d) are as follows:

   $$\begin{aligned}
   (a,b) + (c,d) &= (a+c, b+d)\\
   (a,b) - (c,d) &= (a-c, b-d)\\
   (a,b) \times (c,d) &= (a\times c - b\times d, a\times d + b\times c)\\
   (a,b) \div (c,d) &= \left(\frac{a\times c + b\times d}{c^2 + d^2}, \frac{b\times c + a\times d}{c^2 + d^2}\right)
   \end{aligned}$$

   Also, the absolute value (or magnitude) of a complex number is defined as

   $$\left|(a,b)\right| = \sqrt{a^2 + b^2}$$

   Design, implement, and test a complex number class that represents the real and imaginary parts as double-precision values (data type double) and provides at least the following operations:

   - Constructors for explicit as well as default initialization. The default initial value should be (0.0, 0.0).
   - Arithmetic operations that add, subtract, multiply, and divide two complex numbers. These should be implemented as value-returning functions, each returning a class object.
   - A complex absolute value operation.

- Two operations, `RealPart` and `ImagPart`, that return the real and imaginary parts of a complex number.

4. Design, implement, and test a countdown timer class named `Timer`. This class mimics a real-world timer by counting off seconds, starting from an initial value. When the timer reaches zero, it beeps (by sending the alert character, '\a', to the standard output device). Some appropriate operations might be the following:

- Create a timer, initializing it to a specified number of seconds.
- Start the timer.
- Reset the timer to some value.

When the `Start` operation is invoked, it should repeatedly decrement and output the current value of the timer approximately every second. To delay the program for one second, use a For loop whose body does absolutely nothing; that is, its body is the null statement. Experiment with the number of loop iterations to achieve as close to a one-second delay as you can.

If your C++ system provides functions to clear the screen and to position the cursor anywhere on the screen, you might want to do the following. Begin by clearing the screen. Then, always display the timer value at the same position in the center of the screen. Each output should overwrite the previous value displayed, just like a real-world timer.

Arrays

- To be able to declare a one-dimensional array.
- To be able to perform fundamental operations on a one-dimensional array:
  - Assign a value to an array component.
  - Access a value stored in an array component.
  - Fill an array with data, and process the data in the array.
- To be able to initialize a one-dimensional array in its declaration.
- To be able to pass one-dimensional arrays as arguments to functions.
- To be able to use arrays of records and class objects.
- To be able to apply subarray processing to a given one-dimensional array.
- To be able to declare and use a one-dimensional array with index values that have semantic content.
- To be able to declare a two-dimensional array.
- To be able to perform fundamental operations on a two-dimensional array:
  - Access a component of the array.
  - Initialize the array.
  - Print the values in the array.
  - Process the array by rows.
  - Process the array by columns.
- To be able to declare a two-dimensional array as a parameter.
- To be able to view a two-dimensional array as an array of arrays.
- To be able to declare and process a multidimensional array.

Data structures play an important role in the design process. The choice of data structure directly affects the design because it determines the algorithms used to process the data. In Chapter 11, we saw how the record (struct) and the class give us the ability to refer to an entire group of components by one name. This simplifies the design of many programs.

In many problems, however, a data structure has so many components that it is difficult to process them if each one must have a unique member name. For example, the IntList abstract data type (ADT) we proposed briefly in Chapter 11 represents a collection of up to 100 integer values. If we used a struct or a class to hold these values, we would need to invent 100 different member names, write 100 different input statements to read values into the members, and write 100 different output statements to display the values—an incredibly tedious task! An *array*—the fourth of the structured data types supported by C++—is a data type that allows us to program operations of this kind with ease.

In this chapter, we examine array data types as provided by the C++ language; in Chapter 13, we show how to combine classes and arrays to implement an ADT such as IntList.

12.1 One-Dimensional Arrays

If we wanted to input 1000 integer values and print them in reverse order, we could write a program of this form:

```
//****************************
// ReverseNumbers program
//****************************
#include <iostream>

using namespace std;

int main()
{
    int value0;
    int value1;
    int value2;
      ⋮
    int value999;

    cin >> value0;
    cin >> value1;
    cin >> value2;
      ⋮
    cin >> value999;
```

```
cout << value999 << endl;
cout << value998 << endl;
cout << value997 << endl;
    ⋮
cout << value0 << endl;
return 0;
}
```

This program is over 3000 lines long, and we have to use 1000 separate variables. Note that all the variables have the same name except for an appended number that distinguishes them. Wouldn't it be convenient if we could put the number into a counter variable and use For loops to go from 0 through 999, and then from 999 back down to 0? For example, if the counter variable were `number`, we could replace the 2000 original input/output statements with the following four lines of code (we enclose `number` in brackets to set it apart from `value`):

```
for (number = 0; number < 1000; number++)
    cin >> value[number];
for (number = 999; number >= 0; number--)
    cout << value[number] << endl;
```

This code fragment is correct in C++ *if* we declare `value` to be a *one-dimensional array*, which is a collection of variables—all of the same type—in which the first part of each variable name is the same, and the last part is an *index value* enclosed in square brackets. In our example, the value stored in `number` is called the *index*.

The declaration of a one-dimensional array is similar to the declaration of a simple variable (a variable of a simple data type), with one exception: You must also declare the size of the array. To do so, you indicate within brackets the number of components in the array:

```
int value[1000];
```

This declaration creates an array with 1000 components, all of type `int`. The first component has index value 0, the second component has index value 1, and the last component has index value 999.

Here is the complete ReverseNumbers program, using array notation. This is certainly much shorter than our first version of the program.

```
//****************************
// ReverseNumbers program
//****************************
#include <iostream>

using namespace std;
```

```
int main()
{
    int value[1000];
    int number;

    for (number = 0; number < 1000; number++)
        cin >> value[number];
    for (number = 999; number >= 0; number--)
        cout << value[number] << endl;
    return 0;
}
```

As a data structure, an array differs from a struct or class in two fundamental ways:

1. An array is a *homogeneous* data structure (all components are of the same data type), whereas structs and classes are heterogeneous types (their components may be of different types).

2. A component of an array is accessed by its *position* in the structure, whereas a component of a struct or class is accessed by an identifier (the member name).

Let's now define arrays formally and look at the rules for accessing individual components.

Declaring Arrays

A **one-dimensional array** is a structured collection of components (often called *array elements*) that can be accessed individually by specifying the position of a component with a single index value. (Later in the chapter, we introduce multidimensional arrays, which are arrays that have more than one index value.)

One-dimensional array A structured collection of components, all of the same type, that is given a single name. Each component (array element) is accessed by an index that indicates the component's position within the collection.

Here is a syntax template describing the simplest form of a one-dimensional array declaration:

ArrayDeclaration

DataType ArrayName [ConstIntExpression] ;

In the syntax template, DataType describes what is stored in each component of the array. Array components may be of almost any type, but for now we limit our discussion to atomic components. ConstIntExpression is an integer expression composed only of literal or named constants. This expression, which specifies the number of

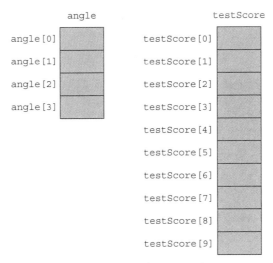

Figure 12-1 *angle* and *testScore* *Arrays*

components in the array, must have a value greater than 0. If the value is *n*, the range of index values is 0 through *n* − 1, not 1 through *n*. For example, the declarations

```
float angle[4];
int   testScore[10];
```

create the arrays shown in Figure 12-1. The `angle` array has four components, each capable of holding one `float` value. The `testScore` array has a total of ten components, all of type `int`.

Accessing Individual Components

Recall that to access an individual component of a struct or class, we use dot notation—the name of the struct variable or class object, followed by a period, followed by the member name. In contrast, to access an individual array component, we write the array name, followed by an expression enclosed in square brackets. The expression specifies which component to access, and the index expression may be as simple as a constant or a variable name or as complex as a combination of variables, operators, and function calls. Whatever the form of the expression, it must result in an integer value. Index expressions can be of type `char`, `short`, `int`, `long`, or `bool` because these are all integral types. Additionally, values of enumeration types can be used as index expressions, with an enumeration value implicitly coerced to an integer.

The simplest form of index expression is a constant. Using our `angle` array, the sequence of assignment statements

```
angle[0] = 4.93;
angle[1] = -15.2;
angle[2] = 0.5;
angle[3] = 1.67;
```

fills the array components one at a time (see Figure 12-2).

Each array component—`angle[2]`, for instance—can be treated exactly the same as a simple variable. For example, we can do the following to the individual component `angle[2]`:

`angle[2] = 9.6;`	Assign it a value.
`cin >> angle[2];`	Read a value into it.
`cout << angle[2];`	Write its contents.
`y = sqrt(angle[2]);`	Pass it as an argument.
`x = 6.8 * angle[2] + 7.5;`	Use it in an arithmetic expression.

Let's look at index expressions that are more complicated than constants. Suppose we declare a 1000-element array of `int` values with the statement

```
int value[1000];
```

and execute the following two statements.

```
value[counter] = 5;
if (value[number+1] % 10 != 0)
    ⋮
```

In the first statement, 5 is stored into an array component. If `counter` is 0, 5 is stored into the first component of the array. If `counter` is 1, 5 is stored into the second place in the array, and so forth.

In the second statement, the expression `number+1` selects an array component. The specific array component accessed is divided by 10 and checked to see if the remainder

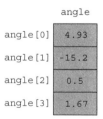

Figure 12-2 `angle` *Array with Values*

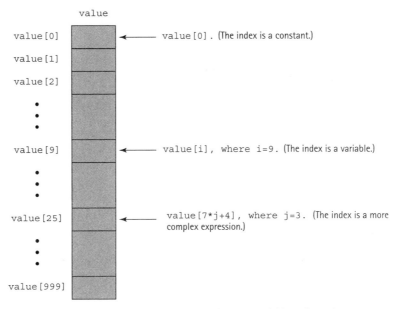

Figure 12-3 *An Index as a Constant, a Variable, and an Arbitrary Expression*

is nonzero. If `number+1` is 0, we are testing the value in the first component; if `number+1` is 1, we are testing the second place; and so on. Figure 12-3 shows the index expression as a constant, a variable, and a more complex expression.

Note that we have seen the use of square brackets before. In earlier chapters, we said that the `string` class allows you to access an individual character within a string:

```
string aString;

aString = "Hello";
cout << aString[1];     // Prints 'e'
```

Although `string` is a class, not an array, the `string` class was written using the advanced C++ technique of *operator overloading* to give the `[]` operator another meaning (string component selection) in addition to its standard meaning (array element selection). The result is that a `string` object is similar to an array of characters but has special properties.

Out-of-Bounds Array Indexes

Given the declaration

```
float alpha[100];
```

the valid range of index values is 0 through 99. What happens if we execute the statement

```
alpha[i] = 62.4;
```

when i is less than 0 or when i is greater than 99? The result is that a memory location outside the array is accessed. C++ does not check for invalid (out-of-bounds) array indexes either at compile time or at run time. If i happens to be 100 in the statement above, the computer stores 62.4 into the next memory location past the end of the array, destroying whatever value was contained there. It is entirely the programmer's responsibility to make sure that an array index does not step off either end of the array.

Out-of-bounds array index   An index value that, in C++, is either less than 0 or greater than the array size minus 1.

Array-processing algorithms often use For loops to step through the array elements one at a time. Here is a loop to zero out our 100-element alpha array (i is an int variable):

```
for (i = 0; i < 100; i++)
    alpha[i] = 0.0;
```

We could also write the first line as

```
for (i = 0; i <= 99; i++)
```

However, C++ programmers commonly use the first version so that the number in the loop test (100) is the same as the array size. With this pattern, it is important to remember to test for *less-than*, not less-than-or-equal.

Initializing Arrays in Declarations

You learned in Chapter 8 that C++ allows you to initialize a variable in its declaration:

```
int delta = 25;
```

The value 25 is called an initializer. You also can initialize an array in its declaration, using a special syntax for the initializer. You specify a list of initial values for the array elements, separate them with commas, and enclose the list within braces:

```
int age[5] = {23, 10, 16, 37, 12};
```

In this declaration, age[0] is initialized to 23, age[1] is initialized to 10, and so on. There must be at least one initial value between the braces. If you specify too many initial values, you get a syntax error message. If you specify too few, the remaining array elements are initialized to zero.

Arrays follow the same rule as simple variables about the time(s) at which initialization occurs. A static array (one that is either global or declared as static within a block) is initialized once only, when control reaches its declaration. An automatic array (one that is local and not declared as static) is reinitialized each time control reaches its declaration.

An interesting feature of C++ is that you are allowed to omit the size of an array when you initialize it in a declaration:

```
float temperature[] = {0.0, 112.37, 98.6};
```

The compiler figures out the size of the array (here, 3) according to how many initial values are listed. In general, this feature is not particularly useful. In Chapter 13, though, we'll see that it can be convenient for initializing certain kinds of char arrays called C strings.

(Lack of) Aggregate Array Operations

In Chapter 11, we defined an aggregate operation as an operation on a data structure as a whole. Some programming languages allow aggregate operations on arrays, but C++ does not. If x and y are declared as

```
int x[50];
int y[50];
```

there is no aggregate assignment of y to x:

```
x = y;    // Not valid
```

To copy array y into array x, you must do it yourself, element by element:

```
for (index = 0; index < 50; index++)
    x[index] = y[index];
```

Similarly, there is no aggregate comparison, I/O, or arithmetic for arrays:

```
if (x == y)   // Not valid
   ⋮
cout << x;    // Not valid
x = x + y;    // Not valid
```

(C++ allows one exception for I/O, which we discuss in Chapter 13. Aggregate I/O is permitted for C strings, which are special kinds of char arrays.) Finally, it's not possible to return an entire array as the value of a value-returning function:

```
return x;    // Not valid
```

484 | Chapter 12: Arrays

The only thing you can do to an array as a whole is to pass it as an argument to a function:

```
DoSomething(x);
```

Passing an array as an argument gives the function access to the entire array. The following table compares arrays, structs, and classes with respect to aggregate operations.

Aggregate Operation	Arrays	Structs and Classes
I/O	No (except C strings)	No
Assignment	No	Yes
Arithmetic	No	No
Comparison	No	No
Argument passage	By reference only	By value or by reference
Return as a function's return value	No	Yes

Later in the chapter, we look in detail at passing arrays as arguments.

Examples of Declaring and Accessing Arrays

We now look in detail at some specific examples of declaring and accessing arrays. Here are some declarations that a program might use to analyze occupancy rates in an apartment building:

```
const int BUILDING_SIZE = 350;   // Number of apartments

int occupants[BUILDING_SIZE];    // occupants[i] is the number of
                                 //   occupants in apartment i
int totalOccupants;              // Total number of occupants
int counter;                     // Loop control and index variable
```

occupants is a 350-element array of integers (see Figure 12-4). occupants[0] = 3 if the first apartment has three occupants; occupants[1] = 5 if the second apartment has five occupants; and so on. If values have been stored into the array, then the following code totals the number of occupants in the building.

```
totalOccupants = 0;
for (counter = 0; counter < BUILDING_SIZE; counter++)
    totalOccupants = totalOccupants + occupants[counter];
```

The first time through the loop, counter is 0. We add the contents of totalOccupants (that is, 0) to the contents of occupants[0], storing the result into totalOccupants. Next, counter becomes 1 and the loop test occurs. The second loop iteration

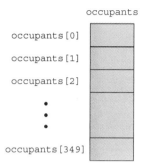

Figure 12-4 *occupants Array*

adds the contents of `totalOccupants` to the contents of `occupants[1]`, storing the result into `totalOccupants`. Now `counter` becomes 2 and the loop test is made. Eventually, the loop adds the contents of `occupants[349]` to the sum and increments `counter` to 350. At this point, the loop condition is false, and control exits the loop.

Note how we used the named constant `BUILDING_SIZE` in both the array declaration and the For loop. When constants are used in this manner, changes are easy to make. If the number of apartments changes from 350 to 400, we need to change only one line: the `const` declaration of `BUILDING_SIZE`. If we had used the literal value 350 in place of `BUILDING_SIZE`, we would need to update several of the statements in the code above, and probably many more throughout the rest of the program.

Because an array index is an integer value, we access the components by their position in the array—that is, the first, the second, the third, and so on. Using an `int` index is the most common way of thinking about an array. C++, however, provides more flexibility by allowing an index to be of any integral type or enumeration type. (The index expression still must evaluate to an integer in the range from 0 through one less than the array size.) The next example shows an array in which the indexes are values of an enumeration type.

```
enum Drink {ORANGE, COLA, ROOT_BEER, GINGER_ALE, CHERRY, LEMON};

float salesAmt[6]; // Array of 6 floats, to be indexed by Drink type
Drink flavor;       // Variable of the index type
```

`Drink` is an enumeration type in which the enumerators `ORANGE`, `COLA`, ..., `LEMON` have internal representations 0 through 5, respectively. `salesAmt` is a group of six `float` components representing dollar sales figures for each kind of drink (see Figure 12-5). The following code prints the values in the array (see Chapter 10 to review how to increment values of enumeration types in For loops).

```
for (flavor = ORANGE; flavor <= LEMON; flavor = Drink(flavor + 1))
    cout << salesAmt[flavor] << endl;
```

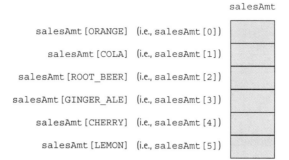

salesAmt

salesAmt[ORANGE]   (i.e., salesAmt[0])

salesAmt[COLA]   (i.e., salesAmt[1])

salesAmt[ROOT_BEER]   (i.e., salesAmt[2])

salesAmt[GINGER_ALE]   (i.e., salesAmt[3])

salesAmt[CHERRY]   (i.e., salesAmt[4])

salesAmt[LEMON]   (i.e., salesAmt[5])

Figure 12-5 *salesAmt Array*

Here is one last example.

```
const int NUM_STUDENTS = 10;

char grade[NUM_STUDENTS];      // Array of 10 student letter grades
int  idNumber;                 // Student ID number (0 through 9)
```

The grade array is pictured in Figure 12-6. Values are shown in the components, which implies that some processing of the array has already occurred. Following are some simple examples showing how the array might be used.

grade

grade[0]	'F'
grade[1]	'B'
grade[2]	'C'
grade[3]	'A'
grade[4]	'F'
grade[5]	'C'
grade[6]	'A'
grade[7]	'A'
grade[8]	'C'
grade[9]	'B'

Figure 12-6 *grade Array with Values*

`cin >> grade[2];`	Reads the next nonwhitespace character from the input stream and stores it into the component in `grade` indexed by 2.
`grade[3] = 'A';`	Assigns the character 'A' to the component in `grade` indexed by 3.
`idNumber = 5;`	Assigns 5 to the index variable `idNumber`.
`grade[idNumber] = 'C';`	Assigns the character 'C' to the component of `grade` indexed by `idNumber` (that is, by 5).

`for (idNumber = 0; idNumber < NUM_STUDENTS;`
`    idNumber++)`
`    cout << grade[idNumber];`
	Loops through the `grade` array, printing each component. For this loop, the output would be FBCAFCAACB.

`for (idNumber = 0; idNumber < NUM_STUDENTS;`
`    idNumber++)`
`    cout << "Student " << idNumber`
`        << " Grade " << grade[idNumber]`
`        << endl;`
	Loops through `grade`, printing each component in a more readable form.

In the last example, `idNumber` is used as the index, but it also has semantic content—it is the student's identification number. The output would be

```
Student 0 Grade F
Student 1 Grade B
   ⋮
Student 9 Grade B
```

Passing Arrays as Arguments

In Chapter 8, we said that if a variable is passed to a function and it is not to be changed by the function, then the variable should be passed by value instead of by reference. We specifically excluded stream variables (such as those representing data files) from this rule and said that there would be one more exception. Arrays are this exception.

By default, C++ simple variables are always passed by value. To pass a simple variable by reference, you must append an ampersand (&) to the data type name in the function's parameter list:

```
int SomeFunc( float param1,    // Pass-by-value
              char& param2 )   // Pass-by-reference
{
    ⋮
}
```

It is impossible to pass a C++ array by value; arrays are *always* passed by reference. Therefore, you never use & when declaring an array as a parameter. When an array is passed as an argument, its **base address**—the memory address of the first element of the array—is sent to the function. The function then knows where the caller's actual array is located and can access any element of the array.

Base address The memory address of the first element of an array.

Here is a C++ function that will zero out a one-dimensional float array of any size:

```
void ZeroOut( /* out */ float arr[],
              /* in */  int    numElements )
{
    int i;

    for (i = 0; i < numElements; i++)
        arr[i] = 0.0;
}
```

In the parameter list, the declaration of arr does not include a size within the brackets. If you include a size, the compiler ignores it. The compiler only wants to know that it is a float array, not a float array of any particular size. Therefore, you must include a second parameter—the number of array elements—in order for the For loop to work correctly.

The calling code can invoke the ZeroOut function for a float array of any size. The following code fragment makes function calls to zero out two arrays of different sizes. Notice how an array parameter is declared in a function prototype.

```
void ZeroOut( float[], int );   // Function prototype
  ⋮
int main()
{
    float velocity[30];
    float refractionAngle[9000];
      ⋮
    ZeroOut(velocity, 30);
    ZeroOut(refractionAngle, 9000);
      ⋮
}
```

With simple variables, passing by value prevents a function from modifying the caller's argument. Although you cannot pass arrays by value in C++, you can still prevent the function from modifying the caller's array. To do so, you use the reserved word const in the declaration of the parameter. The following is a function that copies one int array into another. The first parameter—the destination array—is expected to be modified, but the second array is not.

```
void Copy( /* out */        int destination[],
           /* in */  const int source[],
           /* in */        int size          )
{
    int i;

    for (i = 0; i < size; i++)
        destination[i] = source[i];
}
```

The word `const` guarantees that any attempt to modify the `source` array within the `Copy` function results in a compile-time error.

One final remark about argument passage: It is a common mistake to pass an array *element* to a function when passing the entire array was intended. For example, our `ZeroOut` function expects the base address of a `float` array to be sent as the first argument. In the following code fragment, the function call is an error.

```
float velocity[30];
  ⋮
ZeroOut(velocity[30], 30);   // Error
```

First of all, `velocity[30]` denotes a single array element—one floating-point number—and not an entire array. Furthermore, there is no array element with an index of 30. The indexes for the `velocity` array run from 0 through 29.

Assertions About Arrays

In assertions written as comments, we often need to refer to a range of array elements:

```
// Assert: alpha[i] through alpha[j] have been printed
```

To specify such ranges, it is more convenient to use an abbreviated notation consisting of two dots:

```
// Assert: alpha[i]..alpha[j] have been printed
```

or, more briefly:

```
// Assert: alpha[i..j] have been printed
```

Note that this dot-dot notation is not valid syntax in C++ language statements. We are talking only about comments in a program.

As an example of the use of this notation, here is how we would write the precondition and postcondition for our `ZeroOut` function:

```
void ZeroOut( /* out */ float arr[],
              /* in */  int   numElements )
```

```
// Precondition:
//     numElements is assigned
// Postcondition:
//     arr[0..numElements-1] == 0.0

{
    int i;

    for (i = 0; i < numElements; i++)
        arr[i] = 0.0;
}
```

Using Typedef with Arrays

In Chapter 10, we discussed the Typedef statement as a way of giving an additional name to an existing data type. We said that before `bool` became a built-in type in C++, programmers often used a Typedef statement such as the following:

```
typedef int Boolean;
```

We can also use Typedef to give a name to an array type. Here's an example:

```
typedef float FloatArr[100];
```

This statement says that the type `FloatArr` is the same as the type "100-element array of `float`." (Notice that the array size in brackets comes at the very end of the statement.) We can now declare variables to be of type `FloatArr`:

```
FloatArr angle;
FloatArr velocity;
```

The compiler essentially translates these declarations into

```
float angle[100];
float velocity[100];
```

In this book, we don't often use Typedefs to give names to one-dimensional array types. However, when we discuss multidimensional arrays later in the chapter, we'll see that the technique can come in handy.

12.2 Arrays of Records and Class Objects

Although arrays with atomic components are very common, many applications require a collection of records or class objects. For example, a business needs a list of parts records, and a teacher needs a list of students in a class. Arrays are ideal for these applications. We simply define an array whose components are records or class objects.

Arrays of Records

Let's define a grade book to be a collection of student records as follows:

```cpp
const int MAX_STUDENTS = 150;

enum GradeType {A, B, C, D, F};

struct StudentRec
{
    string      stuName;
    float       gpa;
    int         examScore[4];
    GradeType   courseGrade;
};

StudentRec  gradeBook[MAX_STUDENTS];
int         count;
```

This data structure can be visualized as shown in Figure 12-7.

An element of `gradeBook` is selected by an index. For example, `gradeBook[2]` is the third component in the array `gradeBook`. Each component of `gradeBook` is a record of type `StudentRec`. To access the course grade of the third student, we use the following expression:

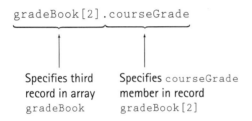

This page visualizes:

Specifies third record in array `gradeBook` — `gradeBook[2]`

Specifies `courseGrade` member in record `gradeBook[2]`

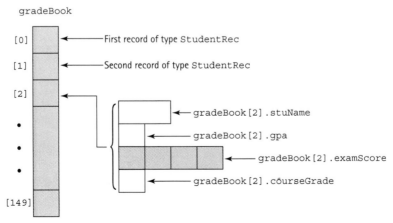

Figure 12-7 *gradeBook Array with Records as Elements*

The record component `gradeBook[2].examScore` is an array. We can access the individual elements in this component just as we would access the elements of any other array: We give the name of the array followed by the index, which is enclosed in brackets.

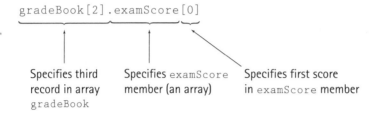

The following code fragment prints the name of each student in the class:

```
for (count = 0; count < MAX_STUDENTS; count++)
    cout << gradeBook[count].stuName << endl;
```

Arrays of Class Objects

The syntax for declaring and using arrays of class objects is the same as for arrays of structs. Given the `TimeType` class of Chapter 11, we can maintain a collection of ten appointment times by starting with the declaration

```
TimeType appointment[10];
```

This statement creates a ten-element array named `appointment`, in which each element is a `TimeType` object. The following statements set the first two appointment times to 8:45:00 and 10:00:00.

```
appointment[0].Set(8, 45, 0);
appointment[1].Set(10, 0, 0);
```

To output all ten appointment times, we would write

```
for (index = 0; index < 10; index++)
{
    appointment[index].Write();
    cout << endl;
}
```

Recall that the `TimeType` class has two constructors defined for it. One is the default (parameterless) constructor, which sets the time for a newly created object to

00:00:00. The other is a parameterized constructor with which the client code can specify an initial time when the class object is created. How are constructors handled when you declare an array of class objects? Here is the rule in C++:

If a class has at least one constructor, and an array of class objects is declared:

```
SomeClass arr[50];
```

then one of the constructors *must* be the default (parameterless) constructor. This constructor is invoked for each element of the array.

Therefore, with our declaration of the `appointment` array

```
TimeType appointment[10];
```

the default constructor is called for all ten array elements, setting each time to an initial value of 00:00:00.

12.3 Special Kinds of Array Processing

Two types of array processing occur especially often: using only part of the declared array (a subarray) and using index values that have specific meaning within the problem (indexes with semantic content). We describe both of these methods briefly here and give further examples in the remainder of the chapter.

Subarray Processing

The *size* of an array—the declared number of array components—is established at compile time. We have to declare it to be as big as it would ever need to be. Because the exact number of values to be put into the array often depends on the data itself, however, we may not fill all of the array components with values. The problem is that to avoid processing empty ones, we must keep track of how many components are actually filled.

As values are put into the array, we keep a count of how many components are filled. We then use this count to process only components that have values stored in them. Any remaining places are not processed. For example, if there are 250 students in a class, a program to analyze test grades would set aside 250 locations for the grades. However, some students may be absent on the day of the test. So the number of test grades must be counted, and that number, rather than 250, is used to control the processing of the array.

If the number of data items actually stored in an array is less than its declared size, functions that receive array parameters must also receive the number of data items as a parameter. For example,

```
void Print( /* in */ const char grade[],    // Array for up to
                                             //    250 students
           /* in */         int  numGrades ) // Number of grades
                                             //    actually in array
```

The first Programming Example at the end of this chapter demonstrates the technique of subarray processing.

Indexes with Semantic Content

In some problems, an array index has meaning beyond simple position; that is, the index has *semantic content*. An example is the `salesAmt` array we showed earlier. This array is indexed by a value of enumeration type `Drink`. The index of a specific sales amount is the kind of soft drink sold; for example, `salesAmt[ROOT_BEER]` is the dollar sales figure for root beer.

The next section gives additional examples of indexes with semantic content.

12.4 Two-Dimensional Arrays

A one-dimensional array is used to represent items in a list or sequence of values. In many problems, however, the relationships between data items are more complex than a simple list. A **two-dimensional array** is used to represent items in a table with rows and columns, provided each item in the table is of the same data type. Two-dimensional arrays are useful for representing board games, such as chess, tic-tac-toe, or Scrabble, and in computer graphics, where the screen is thought of as a two-dimensional array. A component in a two-dimensional array is accessed by specifying the row and column indexes of the item in the array. This is a familiar task. For example, if you want to find a street on a map, you look up the street name on the back of the map to find the coordinates of the street, usually a letter and a number. The letter specifies a column to look on, and the number specifies a row. You find the street where the row and column meet.

Two-dimensional array A collection of components, all of the same type, structured in two dimensions. Each component is accessed by a pair of indexes that represent the component's position in each dimension.

Figure 12-8 shows a two-dimensional array with 100 rows and 9 columns. The rows are accessed by an integer ranging from 0 through 99; the columns are accessed by an integer ranging from 0 through 8. Each component is accessed by a row-column pair— for example, 0, 5.

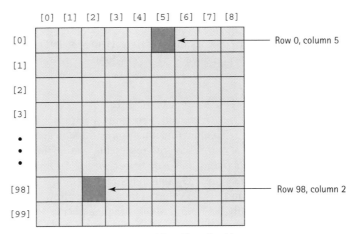

Figure 12-8 *A Two-Dimensional Array*

A two-dimensional array is declared in exactly the same way as a one-dimensional array, except that sizes must be specified for two dimensions. Following is an example of declaring an array with more than one dimension.

```
const int NUM_ROWS = 100;
const int NUM_COLS = 9;
   :
float alpha[NUM_ROWS][NUM_COLS];
```

First dimension   Second dimension

This example declares `alpha` to be a two-dimensional array, all of whose components are `float` values. The declaration creates the array that is pictured in Figure 12-8.

To access an individual component of the `alpha` array, two expressions (one for each dimension) are used to specify its position. Each expression is in its own pair of brackets next to the name of the array:

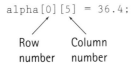

```
alpha[0][5] = 36.4;
```

Row number   Column number

As with one-dimensional arrays, each index expression must result in an integer value.

Let's look now at some examples. Here is the declaration of a two-dimensional array with 364 integer components (52 × 7 = 364):

```
int hiTemp[52][7];
```

hiTemp is an array with 52 rows and 7 columns. Each place in the array (each component) can contain any int value. Our intention is that the array contains high temperatures for each day in a year. Each row represents one of the 52 weeks in a year, and each column represents one of the 7 days in a week. (To keep the example simple, we ignore the fact that there are 365–and sometimes 366–days in a year.) The expression hiTemp[2][6] refers to the int value in the third row (row 2) and the seventh column (column 6). Semantically, hiTemp[2][6] is the temperature for the seventh day of the third week. The code fragment shown in Figure 12-9 would print the temperature values for the third week.

Another representation of the same data might be as follows:

```
enum DayType
{
    MONDAY, TUESDAY, WEDNESDAY, THURSDAY, FRIDAY, SATURDAY, SUNDAY
};

int hiTemp[52][7];
```

Here, hiTemp is declared the same as before, but we can use an expression of type DayType for the column index. hiTemp[2][SUNDAY] corresponds to the same component as hiTemp[2][6] in the first example. (Recall that enumerators such as MONDAY,

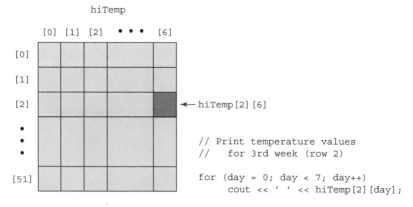

Figure 12-9 *hiTemp Array*

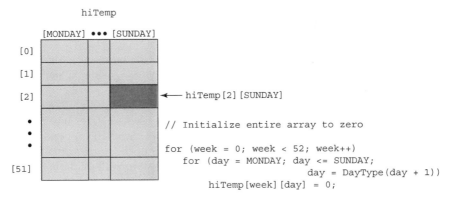

Figure 12-10 *hiTemp Array (Alternate Form)*

TUESDAY, ... are represented internally as the integers 0, 1, 2, ...) If `day` is of type `Day-Type` and `week` is of type `int`, the code fragment shown in Figure 12-10 sets the entire array to 0. (Notice that by using `DayType`, the temperature values in the array begin with the first Monday of the year, not necessarily with January 1.)

Another way of looking at a two-dimensional array is to see it as a structure in which each component has two features. For example, in the following code,

```
enum Colors {RED, ORANGE, YELLOW, GREEN, BLUE, INDIGO, VIOLET};
enum Makes
{
    FORD, TOYOTA, HYUNDAI, JAGUAR, CITROEN, BMW, FIAT, SAAB
};
const int NUM_COLORS = 7;
const int NUM_MAKES = 8;

float crashRating[NUM_COLORS][NUM_MAKES];   // Array of crash
                                            // likelihoods by color
                                            // and make
    ⋮
crashRating[BLUE][JAGUAR] = 0.83;           // Blue Jaguars have a crash
                                            //    likelihood of 0.83
crashRating[RED][FORD] = 0.19;              // Red Fords have a crash
                                            //    likelihood of 0.19
```

the data structure uses one dimension to represent the color and the other to represent the make of automobile. In other words, both indexes have semantic content—a concept we discussed in the previous section.

12.5 Processing Two–Dimensional Arrays

Processing data in a two-dimensional array generally means accessing the array in one of four patterns: randomly, along rows, along columns, or throughout the entire array. Each of these may also involve subarray processing.

The simplest way to access a component is to look directly in a given location. For example, a user enters map coordinates that we use as indexes into an array of street names to access the desired name at those coordinates. This process is referred to as *random access* because the user may enter any set of coordinates at random.

There are many cases in which we might wish to perform an operation on all the elements of a particular row or column in an array. Consider the `hiTemp` array defined previously, in which the rows represent weeks of the year and the columns represent days of the week. If we wanted the average high temperature for a given week, we would sum the values in that row and divide by 7. If we wanted the average for a given day of the week, we would sum the values in that column and divide by 52. The former case is access by row; the latter case is access by column.

Now suppose that we wish to determine the average for the year. We must access every element in the array, sum them, and divide by 364. In this case, the order of access—by row or by column—is not important. (The same is true when we initialize every element of an array to zero.) This is access throughout the array.

There are times when we must access every array element in a particular order, either by rows or by columns. For example, if we wanted the average for every week, we would run through the entire array, taking each row in turn. However, if we wanted the average for each day of the week, we would run through the array a column at a time.

Let's take a closer look at these patterns of access by considering four common examples of array processing.

1. Sum the rows.
2. Sum the columns.
3. Initialize the array to all zeros (or some special value).
4. Print the array.

First, let's define some constants and variables using general identifiers, such as `row` and `col`, rather than problem-dependent identifiers. Then let's look at each algorithm in terms of generalized two-dimensional array processing.

```
const int NUM_ROWS = 50;
const int NUM_COLS = 50;

int arr[NUM_ROWS][NUM_COLS];    // A two-dimensional array
int row;                        // A row index
int col;                        // A column index
int total;                      // A variable for summing
```

Sum the Rows

Suppose we want to sum row number 3 (the fourth row) in the array and print the result. We can do this easily with a For loop:

```
total = 0;
for (col = 0; col < NUM_COLS; col++)
    total = total + arr[3][col];
cout << "Row sum: " << total << endl;
```

This For loop runs through each column of `arr`, while keeping the row index fixed at 3. Every value in row 3 is added to `total`.

Now suppose we want to sum and print two rows—row 2 and row 3. We can use a nested loop and make the row index a variable:

```
for (row = 2; row < 4; row++)
{
    total = 0;
    for (col = 0; col < NUM_COLS; col++)
        total = total + arr[row][col];
    cout << "Row sum: " << total << endl;
}
```

The outer loop controls the rows, and the inner loop controls the columns. For each value of `row`, every column is processed; then the outer loop moves to the next row. In the first iteration of the outer loop, `row` is held at 2 and `col` goes from 0 through NUM_COLS-1. Therefore, the array is accessed in the following order:

```
arr[2][0]   [2][1]   [2][2]   [2][3] ... [2][NUM_COLS-1]
```

In the second iteration of the outer loop, `row` is incremented to 3, and the array is accessed as follows:

```
arr[3][0]   [3][1]   [3][2]   [3][3] ... [3][NUM_COLS-1]
```

We can generalize this row processing to run through every row of the array by having the outer loop run from 0 through NUM_ROWS-1. However, if we want to access only part of the array (subarray processing), given variables declared as

```
int rowsFilled;    // Data is in 0..rowsFilled-1
int colsFilled;    // Data is in 0..colsFilled-1
```

then we write the code fragment as follows:

```
for (row = 0; row < rowsFilled; row++)
{
```

```
        total = 0;
        for (col = 0; col < colsFilled; col++)
            total = total + arr[row][col];
        cout << "Row sum: " << total << endl;
}
```

Figure 12-11 illustrates subarray processing by row.

Sum the Columns

Suppose we want to sum and print each column. The code to perform this task follows. Again, we have generalized the code to sum only the portion of the array that contains valid data.

```
for (col = 0; col < colsFilled; col++)
{
    total = 0;
    for (row = 0; row < rowsFilled; row++)
        total = total + arr[row][col];
    cout << "Column sum: " << total << endl;
}
```

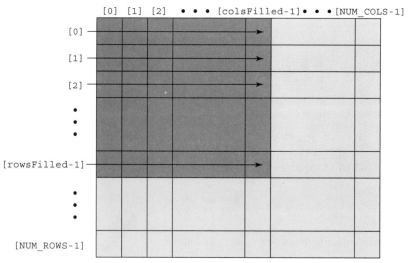

Figure 12-11 *Partial Array Processing by Row*

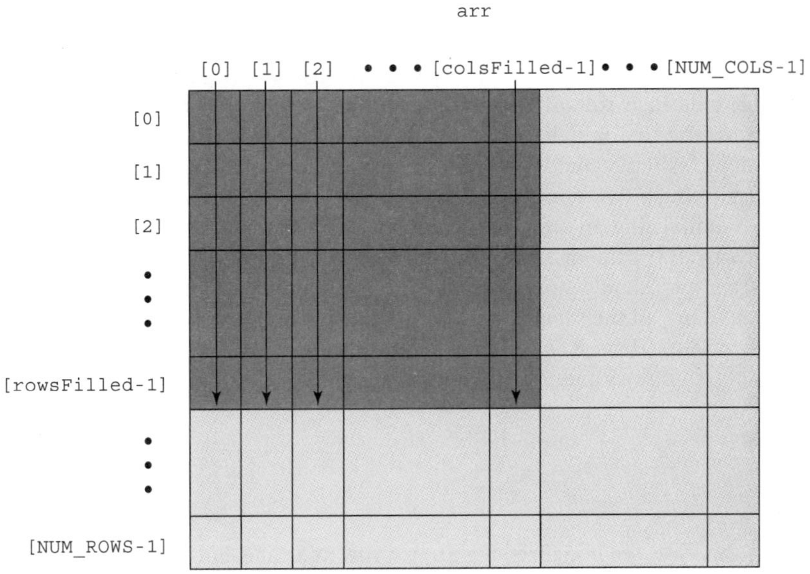

arr

Figure 12-12 *Partial Array Processing by Column*

In this case, the outer loop controls the column, and the inner loop controls the row. All the components in the first column are accessed and summed before the outer loop index changes and the components in the second column are accessed. Figure 12-12 illustrates subarray processing by column.

Initialize the Array

As with one-dimensional arrays, we can initialize a two-dimensional array either by initializing it in its declaration or by using assignment statements. If the array is small, it is simplest to initialize it in its declaration. To initialize a two-row by three-column array to look like this:

```
14    3   -5
 0   46    7
```

we can use the following declaration.

```
int arr[2][3] =
{
    {14, 3, -5},
    {0, 46, 7}
};
```

In this declaration, the initializer list consists of two items, each of which is itself an initializer list. The first inner initializer list stores 14, 3, and –5 into row 0 of the array; the second stores 0, 46, and 7 into row 1. The use of two initializer lists makes sense if you think of each row of the two-dimensional array as a one-dimensional array of three ints. The first initializer list initializes the first array (the first row), and the second list initializes the second array (the second row). Later in the chapter, we revisit this notion of viewing a two-dimensional array as an array of arrays.

Initializing an array in its declaration is impractical if the array is large. For a 100-row by 100-column array, you don't want to list 10,000 values. If the values are all different, you should store them into a file and input them into the array at run time. If the values are all the same, the usual approach is to use nested For loops and an assignment statement. Here is a general-purpose code segment that zeros out an array with NUM_ROWS rows and NUM_COLS columns:

```
for (row = 0; row < NUM_ROWS; row++)
    for (col = 0; col < NUM_COLS; col++)
        arr[row][col] = 0;
```

In this case, we initialized the array a row at a time, but we could just as easily have run through each column instead. The order doesn't matter as long as we access every element.

Print the Array

If we wish to print out an array with one row per line, then we have another case of row processing:

```
#include <iomanip>    // For setw()
    ⋮
for (row = 0; row < NUM_ROWS; row++)
{
    for (col = 0; col < NUM_COLS; col++)
        cout << setw(15) << arr[row][col];
    cout << endl;
}
```

This code fragment prints the values of the array in columns that are 15 characters wide. As a matter of proper style, this fragment should be preceded by code that prints headings over the columns to identify their contents.

Almost all processing of data stored in a two-dimensional array involves either processing by row or processing by column. In most of our examples, the index type has been int, but the pattern of operation of the loops is the same no matter what types the indexes are.

The looping patterns for row processing and column processing are so useful that we summarize them next. To make them more general, we use minRow for the first row number and minCol for the first column number. Remember that row processing has the row index in the outer loop, and column processing has the column index in the outer loop.

Row Processing

```
for (row = minRow; row < rowsFilled; row++)
    for (col = minCol; col < colsFilled; col++)
        ⋮              // Whatever processing is required
```

Column Processing

```
for (col = minCol; col < colsFilled; col++)
    for (row = minRow; row < rowsFilled; row++)
        ⋮              // Whatever processing is required
```

12.6 Passing Two-Dimensional Arrays as Arguments

Earlier in the chapter, we said that when one-dimensional arrays are declared as parameters in a function, the size of the array usually is omitted from the square brackets:

```
void SomeFunc( /* inout */ float alpha[],
               /* in */    int   size   )
{
    ⋮
}
```

If you include a size in the brackets, the compiler ignores it. As you learned, the base address of the caller's argument (the memory address of the first array element) is passed to the function. The function works for an argument of any size. Because the function cannot know the size of the caller's array, we either pass the size as an argument—as in SomeFunc above—or use a named constant if the function always operates on an array of a certain size.

When a two-dimensional array is passed as an argument, again the base address of the caller's array is sent to the function. But you cannot leave off the sizes of both of the array dimensions. You can omit the size of the first dimension (the number of rows) but not the second (the number of columns). Here is the reason.

In the computer's memory, C++ stores two-dimensional arrays in row order. Thinking of memory as one long line of memory cells, the first row of the array is followed by the second row, which is followed by the third, and so on (see Figure 12-13). To locate beta[1][0] in this figure, a function that receives beta's base address must be able to know that there are four elements in each row—that is, that the array consists of four columns. Therefore, the declaration of a parameter must always state the number of columns:

```
void AnotherFunc( /* inout */ int beta[][4] )
```

MEMORY

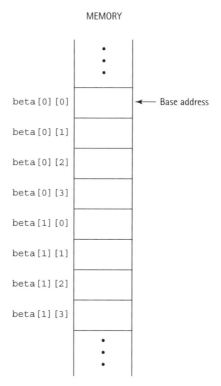

Figure 12-13 *Memory Layout for a Two-Row by Four-Column Array*

Furthermore, the number of columns declared for the parameter must be *exactly* the same as the number of columns in the caller's array. As you can tell from Figure 12-13, if there is any discrepancy in the number of columns, the function will access the wrong array element in memory.

Our AnotherFunc function works for a two-dimensional array of any number of rows, as long as it has exactly four columns. In practice, we seldom write programs that use arrays with a varying number of rows but the same number of columns. To avoid problems with mismatches in argument and parameter sizes, it's practical to use a Typedef statement to define a two-dimensional array type and then declare both the argument and the parameter to be of that type. For example, we might make the declarations

```
const int NUM_ROWS = 10;
const int NUM_COLS = 20;
typedef int ArrayType[NUM_ROWS][NUM_COLS];
```

and then write the following general-purpose function that initializes all elements of an array to a specified value:

```
void Initialize( /* out */ ArrayType arr,       // Array to initialize
                 /* in */  int       initVal)  // Initial value

// Initializes each element of arr to initVal

// Precondition:
//     initVal is assigned
// Postcondition:
//     arr[0..NUM_ROWS-1][0..NUM_COLS-1] == initVal

{
    int row;
    int col;

    for (row = 0; row < NUM_ROWS; row++)
        for (col = 0; col < NUM_COLS; col++)
            arr[row][col] = initVal;
}
```

The calling code could then declare and initialize one or more arrays of type `ArrayType` by making calls to the `Initialize` function. For example,

```
ArrayType delta;
ArrayType gamma;

Initialize(delta, 0);
Initialize(gamma, -1);
  ⋮
```

12.7 Another Way of Defining Two-Dimensional Arrays

We hinted earlier that a two-dimensional array can be viewed as an array of arrays. This view is supported by C++ in the sense that the components of a one-dimensional array do not have to be atomic. The components can themselves be structured—structs, class objects, even arrays. For example, our `hiTemp` array could be declared as follows.

```
typedef int WeekType[7];    // Array type for 7 temperature readings

WeekType hiTemp[52];        // Array of 52 WeekType arrays
```

With this declaration, the 52 components of the hiTemp array are one-dimensional arrays of type WeekType. In other words, hiTemp has two dimensions. We can refer to each row as an entity: hiTemp[2] refers to the array of temperatures for week 2. We can also access each individual component of hiTemp by specifying both indexes: hiTemp[2][0] accesses the temperature on the first day of week 2.

Does it matter which way we declare a two-dimensional array? Not to C++. The choice should be based on readability and understandability. Sometimes the features of the data are shown more clearly if both indexes are specified in a single declaration. At other times, the code is clearer if one dimension is defined first as a one-dimensional array type.

Here is an example of when it is advantageous to define a two-dimensional array as an array of arrays. If the rows have been defined first as a one-dimensional array type, each row can be passed to a function whose parameter is a one-dimensional array of the same type. For example, the following function calculates and returns the maximum value in an array of type WeekType.

```
int Maximum( /* in */ const WeekType data )   // Array to be examined

// Precondition:
//     data[0..6] are assigned
// Postcondition:
//     Function value == maximum value in data[0..6]

{
    int max;       // Temporary max. value
    int index;     // Loop control and index variable

    max = data[0];
    for (index = 1; index < 7; index++)
        if (data[index] > max)
            max = data[index];
    return max;
}
```

Our two-part declaration of hiTemp permits us to call Maximum using a component of hiTemp as follows.

```
highest = Maximum(hiTemp[20]);
```

Row 20 of hiTemp is passed to Maximum, which treats it like any other one-dimensional array of type WeekType (see Figure 12-14). It makes sense to pass the row as an argument because both it and the function parameter are of the same named type, WeekType.

With hiTemp declared as an array of arrays, we can output the maximum temperature of each week of the year with the following code:

hiTemp

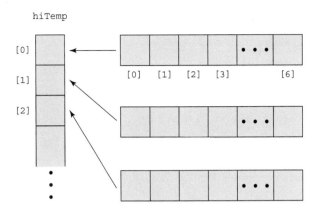

The components of `hiTemp`
are one-dimensional arrays
of type `WeekType`.

Figure 12-14 *A One-Dimensional Array of One-Dimensional Arrays*

```
cout << " Week   Maximum" << endl
     << "Number Temperature" << endl;
for (week = 0; week < 52; week++)
   cout << setw(6) << week
        << setw(9) << Maximum(hiTemp[week]) << endl;
```

12.8 Multidimensional Arrays

C++ does not place a limit on the number of dimensions that an array can have. We can generalize our definition of an **array** to cover all cases.

> **Array** A collection of components, all of the same type, ordered on *N* dimensions (*N* ≥ 1). Each component is accessed by *N* indexes, each of which represents the component's position within that dimension.

You might have guessed by now that you can have as many dimensions as you want. How many should you have in a particular case? Use as many as there are features that describe the components in the array.

Take, for example, a chain of department stores. Monthly sales figures must be kept for each item by store. There are three important pieces of information about each item: the month in which it was sold, the store from which it was purchased, and the item number. We can define an array type to summarize this data as follows:

```
const int NUM_ITEMS = 100;
const int NUM_STORES = 10;
```

```
typedef int SalesType[NUM_STORES][12][NUM_ITEMS];

SalesType sales;    // Array of sales figures
int        item;
int        store;
int        month;
int        numberSold;
int        currentMonth;
```

A graphic representation of the `sales` array is shown in Figure 12-15.

The number of components in `sales` is 12,000 (10 × 12 × 100). If sales figures are available only for January through June, then half the array is empty. If we want to process the data in the array, we must use subarray processing. The following program fragment sums and prints the total number of each item sold this year to date by all stores.

```
for (item = 0; item < NUM_ITEMS; item++)
{
    numberSold = 0;
    for (store = 0; store < NUM_STORES; store++)
        for (month = 0; month <= currentMonth; month++)
            numberSold = numberSold + sales[store][month][item];
    cout << "Item #" << item << " Sales to date = " << numberSold
        << endl;
}
```

Because `item` controls the outer For loop, we are summing each item's sales by `month` and `store`. If we want to find the total sales for each store, we use `store` to control the outer For loop, summing its sales by `month` and `item` with the inner loops.

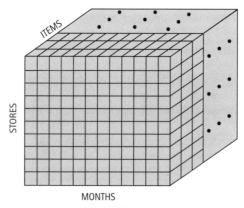

Figure 12-15 *Graphical Representation of* `sales` *Array*

```
for (store = 0; store < NUM_STORES; store++)
{
    numberSold = 0;
    for (item = 0; item < NUM_ITEMS; item++)
        for (month = 0; month <= currentMonth; month++)
            numberSold = numberSold + sales[store][month][item];
    cout << "Store #" << store << " Sales to date = " << numberSold
        << endl;
}
```

It takes two loops to access each component in a two-dimensional array; it takes three loops to access each component in a three-dimensional array. The task to be accomplished determines which index controls the outer loop, the middle loop, and the inner loop. If we want to calculate monthly sales by store, month controls the outer loop and store controls the middle loop. If we want to calculate monthly sales by item, month controls the outer loop and item controls the middle loop.

If we want to keep track of the departments that sell each item, we can add a fourth dimension.

```
enum Departments {A, B, C, D, E, F, G};
const int NUM_DEPTS = 7;
typedef int SalesType[NUM_STORES][12][NUM_ITEMS][NUM_DEPTS];
```

How would we visualize this new structure? Not very easily! Fortunately, we do not have to visualize a structure in order to use it. If we want the number of sales in store 1 during June for item number 4 in department C, we simply access the array element

```
sales[1][5][4][C]
```

When a multidimensional array is declared as a parameter in a function, C++ requires you to state the sizes of all dimensions except the first. For our four-dimensional version of SalesType, a function heading would look either like this:

```
void DoSomething( /* inout */ int arr[][12][NUM_ITEMS][NUM_DEPTS] )
```

or, better yet, like this:

```
void DoSomething( /* inout */ SalesType arr )
```

The second version is the safest (and the most uncluttered to look at). It ensures that the sizes of all dimensions of the parameter match those of the argument exactly. With the first version, the reason that you must declare the sizes of all but the first dimension is the same as we discussed earlier for two-dimensional arrays. Because arrays are stored linearly in memory (one array element after another), the compiler must use this size information to locate correctly an element that lies within the array.

Programming Example

Comparison of Two Lists

Problem   You are writing a program for an application that does not tolerate erroneous input data. Therefore, the data values are prepared by entering them twice into one file. The file contains two lists of positive integer numbers, separated by a negative number. These two lists of numbers should be identical; if they are not, then a data entry error has occurred. For example, if the input file contains the sequence of numbers 17, 14, 8, –5, 17, 14, 8, then the two lists of three numbers are identical. However, the sequence 17, 14, 8, –5, 17, 12, 8 shows a data entry error.

You decide to write a separate program to compare the lists and print out any pairs of numbers that are not the same. The exact number of integers in each list is unknown, but each list has no more than 500.

Input   A file (`dataFile`) containing two lists of positive integers. The lists are separated by a negative integer, and both lists have the same number of integers.

Output   A statement that the lists are identical, or a list of the pairs of values that do not match.

Discussion   Because the lists are in the same file, the first list has to be read and stored until the negative number is read. Then the second list can be read and compared with the first list.

If we were checking the lists by hand, we would write the numbers from the first list on a pad of paper, one per line. The line number would correspond to the number's position in the list; that is, the first number would be on the first line, the second number on the second line, and so on. The first number in the second list would then be compared to the number on the first line, the second number to the number on the second line, and so forth.

We use an array named `firstList` to represent the pad of paper. Its declaration looks like this:

```
const int MAX_NUMBER = 500;    // Maximum in each list

int firstList[MAX_NUMBER];     // Holds first list
```

Because the first array component has index 0, we must think of our pad of paper as having its lines numbered from 0, not 1.

Assumption   The two lists to be compared have the same number of integers.

Data Structures   A one-dimensional `int` array (`firstList`) to hold the first list of numbers. If `numVals` is the actual number of values in each list, only positions 0 through `numVals` – 1 of the array will be filled (see Figure 12-16).

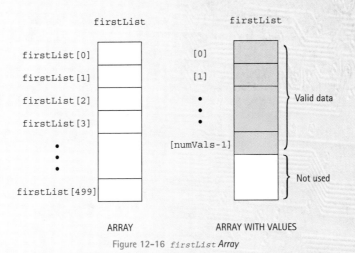

Figure 12-16 *firstList Array*

(The following program is written in ISO/ANSI standard C++. If you are working with pre-standard C++, see the alternate version of the program in the PRE_STD directory of the program disk, available at the publisher's Web site, www.jbpub.com/disks.)

```cpp
//*******************************************************************
// CheckLists program
// There are two lists of positive integers in a data file,
// separated by a negative integer.  This program compares the two
// lists.  If they are identical, a message is printed.  If not,
// nonmatching pairs are printed.  Assumption: The number of values
// in both lists is the same and is <= 500
//*******************************************************************
#include <iostream>
#include <iomanip>     // For setw()
#include <fstream>     // For file I/O
#include <string>      // For string class

using namespace std;

const int MAX_NUMBER = 500;      // Maximum in each list

void CompareLists( const int[], int, ifstream&, bool& );
void OpenForInput( ifstream& );
void ReadFirstList( int[], int&, ifstream& );
```

```
int main()
{
    int      firstList[MAX_NUMBER];   // Holds first list
    bool     allOK;                    // True if lists are identical
    int      numVals;                  // No. of values in first list
    ifstream dataFile;                 // Input file

    OpenForInput(dataFile);
    if ( !dataFile )
        return 1;

    ReadFirstList(firstList, numVals, dataFile);
    allOK = true;
    CompareLists(firstList, numVals, dataFile, allOK);
    if (allOK)
        cout << "The two lists are identical" << endl;
    return 0;
}

//**********************************************************************

void OpenForInput( /* inout */ ifstream& someFile )    // File to be
                                                        // opened
// Prompts the user for the name of an input file
// and attempts to open the file
{
    .
    .         (Same as in Graph program of Chapter 7)
    .
}

//**********************************************************************

void ReadFirstList(
        /* out */   int      firstList[],    // Filled first list
        /* out */   int&     numVals,        // Number of values
        /* inout */ ifstream& dataFile   )   // Input file

// Reads the first list from the data file
// and counts the number of values in the list

// Precondition:
//      dataFile has been successfully opened for input
//   && The no. of input values in the first list <= MAX_NUMBER
```

```
// Postcondition:
//     numVals == number of input values in the first list
//     && firstList[0..numVals-1] contain the input values

{
    int counter;     // Index variable
    int number;      // An input value

    counter = 0;
    dataFile >> number;
    while (number >= 0)
    {
        firstList[counter] = number;
        counter++;
        dataFile >> number;
    }
    numVals = counter;
}

//**********************************************************************

void CompareLists(
    /* in */      const int      firstList[],   // 1st list of numbers
    /* in */            int      numVals,        // Number in 1st list
    /* inout */         ifstream& dataFile,      // Input file
    /* inout */         bool&     allOK       )  // True if lists match

// Reads the second list of numbers
// and compares it to the first list

// Precondition:
//     allOK is assigned
//     && numVals <= MAX_NUMBER
//     && firstList[0..numVals-1] are assigned
//     && The two lists have the same number of values
// Postcondition:
//     Values from the second list have been read from the
//     input file
//     && IF all values in the two lists match
//         allOK == allOK@entry
//     ELSE
//         allOK == false
//         && The positions and contents of mismatches have been
//         printed
```

```
{
    int counter;    // Loop control and index variable
    int number;     // An input value

    for (counter = 0; counter < numVals; counter++)
    {
        dataFile >> number;
        if (number != firstList[counter])
        {
            allOK = false;
            cout << "Position " << counter << ": "
                 << setw(4) << firstList[counter] << " != "
                 << setw(4) << number << endl;
        }
    }
}
```

Testing   The program is run with two sets of data, one in which the two lists are identical and one in which there are errors. The data and the results from each are shown below.

Data Set 1	Data Set 2
21	21
32	32
76	76
22	22
21	21
-4	-4
21	21
32	32
76	176
22	12
21	21

Output

The two lists are identical.

Output

Position 2: 76 != 176
Position 3: 22 != 12

Programming Example

City Council Election

Problem   There has just been a hotly contested city council election. In four voting precincts, citizens have cast their ballots for four candidates. Let's do an analysis of the votes for the four candidates by precinct. We want to know how many votes each candidate received in each precinct, how many total votes each candidate received, and how many total votes were cast in each precinct.

Input   An arbitrary number of votes in a file `voteFile`, with each vote represented as a pair of numbers: a precinct number (1 through 4) and a candidate number (1 through 4); and candidate names, entered from the keyboard (to be used for printing the output).

Output   The following three items, written to a file `reportFile`: a tabular report showing how many votes each candidate received in each precinct, the total number of votes for each candidate, and the total number of votes in each precinct.

Discussion   The data consists of a pair of numbers for each vote. The first number is the precinct number; the second number is the candidate number.

   If we were doing the analysis by hand, our first task would be to go through the data, counting how many people in each precinct voted for each candidate. We would probably create a table with precincts down the side and candidates across the top. Each vote would be recorded as a hash mark in the appropriate row and column (see Figure 12-17).

   When all of the votes had been recorded, a sum of each column would tell us how many votes each candidate had received. A sum of each row would tell us how many people had voted in each precinct.

   As is so often the case, we can use this by-hand algorithm directly in our program. We can create a two-dimensional array in which each component is a counter for the number of votes for a particular candidate in each precinct; for example, the value indexed by `[2] [1]` would be the counter for the votes in precinct 2 for candidate 1. Well, not quite. C++ arrays are indexed beginning at 0, so the correct array component would be indexed by `[1] [0]`. When we input a precinct number and candidate number, we must remember to subtract 1

Precinct	Smith	Jones	Adams	Smiley
1	⁜⁜⁜⁜ //	//	⁜⁜⁜⁜ ⁜⁜⁜⁜ //	⁜⁜⁜⁜
2	⁜⁜⁜⁜ ⁜⁜⁜⁜	//	⁜⁜⁜⁜	///
3	//	⁜⁜⁜⁜ ///	⁜⁜⁜⁜ ⁜⁜⁜⁜ ⁜⁜⁜⁜	///
4	⁜⁜⁜⁜	⁜⁜⁜⁜ ///	⁜⁜⁜⁜ ⁜⁜⁜⁜	//

Figure 12-17 *Vote-Counting Table*

from each before indexing into the array. Likewise, we must add 1 to an array index that represents a precinct number or candidate number before printing it out.

Data Structures:

A two-dimensional array named `votes`, where the rows represent precincts and the columns represent candidates

A one-dimensional array of strings containing the names of the candidates, to be used for printing (see Figure 12-18).

In the program that follows, we use the named constants `NUM_PRECINCTS` and `NUM_CANDIDATES` in place of the literal constants 4 and 4.

Note that each candidate's name is stored in the slot in the `name` array corresponding to his or her candidate number (minus 1). These names are useful when the totals are printed.

(The following program is written in ISO/ANSI standard C++. If you are working with pre-standard C++, see the alternate version of the program in the PRE_STD directory of the program disk, available at the publisher's Web site, `www.jbpub.com/disks`.)

```
//*********************************************************************
// Election program
// This program reads votes represented by precinct number and
// ballot position from a data file, calculates the sums per
// precinct and per candidate, and writes all totals to an
// output file
//*********************************************************************
#include <iostream>
#include <iomanip>      // For setw()
#include <fstream>      // For file I/O
#include <string>       // For string class
```

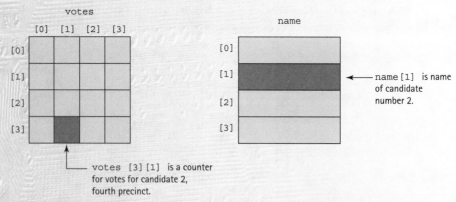

Figure 12-18 *Data Structures for Election Program*

```cpp
using namespace std;

const int NUM_PRECINCTS = 4;
const int NUM_CANDIDATES = 4;

typedef int VoteArray[NUM_PRECINCTS][NUM_CANDIDATES];
                                // 2-dimensional array type
                                //   for votes
void GetNames( string[] );
void OpenForInput( ifstream& );
void OpenForOutput( ofstream& );
void WritePerCandidate( const VoteArray, const string[],
                        ofstream& );
void WritePerPrecinct( const VoteArray, ofstream& );
void WriteReport( const VoteArray, const string[], ofstream& );
void ZeroVotes( VoteArray );

int main()
{
    string     name[NUM_CANDIDATES];  // Array of candidate names
    VoteArray votes;               // Totals for precincts vs. candidates
    int        candidate;          // Candidate number input from voteFile
    int        precinct;           // Precinct number input from voteFile
    ifstream   voteFile;           // Input file of precincts, candidates
    ofstream   reportFile;         // Output file receiving summaries

    OpenForInput(voteFile);
    if ( !voteFile )
        return 1;
    OpenForOutput(reportFile);
    if ( !reportFile )
        return 1;

    GetNames(name);
    ZeroVotes(votes);

    // Read and tally votes

    voteFile >> precinct >> candidate;
    while (voteFile)
    {
        votes[precinct-1][candidate-1]++;
        voteFile >> precinct >> candidate;
    }
```

```
        // Write results to report file

        WriteReport(votes, name, reportFile);
        WritePerCandidate(votes, name, reportFile);
        WritePerPrecinct(votes, reportFile);
        return 0;
}

//**********************************************************************

void OpenForInput( /* inout */ ifstream& someFile )    // File to be
                                                        // opened
// Prompts the user for the name of an input file
// and attempts to open the file

{
    .
    .        (Same as in previous chapters)
    .
}

//**********************************************************************

void OpenForOutput( /* inout */ ofstream& someFile )   // File to be
                                                        // opened
// Prompts the user for the name of an output file
// and attempts to open the file

{
    .
    .        (Similar to OpenForInput function)
    .
}

//**********************************************************************

void GetNames( /* out */ string name[] )    // Array of candidate
                                             //    names
// Reads the candidate names from standard input

// Postcondition:
//     The user has been prompted to enter the candidate names
//     && name[0..NUM_CANDIDATES-1] contain the input names,
//     truncated to 10 characters each
```

```
{
    string inputStr;      // An input string
    int    candidate;     // Loop counter

    cout << "Enter the names of the candidates, one per line,"
         << endl << "in the order they appear on the ballot."
         << endl;

    for (candidate = 0; candidate < NUM_CANDIDATES; candidate++)
    {
        cin >> inputStr;
        name[candidate] = inputStr.substr(0, 10);
    }
}


//***********************************************************************

void ZeroVotes( /* out */ VoteArray votes )  // Array of vote totals

// Zeros out the votes array

// Postcondition:
//    All votes[0..NUM_PRECINCTS-1][0..NUM_CANDIDATES-1] == 0

{
    int precinct;      // Loop counter
    int candidate;     // Loop counter

    for (precinct = 0; precinct < NUM_PRECINCTS; precinct++)
        for (candidate = 0; candidate < NUM_CANDIDATES; candidate++)
            votes[precinct][candidate] = 0;
}


//***********************************************************************

void WriteReport(
    /* in */      const VoteArray votes,       // Total votes
    /* in */      const string    name[],      // Candidate names
    /* inout */        ofstream& reportFile )   // Output file

// Writes the vote totals in tabular form to the report file

// Precondition:
//    votes[0..NUM_PRECINCTS-1][0..NUM_CANDIDATES] are assigned
//    && name[0..NUM_CANDIDATES-1] are assigned
```

```
// Postcondition:
//      The name array has been output across one line, followed by
//      the votes array, one row per line

{
    int precinct;        // Loop counter
    int candidate;       // Loop counter

    // Set up headings

    reportFile << "              ";
    for (candidate = 0; candidate < NUM_CANDIDATES; candidate++)
        reportFile << setw(12) << name[candidate];
    reportFile << endl;

    // Print array by row

    for (precinct = 0; precinct < NUM_PRECINCTS; precinct++)
    {
        reportFile << "Precinct" << setw(4) << precinct + 1;
        for (candidate = 0; candidate < NUM_CANDIDATES; candidate++)
            reportFile << setw(12) << votes[precinct][candidate];
        reportFile << endl;
    }
    reportFile << endl;
}

//*********************************************************************

void WritePerCandidate(
        /* in */     const VoteArray votes,      // Total votes
        /* in */     const string    name[],     // Candidate names
        /* inout */          ofstream& reportFile )  // Output file

// Sums the votes per person and writes the totals to the
// report file

// Precondition:
//      votes[0..NUM_PRECINCTS-1][0..NUM_CANDIDATES] are assigned
//   && name[0..NUM_CANDIDATES-1] are assigned
// Postcondition:
//      For each person i, name[i] has been output,
//      followed by the sum
//      votes[0][i] + votes[1][i] + ... + votes[NUM_PRECINCTS-1][i]
```

```
{
    int precinct;       // Loop counter
    int candidate;      // Loop counter
    int total;          // Total votes for a candidate

    for (candidate = 0; candidate < NUM_CANDIDATES; candidate++)
    {
        total = 0;

        // Compute column sum

        for (precinct = 0; precinct < NUM_PRECINCTS; precinct++)
            total = total + votes[precinct][candidate];

        reportFile << "Total votes for"
                   << setw(10) << name[candidate] << ":"
                   << setw(3) << total << endl;
    }
    reportFile << endl;
}


//**********************************************************************

void WritePerPrecinct(
        /* in */     const VoteArray votes,       // Total votes
        /* inout */      ofstream& reportFile )    // Output file

// Sums the votes per precinct and writes the totals to the
// report file

// Precondition:
//     votes[0..NUM_PRECINCTS-1][0..NUM_CANDIDATES] are assigned
// Postcondition:
//     For each precinct i, the value i+1 has been output,
//     followed by the sum
//     votes[i][0] + votes[i][1] + ... + votes[i][NUM_CANDIDATES-1]

{
    int precinct;       // Loop counter
    int candidate;      // Loop counter
    int total;          // Total votes for a precinct
```

```
        for (precinct = 0; precinct < NUM_PRECINCTS; precinct++)
        {
            total = 0;

            // Compute row sum

            for (candidate = 0; candidate < NUM_CANDIDATES; candidate++)
                total = total + votes[precinct][candidate];

            reportFile << "Total votes for precinct"
                       << setw(3) << precinct + 1 << ':'
                       << setw(3) << total << endl;
        }
    }
```

Testing   This program was executed with the data listed below. (We list the data in three columns to save space.) The names of the candidates entered from the keyboard were Smith, Jones, Adams, and Smiley. In this data set, there is at least one vote for each candidate in each precinct.

Input Data

1 1	3 1	3 3
1 1	4 3	4 4
1 2	3 4	4 4
1 2	3 2	4 3
1 3	3 3	4 4
1 4	2 1	4 4
2 2	2 3	4 1
2 2	4 3	4 2
2 3	4 4	2 4
2 1	3 2	4 4

The output, which was written to file `reportFile`, is shown below.

		Jones	Smith	Adams	Smiley
Precinct	1	2	2	1	1
Precinct	2	2	2	2	1
Precinct	3	1	2	2	1
Precinct	4	1	1	3	6

```
Total votes for    Jones:   6
Total votes for    Smith:   7
Total votes for    Adams:   8
Total votes for    Smiley:  9
```

```
Total votes for precinct  1:  6
Total votes for precinct  2:  7
Total votes for precinct  3:  6
Total votes for precinct  4: 11
```

Testing and Debugging

One-Dimensional Arrays

The most common error in processing arrays is an out-of-bounds array index. That is, the program attempts to access a component using an index that is either less than 0 or greater than the array size minus 1. For example, given the declarations

```
char line[100];
int  counter;
```

the following For statement would print the 100 elements of the `line` array and then print a 101st value—the value that resides in memory immediately beyond the end of the array.

```
for (counter = 0; counter <= 100; counter++)
    cout << line[counter];
```

This error is easy to detect, because 101 characters get printed instead of 100. The loop test should be `counter < 100`. But you won't always use a simple For statement when accessing arrays. Suppose we read data into the `line` array in another part of the program. Let's use a While statement that reads to the newline character:

```
counter = 0;
cin.get(ch);
while (ch != '\n')
{
    line[counter] = ch;
    counter++;
    cin.get(ch);
}
```

This code seems reasonable enough, but what if the input line has more than 100 characters? After the hundredth character is read and stored into the array, the loop continues to execute with the array index out of bounds. Characters are stored into memory locations past the end of the array, wiping out other data values (or even machine language instructions in the program!).

The moral is: When processing arrays, give special attention to the design of loop termination conditions. Always ask yourself if the loop could possibly keep running after the last array component has been processed.

Whenever an array index goes out of bounds, the first suspicion should be a loop that fails to terminate properly. The second thing to check is any array access involving an index that is based on input data or a calculation. When an array index is input as data, a data validation check is an absolute necessity.

Complex Structures

As we have demonstrated in many examples in this chapter and the last, it is possible to combine data structures in various ways: structs whose components are structs, structs whose components are arrays, arrays whose components are structs or class objects, arrays whose components are arrays (multidimensional arrays), and so forth. When arrays, structs, and class objects are combined, there can be confusion about precisely where to place the operators for array element selection ([]) and struct or class member selection (.).

To summarize the correct placement of these operators, let's use the StudentRec type we introduced in this chapter:

```
struct StudentRec
{
    string      stuName;
    float       gpa;
    int         examScore[4];
    GradeType   courseGrade;
};
```

If we declare a variable of type StudentRec,

```
StudentRec student;
```

then what is the syntax for selecting the first exam score of the student (that is, for selecting element 0 of the examScore member of student)? The dot operator is a binary (two-operand) operator; its left operand denotes a struct variable, and its right operand is a member name:

StructVariable . MemberName

The [] operator is a unary (one-operand) operator; it comes immediately after an expression denoting an array:

Array [IndexExpression]

Therefore, the expression

```
student
```

denotes a struct variable, the expression

```
student.examScore
```

denotes an array, and the expression

```
student.examScore[0]
```

denotes an integer—the integer located in element 0 of the `student.examScore` array.

With arrays of structs or class objects, again you have to be sure that the [] and . operators are in the proper positions. Given the declaration

```
StudentRec gradeBook[150];
```

we can access the `gpa` member of the first element of the `gradeBook` array with the expression

```
gradeBook[0].gpa
```

The index `[0]` is correctly attached to the identifier `gradeBook` because `gradeBook` is the name of an array. Furthermore, the expression

```
gradeBook[0]
```

denotes a struct, so the dot operator selects the `gpa` member of this struct.

Multidimensional Arrays

Errors with multidimensional arrays usually fall into two major categories: index expressions that are out of order and index range errors.

Suppose we have an array that holds the votes cast in an election for ten candidates in four different precincts:

```
int votes[4][10];
```

The first dimension represents the precincts, and the second represents the candidates. An example of the first kind of error—incorrect order of the index expressions—would be to print out the `votes` array as follows.

```
for (precinct = 0; precinct < 4; precinct++)
{
    for (candidate = 0; candidate < 10; candidate++)
        cout << setw(4) << votes[candidate][precinct];
    cout << endl;
}
```

The output statement specifies the array indexes in the wrong order. The loops march through the array with the first index ranging from 0 through 9 (instead of 0 through 3) and the second index ranging from 0 through 3 (instead of 0 through 9). The effect of executing this code may vary from system to system. The program may output the wrong array components and continue executing, or the program may crash with a memory access error.

An example of the second kind of error—an incorrect index range in an otherwise correct loop—can be seen in this code:

```
for (precinct = 0; precinct < 10; precinct++)
{
    for (candidate = 0; candidate < 4; candidate++)
        cout << setw(4) << votes[precinct][candidate];
    cout << endl;
}
```

Here, the output statement correctly uses `precinct` for the first index and `candidate` for the second. However, the For statements use incorrect upper limits for the index variables. As with the preceding example, the effect of executing this code is undefined but is certainly wrong. A valuable way to prevent this kind of error is to use named constants, such as NUM_PRECINCTS and NUM_CANDIDATES, instead of the literals 10 and 4. You are much more likely to spot an error (or to avoid making an error in the first place) if you write something like this:

```
for (precinct = 0; precinct < NUM_PRECINCTS; precinct++)
```

than if you use a literal constant as the upper limit for the index variable.

Testing and Debugging Hints

1. When an individual component of a one-dimensional array is accessed, the index must be within the range 0 through the array size minus 1. Attempting to use an index value outside this range causes your program to access memory locations outside the array.

2. The individual components of an array are themselves variables of the component type. When values are stored into an array, they should either be of the component type or be explicitly converted to the component type; otherwise, implicit type coercion occurs.

3. C++ does not allow aggregate operations on arrays. There is no aggregate assignment, aggregate comparison, aggregate I/O, or aggregate arithmetic. You must write code to do all of these operations, one array element at a time.

4. Omitting the size of a one-dimensional array in its declaration is permitted only in two cases: (1) when an array is declared as a parameter in a function heading and

(2) when an array is initialized in its declaration. In all other declarations, you *must* specify the size of the array with a constant integer expression.

5. If an array parameter is incoming-only, declare the parameter as `const` to prevent the function from modifying the caller's argument accidentally.

6. Don't pass an individual array component as an argument when the function expects to receive the base address of an entire array.

7. The size of an array is fixed at compile time, but the number of values actually stored there is determined at run time. Therefore, an array must be declared to be as large as it could ever be for the particular problem. Subarray processing is used to process only the components that have data in them.

8. When functions perform subarray processing on a one-dimensional array, pass both the array name and the number of data items actually stored in the array.

9. With multidimensional arrays, use the proper number of indexes when referencing an array component, and make sure the indexes are in the correct order.

10. In loops that process multidimensional arrays, double-check the upper and lower bounds on each index variable to be sure they are correct for that dimension of the array.

11. When declaring a multidimensional array as a parameter, you must state the sizes of all but the first dimension. Also, these sizes must agree exactly with the sizes of the caller's argument.

12. To eliminate the chances of the size mismatches referred to in Item 11, use a Typedef statement to define a multidimensional array type. Declare both the argument and the parameter to be of this type.

Summary

The one-dimensional array is a homogeneous data structure that gives a name to a sequential group of like components. Each component is accessed by its relative position within the group (rather than by name, as in a struct or class), and each component is a variable of the component type. To access a particular component, we give the name of the array and an index that specifies which component of the group we want. The index can be an expression of any integral type, as long as it evaluates to an integer from 0 through the array size minus 1. Array components can be accessed in random order directly, or they can be accessed sequentially by stepping through the index values one at a time.

Two-dimensional arrays are useful for processing information that is represented naturally in tabular form. Processing data in two-dimensional arrays usually takes one of two forms: processing by row or processing by column. An array of arrays, which is useful if rows of the array must be passed as arguments, is an alternative way of defining a two-dimensional array.

A multidimensional array is a collection of like components that are ordered on more than one dimension. Each component is accessed by a set of indexes, one for each dimension, that represents the component's position on the various dimensions. Each index may be thought of as describing a feature of a given array component.

Quick Check

1. Declare a one-dimensional array named `quizAnswer` that contains 12 components indexed by the integers 0 through 11. The component type is `bool`. (pp. 476–479)

2. Given the declarations

```
const int SIZE = 30;

char firstName[SIZE];
```

   a. Write an assignment statement that stores 'A' into the first component of array `firstName`. (pp. 479–481)
   b. Write an output statement that prints the value of the fourteenth component of array `firstName`. (pp. 479–481)
   c. Write a For statement that fills array `firstName` with blanks. (p. 482)

3. Declare a five-element one-dimensional `int` array named `oddNums`, and initialize it (in its declaration) to contain the first five odd integers, starting with 1. (pp. 482–483)

4. Give the function heading for a void function named `SomeFunc`, where
   a. `SomeFunc` has a single parameter: a one-dimensional `float` array x that is an Inout parameter.
   b. `SomeFunc` has a single parameter: a one-dimensional `float` array x that is an In parameter.
   (pp. 487–489)

5. Given the declaration

```
StudentRec gradeBook[150];
```

   where `StudentRec` is the `struct` type defined in this chapter, do the following.
   a. Write an assignment statement that records the fact that the tenth student has a grade point average of 3.25.
   b. Write an assignment statement that records the fact that the fourth student scored 78 on the third exam. (pp. 490–492)

6. Given the declarations in Question 2 and the following program fragment, which reads characters into array `firstName` until a blank is encountered, write a For statement that prints out the portion of the array that is filled with input data. (pp. 493–494)

```
n = 0;
cin.get(letter);
while (letter != ' ')
```

```
    {
        firstName[n] = letter;
        n++;
        cin.get(letter);
    }
```

7. Define an enumeration type for the musical notes A through G (excluding sharps and flats). Then declare a one-dimensional array in which the index values represent musical notes, and the component type is `float`. Finally, show an example of a For loop that prints out the contents of the array. (p. 494)

8. Declare a two-dimensional array, named `plan`, with 30 rows and 10 columns. The component type of the array is `float`. (p. 494–497)

9. a. Assign the value 27.3 to the component in row 13, column 7 of the array `plan` from Question 8. (pp. 494–497)

   b. Nested For loops can be used to sum the values in each row of array `plan`. What range of values would the outer For loop count through to do this? (pp. 499–500)

   c. Nested For loops can be used to sum the values in each column of array `plan`. What range of values would the outer For loop count through to do this? (pp. 500–501)

   d. Write a program fragment that initializes array `plan` to all zeros. (pp. 501–502)

   e. Write a program fragment that prints the contents of array `plan`, one row per line of output. (pp. 502–503)

10. Suppose array `plan` is passed as an argument to a function in which the corresponding parameter is named `someArray`. What would the declaration of `someArray` look like in the parameter list? (pp. 503–505)

11. Given the declarations

    ```
    typedef int OneDimType[100];

    OneDimType twoDim[40];
    ```

    rewrite the declaration of `twoDim` without referring to type `OneDimType`. (pp. 505–507)

12. Given the declarations

    ```
    const int SIZE = 10;
    typedef char FourDim[SIZE][SIZE][SIZE][SIZE-1];

    FourDim quick;
    ```

    a. How many components does array `quick` contain? (pp. 507–509)

    b. Write a program fragment that fills array `quick` with blanks. (pp. 507–509)

Answers

1. ```
   bool quizAnswer[12];
   ```
2. a. ```
      firstName[0] = 'A';
      ```
   b. ```
      cout << firstName[13];
      ```
   c. ```
      for (index = 0; index < SIZE; index++)
          firstName[index] = ' ';
      ```
3. ```
   int oddNums[5] = {1, 3, 5, 7, 9};
   ```
4. a. ```
      void SomeFunc(float x[])
      ```
   b. ```
      void SomeFunc( const float x[] )
      ```
5. a. ```
      gradeBook[9].gpa = 3.25;
      ```
   b. ```
      gradeBook[3].examScore[2] = 78;
      ```
6. ```
   for (index = 0; index < n; index++)
       cout << firstName[index];
   ```
7. ```
   enum NoteType {A, B, C, D, E, F, G};
   float noteVal[7];
   NoteType index;
   for (index = A; index <= G; index = NoteType(index + 1))
       cout << noteVal[index] << endl;
   ```
8. ```
   float plan[30][10];
   ```
9. a. ```
      plan[13][7] = 27.3;
      ```
   b. ```
      for (row = 0; row < 30; row++)
      ```
   c. ```
      for (col = 0; col < 10; col++)
      ```
   d. ```
      for (row = 0; row < 30; row++)
          for (col = 0; col < 10; col++)
              plan[row][col] = 0.0;
      ```
   e. ```
      for (row = 0; row < 30; row++)
      {
          for (col = 0; col < 10; col++)
              cout << setw(8) << plan[row][col];
          cout << endl;
      }
      ```
10. **Either**

    ```
    float someArray[30][10]
    ```

    or

    ```
    float someArray[][10]
    ```

11. ```
    int twoDim[40][100];
    ```
12. a. **Nine thousand** ($10 \times 10 \times 10 \times 9$)
    b. ```
       for (dim1 = 0; dim1 < SIZE; dim1++)
           for (dim2 = 0; dim2 < SIZE; dim2++)
               for (dim3 = 0; dim3 < SIZE; dim3++)
                   for (dim4 = 0; dim4 < SIZE - 1; dim4++)
                       quick[dim1][dim2][dim3][dim4] = ' ';
       ```
       ```

Exam Preparation Exercises

1. Every component in an array must have the same type, and the number of components is fixed at compile time. (True or False?)

2. The components of an array must be of an integral or enumeration type. (True or False?)

3. Declare one-dimensional arrays according to the following descriptions.
   a. A 24-element `float` array
   b. A 500-element `int` array
   c. A 50-element double-precision floating-point array
   d. A 10-element `char` array

4. Write a code fragment to do the following tasks:
   a. Declare a constant named `CLASS_SIZE` representing the number of students in a class.
   b. Declare a one-dimensional array `quizAvg` of size `CLASS_SIZE` whose components will contain floating-point quiz score averages.

5. Write a code fragment to do the following tasks:
   a. Declare an enumeration type `BirdType` made up of bird names.
   b. Declare a one-dimensional `int` array `sightings` that is to be indexed by `BirdType`.

6. Given the declarations

   ```
   const int SIZE = 100;

   enum Colors
   {
       BLUE, GREEN, GOLD, ORANGE, PURPLE, RED, WHITE, BLACK
   };

   int     count[8];
   Colors cIndex;                  // Index for count array
   Colors rainbow[SIZE];
   int     rIndex;                 // Index for rainbow array
   ```

   write code fragments to do the following tasks:
   a. Set `count` to all zeros.
   b. Set `rainbow` to all `WHITE`.
   c. Count the number of times `GREEN` appears in `rainbow`.
   d. Print the value in `count` indexed by `BLUE`.
   e. Total the values in `count`.

7. What is the output of the following program? The data for the program is given below it.

   ```
   #include <iostream>

   using namespace std;
   ```

```
int main()
{
    int a[100];
    int b[100];
    int j;
    int m;
    int sumA = 0;
    int sumB = 0;
    int sumDiff = 0;

    cin >> m;
    for (j = 0; j < m; j++)
    {
        cin >> a[j] >> b[j];
        sumA = sumA + a[j];
        sumB = sumB + b[j];
        sumDiff = sumDiff + (a[j] - b[j]);
    }
    for (j = m - 1; j >= 0; j--)
        cout << a[j] << ' ' << b[j] << ' '
             << a[j] - b[j] << endl;
    cout << endl;
    cout << sumA << ' ' << sumB << ' ' << sumDiff << endl;
    return 0;
}
```

Data

```
    5
11  15
19  14
 4   2
17   6
 1   3
```

8. A person wrote the following code fragment, intending to print 10 20 30 40.

```
int arr[4] = {10, 20, 30, 40};
int index;

for (index = 1; index <= 4; index++)
    cout << ' ' << arr[index];
```

Instead, the code printed 20 30 40 24835. Explain the reason for this output.

9. Given the declarations

```
int sample[8];
int i;
int k;
```

show the contents of the array `sample` after the following code segment is executed. Use a question mark to indicate any undefined values in the array.

```
for (k = 0; k < 8; k++)
    sample[k] = 10 - k;
```

10. Using the same declarations given for Exercise 9, show the contents of the array `sample` after the following code segment is executed.

```
for (i = 0; i < 8; i++)
    if (i <= 3)
        sample[i] = 1;
    else
        sample[i] = -1;
```

11. Using the same declarations given for Exercise 9, show the contents of the array `sample` after the following code segment is executed.

```
for (k = 0; k < 8; k++)
    if (k % 2 == 0)
        sample[k] = k;
    else
        sample[k] = k + 100;
```

12. What are the two basic differences between a record and an array?

13. If the members of a record are all the same data type, an array data structure could be used instead. (True or False?)

14. For each of the following descriptions of data, determine which general type of data structure (array, record, array of records, or hierarchical record) is appropriate.
    a. A payroll entry with a name, address, and pay rate.
    b. A person's address.
    c. An inventory entry for a part.
    d. A list of addresses.
    e. A list of hourly temperatures.
    f. A list of passengers on an airliner, including names, addresses, fare class, and seat assignment.
    g. A departmental telephone directory with last name and extension number.

15. Given the declarations

```
const int NUM_SCHOOLS = 10;
const int NUM_SPORTS = 3;
enum SportType {FOOTBALL, BASKETBALL, VOLLEYBALL};

int    kidsInSports[NUM_SCHOOLS][NUM_SPORTS];
float costOfSports[NUM_SPORTS][NUM_SCHOOLS];
```

answer the following questions:
    a. What is the number of rows in `kidsInSports`?
    b. What is the number of columns in `kidsInSports`?

c. What is the number of rows in `costOfSports`?

d. What is the number of columns in `costOfSports`?

e. How many components does `kidsInSports` have?

f. How many components does `costOfSports` have?

g. What kind of processing (row or column) would be needed to total the amount of money spent on each sport?

h. What kind of processing (row or column) would be needed to total the number of children participating in sports at a particular school?

16. Given the following code segments, draw the arrays and their contents after the code is executed. Indicate any undefined values with the letter U.

a.
```
int exampleA[4][3];
int i, j;

for (i = 0; i < 4; i++)
    for (j = 0; j < 3; j++)
        exampleA[i][j] = i * j;
```

b.
```
int exampleB[4][3];
int i, j;

for (i = 0; i < 3; i++)
    for (j = 0; j < 3; j++)
        exampleB[i][j] = (i + j) % 3;
```

c.
```
int exampleC[8][2];
int i, j;

exampleC[7][0] = 4;
exampleC[7][1] = 5;
for (i = 0; i < 7; i++)
{
    exampleC[i][0] = 2;
    exampleC[i][1] = 3;
}
```

17. a. Define enumeration types for the following:
    `TeamType` made up of classes (freshman, sophomore, etc.) on your campus
    `ResultType` made up of game results (won, lost, or tied)

    b. Using Typedef, declare a two-dimensional integer array type named `Outcome`, intended to be indexed by `TeamType` and `ResultType`.

    c. Declare an array variable `standings` to be of type `Outcome`.

    d. Give a C++ statement that increases the number of freshman wins by 1.

18. The following code fragment includes a call to a function named `DoSomething`.

```
typedef float ArrType[100][20];

ArrType x;
    ⋮
DoSomething(x);
```

Indicate whether each of the following would be valid or invalid as the function heading for DoSomething.

a. `void DoSomething( /* inout */ ArrType arr )`
b. `void DoSomething( /* inout */ float arr[100][20] )`
c. `void DoSomething( /* inout */ float arr[100][] )`
d. `void DoSomething( /* inout */ float arr[][20] )`
e. `void DoSomething( /* inout */ float arr[][] )`
f. `void DoSomething( /* inout */ float arr[][10] )`

19. Declare the two-dimensional array variables described below. Use proper style.
    a. An array with five rows and six columns that contains Boolean values.
    b. An array, indexed from 0 through 39 and 0 through 199, that contains `float` values.
    c. A `char` array with rows indexed by a type

       ```
       enum FruitType {LEMON, PEAR, APPLE, ORANGE};
       ```

       and columns indexed by the integers 0 through 15.

20. A logging operation keeps records of 37 loggers' monthly production for purposes of analysis, using the following array structure:

    ```
    const int NUM_LOGGERS = 37;

    int logsCut[NUM_LOGGERS][12];   // Logs cut per logger per month
    int monthlyHigh;
    int monthlyTotal;
    int yearlyTotal;
    int high;
    int month;
    int bestMonth;
    int logger;
    int bestLogger;
    ```

    a. The following statement assigns the January log total for logger number 7 to `monthlyTotal`. (True or False?)

       ```
       monthlyTotal = logsCut[7][0];
       ```

    b. The following statements compute the yearly total for logger number 11. (True or False?)

       ```
       yearlyTotal = 0;
       for (month = 0; month < NUM_LOGGERS; month++)
           yearlyTotal = yearlyTotal + logsCut[month][10];
       ```

    c. The following statements find the best logger (most logs cut) in March. (True or False?)

       ```
       monthlyHigh = 0;
       for (logger = 0; logger < NUM_LOGGERS; logger++)
           if (logsCut[logger][2] > monthlyHigh)
       ```

```
        {
            bestLogger = logger;
            monthlyHigh = logsCut[logger][2];
        }
```

d. The following statements find the logger with the highest monthly production and the logger's best month. (True or False?)

```
high = -1;
for (month = 0; month < 12; month++)
    for (logger = 0; logger < NUM_LOGGERS; logger++)
        if (logsCut[logger][month] > high)
        {
            high = logsCut[logger][month];
            bestLogger = logger;
            bestMonth = month;
        }
```

21. Declare the `float` array variables described below. Use proper style.
    a. A three-dimensional array in which the first dimension is indexed from 0
       through 9, the second dimension is indexed by an enumeration type repre-
       senting the days of the week, and the third dimension is indexed from 0
       through 20.
    b. A four-dimensional array in which the first two dimensions are indexed from
       0 through 49, and the third and fourth are indexed by any valid ASCII char-
       acter.

Programming Warm-up Exercises

Use the following declarations in Exercises 1–7. You may declare any other variables
that you need.

```
const int NUM_STUDS = 100;   // Number of students

bool failing[NUM_STUDS];
bool passing[NUM_STUDS];
int  grade;
int  score[NUM_STUDS];
```

1. Write a C++ function that initializes all components of `failing` to `false`. The
   `failing` array is a parameter.
2. Write a C++ function that has `failing` and `score` as parameters. Set the components of `failing` to `true` wherever the corresponding value in `score` is less
   than 60.
3. Write a C++ function that has `passing` and `score` as parameters. Set the components of `passing` to `true` wherever the corresponding value in `score` is
   greater than or equal to 60.

4. Write a C++ value-returning function `PassTally` that takes `passing` as a parameter and reports how many components in `passing` are `true`.

5. Write a C++ value-returning function `Error` that takes `passing` and `failing` as parameters. `Error` returns `true` if any corresponding components in `passing` and `failing` are the same.

6. Write a C++ value-returning function that takes `grade` and `score` as parameters. The function reports how many values in `score` are greater than or equal to `grade`.

7. Write a C++ function that takes `score` as a parameter and reverses the order of the components in `score`; that is, `score[0]` goes into `score[NUM_STUDS-1]`, `score[1]` goes into `score[NUM_STUDS-2]`, and so on.

8. Write a program segment to read in a set of part numbers and associated unit costs. Use an array of structs with two members, `number` and `cost`, to represent each pair of input values. Assume the end-of-file condition terminates the input.

9. Below is the specification of a "safe array" class, which halts the program if an array index goes out of bounds. (Recall that C++ does not check for out-of-bounds indexes when you use built-in arrays.)

```
const int MAX_SIZE = 200;

class IntArray
{
public:
    int ValueAt( /* in */ int i ) const;
        // Precondition:
        //      i is assigned
        // Postcondition:
        //      IF i >= 0  &&  i < declared size of array
        //          Function value == value of array element
        //                              at index i
        //      ELSE
        //          Program has halted with error message

    void Store( /* in */ int val,
                /* in */ int i   );
        // Precondition:
        //      val and i are assigned
        // Postcondition:
        //      IF i >= 0  &&  i < declared size of array
        //          val is stored in array element i
        //      ELSE
        //          Program has halted with error message

    IntArray( /* in */ int arrSize );
        // Precondition:
        //      arrSize is assigned
```

```
                        // Postcondition:
                        //     IF arrSize >= 1  &&  arrSize <= MAX_SIZE
                        //         Array created with all array elements == 0
                        //     ELSE
                        //         Program has halted with error message
            private:
                int arr[MAX_SIZE];
                int size;
            };
```

Implement each member function as it would appear in the implementation file. To halt the program, use the `exit` function supplied by the C++ standard library through the header file `cstdlib` (see Appendix C).

10. Write a C++ value-returning function that returns `true` if all the values in a certain subarray of a two-dimensional array are positive, and returns `false` otherwise. The array (of type `ArrayType`), the number of columns in the subarray, and the number of rows in the subarray should be passed as arguments.

11. Write a C++ function `Copy` that takes a two-dimensional `int` array `data`, defined to be NUM_ROWS by NUM_COLS, and copies the values into a second array `data2`, defined the same way. `data` and `data2` are of type `TwoDimType`. The constants NUM_ROWS and NUM_COLS may be accessed globally.

12. Write a C++ function that finds the largest value in a two-dimensional `float` array of 50 rows and 50 columns.

13. Using the declarations in Exam Preparation Exercise 15, write functions, in proper style, to do the following tasks. Only constants may be accessed globally.
    a. Determine which school spent the most money on football.
    b. Determine which sport the last school spent the most money on.
    c. Determine which school had the most students playing basketball.
    d. Determine in which sport the third school had the most students participating.
    e. Determine the total amount spent by all the schools on volleyball.
    f. Determine the total number of students who played any sport. (Assume that each student played only one sport.)
    g. Determine which school had the most students participating in sports.
    h. Determine which was the most popular sport in terms of money spent.
    i. Determine which was the most popular sport in terms of student participation.

14. Given the following declarations

```
const int NUM_DEPTS = 100;
const int NUM_STORES = 10;
const int NUM_MONTHS = 12;

typedef int SalesType[NUM_STORES][NUM_MONTHS][NUM_DEPTS];
```

write a C++ function to initialize an array of type `SalesType` to 0. The constants `NUM_STORES`, `NUM_MONTHS`, and `NUM_DEPTS` may be accessed globally. The array should be a parameter.

15. Sales figures are kept on items sold by store, by department, and by month. Write a C++ function to calculate and print the total number of items sold during the year by each department in each store. The data is stored in an array of type `SalesType` as defined in Programming Warm-up Exercise 14. The array containing the data should be a parameter. The constants `NUM_STORES`, `NUM_MONTHS`, and `NUM_DEPTS` may be accessed globally.

16. Write a C++ value-returning function that returns the sum of the elements in a specified row of a two-dimensional array. The array, the number of filled-in columns, and which row is to be totaled should be parameters.

17. In the CheckLists program, the `ReadFirstList` function declares a parameter `firstList`. Would it be all right to prefix the declaration of `firstList` with the word `const`? Explain.

18. Modify the CheckLists program so that it works even if the lists are not the same length or they contain more than 500 values. Print appropriate error messages and stop the comparison.

Programming Problems

1. The local baseball team is computerizing its records. You are to write a program that computes batting averages. There are 20 players on the team, identified by the numbers 1 through 20. Their batting records are coded in a file as follows. Each line contains four numbers: the player's identification number and the number of hits, walks, and outs he or she made in a particular game. Here is a sample:

```
3   2   1   1
```

The example above indicates that during a game, player number 3 was at bat four times and made 2 hits, 1 walk, and 1 out. For each player there are several lines in the file. Each player's batting average is computed by adding the player's total number of hits and dividing by the total number of times at bat. A walk does not count as either a hit or a time at bat when the batting average is being calculated. Your program prints a table showing each player's identification number, batting average, and number of walks. (Be careful: The players' identification numbers are 1 through 20, but C++ array indexes start at 0.)

2. Write a program that calculates the mean and standard deviation of integers stored in a file. The output should be of type `float` and should be properly labeled and formatted to two decimal places. The formula for calculating the mean of a series of integers is to add all the numbers, then divide by the number

of integers. Expressed in mathematical terms, the mean $\overline{X}$ of N numbers X_1, X_2, ... X_N is

$$\overline{X} = \frac{\sum\limits_{i=1}^{N} X_i}{N}$$

To calculate the standard deviation of a series of integers, subtract the mean from each integer (you may get a negative number) and square the result, add all these squared differences, divide by the number of integers minus 1, then take the square root of the result. Expressed in mathematical terms, the standard deviation S is

$$S = \sqrt{\frac{\sum\limits_{i=1}^{N} (X_i - \overline{X})^2}{N-1}}$$

3. One of the local banks is gearing up for a big advertising campaign and would like to see how long its customers are waiting for service at drive-up windows. Several employees have been asked to keep accurate records for the 24-hour drive-up service. The collected information, which is read from a file, consists of the time the customer arrived in hours, minutes, and seconds; the time the customer actually was served; and the ID number of the teller. Write a program that does the following:

a. Reads in the wait data.

b. Computes the wait time in seconds.

c. Calculates the mean, standard deviation (defined in Programming Problem 2), and range.

d. Prints a single-page summary showing the values calculated in part c.

Input

The first data line contains a title.

The remaining lines each contain a teller ID, an arrival time, and a service time. The times are broken up into integer hours, minutes, and seconds according to a 24-hour clock.

Processing

Calculate the mean and the standard deviation.

Locate the shortest wait time and the longest wait time for any number of records up to 100.

Output

The input data (echo print).

The title.

The following values, all properly labeled: number of records, mean, standard deviation, and range (minimum and maximum).

4. Your history professor has so many students in her class that she has trouble determining how well the class does on exams. She has discovered that you are a computer whiz and has asked you to write a program to perform some simple statistical analyses on exam scores. Your program must work for any class size up to 100. Write and test a computer program that does the following:

   a. Reads the test grades from file inData.
   b. Calculates the class mean, standard deviation (defined in Programming Problem 2), and percentage of the test scores falling in the ranges <10, 10–19, 20–29, 30–39, ... , 80–89, and >90.
   c. Prints a summary showing the mean and the standard deviation, as well as a histogram showing the percentage distribution of test scores.

   Input

   The first data line contains the number of exams to be analyzed and a title for the report.
   The remaining lines have ten test scores on each line until the last line, and one to ten scores on the last. The scores are all integers.

   Output

   The input data as they are read.
   A report consisting of the title that was read from the data, the number of scores, the mean, the standard deviation (all clearly labeled), and the histogram.

5. The final exam in your psychology class consists of 30 multiple-choice questions. Your instructor says that if you write the program to grade the finals, you won't have to take the exam.

   Input

   The first data line contains the key to the exam. The correct answers are the first 30 characters; they are followed by an integer number that says how many students took the exam (call it *n*).
   The next *n* lines contain student answers in the first 30 character positions, followed by the student's name in the next 10 character positions.

   Output

   For each student—the student's name; followed by the number of correct answers; followed by PASS if the number correct is 60 percent or better, or FAIL otherwise.

6. Write an interactive program that plays tic-tac-toe. Represent the board as a 3 × 3 character array. Initialize the array to blanks and ask each player in turn to input a position. The first player's position is marked on the board with an *O*, and the second player's position is marked with an *X*. Continue the process until a player wins or the game is a draw. To win, a player must have three marks in a row, in a column, or on a diagonal. A draw occurs when the board is full and no one has won.

Each player's position should be input as indexes into the tic-tac-toe board—that is, a row number, a space, and a column number. Make the program user-friendly.

After each game, print out a diagram of the board showing the ending positions. Keep a count of the number of games each player has won and the number of draws. Before the beginning of each game, ask each player if he or she wishes to continue. If either player wishes to quit, print out the statistics and stop.

7. Photos taken in space by the Galileo spacecraft are sent back to earth as a stream of numbers. Each number represents a level of brightness. A large number represents a high brightness level, and a small number represents a low level. Your job is to take a matrix (a two-dimensional array) of the numbers and print it as a picture.

One approach to generating a picture is to print a dark character (such as a $) when the brightness level is low, and to print a light character (such as a blank or a period) when the level is high. Unfortunately, errors in transmission sometimes occur. Thus, your program should first attempt to find and correct these errors. Assume a value is in error if it differs by more than 1 from each of its four neighboring values. Correct the erroneous value by giving it the average of its neighboring values, rounded to the nearest integer.

Example:

```
    5        The 2 would be regarded as an error and would be given
4   2   5    a corrected value of 5.
    5
```

Note that values on the corners or boundaries of the matrix have to be processed differently than the values on the interior. Your program should print an image of the uncorrected picture and then an image of the corrected picture.

8. In competitive diving, each diver makes three dives of varying degrees of difficulty. Nine judges score each dive from 0 through 10 in steps of 0.5. The total score is obtained by discarding the lowest and highest of the judges' scores, adding the remaining scores, and then multiplying the scores by the degree of difficulty. The divers take turns, and when the competition is finished, they are ranked according to score. Write a program to calculate the outcome of a competition, using the following input and output specifications.

Input

Number of divers

Diver's name (ten characters), difficulty (`float`), and judges' ratings (nine `floats`)

There is a line of data for each diver for each dive. All the data for Dive 1 are grouped together, then all for Dive 2, then all for Dive 3.

Output

The input data, echo printed in tabular form with appropriate headings—for example, Name, Difficulty, judge's number (1–9)

A table that contains the following information:

Name   Dive 1   Dive 2   Dive 3   Total

where Name is the diver's name; Dive 1, Dive 2, and Dive 3 are the total points received for a single dive, as described above; and Total is the overall total

Array-Based Lists

- ■ To be able to insert a value into a list.

- ■ To be able to delete a specific value from a list.

- ■ To be able to search for a specific value in a list.

- ■ To be able to sort the components of a list into ascending or descending order.

- ■ To be able to insert a value into a sorted list.

- ■ To be able to delete a specific value from a sorted list.

- ■ To be able to search for a specific value in a sorted list using a linear search.

- ■ To be able to search for a specific value using a binary search.

- ■ To be able to declare and use C strings.

Chapter 12 introduced the array, a data structure that is a collection of components of the same type given a single name. In general, a one-dimensional array is a structure used to hold a list of items. In this chapter, we examine algorithms that build and manipulate data stored as a list in a one-dimensional array. These algorithms are implemented as general-purpose functions that can be modified easily to work with many kinds of lists.

We also consider the *C string*, a special kind of built-in one-dimensional array that is used for storing character strings. We conclude with a programming example that uses list algorithms developed in this chapter.

13.1 The List as an Abstract Data Type

As defined in Chapter 12, a one-dimensional array is a built-in data structure that consists of a fixed number of homogeneous components. One use for an array is to store a list of values. A list may contain fewer values than the number of places reserved in the array. In Chapter 12's Comparison of Two Lists Programming Example, we used a variable numVals to keep track of the number of values currently stored in the array, and we employed subarray processing to prevent processing array components that were not part of the list of values. In Figure 12-16, you can see that the *array* goes from firstList[0] through firstList[499], but the *list* stored in the array goes from firstList[0] through firstList[numVals-1]. The number of places in the array is fixed, but the number of values in the list stored there may vary.

For a moment, let's think of the concept of a list not in terms of arrays but as a separate data type. We can define a **list** as a varying-length, linear collection of homogeneous components. That's quite a mouthful. By *linear* we mean that each component (except the first) has a unique component that comes before it and each component (except the last) has a unique component that comes after it. The length of a list—the number of values currently stored in the list—can vary during the execution of the program.

List   A variable-length, linear collection of homogeneous components.

Length   The number of values currently stored in a list.

Like any data type, a list must have associated with it a set of allowable operations. What kinds of operations would we want to define for a list? Here are some possibilities: create a list, add an item to a list, delete an item from a list, print a list, search a list for a particular value, sort a list into alphabetical or numerical order, and so on. When we define a data type formally—by specifying its properties and the operations that preserve those properties—we are creating an abstract data type (ADT). In fact, in Chapter 11 we proposed an ADT named IntList, a data type for a list of up to 100 integer values. At the time, we did not implement this ADT because we did not have at our disposal a suitable concrete data representation. Now that we are familiar with the idea of using a one-dimensional array to represent a list, we can combine C++ classes and arrays to implement list ADTs.

Let's generalize the IntList ADT by (a) allowing the components to be of *any* simple type or of type string, (b) replacing the maximum length of 100 with a maximum of

MAX_LENGTH, a defined constant, and (c) including a wider variety of allowable operations. Here is the specification of the more general ADT:

TYPE
 List
DOMAIN
 Each instance of type List is a collection of up to MAX_LENGTH components,
   each of type ItemType.
OPERATIONS
 Create an initially empty list.
 Report whether the list is empty (true or false).
 Report whether the list is full (true or false).
 Return the current length of the list.
 Insert an item into the list.
 Delete an item from the list.
 Search for a specified item, returning true or false according to whether the
   item is present in the list.
 Sort the list into ascending order.
 Print the list.

We can use a C++ class named List to represent the List ADT in our programs. For
the concrete data representation, we use two items: a one-dimensional array to hold the
list items, and an int variable that stores the current length of the list. When we compile the List class, we need to supply definitions for MAX_LENGTH and ItemType:

```
const int MAX_LENGTH = [        ];   // Maximum possible number of
                                     //    components needed
typedef [        ] ItemType;         // Type of each component
                                     //    (a simple type or the
                                     //     string class)
```

Here is the specification file for our List ADT. Notice that we use 50 for
MAX_LENGTH and int for ItemType. Notice also that the abstract operation *Create an
initially empty list* is implemented as the class constructor List().

```
//*****************************************************************
// SPECIFICATION FILE (list.h)
// This file gives the specification of a list abstract data type.
// The list components are not assumed to be in order by value
//*****************************************************************

const int MAX_LENGTH = 50;      // Maximum possible number of
                                //    components needed
typedef int ItemType;           // Type of each component
                                //    (a simple type or string class)
```

```
class List
{
public:
    bool IsEmpty() const;
        // Postcondition:
        //      Function value == true, if list is empty
        //                     == false, otherwise

    bool IsFull() const;
        // Postcondition:
        //      Function value == true, if list is full
        //                     == false, otherwise

    int Length() const;
        // Postcondition:
        //      Function value == length of list

    void Insert( /* in */ ItemType item );
        // Precondition:
        //      NOT IsFull()
        //   && item is assigned
        // Postcondition:
        //      item is in list
        //   && Length() == Length()@entry + 1

    void Delete( /* in */ ItemType item );
        // Precondition:
        //      NOT IsEmpty()
        //   && item is assigned
        // Postcondition:
        //      IF item is in list at entry
        //          First occurrence of item is no longer in list
        //       && Length() == Length()@entry - 1
        //      ELSE
        //          List is unchanged

    bool IsPresent( /* in */ ItemType item ) const;
        // Precondition:
        //      item is assigned
        // Postcondition:
        //      Function value == true, if item is in list
        //                     == false, otherwise

    void SelSort();
        // Postcondition:
        //      List components are in ascending order of value
```

```
      void Print() const;
         // Postcondition:
         //     All components (if any) in list have been output

      List();
         // Constructor
         // Postcondition:
         //     Empty list is created
private:
   int     length;
   ItemType data[MAX_LENGTH];
};
```

The private part of the class declaration shows our data representation of a list: an int variable and an array (see Figure 13-1). However, notice that the preconditions and postconditions of the member functions mention nothing about an array. The abstraction is a list, not an array. The user of the class is interested only in manipulating lists

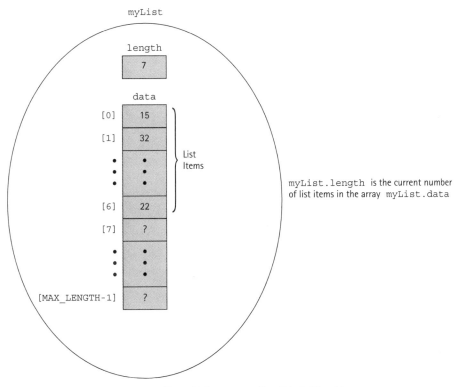

Figure 13-1 *myList, a Class Object of Type* List

of items and does not care how we implement a list. If we change to a different data representation, neither the public interface nor the client code needs to be changed.

We now consider how to implement each of the ADT operations, given that the list items are stored in an array. Before we do so, however, we must distinguish between lists whose components must always be kept in alphabetical or numerical order (*sorted lists*) and lists in which the components are not arranged in any particular order (*unsorted lists*). We begin with unsorted lists.

13.2 Unsorted Lists

Basic Operations

As we discussed in Chapter 11, an ADT is typically implemented in C++ by using a pair of files: the specification file (such as the preceding `list.h` file) and the implementation file, which contains the implementations of the class member functions. Here is how the implementation file `list.cpp` starts out:

```
//******************************************************************
// IMPLEMENTATION FILE (list.cpp)
// This file implements the List class member functions
// List representation: a one-dimensional array and a length
//                      variable
//******************************************************************
#include "list.h"
#include <iostream>

using namespace std;

// Private members of class:
//    int      length;               Length of the list
//    ItemType data[MAX_LENGTH];     Array holding the list
```

Let's look now at the implementations of the basic list operations.

Creating an Empty List   As Figure 13-1 shows, the list exists in the array elements `data[0]` through `data[length-1]`. To create an empty list, it is sufficient to set the `length` member to 0. We do not need to store any special values into the `data` array to make the list empty, because only those values in `data[0]` through `data[length-1]` are processed by the list algorithms.

In the `List` class, the appropriate place to initialize the list to be empty is the class constructor:

```
List::List()

// Constructor
```

```
// Postcondition:
//      length == 0

{

    length = 0;
}
```

One thing you will notice as we go through the List member functions is that the *implementation assertions* (the preconditions and postconditions appearing in the implementation file) are often stated differently from the *abstract assertions* (those located in the specification file). Abstract assertions are written in terms that are meaningful to the user of the ADT; implementation details should not be mentioned. In contrast, implementation assertions can be made more precise by referring directly to variables and algorithms in the implementation code. For the List class constructor, the abstract postcondition is simply that an empty list has been created. On the other hand, the implementation postcondition (length == 0) is phrased in terms of our private data representation.

The IsEmpty Operation This operation returns true if the list is empty and false if the list is not empty. Using our convention that length equals 0 if the list is empty, the implementation of this operation is straightforward.

```
bool List::IsEmpty() const

// Reports whether list is empty

// Postcondition:
//      Function value == true, if length == 0
//                     == false, otherwise

{

    return (length == 0);
}
```

The IsFull Operation The list is full if there is no more room in the array holding the list items—that is, if the list length equals MAX_LENGTH.

```
bool List::IsFull() const

// Reports whether list is full

// Postcondition:
//      Function value == true, if length == MAX_LENGTH
//                     == false, otherwise
```

```
{
    return (length == MAX_LENGTH);
}
```

The Length Operation This operation simply returns to the client the current length of the list.

```
int List::Length() const

// Returns current length of list

// Postcondition:
//      Function value == length

{
    return length;
}
```

The Print Operation To output the components of the list, we can simply use a For loop that steps through the `data` array, printing each array element in sequence.

```
void List::Print() const

// Prints the list

// Postcondition:
//      Contents of data[0..length-1] have been output

{
    int index;      // Loop control and index variable

    for (index = 0; index < length; index++)
        cout << data[index] << endl;
}
```

Insertion and Deletion

To devise an algorithm for inserting a new item into the list, we first observe that we are working with an unsorted list and that the values do not have to be maintained in any particular order. Therefore, we can store a new value into the next available position in the array—data[length]—and then increment `length`. This algorithm brings up a question: Do we need to check that there is room in the list for the new item? We have two choices. The `Insert` function can test `length` against MAX_LENGTH and return an error flag if there isn't any room, or we can let the client code make the test before calling `Insert` (that is, make it a precondition that the list is not full). We have chosen the second approach. The client can use the `IsFull` operation to make sure the precondition is true. If the client fails to satisfy the precondition, the contract between client and function is broken, and the function is not required to satisfy the postcondition.

```
void List::Insert( /* in */ ItemType item )

// Inserts item into the list

// Precondition:
//     length < MAX_LENGTH
//   && item is assigned
// Postcondition:
//     data[length@entry] == item
//   && length == length@entry + 1

{
    data[length] = item;
    length++;
}
```

Deleting a component from a list consists of two parts: finding the component and removing it from the list. Before we can write the algorithm, we must know what to do if the component is not there. *Delete* can mean "Delete, if it's there" or "Delete, it *is* there." We assume the first meaning; the code for the first definition works for the second as well but is not as efficient. We must start at the beginning of the list and search for the value to be deleted. If we find it, how do we remove it? We take the last value in the list (the one stored in `data[length-1]`), put it where the item to be deleted is located, and then decrement `length`. Moving the last item from its original position is appropriate only for an unsorted list because we don't need to preserve the order of the items in the list.

The definition "Delete, if it's there" requires a searching loop with a compound condition. We examine each component in turn and stop looking when we find the item to be deleted or when we have looked at all the items and know that it is not there.

```
void List::Delete( /* in */ ItemType item )

// Deletes item from the list, if it is there

// Precondition:
//     length > 0
//   && item is assigned
// Postcondition:
//     IF item is in data array at entry
//          First occurrence of item is no longer in array
```

```
//          && length == length@entry - 1
//      ELSE
//          length and data array are unchanged

{

    int index = 0;     // Index variable

    while (index < length && item != data[index])
        index++;

    if (index < length)
    {                                           // Remove item
        data[index] = data[length-1];
        length--;
    }
}
```

Sequential Search

In the `Delete` function, the algorithm we used to search for the item to be deleted is known as a *sequential* or *linear search* in an unsorted list. We use the same algorithm to implement the `IsPresent` function of the `List` class.

```
bool List::IsPresent( /* in */ ItemType item ) const

// Searches the list for item, reporting whether it was found

// Precondition:
//      item is assigned
// Postcondition:
//      Function value == true, if item is in data[0..length-1]
//                     == false, otherwise

{

    int index = 0;     // Index variable

    while (index < length && item != data[index])
        index++;

    return (index < length);
}
```

This algorithm is called a sequential search because we start at the beginning of the list and look at each item in sequence. We stop the search as soon as we find the item we are looking for (or when we reach the end of the list, concluding that the desired item is not present in the list).

We can use this algorithm in any program requiring a list search. In the form shown, it searches a list of `ItemType` components, provided that `ItemType` is an integral type or the `string` class. To use the function with a list of floating-point values, we must modify it so that the While statement tests for near equality rather than exact equality (for the reasons discussed in Chapter 10). In the following statement, we assume that `EPSILON` is defined as a global constant.

```
while (index < length && fabs(item - data[index]) >= EPSILON)
    index++;
```

The sequential search algorithm finds the first occurrence of the searched-for item. How would we modify it to find the last occurrence? We would initialize `index` to `length-1` and decrement `index` each time through the loop, stopping when we found the item we wanted or when `index` became –1.

Sorting

Although we are implementing an unsorted list ADT, there are times when the user of the `List` class may want to rearrange the list components into a certain order just before calling the `Print` function. For example, the user might want to put a list of stock numbers into either ascending or descending order, or the user might want to put a list of words into alphabetical order. In software development, arranging list items into order is a very common operation and is known as **sorting**.

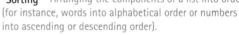

Sorting Arranging the components of a list into order (for instance, words into alphabetical order or numbers into ascending or descending order).

If you were given a sheet of paper with a column of 20 numbers on it and were asked to write the numbers in ascending order, you would probably do the following:

1. Make a pass through the list, looking for the smallest number.

2. Write it on the paper in a second column.

3. Cross the number off the original list.

4. Repeat the process, always looking for the smallest number remaining in the original list.

5. Stop when all the numbers have been crossed off.

We can implement this algorithm directly in C++, but we need two arrays—one for the original list and a second for the sorted list. If the list is large, we might not have enough memory for two copies of it. Also, how do we "cross off" an array component? We could simulate crossing off a value by replacing it with some dummy value like `INT_MAX`. That is, we would set the value of the crossed-off variable to something that would not interfere with the processing of the rest of the components. However, a slight variation of our hand-done algorithm allows us to sort the components *in place*. We do not have to use a second array; we can put a value into its proper place in the list by having it swap places with the component currently in that position.

We can state the algorithm as follows. We search for the smallest value in the list and exchange it with the component in the first position in the list. We search for the next-smallest value in the list and exchange it with the component in the second position in the list. This process continues until all the components are in their proper places.

```
FOR count going from 0 through length−2
  Find minimum value in data[count .. length−1]
  Swap minimum value with data[count]
```

Figure 13-2 illustrates how this algorithm works.

Observe that we perform length−1 passes through the list because count runs from 0 through length−2. The loop does not need to be executed when count equals length−1 because the last value, data[length-1], is in its proper place after the preceding components have been sorted.

This sort, known as the *straight selection sort,* belongs to a class of sorts called selection sorts. There are many types of sorting algorithms. Selection sorts are characterized by finding the smallest (or largest) value left in the unsorted portion at each iteration and swapping it with the value indexed by the iteration counter. Swapping the contents of two variables requires a temporary variable so that no values are lost (see Figure 13-3).

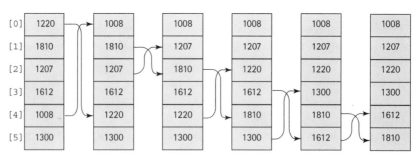

Figure 13-2 *Straight Selection Sort*

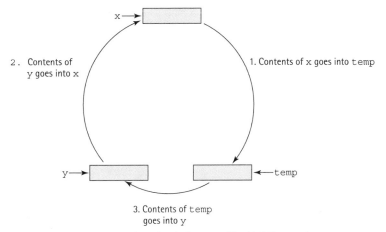

2 . Contents of
y goes into x

1. Contents of x goes into temp

3. Contents of temp
goes into y

Figure 13-3   *Swapping the Contents of Two Variables, x and y*

Here is the code for the sorting operation of the List class:

```
void List::SelSort()

// Sorts list into ascending order

// Postcondition:
//      data array contains the same values as data@entry,
//      rearranged into ascending order

{
   ItemType temp;              // Temporary variable
   int      passCount;         // Loop control variable
   int      searchIndx;        // Loop control variable
   int      minIndx;           // Index of minimum so far

   for (passCount = 0; passCount < length - 1; passCount++)
   {
      minIndx = passCount;

      // Find the index of the smallest component
      // in data[passCount..length-1]
```

```
          for (searchIndx = passCount + 1; searchIndx < length;
                                                        searchIndx++)
            if (data[searchIndx] < data[minIndx])
               minIndx = searchIndx;

          // Swap data[minIndx] and data[passCount]

          temp = data[minIndx];
          data[minIndx] = data[passCount];
          data[passCount] = temp;
       }
   }
```

Note that with each pass through the outer loop, we are looking for the minimum value in the rest of the list (`data[passCount]` through `data[length-1]`). Therefore, `minIndx` is initialized to `passCount` and the inner loop runs from `searchIndx` equal to `passCount+1` through `length-1`. Upon exit from the inner loop, `minIndx` contains the position of the smallest value. (Note that the If statement is the only statement in the loop.)

Note also that we may swap a component with itself, which occurs if no value in the remaining list is smaller than `data[passCount]`. We could avoid this unnecessary swap by checking to see if `minIndx` is equal to `passCount`. Because this comparison would be made during each iteration of the outer loop, it is more efficient not to check for this possibility and just to swap something with itself occasionally. If the components we are sorting are much more complex than simple numbers, we might reconsider this decision.

This algorithm sorts the components into ascending order. To sort them into descending order, we would scan for the maximum value instead of the minimum value. To do so, we would simply change the relational operator in the inner loop from < to >. Of course, `minIndx` would no longer be an appropriate identifier and should be changed to `maxIndx`.

By providing the user of the `List` class with a sorting operation, we have not turned our unsorted list ADT into a sorted list ADT. The `Insert` and `Delete` algorithms we wrote do not preserve ordering by value. `Insert` places a new item at the end of the list, regardless of its value, and `Delete` moves the last item to a different position in the list. After `SelSort` has executed, the list items remain in sorted order only until the next insertion or deletion takes place. We now look at a sorted list ADT in which all the list operations cooperate to preserve the sorted order of the list components.

13.3 Sorted Lists

In the `List` class, the `IsPresent` algorithm assumes that the list to be searched is unsorted. A drawback to searching an unsorted list is that we must scan the entire list to discover that the search item is not there. Think what it would be like if your city telephone book contained people's names in random rather than alphabetical order. To look up Mary Anthony's phone number, you would have to start with the first name in the phone book and scan sequentially, page after page, until you found it. In the worst case, you might have to examine tens of thousands of names only to find out that Mary's name is not in the book.

Of course, telephone books *are* alphabetized, and the alphabetical ordering makes searching easier. If Mary Anthony's name is not in the book, you discover this fact quickly by starting with the A's and stopping the search as soon as you have passed the place where her name should be.

Let's define a sorted list ADT in which the components always remain in order by value, no matter what operations are applied. Below is the slist.h file that contains the declaration of a SortedList class.

```cpp
//*********************************************************************
// SPECIFICATION FILE (slist.h)
// This file gives the specification of a sorted list abstract data
// type.  The list components are maintained in ascending order
// of value
//*********************************************************************

const int MAX_LENGTH = 50;       // Maximum possible number of
                                 //   components needed
                                 // Requirement:
                                 //   MAX_LENGTH <= INT_MAX/2
typedef int ItemType;            // Type of each component
                                 //   (a simple type or string class)

class SortedList
{
public:
    bool IsEmpty() const;
        // Postcondition:
        //     Function value == true, if list is empty
        //                    == false, otherwise

    bool IsFull() const;
        // Postcondition:
        //     Function value == true, if list is full
        //                    == false, otherwise

    int Length() const;
        // Postcondition:
        //     Function value == length of list

    void Insert( /* in */ ItemType item );
        // Precondition:
        //     NOT IsFull()
```

```
              //  && item is assigned
              // Postcondition:
              //     item is in list
              //  && Length() == Length()@entry + 1
              //  && List components are in ascending order of value

      void Delete( /* in */ ItemType item );
              // Precondition:
              //     NOT IsEmpty()
              //  && item is assigned
              // Postcondition:
              //     IF item is in list at entry
              //          First occurrence of item is no longer in list
              //       && Length() == Length()@entry - 1
              //       && List components are in ascending order of value
              //     ELSE
              //          List is unchanged

      bool IsPresent( /* in */ ItemType item ) const;
              // Precondition:
              //     item is assigned
              // Postcondition:
              //     Function value == true, if item is in list
              //                     == false, otherwise

      void Print() const;
              // Postcondition:
              //     All components (if any) in list have been output

      SortedList();
              // Constructor
              // Postcondition:
              //     Empty list is created
  private:
      int       length;
      ItemType  data[MAX_LENGTH];
      void      BinSearch( ItemType, bool&, int& ) const;
  };
```

How does the declaration of SortedList differ from the declaration of our original List class? Apart from a few changes in the documentation comments, there are only two differences:

1. The SortedList class does not supply a sorting operation to the client. Such an operation is needless, because the list components are assumed to be kept in sorted order at all times.

2. The SortedList class has an additional class member in the private part: a Bin-Search function. This function is an auxiliary ("helper") function that is used only by other class member functions and is inaccessible to clients. We discuss its purpose when we examine the class implementation.

Let's look at what changes, if any, are required in the algorithms for the ADT operations, given that we are now working with a sorted list instead of an unsorted list.

Basic Operations

The algorithms for the class constructor, IsEmpty, IsFull, Length, and Print are identical to those in the List class. The constructor sets the private data member length to 0, IsEmpty reports whether length equals 0, IsFull reports whether length equals MAX_LENGTH, Length returns the value of length, and Print outputs the list items from first to last.

Insertion

To add a new value to an already sorted list, we could store the new value at data[length], increment length, and sort the array again. However, such a solution is *not* efficient. Inserting five new items results in five separate sorting operations.

If we were to insert a value by hand into a sorted list, we would write the new value out to the side and draw a line showing where it belongs. To find this position, we start at the top and scan the list until we find a value greater than the one we are inserting. The new value goes in the list just before that point.

We can use a similar process in our Insert function. We find the proper place in the list using the by-hand algorithm. Instead of writing the value to the side, we shift all the values larger than the new one down one place to make room for it. The main algorithm is expressed as follows, where item is the value being inserted.

```
WHILE place not found AND more places to look
  IF item > current component in list
      Increment current position
  ELSE
      Place found
Shift remainder of list down
Insert item
Increment length
```

Assuming that index is the place where item is to be inserted, the algorithm for Shift List Down is

Set data[length]   =   data[length–1]
Set data[length–1]   =   data[length–2]
  ⋮   ⋮
Set data[index+1]   =   data[index]

This algorithm is illustrated in Figure 13-4.

This algorithm is based on how we would accomplish the task by hand. Often, such an adaptation is the best way to solve a problem. However, in this case, further thought reveals a slightly better way. Notice that we search from the front of the list (people always do), and we shift down from the end of the list upward. We can combine the searching and shifting by beginning at the *end* of the list.

If item is the new item to be inserted, compare item to the value in data[length-1]. If item is *less*, put data[length-1] into data[length] and com-

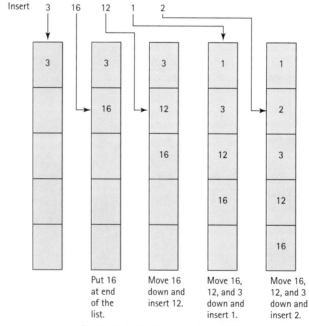

Figure 13-4   *Inserting into a Sorted List*

pare item to the value in data[length-2]. This process continues until you find the place where item is greater than or equal to the item in the list. Store item directly below it. Here is the algorithm:

```
Set index = length - 1
WHILE index ≥ 0 AND item < data[index]
  Set data[index + 1] = data[index]
  Decrement index
Set data[index + 1] = item
Increment length
```

What about duplicates? The algorithm continues until an item is found that is less than the one we are inserting. Therefore, the new item is inserted below a duplicate value (if one is there). Here is the code:

```cpp
void SortedList::Insert( /* in */ ItemType item )

// Inserts item into the list

// Precondition:
//     length < MAX_LENGTH
//  && data[0..length-1] are in ascending order
//  && item is assigned
// Postcondition:
//     item is in the list
//  && length == length@entry + 1
//  && data[0..length-1] are in ascending order

{
    int index;    // Index and loop control variable

    index = length - 1;
    while (index >= 0 && item < data[index])
    {
        data[index+1] = data[index];
        index--;
    }
    data[index+1] = item;          // Insert item
    length++;
}
```

Notice that this algorithm works even if the list is empty. When the list is empty, `length` is 0 and the body of the While loop is not entered. So `item` is stored into `data[0]`, and `length` is incremented to 1. Does the algorithm work if `item` is the smallest? The largest? Let's see. If `item` is the smallest, the loop body is executed `length` times, and `index` is -1. Thus, `item` is stored into position 0, where it belongs. If `item` is the largest, the loop body is not entered. The value of `index` is still `length` - 1, so `item` is stored into `data[length]`, where it belongs.

This algorithm is the basis for another general-purpose sorting algorithm—an *insertion sort*. In an insertion sort, values are inserted one at a time into a list that was originally empty. An insertion sort is often used when input data must be sorted; each value is put into its proper place as it is read. We use this technique in the Programming Example at the end of this chapter.

Sequential Search

When we search for an item in an unsorted list, we won't discover that the item is missing until we reach the end of the list. If the list is already sorted, we know that an item is missing when we pass the place where it should be in the list. For example, if a list contains the values

7
11
13
76
98
102

and we are looking for 12, we need only compare 12 with 7, 11, and 13 to know that 12 is not in the list.

If the search item is greater than the current list component, we move on to the next component. If the item is equal to the current component, we have found what we are looking for. If the item is less than the current component, then we know that it is not in the list. In either of the last two cases, we stop looking. We can restate this algorithmically with the following code, in which `found` is set to `true` if the search item was found.

```
// Sequential search in a sorted list

index = 0;
while (index < length && item > data[index])
    index++;

found = (index < length && item == data[index]);
```

On average, searching a sorted list in this way takes the same number of iterations to find an item as searching an unsorted list. The advantage of this new algorithm is that we find out sooner if an item is missing. Thus, it is slightly more efficient; however, it works only on a sorted list.

We do not use this algorithm to implement the `SortedList::IsPresent` function. There is a better algorithm, which we look at next.

Binary Search

There is a second search algorithm on a sorted list that is considerably faster both for finding an item and for discovering that an item is missing. This algorithm is called a *binary search*. A binary search is based on the principle of successive approximation. The algorithm divides the list in half (divides by 2—that's why it's called *binary* search) and decides which half to look in next. Division of the selected portion of the list is repeated until the item is found or it is determined that the item is not in the list.

This method is analogous to the way in which we look up a word in a dictionary. We open the dictionary in the middle and compare the word with one on the page that we turned to. If the word we're looking for comes before this word, we continue our search in the left-hand section of the dictionary. Otherwise, we continue in the right-hand section of the dictionary. We repeat this process until we find the word. If it is not there, we realize that either we have misspelled the word or our dictionary isn't complete.

The algorithm for a binary search is given below. The list of values is in the array data, and the value being looked for is item (see Figure 13-5).

1. Compare item to data[middle]. If item = data[middle], then we have found it. If item < data[middle], then look in the first half of data. If item > data[middle], then look in the second half of data.

2. Redefine data to be the half of data that we search next, and repeat Step 1.

3. Stop when we have found item or know it is missing. We know it's missing when there is nowhere else to look and we still have not found it.

With each comparison, at best, we find the item for which we are searching; at worst, we eliminate half of the remaining list from consideration.

We need to keep track of the first possible place to look (first) and the last possible place to look (last). At any one time, we are looking only in data[first] through data[last]. When the function begins, first is set to 0 and last is set to length-1 to encompass the entire list.

Our previous search algorithms have been Boolean operations. They just answer the question, Is this item in the list? Let's code the binary search as a void function that not only asks if the item is in the list but also asks which one it is (if it's there). To do so, we

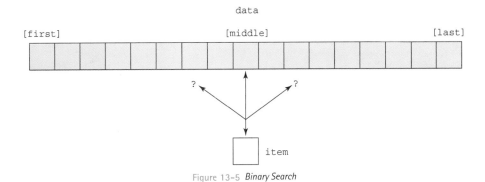

Figure 13-5 *Binary Search*

need to add two parameters to the parameter list: a Boolean flag `found` (to tell us whether the item is in the list) and an integer variable `position` (to tell us which item it is). If `found` is `false`, `position` is undefined.

```
void SortedList::BinSearch(
      /* in */   ItemType item,              // Item to be found
      /* out */  bool&    found,             // True if item is found
      /* out */  int&     position ) const   // Location if found

// Searches list for item, returning the index
// of item if item was found.

// Precondition:
//    length <= INT_MAX / 2
//  && data[0..length-1] are in ascending order
//  && item is assigned
// Postcondition:
//    IF item is in the list
//       found == true  &&  data[position] contains item
//    ELSE
//       found == false  &&  position is undefined

{
    int first = 0;             // Lower bound on list
    int last = length - 1;     // Upper bound on list
    int middle;                // Middle index

    found = false;
    while (last >= first && !found)
    {
        middle = (first + last) / 2;
        if (item < data[middle])
            // Assert: item is not in data[middle..last]
            last = middle - 1;
        else if (item > data[middle])
            // Assert: item is not in data[first..middle]
            first = middle + 1;
        else
            // Assert: item == data[middle]
            found = true;
    }
    if (found)
        position = middle;
}
```

Should `BinSearch` be a public member of the `SortedList` class? No. The function returns the index of the array element where the item was found. An array index is useless to a client of `SortedList`. The array containing the list items is encapsulated within the private part of the class and is inaccessible to clients. If you review the `SortedList` class declaration, you'll see that `BinSearch` is a *private*, not public, class member. We intend to use it as a helper function when we implement the public operations `IsPresent` and `Delete`.

Let's do a code walk-through of the binary search algorithm. The value being searched for is 24. Figure 13-6a shows the values of `first`, `last`, and `middle` during the first iteration. In this iteration, 24 is compared with 103, the value in `data[middle]`. Because 24 is less than 103, `last` becomes `middle-1` and `first` stays the same. Figure 13-6b shows the situation during the second iteration. This time, 24 is compared with 72, the value in `data[middle]`. Because 24 is less than 72, `last` becomes `middle-1` and `first` again stays the same.

In the third iteration (Figure 13-6c), `middle` and `first` are both 0. The value 24 is compared with 12, the value in `data[middle]`. Because 24 is greater than 12, `first` becomes `middle+1`. In the fourth iteration (Figure 13-6d), `first`, `last`, and `middle` are all the same. Again, 24 is compared with the value in `data[middle]`. Because 24 is less than 64, `last` becomes `middle-1`. Now that `last` is less than `first`, the process stops; `found` is `false`.

The binary search is the most complex algorithm that we have examined so far. The following table shows `first`, `last`, `middle`, and `data[middle]` for searches of the values 106, 400, and 406, using the same data as in the previous example. Examine the results in this table carefully.

item	first	last	middle	data[middle]	Termination of Loop
106	0	10	5	103	
	6	10	8	200	
	6	7	6	106	found = true
400	0	10	5	103	
	6	10	8	200	
	9	10	9	300	
	10	10	10	400	found = true
406	0	10	5	103	
	6	10	8	200	
	9	10	9	300	
	10	10	10	400	
	11	10			last < first
					found = false

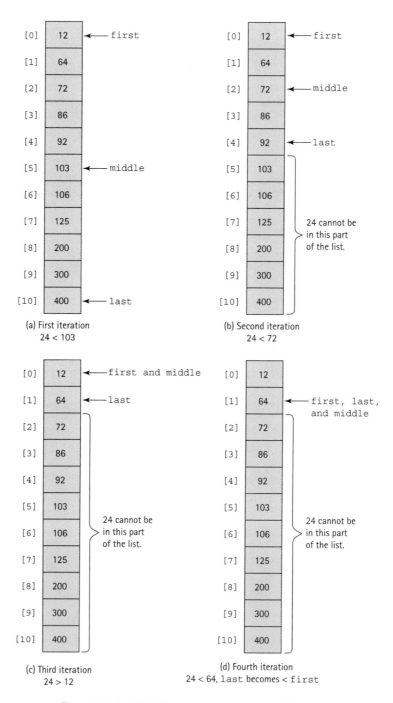

Figure 13-6 *Code Walk-Through of* `BinSearch` *Function (Search Item Is 24)*

The calculation

```
middle = (first + last) / 2;
```

explains why the function precondition restricts the value of `length` to `INT_MAX/2`. If the item being searched for happens to reside in the last position of the list (for example, when `item` equals 400 in our sample list), then `first + last` equals `length + length`. If `length` is greater than `INT_MAX/2`, the sum `length + length` would produce an integer overflow.

Notice in the table that whether we searched for 106, 400, or 406, the loop never executed more than four times. It never executes more than four times in a list of 11 components because the list is being cut in half each time through the loop. The table below compares a sequential search and a binary search in terms of the average number of iterations needed to find an item.

	Average Number of Iterations	
Length of List	Sequential Search	Binary Search
10	5.5	2.9
100	50.5	5.8
1000	500.5	9.0
10,000	5000.5	12.4

If the binary search is so much faster, why not use it all the time? It certainly is faster in terms of the number of times through the loop, but more computations are performed within the binary search loop than in the other search algorithms. So if the number of components in the list is small (say, less than 20), the sequential search algorithms are faster because they perform less work at each iteration. As the number of components in the list increases, the binary search algorithm becomes relatively more efficient. Remember, however, that the binary search requires the list to be sorted, and sorting takes time. Keep three factors in mind when you are deciding which search algorithm to use:

1. The length of the list to be searched

2. Whether or not the list is already sorted

3. The number of times the list is to be searched

Given the `BinSearch` function (a private member of the `SortedList` class), it's easy to implement the `IsPresent` function (a public member of the class).

```
bool SortedList::IsPresent( /* in */ ItemType item ) const

// Searches the list for item, reporting whether it was found

// Precondition:
//      length <= INT_MAX / 2
//   && data[0..length-1] are in ascending order
//   && item is assigned
// Postcondition:
//      Function value == true, if item is in data[0..length-1]
//                     == false, otherwise

{
    bool found;         // True if item is found
    int position;       // Required (but unused) argument for
                        //   the call to BinSearch

    BinSearch(item, found, position);
    return found;
}
```

The body of IsPresent calls BinSearch, obtaining the result of the search in the variables found and position. Like the children's game of Pass It On, IsPresent receives the value of found from BinSearch and simply passes it on to the client (via the return statement). The body of IsPresent is not interested in where the item was found, so it ignores the value returned in the position argument. Why did we include this third argument when we designed BinSearch? The answer is that the Delete operation, which we look at next, calls BinSearch and *does* use the position argument.

Deletion

In the List::Delete function, we deleted an item by moving up the last component in the list to fill the deleted item's position. Although this algorithm is fine for unsorted lists, it won't work for sorted lists. Moving the last component to an arbitrary position in the list is almost certain to disturb the sorted order of the components. We need a new algorithm for sorted lists.

Let's call BinSearch to tell us the position of the item to be deleted. Then we can "squeeze out" the deleted item by shifting up all the remaining array elements by one position:

BinSearch(item, found, position)
IF found
 Shift remainder of list up
 Decrement length

The algorithm for Shift List Up is

Set data[position]   =   data[position+1]
Set data[position+1]   =   data[position+2]
  ⋮   ⋮
Set data[length–2]   =   data[length–1]

Here is the coded version of this algorithm:

```
void SortedList::Delete( /* in */ ItemType item )

// Deletes item from the list, if it is there

// Precondition:
//     0 < length <= INT_MAX/2
//  && data[0..length-1] are in ascending order
//  && item is assigned
// Postcondition:
//     IF item is in data array at entry
//         First occurrence of item is no longer in array
//      && length == length@entry - 1
//      && data[0..length-1] are in ascending order
//     ELSE
//         length and data array are unchanged
```

```
{
    bool found;        // True if item is found
    int position;      // Position of item, if found
    int index;         // Index and loop control variable

    BinSearch(item, found, position);
    if (found)
    {
        // Shift data[position..length-1] up one position

        for (index = position; index < length - 1; index++)
            data[index] = data[index+1];
        length--;
    }
}
```

Now let's turn our attention to another example of array-based lists—a special kind of array that is useful when working with alphanumeric character data.

13.4 Understanding Character Strings

Ever since Chapter 2, we have been using the `string` class to store and manipulate character strings.

```
string name;

name = "James Smith";
len = name.length();
    ⋮
```

In some contexts, we think of a string as a single unit of data. In other contexts, we treat it as a group of individually accessible characters. In particular, we think of a string as a variable-length, linear collection of homogeneous components (of type `char`). Does this sound familiar? It should. As an abstraction, a string is a list of characters that, at any moment in time, has a length associated with it.

Thinking of a string as an ADT, how would we implement the ADT? There are many ways to implement strings. Programmers have specified and implemented their own string classes—the `string` class from the standard library, for instance. And the C++ language has its own built-in notion of a string: the **C string**. In C++, a string constant (or string literal, or literal string) is a sequence of characters enclosed by double quotes:

C string In C and C++, a null-terminated sequence of characters stored in a `char` array.

```
"Hi"
```

A string constant is stored as a `char` array with enough components to hold each specified character plus one more—the *null character*. The null character, which is the first character in both the ASCII and EBCDIC character sets, has internal representation 0. In C++, the escape sequence \0 stands for the null character. When the compiler encounters the string "Hi" in a program, it stores the three characters 'H', 'i', and '\0' into a three-element, anonymous (unnamed) `char` array as follows:

The C string is the only kind of C++ array for which there exists an aggregate constant—the string constant. Notice that in a C++ program, the symbols 'A' denote a single character, whereas the symbols "A" denote two: the character 'A' and the null character.*

In addition to C string constants, we can create C string *variables*. To do so, we explicitly declare a `char` array and store into it whatever characters we want to, finishing with the null character. Here's an example:

```
char myStr[8];    // Room for 7 significant characters plus '\0'

myStr[0] = 'H';
myStr[1] = 'i';
myStr[2] = '\0';
```

In C++, all C strings (constants or variables) are assumed to be null-terminated. This convention is agreed upon by all C++ programmers and standard library functions. The null character serves as a sentinel value; it allows algorithms to locate the end of the string. For example, here is a function that determines the length of any C string, not counting the terminating null character:

```
int StrLength( /* in */ const char str[] )
{
    int i = 0;    // Index variable

    while (str[i] != '\0')
        i++;
    return i;
}
```

---

*C *string* is not an official term used in C++ language manuals. Such manuals typically use the term *string*. However, we use C *string* to distinguish between the general concept of a string and the built-in array representation defined by the C and C++ languages.

The value of i is the correct value for this function to return. If the array being examined is

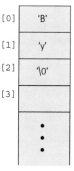

then i equals 2 at loop exit. The string length is therefore 2.

The argument to the StrLength function can be a C string variable, as in the function call

```
cout << StrLength(myStr);
```

or it can be a string constant:

```
cout << StrLength("Hello");
```

In the first case, the base address of the myStr array is sent to the function, as we discussed in Chapter 12. In the second case, a base address is also sent to the function—the base address of the unnamed array that the compiler has set aside for the string constant.

There is one more thing we should say about our StrLength function. A C++ programmer would not actually write this function. The standard library supplies several string-processing functions, one of which is named strlen and does exactly what our StrLength function does. Later in the chapter, we look at strlen and other library functions.

Initializing C Strings

In Chapter 12, we showed how to initialize an array in its declaration by specifying a list of initial values within braces, like this:

```
int delta[5] = {25, -3, 7, 13, 4};
```

To initialize a C string variable in its declaration, you could use the same technique:

```
char message[8] = {'W', 'h', 'o', 'o', 'p', 's', '!', '\0'};
```

However, C++ allows a more convenient way to initialize a C string. You can simply initialize the array by using a string constant:

```
char message[8] = "Whoops!";
```

This shorthand notation is unique to C strings because there is no other kind of array for which there are aggregate constants.

We said in Chapter 12 that you can omit the size of an array when you initialize it in its declaration (in which case, the compiler determines its size). This feature is often used with C strings because it keeps you from having to count the number of characters. For example,

```
char promptMsg[] = "Enter a positive number:";   // Size is 25
char errMsg[] = "Value must be positive.";       // Size is 24
```

Be very careful about one thing: C++ treats initialization (in a declaration) and assignment (in an assignment statement) as two distinct operations. Different rules apply. Remember that array initialization is legal, but aggregate array assignment is not.

```
char myStr[20] = "Hello";    // OK
    ⋮
myStr = "Howdy";             // Not allowed
```

C String Input and Output

In Chapter 12, we emphasized that C++ does not allow aggregate assignment, aggregate comparison, or aggregate arithmetic on arrays. We also see that aggregate input/output of arrays is not possible, with one exception: C strings. Let's look first at output.

To output the contents of an array that is *not* a C string, you aren't allowed to do this:

```
int alpha[100];
    ⋮
cout << alpha;    // Not allowed
```

Instead, you must write a loop and print the array elements one at a time. However, aggregate output of a null-terminated `char` array (that is, a C string) is valid. The C string can be a constant (as we've been doing since Chapter 2):

```
cout << "Results are:";
```

or it can be a variable:

```
char msg[8] = "Welcome";
    ⋮
cout << msg;
```

In both cases, the insertion operator (<<) outputs each character in the array until the null character is found. It is up to you to double-check that the terminating null character is present in the array. If not, the << operator will march through the array and into the rest of memory, printing out bytes until—just by chance—it encounters a byte whose integer value is 0.

To input C strings, we have several options. The first is to use the extraction operator (>>), which behaves exactly the same as with `string` class objects. When reading input characters into a C string variable, the >> operator skips leading whitespace characters and then reads successive characters into the array, stopping at the first trailing whitespace character (which is not consumed, but remains as the first character waiting in the input stream). The >> operator also takes care of adding the null character to the end of the string. For example, assume we have the following code:

```
char firstName[31];    // Room for 30 characters plus '\0'
char lastName[31];

cin >> firstName >> lastName;
```

If the input stream initially looks like this (where □ denotes a blank):

```
□□John□Smith□□□25
```

then our input statement stores 'J', 'o', 'h', 'n', and '\0' into `firstName[0]` through `firstName[4]`; stores 'S', 'm', 'i', 't', 'h', and '\0' into `lastName[0]` through `lastName[5]`; and leaves the input stream as

```
□□□25
```

The >> operator, however, has two potential drawbacks.

1. If the array isn't large enough to hold the sequence of input characters (and the '\0'), the >> operator will continue to store characters into memory past the end of the array.
2. The >> operator cannot be used to input a string that has blanks within it. (It stops reading as soon as it encounters the first whitespace character.)

To cope with these limitations, we can use a variation of the `get` function, a member of the `istream` class. We have used the `get` function to input a single character, even if it is a whitespace character:

```
cin.get(inputChar);
```

The `get` function also can be used to input C strings, in which case the function call requires two arguments. The first is the array name and the second is an `int` expression.

```
cin.get(myStr, charCount + 1);
```

The `get` function does not skip leading whitespace characters and continues until it either has read `charCount` characters or it reaches the newline character '\n', whichever comes first. It then appends the null character to the end of the string. With the statements

```
char oneLine[81];    // Room for 80 characters plus '\0'
   ⋮
cin.get(oneLine, 81);
```

the `get` function reads and stores an entire input line (to a maximum of 80 characters), embedded blanks and all. If the line has fewer than 80 characters, reading stops at '\n' but does not consume it. The newline character is now the first one waiting in the input stream. To read two consecutive lines worth of strings, it is necessary to consume the newline character:

```
char dummy;
   ⋮
cin.get(string1, 81);
cin.get(dummy);          // Eat newline before next "get"
cin.get(string2, 81);
```

The first function call reads characters up to, but not including, the '\n'. If the input of `dummy` were omitted, then the input of `string2` would read *no* characters because '\n' would immediately be the first character waiting in the stream.

Finally, the `ignore` function—introduced in Chapter 4—can be useful in conjunction with the `get` function. Recall that the statement

```
cin.ignore(200, '\n');
```

says to skip at most 200 input characters but stop if a newline was read. (The newline character *is* consumed by this function.) If a program inputs a long string from the user but only wants to retain the first four characters of the response, here is a way to do it:

```
char response[5];        // Room for 4 characters plus '\0'

cin.get(response, 5);    // Input at most 4 characters
cin.ignore(100, '\n');   // Skip remaining chars up to and
                         //    including '\n'
```

The value 100 in the last statement is arbitrary. Any "large enough" number will do.

Here is a table that summarizes the differences between the >> operator and the get function when reading C strings:

Statement	Skips Leading Whitespace?	Stops Reading When?
cin >> inputStr;	Yes	At the first trailing whitespace character (which is *not* consumed)
cin.get(inputStr, 21);	No	When either 20 characters are read or '\n' is encountered (which is *not* consumed)

Finally, we revisit a topic that came up in Chapter 4. Certain library functions and member functions of system-supplied classes require C strings as arguments. An example is the ifstream class member function named open. To open a file, we pass the name of the file as a C string, either a constant or a variable:

```
ifstream file1;
ifstream file2;
char     fileName[51];    // Max. 50 characters plus '\0'

file1.open("students.dat");
cin.get(fileName, 51);              // Read at most 50 characters
cin.ignore(100, '\n');              // Skip rest of input line
file2.open(fileName);
```

As discussed in Chapter 4, if our file name is contained in a string class object, we still can use the open function, *provided* we use the string class member function named c_str to convert the string to a C string:

```
ifstream inFile;
string   fileName;

cin >> fileName;
inFile.open(fileName.c_str());
```

Comparing these two code segments, you can observe a major advantage of the string class over C strings: A string in a string class object has unbounded length, whereas the length of a C string is bounded by the array size, which is fixed at compile time.

C String Library Routines

Through the header file `cstring`, the C++ standard library provides a large assortment of C string operations. In this section, we discuss three of these library functions: `strlen`, which returns the length of a string; `strcmp`, which compares two strings using the relations less-than, equal, and greater-than; and `strcpy`, which copies one string to another. Here is a summary of `strlen`, `strcmp`, and `strcpy`:

Header File	Function	Function Value	Effect
`<cstring>`	`strlen(str)`	Integer length of `str` (excluding '\0')	Computes length of `str`
`<cstring>`	`strcmp(str1, str2)`	An integer < 0, if `str1` < `str2` The integer 0, if `str1` = `str2` An integer > 0, if `str1` > `str2`	Compares `str1` and `str2`
`<cstring>`	`strcpy(toStr, fromStr)`	Base address of `toStr` (usually ignored)	Copies `fromStr` (including '\0') to `toStr`, overwriting what was there; `toStr` must be large enough to hold the result

The `strlen` function is similar to the `StrLength` function we wrote earlier. It returns the number of characters in a C string prior to the terminating '\0'. Here's an example of a call to the function:

```
#include <cstring>
   ⋮
char subject[] = "Computer Science";

cout << strlen(subject);    // Prints 16
```

The `strcpy` routine is important because aggregate assignment with the = operator is not allowed on C strings. In the following code fragment, we show the wrong way and the right way to perform a string copy.

```
#include <cstring>
   ⋮
char myStr[100];
   ⋮
myStr = "Abracadabra";           // Not legal
strcpy(myStr, "Abracadabra");    // Legal
```

In strcpy's argument list, the destination string is the one on the left, just as an assignment operation transfers data from right to left. It is the caller's responsibility to make sure that the destination array is large enough to hold the result.

The strcpy function is technically a value-returning function; it not only copies one C string to another, but also returns as a function value the base address of the destination array. The reason why the caller would want to use this function value is not at all obvious, and we don't discuss it here. Programmers nearly always ignore the function value and simply invoke strcpy as if it were a void function (as we did above). You may wish to review the special box in Chapter 8 entitled "Ignoring a Function Value."

The strcmp function is used for comparing two strings. The function receives two C strings as parameters and compares them in *lexicographic* order (the order in which they would appear in a dictionary)—the same ordering used in comparing string class objects. Given the function call strcmp(str1, str2), the function returns one of the following int values: a negative integer, if str1 < str2 lexicographically; the value 0, if str1 = str2; or a positive integer, if str1 > str2. The precise values of the negative integer and the positive integer are unspecified. You simply test to see if the result is less than 0, 0, or greater than 0. Here is an example:

```
if (strcmp(str1, str2) < 0)    // If str1 is less than str2 ...
    ⋮
```

We have described only three of the string-handling routines provided by the standard library. These three are the most commonly needed, but there are many more. If you are designing or maintaining programs that use C strings extensively, you should read the documentation on strings for your C++ system.

String Class or C Strings?

When working with string data, should you use a class like string, or should you use C strings? From the standpoints of clarity, versatility, and ease of use, there is no contest. Use a string class. The standard library string class provides strings of unbounded length, aggregate assignment, aggregate comparison, concatenation with the + operator, and so forth.

However, it is still useful to be familiar with C strings. Among the thousands of software products currently in use that are written in C and C++, most (but a declining percentage) use C strings to represent string data. In your next place of employment, if you are asked to modify or upgrade such software, understanding C strings is essential. Additionally, *using* a string class is one thing; *implementing* it is another. Someone must implement the class using a concrete data representation. In your employment, that someone might be you, and the underlying data representation might very well be a C string!

Programming Example

Exam Attendance

Problem   You are the grader for a U.S. government class of 200 students. The instructor has asked you to prepare two lists: students taking an exam and students who have missed it. The catch is that he wants the lists before the exam is over. You decide to write a program for your notebook computer that takes each student's name as the student enters the exam room and prints the lists of absentees and attendees for your instructor.

Input

A list of last names of the students in the class (file `roster`), which was obtained from a
   master list in order of Social Security number
Each student's last name as he or she enters the room (standard input device)
(In this class, there are no duplicate last names.)

Output

A list of those students taking the exam
A list of those students who are absent

Discussion   As each student enters the room, you enter his or her name at the keyboard. Your program scans the list of students for that name and marks that the student is present. When the last student has entered, you can enter a special sentinel name, perhaps "EndData," to signal the program to print the lists.

You can simulate "Mark that the student is present" by maintaining two lists: `notCheckedIn`, which initially contains all the student names, and `thosePresent`, which is initially empty. To mark a student present, delete his or her name from the `notCheckedIn` list and insert it into the `thosePresent` list. After all students have entered the exam room, the two lists contain the names of those absent and those present.

Your program must prepare the initial list of students in `notCheckedIn` from the class roster file, which is ordered by Social Security number. If you enter the names directly from the roster, they will not be in alphabetical order. Does that matter? Yes, in this case it does matter. The size of the class is 200, and the students need to enter the exam room with minimum delay (because most arrive just before the exam starts).

The length of the list and the speed required suggest that a binary search is appropriate. A binary search requires that the list be in sorted order. The names in the input file are not in alphabetical order, so your program must sort them. You can input all the names at once and then sort them using a function like `SelSort`, or you can use an insertion sort, inserting each name into its proper place as it is read. You decide to take the second approach because you can use the `SortedList` class of this chapter directly. This class provides such an `Insert` operation as well as a `BinSearch` operation.

Data Structures and Objects

A `SortedList` object containing names of students not yet checked in (`notCheckedIn`)

A `SortedList` object containing names of students who have checked in (`thosePresent`)

Because our program uses the `SortedList` class, we need

```
#include "slist.h"
```

to insert the appropriate declarations into the program. But we must make sure that `MAX_LENGTH` and `ItemType` in the file `slist.h` are correct for our problem. Our lists should hold up to 200 student names, and the type of each list component is `string`. Thus, we edit `slist.h` as follows:

```
const int MAX_LENGTH = 200;
typedef string ItemType;
```

Then we recompile `slist.cpp` into `slist.obj`. To run our Exam program, we link its object code file with the object code file `slist.obj`.

(The following program is written in ISO/ANSI standard C++. If you are working with pre-standard C++, see the alternate version of the program in the PRE_STD directory of the program disk, available at the publisher's Web site, www.jbpub.com/disks.)

```
//*****************************************************************
// Exam program
// This program compares students who come to take an exam against
// a class roster.  A list of students who took the exam and a list
// of students who missed the exam are printed.
// Assumption: Max. number of student names in roster file is
// MAX_LENGTH, which is defined in slist.h
//*****************************************************************
#include <iostream>
#include <fstream>        // For file I/O
#include <string>         // For string class
#include "slist.h"        // For SortedList class

const string END_DATA = "EndData";      // Sentinel value for
                                        //    student name

void CheckInStudents( SortedList&, SortedList& );
void GetClassRoster( SortedList&, ifstream& );
void OpenForInput( ifstream& );
void Print( SortedList, SortedList );
void ProcessName( string, SortedList&, SortedList& );
```

```
int main()
{
    SortedList notCheckedIn;    // List of students not yet checked in
    SortedList thosePresent;    // List of students present at exam
    ifstream roster;            // Input file to be analyzed

    OpenForInput(roster);
    if ( !roster )
        return 1;

    GetClassRoster(notCheckedIn, roster);
    CheckInStudents(notCheckedIn, thosePresent);
    Print(notCheckedIn, thosePresent);
    return 0;
}


//***********************************************************************

void OpenForInput( /* inout */ ifstream& someFile )     // File to be
                                                        // opened
// Prompts the user for the name of an input file
// and attempts to open the file

{
    .
    .        (Same as in previous chapters)
    .
}


//***********************************************************************

void GetClassRoster(
        /* inout */ SortedList& notCheckedIn,    // List of students
        /* inout */ ifstream&   roster      )    // Roster data file

// Reads the class roster from the data file

// Precondition:
//     notCheckedIn is the empty list
// Precondition:
//     The roster file has been successfully opened for input
//  && The no. of student names in the file <= MAX_LENGTH (defined
//        in slist.h)
```

```
// Postcondition:
//     notCheckedIn contains the student names read from the file

{
    string stuName;       // An input student name

    roster >> stuName;
    while (roster)
    {
        notCheckedIn.Insert(stuName);
        roster >> stuName;
    }
}


//*****************************************************************************

void CheckInStudents(
    /* inout */ SortedList& notCheckedIn,    // List of students
    /* inout */ SortedList& thosePresent )   // List of students

// Inputs student names from standard input,
// marking students present

// Precondition:
//     notCheckedIn contains names of all students in class
//  && thosePresent is empty
// Postcondition:
//     The user has been repeatedly prompted to enter student names
//  && thosePresent contains all the valid input names
//  && notCheckedIn contains all student names except the valid
//        input names
//  && For all input names not found in the notCheckedIn list,
//        an error message has been printed

{
    string stuName;     // Name of student who is checking in

    cout << "Enter last name: ";
    cin >> stuName;
    while (stuName != END_DATA)
    {
        ProcessName(stuName, notCheckedIn, thosePresent);
        cout << "Enter last name: ";
        cin >> stuName;
    }
}
```

```
//*********************************************************************

void ProcessName(
        /* in */      string      stuName,      // Input student name
        /* inout */ SortedList& notCheckedIn,   // List of students
        /* inout */ SortedList& thosePresent )  // List of students

// Searches for stuName in the notCheckedIn list.  If stuName
// is found, it is inserted into thosePresent and deleted from
// notCheckedIn.  Otherwise, an error message is printed.

// Precondition:
//      stuName is assigned
// Postcondition:
//      IF stuName is in notCheckedIn@entry
//          stuName is in thosePresent
//       && stuName is not in notCheckedIn
//      ELSE
//          An error message has been printed

{
    if (notCheckedIn.IsPresent(stuName))
    {
        thosePresent.Insert(stuName);
        notCheckedIn.Delete(stuName);
    }
    else
        cout << "Name not on roster." << endl;
}


//*********************************************************************

void Print( /* in */ SortedList notCheckedIn,    // List of students
            /* in */ SortedList thosePresent )   // List of students

// Prints the names of those taking the exam, then the names
// of those who are absent

// Postcondition:
//      Contents of thosePresent and notCheckedIn have been printed

{
    cout << endl << "The following students are taking the exam."
        << endl;
    thosePresent.Print();
```

```
cout << endl << "The following students have missed the exam."
    << endl;
notCheckedIn.Print();
}
```

Testing   The list manipulation operations `Insert`, `Delete`, `IsPresent`, and `Print` must be tested with different sized lists: an empty list, a one-item list, a list of maximum length, and several sizes in between. The `IsPresent` routine must be tested by searching for items that are in the list, items that are not in the list, at least one item that compares less than the first item in the list, at least one item that compares greater than the last item in the list, the last item, and the first item.

In testing the overall logic of the program, names read from the keyboard must be spelled incorrectly as well as correctly. The following data represents a sample data set.

Roster File

```
Dale
MacDonald
Weems
Vitek
Westby
Smith
Jamison
Jones
Kirshen
Gleason
Thompson
Ripley
Lilly
Headington
```

Copy of the Screen During the Run

```
Input file name: roster.dat
Enter last name: Weems
Enter last name: Dale
Enter last name: McDonald
Name not on roster.
Enter last name: MacDonald
Enter last name: Vitek
Enter last name: Westby
Enter last name: Gleason
Enter last name: EndData
```

```
The following students are taking the exam.
Dale
Gleason
MacDonald
Vitek
Weems
Westby

The following students have missed the exam.
Headington
Jamison
Jones
Kirshen
Lilly
Ripley
Smith
Thompson
```

Testing and Debugging

In this chapter, we have discussed, designed, and coded algorithms to construct and manipulate items in a list. In addition to the basic list operations IsFull, IsEmpty, Length, and Print, the algorithms included two sequential searches, a binary search, insertion into sorted and unsorted lists, deletion from sorted and unsorted lists, and a selection sort. We have already tested SortedList::Insert, SortedList::Delete, and SortedList::BinSearch in conjunction with the Programming Example. Now we need to test the other searching algorithms and the functions List::Insert, List::Delete, and List::SelSort. We can use the same scheme that we used to test BinSearch to test the other search algorithms. We should test List::Insert, List::Delete, and List::SelSort with lists containing no components, one component, two components, MAX_LENGTH − 1 components, and MAX_LENGTH components.

When we wrote the precondition that the list was not full for operation List::Insert, we indicated that we could handle the problem another way—we could include an error flag in the function's parameter list. The function would call IsFull and set the error flag. The insertion would not take place if the error flag were set to true. Both options are acceptable ways of handling the problem. The important point is that we clearly state whether the calling code or the called function is to check for the error condition. However, it is the calling code that must decide what to do when an error condition occurs. In other words, if errors are handled by means of preconditions, then the user must write the code to guarantee the preconditions. If errors are handled by flags, then the user must write the code to monitor the error flags.

Testing and Debugging Hints

1. Review the Testing and Debugging Hints for Chapter 12. They apply to all one-dimensional arrays, including C strings.

2. Make sure that every C string is terminated with the null character. String constants are automatically null-terminated by the compiler. On input, the >> operator and the `get` function automatically add the null character. If you store characters into a C string individually or manipulate the array in any way, be sure to account for the null character.

3. Remember that C++ treats C string initialization (in a declaration) as different from C string assignment. Initialization is allowed, but assignment is not.

4. Aggregate input/output is allowed for C strings but not for other array types.

5. If you use the >> operator to input into a C string variable, be sure the array is large enough to hold the null character plus the longest sequence of (nonwhitespace) characters in the input stream.

6. With C string input, the >> operator stops at, *but does not consume,* the first trailing whitespace character. Likewise, if the `get` function stops reading early because it encounters a newline character, the newline character is not consumed.

7. When you use the `strcpy` library function, ensure that the destination array is at least as large as the array from which you are copying.

8. General-purpose functions (such as ADT operations) should be tested outside the context of a particular program, using a test driver.

9. Choose test data carefully so that you test all end conditions and some in the middle. End conditions are those that reach the limits of the structure used to store them. For example, in a list, there should be test data in which the number of components is 0, 1, and MAX_LENGTH, as well as between 1 and MAX_LENGTH.

Summary

This chapter has provided practice in working with lists stored in one-dimensional arrays. We have examined algorithms that insert, delete, search, and sort data stored in a list, and we have written functions to implement these algorithms. We can use these functions again and again in different contexts because they are members of general-purpose C++ classes (List and SortedList) that represent list ADTs.

C strings are a special case of char arrays in C++. The last significant character must be followed by a null character to mark the end of the string. C strings are less versatile than a string class. However, it pays to understand how they work because many existing programs in C and C++ use them, and string classes often use C strings as the underlying data representation.

Quick Check

1. The following code fragment implements the "Delete, if it's there" meaning for the Delete operation in an unsorted list. Change it so that the other meaning is implemented; that is, there is a precondition that the item *is* in the list. (pp. 552–554)

```
index = 0;
while (index < length && item != data[index])
    index++;
if (index < length)
{                                       // Remove item
    data[index] = data[length-1];
    length--;
}
```

2. In a sequential search of an unsorted array of 1000 values, what is the average number of loop iterations required to find a value? What is the maximum number of iterations? (p. 569)

3. The following program fragment sorts list items into ascending order. Change it to sort into descending order. (pp. 555–558)

```
for (passCount = 0; passCount < length - 1; passCount++)
{
    minIndx = passCount;
    for (searchIndx = passCount + 1; searchIndx < length;
                                        searchIndx++)
        if (data[searchIndx] < data[minIndx])
            minIndx = searchIndx;
    temp = data[minIndx];                // Swap
    data[minIndx] = data[passCount];
    data[passCount] = temp;
}
```

4. Describe how the `SortedList::Insert` operation can be used to build a sorted list from unsorted input data. (pp. 561–564)
5. Describe the basic principle behind the binary search algorithm. (pp. 565–568)
6. Using Typedef, define an array data type for a C string of up to 15 characters plus the null character. Declare an array variable of this type, initializing it to your first name. Then use a library function to replace the contents of the variable with your last name (up to 15 characters). (pp. 572–580)

Answers

1.
```
index = 0;
while (item != data[index])
    index++;
data[index] = data[length-1];
length--;
```

2. The average number is 500.5 iterations. The maximum is 1000 iterations. 3. The only required change is to replace the < symbol in the inner loop with a >. As a matter of style, the name `minIndx` should be changed to `maxIndx`. 4. The list initially has a length of 0. Each time a data value is read, insertion adds the value to the list in its correct position. When all the data values have been read, they are in the array in sorted order. 5. The binary search takes advantage of sorted list values, looking at a component in the middle of the list and deciding whether the search value precedes or follows the midpoint. The search is then repeated on the appropriate half, quarter, eighth, and so on, of the list until the value is located.

6.
```
typedef char String15[16];

String15 name = "Anna";

strcpy(name, "Rodriguez");
```

Exam Preparation Exercises

1. What three factors should you consider when you are deciding which search algorithm to use on a list?
2. The following values are stored in an array in ascending order.

   28 45 97 103 107 162 196 202 257

   Applying function `List::IsPresent` to this array, search for the following values and indicate how many comparisons are required to either find the number or find that it is not in the list.

   a. 28
   b. 32
   c. 196
   d. 194
3. Repeat Exercise 2, applying the algorithm for a sequential search in a sorted list (page 564).
4. The following values are stored in an array in ascending order.

   29 57 63 72 79 83 96 104 114 136

   Apply function `SortedList::BinSearch` with item = 114 to this list, and trace the values of `first`, `last`, and `middle`. Indicate any undefined values with a *U*.
5. A binary search is always better to use than a sequential search. (True or False?)
6. a. Using Typedef, define a data type `NameType` for a C string of at most 40 characters plus the null character.
   b. Declare a variable `oneName` to be of type `NameType`.
   c. Declare `employeeName` to be a 100-element array whose elements are C strings of type `NameType`.

7. Given the declarations

```
typedef char NameString[21];
typedef char WordString[11];

NameString firstName;
NameString lastName;
WordString word;
```

mark the following statements valid or invalid. (Assume the header file cstring has been included.)

a.
```
i = 0;
while (firstName[i] != '\0')
{
    cout << firstName[i];
    i++;
}
```

b. `cout << lastName;`

c.
```
if (firstName == lastName)
    n = 1;
```

d.
```
if (strcmp(firstName, lastName) == 0)
    m = 8;
```

e. `cin >> word;`

f. `lastName = word;`

g.
```
if (strcmp(NameString, "Hi") < 0)
    n = 3;
```

h.
```
if (firstName[2] == word[5])
    m = 4;
```

8. Given the declarations

```
typedef char String20[21];
typedef char String30[31];

String20 rodent;
String30 mammal;
```

write code fragments for the following tasks. (If the task is not possible, say so.)

a. Store the string "Moose" into mammal.

b. Copy whatever string is in rodent into mammal.

c. If the string in mammal is greater than "Opossum" lexicographically, increment a variable count.

d. If the string in mammal is less than or equal to "Jackal", decrement a variable count.

e. Store the string "Grey-tipped field shrew" into rodent.

f. Print the length of the string in rodent.

9. Given the declarations

```
const int NUMBER_OF_BOOKS = 200;

typedef char BookName[31];
typedef char PersonName[21];

BookName    bookOut[NUMBER_OF_BOOKS];
PersonName  borrower[NUMBER_OF_BOOKS];
BookName    bookIn;
PersonName  name;
```

mark the following statements valid or invalid. (Assume the header file cstring has been included.)

a. `cout << bookIn;`
b. `cout << bookOut;`
c. `for (i = 0; i < NUMBER_OF_BOOKS; i++)`
   `     cout << bookOut[i] << endl;`
d. `if (bookOut[3] > bookIn)`
   `     cout << bookIn;`
e. `for (i = 0; i < NUMBER_OF_BOOKS; i++)`
   `     if (strcmp(bookIn, bookOut[i]) == 0)`
   `          cout << bookIn << ' ' << borrower[i] << endl;`
f. `bookIn = "Don Quixote";`
g. `cout << name[2];`

10. Write code fragments to perform the following tasks, using the declarations given in Exercise 9. Assume that the books listed in bookOut have been borrowed by the person listed in the corresponding position of borrower.

    a. Write a code fragment to print each book borrowed by name.
    b. Write a code fragment to count the number of books borrowed by name.
    c. Write a code fragment to count the number of copies of bookIn that have been borrowed.
    d. Write a code fragment to count the number of copies of bookIn that have been borrowed by name.

11. The Exam program uses a binary search to search the student list. Assuming a list of 200 students, how many loop iterations are required to determine that a student is absent? How many iterations would be required if we had used the algorithm for a sequential search of a sorted list instead of BinSearch?

Programming Warm-up Exercises

1. Write a C++ Boolean function named Exclusive that has three parameters: item (of type ItemType), list1, and list2 (both of type List as defined in this chapter). The function returns true if item is present in either list1 or list2 but not both.

2. To this chapter's `List` class, we wish to add a value-returning member function named `Occurrences` that receives a single parameter, `item`, and returns the number of times `item` occurs in the list. Write the function definition as it would appear in the implementation file.

3. Repeat Exercise 2 for the `SortedList` class.

4. To this chapter's `List` class, we wish to add a Boolean member function named `GreaterFound` that receives a single parameter, `item`, and searches the list for a value greater than `item`. If such a value is found, the function returns `true`; otherwise, it returns `false`. Write the function definition as it would appear in the implementation file.

5. Repeat Exercise 4 for the `SortedList` class.

6. The `SortedList::Insert` function inserts items into the list in ascending order. Rewrite it so that it inserts items in descending order.

7. Rewrite the `SortedList::Delete` function so that it removes all occurrences of `item` from the list.

8. Modify function `SortedList::BinSearch` so that `position` is where `item` should be inserted when `found` is `false`.

9. Rewrite function `SortedList::Insert` so that it implements the first insertion algorithm discussed for sorted lists. That is, the place where the item should be inserted is found by searching from the beginning of the list. When the place is found, all the items from the insertion point to the end of the list are shifted down one position. (Assume that `BinSearch` has been modified as in Exercise 8.) Write the function definition as it would appear in the implementation file.

10. To the `SortedList` class, we wish to add a member function named `Component` that returns a component of the list if a given position number (`pos`) is in the range 0 through `length` − 1. The function should also return a Boolean flag named `valid` that is `false` if `pos` is outside this range. Write the function definition as it would appear in the implementation file.

11. To the `SortedList` class, we wish to add a Boolean member function named `Equal` that has a single parameter named `otherList`, which is an object of type `SortedList`. This function compares two lists for equality: the one represented by `otherList` and the one represented by the class object for which the function is called. The function returns `true` if the two lists are of the same length and each element in one list equals the corresponding element in the other list. Here is an example of a call to the `Equal` function:

```
if (myList.Equal(yourList))
    ⋮
```

Assume the `Component` function of Exercise 10 has been added as a member of the `SortedList` class. Write the function definition as it would appear in the implementation file.

12. The Exam program assumes that the students have unique last names. Rewrite the program so that it accommodates duplicate last names. Assume now that each line in the `roster` file contains a student's first and last names, with last name first.

13. The Exam program uses an insertion sort, placing each student's name into its proper place in the list as it is input. How would you rewrite the program to input all the names at once and then sort them using `SelSort`?

Programming Problems

1. A company wants to know the percentages of total sales and total expenses attributable to each salesperson. Each person has a pair of data lines. The first line contains his or her name, last name first. The second line contains his or her sales (`int`) and expenses (`float`). Write a program that produces a report with a header line containing the total sales and total expenses. Following this header should be a table with each salesperson's name, percentage of total sales, and percentage of total expenses, sorted by salesperson's name.

   Use one of the list classes developed in this chapter, modifying it as follows. `ItemType` should be a `struct` type that holds one salesperson's information. Therefore, the list is a list of structs. Some member functions of the list class must be modified to accommodate this `ItemType`. For example, comparisons involving list components must be changed to comparisons involving *members* of list components (which are structs). Also, include a `Component` member function in your list class (see Programming Warm-up Exercise 10) to allow the client code to access components of the list.

2. Only authorized shareholders are allowed to attend a stockholders' meeting. Write a program to read a person's name from the keyboard, check it against a list of shareholders, and print a message saying whether or not the person may attend the meeting. The list of shareholders is in a file `inFile` in the following format: first name, blank, last name. Use the end-of-file condition to stop reading the file. The maximum number of shareholders is 1000.

   The user should be prompted to enter his or her name in the same format as is used for the data in the file. If the name does not appear on the list, the program should repeat the instructions on how to enter the name and then tell the user to try again. A message saying that the person may not enter should be printed only after he or she has been given a second chance to enter the name. The prompt to the user should include the message that a *Q* should be entered to end the program.

3. Enhance the program in Problem 2 as follows:
   a. Print a report showing the number of stockholders at the time of the meeting, how many were present at the meeting, and how many people who tried to enter were denied permission to attend.
   b. Follow this summary report with a list of the names of the stockholders, with either *Present* or *Absent* after each name.

4. An advertising company wants to send a letter to all its clients announcing a new fee schedule. The clients' names are on several different lists in the company. The various lists are merged to form one file, `clientNames`, but obviously, the company does not want to send a letter twice to anyone.

Write a program that removes any names appearing on the list more than once. On each line of data, there is a four-digit code number, followed by a blank and then the client's name. For example, Amalgamated Steel is listed as

```
0231 Amalgamated Steel
```

Your program is to output each client's code and name, but no duplicates should be printed.

Use one of the list classes developed in this chapter, modifying it as follows. ItemType should be a `struct` type that holds one company's information. Therefore, the list is a list of structs. Some member functions of the list class must be modified to accommodate this ItemType. For example, comparisons involving list components must be changed to comparisons involving *members* of list components (which are structs).

Object-Oriented
Software Development

- To be able to distinguish between structured (procedural) programming and object-oriented programming.

- To be able to define the characteristics of an object-oriented programming language.

- To be able to create a new C++ class from an existing class by using inheritance.

- To be able to create a new C++ class from an existing class by using composition.

- To be able to distinguish between static and dynamic binding of operations to objects.

- To be able to apply the object-oriented design methodology to solve a problem.

- To be able to take an object-oriented design and code it in C++.

In Chapter 11, we defined the notion of an abstract data type (ADT) and used the C++ class mechanism to incorporate both data and operations into a single data type. In that chapter and Chapter 13, we saw how an object of a given class maintains its own private data and is manipulated by calling its public member functions.

In this chapter, we examine how classes and objects can be used to guide the entire software development process. Although the design phase precedes the implementation phase in the development of software, we reverse the order of presentation in this chapter. We begin with *object-oriented programming*, a topic that includes design but is more about implementation issues. We describe the basic principles, terminology, and programming language features associated with the object-oriented approach. After presenting these fundamental concepts, we look more closely at the design phase—*object-oriented design*.

14.1 Object-Oriented Programming

Until now, we have used functional decomposition (also called *structured design*), in which we decompose a problem into modules, where each module is a self-contained collection of steps that solves one part of the overall problem. The process of implementing a functional decomposition is often called **structured** (or **procedural**) **programming**. Some modules are translated directly into a few programming language instructions, whereas others are coded as functions with or without arguments. The end result is a program that is a collection of interacting functions (see Figure 14-1). Throughout

Structured (procedural) programming The construction of programs that are collections of interacting functions or procedures.

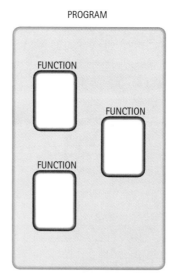

PROGRAM

FUNCTION

FUNCTION

FUNCTION

Figure 14-1 *Program Resulting from Structured (Procedural) Programming*

structured design and structured programming, data is considered a passive quantity to be acted upon by control structures and functions.

In building large software systems, structured design has two important limitations. First, the technique yields an inflexible structure. If the top-level algorithm requires modification, the changes may force many lower-level algorithms to be modified as well. Second, the technique does not lend itself easily to code reuse. By *code reuse* we mean the ability to use pieces of code—either as they are or adapted slightly—in other sections of the program or in other programs. It is rare to be able to take a complicated C++ function and reuse it easily in a different context.

A methodology that often works better for creating large software systems is object-oriented design (OOD), which we introduced briefly in Chapter 4. OOD decomposes a problem into objects—self-contained entities composed of data and operations on the data. The process of implementing an object-oriented design is called **object-oriented programming (OOP)**. The end result is a program that is a collection of interacting objects (see Figure 14-2). In OOD and OOP, data plays a leading role; the primary contribution of algorithms is to implement the operations on objects.

Object-oriented programming (OOP) The use of data abstraction, inheritance, and dynamic binding to construct programs that are collections of interacting objects.

PROGRAM

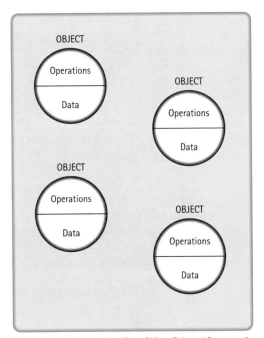

Figure 14-2 *Program Resulting from Object-Oriented Programming*

Several programming languages have been created specifically to support OOD and OOP: C++, Java, Smalltalk, Simula, CLOS, Objective-C, Eiffel, Actor, Object-Pascal, recent versions of Turbo Pascal, and others. These languages, called *object-oriented programming languages*, have facilities for

1. Data abstraction
2. Inheritance
3. Dynamic binding

You have already seen that C++ supports data abstraction through the class mechanism. Some non-OOP languages also have facilities for data abstraction. But only OOP languages support the other two concepts—*inheritance* and *dynamic binding*. Before we define these two concepts, we discuss some of the fundamental ideas and terminology of object-oriented programming.

14.2 Objects

The major principles of OOP originated as far back as the mid-1960s with a language called Simula. However, much of the current terminology of OOP is due to Smalltalk, a language developed in the late 1970s at Xerox's Palo Alto Research Center. In OOP, the term *object* has a very specific meaning: It is a self-contained entity encapsulating data and operations on the data. In other words, an object represents an instance of an ADT. More specifically, an object has an internal *state* (the current values of its private data, called *instance variables*), and it has a set of *methods* (public operations). Methods are the only means by which an object's state can be inspected or modified by another object. An object-oriented program consists of a collection of objects, communicating with one another by *message passing*. If object A wants object B to perform some task, object A sends a message containing the name of the object (B, in this case) and the name of the particular method to execute. Object B responds by executing this method in its own way, possibly changing its state and sending messages to other objects as well.

As you can tell, an object is quite different from a traditional data structure. A C++ struct is a passive data structure that contains only data and is acted upon by a program. In contrast, an object is an active data structure; the data and the code that manipulates the data are bound together within the object. In OOP jargon, an object knows how to manipulate itself.

The vocabulary of Smalltalk has influenced the vocabulary of OOP. The literature of OOP is full of phrases such as "methods," "instance variables," and "sending a message to." Here are some OOP terms and their C++ equivalents:

OOP	C++
Object	Class object or class instance
Instance variable	Private data member
Method	Public member function
Message passing	Function call (to a public member function)

In C++, we define the properties and behavior of objects by using the class mechanism. Within a program, classes can be related to each other in various ways. The three most common relationships are as follows:

1. Two classes are independent of each other and have nothing in common.
2. Two classes are related by *inheritance*.
3. Two classes are related by *composition*.

The first relationship—none—is not very interesting. Let's look at the other two—inheritance and composition.

14.3 Inheritance

In the world at large, it is often possible to arrange concepts into an *inheritance hierarchy*—a hierarchy in which each concept inherits the properties of the concept immediately above it in the hierarchy. For example, we might classify different kinds of vehicles according to the inheritance hierarchy in Figure 14-3. Moving down the hierarchy, each kind of vehicle is more specialized than its *parent* (and all of its *ancestors*)

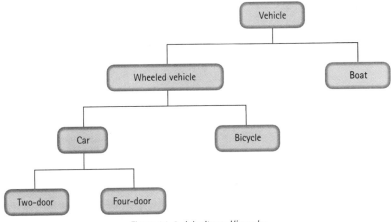

Figure 14-3 *Inheritance Hierarchy*

and is more general than its *child* (and all of its *descendants*). A wheeled vehicle inherits properties common to all vehicles (it holds one or more people and carries them from place to place) but has an additional property that makes it more specialized (it has wheels). A car inherits properties common to all wheeled vehicles but also has additional, more specialized properties (four wheels, an engine, a body, and so forth).

The inheritance relationship can be viewed as an *is-a relationship*. Every two-door car is a car, every car is a wheeled vehicle, and every wheeled vehicle is a vehicle.

Inheritance A mechanism by which one class acquires the properties—the data and operations—of another class.

Base class (superclass) The class being inherited from.

Derived class (subclass) The class that inherits.

In OOP languages, **inheritance** is the mechanism by which one class acquires the properties of another class. You can take an existing class A (called the **base class** or **superclass**) and create from it a new class B (called the **derived class** or **subclass**). The derived class B inherits all the properties of its base class A. In particular, the data and operations defined for A are now also defined for B. (Notice the is-a relationship—every B is also an A.) The idea, next, is to specialize class B, usually by adding specific properties to those already inherited from A. Let's look at an example in C++.

Deriving One Class from Another

Suppose that someone has already written a Time class with the following specification, abbreviated by omitting the preconditions and postconditions:

```
class Time
{
public:
    void Set( /* in */ int hours,
              /* in */ int minutes,
              /* in */ int seconds );
    void Increment();
    void Write() const;
    Time( /* in */ int initHrs,        // Constructor
          /* in */ int initMins,
          /* in */ int initSecs );
    Time();                            // Default constructor,
private:                               //    setting time to 0:0:0
    int hrs;
    int mins;
    int secs;
};
```

This class is the same as our TimeType class of Chapter 11, simplified by omitting the Equal and LessThan member functions. Figure 14-4 displays a *class interface diagram* for the Time class. The public interface, shown as ovals in the side of the large circle, consists of the operations available to client code. The private data items shown in the interior are inaccessible to clients.

Suppose that we want to modify the `Time` class by adding, as private data, a variable of an enumeration type indicating the (American) time zone—EST for Eastern Standard Time, CST for Central Standard Time, MST for Mountain Standard Time, PST for Pacific Standard Time, EDT for Eastern Daylight Time, CDT for Central Daylight Time, MDT for Mountain Daylight Time, or PDT for Pacific Daylight Time. We'll need to modify the `Set` function and the class constructors to accommodate a time zone value. And the `Write` function should print the time in the form

```
12:34:10 CST
```

The `Increment` function, which advances the time by one second, does not need to be changed.

To add these time zone features to the `Time` class, the conventional approach would be to obtain the source code found in the `time.cpp` implementation file, analyze in detail how the class is implemented, then modify and recompile the source code. This process has several drawbacks. If `Time` is an off-the-shelf class on a system, the source code for the implementation is probably unavailable. Even if it is available, modifying it may introduce bugs into a previously debugged solution. Access to the source code also violates a principal benefit of abstraction: Users of an abstraction should not need to know how it is implemented.

In C++, there is a far quicker and safer way in which to add time zone features: Use inheritance. Let's derive a new class from the `Time` class and then specialize it. This

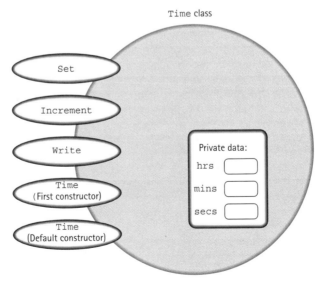

Figure 14-4 *Class Interface Diagram for* `Time` *Class*

new, extended time class—call it `ExtTime`—inherits the members of its base class, `Time`. Here is the declaration of `ExtTime`:

```
enum ZoneType {EST, CST, MST, PST, EDT, CDT, MDT, PDT};

class ExtTime : public Time
{
public:
    void Set( /* in */ int      hours,
              /* in */ int      minutes,
              /* in */ int      seconds,
              /* in */ ZoneType timeZone );
    void Write() const;
    ExtTime( /* in */ int      initHrs,      // Constructor
             /* in */ int      initMins,
             /* in */ int      initSecs,
             /* in */ ZoneType initZone );

    ExtTime();                                // Default constructor,
                                              //   setting time to
private:                                      //   0:0:0 EST
    ZoneType zone;
};
```

The opening line

```
class ExtTime : public Time
```

states that `ExtTime` is derived from `Time`. The reserved word `public` declares `Time` to be a *public base class* of `ExtTime`. This means that all public members of `Time` (except constructors) are also public members of `ExtTime`. In other words, `Time`'s member functions `Set`, `Increment`, and `Write` can also be invoked for `ExtTime` objects.* However, the public part of `ExtTime` specializes the base class by reimplementing (redefining) the inherited functions `Set` and `Write` and by providing its own constructors.

The private part of `ExtTime` declares that a new private member is added: `zone`. The private members of `ExtTime` are therefore `hrs`, `mins`, `secs` (all inherited from

---

*If a class declaration omits the word `public` and begins as

`class DerivedClass : BaseClass`

or if it explicitly uses the word `private`,

`class DerivedClass : private BaseClass`

then `BaseClass` is called a *private base class* of `DerivedClass`. Public members of `BaseClass` are *not* public members of `DerivedClass`. That is, clients of `DerivedClass` cannot invoke `BaseClass` operations on `DerivedClass` objects. We do not work with private base classes in this book.

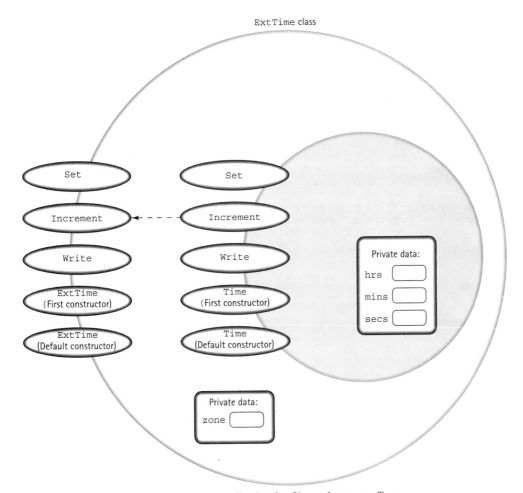

Figure 14-5 *Class Interface Diagram for* ExtTime *Class*

Time), and zone. Figure 14-5 pictures the relationship between the ExtTime and Time classes.

This diagram shows that each ExtTime object has a Time object as a *subobject.* Every ExtTime is a Time, and more. C++ uses the terms *base class* and *derived class* instead of *superclass* and *subclass.* The terms *superclass* and *subclass* can be confusing because the prefix *sub-* usually implies something smaller than the original (for example, a subset of a mathematical set). In contrast, a subclass is often "bigger" than its superclass—that is, it has more data and/or functions.

In Figure 14-5, you see an arrow between the two ovals labeled Increment. Because Time is a public base class of ExtTime, and because Increment is not redefined by ExtTime, the Increment function available to clients of ExtTime is the same as the one inherited from Time. We use the arrow between the corresponding ovals to indicate this fact. (Notice in the diagram that Time's constructors are operations on Time, not on ExtTime. The ExtTime class must have its own constructors.)

Inheritance and Accessibility

With C++, it is important to understand that inheritance does not imply accessibility. Although a derived class inherits the members of its base class, both private and public, it cannot access the private members of the base class. Figure 14-5 shows the variables hrs, mins, and secs to be encapsulated within the Time class. Neither external client code nor ExtTime member functions can refer to these three variables directly. If a derived class were able to access the private members of its base class, any programmer could derive a class from another and then write code to directly inspect or modify the private data, defeating the benefits of encapsulation and information hiding.

Specification of the ExtTime Class

Below is the fully documented specification of the ExtTime class. Notice that the preprocessor directive

```
#include "time.h"
```

is necessary for the compiler to verify the consistency of the derived class with its base class.

```
//***********************************************************************
// SPECIFICATION FILE (exttime.h)
// This file gives the specification of an ExtTime abstract data
// type.  The Time class is a public base class of ExtTime, so
// public operations of Time are also public operations of ExtTime.
//***********************************************************************
#include "time.h"

enum ZoneType {EST, CST, MST, PST, EDT, CDT, MDT, PDT};

class ExtTime : public Time
{
public:
    void Set( /* in */ int       hours,
              /* in */ int       minutes,
              /* in */ int       seconds,
              /* in */ ZoneType timeZone );
        // Precondition:
        //     0 <= hours <= 23  &&  0 <= minutes <= 59
        //  && 0 <= seconds <= 59  &&  timeZone is assigned
```

```
    // Postcondition:
    //      Time is set according to the incoming parameters

  void Write() const;
    // Postcondition:
    //      Time has been output in the form HH:MM:SS ZZZ
    //      where ZZZ is the time zone

  ExtTime( /* in */ int      initHrs,
           /* in */ int      initMins,
           /* in */ int      initSecs,
           /* in */ ZoneType initZone );
    // Precondition:
    //      0 <= initHrs <= 23  &&  0 <= initMins <= 59
    //   && 0 <= initSecs <= 59  &&  initZone is assigned
    // Postcondition:
    //      Class object is constructed
    //   && Time is set according to the incoming parameters

  ExtTime();
    // Postcondition:
    //      Class object is constructed
    //   && Time is 0:0:0 Eastern Standard Time
private:
  ZoneType zone;
};
```

With this new class, the programmer can set the time with a time zone (via a class constructor or the redefined Set function), output the time with its time zone (via the redefined Write function), and increment the time by one second (via the inherited Increment function):

```
// Client code:

#include "exttime.h"
   ⋮
ExtTime time1(8, 35, 0, PST);
ExtTime time2;                    // Default constructor called

time2.Write();                    // Outputs 0:0:0 EST
cout << endl;

time2.Set(16, 49, 23, CDT);
time2.Write();                    // Outputs 16:49:23 CDT
cout << endl;
```

```
time1.Increment();
time1.Increment();
time1.Write();                          // Outputs 08:35:02 PST
cout << endl;
    ⋮
```

Implementation of the `ExtTime` Class

The implementation of the `ExtTime` class needs to deal only with the new features that are different from `Time`. Specifically, we must write code to redefine the `Set` and `Write` functions and we must write the two constructors.

With derived classes, constructors are subject to special rules. At run time, the base class constructor is implicitly called first, before the body of the derived class's constructor executes. Additionally, if the base class constructor requires arguments, these arguments must be passed by the derived class's constructor. To see how these rules pertain, let's examine the implementation file `exttime.cpp` (see Figure 14-6).

Figure 14-6 *ExtTime Implementation File*

```
//*********************************************************************
// IMPLEMENTATION FILE (exttime.cpp)
// This file implements the ExtTime member functions.
// The Time class is a public base class of ExtTime
//*********************************************************************
#include "exttime.h"
#include <iostream>
#include <string>

using namespace std;

// Additional private members of class:
//      ZoneType zone;


//*********************************************************************


ExtTime::ExtTime( /* in */ int      initHrs,
                  /* in */ int      initMins,
                  /* in */ int      initSecs,
                  /* in */ ZoneType initZone )

     : Time(initHrs, initMins, initSecs)

// Constructor
```

(continued)

Figure 14-6 *(continued)*

```
// Precondition:
//     0 <= initHrs <= 23  &&  0 <= initMins <= 59
//  && 0 <= initSecs <= 59  &&  initZone is assigned
// Postcondition:
//     Time is set according to initHrs, initMins, and initSecs
//     (via call to base class constructor)
//  && zone == initZone

{
    zone = initZone;
}

//*******************************************************************


ExtTime::ExtTime()

// Default constructor

// Postcondition:
//     Time is 0:0:0 (via implicit call to base class's
//     default constructor)
//  && zone == EST

{
    zone = EST;
}

//*******************************************************************


void ExtTime::Set( /* in */ int      hours,
                   /* in */ int      minutes,
                   /* in */ int      seconds,
                   /* in */ ZoneType timeZone )

// Precondition:
//     0 <= hours <= 23  &&  0 <= minutes <= 59
//  && 0 <= seconds <= 59  &&  timeZone is assigned
// Postcondition:
//     Time is set according to hours, minutes, and seconds
//  && zone == timeZone
```

(continued)

Figure 14-6 *(continued)*

```
{
    Time::Set(hours, minutes, seconds);
    zone = timeZone;
}

//*********************************************************************

void ExtTime::Write() const

// Postcondition:
//     Time has been output in the form HH:MM:SS ZZZ
//     where ZZZ is the time zone

{
    static string zoneString[8] =
    {
        "EST", "CST", "MST", "PST", "EDT", "CDT", "MDT", "PDT"
    };

    Time::Write();
    cout << ' ' << zoneString[zone];
}
```

In the first constructor in Figure 14-6, notice the syntax by which a constructor passes arguments to its base class constructor:

```
ExtTime::ExtTime( /* in */ int      initHrs,
                  /* in */ int      initMins,
                  /* in */ int      initSecs,
                  /* in */ ZoneType initZone )

    : Time(initHrs, initMins, initSecs)      ←  Constructor initializer

{
    zone = initZone;
}
```

After the parameter list to the ExtTime constructor (but before its body), you insert what is called a *constructor initializer*—a colon and then the name of the base class along with the arguments to *its* constructor. When an ExtTime object is created with a declaration such as

```
ExtTime time1(8, 35, 0, PST);
```

the `ExtTime` constructor receives four arguments. The first three are simply passed along to the `Time` class constructor by means of the constructor initializer. After the `Time` class constructor has executed (creating the base class subobject as shown in Figure 14-5), the body of the `ExtTime` constructor executes, setting `zone` equal to the fourth argument.

The second constructor in Figure 14-6 (the default constructor) does not need a constructor initializer; there are no arguments to pass to the base class's default constructor. When an `ExtTime` object is created with the declaration

```
ExtTime time2;
```

the `ExtTime` class's default constructor first implicitly calls `Time`'s default constructor, after which its body executes, setting `zone` to `EST`.

Next, look at the `Set` function in Figure 14-6. This function reimplements the `Set` function inherited from the base class. Consequently, there are two distinct `Set` functions, one a public member of the `Time` class, the other a public member of the `Ext-Time` class. Their full names are `Time::Set` and `ExtTime::Set`. In Figure 14-6, the `ExtTime::Set` function begins by "reaching up" into its base class and calling `Time::Set` to set the hours, minutes, and seconds. (Remember that a class derived from `Time` cannot access the private data `hrs`, `mins`, and `secs` directly; these variables are private to the `Time` class.) The function then finishes by assigning a value to `ExtTime`'s private data, the `zone` variable.

The `Write` function in Figure 14-6 uses a similar strategy. It reaches up into its base class and invokes `Time::Write` to output the hours, minutes, and seconds. Then it outputs a string corresponding to the time zone. (Recall that a value of enumeration type cannot be output directly in C++. If we were to print the value of `zone` directly, the output would be an integer from 0 through 7—the internal representations of the `Zone-Type` values.) The `Write` function establishes an array of eight strings and selects the correct string by using `zone` to index into the array. Why is `zoneString` declared to be `static`? Remember that by default, local variables in C++ are automatic variables—that is, memory is allocated for them when the function begins execution and is deallocated when the function returns. With `zoneString` declared as `static`, the array is allocated once only, when the program begins execution, and remains allocated until the program terminates. From function call to function call, the computer does not waste time creating and destroying the array.

Now we can compile the file `exttime.cpp` into an object code file, say, `ext-time.obj`. After writing a test driver and compiling it into `test.obj`, we obtain an executable file by linking three object files:

1. `test.obj`

2. `exttime.obj`

3. `time.obj`

We can then test the resulting program.

The remarkable thing about derived classes and inheritance is that modification of the base class is unnecessary. The source code for the implementation of the Time class may be unavailable. Yet variations of this ADT can continue to be created without that source code, in ways the creator never even considered. Through classes and inheritance, OOP languages facilitate code reuse. A class such as Time can be used as-is in many different contexts, or it can be adapted to a particular context by using inheritance. Inheritance allows us to create *extensible* data abstractions—a derived class typically extends the base class by including additional private data or public operations or both.

Avoiding Multiple Inclusion of Header Files

We saw that the specification file exttime.h begins with an #include directive to insert the file time.h:

```
#include "time.h"

enum ZoneType {EST, CST, MST, PST, EDT, CDT, MDT, PDT};

class ExtTime : public Time
{
    ⋮
};
```

Now think about what happens if a programmer using the ExtTime class already has included time.h for other purposes, overlooking the fact that exttime.h also includes it:

```
#include "time.h"
#include "exttime.h"
```

The preprocessor inserts the file time.h, then exttime.h, and then time.h a second time (because exttime.h also includes time.h). The result is a compile-time error, because the Time class is defined twice.

The widely used solution to this problem is to write time.h this way:

```
#ifndef TIME_H
#define TIME_H
class Time
{
    ⋮
};
#endif
```

The lines beginning with "#" are directives to the preprocessor. TIME_H (or any identifier you wish to use) is a preprocessor identifier, not a C++ program identifier. In effect, these directives say:

If the preprocessor identifier TIME_H is not already defined, then

  1. define TIME_H as an identifier known to the preprocessor,

and

  2. let the declaration of the Time class pass through to the compiler.

If a subsequent #include "time.h" is encountered, the test #ifndef TIME_H will fail. The Time class declaration will not pass through to the compiler a second time.

14.4 Composition

Earlier we said that two classes typically exhibit one of the following relationships: They are independent of each other, they are related by inheritance, or they are related by **composition**. Composition (or **containment**) is the relationship in which the internal data of one class A includes an object of another class B. Stated another way, a B object is contained within an A object.

> **Composition (containment)**   A mechanism by which the internal data (the state) of one class includes an object of another class.

C++ does not have (or need) any special language notation for composition. You simply declare an object of one class to be one of the data members of another class. Let's look at an example.

Design of a TimeCard Class

You are developing a program to manage a factory's payroll. Employees are issued time cards containing their ID numbers. When reporting for work, an employee "punches in" by inserting the card into a clock, which punches the current time onto the card. When leaving work, the employee takes a new card and "punches out" to record the departure time. For your program, you decide that you need a TimeCard ADT to represent an employee's time card. The abstract data consists of an ID number and a time. The abstract operations include Punch the Time, Print the Time Card Data, constructor operations, and others. To implement the ADT, you must choose a concrete data representation for the abstract data and you must implement the operations. Assuming an employee ID number is a large integer value, you choose the long data type to represent the ID number. To represent time, you remember that one of your friends has already written and debugged a Time class (we'll use the one from earlier in this chapter). At this point, you create a TimeCard class declaration as follows:

```
#include "time.h"
  ⋮
class TimeCard
{
```

```
public:
    void Punch( /* in */ int hours,
                /* in */ int minutes,
                /* in */ int seconds );
    void Print() const;
     ⋮
    TimeCard( /* in */ long idNum,
              /* in */ int  initHrs,
              /* in */ int  initMins,
              /* in */ int  initSecs );
    TimeCard();
private:
    long id;
    Time timeStamp;
};
```

In designing the `TimeCard` class, you have used composition; a `TimeCard` object is composed of a `Time` object (and a `long` variable). Composition creates a *has-a relationship*—a `TimeCard` object *has a* `Time` object as a subobject (see Figure 14-7).

Implementation of the `TimeCard` Class

The private data of `TimeCard` consists of a `long` variable named `id` and a `Time` object named `timeStamp`. The `TimeCard` member functions can manipulate `id` by using ordinary built-in operations, but they must manipulate `timeStamp` through the member functions defined for the `Time` class. For example, you could implement the `Print` and `Punch` functions as follows:

```
void TimeCard::Print() const
{
    cout << "ID: "  << id << " Time: " ;
    timeStamp.Write();
}


void TimeCard::Punch( /* in */ int hours,
                      /* in */ int minutes,
                      /* in */ int seconds )
{
    timeStamp.Set(hours, minutes, seconds);
}
```

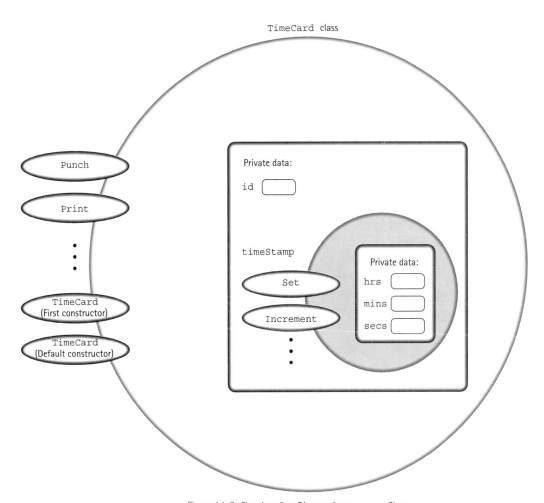

Figure 14-7 *Class Interface Diagram for* TimeCard *Class*

Implementing the class constructors is a bit more complicated to describe. Let's start with an implementation of the first constructor shown in the TimeCard class declaration:

```
TimeCard::TimeCard( /* in */ long idNum,
                    /* in */ int  initHrs,
                    /* in */ int  initMins,
                    /* in */ int  initSecs )
```

```
    : timeStamp(initHrs, initMins, initSecs)     ← Constructor initializer

{
    id = idNum;
}
```

This is the second time we've seen the unusual notation—the constructor initializer—inserted between the parameter list and the body of a constructor. The first time was when we implemented the parameterized `ExtTime` class constructor (Figure 14-6). There, we used the constructor initializer to pass some of the incoming arguments to the base class constructor. Here, we use a constructor initializer to pass some of the arguments to a member object's (`timeStamp`'s) constructor. Whether you are using inheritance or composition, the purpose of a constructor initializer is the same: to pass arguments to another constructor. The only difference is the following: With inheritance, you specify the name of the *base class* prior to the argument list, as follows.

```
ExtTime::ExtTime( /* in */ int       initHrs,
                  /* in */ int       initMins,
                  /* in */ int       initSecs,
                  /* in */ ZoneType  initZone )

    : Time(initHrs, initMins, initSecs)
```

With composition, you specify the name of the *member object* prior to the argument list:

```
TimeCard::TimeCard( /* in */ long idNum,
                    /* in */ int  initHrs,
                    /* in */ int  initMins,
                    /* in */ int  initSecs )

    : timeStamp(initHrs, initMins, initSecs)
```

Furthermore, if a class has several members that are objects of classes with parameterized constructors, you form a list of constructor initializers separated by commas:

```
SomeClass::SomeClass( ... )

    : memberObject1(arg1, arg2), memberObject2(arg3)
```

Having discussed both inheritance and composition, we can give a complete description of the order in which constructors are executed:

Given a class X, if X is a derived class, its base class constructor is executed first. Next, constructors for member objects (if any) are executed. Finally, the body of X's constructor is executed.

When a `TimeCard` object is created, the constructor for its `timeStamp` member is first invoked. After the `timeStamp` object is constructed, the body of `TimeCard`'s constructor is executed, setting the `id` member equal to `idNum`.

The second constructor shown in the `TimeCard` class declaration—the default constructor—has no parameters and could be implemented as follows:

```
TimeCard::TimeCard()
{
    id = 0;
}
```

In this case, what happened to construction of the `timeStamp` member object? We didn't include a constructor initializer, so the `timeStamp` object is first constructed using the *default* constructor of the `Time` class, after which the body of the `TimeCard` constructor is executed. The result is a time card having a time stamp of 0:0:0 and an ID number of 0.

14.5 Dynamic Binding and Virtual Functions

Early in the chapter, we said that object-oriented programming languages provide language features that support three concepts: data abstraction, inheritance, and dynamic binding. The phrase *dynamic binding* means, more specifically, *dynamic binding of an operation to an object.* To explain this concept, let's begin with an example.

Given the `Time` and `ExtTime` classes of this chapter, the following code creates two class objects and outputs the time represented by each.

```
Time    startTime(8, 30, 0);
ExtTime endTime(10, 45, 0, CST);

startTime.Write();
cout << endl;
endTime.Write();
cout << endl;
```

This code fragment invokes two different `Write` functions, even though the functions appear to have the same name. The first function call invokes the `Write` function of the `Time` class, printing out three values: hours, minutes, and seconds. The second call invokes the `Write` function of the `ExtTime` class, printing out four values: hours, minutes, seconds, and time zone. In this code fragment, the compiler uses **static** (compile-time) **binding** of the operation (`Write`) to the appropriate object. The compiler can easily determine which `Write` function to call by checking the data type of the associated object.

> **Static binding** The compile-time determination of which function to call for a particular object.

In some situations, the compiler cannot determine the type of an object, and the binding of an operation to an object must occur at run time. One situation, which we look at now, involves passing class objects as arguments.

The basic C++ rule for passing class objects as arguments is that the argument and its corresponding parameter must be of identical type. With inheritance, though, C++ relaxes the rule. You may pass an object of a child class *C* to an object of its parent class *P*, but not the other way around—that is, you cannot pass an object of type *P* to an object of type *C*. More generally, you can pass an object of a descendant class to an object of any of its ancestor classes. This rule has a tremendous benefit—it allows us to write a single function that applies to any descendant class instead of writing a different function for each. For example, we could write a fancy `Print` function that takes as an argument an object of type `Time` or any class descended from `Time`:

```
void Print( /* in */ Time someTime )
{
    cout << "*************************" << endl;
    cout << "** The time is ";
    someTime.Write();
    cout << endl;
    cout << "*************************" << endl;
}
```

Given the code fragment

```
Time    startTime(8, 30, 0);
ExtTime endTime(10, 45, 0, CST);

Print(startTime);
Print(endTime);
```

the compiler lets us pass either a `Time` object or an `ExtTime` object to the `Print` function. Unfortunately, the output is not what we would like. When `endTime` is printed, the time zone `CST` is missing from the output. Let's see why.

The Slicing Problem

Our `Print` function uses passing by value for the parameter `someTime`. Passing by value sends a copy of the argument to the parameter. Whenever you pass an object of a child class to an object of its parent class using a pass by value, only the data members they have in common are copied. Remember that a child class is often "larger" than its parent—that is, it contains additional data members. For example, a `Time` object has three data members (`hrs`, `mins`, and `secs`), but an `ExtTime` object has four data members (`hrs`, `mins`, `secs`, and `zone`). When the larger class object is copied to the smaller parameter using a pass by value, the extra data members are discarded or "sliced off." This situation is called the *slicing problem* (see Figure 14-8).

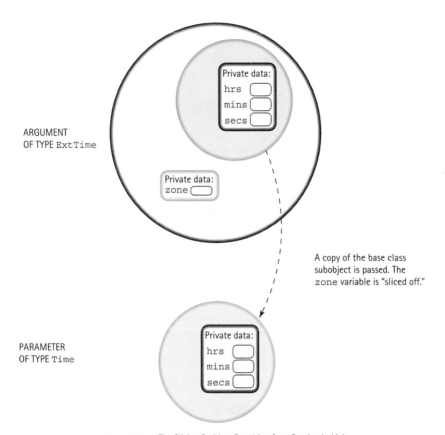

ARGUMENT
OF TYPE ExtTime

A copy of the base class
subobject is passed. The
zone variable is "sliced off."

PARAMETER
OF TYPE Time

Figure 14-8 *The Slicing Problem Resulting from Passing by Value*

(The slicing problem also occurs with assignment operations. In the statement

```
parentClassObject = childClassObject;
```

only the data members that the two objects have in common are copied. Additional data members contained in childClassObject are not copied.)

With passing by reference, the slicing problem does not occur because the *address* of the caller's argument is sent to the function. Let's change the heading of our Print function so that someTime is a reference parameter:

```
void Print( /* in */ Time& someTime )
```

Now when we pass endTime as the argument, its address is sent to the function. Its time zone member is not sliced off because no copying takes place. But to our dismay, the Print function *still* prints only three of endTime's data members—hours, minutes, and seconds.

Within the Print function, the difficulty is that static binding is used in the statement

```
someTime.Write();
```

The compiler must generate machine language code for the Print function at compile time, but the type of the actual argument (Time or ExtTime) isn't known until run time. How can the compiler know which Write function to use—Time::Write or ExtTime::Write? The compiler cannot know, so it uses Time::Write because the parameter someTime is of type Time. Therefore, the Print function always prints just three values—hours, minutes, and seconds—regardless of the type of the argument. Fortunately, C++ provides a very simple solution to our problem: *virtual functions.*

Virtual Functions

Suppose we make one small change to our Time class declaration: We begin the declaration of the Write function with the reserved word virtual.

```
class Time
{
public:
    ⋮
    virtual void Write() const;
    ⋮
private:
    ⋮
};
```

Dynamic binding The run-time determination of which function to call for a particular object.

Declaring a member function to be virtual instructs the compiler to generate code that guarantees **dynamic (run-time) binding** of a function to an object. That is, the determination of which function to call is postponed until run time. (Note that to make Write a virtual function, the word virtual appears in one place only—the Time class declaration. It does not appear in the Write function definition that is located in the time.cpp file, nor does it appear in any descendant class—such as ExtTime—that redefines the Write function.)

Virtual functions work in the following way. If a class object is passed *by reference* to some function, and if the body of that function contains a statement

```
param.MemberFunc( ... );
```

then

1. If `MemberFunc` is not a virtual function, the type of the *parameter* determines which function to call. (Static binding is used.)
2. If `MemberFunc` is a virtual function, the type of the *argument* determines which function to call. (Dynamic binding is used.)

With just one word—`virtual`—the difficulties we encountered with our `Print` function disappear entirely. If we declare `Write` to be a virtual function in the `Time` class, the function

```
void Print( /* in */ Time& someTime )
{
    ⋮
    someTime.Write();
    ⋮
}
```

works correctly for arguments either of type `Time` or of type `ExtTime`. The correct `Write` function (`Time::Write` or `ExtTime::Write`) is invoked because the argument carries the information necessary at run time to choose the appropriate function. Deriving a new and unanticipated class from `Time` presents no complications. If this new class redefines the `Write` function, then our `Print` function still works correctly. Dynamic binding ensures that each object knows how to print itself, and the appropriate version will be invoked. In OOP terminology, `Write` is a **polymorphic operation**—an operation that has multiple meanings depending on the type of the object to which it is bound at run time.

Polymorphic operation An operation that has multiple meanings depending on the type of the object to which it is bound at run time.

Here are some things to know about using virtual functions in C++:

1. To obtain dynamic binding, you must use passing by reference when passing a class object to a function. If you use passing by value, the compiler does not use the `virtual` mechanism; instead, member slicing and static binding occur.
2. In the declaration of a virtual function, the word `virtual` appears only in the base class, not in any derived class.
3. If a base class declares a virtual function, it *must* implement that function, even if the body is empty.
4. A derived class is not required to provide its own reimplementation of a virtual function. In this case, the base class's version is used by default.
5. A derived class cannot redefine the function return type of a virtual function.

14.6 Object-Oriented Design

We have looked at language features that let us implement an object-oriented design. Now let's turn to the phase that precedes implementation—OOD itself.

A computer program usually models some real-life activity or concept. A banking program models the real-life activities associated with a bank. A spreadsheet program models a real spreadsheet, a large paper form used by accountants and financial planners. A robotics program models human perception and human motion.

Nearly always, the aspect of the world that we are modeling (the *application domain* or *problem domain*) consists of objects—checking accounts, bank tellers, spreadsheet rows, spreadsheet columns, robot arms, robot legs. The computer program that solves the real-life problem also includes objects (the *solution domain*)—counters, lists, menus, windows, and so forth. OOD is based on the philosophy that programs are easier to write and understand if the major objects in a program correspond closely to the objects in the problem domain.

There are many ways in which to perform object-oriented design. Different authors advocate different techniques. Our purpose is not to choose one particular technique or to present a summary of all the techniques. Rather, our purpose is to describe a three-step process that captures the essence of OOD:

1. Identify the objects and operations.
2. Determine the relationships among objects.
3. Design the driver.

In this section, we do not show a complete example of an object-oriented design of a problem solution—we save that for the Programming Example at the end of the chapter. Instead, we describe the important issues involved in each of the three steps.

Step 1: Identify the Objects and Operations

Recall that structured design (functional decomposition) begins with identification of the major actions the program is to perform. In contrast, OOD begins by identifying the major objects and the associated operations on those objects. In both design methods, it is often difficult to see where to start.

To identify solution-domain objects, a good way to start is to look at the problem domain. More specifically, go to the problem definition and look for important nouns and verbs. The nouns (and noun phrases) may suggest objects; the verbs (and verb phrases) may suggest operations. For example, the problem definition for a banking program might include the following sentences:

... The program must handle a customer's savings account. The customer is allowed to deposit funds into the account and withdraw funds from the account, and the bank must pay interest on a quarterly basis. ...

In these sentences, the key nouns are

Savings account
Customer

and the key verb phrases are

Deposit funds
Withdraw funds
Pay interest

Although we are working with a very small portion of the entire problem definition, the list of nouns suggests two potential objects: `savingsAccount` and `customer`. The operations on a `savingsAccount` object are suggested by the list of verb phrases—namely, `Deposit`, `Withdraw`, and `PayInterest`. What are the operations on a `customer` object? We would need more information from the rest of the problem definition in order to answer this question. In fact, `customer` may not turn out to be a useful object at all. The nouns-and-verbs technique is only a starting point—it points us to *potential* objects and operations.

Determining which nouns and verbs are significant is one of the most difficult aspects of OOD. There are no cookbook formulas for doing so, and there probably never will be. Not all nouns become objects, and not all verbs become operations. The nouns-and-verbs technique is imperfect, but it does give us a first approximation to a solution.

The solution domain includes not only objects drawn from the problem domain but also *implementation-level* objects. These are objects that do not model the problem domain but are used in building the program itself. In systems with graphical user interfaces—Microsoft Windows or the Macintosh operating system, for example—a program may need several kinds of implementation-level objects: window objects, menu objects, objects that respond to mouse clicks, and so on. Objects such as these are often available in class libraries so that we don't need to design and implement them from scratch each time we need them in different programs.

Step 2: Determine the Relationships Among Objects

After selecting potential objects and operations, the next step is to examine the relationships among the objects. In particular, we want to see whether certain objects might be related either by inheritance or by composition. Inheritance and composition relationships not only pave the way for code reuse—as we emphasized in our discussion of OOP—but also simplify the design and allow us to model the problem domain more accurately. For example, the banking problem may require several kinds of savings accounts—one for general customers, another for preferred customers, and another for children under the age of 12. If these are all variations on a basic savings account, the is-a relationship (and, therefore, inheritance) is probably appropriate. Starting with a `SavingsAccount` class that provides operations common to any savings account, we could design each of the other accounts as a child class of `SavingsAccount`, concentrating our efforts only on the properties that make each one different from the parent class.

Sometimes the choice between inheritance and composition is not immediately clear. Earlier we wrote a `TimeCard` class to represent an employee's time card. Given an existing `Time` class, we used composition to relate `TimeCard` and `Time`—the private part of the `TimeCard` class was composed of a `Time` object (and an ID number). We could also have used inheritance. We could have derived class `TimeCard` from `Time` (inheriting the hours, minutes, and seconds members) and then specialized it by adding an extra data member (the ID number) and the extra operations of `Punch`, `Print`, and so forth. Both inheritance and composition give us four private data members: hours, minutes, seconds, and ID number. However, the use of inheritance means that all of the `Time` operations are also valid for `TimeCard` objects. A user of the `TimeCard` class could—either intentionally or accidentally—invoke operations such as `Set` and `Increment`, which are not appropriate operations on a time card. Furthermore, inheritance leads to a confused design in this example. It is not true that a `TimeCard` *is a* `Time`; rather, a `TimeCard` *has a* `Time` (and an ID number). In general, the best design strategy is to use inheritance for is-a relationships and composition for has-a relationships.

Step 3: Design the Driver

The final step is to design the driver—the top-level algorithm. In OOD, the driver is the glue that puts the objects (along with their operations) together. When implementing the design in C++, the driver becomes the `main` function.

Notice that structured design *begins* with the design of the top-level algorithm, whereas OOD *ends* with the top-level algorithm. In OOD, most of the control flow has already been designed in Steps 1 and 2; the algorithms are located within the operations on objects. As a result, the driver often has very little to do but process user commands or input some data and then delegate tasks to various objects.

The Iterative Nature of Object-Oriented Design

Software developers, researchers, and authors have proposed many different strategies for performing OOD. Common to nearly all of these strategies are three fundamental steps:

1. Identify the objects and operations.
2. Determine the relationships among objects.
3. Design the driver.

Experience with large software projects has shown that these three steps are not necessarily sequential—Step 1, Step 2, Step 3, then we are done. In practice, Step 1 occurs first, but only as a first approximation. During Steps 2 and 3, new objects or operations may be discovered, leading us back to Step 1 again. It is realistic to think of Steps 1 through 3 not as a sequence but as a loop.

Furthermore, each step is an iterative process within itself. Step 1 may entail working and reworking our view of the objects and operations. Similarly, Steps 2 and 3 often involve experimentation and revision. In any step, we may conclude that a potential object is not useful after all. Or we might decide to add or eliminate operations on a particular object.

There is always more than one way to solve a problem. Iterating and reiterating through the design phase leads to insights that produce a better solution.

14.7 Implementing the Design

In OOD, when we first identify an object, it is an *abstract object*. We do not immediately choose an exact data representation for that object. Similarly, the operations on objects begin as *abstract operations*, because there is no initial attempt to provide algorithms for these operations.

Eventually, we have to implement the objects and operations. For each abstract object, we must

- Choose a suitable data representation.
- Create algorithms for the abstract operations.

To select a data representation for an object, the C++ programmer has three options:

1. Use a built-in data type.
2. Use an existing ADT.
3. Create a new ADT.

For a given object, a good rule of thumb is to consider these three options in the order listed. A built-in type is the most straightforward to use and understand, and operations on these types are already defined by the language. If a built-in type is not adequate to represent an object, you should survey available ADTs in a class library (either the system's or your own) to see if any are a good match for the abstract object. If no suitable ADT exists, you must design and implement a new ADT to represent the object.

Fortunately, even if you must resort to Option 3, the mechanisms of inheritance and composition allow you to combine Options 2 and 3. When we needed an ExtTime class earlier in the chapter, we used inheritance to build on an existing Time class. And when we created a TimeCard class, we used composition to include a Time object in the private data.

In addition to choosing a data representation for the abstract object, we must implement the abstract operations. With OOD, the algorithms that implement the abstract operations are often short and straightforward. We have seen numerous examples in this chapter and in Chapters 11 and 13 in which the code for ADT operations is only a few lines long. But this is not always the case. If an operation is extremely complex, it may be best to treat the operation as a new problem and use functional decomposition on the control flow. In this situation, it is appropriate to apply both functional decomposition and object-oriented methodologies together. Experienced programmers are familiar with both methodologies and use them either independently or in combination with each other. However, the software development community is becoming increasingly convinced that although functional decomposition is important for designing low-level algorithms and operations on ADTs, the future in developing huge software systems lies in OOD and OOP.

Programming Example

Time Card Lookup

Problem In this chapter, we talked about a factory that is computerizing its employee time card information. Work on the software has already begun, and you have been hired to join the effort. Each morning after the employees have punched in, the time card data (ID number and time stamp) for all employees is written to a file named `punchInFile`. Your task is to write a program that inputs the data from this file and allows the user to look up the time stamp (punch-in time) for any employee. The program should prompt the user for an ID number, look up that employee's time card information, and print it out. This interactive lookup process is repeated until the user types a negative number for the employee ID. The factory has, at most, 500 employees. If `punchInFile` contains more than 500 time cards, the excess time cards should be ignored and a warning message printed.

Input Employee time card information (file stream `punchInFile`) and a sequence of employee ID numbers to be looked up (standard input device).

Each line in `punchInFile` contains an employee's ID number (`long` integer) and the time he or she punched in (three integers—hours, minutes, and seconds):

```
246308 7 45 50
129336 8 15 29
```

The end-of-file condition signals the end of the input data.

Interactive input from the user consists of employee ID numbers, entered one at a time in response to a prompt. A negative ID number signals the end of the interactive input.

Output For each employee ID that is input from the user, the corresponding time at which the employee punched in (or a message if the program cannot find a time card for the employee).

Below is a sample of the run-time dialogue. The user's input is highlighted.

```
Enter an employee ID (negative to quit): 129336
ID: 129336 Time: 08:15:29

Enter an employee ID (negative to quit): 222000
222000 has not punched in yet.

Enter an employee ID (negative to quit): -3
```

Discussion We begin our design by identifying objects and their associated operations. The best place to start is by examining the problem domain. In object-oriented fashion, we search for important nouns and noun phrases in the problem definition. Here is a list of candidate objects (potential objects):

Factory
Employee
File `punchInFile`
ID number
Time card
Time stamp (punch-in time)
User

Reviewing this list, we conclude that the first two candidates and the last—factory, employee, and user—are probably not objects in the solution domain. In the problem we are to solve, these candidates have no useful properties or interesting operations. Thus, we pare down our list of potential objects to the following:

File `punchInFile`
ID number
Time card
Time stamp

To determine operations on these objects, we look for significant verb phrases in the problem definition. Here are some possibilities:

Punch a time card
Input data from the file
Look up time card information
Print out time card information
Input an employee ID

To associate these operations with the appropriate objects, let's make an *object table* as follows:

Object	Operation
File `punchInFile`	Input data from the file
ID number	Input an employee ID
Time card	Punch a time card, Look up time card information, Print out time card information
Time stamp	—

Analyzing the object table, we see that something is not quite right. "Look up time card information" is not an operation on a single time card—it's more properly an operation that applies to a *collection* of time cards. We're missing an object that represents a list of time cards. That is, the program should read all the time cards from the data file and store them into a list. From this list, our program can look up the time card that matches a particular employee ID. Notice that this new object—the time card list—is an implementation-level object rather than a problem-domain object. This object is not readily apparent in the problem domain, yet we need it in order to design and implement the program.

Another thing we notice in the object table is the absence of any operations on the time stamp object. A little thought should convince us that this object simply represents the time of day. As with the `Time` class we discussed in this chapter, suitable operations might be to set the time and to print the time.

Here is a revised object table that includes the time card list object and refines the operations that might be suitable for each object:

Object	Operation
File `punchInFile`	Open the file, Input data from the file
ID number	Input an employee ID, Print an employee ID
Time card	Set the ID number on a time card, Inspect the ID number on a time card, Punch the time stamp on a time card, Inspect the time stamp on a time card, Print the time card information
Time card list	Read all time cards into the list, Look up time card information
Time stamp	Set the time of day, Print the time

The second major step in OOD is to determine the relationships among the objects. Specifically, we're looking for inheritance and composition relationships. Our object table does not reveal any inheritance relationships. Using *is-a* as a guide, we cannot say that a time card is a kind of time stamp or vice versa, that a time card list is a kind of time card or vice versa, and so on. However, we find several composition relationships. Using *has-a* as a guide, we see that a time card has a time stamp as part of its state, a time card has an ID number as part of its state, and a time card list has several time cards as part of its state (see Figure 14-9). Discovery of these relationships helps us to further refine the design (and implementation) of the objects.

Now that we have determined a reasonable set of objects and operations, let's look at each object in detail. Keep in mind that the decisions we have made are not necessarily final. Remember that OOD is an iterative process, characterized by experimentation and revision.

The `punchInFile` Object This object represents an ordinary kind of input file with the ordinary operations of opening the file and reading from the file. No further design of this object is necessary. To implement the object, the obvious choice for a data representation is the `ifstream` class supplied by the C++ standard library. The `ifstream` class provides operations for opening and reading from a file, so we don't need to implement these operations ourselves.

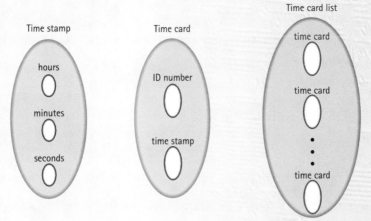

Figure 14-9 *Composition Relationships Among Objects*

The ID Number Object   This object merely represents an integer number (possibly large), and the only abstract operations we have identified are input and output. Therefore, the built-in long type is the most straightforward data representation. To implement the abstract operations of input and output, we can simply use the << and >> operators.

The Time Stamp Object   The time stamp object represents a time of day. There is no built-in type we can use as a data representation, but we can use an existing class—the Time class we worked with earlier in the chapter. The complete specification of the Time class appears below.

```
//******************************************************************
// SPECIFICATION FILE (time.h)
// This file gives the specification of a Time abstract data type
//******************************************************************
#ifndef TIME_H
#define TIME_H

class Time
{
public:
    void Set( /* in */ int hours,
              /* in */ int minutes,
              /* in */ int seconds );
```

```
                    // Precondition:
                    //      0 <= hours <= 23   && 0 <= minutes <= 59
                    //   && 0 <= seconds <= 59
                    // Postcondition:
                    //      Time is set according to the incoming parameters

            void Increment();
                    // Postcondition:
                    //      Time has been advanced by one second, with
                    //      23:59:59 wrapping around to 0:0:0

            void Write() const;
                    // Postcondition:
                    //      Time has been output in the form HH:MM:SS

        Time( /* in */ int initHrs,
              /* in */ int initMins,
              /* in */ int initSecs );
                    // Precondition:
                    //      0 <= initHrs <= 23   && 0 <= initMins <= 59
                    //   && 0 <= initSecs <= 59
                    // Postcondition:
                    //      Class object is constructed
                    //   && Time is set according to the incoming parameters

        Time();
                    // Postcondition:
                    //      Class object is constructed  && Time is 0:0:0
    private:
        int hrs;
        int mins;
        int secs;
    };
    #endif
```

(We surround the code with the preprocessor directives)

```
    #ifndef TIME_H
    #define TIME_H
        ⋮
    #endif
```

to prevent multiple inclusion of the Time class declaration in cases where a new class is created from Time by inheritance or composition. You may wish to review the section "Avoiding Multiple Inclusion of Header Files" in this chapter.)

You have already seen the implementations of the Time class member functions. They are the same as in the TimeType class of Chapter 11.

By declaring a time stamp object to be of type `Time`, we can simply implement our time stamp operations as calls to the `Time` class member functions:

```
Time timeStamp;

timeStamp.Set(hours, minutes, seconds);
timeStamp.Write();
```

Notice that the abstract operations we listed for a time stamp do not include an increment operation. Should we rewrite the `Time` class to eliminate the `Increment` function? No. Wherever possible, we want to reuse existing code. Let's use the `Time` class as it exists. The presence of the `Increment` function does no harm. We simply have no need to invoke it on behalf of a time stamp object.

Testing Testing the `Time` class amounts to testing each of its member functions. In the Testing and Debugging section of Chapter 11, we described at length how to test a similar class, `TimeType`. `Time` is identical to `TimeType` except for the absence of two member functions, `Equal` and `LessThan`.

The Time Card Object A time card object represents a pair of values: an employee ID number and a time stamp. The abstract operations are those we listed in our object table. There is no built-in type or existing C++ class that we can use directly to represent a time card, so we'll design a new class. (We sketched a `TimeCard` class earlier in the chapter, but it was not complete.)

Here is a possible specification of the class. Notice that we have added a new operation that did not appear in our object table: a class constructor.

```
//*********************************************************************
// SPECIFICATION FILE (timecard.h)
// This file gives the specification of a TimeCard ADT
//*********************************************************************
#ifndef TIMECARD_H
#define TIMECARD_H

#include "time.h"

class TimeCard
{
public:
    void Punch( /* in */ int hours,
                /* in */ int minutes,
                /* in */ int seconds );
      // Precondition:
      //     0 <= hours <= 23  &&  0 <= minutes <= 59
```

```
    //    && 0 <= seconds <= 59
    // Postcondition:
    //       Time is punched according to the incoming parameters

void SetID( /* in */ long idNum );
    // Precondition:
    //       idNum is assigned
    // Postcondition:
    //       ID number on the time card is idNum

long IDPart() const;
    // Postcondition:
    //       Function value == ID number on the time card

Time TimePart() const;
    // Postcondition:
    //       Function value == time stamp on the time card

void Print() const;
    // Postcondition:
    //       Time card has been output in the form
    //          ID: 235658 Time: 08:14:25

TimeCard();
    // Postcondition:
    //       Class object is constructed with an ID number of 0
    //       and a time of 0:0:0
private:
    long id;
    Time timeStamp;
};
#endif
```

The private part of this class declaration shows very clearly the composition relationship we proposed earlier—namely, that a time card object is composed of an ID number object and a time stamp object.

To implement the abstract operations on a time stamp, we must implement the Time-Card class member functions. Earlier in the chapter, we showed how to implement the constructor, Punch, and Print functions, so we do not repeat the discussion here. Now we must implement SetID, IDPart, and TimePart. These are easy. The body of SetID merely sets the private variable id equal to the incoming parameter, idNum:

```
id = idNum;
```

The body of `IDPart` needs only to return the current value of `id`, and the body of `TimePart` simply returns the current value of the private object `timeStamp`. Here is the implementation file containing the definitions of all the `TimeCard` member functions:

```cpp
//******************************************************************
// IMPLEMENTATION FILE (timecard.cpp)
// This file implements the TimeCard class member functions
//******************************************************************
#include "timecard.h"
#include <iostream>

using namespace std;

// Private members of class:
//     long id;
//     Time timeStamp;


//******************************************************************

TimeCard::TimeCard()

// Default constructor

// Postcondition:
//     Time is 0:0:0 (via implicit call to timeStamp object's
//     default constructor)
//   && id == 0

{
    id = 0;
}

//******************************************************************

void TimeCard::Punch( /* in */ int hours,
                      /* in */ int minutes,
                      /* in */ int seconds )

// Precondition:
//     0 <= hours <= 23  &&  0 <= minutes <= 59
//  && 0 <= seconds <= 59
// Postcondition:
//     Time is punched according to hours, minutes, and seconds
```

```
{
    timeStamp.Set(hours, minutes, seconds);
}

//**********************************************************************

void TimeCard::SetID( /* in */ long idNum )

// Precondition:
//      idNum is assigned
// Postcondition:
//      id == idNum

{
    id = idNum;
}

//**********************************************************************

long TimeCard::IDPart() const

// Postcondition:
//      Function value == id

{
    return id;
}

//**********************************************************************

Time TimeCard::TimePart() const

// Postcondition:
//      Function value == timeStamp

{
    return timeStamp;
}

//**********************************************************************

void TimeCard::Print() const

// Postcondition:
//      Time card has been output in the form
```

```
//        ID: 235658 Time: 08:14:25

{
    cout << "ID: " << id << " Time: ";
    timeStamp.Write();
}
```

Testing   These functions are all very easy to test. Because the `Time` class has already been tested and debugged, the `Punch` function (which calls `Time::Set`) and the `Print` function (which calls `Time::Write`) should work correctly. Also, none of the `TimeCard` member functions use loops or branching, so it is sufficient to write a single test driver that calls each of the member functions, supplying argument values that satisfy the preconditions.

The Time Card List Object   This object represents a list of time cards. Once again, we'll write a new C++ class for this list because no built-in type or existing class will do.

In Chapter 13, we introduced the list as an ADT and examined typical list operations: insert an item into the list, delete an item, report whether the list is full, and so forth. Should we include all these operations when designing our list of time cards? Probably not. It's unlikely that a list of time cards would be considered general-purpose enough to warrant the effort. Let's stick to the operations we listed in the object table:

Read all time cards into the list
Look up time card information

To choose a data representation for the list, let's review the relationships among the objects in our program. We said that the time card list object is composed of time card objects. Therefore, we can use a 500-element array of `TimeCard` class objects to represent the list, along with an integer variable indicating the length of the list (the number of array elements that are actually in use).

Before we write the specification of the `TimeCardList` class, let's review the operations once more. The lookup operation must search the array for a particular time card. Because the array is potentially very large (500 elements), a binary search is better than a sequential search. However, a binary search requires the array elements to be in sorted order. We must either insert each time card into its proper place as it is read from the data file or sort the time cards after they have been read. Chapter 13's Exam Attendance case study used the former approach. For variety, let's take the latter approach and add another operation—a sorting operation. (We'll use the selection sort we developed in Chapter 13.) Finally, we need one more operation to initialize the private data: a class constructor. Here is the resulting class specification:

```
//******************************************************************
// SPECIFICATION FILE (tclist.h)
// This file gives the specification of TimeCardList, an ADT for a
// list of TimeCard objects.
```

```
//***********************************************************************
#ifndef TCLIST_H
#define TCLIST_H

#include "timecard.h"
#include <fstream>

using namespace std;

const int MAX_LENGTH = 500;    // Maximum number of time cards

class TimeCardList
{
public:
    void ReadAll( /* inout */ ifstream& inFile );
        // Precondition:
        //     inFile has been opened for input
        // Postcondition:
        //     List contains at most MAX_LENGTH employee time cards
        //     as read from inFile. (Excess time cards are ignored
        //     and a warning message is printed)

    void SelSort();
        // Postcondition:
        //     List components are in ascending order of employee ID

    void BinSearch( /* in */  long       idNum,
                    /* out */ bool&      found,
                    /* out */ TimeCard&  card  ) const;
        // Precondition:
        //     List components are in ascending order of employee ID
        //  && idNum is assigned
        // Postcondition:
        //     IF time card for employee idNum is in list
        //         found == true  &&  card == time card for idNum
        //     ELSE
        //         found == false  &&  value of card is undefined

    TimeCardList();
        // Postcondition:
        //     Empty list created
```

```
private:
    int       length;
    TimeCard data[MAX_LENGTH];
};
#endif
```

The `BinSearch` function is a little different from the one we presented in Chapter 13. There, it was a private member function that returned the index of the array element where the item was found. Here, `BinSearch` is a public member function that returns the entire time card to the client.

Now we must implement the `TimeCardList` member functions. Let's begin with the class constructor. Remember that when a class X is composed of objects of other classes, the constructors for those objects are executed before the body of X's constructor is executed. When the `TimeCardList` constructor is called, all 500 `TimeCard` objects in the private `data` array are first constructed. These objects are constructed via implicit calls to the `Time-Card` class's default constructor. (Recall from Chapter 12 that an array of class objects is constructed using the class's default constructor, not a parameterized constructor.) After the `data` array elements are constructed, there is nothing left to do but to set the private variable `length` equal to 0:

```
TimeCardList::TimeCardList()

// Postcondition:
//      Each element of data array has an ID number of 0
//      and a time of 0:0:0 (via implicit call to each array
//      element's default constructor)
//   && length == 0

{
    length = 0;
}
```

To implement the `ReadAll` member function, we use a loop that reads each employee's data (ID number and hours, minutes, and seconds of the punch-in time) and stores the data into the next unused element of the `data` array. The loop terminates either when end-of-file occurs or when the length of the array reaches `MAX_LENGTH`. After exiting the loop, we are to print a warning message if more data exists in the file (that is, if end-of-file has not occurred).

The implementation of the `SelSort` member function has to be slightly different from the one we developed in Chapter 13. Remember that `SelSort` finds the minimum value in the list and swaps it with the value in the first place in the list. Then the next-smallest value in the list is swapped with the value in the second place. This process continues until all the values are in order. The location in this algorithm that we must change is where the minimum value is determined. Instead of comparing two time cards in the list (which doesn't make any sense), we compare the *ID numbers* on the time cards. To inspect the ID number on a time card, we use the function `IDPart` provided by the `TimeCard` class. The statement that did the comparison in the original `SelSort` function must be changed from

```
if (data[searchIndx] < data[minIndx])
```

to

```
if (data[searchIndx].IDPart() < data[minIndx].IDPart())
```

We must make a similar change in the `BinSearch` function. The original version in Chapter 13 compared the search item with list components directly. Here, we cannot compare the search item (an ID number of type `long`) with a list component (an object of type `TimeCard`). Again, we must use the `IDPart` function to inspect the ID number on a time card.

Below is the implementation file for the `TimeCardList` class.

```
//*********************************************************************
// IMPLEMENTATION FILE (tclist.cpp)
// This file implements the TimeCardList class member functions.
// List representation: an array of TimeCard objects and an
// integer variable giving the current length of the list
//*********************************************************************
#include "tclist.h"
#include <iostream>

using namespace std;

// Private members of class:
//     int     length;            Current length of list
//     TimeCard data[MAX_LENGTH];    Array of TimeCard objects


//*********************************************************************


TimeCardList::TimeCardList()

// Default constructor

// Postcondition:
//     Each element of data array has an ID number of 0
//     and a time of 0:0:0 (via implicit call to each array
//     element's default constructor)
//     && length == 0

{
    length = 0;
}
```

```
//*************************************************************************

void TimeCardList::ReadAll( /* inout */ ifstream& inFile )

// Precondition:
//     inFile has been opened for input
// Postcondition:
//     data[0..length-1] contain employee time cards as read
//     from inFile
// && 0 <= length <= MAX_LENGTH
// && IF inFile contains more than MAX_LENGTH time cards
//          Warning message has been printed and excess time cards
//          are ignored

{
    long idNum;       // Employee ID number
    int  hours;       // Employee punch-in time
    int  minutes;
    int  seconds;

    inFile >> idNum >> hours >> minutes >> seconds;
    while (inFile && length < MAX_LENGTH)
    {
        data[length].SetID(idNum);
        data[length].Punch(hours, minutes, seconds);
        length++;
        inFile >> idNum >> hours >> minutes >> seconds;
    }
    if (inFile)
        // Assert: inFile is not at end-of-file
        cout << "More than " << MAX_LENGTH << " time cards "
            << "in input file.  Remainder are ignored." << endl;
}


//*************************************************************************

void TimeCardList::SelSort()

// Postcondition:
//     data array contains the same values as data@entry,
//     rearranged into ascending order of employee ID
```

```
    {
        TimeCard temp;          // Used for swapping
        int      passCount;     // Loop control variable
        int      searchIndx;    // Loop control variable
        int      minIndx;       // Index of minimum so far

        for (passCount = 0; passCount < length - 1; passCount++)
        {
            minIndx = passCount;

            // Find the index of the smallest component
            // in data[passCount..length-1]

            for (searchIndx = passCount + 1; searchIndx < length;
                                                        searchIndx++)
                if (data[searchIndx].IDPart() < data[minIndx].IDPart())
                    minIndx = searchIndx;

            // Swap data[minIndx] and data[passCount]

            temp = data[minIndx];
            data[minIndx] = data[passCount];
            data[passCount] = temp;
        }
    }


//***********************************************************************

    void TimeCardList::BinSearch( /* in */  long       idNum,
                                  /* out */ bool&      found,
                                  /* out */ TimeCard& card  ) const

// Precondition:
//     data[0..length-1] are in ascending order of employee ID
//  && idNum is assigned
// Postcondition:
//     IF time card for employee idNum is in list at position i
//         found == true  &&  card == data[i]
//     ELSE
//         found == false  &&  value of card is undefined

    {
        int first = 0;          // Lower bound on list
        int last = length - 1;  // Upper bound on list
        int middle;             // Middle index
```

```
        found = false;
        while (last >= first && !found)
        {
            middle = (first + last) / 2;
            if (idNum < data[middle].IDPart())
                // Assert: idNum is not in data[middle..last]
                last = middle - 1;
            else if (idNum > data[middle].IDPart())
                // Assert: idNum is not in data[first..middle]
                first = middle + 1;
            else
                // Assert: idNum is in data[middle]
                found = true;
        }
        if (found)
            card = data[middle];
}
```

Testing If we step back and think about it, we realize that if we write a test driver for the `TimeCardList` class, we will have written the main driver for the entire program! The big picture is that our program is to read in all the file data (function `ReadAll`), sort the time cards into order (function `SelSort`), and look up the time card information for various employees (function `BinSearch`). Therefore, we defer a discussion of testing until we have looked at the main driver.

The Driver The final step in OOD is to design the driver—the top-level algorithm. As is usually the case in OOD, the driver has very little to do but coordinate the objects that have already been designed.

The PunchIn program showing the implementation of the driver follows. We use

```
#include "timecard.h"
```

to insert the `TimeCard` class declaration into the program, and we use

```
#include "tclist.h"
```

to insert the `TimeCardList` class declaration. (Recall that `tclist.h` also happens to `#include` the header file `timecard.h`. Thus, `timecard.h` gets inserted into our program twice. If we had not used the `#ifndef` directive at the beginning of `timecard.h`, we would now get a compile-time error for declaring the `TimeCard` class twice.)

To run the program, we link its object code file with the object code files `tclist.obj`, `timecard.obj`, and `time.obj`.

(The following program is written in ISO/ANSI standard C++. If you are working with pre-standard C++, see the alternate version of the program in the PRE_STD directory of the program disk, available at the publisher's Web site, www.jbpub.com/disks.)

```cpp
//*********************************************************************
// PunchIn program
// A data file contains time cards for employees who have punched
// in for work.  This program reads in the time cards from the
// input file, then reads employee ID numbers from the standard
// input.  For each ID number, the program looks up the employee's
// punch-in time and displays it to the user
//*********************************************************************
#include <iostream>
#include <fstream>       // For file I/O
#include <string>        // For string class
#include "timecard.h"    // For TimeCard class
#include "tclist.h"      // For TimeCardList class

void GetID( long& );
void OpenForInput( ifstream& );

int main()
{
    ifstream     punchInFile;    // Input file of time cards
    TimeCardList punchInList;    // List of time cards
    TimeCard     punchInCard;    // A single time card
    long         idNum;          // Employee ID number
    bool         found;          // True if idNum found in list

    OpenForInput(punchInFile);
    if ( !punchInFile )
        return 1;

    punchInList.ReadAll(punchInFile);
    punchInList.SelSort();

    GetID(idNum);
    while (idNum >= 0)
    {
        punchInList.BinSearch(idNum, found, punchInCard);
        if (found)
        {
            punchInCard.Print();
            cout << endl;
        }
```

```
        else
            cout << idNum << " has not punched in yet." << endl;
        GetID(idNum);
    }
    return 0;
}
```

```
//*********************************************************************

void OpenForInput( /* inout */ ifstream& someFile )        // File to be
                                                            // opened
// Prompts the user for the name of an input file
// and attempts to open the file

// Postcondition:
//      The user has been prompted for a file name
//   && IF the file could not be opened
//          An error message has been printed
// Note:
//      Upon return from this function, the caller must test
//      the stream state to see if the file was successfully opened

{
    •
    •    (Same as in previous chapters)
    •

}
```

```
//*********************************************************************

void GetID( /* out */ long& idNum )      // Employee ID number

// Prompts for and reads an employee ID number

// Postcondition:
//      idNum == value read from standard input

{
    cout << endl;
    cout << "Enter an employee ID (negative to quit): ";
    cin >> idNum;
}
```

Testing To test this program, we begin by preparing an input file that contains time card information for, say, five employees. The data should be in random order of employee ID to verify that the sorting routine works properly. Using this input file, we run the program and supply the following interactive input: the ID numbers of all five employees in the data file (the program should print their punch-in times), a few ID numbers that are not in the data file (the program should print the message that these employees have not checked in yet), and a negative ID number (the program should quit). If the program tells us that one of the five employees in the data file has not checked in yet or prints a punch-in time for one of the employees not in the data file, the fault clearly lies with the punchInList object—the object responsible for reading the file, sorting, and searching. Using a hand trace, the system debugger, or debug output statements, we should check the TimeCardList member functions in the following order: ReadAll (to verify that the file data was read into the list correctly), SelSort (to confirm that the time card information ends up in ascending order of ID number), then BinSearch (to ensure that items in the list are indeed found and that items not in the list are reported as not there).

One more thing needs to be tested. If the data file contains more than MAX_LENGTH time cards, the ReadAll function should print a warning message and ignore the excess time cards. To test this feature, we obviously don't want to create an input file with over 500 time cards. Instead, we go into tclist.h and change the const definition of MAX_LENGTH from 500 to a more manageable value—3, for example. We then recompile only tclist.cpp and relink all four object code files. When we run the program, it should read only the first three time cards from the file, print a warning message, and work with a list of only three time cards. Here is a sample run of the program using 3 as the value of MAX_LENGTH:

Input File

```
398405 7 45 04
290387 7 48 10
193847 7 53 20
938473 7 55 14
837485 8 00 00
385473 8 05 45
573920 8 12 13
483948 8 14 45
```

Copy of the Screen During the Run

```
Input file name: punchin.dat
More than 3 time cards in input file.  Remainder are ignored.

Enter an employee ID (negative to quit): 398405
ID: 398405 Time: 07:45:04

Enter an employee ID (negative to quit): 193847
ID: 193847 Time: 07:53:20

Enter an employee ID (negative to quit): 290387
ID: 290387 Time: 07:48:10
```

```
Enter an employee ID (negative to quit): 938473
938473 has not punched in yet.

Enter an employee ID (negative to quit): 111111
111111 has not punched in yet.

Enter an employee ID (negative to quit): -5
```

After testing this aspect of the program, we must not forget to change the value of MAX_LENGTH back to 500, recompile `tclist.cpp`, and relink the object code files.

Testing and Debugging

Testing and debugging an object-oriented program is largely a process of testing and debugging the C++ classes on which the program is built. The top-level driver also needs testing, but this testing is usually uncomplicated—OOD tends to result in a simple driver.

To review how to test a C++ class, you should refer back to the Testing and Debugging section of Chapter 11. There we walked through the process of testing each member function of a class.

When an object-oriented program uses inheritance and composition, the order in which you test the classes is, in a sense, predetermined. If class X is derived from class Y or contains an object of class Y, you cannot test X until you have designed and implemented Y. Thus, it makes sense to test and debug the lower-level class (class Y) before testing class X. This chapter's Programming Example demonstrated this sequence of testing. We tested the lowest level class—the Time class—first. Next, we tested the TimeCard class, which contains a Time object. Finally, we tested the TimeCardList class, which contains an array of TimeCard objects. The general principle is that if class X is built on class Y (through inheritance or composition), the testing of X is simplified if Y is already tested and is known to behave correctly.

Testing and Debugging Hints

1. Review the Testing and Debugging Hints for Chapter 11. They apply to the design and testing of C++ classes, which are at the heart of OOP.

2. When using inheritance, don't forget to include the word `public` when declaring the derived class:

```
class DerivedClass : public BaseClass
{
  ⋮
};
```

The word `public` makes `BaseClass` a public base class of `DerivedClass`. That is, clients of `DerivedClass` can apply any public `BaseClass` operation (except constructors) to a `DerivedClass` object.

3. The header file containing the declaration of a derived class must `#include` the header file containing the declaration of the base class.

4. Although a derived class inherits the private and public members of its base class, it cannot directly access the inherited private members.

5. If a base class has a constructor, it is invoked before the body of the derived class's constructor is executed. If the base class constructor requires arguments, you must pass these arguments using a constructor initializer:

```
DerivedClass::DerivedClass( ... )
    : BaseClass(arg1, arg2)
{
  ⋮
}
```

If you do not include a constructor initializer, the base class's default constructor is invoked.

6. If a class has a member that is an object of another class and this member object's constructor requires arguments, you must pass these arguments using a constructor initializer:

```
SomeClass::SomeClass( ... )
    : memberObject(arg1, arg2)
{
  ⋮
}
```

If there is no constructor initializer, the member object's default constructor is invoked.

7. To obtain dynamic binding of an operation to an object when passing class objects as arguments, you must
   - Pass the object by reference, not by value.
   - Declare the operation to be `virtual` in the base class declaration.

8. If a base class declares a virtual function, it *must* implement that function even if the body is empty.

9. A derived class cannot redefine the function return type of a virtual function.

Summary

Object-oriented design (OOD) decomposes a problem into objects—self-contained entities in which data and operations are bound together. In OOD, data is treated as an active, rather than passive, quantity. Each object is responsible for one part of the solution, and the objects communicate by invoking each other's operations.

OOD begins by identifying potential objects and their operations. Examining objects in the problem domain is a good way to begin the process. The next step is to determine the relationships among the objects using inheritance (to express is-a relationships) and composition (to express has-a relationships). Finally, a driver algorithm is designed to coordinate the overall flow of control.

Object-oriented programming (OOP) is the process of implementing an object-oriented design by using language mechanisms for data abstraction, inheritance, and dynamic binding. Inheritance allows any programmer to take an existing class (the base class) and create a new class (the derived class) that inherits the data and operations of the base class. The derived class then specializes the base class by adding new private data, adding new operations, or reimplementing inherited operations—all without analyzing and modifying the implementation of the base class in any way. Dynamic binding of operations to objects allows objects of many different derived types to respond to a single function name, each in its own way. Together, inheritance and dynamic binding have been shown to dramatically reduce the time and effort required to customize existing ADTs. The result is truly reusable software components whose applications and lifetimes extend beyond those conceived of by the original creator.

Quick Check

1. Fill in the blanks: Structured (procedural) programming results in a program that is a collection of interacting _____, whereas OOP results in a program that is a collection of interacting _____. (pp. 598–601)
2. Name the three language features that characterize object-oriented programming languages. (pp. 598–601)
3. Given the class declaration

```
class Point
{
public:
    int X_Coord() const;      // Return the x-coordinate
    int Y_Coord() const;      // Return the y-coordinate
    Point( /* in */ int initX,  // Constructor
           /* in */ int initY );
private:
    int x;
    int y;
};
```

and the type declaration

```
enum StatusType {ON, OFF};
```

declare a class `Pixel` that inherits from class `Point`. Class `Pixel` has an additional data member of type `StatusType` named `status`; it has an additional member function `CurrentStatus` that returns the value of `status`; and it supplies its own constructor that receives three parameters. (pp. 601–608)

4. Write a client statement that creates a `Pixel` object named `onePixel` with an initial (*x*, *y*) position of (3, 8) and a status of `OFF`. (pp. 601–608)
5. Assuming `somePixel` is an object of type `Pixel`, write client code that prints out the current *x*- and *y*-coordinates and status of `somePixel`. (pp. 601–608)
6. Write the function definitions for the `Pixel` class constructor and the `CurrentStatus` function. (pp. 608–613)
7. Fill in the private part of the following class declaration, which uses composition to define a `Line` object in terms of two `Point` objects. (pp. 613–614)

```
class Line
{
public:
    Point StartingPoint() const;    // Return line's starting
                                    //     point
    Point EndingPoint() const;      // Return line's ending point
    float Length() const;           // Return length of the line
    Line( /* in */ int startX,      // Constructor
          /* in */ int startY,
          /* in */ int endX,
          /* in */ int endY   );
private:


};
```

8. Write the function definition for the `Line` class constructor. (pp. 614–617)
9. What is the difference between static and dynamic binding of an operation to an object? (pp. 617–621)
10. Although there are many specific techniques for performing OOD, this chapter uses a three-step process. What are these three steps? (pp. 622–624)
11. When selecting a data representation for an abstract object, what three choices does the C++ programmer have? (p. 625)

Answers   1. functions, objects 2 Data abstraction, inheritance, dynamic binding

3.
```
    class Pixel : public Point
    {
    public:
        StatusType CurrentStatus() const;
        Pixel( /* in */ int        initX,
               /* in */ int        initY,
               /* in */ StatusType initStatus );
    private:
        StatusType status;
    };
```

4. `Pixel onePixel(3, 8, OFF);`

5.
```
    cout << "x-coordinate: " << somePixel.X_Coord() << endl;
    cout << "y-coordinate: " << somePixel.Y_Coord() << endl;
    if (somePixel.CurrentStatus() == ON)
        cout << "Status: on" << endl;
    else
        cout << "Status: off" << endl;
```

6.
```
    Pixel::Pixel( /* in */ int        initX,
                  /* in */ int        initY,
                  /* in */ StatusType initStatus )

        : Point(initX, initY)              // Constructor initializer
    {
        status = initStatus;
    }
```

7.
```
    Point startPt;
    Point endPt;
```

8.
```
    Line::Line( /* in */ int startX,
                /* in */ int startY,
                /* in */ int endX,
                /* in */ int endY   )

        : startPt(startX, startY), endPt(endX, endY)
    {
        // Empty body--nothing more to do
    }
```

9. With static binding, the determination of which function to call for an object occurs at compile time. With dynamic binding, the determination of which function to call for an object occurs at run time. 10. Identify the objects and operations, determine the relationships among the objects, and design the driver. 11. Use a built-in data type, use an existing ADT, or create a new ADT.

Exam Preparation Exercises

1. Define the following terms:

   structured design   method (of an object)

   code reuse   is-a relationship

   state (of an object)   has-a relationship

   instance variable (of an object)

2. In C++, inheritance allows a derived class to directly access all of the functions and data of its base class. (True or False?)

3. Given an existing class declaration

   ```
   class Sigma
   {
   public:
       void Write() const;
         ⋮
   private:
       int n;
   };
   ```

   a programmer derives a new class `Epsilon` as follows:

   ```
   class Epsilon : Sigma
   {
   public:
       void Twist();
       Epsilon( /* in */ float initVal );
   private:
       float x;
   };
   ```

   Then the following client code results in a compile-time error:

   ```
   Epsilon someObject(4.8);

   someObject.Write();    // Error
   ```

   a. Why is the call to the `Write` function erroneous?
   b. How would you fix the problem?

4. Consider the following two class declarations:

   ```
   class Abc
   {
   public:
       void DoThis();
   private:
       void DoThat();
       int   alpha;
       int   beta;
   };
   ```

```
class Xyz : public Abc
{
public:
    void TryIt();
private:
    int gamma;
};
```

For *each* class, do the following:
a. List all private data members.
b. List all private data members that the class's member functions can reference directly.
c. List all functions that the class's member functions can invoke.
d. List all member functions that a client of the class may legally invoke.

5. A class X uses both inheritance and composition as follows. X is derived from class Y and has a member that is an object of class Z. When an object of class X is created, in what order are the constructors for classes X, Y, and Z executed?

6. With argument passing in C++, you can pass an object of an ancestor class to a parameter that is an object of a descendant class. (True or False?)

7. Define the following terms associated with object-oriented design:
problem domain
solution domain
implementation-level object

8. Mark each of the following statements as True or False.
a. Every noun and noun phrase in a problem definition becomes an object in the solution domain.
b. For a given problem, there are usually more objects in the solution domain than in the problem domain.
c. In the three-step process for performing object-oriented design, all decisions made during each step are final.

9. For each of the following design methodologies, at what general time (beginning, middle, end) is the driver—the top-level algorithm—designed?
a. Object-oriented design
b. Structured design

10. Fill in each blank below with either *is-a* or *has-a*.
In general, the best strategy in object-oriented design is to use inheritance for _____ relationships and composition for _____ relationships.

Programming Warm-up Exercises

1. For the Line class of Quick Check Question 7, implement the StartingPoint and EndingPoint member functions.

2. For the `Line` class of Quick Check Question 7, implement the `Length` member function. *Hint:* The distance between two points (x_1, y_1) and (x_2, y_2) is

$$\sqrt{(x_1 - x_2)^2 + (y_1 - y_2)^2}$$

3. The following class represents a person's mailing address in the United States.

```
class Address
{
public:
    void Write() const;
    Address( /* in */ string newStreet,
             /* in */ string newCity,
             /* in */ string newState,
             /* in */ string newZip   );
private:
    string street;
    string city;
    string state;
    string zipCode;
};
```

Using inheritance, we want to derive an international address class, `InterAddress`, from the `Address` class. For this exercise, an international address has all the attributes of a U.S. address plus a country code (a string indicating the name of the country). The public operations of `InterAddress` are `Write` (which reimplements the `Write` function inherited from `Address`) and a class constructor that receives five parameters (street, city, state, zip code, and country code). Write a class declaration for the `InterAddress` class.

4. Implement the `InterAddress` class constructor.

5. Implement the `Write` function of the `InterAddress` class.

6. Write a global function `PrintAddress` that takes a single parameter and uses dynamic binding to print either a U.S. address or an international address. Make the necessary change(s) in the declaration of the `Address` class so that `PrintAddress` executes correctly.

7. In Chapter 11, we developed a `TimeType` class (page 436) and a `DateType` class (page 442). Using composition, we want to create a `TimeAndDay` class that contains both a `TimeType` object and a `DateType` object. The public operations of the `TimeAndDay` class should be `Set` (with six parameters to set the time and day), `Increment`, `Write`, and a default constructor. Write a class declaration for the `TimeAndDay` class.

8. Implement the `TimeAndDay` default constructor.

9. Implement the `Set` function of the `TimeAndDay` class.

10. Implement the `Increment` function of the `TimeAndDay` class. (*Hint:* If the time part is incremented to midnight, increment the date part.)
11. Implement the `Write` function of the `TimeAndDay` class.
12. Revise the `TimeCardList` class by removing the `SelSort` function and modifying `ReadAll` so that it inserts each time card into its proper place in the list as it is read from the input file. Give both the specification and the implementation of the revised class.

Programming Problems

1. Your parents are thinking of opening a video rental store. Because they are helping with your tuition, they ask you to write a program to handle their inventory.

   What are the major objects in a rental store? They are the items to be rented and the people who rent them. You begin with the abstraction of the items to be rented—video tapes. To determine the characteristics of a video object, you jot down a list of questions.

   - Should the object be one physical video tape, or should it be a title (to allow for multiple copies of a video)?
   - What information about each title should be kept?
   - Should the object contain a place for the card number of the person who has it rented?
   - If there are multiple copies, is it important to keep track of specific copies?
   - What operations should a video object be able to execute?

   You decide that the basic object is the title, not an individual tape. The number of copies owned can be a data member of the object. Other data members should include the title, the movie stars, the producer, the director, and the production company. The system eventually must be able to track who has rented which videos, but this is not a property of the video object itself. You'll worry about how to represent the "has rented" object later. For now, who has which specific copy is not important.

   The video object must have operations to initialize it and access the various data members. In addition, the object should adjust the number of copies (up or down), determine if a copy is available, check in a copy, and check out a copy. Because you will need to create a list of videos later, you decide to include operations that compare titles and print titles.

   You decide to stop at this point, implement the video object, and test it before going on to the rest of the design.

2. Having completed the design and testing of the video object in Programming Problem 1, you are ready to continue with the original problem. Write a program to do the following tasks.
   a. Create a list of video objects.
   b. Search the list for a particular title.
   c. Determine if there are any copies of a particular video currently in the store.
   d. Print the list of video titles.

3. Now that the video inventory is under control, determine the characteristics of the customer and define a customer object. Write the operations and test them. Using this representation of a customer, write a program to do the following tasks.

   a. Create a list of customers.
   b. Search the list by customer name.
   c. Search the list by customer identification number.
   d. Print the list of customer names.

4. Combine the list of video objects and the list of customer objects into a program with the following capabilities.

   a. Check out a video.
   b. Check in a video.
   c. Determine how many videos a customer has (by customer identification number).
   d. Determine which customers have a certain video checked out (by title). (*Hint:* Create a hasVideo object that has a video title and a customer number.)

Recursion

- To be able to identify the base case(s) and the general case in a recursive definition.

- To be able to write a recursive algorithm for a problem involving only simple variables.

- To be able to write a recursive algorithm for a problem involving structured variables.

> **Recursive call**   A function call in which the function being called is the same as the one making the call.

In C++, any function can call another function. A function can even call itself! When a function calls itself, it is making a **recursive call**. The word *recursive* means "having the characteristic of coming up again, or repeating." In this case, a function call is being repeated by the function itself. Recursion is a powerful technique that can be used in place of iteration (looping).

Recursive solutions are generally less efficient than iterative solutions to the same problem. However, some problems lend themselves to simple, elegant, recursive solutions and are exceedingly cumbersome to solve iteratively. Some programming languages are especially oriented to recursive algorithms—LISP is one of these. C++ lets us implement both iterative and recursive algorithms.

Our examples are broken into two groups: problems that use only simple variables and problems that use structured variables. If you are studying recursion before reading Chapters 11 and 12 on structured data types, then cover only the first set of examples and leave the rest until you have completed the chapters on structured data types.

15.1   What Is Recursion?

You may have seen a set of gaily painted Russian dolls that fit inside one another. Inside the first doll is a smaller doll, inside of which is an even smaller doll, inside of which is yet a smaller doll, and so on. A recursive algorithm is like such a set of Russian dolls. It reproduces itself with smaller and smaller examples of itself until a solution is found—that is, until there are no more dolls. The recursive algorithm is implemented by using a function that makes recursive calls to itself.

In Chapter 8, we wrote a function named Power that calculates the result of raising an integer to a positive power. If X is an integer and N is a positive integer, the formula for X^N is

$$x^N = \underbrace{X \times X \times X \times X \times \ldots \times X}_{N \text{ times}}$$

We could also write this formula as

$$x^N = X \times \underbrace{\left(X \times X \times \ldots \times X\right)}_{(N-1) \text{ times}}$$

or even as

$$x^N = X \times X \times \underbrace{\left(X \times X \times \ldots \times X\right)}_{(N-2) \text{ times}}$$

In fact, we can write the formula most concisely as

$$X^N = X \times X^{N-1}$$

This definition of X^N is a classic **recursive definition**—that is, a definition given in terms of a smaller version of itself.

> **Recursive definition** A definition in which something is defined in terms of smaller versions of itself.

X^N is defined in terms of multiplying X times X^{N-1}. How is X^{N-1} defined? Why, as $X \times X^{N-2}$, of course! And X^{N-2} is $X \times X^{N-3}$; X^{N-3} is $X \times X^{N-4}$; and so on. In this example, "in terms of smaller versions of itself" means that the exponent is decremented each time.

When does the process stop? When we have reached a case for which we know the answer without resorting to a recursive definition. In this example, it is the case where N equals 1: X^1 is X. The case (or cases) for which an answer is explicitly known is called the **base case**. The case for which the solution is expressed in terms of a smaller version of itself is called the **recursive** or **general case**. A **recursive algorithm** is an algorithm that expresses the solution in terms of a call to itself, a recursive call. A recursive algorithm must terminate; that is, it must have a base case.

> **Base case** The case for which the solution can be stated nonrecursively.
>
> **General case** The case for which the solution is expressed in terms of a smaller version of itself; also known as *recursive case*.
>
> **Recursive algorithm** A solution that is expressed in terms of (a) smaller instances of itself and (b) a base case.

Figure 15-1 shows a recursive version of the Power function with the base case and the recursive call marked. The function is embedded in a program that reads in a number and an exponent and prints the result.

Figure 15-1 *Power Function*

```
//*********************************************************************
// Exponentiation program
//*********************************************************************
#include <iostream>

using namespace std;

int Power( int, int );

int main()
{
    int number;           // Number that is being raised to power
    int exponent;         // Power the number is being raised to
```

(continued)

Figure 15-1 *(continued)*

```
    cin >> number >> exponent;
    cout << Power(number, exponent);  <———————— // Nonrecursive call
    return 0;
}


//*********************************************************************

int Power( /* in */ int x,    // Number that is being raised to power
           /* in */ int n )   // Power the number is being raised to

// Computes x to the n power by multiplying x times the result of
// computing x to the n - 1 power.

// Precondition:
//     x is assigned   &&   n > 0
// Postcondition:
//     Function value == x raised to the power n
// Note:
//     Large exponents may result in integer overflow

{
    if (n == 1)
        return x;  <————————————————————————————— // Base case
    else
        return x * Power(x, n - 1);  <———————————— // Recursive call
}
```

Each recursive call to Power can be thought of as creating a completely new copy of the function, each with its own copies of the parameters x and n. The value of x remains the same for each version of Power, but the value of n decreases by 1 for each call until it becomes 1.

Let's trace the execution of this recursive function, with number equal to 2 and exponent equal to 3. We use a new format to trace recursive routines: We number the calls and then discuss what is happening in paragraph form.

Call 1: Power is called by main, with number equal to 2 and exponent equal to 3. Within Power, the parameters x and n are initialized to 2 and 3, respectively. Because n is not equal to 1, Power is called recursively with x and n − 1 as arguments. Execution of Call 1 pauses until an answer is sent back from this recursive call.

Call 2: x is equal to 2 and n is equal to 2. Because n is not equal to 1, the function Power is called again, this time with x and n − 1 as arguments. Execution of Call 2 pauses until an answer is sent back from this recursive call.

Call 3: x is equal to 2 and n is equal to 1. Because n equals 1, the value of x is to be returned. This call to the function has finished executing, and the function return value (which is 2) is passed back to the place in the statement from which the call was made.

Call 2: This call to the function can now complete the statement that contained the recursive call because the recursive call has returned. Call 3's return value (which is 2) is multiplied by x. This call to the function has finished executing, and the function return value (which is 4) is passed back to the place in the statement from which the call was made.

Call 1: This call to the function can now complete the statement that contained the recursive call because the recursive call has returned. Call 2's return value (which is 4) is multiplied by x. This call to the function has finished executing, and the function return value (which is 8) is passed back to the place in the statement from which the call was made. Because the first call (the nonrecursive call in main) has now completed, this is the final value of the function Power.

This trace is summarized in Figure 15-2. Each box represents a call to the Power function. The values for the parameters for that call are shown in each box.

What happens if there is no base case? We have **infinite recursion**, the recursive equivalent of an infinite loop. For example, if the condition

> **Infinite recursion**   The situation in which a function calls itself over and over endlessly.

```
if (n == 1)
```

were omitted, Power would be called over and over again. Infinite recursion also occurs if Power is called with n less than or equal to 0.

In actuality, recursive calls can't go on forever. Here's the reason. When a function is called, either recursively or nonrecursively, the computer system creates temporary storage for the parameters and the function's (automatic) local variables. This temporary storage is a region of memory called the *run-time stack*. When the function returns, its parameters and local variables are released from the run-time stack. With infinite recursion, the recursive function calls never return. Each time the function calls itself, a little more of the run-time stack is used to store the new copies of the variables. Eventually,

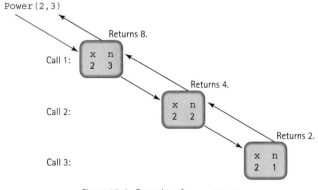

Figure 15-2 *Execution of Power(2, 3)*

all the memory space on the stack is used. At that point, the program crashes with an error message such as "STACK OVERFLOW" (or the computer may simply hang).

Let's organize what we have done in our `Power` function into an outline for writing recursive algorithms.

1. Understand the problem. (We threw this in for good measure; it is always the first step.)
2. Determine the base case(s).
3. Determine the recursive case(s).

We have used the power algorithm to demonstrate recursion because it is easy to visualize. In practice, one would never want to calculate this function using the recursive solution. The iterative solution is simpler and much more efficient because starting a new iteration of a loop is a faster operation than calling a function. If we compare the code for the iterative and recursive versions of the power problem, we see that the iterative version has a local variable, whereas the recursive version has none. There are usually fewer local variables in a recursive routine than in an iterative routine. Also, the iterative version always has a loop, whereas the recursive version always has a selection statement—either an If or a Switch.

In the next section, we examine a more complicated problem—one in which the recursive solution is not immediately apparent.

15.2 Towers of Hanoi

One of your first toys may have been three pegs with colored circles of different diameters. If so, you probably spent countless hours moving the circles from one peg to another. If we put some constraints on how the circles or discs can be moved, we have an adult game called the Towers of Hanoi. When the game begins, all the circles are on the first peg in order by size, with the smallest on the top. The object of the game is to move the circles, one at a time, to the third peg. The catch is that a circle cannot be placed on top of one that is smaller in diameter. The middle peg can be used as an auxiliary peg, but it must be empty at the beginning and at the end of the game.

To get a feel for how this might be done, let's look at some sketches of what the configuration must be at certain points if a solution is possible. We use four circles or discs. The beginning configuration is:

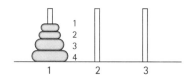

To move the largest circle (circle 4) to peg 3, we must move the three smaller circles to peg 2. Then circle 4 can be moved into its final place:

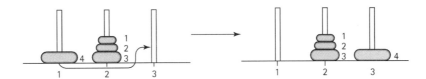

Let's assume we can do this. Now, to move the next largest circle (circle 3) into place, we must move the two circles on top of it onto an auxiliary peg (peg one in this case):

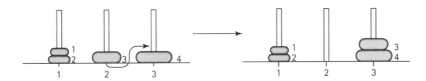

To get circle 2 into place, we must move circle 1 to another peg, freeing circle 2 to be moved to its place on peg 3:

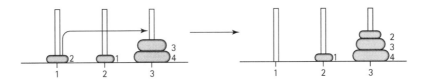

The last circle (circle 1) can now be moved into its final place, and we are finished:

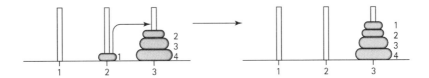

Notice that to free circle 4, we had to move three circles to another peg. To free circle 3, we had to move two circles to another peg. To free circle 2, we had to move one circle to another peg. This sounds like a recursive algorithm: To free the nth circle, we have to move $n - 1$ circles. Each stage can be thought of as beginning again with three pegs, but with one less circle each time. Let's see if we can summarize this process, using n instead of an actual number.

Get N Circles Moved from Peg 1 to Peg 3

> Get n – 1 circles moved from peg 1 to peg 2
> Move nth circle from peg 1 to peg 3
> Get n – 1 circles moved from peg 2 to peg 3

This algorithm certainly sounds simple; surely there must be more. But this really is all there is to it.

Let's write a recursive function that implements this algorithm. We can't actually move discs, of course, but we can print out a message to do so. Notice that the beginning peg, the ending peg, and the auxiliary peg keep changing during the algorithm. To make the algorithm easier to follow, we call the pegs `beginPeg`, `endPeg`, and `auxPeg`. These three pegs, along with the number of circles on the beginning peg, are the parameters of the function.

We have the recursive or general case, but what about a base case? How do we know when to stop the recursive process? The clue is in the expression "Get *n* circles moved." If we don't have any circles to move, we don't have anything to do. We are finished with that stage. Therefore, when the number of circles equals 0, we do nothing (that is, we simply return).

```
void DoTowers(
    /* in */ int circleCount,    // Number of circles to move
    /* in */ int beginPeg,       // Peg containing circles to move
    /* in */ int auxPeg,         // Peg holding circles temporarily
    /* in */ int endPeg      )   // Peg receiving circles being moved
{
    if (circleCount > 0)
    {
        // Move n - 1 circles from beginning peg to auxiliary peg

        DoTowers(circleCount - 1, beginPeg, endPeg, auxPeg);
        cout << "Move circle from peg " << beginPeg
             << " to peg " << endPeg << endl;

        // Move n - 1 circles from auxiliary peg to ending peg

        DoTowers(circleCount - 1, auxPeg, beginPeg, endPeg);
    }
}
```

It's hard to believe that such a simple algorithm actually works, but we'll prove it to you. Following is a driver program that calls the `DoTowers` function. Output statements have been added so you can see the values of the arguments with each recursive call.

Because there are two recursive calls within the function, we have indicated which recursive statement issued the call.

```cpp
//*****************************************************************
// TestTowers program
// This program, a test driver for the DoTowers function, reads in
// a value from standard input and passes this value to DoTowers
//*****************************************************************
#include <iostream>
#include <iomanip>     // For setw()

using namespace std;

void DoTowers( int, int, int, int );

int main()
{
    int circleCount;    // Number of circles on starting peg

    cout << "Input number of circles: ";
    cin >> circleCount;
    cout << "OUTPUT WITH " << circleCount << " CIRCLES" << endl
         << endl;
    cout << "CALLED FROM  #CIRCLES" << setw(8) << "BEGIN"
         << setw(8) << "AUXIL." << setw(5) << "END"
         << "    INSTRUCTIONS" << endl
         << endl;
    cout << "Original    :";
    DoTowers(circleCount, 1, 2, 3);
    return 0;
}


//*****************************************************************

void DoTowers(
    /* in */ int circleCount,    // Number of circles to move
    /* in */ int beginPeg,       // Peg containing circles to move
    /* in */ int auxPeg,         // Peg holding circles temporarily
    /* in */ int endPeg      )   // Peg receiving circles being moved

// This recursive function moves circleCount circles from beginPeg
// to endPeg.  All but one of the circles are moved from beginPeg
// to auxPeg, then the last circle is moved from beginPeg to endPeg,
// and then the circles are moved from auxPeg to endPeg.
```

```
// The subgoals of moving circles to and from auxPeg are what
// involve recursion

// Precondition:
//      All parameters are assigned  &&  circleCount >= 0
// Postcondition:
//      The values of all parameters have been printed
//   && IF circleCount > 0
//          circleCount circles have been moved from beginPeg to
//          endPeg in the manner detailed above
//      ELSE
//          No further actions have taken place

{

    cout << setw(6) << circleCount << setw(9) << beginPeg
        << setw(7) << auxPeg << setw(7) << endPeg << endl;
    if (circleCount > 0)
    {
        cout << "From  first:";
        DoTowers(circleCount - 1, beginPeg, endPeg, auxPeg);
        cout << setw(58) << "Move circle " << circleCount
            << " from " << beginPeg << " to " << endPeg << endl;
        cout << "From second:";
        DoTowers(circleCount - 1, auxPeg, beginPeg, endPeg);
    }
}
```

The output from a run with three circles follows. "Original" means that the parameters listed beside it are from the nonrecursive call, which is the first call to DoTowers. "From first" means that the parameters listed are for a call issued from the first recursive statement. "From second" means that the parameters listed are for a call issued from the second recursive statement. Notice that a call cannot be issued from the second recursive statement until the preceding call from the first recursive statement has completed execution.

```
OUTPUT WITH 3 CIRCLES

CALLED FROM  #CIRCLES   BEGIN  AUXIL.   END    INSTRUCTIONS

Original   :     3        1      2       3
From  first:     2        1      3       2
From  first:     1        1      2       3
From  first:     0        1      3       2
                                                Move circle 1 from 1 to 3
```

```
From second:      0          2        1        3
                                               Move circle 2 from 1 to 2
From second:      1          3        1        2
From  first:      0          3        2        1
                                               Move circle 1 from 3 to 2
From second:      0          1        3        2
                                               Move circle 3 from 1 to 3
From second:      2          2        1        3
From  first:      1          2        3        1
From  first:      0          2        1        3
                                               Move circle 1 from 2 to 1
From second:      0          3        2        1
                                               Move circle 2 from 2 to 3
From second:      1          1        2        3
From  first:      0          1        3        2
                                               Move circle 1 from 1 to 3
From second:      0          2        1        3
```

15.3 Recursive Algorithms with Structured Variables

In our definition of a recursive algorithm, we said there were two cases: the recursive or general case, and the base case. In the general case for all our algorithms so far, an argument was expressed in terms of a smaller value each time. When structured variables are used, the recursive case is often in terms of a smaller structure rather than a smaller value; the base case occurs when there are no values left to process in the structure.

We examine a recursive algorithm for printing the contents of a one-dimensional array of n elements to show what we mean.

Print Array

> IF more elements
>   Print the value of the first element
>   Print array of n-1 elements

The recursive case is to print the values in an array that is one element "smaller"; that is, the size of the array decreases by 1 with each recursive call. The base case is when the size of the array becomes 0—that is, when there are no more elements to print.

Our arguments must include the index of the first element (the one to be printed). How do we know when there are no more elements to print (that is, when the size of the array to be printed is 0)? We know we have printed the last element in the array when the index of the next element to be printed is beyond the index of the last element in the array. Therefore, the index of the last array element must be passed as an argument. We call the indexes `first` and `last`. When `first` is greater than `last`, we are finished. The name of the array is `data`.

```
void Print( /* in */ const int data[],    // Array to be printed
            /* in */           int first,  // Index of first element
            /* in */           int last  ) // Index of last element
{
    if (first <= last)
    {                                                    // Recursive case
        cout << data[first] << endl;
        Print(data, first + 1, last);
    }
    // Empty else-clause is the base case
}
```

Figure 15-3 illustrates execution of the function call

data

[0]	23
[1]	44
[2]	52
[3]	61
[4]	77

```
Print(data, 0, 4);
```

using the array shown at the left. Notice that the array gets smaller with each recursive call (`data[first]` through `data[last]`). Also, if we want to print the array elements in reverse order recursively, all we have to do is interchange the two statements within the If statement.

Notice also that once the deepest call (the call with the highest number) was reached, each of the calls before it returned without doing anything. When no statements are executed after the return from the recursive call to the function, the recursion is known as **tail recursion**. Tail recursion often indicates that the problem could be solved more easily using iteration. We used the array example because it made the recursive process easy to visualize; in practice, an array should be printed iteratively.

Tail recursion A recursive algorithm in which no statements are executed after the return from the recursive call.

15.4 Recursion or Iteration?

Recursion and iteration are alternative ways of expressing repetition in a program. When iterative control structures are used, processes are made to repeat by embedding code in a looping structure such as a While, For, or Do-While. In recursion, a process is made to repeat by having a function call itself. A selection statement is used to control the repeated calls.

Print(data, 0, 4)

data, which is the array, is not shown in the boxes.

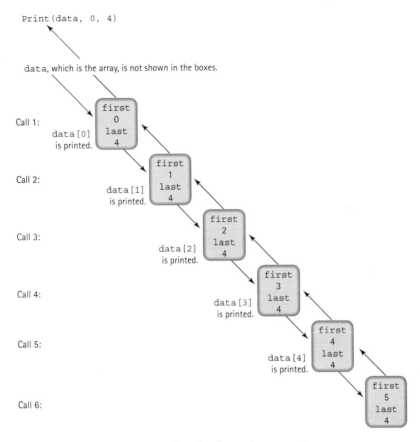

Call 1:
data[0] is printed.
first 0 last 4

Call 2:
data[1] is printed.
first 1 last 4

Call 3:
data[2] is printed.
first 2 last 4

Call 4:
data[3] is printed.
first 3 last 4

Call 5:
data[4] is printed.
first 4 last 4

Call 6:
first 5 last 4

Figure 15-3 *Execution of* Print(data, 0, 4)

Which is better to use—recursion or iteration? There is no simple answer to this question. The choice usually depends on two issues: efficiency and the nature of the problem being solved.

Historically, the quest for efficiency, in terms of both execution speed and memory usage, has favored iteration over recursion. Each time a recursive call is made, the system must allocate stack space for all parameters and (automatic) local variables. The overhead involved in any function call is time-consuming. On early, slow computers with limited memory capacity, recursive algorithms were visibly—sometimes painfully—slower than the iterative versions. However, studies have shown that on modern, fast computers, the overhead of recursion is often so small that the increase in computation time is almost unnoticeable to the user. Except in cases where efficiency is absolutely critical, then, the choice between recursion and iteration more often depends on the second issue—the nature of the problem being solved.

Consider the power algorithm we discussed earlier in the chapter. In this case, an iterative solution was obvious and easy to devise. We imposed a recursive solution on this problem only to demonstrate how recursion works. As a rule of thumb, if an iterative solution is more obvious or easier to understand, use it; it will be more efficient. However, there are problems for which the recursive solution is more obvious or easier to devise, such as the Towers of Hanoi problem. (It turns out that Towers of Hanoi is surprisingly difficult to solve using iteration.) Computer science students should be aware of the power of recursion. If the definition of a problem is inherently recursive, then a recursive solution should certainly be considered.

Testing and Debugging

Recursion is a powerful technique when used correctly. Improperly used, recursion can cause errors that are difficult to diagnose. The best way to debug a recursive algorithm is to construct it correctly in the first place. To be realistic, however, we give a few hints about where to look if an error occurs.

Testing and Debugging Hints

1. Be sure there is a base case. If there is no base case, the algorithm continues to issue recursive calls until all memory has been used. An error message such as "STACK OVERFLOW" indicates that the base case is missing.

2. Be sure you have not used a While structure. The basic structure in a recursive algorithm is the If statement. There must be at least two cases: the recursive case and the base case. If the base case does nothing, the else-clause is omitted. The selection structure, however, must be there. If a While statement is used in a recursive algorithm, the While statement usually should not contain a recursive call.

3. As with nonrecursive functions, do not reference global variables directly within a recursive function unless you have justification for doing so.

4. Parameters that relate to the size of the problem must be value parameters, not reference parameters. The arguments that relate to the size of the problem are usually expressions. Arbitrary expressions can be passed only to value parameters.

5. Use your system's debugger program (or use debug output statements) to trace a series of recursive calls. Inspecting the values of parameters and local variables often helps to locate errors in a recursive algorithm.

Summary

A recursive algorithm is expressed in terms of a smaller instance of itself. It must include a recursive case, for which the algorithm is expressed in terms of itself, and a base case, for which the algorithm is expressed in nonrecursive terms.

In many recursive problems, the smaller instance refers to a numeric argument that is being reduced with each call. In other problems, the smaller instance refers to the size of the data structure being manipulated. The base case is the one in which the size of the problem (value or structure) reaches a point for which an explicit answer is known.

In the example for printing the array, the size of the problem was the size of the array being printed. When the array size became 0, the printing process was complete.

In the Towers of Hanoi game, the size of the problem was the number of discs to be moved. When there was only one left on the beginning peg, it could be moved to its final destination.

Quick Check

1. What distinguishes the base case from the recursive case in a recursive algorithm? (pp. 656–657)
2. What is the base case in the Towers of Hanoi algorithm? (pp. 660–664)
3. In working with simple variables, the recursive case is often stated in terms of a smaller value. What is typical of the recursive case in working with structured variables? (pp. 665–666)

Answers   1. The base case is the simplest case, the case for which the solution can be stated nonrecursively. 2. When there are no more circles left to move. 3. It is often stated in terms of a smaller structure.

Exam Preparation Exercises

1. Recursion is an example of
   a. selection
   b. a data structure
   c. repetition
   d. data-flow programming
2. A void function can be recursive, but a value-returning function cannot. (True or False?)
3. When a function is called recursively, the arguments and automatic local variables of the calling version are saved until its execution is resumed. (True or False?)
4. Given the recursive formula $F(N) = -F(N - 2)$, with base case $F(0) = 1$, what are the values of $F(4)$, $F(6)$, and $F(5)$? (If any of the values are undefined, say so.)
5. What algorithm error(s) leads to infinite recursion?
6. What control structure appears most commonly in a recursive function?

7. If you develop a recursive algorithm that employs tail recursion, what should you consider?
8. A recursive algorithm depends on making something smaller. When the algorithm works on a data structure, what may become smaller?
   a. Distance from a position in the structure.
   b. The data structure.
   c. The number of variables in the recursive function.
9. Given the following input:

```
15
23
21
19
```

what is the output of the following program?

```cpp
#include <iostream>

using namespace std;

void PrintNums();

int main()
{
    PrintNums();
    cout << endl;
    return 0;
}

//****************************************

void PrintNums()
{
    int n;

    cin >> n;
    if (cin)                    // If not EOF...
    {
        cout << n << ' ';
        PrintNums();
        cout << n << ' ';
    }
}
```

Programming Warm-up Exercises

1. Write a C++ value-returning function that implements the recursive formula $F(N) = F(N - 1) + F(N - 2)$ with base cases $F(0) = 1$ and $F(1) = 1$.

2. Add whatever is necessary to fix the following function so that Func(3) equals 10.

```
int Func ( /* in */ int n )
{
    return Func(n - 1) + 3;
}
```

3. Rewrite the following DoubleSpace function without using recursion.

```
void DoubleSpace( /* inout */ ifstream& inFile )
{
    char ch;

    inFile.get(ch);
    if (inFile)              // If not EOF...
    {
        cout << ch;
        if (ch == '\n')
            cout << endl;
        DoubleSpace();
    }
}
```

4. Rewrite the following PrintSquares function using recursion.

```
void PrintSquares()
{
    int count;

    for (count = 1; count <= 10; count++)
        cout << count << ' ' << count * count;
}
```

5. Write a recursive value-returning function that sums the integers from 1 through N.

6. Rewrite the following function so that it is recursive.

```
void PrintSqRoots( /* in */ int n )
{
    int i;

    for (i = n; i > 0; i--)
        cout << i << ' ' << sqrt(double(i)) << endl;
}
```

Programming Problems

1. Use recursion to solve the following problem.

   A *palindrome* is a string of characters that reads the same forward and backward. Write a program that reads in strings of characters and determines if each string is a palindrome. Each string is on a separate input line. Echo print each string, followed by "Is a palindrome" if the string is a palindrome or "Is not a palindrome" if the string is not a palindrome. For example, given the input string

   ```
   Able was I, ere I saw Elba.
   ```

   the program would print "Is a palindrome." In determining whether a string is a palindrome, consider uppercase and lowercase letters to be the same and ignore punctuation characters.

2. Write a program to place eight queens on a chessboard in such a way that no queen is attacking any other queen. This is a classic problem that lends itself to a recursive solution. The chessboard should be represented as an 8 × 8 Boolean array. If a square is occupied by a queen, the value is true; otherwise, the value is false. The status of the chessboard when all eight queens have been placed is the solution.

3. A maze is to be represented by a 10 × 10 array of an enumeration type composed of three values: PATH, HEDGE, and EXIT. There is one exit from the maze. Write a program to determine if it is possible to exit the maze from a given starting point. You may move vertically or horizontally in any direction that contains PATH; you may not move to a square that contains HEDGE. If you move into a square that contains EXIT, you have exited.

   The input data consists of two parts: the maze and a series of starting points. The maze is entered as ten lines of ten characters (P, H, and E). Each succeeding line contains a pair of integers that represents a starting point (that is, row and column numbers). Continue processing entry points until end-of-file occurs.

Appendix A   Reserved Words

and	double	not	this
and_eq	dynamic_cast	not_eq	throw
asm	else	operator	true
auto	enum	or	try
bitand	explicit	or_eq	typedef
bitor	export	private	typeid
bool	extern	protected	typename
break	false	public	union
case	float	register	unsigned
catch	for	reinterpret_cast	using
char	friend	return	virtual
class	goto	short	void
compl	if	signed	volatile
const	inline	sizeof	wchar_t
const_cast	int	static	while
continue	long	static_cast	xor
default	mutable	struct	xor_eq
delete	namespace	switch	
do	new	template	

Appendix B
Operator Precedence

The following table summarizes C++ operator precedence. Several operators are not discussed in this book (typeid, the comma operator, ->*, and .*, for instance).

In the table, the operators are grouped by precedence level (highest to lowest), and a horizontal line separates each precedence level from the next-lower level.

In general, the binary operators group from left to right; the unary operators, from right to left; and the ?: operator, from right to left. Exception: The assignment operators group from right to left.

Precedence (highest to lowest)		
Operator	**Associativity**	**Remarks**
`: :`	Left to right	Scope resolution (binary)
`: :`	Right to left	Global access (unary)
`( )`	Left to right	Function call and function-style cast
`[]   ->   .`	Left to right	
`++   - -`	Right to left	++ and - - as postfix operators
`typeid   dynamic_cast`	Right to left	
`static_cast   const_cast`	Right to left	
`reinterpret_cast`	Right to left	
`++   - -   !` Unary + Unary -	Right to left	++ and - - as prefix operators
`~` Unary * Unary &	Right to left	
`(cast)   sizeof   new   delete`	Right to left	
`->*   .*`	Left to right	
`*   /   %`	Left to right	
`+   -`	Left to right	
`<<   >>`	Left to right	
`<   <=   >   >=`	Left to right	
`==   !=`	Left to right	
`&`	Left to right	
`^`	Left to right	
`|`	Left to right	
`&&`	Left to right	
`||`	Left to right	
`? :`	Right to left	
`=   +=   -=   *=   /=   %=`	Right to left	
`<<=   >>=   &=   |=   ^=`	Right to left	
`throw`	Right to left	
`,`	Left to right	The sequencing operator, not the separator

Appendix C
A Selection of Standard
Library Routines

The C++ standard library provides a wealth of data types, functions, and named constants. This appendix details only some of the more widely used library facilities. It is a good idea to consult the manual for your particular system to see what other types, functions, and constants the standard library provides.

This appendix is organized alphabetically according to the header file your program must #include. For example, to use a mathematics routine such as sqrt, you would #include the header file cmath as follows:

```
#include <cmath>
using namespace std;
  ⋮
y = sqrt(x);
```

Note that every identifier in the standard library is defined to be in the namespace std. Without the using directive above, you would write

```
y = std::sqrt(x);
```

C.1 The Header File cassert

assert(booleanExpr)
  Argument: A logical (Boolean) expression
  Effect: If the value of booleanExpr is true, execution of the program simply continues. If the value is false, execution terminates with a message stating the Boolean expression, the name of the source code file, and the line number in the file.
  Function return value: None (a void function)
  Note: If the preprocessor directive #define NDEBUG is placed before the directive #include <cassert>, all assert statements are ignored.

C.2 The Header File `cctype`

`isalnum(ch)`
Argument: A `char` value `ch`
Function return value: An `int` value that is
- nonzero (`true`), if `ch` is a letter or a digit character ('A'–'Z', 'a'–'z', '0'–'9')
- 0 (`false`), otherwise

`isalpha(ch)`
Argument: A `char` value `ch`
Function return value: An `int` value that is
- nonzero (`true`), if `ch` is a letter ('A'–'Z', 'a'–'z')
- 0 (`false`), otherwise

`iscntrl(ch)`
Argument: A `char` value `ch`
Function return value: An `int` value that is
- nonzero (`true`), if `ch` is a control character (in ASCII, a character with the value 0–31 or 127)
- 0 (`false`), otherwise

`isdigit(ch)`
Argument: A `char` value `ch`
Function return value: An `int` value that is
- nonzero (`true`), if `ch` is a digit character ('0'–'9')
- 0 (`false`), otherwise

`isgraph(ch)`
Argument: A `char` value `ch`
Function return value: An `int` value that is
- nonzero (`true`), if `ch` is a nonblank printable character (in ASCII, '!' through '~')
- 0 (`false`), otherwise

`islower(ch)`
Argument: A `char` value `ch`
Function return value: An `int` value that is
- nonzero (`true`), if `ch` is a lowercase letter ('a'–'z')
- 0 (`false`), otherwise

`isprint(ch)`
Argument: A `char` value `ch`
Function return value: An `int` value that is
- nonzero (`true`), if `ch` is a printable character, including the blank (in ASCII, ' ' through '~')
- 0 (`false`), otherwise

`ispunct(ch)`
Argument: A `char` value `ch`
Function return value: An `int` value that is
- nonzero (`true`), if `ch` is a punctuation character (equivalent to `isgraph(ch) && !isalnum(ch)`)
- 0 (`false`), otherwise

`isspace(ch)`
Argument: A `char` value `ch`
Function return value: An `int` value that is
- nonzero (`true`), if `ch` is a whitespace character (blank, newline, tab, carriage return, form feed)
- 0 (`false`), otherwise

`isupper(ch)`
Argument: A `char` value `ch`
Function return value: An `int` value that is
- nonzero (`true`), if `ch` is an uppercase letter ('A'–'Z')
- 0 (`false`), otherwise

`tolower(ch)`
Argument: A `char` value `ch`
Function return value: A character that is
- the lowercase equivalent of `ch`, if `ch` is an uppercase letter
- `ch`, otherwise

`toupper(ch)`
Argument: A `char` value `ch`
Function return value: A character that is
- the uppercase equivalent of `ch`, if `ch` is a lowercase letter
- `ch`, otherwise

C.3 The Header File `cfloat`

This header file supplies named constants that define the characteristics of floating-point numbers on your particular machine. Among these constants are the following:

FLT_DIG	Approximate number of significant digits in a `float` value
FLT_MAX	Maximum positive `float` value
FLT_MIN	Minimum positive `float` value
DBL_DIG	Approximate number of significant digits in a `double` value
DBL_MAX	Maximum positive `double` value
DBL_MIN	Minimum positive `double` value
LDBL_DIG	Approximate number of significant digits in a `long double` value
LDBL_MAX	Maximum positive `long double` value
LDBL_MIN	Minimum positive `long double` value

C.4 The Header File `climits`

This header file supplies named constants that define the limits of integer values on your particular machine. Among these constants are the following:

CHAR_BITS	Number of bits in a byte (8, for example)
CHAR_MAX	Maximum `char` value
CHAR_MIN	Minimum `char` value
SHRT_MAX	Maximum `short` value
SHRT_MIN	Minimum `short` value
INT_MAX	Maximum `int` value
INT_MIN	Minimum `int` value
LONG_MAX	Maximum `long` value
LONG_MIN	Minimum `long` value
UCHAR_MAX	Maximum `unsigned char` value
USHRT_MAX	Maximum `unsigned short` value
UINT_MAX	Maximum `unsigned int` value
ULONG_MAX	Maximum `unsigned long` value

C.5 The Header File `cmath`

In the following `math` routines,

1. Error handling for incalculable or out-of-range results is system dependent.
2. All arguments and function return values are technically of type `double`. However, `float` values may be passed to the functions.

`acos(x)`
Argument: A floating-point expression x, where $-1.0 \le x \le 1.0$
Function return value: Arc cosine of x, in the range 0.0 through π

`asin(x)`
Argument: A floating-point expression x, where $-1.0 \le x \le 1.0$
Function return value: Arc sine of x, in the range $-\pi/2$ through $\pi/2$

`atan(x)`
Argument: A floating-point expression x
Function return value: Arc tangent of x, in the range $-\pi/2$ through $\pi/2$

`ceil(x)`
Argument: A floating-point expression x
Function return value: "Ceiling" of x (the smallest whole number $\ge$ x)

`cos(angle)`
Argument: A floating-point expression `angle`, measured in radians
Function return value: Trigonometric cosine of `angle`

`cosh(x)`
Argument: A floating-point expression x
Function return value: Hyperbolic cosine of x

`exp(x)`
Argument: A floating-point expression x
Function return value: The value e(2.718...) raised to the power x

`fabs(x)`
Argument: A floating-point expression x
Function return value: Absolute value of x

`floor(x)`
Argument: A floating-point expression x
Function return value: "Floor" of x (the largest whole number $\le$ x)

log(x)
> *Argument:* A floating-point expression x, where x > 0.0
> *Function return value:* Natural logarithm (base *e*) of x

log10(x)
> *Argument:* A floating-point expression x, where x > 0.0
> *Function return value:* Common logarithm (base 10) of x

pow(x, y)
> *Arguments:* Floating-point expressions x and y. If x = 0.0, y must be positive; if x ≤ 0.0, y must be a whole number
> *Function return value:* x raised to the power y

sin(angle)
> *Argument:* A floating-point expression angle, measured in radians
> *Function return value:* Trigonometric sine of angle

sinh(x)
> *Argument:* A floating-point expression x
> *Function return value:* Hyperbolic sine of x

sqrt(x)
> *Argument:* A floating-point expression x, where x ≥ 0.0
> *Function return value:* Square root of x

tan(angle)
> *Argument:* A floating-point expression angle, measured in radians
> *Function return value:* Trigonometric tangent of angle

tanh(x)
> *Argument:* A floating-point expression x
> *Function return value:* Hyperbolic tangent of x

C.6 The Header File cstdlib

abs(i)
> *Argument:* An int expression i
> *Function return value:* An int value that is the absolute value of i

atof(str)
> *Argument:* A C string (null-terminated char array) str representing a floating-point number, possibly preceded by whitespace characters and a '+' or '-'

| *Function return value:* | A `double` value that is the floating-point equivalent of the characters in `str` |
| *Note:* | Conversion stops at the first character in `str` that is inappropriate for a floating-point number. If no appropriate characters were found, the return value is system dependent. |

`atoi(str)`

Argument:	A C string (null-terminated `char` array) `str` representing an integer number, possibly preceded by whitespace characters and a '+' or '−'
Function return value:	An `int` value that is the integer equivalent of the characters in `str`
Note:	Conversion stops at the first character in `str` that is inappropriate for an integer number. If no appropriate characters were found, the return value is system dependent.

`atol(str)`

Argument:	A C string (null-terminated `char` array) `str` representing a long integer, possibly preceded by whitespace characters and a '+' or '−'
Function return value:	A `long` value that is the long integer equivalent of the characters in `str`
Note:	Conversion stops at the first character in `str` that is inappropriate for a `long` integer number. If no appropriate characters were found, the return value is system dependent.

`exit(exitStatus)`

Argument:	An `int` expression `exitStatus`
Effect:	Program execution terminates immediately with all files properly closed
Function return value:	None (a void function)
Note:	By convention, `exitStatus` is 0 to indicate normal program completion and is nonzero to indicate an abnormal termination.

`labs(i)`

| *Argument:* | A `long` expression `i` |
| *Function return value:* | A `long` value that is the absolute value of `i` |

`rand()`

Argument:	None
Function return value:	A random `int` value in the range 0 through `RAND_MAX`, a constant defined in `cstdlib` (`RAND_MAX` is usually the same as `INT_MAX`)
Note:	See `srand` on the next page.

srand(seed)
Argument: An int expression seed, where seed ≥ 0
Effect: Using seed, the random number generator is initialized in
                               preparation for subsequent calls to the rand function.
Function return value: None (a void function)
Note: If srand is not called before the first call to rand, a seed
                               value of 1 is assumed.

C.7 The Header File cstring

The header file cstring (not to be confused with the header file named string) supports manipulation of C strings (null-terminated char arrays).

strcat(toStr, fromStr)
Arguments: C strings (null-terminated char arrays) toStr and fromStr,
                               where toStr must be large enough to hold the result
Effect: fromStr, including the null character '\0', is concatenated
                               (joined) to the end of toStr.
Function return value: The base address of toStr
Note: Programmers usually ignore the function return value, using
                               the syntax of a void function call rather than a value-return-
                               ing function call.

strcmp(str1, str2)
Arguments: C strings (null-terminated char arrays) str1 and str2
Function return value: An int value < 0, if str1 < str2 lexicographically
                               The int value 0, if str1 = str2 lexicographically
                               An int value > 0, if str1 > str2 lexicographically

strcpy(toStr, fromStr)
Arguments: toStr is a char array and fromStr is a C string (null-termi-
                               nated char array), and toStr must be large enough to hold
                               the result
Effect: fromStr, including the null character '\0', is copied to toStr,
                               overwriting what was there.
Function return value: The base address of toStr
Note: Programmers usually ignore the function return value, using
                               the syntax of a void function call rather than a value-return-
                               ing function call.

strlen(str)
Argument: A C string (null-terminated char array) str
Function return value: An int value ≥ 0 that is the length of str (excluding the '\0')

C.8 The Header File `string`

This header file supplies a programmer-defined data type (specifically, a *class*) named `string`. Associated with the `string` type are a data type `string::size_type` and a named constant `string::npos`, defined as follows:

`string::size_type`	An unsigned integer type related to the number of characters in a string
`string::npos`	The maximum value of type `string::size_type`

There are dozens of functions associated with the `string` type. Below are several of the most important ones. In the descriptions, `s` is assumed to be a variable (an *object*) of type `string`.

`s.c_str()`
    Arguments: None
    Function return value: The base address of a C string (null-terminated `char` array) corresponding to the characters stored in `s`

`s.find(arg)`
    Argument: An expression of type `string` or `char`, or a C string (such as a literal string)
    Function return value: A value of type `string::size_type` that gives the starting position in `s` where `arg` was found. If `arg` was not found, the return value is `string::npos`.
    Note: Positions of characters within a string are numbered starting at 0.

`getline(inStream, s)`
    Arguments: An input stream `inStream` (of type `istream` or `ifstream`) and a `string` object `s`
    Effect: Characters are input from `inStream` and stored into `s` until the newline character is encountered. (The newline character is consumed but not stored into `s`.)
    Function return value: Although the function technically returns a value (which we do not discuss here), programmers usually invoke the function as though it were a void function.

`s.length()`
    Arguments: None
    Function return value: A value of type `string::size_type` that gives the number of characters in the string

`s.size()`
    Arguments: None
    Function return value: The same as `s.length()`

```
s.substr(pos, len)
```

Arguments:	Two unsigned integers, pos and len, representing a position and a length. The value of pos must be less than s.length().
Function return value:	A temporary string object that holds a substring of at most len characters, starting at position pos of s. If len is too large, it means "to the end" of the string in s.
Note:	Positions of characters within a string are numbered starting at 0.

Appendix D
Using This Book with a
Prestandard Version of C++

D.1 The string Type

Prior to the ISO/ANSI C++ language standard, the standard library did not provide a string data type. For readers with prestandard compilers, the authors of this book have created a data type named StrType that mimics a subset of the standard string type. The subset is sufficient to match the string operations displayed throughout this book.

The files related to StrType are available for download from the publisher's Web site (www.jbpub.com). Among the files is one called README.TXT, which explains how to compile the source code and link it with the programs you write. Another file is the header file strtype.h, which contains important declarations that define the StrType type. Programs that use StrType must #include this header file:

```
#include "strtype.h"
```

In the #include directive, you cannot place the file name in angle brackets (< >). Instead, you enclose the file name in double quotes (" "). The double quotes tell the preprocessor to look for the file in the programmer's current directory. Therefore, to use StrType in your program, you must (a) verify that the file strtype.h is in the directory in which you are currently working on your program, and (b) make sure your program uses the directive

```
#include "strtype.h"
```

Additional directions are given in README.TXT.

Throughout this book you can use StrType instead of the string data type as follows. First, in your variable declarations, substitute the word StrType for string as the name of the data type. Second, change the directive #include <string> to #include "strtype.h". For example, instead of

```
#include <string>
⋮
string lastName;
```

you would write

```
#include "strtype.h"
⋮
StrType lastName;
```

Finally, there is a restriction on performing input into StrType variables. Chapter 4 discusses the use of the >> operator and the getline function to input characters into a string variable. Using >> with StrType variables, at most 1023 characters can be read and stored into one variable. In practice, however, it would be extremely rare for an input string to consist of that many characters. Input using getline is also restricted to 1023 characters. In the function call

```
getline(cin, myString);
```

in which myString is a StrType variable, the getline function does not skip leading whitespace characters and continues until it either has read 1023 characters or it reaches the newline character '\n', whichever comes first. Note that for an input line of 1023 characters or less, the newline character *is* consumed (but is not stored into myString).

D.2 Standard Header Files and Namespaces

Historically, the standard header files in both C and C++ had file names ending in .h (meaning "header file"). Certain header files—for example, `iostream.h` and `fstream.h`—related specifically to C++. Others, such as `math.h` and `string.h`, were carried over from the C standard library and were available to both C and C++ programs. When you used an `#include` directive such as

```
#include <math.h>
```

near the beginning of your program, all identifiers declared in `math.h` were introduced into your program in global scope (as discussed in Chapter 8). With the advent of the *namespace* mechanism in ISO/ANSI standard C++ (see Chapter 2 and, in more detail, Chapter 8), all of the standard header files were modified so that identifiers are declared within a namespace called `std`. In standard C++, when you `#include` a standard header file, the identifiers therein are not automatically placed into global scope.

To preserve compatibility with older versions of C++ that still need the original files `iostream.h`, `math.h`, and so forth, the new standard header files are renamed as follows: The C++-related header files have the .h removed, and the header files from the C library have the .h removed *and* the letter c inserted at the beginning. Here is a list of the old and new names for some of the most commonly used header files.

Old Name	New Name
iostream.h	iostream
iomanip.h	iomanip
fstream.h	fstream
assert.h	cassert
ctype.h	cctype
float.h	cfloat
limits.h	climits
math.h	cmath
stddef.h	cstddef
stdlib.h	cstdlib
string.h	cstring

Be careful: The last entry in the list above refers to the C language concept of a string and is unrelated to the `string` type defined in the C++ standard library.

If you are working with a prestandard compiler that does not recognize the new header file names or namespaces, simply substitute the old header file names for the new ones as you encounter them in the book. For example, where we have written

```
#include <iostream>
using namespace std;
```

you would write

```
#include <iostream.h>
```

D.3 The `fixed` and `showpoint` Manipulators

Chapter 3 introduces five manipulators for formatting the output: `endl`, `setw`, `fixed`, `showpoint`, and `setprecision`. If you are using a prestandard compiler with the header file `iostream.h`, the `fixed` and `showpoint` manipulators may not be available.

In place of the following code shown in Chapter 3,

```
#include <iostream>
using namespace std;
   ⋮
cout << fixed << showpoint;          // Set up floating-pt.
                                     //   output format
```

you can substitute the following code:

```
#include <iostream.h>
   ⋮
cout.setf(ios::fixed, ios::floatfield);
cout.setf(ios::showpoint);
```

These two statements employ some advanced C++ notation. Our advice is simply to use the statements just as you see them and not worry about the details.

Note: If your compiler complains about the syntax `ios::fixed`, `ios::floatfield`, or `ios::showpoint`, you may have to replace `ios` with `ios_base` as follows:

```
cout.setf(ios_base::fixed, ios_base::floatfield);
cout.setf(ios_base::showpoint);
```

D.4 The `bool` Type

Before the ISO/ANSI C++ language standard, C++ did not have a `bool` data type. Some prestandard compilers implemented the `bool` type before the standard was approved, but others did not.

In versions of C++ without the `bool` type, the value 0 represents *false*, and any nonzero value represents *true*. It is customary in pre–standard C++ to use the `int` type to represent Boolean data:

```
int dataOK;
  ⋮
dataOK = 1;    // Store "true" into dataOK
  ⋮
dataOK = 0;    // Store "false" into dataOK
```

To make the code more self-documenting, many pre–standard C++ programmers define their own Boolean data type by using a *Typedef statement*. This statement allows you to introduce a new name for an existing data type:

```
typedef int bool;
```

All this statement does is tell the compiler to substitute the word `int` for every occurrence of the word `bool` in the rest of the program.

With the Typedef statement and declarations of two named constants, `true` and `false`, the code at the beginning of this discussion becomes the following:

```
typedef int bool;
const int true = 1;
const int false = 0;
  ⋮
bool dataOK;
  ⋮
dataOK = true;
  ⋮
dataOK = false;
```

Throughout the book, our programs use the words `bool`, `true`, and `false` when manipulating Boolean data. If your compiler recognizes `bool` as a built-in type, there is nothing you need to do. Otherwise, here are three steps you can take.

1. Use your system's editor to create a file containing the following lines:

```
#ifndef BOOL_H
#define BOOL_H
typedef int bool;
const int true = 1;
const int false = 0;
#endif
```

Don't worry about the meaning of the first, second, and last lines. They are explained in Chapter 14. Simply type the lines as you see them above.

2. Save the file you created in Step 1, giving it the name `bool.h`. Save this file into the same directory in which you work on your C++ programs.

3. Near the top of every program in which you need `bool` variables, type the line

```
#include "bool.h"
```

Be sure to surround the file name with double quotes, not angle brackets (< >). The quotes tell the preprocessor to look for `bool.h` in your current directory rather than the C++ system directory.

With `bool`, `true`, and `false` defined in this fashion, the programs in this book run correctly, and you can use `bool` in your own programs, even if it is not a built-in type.

Appendix E
Character Sets

The following charts show the ordering of characters in two widely used character sets: ASCII (American Standard Code for Information Interchange) and EBCDIC (Extended Binary Coded Decimal Interchange Code). The internal representation for each character is shown in decimal. For example, the letter A is represented internally as the integer 65 in ASCII and as 193 in EBCDIC. The space (blank) character is denoted by a "□".

Left Digit(s)	Right Digit	ASCII									
		0	1	2	3	4	5	6	7	8	9
0		NUL	SOH	STX	ETX	EOT	ENQ	ACK	BEL	BS	HT
1		LF	VT	FF	CR	SO	SI	DLE	DC1	DC2	DC3
2		DC4	NAK	SYN	ETB	CAN	EM	SUB	ESC	FS	GS
3		RS	US	☐	!	"	#	$	%	&	'
4		(	)	*	+	,	−	.	/	0	1
5		2	3	4	5	6	7	8	9	:	;
6		<	=	>	?	@	A	B	C	D	E
7		F	G	H	I	J	K	L	M	N	O
8		P	Q	R	S	T	U	V	W	X	Y
9		Z	[	\	]	^	_	`	a	b	c
10		d	e	f	g	h	i	j	k	l	m
11		n	o	p	q	r	s	t	u	v	w
12		x	y	z	{	|	}	~	DEL		

Codes 00–31 and 127 are the following nonprintable control characters:

NUL	Null character	VT	Vertical tab	SYN	Synchronous idle
SOH	Start of header	FF	Form feed	ETB	End of transmitted block
STX	Start of text	CR	Carriage return	CAN	Cancel
ETX	End of text	SO	Shift out	EM	End of medium
EOT	End of transmission	SI	Shift in	SUB	Substitute
ENQ	Enquiry	DLE	Data link escape	ESC	Escape
ACK	Acknowledge	DC1	Device control one	FS	File separator
BEL	Bell character (beep)	DC2	Device control two	GS	Group separator
BS	Back space	DC3	Device control three	RS	Record separator
HT	Horizontal tab	DC4	Device control four	US	Unit separator
LF	Line feed	NAK	Negative acknowledge	DEL	Delete

Left Digit(s)	Right Digit	EBCDIC								
		0	1	2	3	4	5	6	7	8	9
6						□					
7						¢	.	<	(	+	|
8		&									
9		!	$	*	)	;	¬	−	/		
10								^	,	%	_
11		>	?								
12			`	:	#	@	'	=	"		a
13		b	c	d	e	f	g	h	i		
14							j	k	l	m	n
15		o	p	q	r						
16			~	s	t	u	v	w	x	y	z
17									\	{	}
18		[	]								
19					A	B	C	D	E	F	G
20		H	I								J
21		K	L	M	N	O	P	Q	R		
22								S	T	U	V
23		W	X	Y	Z						
24		0	1	2	3	4	5	6	7	8	9

In the EBCDIC table, nonprintable control characters—codes 00-63, 250-255, and those for which empty spaces appear in the chart—are not shown.

Appendix F
Program Style, Formatting, and Documentation

Useful programs have very long lifetimes, during which they must be modified and updated. Good style and documentation are essential if another programmer is to understand and work with your program.

F.1 General Guidelines

Style is of benefit only for a human reader of your program—differences in style make no difference to the computer. Good style includes the use of meaningful variable names, comments, and indentation of control structures, all of which help others to understand and work with your program. Perhaps the most important aspect of program style is consistency. If the style within a program is not consistent, then it becomes misleading and confusing.

F.2 Comments

Comments are extra information included to make a program easier to understand. You should include a comment anywhere the code is difficult to understand. However, don't overcomment. Too many comments in a program can obscure the code and be a source of distraction.

In our style, there are four basic types of comments: headers, declarations, in-line, and sidebar.

Header comments appear at the top of the program and should include your name, the date that the program was written, and its purpose. It is also useful to include sections describing input, output, and assumptions. Think of the header comments as the reader's introduction to your program. Here is an example:

```
// This program computes the sidereal time for a given date and
// solar time.
//
// Written By: Your Name
//
// Date Completed: 4/8/02
//
// Input: A date and time in the form MM DD YYYY HH MM SS
//
// Output: Sidereal time in the form HH MM SS
//
// Assumptions: Solar time is specified for a longitude of 0
//      degrees (GMT, UT, or Z time zone)
```

Header comments should also be included for all user-defined functions (see Chapters 7 and 8).

Declaration comments accompany the constant and variable declarations in the program. Anywhere that an identifier is declared, it is helpful to include a comment that explains its purpose. For example:

```
const float E = 2.71828;    // The base of the natural logarithms

float deltaX;               // The difference in the x direction
float deltaY;               // The difference in the y direction
```

Notice that aligning the comments gives the code a neater appearance and is less distracting.

In-line comments are used to break long sections of code into shorter, more comprehensible fragments. It is generally a good idea to surround in-line comments with blank lines to make them stand out. For example:

```
// Prepare file for reading

scoreFile.open("scores.dat");

// Get data

scoreFile >> test1 >> weight1;
scoreFile >> test2 >> weight2;
scoreFile >> test3 >> weight3;

// Print heading

cout << "Test Score   Weight" << endl;
```

Even if comments are not used, blank lines can be inserted wherever there is a logical break in the code that you would like to emphasize.

Sidebar comments appear to the right of executable statements and are used to shed light on the purpose of the statement. Sidebar comments are often just pseudocode statements from the lowest levels of your design. If a complicated C++ statement requires some explanation, the pseudocode statement should be written to the right of the C++ statement. For example:

```
while (file1 && file2)    // While neither file is empty...
{
    ⋮
```

In addition to the four main types of comments that we have discussed, there are some miscellaneous comments that we should mention. After the `main` function, we recommend using a row of asterisks (or dashes or equal signs or ...) in a comment before and after each function to help it to stand out. For example:

```
//****************************************************************

void PrintSecondHeading()
{
    ⋮
}

//****************************************************************
```

In this text, we use C++'s alternative comment form

```
/* Some comment */
```

to document the flow of information for each parameter of a function:

```
void GetData( /* out */ int age,          // Patient's age
              /* out */ int weight )       // Patient's weight
{
    ⋮
}

void Print( /* in */     float val,        // Value to be printed
            /* inout */ int&  count )       // Number of lines printed
                                            //   so far
{
    ⋮
}
```

(Chapter 7 describes the purpose of labeling each parameter as `/* in */`, `/* out */`, or `/* inout */`.)

Programmers sometimes place a comment after the right brace of a block (compound statement) to indicate which control structure the block belongs to:

```
while (num >= 0)
{
    ⋮
    if (num == 25)
    {
        ⋮
    } // if
} // while
```

Attaching comments in this fashion can help to clarify the code and aid in debugging mismatched braces.

F.3 Identifiers

The most important consideration in choosing a name for a data item or a function is that the name convey as much information as possible about what the data item is or what the function does. The name should also be readable in the context in which it is used. For example, the following names convey the same information but one is more readable than the other:

```
datOfInvc        invoiceDate
```

Although an identifier may be a series of words, very long identifiers can become quite tedious and can make the program difficult to read. The best approach to designing an identifier is to try writing out different names until you reach an acceptable compromise—and then write an especially informative declaration comment next to the declaration.

F.4 Formatting Lines and Expressions

C++ allows you to break a long statement in the middle and continue onto the next line. (However, you cannot split a line in the middle of an identifier, a literal constant, or a string.) When you must split a line, it's important to choose a breaking point that is logical and readable. Compare the readability of the following code fragments.

```
cout << "For a radius of " << radius << " the diameter of the cir"
        << "cle is " << diameter << endl;
cout << "For a radius of " << radius
        << " the diameter of the circle is " << diameter << endl;
```

When writing expressions, keep in mind that spaces improve readability. Usually you should include one space on either side of the = operator and most other operators. Occasionally, spaces are left out to emphasize the order in which operations are performed. Here are some examples:

```
if (x+y > y+z)
    maximum = x + y;
else
    maximum = y + z;
hypotenuse = sqrt(a*a + b*b);
```

F.5 Indentation

The purpose of indenting statements in a program is to provide visual cues to the reader and to make the program easier to debug. When a program is properly indented, the way the statements are grouped is immediately obvious. Compare the following two program fragments:

```
while (count <= 10)              while (count <= 10)
{                                {
cin >> num;                          cin >> num;
if (num == 0)                        if (num == 0)
{                                    {
count++;                                 count++;
num = 1;                                 num = 1;
}                                    }
cout << num << endl;                 cout << num << endl;
cout << count << endl;               cout << count << endl;
}                                }
```

As a basic rule in this text, each nested or lower-level item is indented by four spaces. Exceptions to this rule are parameter declarations and statements that are split across two or more lines. Indenting by four spaces is a matter of personal preference. Some people prefer to indent by three, five, or even more than five spaces.

Glossary

Abstract data type A data type whose properties (domain and operations) are specified independently of any particular implementation.

Abstraction barrier The invisible wall around a class object that encapsulates implementation details. The wall can be breached only through the public interface.

Aggregate operation An operation on a data structure as a whole, as opposed to an operation on an individual component of the data structure.

Algorithm A step-by-step procedure for solving a problem in a finite amount of time.

Anonymous type A type that does not have an associated type identifier.

Argument A variable or expression listed in a call to a function; also called *actual argument* or *actual parameter*.

Argument list A mechanism by which functions communicate with each other.

Arithmetic/logic unit (ALU) The component of the central processing unit that performs arithmetic and logical operations.

Array A collection of components, all of the same type, ordered on N dimensions ($N \geq$ 1). Each component is accessed by N indexes, each of which represents the component's position within that dimension.

Assignment expression A C++ expression with (1) a value and (2) the side effect of storing the expression value into a memory location.

Assignment statement A statement that stores the value of an expression into a variable.

Automatic variable A variable for which memory is allocated and deallocated when control enters and exits the block in which it is declared.

Auxiliary storage device A device that stores data in encoded form outside the computer's main memory.

Base address The memory address of the first element of an array.

Base case The case for which the solution can be stated nonrecursively.

Base class (superclass) The class being inherited from.

Binary operator An operator that has two operands.

Black box An electrical or mechanical device whose inner workings are hidden from view.

C string In C and C++, a null-terminated sequence of characters stored in a `char` array.

Central processing unit (CPU) The part of the computer that executes the instructions (program) stored in memory; made up of the arithmetic/logic unit and the control unit.

Class A structured type in a programming language that is used to represent an abstract data type.

Class member A component of a class. Class members may be either data or functions.

Class object (class instance) A variable of a `class` type.

Client Software that declares and manipulates objects of a particular class.

Compiler A program that translates a high-level language into machine code.

Composition (containment) A mechanism by which the internal data (the state) of one class includes an object of another class.

Computer A programmable device that can store, retrieve, and process data.

Computer program A sequence of instructions to be performed by a computer.

Computer programming The process of planning a sequence of steps for a computer to follow.

Control abstraction The separation of the logical properties of an action from its implementation.

Control structure A statement used to alter the normally sequential flow of control.

Control unit The component of the central processing unit that controls the actions of the other components so that instructions (the program) are executed in the correct sequence.

Count-controlled loop A loop that executes a specified number of times.

Data Information in a form a computer can use.

Data abstraction The separation of a data type's logical properties from its implementation.

Data flow The flow of information from the calling code to a function and from the function back to the calling code.

Data representation The concrete form of data used to represent the abstract values of an abstract data type.

Data type A specific set of data values, along with a set of operations on those values.

Declaration A statement that associates an identifier with a data object, a function, or a data type so that the programmer can refer to that item by name.

Demotion (narrowing) The conversion of a value from a "higher" type to a "lower" type according to a programming language's precedence of data types. Demotion may cause corruption of data.

Derived class (subclass) The class that inherits.

Documentation The written text and comments that make a program easier for others to understand, use, and modify.

Driver A simple `main` function that is used to call a function being tested. The use of a driver permits direct control of the testing process.

Dynamic binding The run-time determination of which function to call for a particular object.

Editor An interactive program used to create and modify source programs or data.

Encapsulation Hiding a module implementation in a separate block with a formally specified interface.

Enumeration type A user-defined data type whose domain is an ordered set of literal values expressed as identifiers.

Enumerator One of the values in the domain of an enumeration type.

Evaluate To compute a new value by performing a specified set of operations on given values.

Event counter A variable that is incremented each time a particular event occurs.

Event-controlled loop A loop that terminates when something happens inside the loop body to signal that the loop should be exited.

Expression An arrangement of identifiers, literals, and operators that can be evaluated to compute a value of a given type.

Expression statement A statement formed by appending a semicolon to an expression.

External representation The printable (character) form of a data value.

Field (member, in C++) A component of a record.

Function A subprogram in C++.

Function call (function invocation) The mechanism that transfers control to a function.

Function call (to a void function) A statement that transfers control to a void function. In C++, this statement is the name of the function, followed by a list of arguments.

Function definition A function declaration that includes the body of the function.

Function prototype A function declaration without the body of the function.

Function value type The data type of the result value returned by a function.

Functional decomposition A technique for developing software in which the problem is divided into more easily handled subproblems, the solutions of which create a solution to the overall problem.

General case The case for which the solution is expressed in terms of a smaller version of itself; also known as *recursive case*.

Hardware The physical components of a computer.

Hierarchical record A record in which at least one of the components is itself a record.

Identifier A name associated with a function or data object and used to refer to that function or data object.

Infinite recursion The situation in which a function calls itself over and over endlessly.

Information Any knowledge that can be communicated.

Information hiding The encapsulation and hiding of implementation details to keep the user of an abstraction from depending on or incorrectly manipulating these details.

Inheritance A mechanism by which one class acquires the properties—the data and operations—of another class.

Input/output (I/O) devices The parts of the computer that accept data to be processed (input) and present the results of that processing (output).

Interactive system A system that allows direct communication between user and computer.

Interface A shared boundary that permits independent systems to meet and act on or communicate with each other. Also, the formal description of the purpose of a subprogram and the mechanism for communicating with it.

Internal representation The form in which a data value is stored inside the memory unit.

Iteration   An individual pass through, or repetition of, the body of a loop.

Iteration counter   A counter variable that is incremented with each iteration of a loop.

Length   The number of values currently stored in a list.

Lifetime   The period of time during program execution when an identifier has memory allocated to it.

List   A variable-length, linear collection of homogeneous components.

Literal value   Any constant value written in a program.

Local variable   A variable declared within a block and not accessible outside of that block.

Loop   A control structure that causes a statement or group of statements to be executed repeatedly.

Loop entry   The point at which the flow of control reaches the first statement inside a loop.

Loop exit   The point at which the repetition of the loop body ends and control passes to the first statement following the loop.

Loop test   The point at which the While expression is evaluated and the decision is made either to begin a new iteration or skip to the statement immediately following the loop.

Machine language   The language, made up of binary-coded instructions, that is used directly by the computer.

Member selector   The expression used to access components of a struct or class variable. It is formed by using the struct or class variable name and the member name, separated by a dot (period).

Memory unit   Internal data storage in a computer.

Mixed type expression   An expression that contains operands of different data types; also called *mixed mode expression.*

Name precedence   The precedence that a local identifier in a function has over a global identifier with the same name in any references that the function makes to that identifier; also called *name hiding.*

Named constant (symbolic constant)   A location in memory, referenced by an identifier, that contains a data value that cannot be changed.

Named type   A user-defined type whose declaration includes a type identifier that gives a name to the type.

Nonlocal identifier   With respect to a given block, any identifier declared outside that block.

Object-oriented design (OOD)   A technique for developing software in which the solution is expressed in terms of objects—self-contained entities composed of data and operations on that data.

Object-oriented programming (OOP)   The use of data abstraction, inheritance, and dynamic binding to construct programs that are collections of interacting objects.

Object program   The machine language version of a source program.

One-dimensional array   A structured collection of components, all of the same type, that is given a single name. Each component (array element) is accessed by an index that indicates the component's position within the collection.

Operating system A set of programs that manages all of the computer's resources.

Out-of-bounds array index An index value that, in C++, is either less than 0 or greater than the array size minus 1.

Parameter A variable declared in a function heading; also called *formal argument* or *formal parameter.*

Peripheral device An input, output, or auxiliary storage device attached to a computer.

Polymorphic operation An operation that has multiple meanings depending on the type of the object to which it is bound at run time.

Postcondition An assertion that must be true after a module has executed.

Precision The maximum number of significant digits.

Precondition An assertion that must be true before a module begins executing.

Programming Planning or scheduling the performance of a task or an event.

Programming language A set of rules, symbols, and special words used to construct a computer program.

Promotion (widening) The conversion of a value from a "lower" type to a "higher" type according to a programming language's precedence of data types.

Range of values The interval within which values of a numeric type must fall, specified in terms of the largest and smallest allowable values.

Record (structure, in C++) A structured data type with a fixed number of components that are accessed by name. The components may be heterogeneous (of different types).

Recursive algorithm A solution that is expressed in terms of (a) smaller instances of itself and (b) a base case.

Recursive call A function call in which the function being called is the same as the one making the call.

Recursive definition A definition in which something is defined in terms of smaller versions of itself.

Reference parameter A parameter that receives the location (memory address) of the caller's argument.

Representational error Arithmetic error that occurs when the precision of the true result of an arithmetic operation is greater than the precision of the machine.

Reserved word A word that has special meaning in C++; it cannot be used as a programmer-defined identifier.

Scope The region of program code where it is legal to reference (use) an identifier.

Scope rules The rules that determine where in the program an identifier may be accessed, given the point where that identifier is declared.

Self-documenting code Program code containing meaningful identifiers as well as judiciously used clarifying comments.

Semantics The set of rules that determines the meaning of instructions written in a programming language.

Short-circuit (conditional) evaluation Evaluation of a logical expression in left-to-right order with evaluation stopping as soon as the final truth value can be determined.

Side effect Any effect of one function on another that is not a part of the explicitly defined interface between them.

Significant digits Those digits from the first nonzero digit on the left to the last nonzero digit on the right (plus any 0 digits that are exact).

Simple (atomic) data type A data type in which each value is atomic (indivisible).

Software Computer programs; the set of all programs available on a computer.

Software engineering The application of traditional engineering methodologies and techniques to the development of software.

Software piracy The unauthorized copying of software for either personal use or use by others.

Sorting Arranging the components of a list into order (for instance, words into alphabetical order or numbers into ascending or descending order).

Source program A program written in a high-level programming language.

Static binding The compile-time determination of which function to call for a particular object.

Static variable A variable for which memory remains allocated throughout the execution of the entire program.

Structured data type A data type in which each value is a collection of components and whose organization is characterized by the method used to access individual components. The allowable operations on a structured data type include the storage and retrieval of individual components.

Structured (procedural) programming The construction of programs that are collections of interacting functions or procedures.

Stub A dummy function that assists in testing part of a program. A stub has the same name and interface as a function that actually would be called by the part of the program being tested, but it is usually much simpler.

Switch expression The expression whose value determines which switch label is selected. It cannot be a floating-point or string expression.

Syntax The formal rules governing how valid instructions are written in a programming language.

Tail recursion A recursive algorithm in which no statements are executed after the return from the recursive call.

Termination condition The condition that causes a loop to be exited.

Test plan A document that specifies how a program is to be tested.

Test plan implementation Using the test cases specified in a test plan to verify that a program outputs the predicted results.

Testing the state of a stream The act of using a C++ stream object in a logical expression as if it were a Boolean variable; the result is `true` if the last I/O operation on that stream succeeded, and `false` otherwise.

Two-dimensional array A collection of components, all of the same type, structured in two dimensions. Each component is accessed by a pair of indexes that represent the component's position in each dimension.

Type casting The explicit conversion of a value from one data type to another; also called type conversion.

Type coercion   The implicit (automatic) conversion of a value from one data type to another.

Unary operator   An operator that has just one operand.

Value parameter   A parameter that receives a copy of the value of the corresponding argument.

Value-returning function   A function that returns a single value to its caller and is invoked from within an expression.

Variable   A location in memory, referenced by an identifier, that contains a data value that can be changed.

Virus   A computer program that replicates itself, often with the goal of spreading to other computers without authorization, and possibly with the intent of doing harm.

Void function (procedure)   A function that does not return a function value to its caller and is invoked as a separate statement.

Answers to Selected Exercises

Chapter 2   Exam Preparation Exercises

1. a. invalid   b. valid   c. valid   d. invalid   e. valid   f. invalid   g. valid   h. invalid
3. program—15; algorithm—14; compiler—3; identifier—1; compilation phase—12; execution phase—10; variable—11; constant—2; memory—13; syntax—6; semantics—8; block—7
4. a. reserved   b. programmer-defined   c. programmer-defined   d. reserved   e. programmer-defined
7. a. `s1 = blues2 = bird`
   b. `Result:bluebird`
   c. `Result:  bluebird`
   d. `Result:  blue bird`
8. `A rolling`
   `stone`
                    ← One blank line
   `gathers`

                    ← Three blank lines

   `nomoss`
11. False
14. `1425B Elm St.`
    `Amaryllis, Iowa`

Chapter 2   Programming Warm-up Exercises

2. `cout << "The moon" << endl;`
   `cout << "is" << endl;`
   `cout << "blue." << endl;`
3. `string make;`
   `string model;`
   `string color;`
   `string plateType;`
   `char   classification;`

Chapter 3   Exam Preparation Exercises

3. a. Floating point: 13.3333   b. Integer: 2   c. Integer: 5   d. Floating point: 13.75
   e. Integer: −4   f. Integer: 1   g. Illegal: 10.0 / 3.0 is a floating-point expression, but the % operator requires integer operands.
6. `Cost is`
   `300`
   `Price is 30Cost is 300`
   `Grade A costs`
   `300`
9. a. `iostream`   b. `cstdlib`   c. `cmath`   d. `iostream`   e. `iostream` and `iomanip`
14. False
15. The named constants make the program easier to read and understand. Also, to change one of the constants, you only need to change one line (the constant declaration) instead of changing every occurrence of the literal constant throughout the program.

Chapter 3   Programming Warm-up Exercises

1. Only one line needs to be changed. In the following declaration, change 10 to 15:

    ```
    const int LBS = 10;
    ```

2. `sum = n * (n + 1) / 2;`

5.  ```
    discriminant = sqrt(b * b - 4.0 * a * c);
    denominator = 2.0 * a;
    solution1 = (-b + discriminant) / denominator;
    solution2 = (-b - discriminant) / denominator;
    ```

9. The expression is `sentence.find("res")`. The first occurrence of the string "res" occurs at position 12.

11. Declare a constant `ROUND_FACTOR` (defined to be equal to the desired rounding factor, such as 100.0 for hundredths) and replace every occurrence of 10.0 with `ROUND_FACTOR`.

Chapter 4   Exam Preparation Exercises

2. a. `int1` contains 17, `int2` contains 13, and `int3` contains 7.

    b. The leftover values remain waiting in the input stream. These values will be read by subsequent input statements (or they will be ignored if no more input statements are executed).

6. True

8. `123  147`

13. Errors in the program are as follows:

    ■ The declaration of `outData` is missing:

    ```
    ofstream outData;
    ```

    ■ The opening of the input file is missing:

    ```
    inData.open("myfile.dat");
    ```

    ■ The statement

    ```
    cin >> n;
    ```

    does not read from the input file. Change `cin` to `inData`.

14. With the corrected version of the program in Exercise 13, file stream `inData` will still contain the value 144 after the program is executed. File stream `outData` will contain 144, followed by a newline character.

18. False. Class member functions are invoked by using dot notation.

19. Get Length and Width, Get Wood Cost, and Get Canvas Cost are input modules. Compute Dimensions and Costs is a computational module. Print Dimensions and Costs is an output module.

Chapter 4   Programming Warm-up Exercises

1. `cin >> ch1 >> ch2 >> ch3;`

3. `cin >> length1 >> height1 >> length2 >> height2;`

4. In the following, the value 100 is arbitrary. Any value greater than 4 will work.

    ```
    cin.get(chr1);
    cin.ignore(100, '\n');
    cin.get(chr2);
    cin.ignore(100, '\n');
    cin.get(chr3);
    cin.ignore(100, '\n');
    ```
    ```

8. ```
#include <iostream>
#include <fstream>

using namespace std;

int main()
{
    int   val1;
    int   val2;
    int   val3;
    int   val4;
    ifstream dataIn;
    ofstream resultsOut;

    dataIn.open("myinput.dat");
    resultsOut.open("myoutput.dat");
    dataIn >> val1 >> val2 >> val3 >> val4;
    resultsOut << val1 << val2 << val3 << val4 << endl;
    return 0;
}
```

10. Note that the problem statement said nothing about getting into the car, adjusting seatbelts, checking the mirror, or driving away. Presumably those tasks, along with starting the car, are subtasks of a larger design such as "Go to the store." Here we are concerned only with starting the car itself.

**Main Module**
  Ensure car won't roll.
  Disengage gears.
  Attempt ignition.

**Ensure Car Won't Roll**
  Engage parking brake.
  Turn wheels into curb.

**Disengage Gears**
  Push in clutch with left foot.
  Move gearshift to neutral.
  Release clutch.

**Attempt Ignition**
  Insert key into ignition slot.
  Turn key to ON position.
  Pump accelerator once.
  Turn key to START position.
  Release after engine catches or 5 seconds, whichever comes first.
```

Chapter 5   Exam Preparation Exercises

2. a. No parentheses are needed. b. No parentheses are needed. c. No parentheses are needed.
   d. !(q && q)
6. a. 4   b. 2   c. 5   d. 3   e. 1
9. a. If-Then-Else   b. If-Then   c. If-Then   d. If-Then-Else
10. The error message is printed because there is a semicolon after the right brace of a block (compound statement).
13. Yes
15. No. The data is only valid if each test score is nonnegative. Modifying the code to test whether the sum of the test scores is nonnegative will not catch the following invalid case: test1 = 100, test2 = 80, test3 = -20.

Chapter 5   Programming Warm-up Exercises

2. In the following statement, the outer parentheses are not required but are included for readability.

```
available = (numberOrdered <= (numberOnHand - numberReserved));
```

4. In the following statement, the outer parentheses are not required but are included for readability.

```
leftPage = (pageNumber % 2 == 0);
```

6.
```
if (year % 4 == 0)
    cout << year << " is a leap year." << endl;
else
{
    year = year + 4 - year % 4;
    cout << year << " is the next leap year." << endl;
}
```

7.
```
if (age > 64)
    cout << "Senior voter";
else if (age < 18)
    cout << "Under age";
else
    cout << "Regular voter";
```

9.
```
// This is a nonsense program
if (a > 0)
    if (a < 20)
    {
        cout << "A is in range." << endl;
        b = 5;
    }
    else
    {
        cout << "A is too large." << endl;
        b = 3;
    }
else
    cout << "A is too small." << endl;
cout << "All done." << endl;
```

14. To input and compute the average of four scores, one control structure would need to be changed. The statement

```
if (test1 < 0 || test2 < 0 || test3 < 0)
    dataOK = false;
else
    dataOK = true;
```

would need to be replaced with

```
if (test1 < 0 || test2 < 0 || test3 < 0 || test4 < 0)
    dataOK = false;
else
    dataOK = true;
```

Note that the program would require other changes, but this is the only control structure that would need to be changed.

Chapter 6   Exam Preparation Exercises

3.
```
number = 1;
while (number < 11)
{
    cout << number << endl;
    number++;
}
```

4. Six iterations are performed.

9. Telephone numbers read in as integers have many different values that could be used as sentinels. In the United States, a standard telephone number is a positive seven-digit integer (ignoring area codes) and cannot start with 0, 1, 411, or 911. Therefore, a reasonable sentinel may be negative, greater than 9999999, or less than 2000000.

11. a. (1) Change < to <=. (2) Change 1 to 0. (3) Change 20 to 21.

   b. Changes (1) and (3) make `count` range from 1 through 21. Change (2) makes `count` range from 0 through 20.

Chapter 6   Programming Warm-up Exercises

1.
```
dangerous = false;
while ( !dangerous )
{
    cin >> pressure;
    if (pressure > 510.0)
        dangerous = true;
}
```

or

```
dangerous = false;
while ( !dangerous )
{
    cin >> pressure;
    dangerous = (pressure > 510.0);
}
```

```
2.  count28 = 0;
    loopCount = 1;
    while (loopCount <= 100)
    {
        inputFile >> number;
        if (number == 28)
            count28++;
        loopCount++;
    }
5.  positives = 0;
    negatives = 0;
    cin >> number;
    while (cin)         // While NOT EOF...
    {
        if (number > 0)
            positives++;
        else if (number < 0)
            negatives++;
        cin >> number;
    }
    cout << "Number of positive numbers: " << positives << endl;
    cout << "Number of negative numbers: " << negatives << endl;
6.  sum = 0;
    evenInt = 16;
    while (evenInt <= 26)
    {
        sum = sum + evenInt;
        evenInt = evenInt + 2;
    }
7.  hour = 1;
    minute = 0;
    am = true;
    done = false;
    while ( !done )
    {
        cout << hour << ':';
        if (minute < 10)
            cout << '0';
        cout << minute;
        if (am)
            cout << " A.M." << endl;
        else
            cout << " P.M." << endl;

        minute++;
        if (minute > 59)
        {
            minute = 0;
            hour++;
            if (hour == 13)
                hour = 1;
            else if (hour == 12)
                am = !am;
        }
```

```
        if (hour == 1 && minute == 0 && am)
            done = true;
    }
```

12. a.   In the While loop, check for a negative income amount before processing it:

```
        incFile >> sex >> amount;
        femaleCount = 0;
        femaleSum = 0.0;
        maleCount = 0;
        maleSum = 0.0;

        while (incFile)
        {
            cout << "Sex: " << sex << " Amount: " << amount << endl;

            if (amount < 0.0)                    // Check for invalid salary
                cout << "** Bad data--negative salary **" << endl;
            else
                if (sex == 'F')
                {
                    femaleCount++;
                    femaleSum = femaleSum + amount;
                }
                else
                {
                    maleCount++;
                    maleSum = maleSum + amount;
                }
            incFile >> sex >> amount;
        }
```

13. Set 1:
          Empty file
    Set 2 (no males) :
          F 30000
    Set 3 (no females):
          M 30000
    Set 4 (invalid sex codes and income values):
          F 64000
          R 20000
          M 40000
          F -15000
          M 50000
          G 30000
          M -30000
          F 20000

Chapter 7   Exam Preparation Exercises

4. 5 3 13
    3 3 9
    9 12 30

7. For passing by value, parts (a) through (g) are all valid. For passing by reference, only parts (a) and (c) are valid.

8. 13571 (the memory address of the variable `widgets`).

10. The answers are 12 10 3

11. Variables in `main` just before `Change` is called: a = 10 and b = 7. Variables in `Change` at the moment control enters the function (before any statements are executed): x = 10, y = 7, and the value of b is undefined. Variables in `main` after return from `Change`: a = 10 (x in `Change` is a value parameter, so the argument a is not modified) and b = 17.

Chapter 7   Programming Warm-up Exercises

2.
```
void RocketSimulation( /* in */     float   thrust,
                       /* inout */ float&  weight,
                       /* in */      int     timeStep,
                       /* in */      int     totalTime,
                       /* out */     float&  velocity,
                       /* out */     bool&   outOfFuel )
```

5.
```
void Halve( /* inout */ int& firstNumber,
            /* inout */ int& secondNumber )


// Precondition:
//     firstNumber and secondNumber are assigned
// Postcondition:
//     firstNumber == firstNumber@entry / 2
//  && secondNumber == secondNumber@entry / 2

{
    ⋮

}
```

7. a. Function definition:

```
void ScanHeart( /* out */ bool& normal )

// Postcondition:
//     normal == true, if a normal heart rate (60-80) was input
//                      before EOF occurred
//            == false, otherwise
{
    int heartRate;

    cin >> heartRate;
    while ((heartRate < 60 || heartRate > 80) && cin)
        cin >> heartRate;

    // At loop exit, either (heartRate >= 60 && heartRate <= 80)
    // or EOF occurred

    normal = (heartRate >= 60 && heartRate <= 80);
}
```

b. Function invocation:

```
ScanHeart(normal);
```

8. a. **Function definition:**

```
void Rotate( /* inout */ int& firstValue,
             /* inout */ int& secondValue,
             /* inout */ int& thirdValue  )
// This function takes three parameters and returns their values
// in a shifted order

// Precondition:
//     firstValue, secondValue, and thirdValue are assigned
// Postcondition:
//     firstValue == secondValue@entry
//  && secondValue == thirdValue@entry
//  && thirdValue == firstValue@entry

{
    int temp;     // Temporary holding variable

    // Save value of first parameter

    temp = firstValue;

    // Shift values of next two parameters

    firstValue = secondValue;
    secondValue = thirdValue;

    // Replace value of final parameter with saved value

    thirdValue = temp;
}
```

b. **Test program:**

```
#include <iostream>

using namespace std;

void Rotate( int&, int&, int& );

int main()
{
    int int1;     // First input value
    int int2;     // Second input value
    int int3;     // Third input value

    cout << "Enter three values: ";
    cin >> int1 >> int2 >> int3;

    cout << "Before: " << int1 << ' ' << int2 << ' '
         << int3 << endl;
```

```
        Rotate(int1, int2, int3);
        cout << "After: " << int1 << ' ' << int2 << ' '
            << int3 << endl;
        return 0;
    }
    // The Rotate function, as above, goes here
16. void PrintData( /* in */ int    deptID,
        /* in */ int    storeNum,
        /* in */ float deptSales )
    {
        string bar;    // Bar of asterisks

        cout << setw(12) << "Dept " << deptID << endl;
        cout << setw(3) << storeNum << "    ";
        bar = BarOfAsterisks(deptSales);
        cout << bar << endl;
    }
```

Chapter 8 Exam Preparation Exercises

1. True
5. 1 1
   1 2
   1 3
7. Yes
11. It is risky to use a reference parameter as a parameter of a value-returning function because it provides a mechanism for side effects to escape from the function. A value-returning function usually is designed to return a single result (the function value), which is then used in the expression that called the function. If a value-returning function declares a reference parameter and modifies the parameter (hence, the caller's argument), that function is returning more than one result, which is not obvious from the way the function is invoked. (However, an I/O stream variable *must* be declared as a reference parameter, even in a value-returning function.)

Chapter 8 Programming Warm-up Exercises

```
3. bool NearlyEqual( /* in */ float num1,
                     /* in */ float num2,
                     /* in */ float difference )
5. float CompassHeading( /* in */ float trueCourse,
                         /* in */ float windCorrAngle,
                         /* in */ float variance,
                         /* in */ float deviation    )

    // Precondition:
    //     All parameters are assigned
    // Postcondition:
    //     Function value == trueCourse + windCorrAngle +
    //                       variance + deviation

    {
        return trueCourse + windCorrAngle + variance + deviation;
    }
```

8. Function body for `Hypotenuse` function (assuming the header file `cmath` has been included in order to access the `sqrt` function):

```
{
    return sqrt(side1*side1 + side2*side2);
}
```

13. Below, the type of `costPerOunce` and the function return type are `float` so that the cost can be expressed in terms of dollars and cents (e.g., 1.23 means $1.23). These types could be `int` if the cost were expressed in terms of cents only (e.g., 123 means $1.23).

```
float Postage( /* in */ int     pounds,
               /* in */ int     ounces,
               /* in */ float costPerOunce )

// Precondition:
//     pounds >= 0  &&  ounces >= 0  &&  costPerOunce >= 0.0
// Postcondition:
//     Function value == (pounds * 16 + ounces) * costPerOunce

{
    return (pounds * 16 + ounces) * costPerOunce;
}
```

14. Change the body of `GetData` so that it begins as follows:

```
{
    bool badData;    // True if an input value is invalid

    badData = true;
    while (badData)
    {
        cout << "Enter the number of crew (1 or 2)." << endl;
        cin >> crew;
        badData = (crew < 1 || crew > 2);
        if (badData)
            cout << "Invalid number of crew members." << endl;
    }
    badData = true;
    while (badData)
    {
        cout << "Enter the number of passengers (0 through 8)."
            << endl;
        cin >> passengers;
        badData = (passengers < 0 || passengers > 8);
        if (badData)
            cout << "Invalid number of passengers." << endl;
    }
```

Continue in this manner to validate the closet weight (0–160 pounds), baggage weight (0–525 pounds), and amount of fuel loaded (10–565 gallons).

Chapter 9 Exam Preparation Exercises

2. False
4. False
6. MaryJoeAnneWhoops!
9. 1
13. False

Chapter 9   Programming Warm-up Exercises

1.
```
switch (grade)
{
    case 'A' : sum = sum + 4;
             break;
    case 'B' : sum = sum + 3;
             break;
    case 'C' : sum = sum + 2;
             break;
    case 'D' : sum++;
             break;
    case 'F' : cout << "Student is on probation" << endl;
             break;    // Not required
}
```

2.
```
switch (grade)
{
    case 'A' : sum = sum + 4;
             break;
    case 'B' : sum = sum + 3;
             break;
    case 'C' : sum = sum + 2;
             break;
    case 'D' : sum++;
             break;
    case 'F' : cout << "Student is on probation" << endl;
             break;
    default  : cout << "Invalid letter grade" << endl;
             break;    // Not required
}
```

5.
```
do
{
    cout << "Enter 1, 2, or 3: ";
    cin >> response;
} while (response < 1 || response > 3);
```

6.
```
cin >> ch;
while (cin)
{
    cout << ch;
    cin >> ch;
}
```

10. This solution returns proper results only if the precondition shown in the comments is true. Note that it returns the correct result for $base^0$, which is 1.

```
int Power( /* in */ int base,
           /* in */ int exponent )

// Precondition:
//    base is assigned  &&  exponent >= 0
// && (base to the exponent power) <= INT_MAX
// Postcondition:
//    Function value == base to the exponent power
```

```
        {
            int result = 1;      // Holds intermediate powers of base
            int count;           // Loop control variable

            for (count = 1; count <= exponent; count++)
                result = result * base;
            return result;
        }
12. void GetYesOrNo( /* out */ char& response )    // User response char
        {
            cin >> response;
            while (response != 'y' && response != 'n')
            {
                cout << "Please type y or n: ";
                cin >> response;
            }
        }
    void GetOneAmount( /* out */ float& amount )    // Rainfall amount
                                                    // for one month
        {
            cin >> amount;
            while (amount < 0.0)
            {
                cout << "Amount cannot be negative. Enter again: ";
                cin >> amount;
            }
        }
```

Chapter 10   Exam Preparation Exercises

3. a. sumOfSquares += x * x;
   b. count--;
      or
      --count;
   c. k = (n > 8) ? 32 : 15 * n;
5. Notice that
   the character \ is a backslash.
6. a. 1.4E+12 (to 10 digits)   b. 100.0 (to 10 digits)   c. 3.2E+5 (to 10 digits)
9. a. valid   b. invalid   c. invalid   d. valid
12. False. The angle brackets (< >) should be quotation marks.

Chapter 10   Programming Warm-up Exercises

2. cout << "Hello\tThere\n\n\n\"Ace\"";
6. enum CourseType {CS101, CS200, CS210, CS350, CS375, CS441};
8. enum DayType {MONDAY, TUESDAY, WEDNESDAY, THURSDAY, FRIDAY};
9. DayType CharToDay(/* in */ char ch1,
                      /* in */ char ch2)

   // Precondition:
   //   ch1=='M' OR ch1=='W' OR ch1=='F' OR
   //   (ch1=='T' && ch2=='U') OR (ch1=='T' && ch2=='H')

```
// Postcondition:
//      Function value == MONDAY, if ch1=='M'
//                     == TUESDAY, if (ch1=='T' && ch2=='U')
//                     == WEDNESDAY, if ch1=='W'
//                     == THURSDAY, if (ch1=='T' && ch2=='H')
//                     == FRIDAY, if ch1=='F'

{
    switch (ch1)
    {
        case 'M' : return MONDAY;
        case 'T' : if (ch2 == 'U')
                       return TUESDAY;
                   else
                       return THURSDAY;
        case 'W' : return WEDNESDAY;
        case 'F' : return FRIDAY;
    }
}
```

Chapter 11   Exam Preparation Exercises

2.
```
struct RecType
{
    int   numDependents;
    float salary;
    bool  hasMajorMed;
};
```
7. a. SomeClass and int   b. Func1, Func2, Func3, and someInt   c. object1 and object2   d. Func1, Func2, and Func3   e. Func1 and Func3   f. part (ii)
8. True
11. a. Only myprog.cpp must be recompiled.   b. All of the object (.obj) files must be relinked.   c. Only file2.cpp and file3.cpp must be recompiled.   d. All of the object (.obj) files must be relinked.

Chapter 11   Programming Warm-up Exercises

1. a.
```
enum YearType {FRESHMAN, SOPHOMORE, JUNIOR, SENIOR};
enum SexType {M, F};

struct PersonType
{
    string   name;
    string   ssNumber;
    YearType year;
    float    gpa;
    SexType  sex;
};
```

```
   b.
   PersonType person;
      :
   cout << person.name << endl;
   cout << person.ssNumber << endl;
   switch (person.year)
   {
       FRESHMAN  : cout << "Freshman" << endl;
                    break;
       SOPHOMORE : cout << "Sophomore" << endl;
                    break;
       JUNIOR    : cout << "Junior" << endl;
                    break;
       SENIOR    : cout << "Senior" << endl;
   }
   cout << person.gpa << endl;
   if (person.sex == M)
       cout << "Male" << endl;
   else
       cout << "Female" << endl;
```

3.
```
   enum YearType {FRESHMAN, SOPHOMORE, JUNIOR, SENIOR};
   struct DateType
   {
       int month;
       int year;
   };

   struct StudentType
   {
       string    name;
       long      studentID;
       int       hoursToDate;
       int       coursesToDate;
       DateType  firstEnrolled;
       YearType  year;
       float     gpa;
   };
```

5.
```
   a. if ( !time1.Equal(time2) )
          n = 1;
   b. if (time1.LessThan(time2) || time1.Equal(time2))
          n = 5;
   c. if (time2.LessThan(time1))
          n = 8;
   d. if ( !time1.LessThan(time2) )
          n = 5;
      or
      if (time2.LessThan(time1) || time2.Equal(time1))
          n = 5;
```

7. Function specification (within the TimeType class declaration):

```
   void WriteAmPm() const;
      // Postcondition:
      //     Time has been output in 12-hour form
      //         HH:MM:SS AM  or  HH:MM:SS PM
```

Function definition (omitting the postcondition to save space):

```
void TimeType::WriteAmPm() const
{
    bool am;            // True if AM should be printed
    int tempHrs;        // Value of hours to be printed

    am = (hrs <= 11);
    if (hrs == 0)
        tempHrs = 12;
    else if (hrs >= 13)
        tempHrs = hrs - 12;
    else
        tempHrs = hrs;

    if (tempHrs < 10)
        cout << '0';
    cout << tempHrs << ':';
    if (mins < 10)
        cout << '0';
    cout << mins << ':';
    if (secs < 10)
        cout << '0';
    cout << secs;
    if (am)
        cout << " AM";
    else
        cout << " PM";
}
```

8. Function specification (within the `TimeType` class declaration):

```
long Minus( /* in */ TimeType time2 ) const;
    // Precondition:
    //     This time and time2 represent times in the same day
    // Postcondition:
    //     Function value == (this time) - time2, in seconds
```

Function definition (omitting the precondition and postcondition to save space):

```
long TimeType::Minus( /* in */ TimeType time2 ) const
{
    long thisTimeInSecs;    // This time in seconds since midnight
    long time2InSecs;       // time2 in seconds since midnight

    // Using 3600 seconds per hour and 60 seconds per minute...

    thisTimeInSecs = long(hrs)*3600 + long(mins)*60 + long(secs);
    time2InSecs = long(time2.hrs)*3600 + long(time2.mins)*60 +
                  long(time2.secs);
    return thisTimeInSecs - time2InSecs;
}
```

15. Assuming a variable `areaCode` is of type `int`, one solution is to print a leading zero if the area code is less than 100:

```
if (areaCode < 100)
    cout << '0';
cout << areaCode;
```

Another solution is to declare an area code to be a string rather than an `int`, thereby reading or printing exactly three characters each time I/O takes place.

Chapter 12   Exam Preparation Exercises

1. True
5. a. `enum BirdType {CARDINAL, BLUEJAY, HUMMINGBIRD, ROBIN};`
   b. `int sightings[4];`
7. 1 3 -2
   17 6 11
   4 2 2
   19 14 5
   11 15 -4

   52 40 12

9. `sample` [0] [1] [2] [3] [4] [5] [6] [7]

10	9	8	7	6	5	4	3

14. a. hierarchical record b. record c. record d. array of records e. array f. array of hierarchical records g. array of records
18. a. valid b. valid c. invalid d. valid e. invalid f. invalid
20. a. True b. False c. True d. True

Chapter 12   Programming Warm-up Exercises

1. ```
void Initialize(/* out */ bool failing[])

// Postcondition:
//   failing[0..NUM_STUDS-1] == false

{
    int index;   // Loop control and index variable

    for (index = 0; index < NUM_STUDS; index++)
        failing[index] = false;
}
```

3. ```
void SetPassing( /* inout */     bool passing[],
                 /* in */   const int  score[]   )

// Precondition:
//     score[0..NUM_STUDS-1] are assigned
// Postcondition:
//     For all i, where 0 <= i <= NUM_STUDS-1,
//         IF score[i] >= 60, THEN passing[i] == true
```

```
    {
        int index;    // Loop control and index variable

        for (index = 0; index < NUM_STUDS; index++)
            if (score[index] >= 60)
                passing[index] = true;
    }
```

8. Below, assume the input will never exceed 500 parts.

```
const int MAX_PARTS = 500;

struct PartType
{
    int    number;
    float cost;
};

PartType part[MAX_PARTS];
int      count = 0;

cin >> part[count].number >> part[count].cost;
while (cin)
{
    count++;
    cin >> part[count].number >> part[count].cost;
}
```

11.
```
void Copy( /* in */   const TwoDimType data,
           /* out */        TwoDimType data2 )

// Precondition:
//     data[0..NUM_ROWS-1][0..NUM_COLS-1] are assigned
// Postcondition:
//     data2[0..NUM_ROWS-1][0..NUM_COLS-1] ==
//        corresponding elements of array "data"

{
    int row;      // Loop control and index variable
    int col;      // Loop control and index variable

    for (row = 0; row < NUM_ROWS; row++)
        for (col = 0; col < NUM_COLS; col++)
            data2[row][col] = data[row][col];
}
```

16. Below, assume ArrayType is a two-dimensional integer array type with NUM_ROWS rows and NUM_COLS columns.

```
int RowSum( /* in */ const ArrayType arr,
            /* in */       int        whichRow,
            /* in */       int        colsFilled )

// Precondition:
//     colsFilled <= NUM_COLS  &&  whichRow < NUM_ROWS
//  && arr[whichRow][0..colsFilled-1] are assigned
```

```
// Postcondition:
//     Function value == arr[whichRow][0] + ...
//                     + arr[whichRow][colsFilled-1]


{
    int col;        // Loop control and index variable
    int sum = 0;    // Accumulating sum

    for (col = 0; col < colsFilled; col++)
        sum = sum + arr[whichRow][col];
    return sum;
}
```

17. No. If `firstList` were declared to be a `const` parameter, the compiler would not allow the function body to modify the array. Specifically, the statement

```
firstList[counter] = number;
```

would generate a compile-time error.

Chapter 13   Exam Preparation Exercises

6. a. `typedef char NameType[41];`
    b. `NameType oneName;`
    c. `NameType employeeName[100];`
7. a. valid   b. valid   c. invalid   d. valid   e. valid   f. invalid   g. invalid   h. valid
9. a. valid   b. invalid   c. valid   d. invalid   e. valid   f. invalid   g. valid
11. Using a binary search, the number of loop iterations for an unsuccessful search of 200 items is 8 (because $\log_2 128 = 7$ and $\log_2 256 = 8$). Using a sequential search of a sorted list, the worst-case number of loop iterations is 200, the best case is 1 iteration, and the average is 100.

Chapter 13   Programming Warm-up Exercises

2. `int List::Occurrences( /* in */ ItemType item )`

```
// Precondition:
//     item is assigned
// Postcondition:
//     Function value == number of occurrences of value "item"
//                     in data[0..length-1]


{
    int index;         // Loop control and index variable
    int counter = 0;   // Number of occurrences of item

    for (index = 0; index < length; index++)
        if (data[index] == item)
            counter++;
    return counter;
}
```

8. The `SortedList::BinSearch` function remains the same until the last If statement. This statement should be replaced with the following:

```
if (found)
    position = middle;
else
    position = first;
```

Also, the function postcondition should read as follows:

```
//      IF item is in list
//          found == true  &&  data[position] contains item
//      ELSE
//          found == false  &&  position is where item belongs
```

10.
```
void SortedList::Component(
        /* in */  int       pos,      // Desired position
        /* out */ ItemType& item,     // Item retrieved
        /* out */ bool&     valid )   // True if pos is valid

// Precondition:
//      pos is assigned
// Postcondition:
//      IF 0 <= pos < length
//          valid == true
//      && item == data[pos]
//      ELSE
//          valid == false
{
    valid = (pos >= 0 && pos < length);
    if (valid)
        item = data[pos];
}
```

Chapter 14 Exam Preparation Exercises

2. False
4. *Class Abc:*
   a. The private data members are `alpha` and `beta`.
   b. Functions `DoThis` and `DoThat` can reference `alpha` and `beta` directly.
   c. Functions `DoThis` and `DoThat` can invoke each other directly.
   d. Clients can invoke `DoThis`.

   Class Xyz:
   a. The private data members are `alpha`, `beta`, and `gamma`.
   b. Function `TryIt` can reference only `gamma` directly.
   c. Function `TryIt` can invoke the parent class's `DoThis` function directly. The syntax for the function call is `Abc::DoThis()`.
   d. Clients can invoke `DoThis` and `TryIt`.

8. a. False b. True c. False

Chapter 14   Programming Warm-up Exercises

```
2. #include <cmath>    // For sqrt()
     ⋮
   float Line::Length() const

   // Postcondition:
   //      Function value == length of this line

   {
       float diffX;    // Difference in x coordinates
       float diffY;    // Difference in y coordinates

       diffX = startPt.X_Coord() - endPt.X_Coord();
       diffY = startPt.Y_Coord() - endPt.Y_Coord();
       return sqrt(diffX*diffX + diffY*diffY);
   }
3. class InterAddress : public Address
   {
   public:
       void Write() const;
           // Postcondition:
           //      Address has been output

       InterAddress( /* in */ string newStreet,
                     /* in */ string newCity,
                     /* in */ string newState,
                     /* in */ string newZip,
                     /* in */ string newCountry );
           // Precondition:
           //      All parameters are assigned
           // Postcondition:
           //      Class object is constructed with private data
           //          initialized by the incoming parameters
   private:
       string country;
   };
7. class TimeAndDay
   {
   public:
       void Set( /* in */ int hours,
                 /* in */ int minutes,
                 /* in */ int seconds,
                 /* in */ int month,
                 /* in */ int day,
                 /* in */ int year      );
           // Precondition:
           //      0 <= hours <= 23   &&  0 <= minutes <= 59
           //   && 0 <= seconds <= 59  &&  1 <= month <= 12
           //   && 1 <= day <= maximum no. of days in month
           //   && year > 1582
           // Postcondition:
           //      Time and date are set according to the
           //          incoming parameters
```

```
        void Increment();
           // Postcondition:
           //     Time has been advanced by one second, with
           //       23:59:59 wrapping around to 0:0:0
           //    && IF new time is 0:0:0
           //          Date has been advanced to the next day

        void Write() const;
           // Postcondition:
           //     Time and date have been output in the form
           //       HH:MM:SS  month day, year

        TimeAndDay();
           // Postcondition:
           //     Class object is constructed with a time of 0:0:0
           //     and a date of January 1, 1583
    private:
        TimeType time;
        DateType date;
    };
```

Chapter 15   Exam Preparation Exercises

2. False. Both void functions and value-returning functions can be recursive.
4. $F(4) = 1$, $F(6) = -1$, and $F(5)$ is undefined.
6. A selection control structure—either an If or a Switch statement

Chapter 15   Programming Warm-up Exercises

```
1. int F( /* in */ int n )
   {
       if (n == 0 || n == 1)
           return 1;
       else
           return F(n - 1) + F(n - 2);
   }
3. void DoubleSpace( /* inout */ ifstream& inFile )
   {
       char ch;

       inFile.get(ch);
       while (inFile)              // While not EOF...
       {
           cout << ch;
           if (ch == '\n')
               cout << endl;
           inFile.get(ch);
       }
   }
```

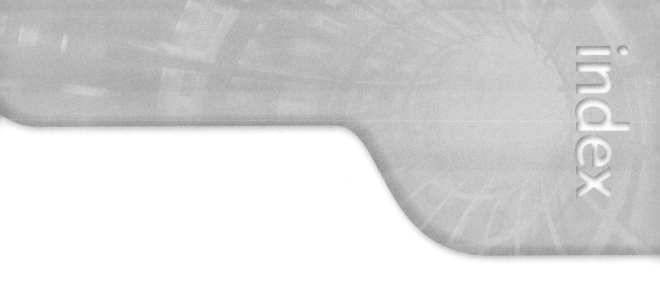

index